School Leadership and Administration

IMPORTANT CONCEPTS, CASE STUDIES, AND SIMULATIONS

FOURTH EDITION

RICHARD A. GORTON
San Diego State University

PETRA E. SNOWDEN
Old Dominion University

Madison, Wisconsin • Indianapolis, Indiana
Melbourne, Australia • Oxford, England

Book Team

Editor *Paul L. Tavenner*
Developmental Editor *Roger Wolkoff*
Production Editor *Deborah DeVries Donner*

Vice President and General Manager *Thomas E. Doran*
Executive Managing Editor *Ed Bartell*
Executive Editor *Edgar J. Laube*
Director of Marketing *Kathy Law Laube*
National Sales Manager *Eric Ziegler*
Marketing Manager *Pamela Cooper*
Advertising Manager *Jodi Rymer*
Managing Editor, Production *Colleen A. Yonda*
Manager of Visuals and Design *Faye M. Schilling*
Production Editorial Manager *Vickie Putman Caughron*
Publishing Services Manager *Karen J. Slaght*
Permissions/Records Manager *Connie Allendorf*

Wm. C. Brown Communications, Inc.

Chairman Emeritus *Wm. C. Brown*
Chairman and Chief Executive Officer *Mark C. Falb*
President and Chief Operating Officer *G. Franklin Lewis*
Corporate Vice President, Operations *Beverly Kolz*
Corporate Vice President, President of WCB Manufacturing *Roger Meyer*

Cover and interior design by Elaine G. Allen

Copyedited by Mary I. Waddell

Library of Congress Catalog Card Number: 91–76558

ISBN 0–697–10317–X

Printed in the United States of America by Wm. C. Brown Communications, Inc., 2460 Kerper Boulevard, Dubuque, IA 52001

10 9 8 7 6 5 4 3 2 1

Contents

Preface

Continued positive reception to the nature and format of the Third Edition of this book, along with the need to update the concept chapters and to expand the case study and in-basket exercises, led to the development of this Fourth Edition. In the newest revision an attempt has been made to maintain the strengths of the Third Edition while updating and presenting new issues and ideas.

In preparing for the revision, a review was conducted of both educational and social science literature on administration, management, and leadership. Although new ideas and data were sought and, when relevant, incorporated into the revision, efforts have been made to continue to utilize important ideas from the past, since considerable useful theory which has been advanced over the years is still not being utilized by many school administrators.

The goal has been to produce an up-to-date text that capitalizes on the best ideas from the past as well as new developments. As a result, the concept chapters have been strengthened, a number of case studies have been added, two new in-baskets have been included (one on the assistant principal), and a new chapter has been added with techniques for most effectively utilizing the case study and in-basket material in this Fourth Edition.

The text—designed to help prospective and experienced administrators and supervisors increase their knowledge and skills—includes concepts, case studies, and simulations. These should be useful for introductory courses in administration or for more advanced courses dealing with theory and problems of school administration, the principalship, supervision, and school-community relations. Use of the Third Edition and pilot-testing of the revision indicate that the book can serve as either a basic or supplementary text in preservice or inservice programs. The Fourth Edition should be especially useful in preparing those individuals who will be evaluated by an assessment center or in helping those who have already been evaluated and now need to improve their skills.

The book comprises two major parts. Part I presents important theoretical concepts and research findings that if adequately understood and appropriately applied can improve educators' problem-solving and leadership effectiveness. These seven concept chapters have been placed in the first half of the book for this Fourth Edition because previous experience with the text suggests that readers need *some* conceptual background before they attempt to address the problems and issues illustrated in the case studies and simulations presented in Part II.

The characters in most of the cases and simulations are depicted as either creating problems through their own actions or as confronting problems. (However, the names used for all characters, schools, and districts identified in the case studies and in-basket exercises are fictitious; any similarity to actual people, schools, or districts is strictly coincidental.) Although this emphasis on school problems reflects a central orientation of the text, the reader should not infer that administrators and others associated with the schools are always creating or facing problems. Nevertheless, it is the *problem* dimension of human behavior in school administration that should be studied, and it is here that preparation and in-service training programs need to be directed if prospective and experienced administrators and supervisors are to be equipped with the skills needed for the future as well as for the present.

It should be noted in regard to the four in-basket exercises that almost no background information is provided about the school and community settings. The intent is to avoid limiting the exercises to a specific setting (e.g., urban vs. rural, elementary vs. secondary) since the text will be used by a variety of universities and school districts with students and administrators from different backgrounds. The resultant text permits greater flexibility in its use, but the instructor or group leader will need to consider what *type* of a school district and community would be most relevant for the participants or the group, and then provide such information as is needed and appropriate. A major advantage of this approach is that the instructor can vary the background information about the setting depending on the characteristics of the people in the group. (Some instructors may wish to use In-Baskets #3, 33, and 34 consecutively.)

In addition, it should be mentioned that the cases in the text are open-ended. While the attempted resolution of subsidiary problems is sometimes described, the administrator in each case is generally left with the need to resolve a major conflict or dilemma. It is recognized that some individuals have mixed feelings about this type of case study, and there is little doubt that an unresolved problem or conflict will demand more thought and effort from the student and the instructor. But the construction of the cases was based on the premise that the student would derive greater benefit from cases requiring a personal resolution to the problem identified than from cases presenting a ready-made solution or alternative solutions. To facilitate such student involvement and use of the social science and administrative concepts presented in Chapters 1 through 7, "Suggested Learning Activities" are presented at the end of each case study.

Users of the text who desire additional insight into the case study and in-basket approaches are encouraged to examine Chapter 8 carefully. This chapter is designed to help users of the case studies and in-basket exercises gain maximum benefits from the materials and activities.

The ultimate goal of this book continues to be that of making a small contribution to improving administrators' preparation and in-service education. Administrator preparation has been periodically indicted as too theoretical and insufficiently grounded in reality, while in-service programs for administrators have frequently been criticized as the reverse. This text attempts to respond constructively to those criticisms by providing a slice of reality (through the presentation of the case studies), theoretical concepts for addressing the issues and problems identified in the cases, and various learning activities for relating the two. It is recognized that the cases and concepts presented may not meet all needs, but the text should be useful to those who would like a single resource for learning about administrative concepts and for examining structured opportunities to apply the concepts to actual problems and issues in school administration and supervision.

Richard A. Gorton

Petra E. Snowden

Acknowledgements

The authors are grateful to many people, including the scholars who stimulated our thinking, the professors who provided useful reactions to previous editions of this book, the practitioners who facilitated the field research for Part 2 of the text, and the students who pilot-tested various aspects of Part 2. We also appreciate the encouragement and assistance of the staff at Brown & Benchmark Publishers, especially Paul Tavenner and Deb Donner.

Finally, we are thankful for the support of our loved ones, without whose patience and understanding this book would not have been possible.

Meet The Authors

Richard A. Gorton received his doctorate from Stanford University, majoring in school administration. His Bachelor's Degree in Political Science and his Master's Degree in Counseling and Guidance were conferred by the University of Iowa. Dr. Gorton's school experience includes teaching, counseling and guidance, and administration. He was Department Chairperson and Professor of Administrative Leadership and Supervision at the University of Wisconsin at Milwaukee. He is currently Senior Professor of Administration, Rehabilitation Counseling and Postsecondary Education at San Diego State University.

A leader in state and national administrator organizations, Dr. Gorton has collaborated on a national study of "the effective principal." Because of his expertise and practical experience, he is frequently called on as a consultant and workshop leader in the areas of teacher and administrator evaluation, in-service education, program evaluation, instructional supervision, student disciplinary problems, school-community relations, problem solving, and conflict resolution.

Dr. Gorton has published two textbooks, two monographs, and over 100 articles, book reviews, and abstracts on a variety of topics related to educational administration and supervision, as well as education in general. Dr. Gorton's other textbook for which he was senior author, *School-Based Leadership, Challenges and Opportunities,* is published by Wm. C. Brown Company and is used in numerous university courses devoted to administrator preparation and by school districts for in-service education. He has also served as senior editor for *The Encyclopedia of School Administration and Supervision.*

Petra E. Snowden received her doctorate from the University of Wisconsin, Milwaukee, where she majored in Urban Education and minored in Educational Administration. Her Master's Degree in German literature and her Bachelor's Degree in French, German, and Secondary Education were also conferred by the University of Wisconsin, Milwaukee. Dr. Snowden is presently Co-director of the Danforth Tidewater Principal Preparation Program and Associate Professor of Educational Administration at Old Dominion University. Her research and writing interests have focused on the areas of staff development and linkages between schools and community service agencies, particularly as these structures affect the lives of vulnerable children and youth.

She founded the Principal Center at Old Dominion University and remains active within school settings by providing professional development seminars on topics such as instructional supervision, mentoring, program evaluation and planning while serving as an assessor, coach, and mentor for the Tidewater NASSP/Assessment Center. Dr. Snowden is active in a number of professional organizations and has presented papers at national, regional, and state conferences on issues pertaining to women in educational administration, the "School as a Care Provider," and school leadership.

In addition, Dr. Snowden served as president of the Hampton Roads YWCA and is an advocate for urban and women's issues. She is the author of numerous articles related to the improvement of school practices and has spoken on a variety of topics pertaining to educational training in community organizations.

Part

1

MAJOR CONCEPTS

in Administration and the Social Sciences: Conceptual Tools for Effective School Leadership

1 Decision Making

The ability to make effective decisions is vital to the successful performance of a school administrator. Herbert Simon has called it the "heart of executive activity" and, more recently, Duncan writes that the one thing "generic" to the job of an administrator is decision making.[1] In addition, reform proposals have called for numerous structural changes and strategic school governance revisions that further underscore the need for successful decision-making skills and improving the process of decision making. The empowerment of teachers by giving them more responsibilities over such issues as hiring, curriculum adoption, staff development and evaluation, and school policies pose decision problems under different conditions for the administrator.

Although intuition and experience can provide a useful basis for decision making, they are seldom sufficient. The effective decision maker must also employ an analytical thought process with greater focus on explaining and predicting the everyday realities that affect educational decision making.

In this chapter, an expansive view of decision making is provided.[2] A set of theoretical constructs that have emerged from the turn of the century to the present will be presented; these constructs, if appropriately applied, can improve a school administrator's decision-making capability. Through careful study and application of the nature and process of decision making, the reader should, as a result, become a better decision maker in schools and school systems.

THE NATURE OF DECISION MAKING

Over the past one hundred years, the process of decision making and the various models and theories associated with that process have been reflected in the research literature on management and educational administration. The aim was to improve performance by making decisions that were cumulatively and successively built on assumptions of choice.

The first model, generally referred to as *rational* or *normative prescriptive,* views decision making as a process that begins with a problem or need that the administrator then logically addresses by engaging in a series of sequential steps, culminating in an effective solution or decision.[3]

The normative prescriptive decision-making approach is concerned with what ought to be done and with prescribing actions designed to produce the best solution. This rational bureaucratic theory assumes that choices are made by administrators to maximize certain desirable values and objectives via rational analysis within a highly structured, bureaucratic system.

The rational theory provided a "scientific" base for the development of modern school systems during the industrial revolution at the turn of the century. Questions of efficiency in school management by growing powerful urban business communities led school decision makers to adhere to the levels of "scientific management" and Weber's ideal type bureaucracy.[4] This rational view assumes that administrators function in a closed system, a bureaucracy, characterized by task specification, rigid adherence to written rules and regulations, and formal hierarchical control. Decision making in this structured context is seen through the lens of the decision maker, a supposedly rational administrator. The decision-making process emphasizes solutions to problems and outcome of choice among alternatives with regard to clearly delineated objectives accomplished by following specific tasks and steps.[5]

Obviously, the school administrators' world and work does not operate in such a logical, sequential, and rational manner as the advocates of the rational bureaucratic decision-making tradition suggest. Various studies, both with school administrators and nonschool executives, have tended to confirm reservations about many of the aspects of the rational normative theory of decision making. Such studies have revealed an organizational environment that is frequently more dynamic, complex, and uncertain for decision makers than the rational bureaucratic or normative prescriptive theory of decision making has recognized.[6] In addition, a number of these studies have raised severe doubts about how rational or sequential most administrators are in their thinking as they proceed to make a decision.[7] In order to protect the image of the educational enterprise and of the school administrator from external interference, the appearance of rationality is frequently applied to the process of decision making. However, this is wrought with ambiguities. Wise, for example, discusses the dangers of "hyperrationalization" in educational organizations as a result of attempts to impose rational standards on nonrational processes.[8]

Normative prescriptive theories have a number of advantages. They specify clearly what should be done in terms of goals, objectives, criteria, and outcomes. They provide the administrator with the challenge of deciding among knowable alternatives by placing highest priority on what is most effective and desirable. And they help to reach agreement on future plans of action. Normative tools such as management by objectives (MBO), management information systems (MIS), and associated models for decision analysis provide a structure for decision making that can assist the administrator in day-to-day managerial tasks. The use of staff time, organizational material, and financial resources can be efficiently and sensibly maximized by the decision maker using a rational decision-making process for budget development, personnel decisions, facility maintenance, scheduling, or plant management. Clearly, rational bureaucratic assumptions accurately reflect the context of many educational decisions.

On the other hand, most administrators who participated in studies that critique the rational normative theory of decision making did not spend much time seeking additional information about the nature of a problem to better understand its causes and possible alternative solutions. Instead, they ignored the need for a decision, apparently hoping the problem would go away, or they took quick action without carefully investigating the nature of the situation. In the latter instances, they typically considered only a narrow set of alternatives, which in most cases, were based primarily on experience rather than reason or analysis and which were not carefully evaluated as to their advantages or disadvantages. The picture that emerges from these studies is that most administrators tend to "muddle through" when faced with a decision, and end up with an action that may have little relationship to the original situation that called for a decision.[9]

A second model, *participatory decision making,* also builds on the assumption of choice. But whereas the rational bureaucratic theory suggests choices are made by the administrator to maximize attainment of objectives, the participatory model assumes choices are made to satisfy constraints. The theory reflects the democratic and administrative norms dating to the work of Mary Parker Follett and constitutes a reaction to the impersonality and rigidity of scientific management beginning in the 1920's.[10] Participatory theories seriously question the definition of decision making as rational choice made solely by an administrator at the apex of an educational hierarchy. Instead, the focus is on consensual decision making, rooted in the values and beliefs of the participants. Assumptions and organizational preconditions for shared decision making include shared goals or values, influence based on professional expertise, open communication, and equal status among participants. Since many of these assumptions (such as shared goals and professional expertise within an organizational structure) are similar to the assumptions governing the rational bureaucratic model, participatory decision making has been viewed as a subset of the bureaucratic approach.

Descriptions of the way administrators *actually* make decisions rather than how they *should* make decisions have contributed to the development of participatory decision-making theory. Led by the pioneering work of Herbert Simon and James March and more recent critiques of the rational approach to decision making, these critics believe that the organizational context in which decisions need to be made reflects much more complexity and uncertainty than the rational theory of decision making seems to acknowledge.[11] These critics also tend to see the decision maker as possessing limited control over the educational enterprise and as being influenced by personality, values, and previous experience more than by reason or intellect. The participatory view of decision making has the administrator rely far less on management controls and more on bonding staff by developing norms which are derived from a shared vision of what is important. These administrators are more likely to view the problem of coordination as cultural rather than management.[12] The benefits of using a participatory decision-making approach in terms of decision outcomes are not conclusive in the research literature. It is not clear, for example, what the direct effect of different obstacles to teacher participation is on decision outcomes and in decision making.[13]

The third model, the *strategic decision-making approach,* views decision choices in an environment where multiple interest groups, conflict, negotiation, limited resources, position authority, and informal power exist. This model incorporates structural elements such as adherence to schedules and policies found in the bureaucratic rational model and aspects of the participatory model, such as seeking consensus via the involvement of many people in the organization. The assumption governing this particular model is that choices the administrator makes are based on comprehensive knowledge and analysis of the internal and external environment.

For strategic decision making to be effective, constraints and obstacles, as well as opportunities and challenges that impact the decision choice, must be identified. Research studies dealing with strategic decision making go beyond the rational procedures prescribed in the bureaucratic model and the shared cooperative elements described in the participatory model. Instead, these studies view decision making in the context of multiple competing interests, problem situations, and influences of power and control.[14] The complexity of decision making is captured in this strategic decision model with many of the nonrational aspects of decision making reflected in the theoretical writings.

The strategic decision-making approach is utilized by the administrator interested in carrying out an educational vision and developing a long range, overall plan that is flexible and subject to amendment. Decisions are governed by a shared philosophy and a shared purpose that ideally come from an empathy to and involvement of people committed to the same holistic purpose. The administrator may discover that despite pure application of the strategic model, decision outcomes are influenced by unexpected events, behaviors, or value orientations. These realities of a world "thriving on chaos" or "organized anarchy" lead us to a description of the fourth model of decision making.[15] For lack of a more sophisticated term we shall refer to this view as *differentiated decision making.*

The differentiated model represents a shift from the traditional paradigm or way of thinking about decision making. This model takes into consideration various focal points or points of emphasis that require the administrator's attention and will affect the decision choice. The administrator can enter the decision-making process at different decision entry points, depending on the type of problem or situation. Hence, this model can also be referred to as "situational decision making." The process may begin with choosing among alternative solutions presented by groups of individuals, or the process may require the administrator to take a risk and decide against conventional mores in order to maximize a long range, educational goal. There are many different situational variables that influence the decision choices an administrator makes.

The new paradigm recognizes situations that permit a linear, structured approach or may require group engagement or careful analysis of the external environment before the administrator takes that existential leap and decides. The decisions do not have to be necessarily goal based, but decision making can focus on the process itself, with the resulting actions having only a tenuous connection to the organizational outcome or the administrator's intention.[16] Ethical considerations, values, organizational culture, and climate are additional elements that impact on decision making. The new paradigm of decision making recognizes the contextual ambiguity and uncertainty within organizations. It builds on the "garbage can model" of decision-making theory of the early 70's that describes a systematic, structured process, operating in an environment consisting of situations that severely limit decision-making capability and decision choices, thus affecting decision outcomes.[17] The new paradigm views effective and efficient performance by an administrator as the desired outcome of decision making.

There is limited research with practical implications for improved decision making in educational organizations faced with financial uncertainty, changing social patterns, technological advances, alternate delivery systems, and educational linkages. There are even fewer studies that provide empirical data and new theories with implications for practice on the symbolic nature of participatory decision making. This latter view of decision making is also incorporated in our new paradigm. The administrator intending to carry out a vision for the school must attempt not only to be performance conscious, but also to determine the connectedness of individual and group participation, motivation, values, and goals to the decision choices. Even questions pertaining to the relationship between a particularly inspiring vision and the appropriate decision-making process must be considered in this paradigm for the 21st century. Empowering teachers, parents or students, embarking on joint ventures with the community, and opening the educational system to change constantly demands reconceiving the paradigm of differentiated decision making.

The main contribution of descriptive and normative decision-making theories has been to develop a better understanding of and appreciation for the complexity, uncertainty, and turbulence of the administrator's organization and environment and for the ways in which the decision maker's personality, values, and past experiences influence the decision choices. The models presented here are not discrete or separate entities but have evolved from each other, one augmenting the other. Together they represent a mature and sophisticated body of knowledge that accepts the complexity of educational decision making and its role in the daily life of the administrator.

Research studies reflect a more interdisciplinary approach with useful implications for practice originating not only in the educational literature but also in sociology and psychology. Suzanne Estler leads us into the artistic dimension of decision making with her apt metaphor, "decision making as drama," and reminds us that the administrator should see beyond any metaphor to the meaning and structure of the underlying assumptions.[18] The degree to which all of the models provide useful implications for practice will be presented in the following sections and explored further in the case studies found in the second part of this book.

THE PROCESS OF DECISION MAKING: IMPORTANT CONCEPTS AND STEPS

Decision making has been defined as ". . . A process influenced by information and values, whereby a perceived problem is explicitly defined, alternative solutions are posed and weighted, and a choice made that subsequently is implemented and evaluated."[19] The process is usually viewed from the perspective of an individual administrator, but decision making also takes place in small committees and in large groups. More recently, the philosophy of school-based management designed to increase the autonomy of the school staff to make school site decisions is gaining hold in school districts across the country.[20] This approach gives greater flexibility to staff, offers increased participation opportunities, and has the ability to provide more immediate services to meet specific needs of students. Some of the problems of school based management are confusion of roles and responsibilities as well as difficulty in adapting to new roles. There could ensue a power struggle among administrators, teachers, and parents, especially if the administrator is not willing to share decision-making authority. Some authorities argue that the individual administrator should not be making many decisions. For example, Griffiths has asserted that, ". . . If the executive is personally making decisions, this means there exists malfunction in the decision process. It is not the function of the chief executive to make decisions; it is his function to monitor the decision-making process to make sure that it performs at the optimum level."[21]

Dade County Public Schools in Miami, the 4th largest school system in the nation, is successfully implementing a school-based management/shared decision-making (SBM/SDM) program which includes decentralizing decision making in order to enhance the leadership of school site administrators and to promote the empowerment of teachers at the work site. Evaluations of shared decision-making procedures are typically conducted by variously named groups of teachers, administrators, noninstructional personnel, parents, and students, supported by grade level or subject interest committees and referred to a central decision-making body. Decisions are normally based on a majority vote with a great deal of opportunity for consultation and consensus resolution of issues, especially in cases where the principal has veto power.[22]

Regardless of whether the decision making occurs individually or in groups, or whether the administrator's role is that of monitor of the process, decision maker or, more likely, both, an administrator must possess a good understanding of the decision-making process in order to be effective in any of these roles. Careful reading and reflection on the following concepts and guidelines should help to accomplish that objective.

Figure 1.1 identifies the major steps in decision making, and the sections that follow describe the concepts involved at each stage. Although the process recommended is based on the rational theory of decision making, every effort will be made in the discussion to present the complexities—as well as the less rational aspects—of decision making. It is, of course, impossible to have a pure, rational process since the administrator cannot enjoy perfect knowledge. Hence, nonrationality becomes a necessity, with aspects of "muddling through." It is only when this necessity becomes a virtue, replacing the search for knowledge and information in decision making, that effective performance suffers.[23]

DEFINING THE SITUATION

The first step an administrator should take when faced with a decision is to define the nature of the situation that seems to require a decision. The importance of this step is underscored by

Figure 1.1 Major Steps in Decision Making.

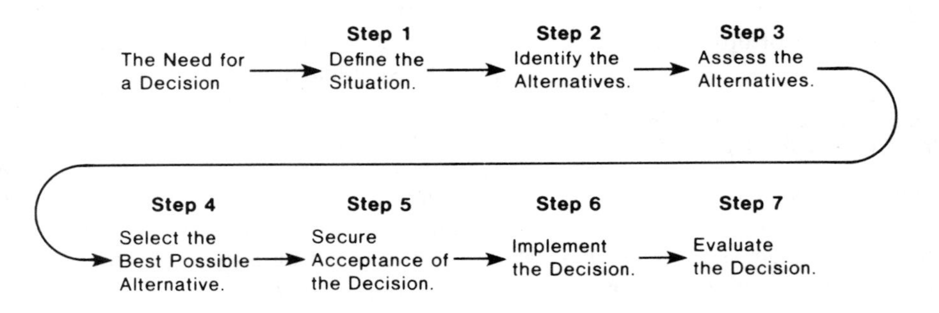

Barnard's observation: ". . . The fine art of executive decision making consists of not deciding questions that are not pertinent, in not deciding prematurely, in not making decisions that cannot be made effectively, and in not making decisions that others should make."[24] If this sage advice were followed more often, more effective administrative decision making would undoubtedly result.

To make effective decisions, including the types of decisions referred to by Barnard, an administrator first needs to attempt to gain a better understanding of the question, problem, or set of circumstances which seems to require an administrative decision.

Except for routine situations, an administrator will not be in the position of possessing sufficient information or understanding at the time the need for a decision first surfaces.

Unfortunately, studies have shown that all too often administrators react too quickly on the basis of assumption, inadequate information, and/or someone else's perception of a situation and immediately begin looking for solutions before the situation has been sufficiently defined.[25]

Of course, in some situations the administrator will be forced to make an on-the-spot decision, and there will be circumstances when the press of time and a lack of available information influences the decision choice. In such instances it will be important for an administrator to be decisive when the situation requires it and to avoid procrastinating in the hope that the perfect solution will at some point surface or that the problem will resolve itself.[26] However, in most situations, particularly those involving important and long-range decisions, an administrator should take sufficient time to investigate and analyze the conditions necessitating a decision in order to reduce the possibility of an ineffective administrative decision.[27] This type of situational or problem analysis is most productively approached by the decision maker's seeking answers to questions such as the following:

1. What is known and unknown about the situation? What other factors must be clarified before a decision can be made?
2. Can anyone else provide additional information or a different perception of the situation? To what extent is the administrator's bias or the biases of others influencing perception of the circumstances necessitating a decision?
3. Who will be affected by a decision?
4. How serious is the problem or question? How soon must a decision be made?

Effective situational and problem analysis is necessary in order to avoid making an incorrect decision based on an inadequate understanding of a situation or problem. Asking relevant questions is the key to effective situational and problem analysis. While there will be time constraints and possibly temptation to seek only the most accessible and interesting information about a situation,[28] the administrator should be trying to obtain the most relevant, accurate, and thorough information available on the situation or problem. A poorly understood problem or situation will almost guarantee an ineffective decision.

IDENTIFYING THE ALTERNATIVES

As a result of defining a problem or situation, the administrator will usually begin to perceive alternative courses of action. A typical mistake made by the inexperienced decision maker is to assume that only two alternatives exist.[29] For example, the principal who is faced with making a decision on a parents' proposal for greater involvement in school affairs may assume there are only two choices: to reject the parents' proposal or to accept their recommendation. However, if the administrator examines the situation further, several additional courses of action may appear. For instance, the administrator could decide to postpone a decision on the parents' proposal until more facts became available, offer a counterproposal to the parents that would incorporate less involvement than the parents have requested but would improve their present circumstances, or perhaps decide not to respond at all to the parents' proposal in the hope that they would take no further action.

What every administrator needs to avoid is the tendency to perceive alternatives in "either-or" terms. In most cases, an administrator will benefit from continuing to examine the problem, probing for that third or fourth alternative. This process requires careful analysis, imagination, and creativity, but it will usually result in an improved decision, one which may consist of a combination or synthesis of two previously identified alternatives, or a totally new approach.

ASSESSING THE ALTERNATIVES

Administrators who fail to assess adequately the feasibility of the various alternatives under consideration may later encounter unanticipated consequences in the process of implementing their decisions.[30] This results, in part, from the ambiguity of information and uncertainty of estimating the consequences of selecting one alternative over another that is characteristic of much decision making.[31] But unanticipated consequences can also occur when an administrator makes certain assumptions about each of the alternatives that turn out to be unjustified. For example, a particular group may react differently than was anticipated, or a key individual may not possess the resources or competencies that are needed, or the extent of supplies required for implementation of the decision may exceed the original estimates. Usually the unanticipated consequences result from the administrator's failure to identify fully and to examine critically the assumptions inherent—although possibly unrecognized—in assessing the original alternatives. As noted previously, it is impossible to reach decisions or to take action without making certain basic assumptions. However, the real danger for an administrator lies in making decisions without prior examination of the assumptions which lie at the heart of the feasibility of each alternative.

In attempting to assess the various alternatives, the administrator needs to anticipate their possible consequences, despite the uncertainty of the results. Such a process may be represented by the following sequence of thought: "If I choose alternative A, then result 1 will probably occur and result 2 will probably not. On the other hand, if I choose alternative B, then result 2 is likely to occur and result 1 is unlikely. However, if I choose alternative C, results 2 and 3 may come about while result 1 is unlikely. . .[32]

As the administrator evaluates each alternative, two important factors should be taken into consideration. The first concern is an assessment of one's own capability and that of the other individuals or groups who will participate in the implementation of a particular course of action. The second involves an assessment of the type of reception the decision will receive from those who will be most affected, e.g., teachers, students, parents, and the general public.

The initial question that an administrator must ask is, "To what extent do I possess the competency, resources, personal influence, or power necessary to implement this alternative?" For instance, an administrator may be interested in initiating a new program of individualized instruction. But before a decision is made to proceed with a plan, a personal inventory must be taken of the technical knowledge and skill for introducing the innovation, of the ability to obtain the necessary resources the new program will require, and of the extent to which personal influence or power are necessary for successfully implementing the decision. Although it may be difficult to evaluate objectively one's own competency, personal influence, or resources, these are the kinds of judgments required for an accurate feasibility assessment of a particular course of action.

A related question that the administrator should ask in assessing the feasibility of each alternative is, "To what extent do the other individuals or groups involved in implementing the decision possess the necessary competency or resources?" The effective implementation of most decisions depends on the capability or resources of people other than the administrator. Too frequently an administrator may assume that teachers, students, or other groups possess the skills, knowledge, or resources required for carrying out certain decisions. However, in the absence of these prerequisites, decisions are usually not implemented effectively, and the people involved may become quite frustrated. Therefore, it is essential that the administrator evaluate the degree to which co-workers possess the competency and resources necessary for successful implementation of a decision.

A second major factor to be considered by the administrator in assessing the feasibility of various alternatives is the type of reception the decision will be given by those most directly affected. Administrative decisions perceived as unsatisfactory may be resisted by those whose cooperation will be needed in the implementation stage.

The administrator should therefore determine how the affected individuals or groups regard the various alternatives. For example, with regard to each alternative, who can be counted upon for support? How solid would that support be? What would be the likelihood that a particular individual or group would reject or actively resist the course of action implied in each alternative? Which individuals or groups could exert sufficient influence or power to overturn a particular decision? Would it be possible for the administrator to change the attitudes of those who might reject or resist a decision? The answers to these questions should help the administrator to ascertain the reception a particular decision will probably be given by those who will be most affected by it.

In trying to understand how various individuals or groups will react to each alternative, the administrator will frequently need to make judgments based on limited experience with those concerned. Although in a few circumstances it may be easy to predict the reactions of certain individuals or groups, it may be necessary in other instances to "float a trial balloon" in order to discover how a group would react to a particular decision.

Regardless of the specific circumstances, however, one cannot overemphasize the need for an administrator to assess objectively and thoroughly in advance the reactions that a particular decision may be given by others. In many situations these reactions may well determine the ultimate fate of any decision. Undoubtedly there will be circumstances when an administrator must or should make a particular kind of decision, regardless of the adverse reactions of those who will be affected by it. However, the administrator should not proceed in ignorance of those attitudes and feelings. The attitudes and feelings of the people who will be affected by a decision will, in most instances, play a major role in determining the fate of any administrative decision and therefore need to be understood and considered carefully.

While the factors discussed thus far should play the major role in determining the feasibility of an alternative, an administrator needs to realize that other variables may unconsciously enter into the decision-making process. Each individual's decision making is affected by prior attitudes about the situation, group, or persons in question.[33] If the administrator's attitude is biased in some way, the administrator may distort the reality of a situation by not considering relevant facts, perceptions, or alternatives. As a result, a decision could be made about an individual or issue which might have been different if it were based on a more objective analysis of the circumstances. It will probably be impossible for an administrator to be completely objective in any situation. However, it is important to be aware of personal biases and to try not to let them significantly affect the decision-making process.

SELECTING A DESIRABLE ALTERNATIVE

If an administrator has followed the previously described guidelines, the best available alternative will usually become apparent.[34] If it does not, then the administrator's steps should be retraced and the assumptions reviewed, beginning with the question of whether or not the problem has been adequately defined. Of course, in most situations there is no ideal alternative, and in some circumstances it is a matter of selecting the least undesirable alternative. However, through diagnosis, objective assessment of alternatives, and a little imagination—which never hurts—the best course of action will generally surface.

IMPLEMENTING THE DECISION

Although some administrators seem to behave as though once they have made a decision, implementation will occur automatically and spontaneously, the process of implementation is more involved than has been frequently recognized.[35] The initial and perhaps most important step in implementing a decision is to secure its acceptance on the part of those who will be most affected. Whether the administrator can gain acceptance of the decision depends on many factors, one of which is the perceived legitimacy of the administrator's position within the organization as a decision maker for the issue, question, or problem under consideration. (We discuss additional factors that determine whether an administrator's decision is accepted in Chapter 3, "Authority, Power, and Influence.") If the individuals or groups who will be affected by a decision perceive the administrator as having the right to make that decision, based on the administrator's position in the organization, the likelihood of having that decision accepted is greatly enhanced. If, on the other hand, those individuals or groups who will be affected by the decision do not perceive the administrator as possessing any more right than anyone else to make the decision in the situation, the possibility of securing acceptance of the administrator's judgment may be severely jeopardized.

The key factor in the acceptance of the principal's decisions is not self-perceived legitimacy but the perceptions of others in regard to the administrator's legitimacy as a decision maker. In securing acceptance of the decision, the principal needs to understand and deal with the perceptions of teachers, parents, students, and other reference groups regarding the administrator's legitimacy as a decision maker. It cannot be assumed that a personal belief in the right to make the decision will engender agreement.

It should be emphasized that even if those affected by the decision do not perceive the administrator as possessing a basic right to make a determination, they may accept the decision if they are persuaded that there is little or nothing they can do to change it or thwart its implementation. For example, although the faculty advisor to the student newspaper may feel that the principal has no right to censor the publication, the decision to screen the content of the newspaper before it is published may be reluctantly accepted, if there is little that can be done to stop the principal. However, if the advisor thinks support can be obtained from the teachers' association's representative in the building, the city newspaper, or the civil liberties union, the advisor may resist the principal's original decision, or at least try to modify its implementation. Also, proponents of teacher and principal empowerment may argue that the administrator is resisting the teacher's expanded role as an inquiring, risk-taking, and contributing professional. The administrator could provide opportunities and the necessary assistance to maintain that teacher's self-esteem without taking ownership of the issue or task, listen with empathy and compassion, and possibly ask for help to solve this problem. Of course, if negative attitudes continue to persist, the administrator will need to take additional steps in resolving the problem.[36]

The administrator encountering negative reactions to a decision can either modify or abandon the original decision, try to enforce the decision against the will of others, or try to change their attitudes. If there is a need to change the attitudes of those who will be affected by the decision, the administrator should recognize that negative attitudes can result from some of the following phenomena:

1. The individual's or group's feeling about the administrator as a person, or about the way in which the decision was made.
2. An incorrect understanding of the way in which the decision will affect the individual or group.
3. Inadequate skill or competency on the part of those who are to carry out the decision.
4. A perception by the individual or group that the decision will cause more personal disadvantages than advantages.
5. An honest disagreement about the merits of the decision, despite the fact that those involved may not feel they would be adversely affected.

An administrator should realize that the reasons people resist a decision or react negatively are complex in nature and need to be analyzed fully. Therefore, when faced with resistance, the administrator should try to diagnose the source of the resistance by thoroughly investigating the various and sometimes subtle reasons why an individual or a group is not accepting the decision. Unfortunately, the administrator is sometimes thrown off balance by a negative reaction to the decision and responds directly to that reaction, rather than trying to explore and understand the reasons for it. However, the administrator is unlikely to be successful in counteracting resistance from others until the underlying causes of the resistance are dealt with.

Rowe and Mason suggest that hidden factors such as the administrator's decision style and that of the staff may affect overall performance. They found that where style is aligned with the requirements of the job, performance is often successful, and where it is not aligned, performance does not meet the person's potential. The authors contend that decision style reflects one's mental predisposition regarding personal objectives, what situations one avoids, what kinds of jobs one enjoys, what things one dislikes, how one communicates, and how one approaches problems and makes decisions. Patterns among these predispositions can be uncovered through the use of a decision style inventory developed by these authors.[37] The administrator attempting to deal with the underlying causes of resistance to a particular decision needs to better understand people's mental predispositions, perceptions, and why they act accordingly, as well as the differences in the way people approach their jobs through the use of such a decision style inventory.

Implementation Steps

If the administrator can obtain acceptance of the decision from those who will be most affected, or if there is a need to proceed in spite of their adverse reactions, the administrator should then attempt to secure the resources and personnel necessary to initiate action. Depending on the nature of the decision, there may be only the need to instruct one individual about what must be done. On the other hand, there may be a need to design and carry out a complicated plan involving many resources, a large number of people, retraining programs, and variables of time and role redefinition. Although the steps which must be taken have been designated by the various terms and have been applied in contexts other than the implementation of a decision, the basic activities include the following:

1. **Planning.** Working out in broad outline the things that need to be done and the methods for doing them to accomplish the purposes set for the enterprise.
2. **Organizing.** Establishing the formal structure of authority through which work subdivisions are arranged, defined, and coordinated for the specific objective.
3. **Staffing.** Selecting and training the staff and maintaining favorable conditions of work.
4. **Directing.** Making decisions and embodying them in orders and instructions; serving as the leaders of the enterprise.
5. **Coordinating.** Interrelating the various parts of the work.
6. **Reporting.** Keeping those to whom the executive is responsible informed as to what is taking place; keeping the executive and the subordinates informed through records, research, and inspection.
7. **Budgeting.** Fiscal planning, accounting, and control.
8. **Evaluation.** Formative and summative.[38]

While the activities listed may be regarded as fundamental to all facets of administration, the writers believe that their application is most appropriate and useful in the implementation of a decision.

CONSTRAINTS AND VALUES

The process of decision making described in the previous section is a logical, rational process which, if followed, should result in improved decision making. However, there are several situational constraints and personal variables that can affect the success of the decision maker's efforts. In addition to the technical expertise required in decision-making and decision-analysis procedures, there are always personal values and ethical factors that will impact an administrator's decision choice. Decisions that are ethically unsound will not have a long commitment from the people who will have to implement the decision in the work setting. Organizational ethics include the development of the administrator as a moral person, the influence of a moral organizational environment and a policy that reflects ethical performance goals.[39]

None of the constraints or personal variables diminishes the need for the administrator to follow the decision-making guidelines previously stated. Nevertheless, these constraints and personal factors must be considered if the administrator is to minimize negative effects. Nutt draws attention to a particular kind of decision made in and for organizations which he calls a "touch decision" in his comprehensive book entitled *Making Tough Decisions.* This type of decision is characterized by situational constraints and personal variables which must be taken into account, including such related dilemmas as ambiguity, conflict, and uncertainty. The authors recommend that administrators investigate future conditions and use sound procedures to gather and analyze information to inform the decision choice they ultimately make. Decision makers who simply focus on conflict management must make assumptions that negate ambiguity and uncertainty, treating tough decisions as if they were easy, frequently resulting in ineffective decision choices. One particular situational constraint, future projection, or the ability of the administrator to anticipate future events and outcomes that may impact on the final decision, requires the administrator to possess specific forecasting skills and techniques.[40]

Many of the difficult decisions an administrator must make deal with future conditions—whether to implement a new multicultural curriculum or install a preschool and after school care program for example. A strategic decision-making process requires the administrator to identify the obstacles or barriers as well as the opportunities or benefits associated with the decision.[41] In addition, thoughtful planning and technical expertise must be utilized by the administrator as a professional decision thinker. This implies expanding the strategic framework to include in the decision choice a concern for the personal values of the staff and community and acknowledging a responsibility to outside constituent groups and the greater society at large.

Situational Constraints

All administrators, even in the best of situations, operate under certain situational constraints. Although the types of constraints may vary from one situation to another, the most typical situational constraints under which administrators operate in a decision-making context are the following:[42]

1. Amount of time available to make a decision.
2. Availability of resources necessary to implement any particular alternative.
3. Amount of information available to make a decision.
4. Ambiguity of the situation, including the alternatives and potential consequences.
5. Degrees of organizational autonomy given for decision making.
6. Expectations of others regarding the nature of the decision-making process and ultimate decision.
7. Amount of tension in the situation.

Each of the factors can act as an important situational constraint on the decision maker and can influence the effectiveness of the final decision on a matter or its implementation. Whether or not the impact of these factors will be negative seems to depend as much on the type of person the administrator is as it does on the nature of the factors. For example, what is perceived as sufficient time, resources, information, and autonomy by one administrator in order to make a particular decision may not be deemed adequate by another administrator in the same situation. A situation characterized by one individual as possessing too much ambiguity, tension, and pressure by an external group for a quick decision may not bother or affect another administrator in the same set of circumstances. These differences reflect variations in personality and capabilities.[43]

However, administrators can also differ in their perceptions of potential constraints. One administrator may perceive strong expectations by a certain reference group to make a quick decision the same week while another administrator in the same situation may not sense the same degree of pressure and may plan to take a month or more to make the decision. In reality, both administrators may be misperceiving the expectations of the reference group, and the effectiveness of the decision may be impaired. Therefore, it is essential for an administrator to test initial perceptions about a potential constraint and to evaluate their validity to make sure they correspond to a reasonable degree with reality.

It also needs to be emphasized in discussing the role of situational constraints in decision making that, assuming the administrator is perceiving them accurately, they need to be analyzed critically to ascertain their potential for modification. For example, the constraint of inadequate time in which to make a thoughtful decision is regularly reported by administrators.[44] There will, of course, be circumstances in which the amount of time available to make a decision may be a real and significant constraint. However, if an administrator is frequently experiencing this problem, and it is seriously affecting the decision making, then an analysis of overall time spent and an evaluation of the order of priorities needs to be conducted. Effective decision making about matters which are out of the ordinary takes time, and while there will be situations in which the administrator must make a quick decision, the necessary time should be set aside for careful and thoughtful decisions on matters of major importance.

Realistically, an administrator will not be able to eliminate or even modify every type of constraint. But if an administrator is to be effective as a decision maker, an effort must be made to analyze the causes and nature of the constraints and attempt to decrease their impact on decision making.

Personal Variables

In addition to situational constraints which can affect the decision-making process, there are numerous personal variables or value considerations which can influence the decision maker and, ultimately, the final decision. These can perhaps be best illustrated by the thoughts expressed by several administrators, along with the attitude or value orientation each represents:

Personal Thoughts	Type of Attitude or Value
1. "I wonder about the risks involved in pursuing this particular alternative."	Risk orientation
2. "If Hank recommends it, I am sure that it would make a good decision."	Attitude toward people
3. "I question whether adopting a 'far out' innovation like the open classroom is good education."	Educational philosophy
4. "This is the type of decision that an educational leader should make."	Concern about status
5. "It seems to me that if we choose that alternative, we can no longer 'call the shots' in that area."	Concern about authority and control

These five examples, of course, are only illustrative of a wide range of possible values and attitudes any administrator might possess and that could play a major role in influencing the type of decision made.

As Lipham and Hoeh have perceptively observed,

> . . . Values serve as a perceptual screen for the decision maker, affecting both his awareness of the problematic state of a system and his screening of information relative to the problem. Second, values condition the screening of possible alternatives . . . Finally, values serve as the criteria against which higher order goals are assessed and projected. . .[45]

While an administrator probably cannot avoid the influence of values and attitudes in making decisions, the administrator should attempt to become more aware of the ethical nature of those values. In his study of chief school administrators, Dexheimer discovered that they were more inclined to engage in nonethical forms of accommodations in critical decision-making activities rather than ethical forms.[46] Although it appears that the study has not been replicated with similar or other administrative positions, it points up the need for every administrator to consider carefully whether the attitudes and values influencing a particular decision are morally and ethically defensible. This will not be an easy task for the decision maker because most individuals are not very conscious of their values and attitudes or how they are affected by them and lack criteria and standards for evaluation.

The emphasis on organizational ethics is found predominantly in writings on business ethics and organizational culture. Studies and articles range in content from business student attitudes before and after taking a course in ethical decision making to identifying ethical business practices after students completed a course on business ethics to models for building ethical organizations.[47] The findings could have implications for an administrator in an educational setting who desires more information on value development and ethical conduct in general.

A problem related to the influence of attitudes and values in decision making is the extent to which they can play a dominant role in compromising the objectivity of the decision maker and short-circuiting the decision-making process. For example, the administrator who has the attitude that, "If Hank recommends it, I am sure that it would make a good decision," is revealing a strong, positive attitude or bias toward the person, Hank. Because of the administrator's attitude in this situation, it will probably be difficult to be objective about evaluating Hank's recommendation or any competing alternative. As a result, the administrator may not engage thoroughly in the various steps of the decision-making process—steps that should include identifying and evaluating objectively all possible alternatives.

Although the administrator's attitude in the previous example is a positive one, at least toward Hank, in another situation involving someone else it may be negative, with the same potential results of compromised objectivity and a superficial decision-making process. Of course, it is not axiomatic that such a decision will be a poor one, and it is recognized that the press of time on an administrator may require taking a "short-cut" through the decision-making process. Unfortunately it is because of the bias of the decision maker and such "short-cuts" that poor decision making frequently results. Therefore, an administrator should make every effort to become more aware of attitudes and values and their influence on the type of decision choices, attempting to reduce that influence when it could compromise objectivity or result in a less thorough and thoughtful decision-making process.

INVOLVING OTHERS

The involvement of individuals and groups, or both, in the decision-making process, who will be either affected by the decision or in some way responsible for implementing a decision, is not a new concept in the social science and school administration literature.[48] Frequently referred to as Participatory Decision Making (PDM), this approach has generated considerable research revealing that PDM can be effective under certain conditions but is a more complex process than typically has been recognized.[49] The following sections will identify appropriate and inappropriate conditions for Participatory Decision Making; the complexities associated with the process will be analyzed and discussed.

The rationale for involving persons other than just the administrator in the decision-making process consists of the following elements:

1. It increases the number of different viewpoints and ideas which might be relevant to the decision being made.
2. It makes for better utilization of the available expertise and problem-solving skills that exist within the school community.
3. It may improve school morale by showing the individuals involved that the administrator values their opinions, giving them greater feelings of professional pride and job satisfaction.
4. It can aid acceptance and implementation of a decision because the people who are involved are more likely to understand the decision and be more committed to its success.
5. It is consistent with a democratic principle of our society which holds that those who are affected by public institutions such as the school should have some voice in how they are run.[50]

Therefore, although frequently given the sole responsibility for making a particular decision, administrators may find it desirable to involve others in the process of arriving at the best determination. The old adage that "two heads are better than one" can be applied to administrative decision making with appreciable advantage under certain conditions.

However, an administrator should not involve others in the decision-making process if the administrator has already decided the outcome. It is certainly appropriate for an administrator to have some tentative ideas about a decision before involving others. But unless those ideas are tentative and there is a willingness to be flexible and open-minded in considering the ideas of others, it would be better not to involve others in the decision- making process. It can be a very frustrating and disillusioning experience for people to be involved by an administrator whose mind is already made up,[51] and who is involving other people only because of trying to project a "democratic" image or to be able to say at a later date, "Well, they were involved, weren't they?" As Lammers has observed, encouraging and allowing participation by others in decisions over which they have little control may be just as damaging, if not more so, than no participation at all.[52]

Variables Influencing Extent of Involvement

Whether or not an administrator should involve others in decision making would appear to depend on a number of factors. Perhaps the most important initial factor is the administrator's attitude toward the people who might be potentially involved in decision making. McGregor has formulated a useful theory relevant to this discussion about administrators' attitudes toward people. McGregor believes that administrative behavior is influenced by two basic attitudes which he refers to as "Theory X and Theory Y."[53] The main characteristics of these two attitudes as they apply to decision making are described below.

Theory X

1. "The average human being has an inherent dislike of work and will avoid it if he can."
2. "Because of this human characteristic of dislike of work, most people must be coerced, controlled, directed, threatened with punishment to get them to put forth adequate effort toward achievement of organizational objectives."
3. "The average human being prefers to be directed, wishes to avoid responsibility, has relatively little ambition and wants security above all."[54]

Theory Y

1. "External control and the threat of punishment are not the only means for bringing about effort toward organizational objectives. Man will exercise self-direction and self-control in the service of objectives to which he is committed."

2. "The average human being learns, under proper conditions, not only to accept but to seek responsibility. Avoidance of responsibility, lack of ambition and emphasis on security are generally consequences of experience, not inherent human characteristics."
3. "The capacity to exercise a relatively high degree of imagination, ingenuity and creativity in the solution of organizational problems is widely, not narrowly, distributed in the population."[55]

Theory X and Theory Y administrators differ markedly in their attitudes toward people. These differences have been found to be related to the extent to which an administrator involves others in school decision making.[56] A major implication of McGregor's Theory and the supporting research is that, unless the administrator's attitude toward other people is one of trust, confidence, and respect, it is unlikely that involvement in administrative decision making will result.

A second major factor that initially seems to influence the administrator as to whether or not to involve others in the decision-making process is the degree of organizational autonomy the administrator has been given by superiors for making decisions. Palmer discovered that the more autonomy administrators were given for making decisions, the more likely they were to consult and involve others in the decision-making process.[57] One implication of Palmer's study is that a certain degree of administrative autonomy and independence from superiors may be a necessary prerequisite for involving others in administrative decision making.

Involvement Considerations

Assuming that an administrator has reasonable autonomy within the organization, is open-minded, and really believes that involving others may help in arriving at the best decision, three basic questions must be considered. (1) *When* should others be involved in decision making? (2) *Who* should be involved? and (3) *How* should they be involved?

With regard to the first question, Bridges has proposed that other individuals or groups should be involved in those administrative decisions that they feel will significantly affect their lives.[58] He theorizes, based on earlier conceptual work by Barnard, that most people possess a zone of indifference. By implication, they also possess a zone of concern. When a particular issue or problem falls within a group's "zone of concern," the members will expect to be involved by the administrator in the decision-making process. If the members are permitted to be involved, they will be self-motivated in their participation because the final determination may affect them in some significant manner. If they are excluded from the decision-making process, they may feel deprived, and dissatisfaction with the administrator or the decision is likely to result.[59]

Although people's zones of concern could potentially vary from one school situation to another (and, for that matter, among the individuals of a group), Schneider found in her study of 23 middle and junior high schools that there existed high levels of teacher interest in becoming involved in such decisions as selecting textbooks and other instructional materials, determining grading procedures, setting and revising school goals, and establishing disciplinary policies in the school.[60]

It should be emphasized that there will undoubtedly be issues or problems which will fall within an individual's or group's "zone of indifference" because these issues are not perceived as important to the group's welfare, or because the decision is one which some feel that the administrator is paid to make and therefore is the administrator's sole responsibility. The administrator, in these situations, will probably not be expected to involve the individual or group in decision making and should not attempt to do so unless no other choice exists. Due to their lack of concern, these individuals or groups will be of little assistance in decision making and, if involved, are likely to feel that they are overinvolved. This could generate a negative attitude toward the administrator and adversely affect the decision-making process.[61]

The goal for the administrator should be to involve people in the process of decision making when their involvement could improve the quality, acceptance, or implementation of the decision, and when the involvement is based on people's desired level of involvement. Also, obviously, not everyone wants to be involved, and not all of the decisions under the province of an administrator will be of concern to other individuals and groups.[62] On the other hand, it would be unwise for the administrator to assume that people really want to have certain decisions made for them, or that they are not concerned about particular issues or problems. Untested assumptions frequently result in unanticipated consequences. The administrator should not rely on assumptions but should actively seek feedback from appropriate others regarding the extent to which they are concerned about various issues and problems and the degree to which they feel their participation is desirable in making decisions.

Involvement Prerequisites

In many situations, the lack of feasibility will preclude participation in the decision-making process by everyone who may desire to do so. Consequently, the administrator will need to determine which individuals or groups should help make a decision in a particular area.

Objectivity would appear to be an important consideration. Individuals who are interested in being involved but who show a particular bias or an ax to grind are not likely to be helpful. Effective decision making requires an open mind and an unbiased examination of the facts and alternatives.

The most desirable criterion for selecting those who should be involved in decision making would appear to be the extent to which they possess the expertise for contributing to an improved decision. Numerous individuals or groups may be interested in participating in decision making, but they may not all possess the expertise necessary to make a positive contribution. As Bridges has pointed out, the interested party should "not only [have] some stake in the outcome but also the capability of contributing to the decision affecting the outcome."[63] Interest and motivation are necessary but not always sufficient conditions for involvement in administrative decision making; the degree to which an individual or group possesses the relevant expertise should also be a consideration. Utilizing the latter criterion, the administrator should identify those students, teachers, parents, or other individuals or groups who can offer special insights, knowledge, or skills for improved decision making. They are the people who can be of considerable assistance to the administrator in arriving at effective decisions.

Levels of Involvement

Having determined that a certain group possesses the necessary motivation, objectivity, and expertise for participating in decision making, an administrator still faces the question of at what level to involve them. Five alternative levels of involvement, each with its underlying assumptions, are presented in Figure 1.2.

As Figure 1.2 shows, the question of how an administrator might involve others in school decision making is a complex one. Several alternatives are usually available, each of which is based on certain assumptions. While there is no formula for easily determining the most appropriate level of involvement by others, the administrator should try to be certain that the assumptions made in reaching this decision are tenable. Although it will be impossible to avoid making assumptions, the administrator should refrain from making those that could restrict valuable input from other people or provide more involvement than others could constructively handle. The initial conceptual work in this area was developed by Robert Tannenbaum and Warren H. Schmidt, as

Figure 1.2 Alternative Levels of Involvement.

Level 1. The administrator makes a tentative decision and utilizes the reactions of other individuals or groups to assess the soundness of his decision. The administrator reserves for himself, however, the final determination on whether or not to proceed with his original decision.

Assumptions

a. The administrator has probably already reached the best decision for the situation.
b. It is unlikely that anyone else could offer a better alternative.
c. There is a possibility that the administrator might yet improve his decision by obtaining the reactions of others.
d. The administrator must make the final determination himself.

Level 2. The administrator describes the problem situation to other individuals or groups and asks them to investigate the various alternatives and to make a recommendation to him on several possible courses of action, listing the advantages and disadvantages of each. The procedures to be used by the individuals or groups investigating the alternatives are specified by the administrator. He will utilize their recommendations to help him make up his mind on the best course of action to follow.

Assumptions

a. The administrator has already adequately defined the nature of the problem.
b. Other people could provide help in identifying the available alternatives.
c. Because of the other participants' inexperience or need for direction, the administrator should specify the procedures they should follow in arriving at their recommendations.
d. The administrator must make the final decision himself.

Level 3. The administrator describes the problem situation to other individuals or groups and asks for help in better defining the nature of the problem, question, or issue, and that he be presented with a recommendation on the best course of action to follow. The administrator specifies the procedures which must be used in arriving at the recommendation and reserves the right to veto the recommended alternative if he doesn't believe it to be in the best interests of the school.

Assumptions

a. Other people could help the administrator to better define the nature of the situation for which a decision is required.
b. Other people could provide help for the administrator in identifying the best available alternative.
c. Because of the other participants' inexperience or need for direction, the administrator should specify the procedures to be followed in arriving at their recommendation.
d. The administrator must make the final decision himself.

Figure 1.2 —*Continued.*

Level 4. The administrator describes the problem situation to other individuals or groups and asks for their help in better defining the nature of the problem, question, or issue, and requests their recommendation on the best course of action to follow. At this level of involvement the administrator specifies no particular procedures to be used in arriving at a recommendation. However, he still reserves the right to reject any recommendation which he believes to be incompatible with the best interests of the school.

Assumptions

a. Other people could help the administrator to better define the nature of the problem and to arrive at a recommendation for the best course of action.
b. The other participants possess sufficient experience and self-direction to determine for themselves the procedures to be used in reaching a recommendation.
c. The administrator must make the final decision himself.

Level 5. The administrator describes the problem situation to other individuals or groups and asks for their help in defining the nature of the problem, question, or issue, and requests them to determine the best alternative. At this level of involvement, the administrator delegates to the other participants the prerogative of determining the procedures to be used in arriving at the best decision and he indicates his willingness to accept whatever decision is finally made.

Assumptions

a. Other people could help the administrator to better define the nature of the problem and arrive at a decision on the best course of action.
b. The other participants are as competent as the administrator to make the final decision.
c. The administrator can delegate the responsibility for making the final decision, and he can accept and support whatever decision is reached by the other participants.

reported in "How to Choose a Leadership Pattern," *Harvard Business Review,* 36 (March–April, 1958): 95–101. The authors have adapted and modified the original model for the purpose of administrative decision making and have added the basic assumptions which undergird each level of involvement.

There is research which suggests that an administrator's choice of the level at which to involve other people is typically based on the individual's attitude toward encouraging the involvement of others in school decision making, the perception of the administrator's immediate superior's attitude toward this question, and the perception of the expectations of others for a certain level of participation in school decision making.[64] The same research indicates that the administrator's own attitude about involving others and the perception of the immediate superior's attitude are the two most important factors influencing the administrator in deciding how to involve others.

However, in view of the evidence presented earlier in this book showing that a growing number of students, teachers, and parents are dissatisfied with their current level of involvement in school decision making, it would seem important for every administrator to give greater consideration to these expectations for more meaningful participation. The challenge for the school administrator is to involve these groups in ways which will permit them to derive satisfaction from their participation and, at the same time, make a contribution to improved decision making in the schools.

Types of Involvement

The most typical approach is for an administrator to analyze a problem or situation calling for a decision with another person or persons in a conference or group setting. Such discussions can be helpful in clarifying the administrator's thinking and obtaining reactions from others.

One systematic example of this approach is the *Quality Circle.*[65] A Quality Circle is a small group of employees such as teachers, secretaries, or any other group performing a common task. They meet weekly or biweekly to analyze problems that impair the effectiveness of the group or reduce the desired quality of a product or outcome of the group or, perhaps, to offer fresh ideas to improve some aspect of their work.[66] A group leader, perhaps an administrator, facilitates group discussion and helps the group to identify and analyze problems, identify and assess alternative solutions, select the most desirable and feasible solution, and develop a decision implementation plan. The decision-making process followed in a Quality Circle is very similar to the process outlined in Figure 1.1.[67]

Although research on the effectiveness of the Quality Circle is limited, the approach is utilized in a number of schools with apparently some success.[68] The assumption that group decisions will be better than the decisions of the most knowledgeable group member is not always proven in the empirical research literature. It is traditionally believed that under most circumstances, the knowledge of the most competent group member represents the upper limit of what a group might reasonably be expected to achieve. However, recent findings from studies that focussed more on contextually relevant and consequential problems to be solved by groups rather than on ad hoc groups using artificial problems and trivial rewards for solving problems demonstrated that groups outperformed their most proficient group member 97% of the time. This finding presents a strong argument for involving groups in problem-solving activities to improve the effectiveness of the decision choice.[69] In addition, the keys to the success of the Quality Circle seem to be a strong commitment from the school board, district administration and from members of the Quality Circle to this type of participatory decision making, as well as a committed group leader equipped with group leadership skills.[70] (These skills are discussed in Chapter 4.) Also, training in group interaction processes and problem-solving methods is essential for the members of the Quality Circle.[71]

While the Quality Circle or other types of group interaction methods of decision making can, under the right conditions, improve the effectiveness of a decision, such conditions are not always present. For example, the people whom the administrator is trying to involve in a Quality Circle may not feel secure in responding to the administrator or to the other members of the group, and, when that occurs, such feelings and thoughts are frequently not revealed. Also, while it is true that in a Quality Circle or in other types of group decision-making situations the people involved may stimulate each other's thinking, it is also true that often in a group discussion it is difficult to engage in the thoughtful, reflective thinking that is important for creative decision making. In addition, in group discussions certain individuals or personalities may dominate, and social relationships may become more important than solving a problem or making the best decision.[72] It should be noted that these problems are not inevitable with the Quality Circle or any other kind of group interaction approach, but their occurrence has led to the consideration of two alternative ways of involving people in the decision-making process.[73]

The first of these is known as the *Delphi Technique*. It is basically a process for generating ideas, reactions, or judgments which could be helpful to the decision maker and includes the following major steps: (1) defining the problem, decision, or question to which reactions of others are sought; (2) identifying those individuals and/or groups whose opinions, judgments, or expert knowledge would be valuable to obtain in the process of making a decision; (3) asking for their responses, usually through the completion of a questionnaire; and (4) summarizing the results of the questionnaire, distributing the results back to the people surveyed, and asking them to review the results and to indicate any changes in their initial responses. This last step is repeated until there is a reasonable consensus on the problem or decision.

The advantage of the Delphi Technique is that it is an excellent approach for involving a large number of people in the decision-making process. The step of writing responses to questions helps people to think through the complexity of a problem and to submit more specific, high quality ideas. The anonymity and isolation of the respondents tend to minimize the influence of status factors and conformity pressures.[74] One disadvantage of the Delphi Technique is that the lack of opportunity for interaction among people asked for their input into the decision-making process can lead to a feeling of detachment and noninvolvement. Furthermore, the lack of opportunity for verbal clarification of responses can cause communication and interpretation problems, while the summarizing of responses does not deal with the problem of conflicting or incompatible ideas.

Another approach to involving people in the decision-making process, the *Nominal Group Technique*, has been developed to avoid or to minimize the possible disadvantages of the Delphi Technique. The Nominal Group Technique (NGT), developed by Andre L. Delbert and Andrew H. Van de Ven in 1968, has been employed in a variety of settings. Its main steps include the following: (1) presenting to a group, verbally or in writing, a question, problem, or task to be addressed by the members of the group; (2) requesting each member in the group to take a period of time, e.g., 10 minutes, to jot down individual ideas, (without talking to anyone else in response to the question, problem, or task); (3) asking each member of the group at the end of the time period to present one of the ideas, recording these ideas on a blackboard or flip chart (at this stage it is important that there be no evaluation of the ideas by anyone); (4) continuing the presentation of ideas in round robin fashion until all the ideas are recorded; (5) discussing briefly each idea, in the sequence in which it is recorded, as to clarity or rationale; and (6) voting privately in writing by rank-ordering or rating the ideas, and then mathematically pooling the outcome of the individual votes.

While the entire process may seem complicated, it is really fairly simple after one has acquired some experience with the various steps. Although NGT does have some disadvantages in that it does not provide as much social interaction as some people may want, and it requires the people involved to hold in abeyance their evaluation of the ideas being presented until later in the process, it nevertheless has tended to be very productive in producing higher quality ideas than either the group discussion or Delphi Technique approaches.[75]

Administrators must also consider their roles in regard to the participation of others in the decision-making process. For example, the administrators could be confined to presenting the initial circumstances calling for a decision and later receiving a group's final recommendation, *or* could attempt to play the role of a resource person for those who are helping reach a decision. The administrator might, alternatively, attempt to influence the final recommendation of the group by playing a dominant role in their deliberations. The question of *which* role the administrator should play while involving others in school decision making is an important one, and the three examples provided are only illustrative of the many possibilities. The administrator's final resolution of this question is sure to influence the nature of the participation by others in the decision-making process.[76]

PREREQUISITES FOR SUCCESS

Assuming that the administrator has selected appropriate participants and methods of involvement, several other factors will determine whether their involvement will result in the mutual satisfaction of both the administrator and participants and whether they will reach a better decision than if the administrator had decided unilaterally. First of all, the administrator must recognize that involving others in decision making increases the complexity and difficulty of the task of making a decision. It increases the number of situational variables with which the administrator will be working and requires a greater degree of competency than if the administrator alone made the decision. To be successful in involving others, an administrator must become competent in the group dynamics and interaction skills we will discuss in more detail in Chapter 4.

Strategic decision making is a popular approach which may be used for training administrators or top executives in business. Most of these training programs focus upon sensing opportunities and problems, diagnosing the situation and generating alternatives, and, of course, making that all important choice. The popularity of various types of training programs at any given moment is reflected in the administration theory currently under discussion. Consequently, the decade of the 90's and beyond is already marked with an emphasis on participatory and group decision-making training for administrators as a result of the research on strategic decision making and teacher empowerment. The group process, collaboration, and teamwork produce better decisions if more people are helping to generate options.[77]

Furthermore, the administrator needs to be certain that the individuals or groups involved are given sufficient training for participation in decision making and adequate information to make a decision. Frequently administrators have attempted to involve students, parents, or teachers in decision making and have become discouraged and discontented because these individuals and groups did not participate fully or productively. When confronted by this type of behavior, the administrator should try to diagnose its cause(s), that might include a lack of skills for participation or insufficient information about the problem.

The administrator also needs to make sure that those involved understand the reason why they are being involved and the purpose, authority, and scope of their participation. Involvement of others tends to run into difficulty when there has not been agreement on the purpose, scope, and authority of that involvement.

The administrator may wish to embark on a strategic planning approach that measures the impact of the decision choices on organizational purposes and performance. This technique of decision analysis is frequently used by administrators and planners to determine the lowest practical level to which a class of decisions should be delegated. Various classes or types of decisions and factors determining the strategic value of the decision category and the impact in measurable, weighted criteria are the major elements of this technique. Dougherty discusses some of the factors that may need to be considered when making a particular decision pertaining to a specific goal or method, such as involving others in decision making: a) *futurity* refers to the length of time after the decision is made before an evaluation of the decision outcome can be made, b) *reversibility* is the ease with which a decision can be reversed, c) *scope* means the extent of the organization affected by the decision, and d) *human impact* indicates the degree of the impact on the people affected by the decision, while e) *frequency* refers to how often the decision would normally be made. The strategic value of each decision category is then numerically calculated. Decision analysis can also be utilized to determine the maximum level of involvement feasible. Any number of criteria can be used to make this determination including "facts available," "competence," "advice available," and "present" or "proposed levels of decision making."[78]

Finally, if the administrator is involving others on a committee whose decision will be only advisory to the administrator, then this needs to be made clear to the committee at the outset. The administrator also needs to provide rewards to those involved throughout the decision-making process in order to keep their spirits up and to show appreciation for their efforts. The time, effort, and contributions of the participants in the decision-making process should not be taken for granted by the administrator if a high level of sustained performance is desired.

ASSESSING DECISION-MAKING EFFECTIVENESS

If a school administrator is to improve as a decision maker, then time will need to be devoted to assessing the effectiveness of the process followed and the quality of the resultant decisions. This will not be an easy task for a variety of reasons. Most school administrators are busy people and, unless a high priority is given to assessing the effectiveness of decision making, the task of assessment is not likely to be accomplished. Also, it is difficult for most decision makers to remain objective about their decisions. After all, once an administrator makes a decision, there is naturally an inclination to have a vested interest in the appearance, if not the reality, of effectiveness. (Involving others in the assessment who do not have that vested interest could increase the objectivity of the evaluation.) An assessment of the decision's effectiveness may threaten to reflect negatively on the administrator. Perhaps the most serious obstacle to the school administrator's self-assessment of decision-making effectiveness is the fact that, unless a decision results in significantly negative consequences, there is seldom any pressure from superiors or anyone else for the administrator to evaluate a decision's effectiveness. Nor are there incentives or rewards for evaluating whether a better decision could have been made.

Despite these difficulties, it is important for the school administrator to assess periodically the effectiveness of decision making if improvement is to continue in this area. Experience in making decisions is not, in itself, a sufficient basis for improvement without reflection upon and assessment of that experience. The checklist presented in Figure 1.3 is proposed for assessing the effectiveness of the decision-making process.[79]

We realize that the administrator will not have the time nor the need to assess the effectiveness of every choice. However, if the administrator is to continue to improve decision-making skills, then periodic assessment of the process and of the quality of decisions will be essential and, in the case of decisions with negative consequences, imperative.

A FINAL NOTE

Effective decision making is a complex process requiring considerable analysis and thought by the administrator. It does not occur in a vacuum but is influenced by situational constraints and the personal values and expertise of the individual making the decision. The process and product of decision making can frequently be improved by the involvement of others, although certain conditions must be met before that involvement will be helpful. While decision making may be the most important administrative process, its effectiveness will depend to a large degree on the understanding and skill with which the administrator utilizes the other administrative practices presented in the next chapters.

Figure 1.3 Checklist for Assessing Decision-Making Effectiveness

	Check one response for each question		
	Yes	No	Uncertain
1. Did you sufficiently investigate the nature of the problem or situation (including causes) that required a decision?	____	____	____
a. Did certain facts later surface that you should have ascertained at the outset?	____	____	____
b. Could facts, which, if known earlier in the decision making process, have improved the quality of the final decision?	____	____	____
c. What additional questions could you or should you have asked when the situation first presented itself that could have provided information leading to a better decision?	____	____	____
d. Do you have good reason for not asking those questions?	____	____	____
2. Did you try to identify more than one or two alternative courses of action to resolving a situation?	____	____	____
a. Did you assume without much thought that only one or two alternatives existed and select the first one that "looked good"?	____	____	____
b. Reflecting upon the decision process you followed, and thinking about the consequences of the decision you made, can you see that there may have been another alternative course of action that might have better resolved the situation or problem?	____	____	____
c. Do you know why the alternative course of action wasn't considered at the time?	____	____	____

Figure 1.3 *—Continued.*

	Check one response for each question		
	Yes	No	Uncertain
3. Did you adequately assess the advantages and disadvantages of the alternatives you considered before making a final decision?	____	____	____
a. Did certain unanticipated consequences develop that adversely affected the consequences of the final decision?	____	____	____
b. Were there problems that occurred that you did not adequately anticipate in choosing the course of action you did?	____	____	____
c. Do you understand now why you didn't sufficiently identify or anticipate those problems?	____	____	____
4. Did you involve to an appropriate extent those individuals and/or groups who could have contributed to an effective decision?	____	____	____
a. Were there people whom you should have involved and whom you would involve if you had to do it over again?	____	____	____
b. Were there people whom you did involve in the decision making process whom you wouldn't involve if you had to do it over again?	____	____	____
c. Have you analyzed how you would have changed the ways in which you involved other people in the decision making process?	____	____	____
5. Did the decision generate resistance?	____	____	____
a. Could that resistance have been anticipated, and steps taken to prevent or reduce it? (Resistance does not automatically mean that the decision was a poor one, but it does have implications for the implementation of the decision, and it may mean that there was room for improvement in the process you followed.)	____	____	____

Figure 1.3 —*Continued.*

	Check one response for each question		
	Yes	No	Uncertain
b. Has the decision been fully implemented by the people who were supposed to implement it?	____	____	____
c. If the decision has not been fully implemented, do you understand why not?	____	____	____
d. Are there certain steps you could have taken (or still could take) to improve implementation?	____	____	____
6. Were the objectives that the decision was intended to achieve accomplished?	____	____	____

Most of the case studies, suggested learning activities, and simulations presented in Part II of the text require the appropriate application of the ideas formed in this chapter on decision making. However, the following exercises should provide the best opportunities for testing your understanding and effective use of decision-making concepts: Cases 16, 25, 47, 48, 50 and 52 and the In-basket exercises.

Notes

1. Herbert A. Simon, *The New Science of Management Decisions* (New York: Harper and Row, 1960); W. Jack Duncan, *Great Ideas in Management* (San Francisco: Jossey Bass, 1989), pp. 69.

2. The major source of insight for the conceptual framework of decision making is found in an excellent article by Suzanne Estler, ''Decision Making,'' *Handbook of Research on Educational Administration,* ed. Norman J. Boyan (New York: Longman, 1988), pp. 305–319.

3. Richard Draft, *Organizational Theory and Design* (San Francisco: West, 1986), pp. 348–349. For classic treatment of rational decision making and problem solving, see Charles H. Kepner and Benjamin B. Tregore, *The Rational Manager* (New York: McGraw-Hill, 1976).

4. Max Weber, *The Theory of Social and Economic Organization,* A. M. Henderson and T. Parson, trans, (Oxford University Press, 1947).

5. G. T. Allison, *Essence of Decision: Explaining the Cuban Missile Crisis* (Boston: Little, Brown, 1971); and Karen S. Cook and Margaret Levi (eds.), *The Limit of Rationality* (Chicago, IL: University of Chicago Press, 1990).

6. For example, see Jon Saphier, Tom Bigda-Peyton, and Geoff Pierson, *How to Make Decisions That Stay Made* (Alexandria, VA: Association for Supervision and Curriculum Development, 1989).

7. For example, see Henry Mintzberg, *The Nature of Managerial Work* (New York: Harper and Row, 1973); H. Fraser and M. Anderson, ''Administrative Decision Making and Quasi Decision Making: An Empirical Study Using the Protocol Method,'' **Planning and Changing** (Winter 1983), pp. 204–213; Ray Cross, ''A Description of Decision-Making Patterns of School Principals,'' **Journal of Educational Research** (January/February 1980), pp. 154–159; Paul C. Nutt, ''Types of Organizational Decision Processes,'' **Administrative Science Quarterly** (September 1984), pp. 414–450. For further discussion see J. G. March, ''Emerging Developments in the Study of Organizations,'' **The Review of Higher Education** (1982), pp. 1–18; J. M. Meyer and B. Rowan, ''The Structure of Educational Organizations,'' in J. W. Meyer, ed. *Environments and Organizations* (San Francisco: Jossey-Bass, 1978).

8. A. Wise, ''Why Educational Policies Often Fail: The Hyperrationalization Hypothesis,'' in J. V. Baldridge and T. Deal, eds. *The Dynamics of Organizational Change in Education* (Berkeley, CA: McCutchan, 1983), pp. 9–113.

9. This label was originally coined by C. E. Lindblom, ''The Science of 'Muddling Through,' '' **Public Administration Review** (Spring 1959), pp. 79–88.

10. N. Gross, "The Scientific Approach to Administration," in D. E. Griffiths, ed. *Behavioral Science and Educational Administration. The 63rd Yearbook of the National Society for the Study of Education* (Chicago: University of Chicago Press, 1964), part 2, pp. 33–72.

11. Herbert A. Simon, *Administrative Behavior,* 3rd ed. (New York: Harper and Row, 1976). Simon's original work on this topic was published in the first edition of this book in 1947. James G. March, "Decision Making Perspectives," in *Perspectives on Organizational Behavior,* ed. Andrew H. Van de Ven and William F. Joyce (New York: John Wiley, 1981), pp. 205–245; Rudi K. Bresser and Ronald C. Bishop, "Dysfunctional Effects of Formal Planning: Two Theoretical Explanations," **Academy of Management Review** (October 1983), pp. 588–599; Donald A. Schon, *The Reflective Practitioner: How Professionals Think in Action* (New York: Basic Books, 1984); M. M. Kennedy, "How Evidence Alters Understanding and Decision," **Educational Evaluation and Policy Analysis** (1984), pp. 207–226. Also see Warren J. Pelson et al., *Tough Choices: The Decision-Making Styles of America's Top 50 CEO's* (Homewood, IL: Dow Jones-Irwin, 1989).

12. William A. Firestone and Bruce L. Wilson, "Using Bureaucratic and Cultural Linkages to Improve Instruction: The Principal's Contribution," **Educational Administration Quarterly,** (1985), pp. 7–30.

13. D. L. Duke, B. K. Showers, and M. Imber, "Teachers and Shared Decision Making: The Costs and Benefits of Involvement," **Educational Administration Quarterly** (1980), pp. 93–106; W. K. Hoy and C. G. Miskel, *Educational Administration: Theory, Research and Practice,* 2nd ed. (New York: Random House, 1982); and, Colin Eden and Jim Radford (eds.), *Tackling Strategic Problems: The Role of Group Decision Support* (Newbury Park, CA: Sage, 1990).

14. M. Gittell, *Limits to Citizen Participation: The Decline of Community Organization* (Beverly Hills, CA: Sage, 1980); F. M. Wirt and M. W. Kirst, *Schools In Conflict* (Berkeley, CA: McCutchan, 1982).

15. For a more in-depth discussion pertaining to this point of view in the private sector see Tom Peters, *Thriving on Chaos: Handbook for a Management Revolution* (New York: Knopf, 1987), and Suzanne Estler's article, "Decision Making," cited elsewhere, focussing on educational administration. Both works provide novel insights into alternate views of decision making and perspectives on leadership and administration in modern organizations.

16. Estler, "Decision Making," pp. 311–317.

17. Michael D. Cohen, James G. March, and John A. Olson, "A Garbage Can Model of Organization Choice," **Administrative Science Quarterly** (March 1972), pp. 1–25.

18. Estler, "Decision Making," p. 317.

19. James Lipham and Marvin L. Fruth, *The Principal and Individually Guided Education* (Reading, MA: Addison-Wesley, 1976), p. 2.

20. Paula A. White, "An Overview of School-Based Management: What Does the Research Say," **National Association of Secondary School Administrators Bulletin** (September 1989); Jerry J. Herman, "A Vision for the Future: Site-Based Strategic Planning," **National Association of Secondary School Administrators Bulletin,** (September 1989); Sharon C. Conley, "Who's On First?: School Reform, Teacher Participation, and the Decision Making Process," **Education and Urban Society** (August 1989), pp. 366–379.

21. Daniel F. Griffiths, *Administrative Theory* (New York: Appleton-Century-Crofts, 1959), p. 73.

22. Peter J. Cistone, Joseph A. Fernandez, and Pat L. Tornillo, Jr., "School-Based Management/Shared Decision Making in Dade County (Miami)," **Education and Urban Society** (August 1989), pp. 393–402.

23. W. Jack Duncan, *Great Ideas in Management,* pp. 88–89.

24. Chester Barnard, *The Functions of the Executive* (Cambridge: Harvard University Press, 1938), p. 194.

25. Fraser and Anderson, "Administrative Decision Making."

26. Donovan Peterson and Kathryn Peterson, "Decisiveness—How Important a Quality Is It for School Administrators?" **National Association of Secondary School Administrators Bulletin** (February 1982), pp. 1–9. For more information on decisiveness in decision making, see O. P. Kharbanda and E. A. Stallworthy, "Managerial Decision Making—Part I: Conventional Techniques," **Management Decision,** (1990), pp. 4–9.

27. Further discussion of this process may be found in an excellent article by Roger Volkema, "Problem Formulation in Planning and Design," **Management Science** (June 1983), pp. 639–652. Also, see Sara Kiesler and Lee Sproull, "Management Response to Changing Environments," **Administrative Science Quarterly** (December 1982), pp. 548–570.

28. Charles A. O'Reilly, "Variations in Decision Makers' Use of Information Sources: The Impact of Quality and Accessibility of Information," **Academy of Management Journal** (December 1982), pp. 756–771.

29. Ray Cross, "A Description of Decision Making Patterns of School Principals," Paper presented at the meeting of the American Educational Research Association, New York, February 1971, pp. 14–15.

30. J. Richard Harrison and James G. March, "Decision Making and Postdecision Surprises," **Administrative Science Quarterly** (March 1984), pp. 26–42.

31. Anna Grandori, "A Prescriptive Contingency of Organizational Decision Making," **Administrative Science Quarterly** (June 1984), pp. 192–209. Also, see Amitai Etzioni, "Normative-Affective Factors: Toward a New Decision-Making Model," **Journal of Economic Psychology** (June 1988), pp. 125–150.

32. For further discussion of this process and associated problems, see R. H. Beach, "Multiple Alternatives in Decision Making: Implications for Educational Planning and Administration," **Planning and Changing** (Summer 1984), pp. 106–113.

33. James M. Lipham et al., *The Principalship: Concepts, Competencies, and Cases* (New York: Longman, 1985), pp. 86–87.

34. James R. Meindl, "The Abundance of Solutions: Some Thoughts for Theoretical and Practical Solution Seekers," **Administrative Science Quarterly** (December 1982), pp. 670–685.

35. William J. Kritek, "Lessons from the Literature on Implementation," **Educational Administration Quarterly** (Fall 1976), pp. 86–102; and Michael Maccoby, *Why Work: Leading the New Generation,* (New York: Simon and Schuster, 1988) Chapter 8.

36. Joseph F. Lagana, "Managing Change and School Improvement Effectively," **National Association of School Administrators Bulletin** (September 1989); Marc Willinger, "Risk Aversion and the Value of Information," **The Journal of Risk and Insurance** (June 1989).

37. Alan J. Rowe and Richard O. Mason, *Managing with Style* (San Francisco: Jossey-Bass, 1987).

38. Luther Gulick and L. Urwick, eds., *Papers on the Science of Administration* (New York: Columbia University Institute of Public Administration, 1937), p. 13. Also see L. Urwick, *The Golden Book of Management,* ed. Arthur P. Brief (New York: Garland Publishing, 1987).

39. Kenneth R. Andrews, "Ethics in Practice," **Harvard Business Review** (September–October, 1989).

40. Paul C. Nutt, *Making Tough Decisions* (New York: Jossey–Bass, 1989).

41. John J. Mauriel, *Strategic Leadership for Schools* (San Francisco: Jossey-Bass, 1989); For additional perspectives on strategic planning, see James M. Hardy, *Managing for Impact in Nonprofit Organizations* (Erwin, Tenn: Essex Press, 1984); and Ben Heirs, *The Professional Decision-Thinker* (New York: Dodd, Mead and Company, 1987).

42. Also, see Richard A. Gorton and Gail Thierbach–Schneider, *School Administration and Supervision: Leadership Challenges and Opportunities,* 3rd ed. (Dubuque, IA: Wm. C. Brown Company Publishers, 1991), pp. 102–110 and 323.

43. For example, see John Hemphill et al., *Administrative Performance and Personality* (New York: Teachers College Press, 1962). For an empirical study on connections between personality types and biases, see Usha C. V. Haley and Stephen A. Stumpf, "Cognitive Trails in Strategic Decision-Making: Linking Theories of Personalities and Cognitions," **Journal of Management Studies** (September 1989), pp. 477–497.

44. Richard A. Gorton and Kenneth E. McIntyre, *The Effective Principal* (Reston, VA: National Association of Secondary School Principals, 1978), pp. 26–30, and William J. Ransom, "Are You a Good Decision Maker?," **Industrial Engineering** (August 1990), p. 20.

45. James M. Lipham and James A. Hoeh, Jr., *The Principalship: Foundations and Functions* (New York: Harper and Row, 1974), p. 158.

46. Roy Dexheimer, "The Ethics of Chief School Administrators: A Study in Accommodation." Paper presented at the meeting of the American Association of School Administrators, Atlantic City, February, 1969.

47. Robert Boyden Lamb, *Running American Business* (New York: Basic Books, 1987). The reader is also referred to an excellent review on this subject by Ralph Kimbrough, *Ethics: A Course of Study for Educational Leaders* (Arlington, VA: American Association of School Administrators, 1985) and to statements of ethics for school administrators developed by various national administrator associations. A copy of these may be obtained by writing to any of the national administrator organizations, such as the National Association of Elementary School Principals, 1625 Duke St., Alexandria, Virginia 22314 or the National Association of Secondary School Principals, 1904 Association Dr., Reston, Virginia 22091. For examples of business ethics, see William R. Wynd and John Mager, "The Business and Society Course: Does It Change Student Attitudes?" **Journal of Business Ethics** (June 1989); Barry Castro, "Business Ethics and Business Education: A Report from a Regional State University," **Journal of Business Ethics** (June 1989); Jeffrey Gandz and Frederick G. Bird, "Designing Ethical Organizations," **Business Quarterly** (August 1989). For a guide on ethical considerations in managerial decision making, see Mary E. Guy, *Ethical Decision Making in Everyday Work Situations* (Westport, CA: Greenwood, 1990).

48. A. Lowin, "Participative Decision Making: A Model, Literature Critique, and Prescriptions for Research," **Organizational Behavior and Human Performance** (February 1968), pp. 68–106; and, William R. Kind et al., *Management Science: A Decision-Support Approach* (Reading, MA: Addison-Wesley, 1990).

49. James A. Conway, "The Myth, Mystery, and Mastery of Participative Decision Making in Education," **Educational Administration Quarterly** (Summer 1984), pp. 11–40.

50. John Lindelow et al., "Participative Decision Making," in *School Leadership: Handbook for Survival,* ed. Stuart C. Smith, et al. (Eugene, OR: Clearinghouse on Educational Management, 1981), pp. 153–155. Also, see Ronald L. Cohen, "Procedural Justice and Participation," **Human Relations** (July 1985), pp. 643–663; and James M. Kouzes and Barry Z. Posner, *The Leadership Challenge: How to Get Extraordinary Things Done in Organizations* (San Francisco: Jossey-Bass, 1987), pp. 161–185.

51. D. L. Duke et al., "Teachers and Shared Decision Making: The Costs and Benefits of Involvement," **Educational Administration Quarterly** (Winter 1980), pp. 93–106.

52. C. J. Lammers, "Power and Participation in Decision Making in Formal Organizations," **American Journal of Sociology** (September 1967), pp. 201–216. Also, see Fred C. Lunenburg and Allan C. Orstein, *Educational Administration* (Belmont, CA: Wadworth, 1991), pp. 174–176.

53. D. McGregor, *The Human Side of Enterprise* (New York: McGraw–Hill, 1960).

54. Ibid., pp. 33–34.

55. Ibid., pp. 47–48.

56. F. C. Tunde Palmer, "The Relationship between Dogmatism, Autonomy, Administrative Style, and Decision Making of Practicing and Aspiring School Principals," Ph.D. Dissertation, University of Toronto, 1974, p. 177.

57. Ibid.

58. Edwin M. Bridges, "A Model for Shared Decision Making in the School Principalship," **Educational Administration Quarterly** (Winter 1967), pp. 49–61. For some additional guidelines for involving others in decision making, see Victor A. Vroom, "A New Look at Managerial Decision Making," **Organizational Dynamics** (Spring 1973), p. 67.

59. J. A. Belasco and J. A. Alluto, "Decision Participation and Teacher Satisfaction," **Educational Administration Quarterly** (Winter 1972), pp. 44–58; and Andrew E. Schwartz and Joy Levin, "Better Group Decision Making," **Supervisory Management** (June 1990), p. 4.

60. Gail Thierbach-Schneider, "Teacher Involvement in Decision Making: Zones of Acceptance, Decision Conditions, and Job Satisfaction," **Journal of Research and Development in Education** (Fall 1984), pp. 25–32.

61. Belasco and Alluto, "Decision Participation."

62. S. R. Hinckley, Jr., "A Closer Look at Participation," **Organizational Dynamics** (Winter 1985), pp. 57–67.

63. Bridges, "Shared Decision Making," p. 52.

64. Richard A. Gorton, "Factors Which are Associated with the Principal's Behavior in Encouraging Teacher Participation in School Decision Making," **Journal of Educational Research** (March 1971), pp. 325–327.

65. For keeping up-to-date on developments with this approach, see the **Quality Circle Journal,** found in many university libraries.

66. David Hawley,"The Quality Circle Concept," **Principal** (November 1985), pp. 41–43.

67. Frank Satterfield, *Managing Quality Circles Effectively,* an ERIC report, Ed. 238–117.

68. S. A. Zahra et al., "Quality Circles for School Districts," **The Educational Forum** (Spring 1985), pp. 323–330.

69. Robert H. Black, Larry K. Michaelsen, and Warren E. Watson, "A Realistic Test of Individual Versus Group Consensus Decision Making," **Journal of Applied Psychology** (October 1989).

70. D. E. Halverson, *An Effective Time and Management Strategy in Quality Circles,* an ERIC report, Ed. 238–113.

71. Mary Bacon, *Team Building in Quality Circles,* an ERIC report, Ed. 238–118.

72. Kenneth H. Price, "Problem Solving Strategies: A Comparison by Solving Phases," **Group and Organizational Studies** (September 1985), pp. 278–299.

73. Richard Gorton is indebted to the authors of the following publication for their ideas on the Delphi Technique and the Nominal Group Techniques: Andre L. Delberg, Andrew H. Van de Ven, and David H. Gustafson, *Group Techniques for Program Planning: A Guide to Nominal Group and Delphi Processes* (Middleton, WI: Greenbriar, 1986).

74. For research on its effectiveness, see Robert E. Erffmeyer and Irving M. Lane, "Quality and Acceptance of an Evaluative Task: The Effects of Four Group Decision Making Formats," **Group and Organizational Studies** (December 1984), pp. 509–529.

75. Jean M. Bartunsk and J. Kenneth Murningham, "The Nominal Group Technique," **Group and Organizational Studies** (September 1984), pp. 417–432.

76. For further discussion of additional ways of involving others in decision making, see I. Adizes and E. Turban, "An Innovative Approach to Group Decision Making," **Personnel** (April 1985), pp. 45–59; and Richard A. Schmuck and Philip J. Runkel, *The Handbook of Organizational Development in Schools* 3rd ed. (Prospect Heights, IL: Waveland Publishing, 1988), pp. 240–292.

77. Beverly Geber, "Decisions, Decisions," **Training** (April 1988).

78. For a more detailed discussion of the technique of decision analysis, see David C. Dougherty, *Strategic Organization Planning: Downsizing for Survival* (New York: Quorum Books, 1989); Geoffrey Gregory, *Decision Analysis* (New York: Plenum Press, 1988); and Richard M. Oliver and John A. Smith (eds.), *Influence Diagrams, Belief Nets, and Decision Analysis* (New York: Wiley, 1990).

79. Stuart L. Hart, "Toward Quality Criteria for Collective Judgments," **Organizational Behavior and Human Decision Processes** (October 1985), pp. 209–228; and, Wayne K. Hoy and Cecil G. Miskel, *Educational Administration: Theory, Research and Practice,* 4th ed. (New York: McGraw-Hill, 1991).

2 Communication

The importance of effective communication practices within an organization cannot be overemphasized. For example, Lysaught believes, "More frequently than not, failures in communication lie at the heart of problems in organization, goal setting, productivity and evaluation."[1] As a result, according to St. John, ". . . No one can manage a modern organization who is not knowledgeable in communication principles and techniques and skilled in their use."[2] Guarino has underscored this point by noting that, "In the area of leadership there is no talent more essential than one's ability to communicate."[3]

Without exception, all of the major national school administrator associations in this country stress the importance of effective communication skills. The National Association of Elementary School Principals for example, identifies communication as one of the leadership proficiencies for elementary and middle school principals, stating, "Of the various proficiencies that make outstanding K–8 principals, few are more important than the ability to communicate effectively."[4] Thus, for any individual to be successful as an administrator or leader, that person must develop effective skills in communication.

COMMUNICATION: THE ADMINISTRATOR'S ROLES

Many school administrators, when they are asked about the importance of communication, tend to see themselves primarily in the role of *communicator* of messages that others need to understand. For example, in a study by Morris and his colleagues, using ethnographic methods, principals were observed spending a great deal of time communicating with students, teachers, parents, superiors, and other individuals associated with the school.[5] Although most of this communication was initiated by the principal, there was no clear indication that the principals in the study had thoughtfully planned their communication or were in control of how much time they spent communicating with various people. Instead, judging from the examples presented in a report of the study, much of the principals' communication seemed unplanned and casual; little effort appeared to have been made by the principals to seek feedback from others or to evaluate what others were telling them.[6] That this problem is not limited to school administrators but is also characteristic of other kinds of managers has been made clear in a study by Luthans and Larsen.[7]

Although it is acknowledged that not all administrator communication can be planned and that it may not always be possible for an administrator to be in control of how much time is spent communicating with different individuals and groups, it would appear that many, if not most, administrators need to improve their communication practices and to adopt additional communication roles.[8] While the administrator as *communicator* is an important role, it is only one of the many communication roles that are essential to the efficient and effective administration of an organization. School administrators also frequently find themselves in the role of *recipient* of messages from others. If the communication to, from, and within an organization is to be efficient and effective, then a school administrator will need to become a *monitor* and *seeker* of communication. In the following sections the different facets of these four communication roles—communicator, recipient, monitor, and seeker—will be discussed, as will factors associated with their effectiveness.

THE ADMINISTRATOR AS A COMMUNICATOR

The school administrator, be it a superintendent, principal, or some other type of administrator, occupies a key position in the organizational hierarchy. In that position, there is a need to communicate with a wide variety of people in a number of different ways about specific situations, problems, or issues. As a communicator, an administrator needs to be aware of six basic aspects of communication:[9]

1. The purpose to be achieved by the message.
2. The person(s) to whom the message is directed.
3. The sender of the message.
4. The content of the message.
5. The alternative channels for communicating the message.
6. The need for feedback or a response to the message.

The Purpose of the Message

The initial task for the administrator who wishes to communicate a message to a particular individual or group is to think carefully about the objectives the communication is to achieve. Is the purpose of the message to inform, to raise questions, to change attitudes, to stimulate action, to inhibit action, to reassure, to solidify support, to clarify, or to achieve some other goal? The administrator may possess a general idea of what the communication is to accomplish, but more time must be spent identifying the specific nature of the objectives the administrator hopes to achieve. As a result of sharpening the focus of the communication goals, the administrator will be in a better position to determine the content of a message and the communication channel to be utilized.

After the specific objectives of the message have been identified and clarified, the administrator should evaluate whether those objectives are attainable. The essential question is whether the goals are reasonable, considering the circumstances. For example, the administrator who has decided to reject a set of demands posed by a militant parent organization may wish to inform the parents about the decision and, at the same time, to dissuade them from taking further action. While the administrator would naturally like to accomplish both goals, is it reasonable to assume that any composed message will effectively do so? The first objective, that of informing the militant parents of the decision, may be achieved without difficulty, but the objective of convincing them that they should take no further action may not be attainable, considering the circumstances. This is not to say that an administrator should restrict communication goals to only those which can be easily achieved. It is suggested, however, that every administrator examine the feasibility of the communication objectives rather than assuming that they will be achieved without difficulty. Such an examination should be conducted after the objectives have been identified—and again after the message has been formulated.

The Recipients of the Message

Every message from the administrator will be interpreted in light of the conditions in which it is received and the characteristics of those who receive it. Depending on the nature of both factors, a message may or may not be successfully communicated. Barriers to effective communication that may be associated with the recipients of the message or the situation in which it is received include:[10]

1. *Lack of Interest.* The administrator may believe that the message planned to be sent is extremely important and that the persons receiving the message should share that attitude. However, the recipients' interest in the contents of the message will depend on their prior attitude toward the sender, the content, and the implications of the message.
2. *Lack of Knowledge.* All communications contain particular words and ideas, requiring a certain background or degree of knowledge. For example, will the parents who receive a message on "alternative programming" fully and accurately understand what is meant by that term? In the absence of that necessary background or knowledge, the recipients may fail to grasp what the administrator is trying to communicate.
3. *The Bias of the Recipients.* The administrator needs to recognize that the content of the message will be filtered through the perceptual value screen of the recipients. Certain words in the message may be misinterpreted, or the purpose of the message may be distorted. Research has shown that people tend to seek messages which are consistent with their own attitudes and values, and that they try to avoid messages which are disconcerting.[11] Although avoidance or misinterpretation of a message cannot always be completely eliminated, the administrator should carefully consider the characteristics of the recipients and the nature of the message in order to reduce the possibilities of being misunderstood.
4. *Social Barriers.* Differences in age, sex, position in the hierarchy, and subculture among the recipients or between them and the sender may pose a communication barrier.[12] For example, a message may be interpreted differently by physical education teachers and social studies teachers; women teachers and men teachers; and new teachers and more experienced ones. Any of these social differences may, in a given set of circumstances, pose a communication problem for the administrator.
5. *The Situation Itself.* Distractions, insufficient time to read the message carefully, and overload of the communication channel through which the message is received are all factors which in a specific situation can pose barriers to effective communication. In many circumstances there is little that the administrator can do to overcome these barriers completely. However, an attempt should be made to take into consideration as much as possible the conditions in which the message will be received.

To minimize the effects of the barriers identified previously, the administrator needs to think about the characteristics of the recipients of the message and the nature of the situation in which it will be received. For example, the following questions may need to be asked, "What kinds of individuals or groups will be receiving the communication? What is their background or knowledge in relation to the topic or idea being communicated? What is their present interest in and attitude toward the topic or the idea being expressed? What is their attitude toward *me* as a communicator of the idea? What characteristics of the *situation* in which the message is being received may prevent or reduce the possibility that the message will be correctly understood and acted upon by the recipients? What characteristics of the individual or groups may cause the message to be misinterpreted or distorted?"

Since the answers to all of these questions may not be readily accessible, it is essential that the administrator make the effort to secure them. This will not be easy. However, success as a communicator will depend in large part on the administrator's knowledge of the situation, the audience for whom the message is intended, and the extent to which that knowledge is taken into consideration in all aspects of the communication process.

The Sender of the Message

In no small measure, an administrator's success as a communicator also depends on the degree of trust that exists between the administrator and the recipients of the message, the prestige of the administrator's position in the organization or community, and the extent to which the individual is perceived as an expert by those who receive the message.[13]

Mutual trust between the communicator and the recipients of the message is very important for effective communication. According to McGregor, trust is the belief that one party will not take an unfair advantage of the other.[14] If an administrator does not trust the recipients of the communication, then this could affect either how the message is framed or how it is delivered. If the recipients of the administrator's message are distrustful, then they are unlikely to believe the message. Mutual trust is a prerequisite to effective communication.

Also important to effective communication is the status of the administrator in the organization or the community.[15] If the administrator is not perceived as being very influential in the organizational hierarchy or as possessing requisite competency in the area in which communication is attempted, it is probable that there will be difficulty in getting others to pay attention to the messages. Certainly, the likelihood that the recipients of a message will change their attitude or behavior on the basis of communication will depend greatly on their perception of the administrator's status in the organization and the recipients' evaluation of that person's expert knowledge in the area under consideration.

However, in addition to these factors, it is important that administrators know and understand themselves as communicators. The administrator might ask, "Am I better at communicating in a one-to-one relationship, or in a group setting? Am I better at communicating verbally or in writing?" (Administrators who would like to improve their ability to give effective speeches and presentations will find suggestions by Ehninger, Murray,[16] and Sigband and Bateman[17] helpful.) The particular circumstances and the objectives an administrator wants to achieve will largely determine the choice of expression. For example, an administrator who wants to establish a secure, mentoring, nurturing climate in the school must know how to communicate successfully with the staff to reach that goal. Staff members use various communication indicators to judge the security of the school climate. Both the actions and the attitude the principal communicates in dealing with the staff will be interpreted as indicators of a secure or insecure climate. Nonverbal communication is as powerful as verbal communication. When nonverbal messages are used without thought and purpose, opportunities to motivate, encourage, and support desired actions may be lost. The resulting negative reaction from the staff may seriously impair the administrator from reaching mutual goals and prevent successful teaching performance.

Knoll suggests that the following communicating behaviors foster a secure climate and subsequently encourage staff performance:

1. Be honest by making open statements about your feelings, attitudes, and reactions to situations.
2. Be tactful and sensitive to staff needs, feelings, and problems, and treat people in a nonthreatening manner.
3. Accept people as they are by respecting individual staff differences, opinions, perceptions, and approaches.
4. Have a positive approach when you greet people, smile at them, and inquire about their health, problems, and joys.

5. Finally, be dependable so that you are trusted by the staff.[18]

There is also the need to analyze and understand personal strengths and weaknesses as a communicator. There are many situations where the administrator will have the opportunity to make a choice regarding the medium for the message. That decision should be based at least in part on an assessment of the administrator's performance as an individual communicator as well as on an evaluation of the effectiveness of the school's communication system and programs.[19]

The Content of the Message

Ideally, all communications from the administrator should be framed and constructed carefully and thoughtfully, although it is recognized that much communication between an administrator and others is spontaneous and casual.[20] Nevertheless, in those situations when the consequences of the verbal or written communication could be significant, the administrator should choose and organize all words with special care. The administrator will want people to regard these messages seriously, for, in many instances, the words will be closely scrutinized and weighed. The administrator should consider the audience for whom they are intended, the specific objectives desired, and the nature of the particular communication channel (e.g., written, verbal) which will be utilized.

For example, the principal who is trying to persuade teachers of the desirability of introducing a particular innovation should select those ideas, facts, or questions that will be most persuasive to the teachers. In constructing the message, the administrator will want to take into consideration the teachers' current attitude towards the innovation, their present knowledge and understanding of the proposed change, their attitude toward the principal as the communicator, and the extent to which the communication medium chosen may limit or facilitate understanding the content of the message.

In order to achieve maximum effectiveness in communicating, the administrator should also critically examine the assumptions made in selecting and organizing the content of the message. Some of the questions that may need to be asked when constructing the message are, "Is the idea clear? Will the words chosen to express the idea achieve the desired goal? How will the receiver perceive the message? Which characteristics of the ideas or words used will be likely to have the intended effect upon the receiver? Which ideas or words could potentially affect the receiver in ways that are not intended? What assumptions am I making?" (For some excellent guidelines on issuing directives and other kinds of messages to subordinates, see St. John and Himstreet and Baty.[21])

Research on communication would indicate that in constructing the content of the messages, particularly those intended to persuade another individual or group, the administrator should (1) concentrate on arousing desire and concern before suggesting appropriate action; (2) place highly desirable communication to the recipients first, followed by less desirable information; (3) acknowledge opposing arguments before presenting a different line of reasoning, unless the recipients are not aware of contrasting arguments to the course of action being recommended (in which case the administrator can proceed with the position on the issue or problem without mentioning the other side); and (4) recognize that fact alone will not change the opinion or attitude of an individual or group whose emotional predisposition runs contrary to the information being presented.[22]

Communication Channels

In communicating a prepared message, in contrast to a spontaneous response, the administrator can

Figure 2.1 Communication Channels.

Communication Channels

Writing	Oral Face-to-Face	Oral Electronic/Visual
• Note	• Individual Conference	• Telephone
• Letter	• Small Group Meetings	• P.A. System
• Memorandum	• Large Group Meetings	• Overhead Projector and Slide Projector
• Community Newspaper	• Social Functions	• Radio
• School Bulletin		• Television
		• Videotapes
		• Electronic Mailboxes

give considerable attention to the communication channels that are available and decide which one would most effectively communicate the message. All too frequently, however, administrators appear to think of only one or two means for communicating their messages. This is unfortunate, since studies such as McCleary's have identified a wide array of possibilities for communication.[23] Figure 2.1 presents a number of these possibilities.

As Figure 2.1 suggests, a wide variety of different kinds of communication channels should be considered. After an administrator has determined which of the communication channels are available in each situation, the best possible means of communicating the message should be reflected. Although this step may appear obvious, administrators too often fail to analyze the strengths and weaknesses of the various communication media available to them. Instead, they habitually write a memo, speak over the public address system, or prepare a staff bulletin instead of carefully and realistically assessing the communication channels which might best serve the needs of each situation. One such alternate approach might be the use of a computer controlled voice message system which could ease communication difficulties between parents and schools, teachers, administrators, and staff. Using a computer, a principal can leave messages on the telephone for as many parents and staff as need to be contacted via this electronic mailbox.[24]

The selection of the appropriate channel of communication should be largely determined by the *content* of the message, the *audience* for whom it is intended, the administrator's *objectives,* and one's *personal strengths and weaknesses as a communicator*. By taking these factors into consideration, an administrator can expect to make more effective decisions in regard to the best medium for conveying a particular message.

When communicating with the public, personal contact is probably most effective; however, the best way to reach a large number of people in a short time is through the media, be it print or broadcast. Newspaper or television coverage gives administrators an opportunity to communicate their story to a large group, although the form that story takes is beyond their control. The right of the press to cover news, and the public's right to know it, will frequently dictate the reporting of newsworthy events in schools—both good and bad. Consequently, the school administrator must work with the media to ensure that the communications to the public are as fair and as accurate as possible. A collegial relationship between the reporter and the administrator, based on trust and mutual respect and understanding, can be developed by providing the press with a steady flow of information and frequent communications, not just at budget time. Honesty, credibility, and respect for reporters' deadlines also contribute to a good working relationship. A principal should get to know reporters personally, understanding that friendships will never prevent the reporting of unfavorable news, since reporters are paid to cover the news. When the inevitable mistakes do occur in the coverage, the school administrator should make it a practice never to take negative reports or mistakes personally.[25]

In becoming aware of different kinds of communication channels, administrators need to recognize that, in a sense, they also represent one type of communication channel. Whether they realize it or not, administrators communicate to people *nonverbally* through facial expressions, gestures, dress, tone of voice, and the physical environment in which they communicate.[26] Through these nonverbal means they can and do (frequently inadvertently) communicate surprise, fear, anger, disgust, disappointment, sadness, happiness, and other kinds of emotions and reactions.

As long as the message communicated through nonverbal means coincides with the message they are communicating in other ways, there is no problem and, in fact, the nonverbal methods can be helpful. However, when the verbal and the nonverbal messages contradict each other, problems can definitely result.[27] For example, if an administrator speaking to a parent is asking for cooperation, while inadvertently conveying dislike through facial expression or tone of voice, then there exists a very real possibility of communicating contradictory messages.

It is not always possible, of course, to be aware of how one is communicating nonverbally, or to control one's nonverbal messages. However, an administrator should make an effort to develop a better understanding of this subtle channel of communication and to be aware of the possibility that an inconsistency between verbal and nonverbal messages could explain certain problems in communication.

The Need for Feedback

Communication should not be regarded as effective just because an administrator sends a message. In order for communication to be effective, it needs to be understood and acted upon in the manner intended by the communicator. To ascertain whether communication is effective, the administrator needs to seek feedback on reactions or responses to the message by those who received it. Without such feedback, the administrator may incorrectly assume that the communication has achieved the desired objective and may be unaware of any problem that has occurred as a result of the communication.

No administrator can afford to wait passively for a response to the communication. As will be discussed later, people don't always voluntarily tell administrators what they think. Therefore, an administrator must personally take the initiative to obtain feedback on the nature of the response to the communication if the intent is to secure an adequate basis for judging the effectiveness of the communication and the need for modifying the message. Specific suggestions for obtaining feedback will be presented in the section, *The Administrator as a Seeker of Communication.*

THE ADMINISTRATOR AS A RECIPIENT OF COMMUNICATION

Thus far, the emphasis has been placed on the administrator's role as a communicator. However, in many cases the administrator is also a recipient of communication. Because administrators occupy an important position in the school organization, they will receive various kinds of written and verbal messages from students, teachers, parents, and other individuals with whom they come into contact.[28] These messages need to be evaluated by the administrator as to their *relevance, substance, significance,* and *implications.* The importance of evaluating communication from subordinates to superiors is underscored by findings from several research studies. For example, a laboratory experiment by Kelly found that low status participants were typically uncritical in their communications to higher status participants and frequently communicated more irrelevant messages than did the high status participants.[29] Kelly's findings were supported by Hurwitz, who discovered in a study of communications between various professional participants that lower status professionals talked less and were less often critical of higher status professionals.[30] And more recent studies confirm this type of communication.[31]

These studies suggest that, due to the administrator's status, subordinates will send few messages that are critical, while, on the other hand, send a number of messages which are laudatory in nature, particularly from those subordinates who are aiming to advance their personal interests. The implication which may be drawn is that the administrator may find it difficult to obtain accurate information from subordinates about proposed or actions already taken. This poses a significant problem for administrators, since they are always in need of valid information. While there is probably no perfect solution to this difficulty, the administrator interested in obtaining complete and honest feedback from subordinates will encourage them to "speak their minds," will avoid reacting negatively to those who do so, even if the message is critical in nature, and will recognize that even under the best circumstances the communication received from subordinates may be less than completely candid.

As a recipient of communication, both verbal and written, the administrator should examine all messages by mentally raising the following questions:

1. Why is the message being sent? What is its purpose, either stated or implied? What does the sender hope to accomplish?
2. What is the factual basis for the message? Which statements in the communication rest on fact, which are based on opinion, and which rely on assumption?
3. What necessary information is not included in the message?
   What questions does the message fail to answer? What additional questions does it raise?
4. What does the message tell the administrator about the sender? What does it reveal about the sender's expectations for the role of the administrator? What does the communication suggest about the sender's perception of or relationship with other people, in or outside the organization?

The messages that an administrator receives will contain facts, perceptions, opinions, and assumptions. In many, if not most instances, a message will contain few confirmed statements of fact, although it should be noted that the observations or opinions offered in a message may be perceived as factual by the sender.[32] While this perception needs to be taken into consideration in responding to a message, the initial task for the administrator is to analyze the communication received, with regard to which aspects of the message appear to be factual and which parts of the content will need to be validated.

In addition, the administrator will want to examine a message for its purpose and the extent to which it provides insight into the sender's personality and the expectations for the behavior of the administrator. All messages are sent for a purpose and are based on an expectation that the administrator will respond in a particular way. It needs to be recognized, however, that the purpose of a message or the sender's expectations and real feelings on a matter may not be stated explicitly.[33] Therefore, the administrator needs to examine each message carefully, trying to "read between the lines" for clues which will offer better information about the true purpose behind the message and the actual behavior expected.

Perhaps one of the most important roles an administrator can play as a recipient of communication is that of listener. In an early study Rankin found that the communication day of an administrator was divided into the following activities: writing—9%, speaking—16%, reading—30%, and listening—45%. This study has often been replicated and shows that listening is the most frequent communication activity, making up almost half of the efforts spent in communication.[34] Much of the communication that administrators receive is verbal, and empathetic, accurate listening is necessary for a valid understanding of what is being communicated.

If an administrator is not a good listener, the very real possibility exists of not fully understanding what is being said. Or, even more seriously, people will avoid expressing themselves because of the administrator's reputation as a "poor listener" or someone who "doesn't care." A recent study found that most people value co-workers and employers who are skilled listeners and who show their interest in others by their focused and genuine empathy.[35] And, while most administrators would probably like to believe that they are good listeners, reports from teachers suggest just the opposite.[36] Actually, most people are probably *not* good listeners and tend, all too frequently, rather than listening, to be waiting for the other party to finish talking so their own views can be expressed. One easy way to demonstrate this phenomenon is for a third party to ask the recipient of a verbal communication to summarize the communicator's message to the latter's satisfaction.

Effective listening is a skill which is not inherited or automatically acquired. It is a skill which must be developed and cultivated. In part, it involves an attitude that indicates the administrator is *interested in* and *cares about* what the other party has to communicate.[37] It is an attitude which cannot be easily fabricated without self-betrayal, and, to be effective, it must be sincerely felt and communicated nonverbally, as well as verbally. Newton recently wrote that people relate to us in large part because of our relative effectiveness in communication, and any person who desires to become a better listener must first have a change in attitude. A person must become more resolved to learn from others and to acknowledge that everyone has something to teach us.[38]

Effective listening also involves avoiding some bad habits and developing good ones, as indicated in Figure 2.2.[39]

Listening is a skill which must be practiced and continually refined. The administrator who is interested in further developing this skill should examine writings on the subject including Nostrand and Shelley's Educational Leadership Listening Model.[40]

THE ADMINISTRATOR AS A MONITOR OF COMMUNICATION

It should be obvious that the school administrator is not the only one in the organization who is sending and receiving communications. For example, within a school, students, teachers, support staff, secretaries, and custodians are all communicating to various people and with one another. Staff communications can set the tone and goals of a school. A positive or negative verbal environment is often reflected in the communication skills teachers and administrators choose to use, be they in the elementary, middle, or high school.

A positive verbal environment can make children or youth feel good about themselves and see the school as a positive influence in their lives. Adults using words to show affection for children and demonstrating a sincere concern for them by using children's interests as a basis for conversation convey a positive message. Teachers or administrators paying superficial attention to what

Figure 2.2 Listening Habits and Recommended Behaviors.

Listening Habits and Recommended Behaviors

To Be Avoided	To Be Developed
Faking attention (pretending to listen) Listening for facts without considering the broader meaning Concentrating on physical appearance and delivery at the expense of verbal content Yielding to distractions Dismissing content as uninteresting Ceasing to listen because the content is difficult to comprehend	Screening out extraneous distractions Concentrating mentally *and* physically on what the other person is saying "Listening with a third ear"—being sensitive to what the person *seems* to be saying . . . or *not* saying Asking questions to draw the other person out and to clarify ideas Responding to the other person nonjudgmentally Summarizing periodically what you think the other person has been saying, and obtaining his reaction to whether or not you accurately heard him.

Recommended Responses	Examples
Showing Attention:	"Yes." "Ah, ah." "I understand." Periodic, slight nodding of the head.
Seeking More Information:	"That's interesting. Could you tell me more about that?"
Seeking Clarification:	"I'm not sure I fully understand. Could you elaborate or give me an example?"
Paraphrasing:	"You seem to be saying . . . Is that correct?"
Reflecting Emotion:	"You seem upset with me. Is this the way you feel?"
Summarizing:	"Let me try to identify the main points you seem to have made, and you let me know if I have missed anything."

children have to say, adults speaking discourteously, and staff members actively discouraging students from talking to them create a negative, verbal communication environment. The administrator must provide a high level of strong leadership in monitoring the communication climate for learning.[41]

In addition, within a school district, communications pass from the people in the district office to the individual schools, and vice versa. There is also the environment external to a school or school district, where special interest groups, parents, community leaders, and others communicate about and to the school and receive messages from those associated with the school or school district. Complex? Indeed! But it is in the best interest of the school administrator to try to monitor (to the extent feasible) the communication networks, both formal and informal,[42] that operate in the organization and community, and to ascertain message distortions of one kind or another. There are numerous examples of these message distortions that we will describe next.

Monitoring communications means that a school administrator should attempt to stay informed about who is communicating with whom and about what, in regard to the school or school district. It will, of course, be impossible for an administrator to always know *all* the different messages that are being sent to, from, and within the school organization. However, by identifying and then establishing open lines of communication with certain key individuals and groups designated as *key communicators,* an administrator should be able to monitor the most important messages emanating from and being sent to the school. The *key communicator* concept has typically been applied to the school's community setting,[43] but in discussing the administrator's role as a monitor of communication, its application is expanded to communication that occurs within the school organization as well.

One of the key communicator groups consists of the school secretaries, especially those who are in a position either to implement a school administrator's directives or to send and receive messages from others in the school organization and community. For example, a principal may have informed the faculty of an "open door" policy and that the principal is always receptive to hearing about teachers' problems and concerns. Despite all good intentions, if the principal's secretary is sending a different message to the teachers, either through nonverbal mannerisms or by overzealous behavior, for example, "The principal can't see you now; The principal is too busy!" then the objectives of the principal's open door policy are unlikely to be achieved.

School secretaries are also key communicators regarding the messages they send to and transmit from parents and the general public. Telephone messages transcribed inaccurately or improperly passed along and the general demeanor of the secretaries in answering school telephones or greeting the public who visit the school are potential problem areas.

An initial question for the school administrator to answer is, "Are the school secretaries sending and transmitting accurate and helpful messages to the people within the school and to those persons who contact the school?" This will not be an easy question to answer. Nevertheless, by getting out of the office frequently, maintaining a high degree of visibility and accessibility, and actively seeking the perceptions of people who have had contact with the school secretaries, an administrator should be able to monitor the communication behavior of these key communicators. If problems are discovered, the school administrator can then attempt to assist the particular individuals who need improvement or, if the problem is widespread, can provide inservice education for all of the secretaries.

Another key group of communicators is represented by department chairpersons or unit leaders in a school. These individuals play what Likert refers to as a "link-pin" role in the school's organizational structure, in that one of the responsibilities of their positions is to transmit messages from the school principal to the teachers in a department or unit, and vice versa.[44] In their role as transmitters, the department chairpersons or unit leaders may be communicating accurately and completely the intent and content of messages from the principal to teachers in their department or unit. Or some of them may be misinterpreting, garbling, omitting essential details, or failing to pass on certain, or many aspects, of the principal's messages. And, of course, the same kinds of problems could be occurring in regard to messages that teachers try to send to the principal through the department chairperson or unit leader. This type of miscommunication may or may not be intentional, but if it occurs, it can negatively influence the operational efficiency and goal achievement of an organization.

To determine whether communication problems are occurring within this group of key communicators, the school administrator should formally and informally survey the teachers in the school to ascertain whether the principal's messages are reaching the teachers as intended, and whether the teachers' messages for the principal are solicited by the department heads and are properly forwarded. Obviously, surveys need to be conducted carefully in order to avoid upsetting the department chairpersons or unit leaders. However, the administrator should recognize that one cannot just *assume* that those communicators are doing their job; some type of periodic assessment will be needed. (For an example of a survey that could be adapted to this purpose, see Davis.[45])

A third group of key communicators is formed by those individuals in the community who are leaders of organizations such as the P.T.A., or special interest groups such as the Junior Chamber of Commerce. According to Kindred and his associates, key communicators need not always be leaders of an organization but can be ". . . barbers, beauticians, bartenders, owners of restaurants, gas station operators, doctors, dentists, letter carriers, or people to whom citizens turn and ask, 'What do you think about . . .' "[46] The latter group would certainly include individuals who engage in informal discussions at the supermarket or local coffee shop, as well as reporters, who are definitely key communicators in a more formal sense.

The first task for a school administrator who wishes to monitor the communications of the key communicators in the community served by the school or school district is to ascertain their identity. The kinds of persons who might be key communicators in one locality may not be influential in a different community. However, the leaders of organizations whose primary purpose is to improve education, such as the P.T.A., or organizations that have a subcommittee devoted to education are likely to be key communicators in any school community. (For more information on this aspect, see Gorton and Thierbach-Schneider.[47]) These are the individuals with whom the administrator should establish open lines of communication. Frequent and informed contact must be maintained, particularly as to whether these key communicators are receiving and sending accurate information about the school or school district.

The other types of key communicators referred to by Kindred—for instance, beauticians—will be more difficult to identify because their communication status and the relevance of their communications about the school may not be obvious. However, if an administrator lives in the community, over time some insight into who these key communicators are can be developed. In addition, an administrator can try to tap the knowledge of those faculty and staff members who live in the school locality as to the identity of key communicators. Once these key communicators have been identified, it is important for the school administrator to develop and maintain open lines of communication with them. It is typically these kinds of key communicators who tend to hear the rumors and gossip about the school. They can be useful in alerting an administrator to this type of communication.

Monitoring the communication occurring within, to, and from an organization will require an alert, energetic, perceptive administrator. It will also require an administrator who is an active *seeker* of communication, a topic which will be addressed in the next section.

THE ADMINISTRATOR AS A SEEKER OF COMMUNICATION

No administrator can afford to limit communication behavior to merely sending, monitoring, and receiving messages. An administrator must also *actively seek* facts, perceptions, and ideas from other people.

Administrators who assume that they will be supplied with all the information needed in order to make a decision, or that all the communications transmitted will be accurate, valid, and complete, are not thinking realistically. Important information may sometimes be withheld because it is thought by others to be of little interest to the administrator or because of fear that the nature of the message might adversely affect their rapport. In order to overcome these barriers to communication, an administrator must make continuous and persistent efforts to learn the attitudes and opinions of co-workers.

For example, after the administrator has initiated messages to others, an attempt must be made to obtain accurate and complete feedback from them on their perceptions of what the intent of the communication *to them* was. It is not enough to merely express decisions, wishes, feelings, instructions, evaluations, or directives for action. The administrator must also ascertain whether the messages have been correctly understood.

In addition, the administrator needs to inquire whether the communications have produced the desired effects. As an illustration, the teachers in a particular situation may have *understood* what the administrator was saying over the public address system, in a memo, or during the faculty meeting, but the crucial question is, "Did the message produce the desired results?" If the answer is negative, the administrator has not necessarily failed to express the message clearly, but obviously the message was not completely successful. As a seeker of communication, the administrator needs to obtain feedback on two dimensions of any message: (1) Was it correctly understood? and (2) Did it produce the desired effect?

The administrator also needs to encourage accurate and full communication throughout the school organization. There is evidence that, in many organizations, communication, particularly formal communication, flows from superior to subordinate; there is frequently little upward or lateral communication.[48] The task for the administrator is to convey to all individuals and groups the need for upward and lateral communication and to develop feasible methods for transmitting this kind of communication. Schmuck and Runkel present several examples of such methods.[49]

In addition, the administrator will need to create a feeling and atmosphere of trust and respect on the part of the people in order to encourage them to communicate more. Unless people feel secure in communicating certain information and feel that what they are communicating will be taken seriously, they are not likely to increase their communication.[50] A principal may need to check out the employee perceptions of the communication climate within the school and determine staff perceptions of the communication relationship between the principal and staff, as well as how these are related to the overall communications climate in the school. A communication audit survey designed to measure perceptions about communication sources, messages, channels, and receivers could be administered to obtain quantitative information. Focus group sessions with all staff could provide extremely useful qualitative information on communication patterns, outcomes, relationships, and content within the school. Results may indicate that a school might improve its communications climate by increasing the amount and frequency of internal communication at all levels or that the communication relationship most in need of attention involves the principal. In order to enhance organizational effectiveness, the principal may discover from such a survey that there is a need to develop strategies that will build personal and organizational trust and that all department heads should meet collectively and individually to develop strategies and techniques needed to improve the school's climate.[51]

If an administrator is to secure the desired kind of feedback in order to perform all aspects of the job effectively, all sources of information will have to be expanded. Many administrator's sources of information are limited, either because of their position in the organizational hierarchy or because of other people's perception of their availability or receptivity to communication. Although an "open door policy" is often proclaimed by administrators, these administrators should realize that the door may not be perceived by everyone as truly open, especially to those with a disturbing or disagreeable message. Consequently, an administrator's contacts may be restricted to only certain kinds of individuals bearing information that is regarded as nonthreatening.

Administrators, therefore, must be careful to avoid the situation of receiving their information, recommendations, evaluations, and reactions from a select group of people who tend to see things in a similar way, either because they share values or because they do not want to impair their relationship. Since administrators need diversity rather than similarity of opinion, additional sources of information providing perceptions of a problem or situation must be developed. Administrators especially need to identify and secure ideas and opinions from those students, teachers, parents, and other professional or community people who may hold *contrasting* sets of values or objectives. In all respects, in order to serve everyone's best interests, administrators must become active seekers of communication from a wide variety of people, utilizing a wide array of communication resources.

For example, communication with others can be greatly expanded and enhanced by linking computers and developing administrative networks. Through a network, teachers and administrators can communicate about faculty meetings, student progress, and parent conferences. Administrative networks can connect every classroom in the school to the principal's office to make regular reporting easy, as well as connect the principal to the superintendent's office or the district's administrative computing system. The computer network streamlines financial management, inventory control, transportation scheduling, word processing, and attendance information for immediate communication to a wide audience. A network communication system also allows principals to communicate with one another, with research organizations, with state departments of education, and with professionals throughout the world, exchanging valuable information on education issues and challenges. Networking is no longer a futuristic concept. Comprehensive networking strategies provide an integrated solution for communicating and sharing information, be it via fiber-optic video delivery or by connecting personal computers, minicomputers, and mainframes.[52]

> Most of the case studies, suggested learning activities, and simulations presented in Part II of the text require the appropriate use of the ideas in this chapter on communication. The following exercises should provide the best opportunities for testing understanding and effective use of communication concepts: Cases 1, 10, 13, 15, 29, 43, and the In-basket exercises.

Notes

1. Jerome P. Lysaught, "Toward a Comprehensive Theory of Communications: A Review of Selected Contributions," **Educational Administration Quarterly** (Summer 1984), p. 102.
2. Walter D. St. John, *A Guide to Effective Communication,* Personal and Organizational Communication Series, an ERIC Report, Ed 057–464, p. 1.
3. Sam Guarino, *Communication for Supervisors* (Columbus, OH: Ohio State University, 1974), p. 1.
4. National Association of Elementary School Principals. *Proficiencies for Principals. Kindergarten through Eighth Grade.* (Alexandria, VA 1986), p. 7. A copy of this document listing additional guidelines for communication proficiency may be obtained by writing directly to the organization. Also see statements from the American Association of School Administrators and The National Association of Secondary School Principals pertaining to the importance of communication skills for administrators.
5. Van Cleve Morris et al., *Principals in Action* (Columbus, OH: Charles E. Merrill, 1984), pp. 33–40 and 54–56.
6. Ibid., pp. 41–49, 58–65, and Chapters 10 and 11.
7. Fred Luthans and Janet Larsen, "How Managers Really Communicate," **Human Relations** (February 1986), pp. 161–178. Also see Eugene V. Donaldson, *Predictable Communication Strategies* (Los Angeles, CA: Outcomes Unlimited, 1990).
8. For suggestions on how administrators can better control the amount of time they spend communicating with individuals and groups, see Stephen Strasser and John Sena, "Why Managers Can't Disengage," **Business Horizons**

(January/February 1986), pp. 26–30. Also see Richard L. Enos (ed.) *Oral and Written Communication* (Newbury Park, CA: Sage, 1990).

9. William J. Seiler et al., *Communication in Business and Professional Organizations* (Reading, MA: Addison-Wesley, 1982), Chap. 1.

10. Richard M. Steers, *Introduction to Organizational Behavior* (Glenview, IL: Scott, Foresman, 1984), pp. 265–267.

11. Mark A. deTurck, "A Transactional Analysis of Compliance Gaining Behavior," **Human Communication Research** (Fall 1985), pp. 54–78; also see Peter F. Oliva, "Helping Teachers Evaluate Themselves," in *Supervision for Today's Schools* (New York: Longman, Inc., 1989), pp. 402–407.

12. Brent D. Ruben, *Communication and Human Behavior* (New York: Macmillian, 1984), Chap. 7; also, see Raymond A. Dumont and John M. Lannon, *Business Communication* (Boston: Little, Brown and Company, 1987), Chapter 2.

13. Rudi Klauss and Bernard M. Bass, *Interpersonal Communications in Organizations* (Orlando, FL: Academic Press, 1982).

14. Douglas McGregor, *The Professional Manager* (New York: McGraw-Hill, 1967), pp. 163–164.

15. Robert A. Snyder and James H. Morris, "Organizational Communication and Performance," **Journal of Applied Psychology** (August 1984), pp. 461–465.

16. Douglas Ehninger et al. *Principals and Types of Speech Communication* (Glenview, IL: Scott, Foresman, 1986). Mary Ellen Murray, "Painless Oral Presentations," **Bulletin of the Association for Business Communication** (June 1989), pp. 13–14.

17. David Bateman and Norman B. Sigband, *Communicating in Business* (Glenview, IL: Scott, Foresman, 1989), Chapters 18 and 19.

18. Marcia K. Knoll, "How to Communicate Successfully: Establishing a Secure Climate," *Supervision for Better Instruction* (Englewood Cliffs, NJ: Prentice-Hall, 1987), pp. 191–201.

19. Walter St. John, "Assessing the Communications Effectiveness of Your School," **The Practitioner** (Reston, VA: National Association of Secondary School Principals, December 1990), pp. 1–12.

20. Peter C. Gronn, "Talk As They Work: The Accomplishment of School Administration," **Administrative Science Quarterly** (March 1983), pp. 1–21; also, see Ray Collins and Brian H. Kleiner, "Orders and Instructions," **Industrial Management and Data Systems** (1989), pp. 3–6.

21. Walter D. St. John, "Plain Speaking," **Personnel Journal** (June 1985), pp. 83–90 and William C. Himstreet and Wayne Murlin Baty, *Business Communications* (Boston: Kent Publishing Co, 1990), Chapter 15.

22. Gerald R. Miller, ed., *Persuasion: New Directions in Theory and Research* (Berkeley, CA: Sage, 1980). Also, see Kenneth J. Tewel, "Improving In-School Communications: A Technique for Principals," **National Association of Secondary School Principals Bulletin** (March 1990), pp. 39–41.

23. Lloyd E. McCleary, "Communications in Large Secondary Schools—A Nationwide Study of Practices and Problems," **National Association of Secondary School Principals Bulletin** (February 1968), pp. 48–61. Also, see Anita M. Pankoke, G. Kent Stewart, and Wynona Winn, "Choices for Effective Communication: Which Channels to Use?," **National Association of Secondary School Principals Bulletin** (November 1990), pp. 53–58.

24. Peter West, "Electronic Mailboxes: Novel Phone Links Close Gap Between Parents and Schools," **Education Week** (March 1989), p. 1.

25. David Coursen and John Thomas, "Communicating," *School Leadership: Handbook for Excellence,* an ERIC Report, EA 020 964, (1989) pp. 252–271.

26. James M. Lipham and Donald C. Franeke, "Nonverbal Behavior of Administrators," **Educational Administration Quarterly** (Spring 1966), pp. 101–109. Also, see James Halleck, "Administrator Nonverbal Communication as Perceived by the Teachers' Ratings of Administrators' Nonverbal Behavior," Ph.D. Dissertation, University of Missouri-Columbus, 1984; and Robin Chandler, "Moving Towards Understanding," **Accountancy** (April 1990), pp. 76–78; and Michael G. Barton, "Manage Words Effectively," **Personnel Journal** (January 1990), pp. 32–40.

27. Joseph A. DeVito, *Human Communication: The Basic Course,* 4th ed. (New York: Harper and Row, 1987), Part 3.

28. Van Cleve Morris et al., *Principals in Action* (Columbus, OH: Charles E. Merrill, 1984), pp. 31–65.

29. H. H. Kelly, "Communication in Experimentally Created Hierarchies," **Human Relations** (1951), pp. 39–56.

30. J. L. Hurwitz et al., "Some Effect of Power on the Relations Between Group Members," in *Group Dynamics in Research and Theory,* ed. Darwin Cartwright and Alvin Zander (New York: Harper and Row, 1960), pp. 800–809.

31. Robert A. Giacalone, "On Slipping When You Thought You Had Your Best Foot Forward," **Group and Organizational Studies** (March 1985), pp. 61–80; and Fred C. Lunenburg and Allan C. Ornstein, *Educational Administration* (Belmont, CA: Wadsworth, 1991), p. 205.

32. Terry Bands, "Toward an Interpersonal Paradigm for Superior Subordinate Communication," Ph.D. Dissertation, University of Denver, 1983. For an empirical study on superior-subordinate communication, see Mel E. Schnake, Michael E. Dumber, Daniel S. Cochran, and Timothy R. Barnett, "Effects of Differences in Superior and Subordinate Perceptions of Superiors' Communication Practices," **The Journal of Business Communications** (Winter 1990), pp. 36–50 and Thomas D. Gougeon et al., "A Quantitative Phenomenological Study of Leadership: Social Control Theory Applied to Actions of School Principals." Paper presented at the Annual Meeting of the American Educational Research Association, April 1990.

33. See the discussion of masked messages in Andrew W. Halpin's *Theory and Research in Administration* (New York: Macmillan, 1966), pp. 258, 270.

34. P. Rankin, "The Importance of Listening Ability," **English Journal** (1928), pp. 623–630; A. D. Wolvin and C. D. Coakley, *Listening Instruction,* an ERIC report, Ed 170–827. These authors confirm the earlier Rankin study in their 1983 report to the Virginia Speech Communication Association.

35. C. Brue, ''Identifying Effective Listening Behaviors Used by Supervisors Involved in Dyadic Conversations with Subordinates.'' Ph.D. Dissertation, University of Texas, Austin, 1988.

36. Richard A. Schmuck and Philip J. Runkel, *The Handbook of Organizational Development in Schools,* 3rd ed. (Prospects Heights, IL: Waveland Printing, 1988), p. 98.

37. Ibid., p. 85.

38. Terry Newton, ''Improving Students' Listening Skills,'' IDEA Paper No. 23, Exchange (Manhattan, Kansas: Center for Faculty Evaluation and Development), September 1990.

39. Ibid., pp. 99–107: Guarino, *Communication for Supervisors,* pp. 48–49.

40. Peter Nostrand and Richard Shelley. *An Educational Leadership Listening Model* (Charlottesville, VA: University of Virginia, 1973); Lois W. Johnson and C. Glenn Pearch, ''Assess and Improve Your Listening Quotient,'' **Business Education Forum** (March 1990), pp. 25–27; and Sonya Hamlin, *How to Talk So People Listen: The Real Key to Job Success* (New York: Harper and Row, 1989).

41. Marjorie J. Kostelnik, Laura C. Stein, and Alice P. Whiren, ''Children's Self-Esteem, the Verbal Environment,'' **Childhood Education** (Fall 1988), pp. 29–32.

42. For an extensive review of research on communication networks, see Rebecca Blair et al., ''Vertical and Network Communication in Organizations,'' in *Organizational Communication,* ed. Robert D. McPhee and Phillip K. Tompkins (Beverly Hills, CA: Sage, 1985), Chap. 2; and, Lawrence F. Frey et al., *Investigating Communication Strategies* (Englewood Cliffs, NJ: Prentice-Hall, 1990).

43. Leslie W. Kindred et al., *The School and Community Relations* (Englewood Cliffs, NJ: Prentice-Hall, 1984), p. 146. Also, see John Thomas, Thomas E. Hart, and Stewart C. Smith, ''Building Coalition'' in *School Leadership: Handbook for Excellence* (1989), pp. 272–290, and Larry Frase and Robert Hetzel, *School Management By Wandering Around* (Lancaster, PA: Technomic Publishing Co., 1990), pp. 86–91.

44. Rensis Likert, *New Patterns of Management* (New York: McGraw-Hill, 1961).

45. Keith Davis, ''Methods of Studying Communication Patterns in Communication,'' **Personal Psychology** (Autumn 1953), pp. 301, 312. For guidelines on surveying faculty about communication, see Kenneth J. Tewel, ''Improving In-School Communications: A Technique for Principals,'' **National Association of Secondary School Administrators Bulletin** (March 1990), pp. 39–41.

46. Kindred et al., *The School and Community Relations,* p. 146.

47. Richard A. Gorton and Gail Thierbach-Schneider, *School Based Leadership: Challenge and Opportunities,* 3rd ed. (Dubuque, IA: Wm. C. Brown, 1991), pp. 516–517.

48. Michael J. Glauser, ''Upward Information Flow in Organizations: Review and Conceptual Analysis,'' **Human Relations** (August 1984), pp. 613–643; also, see Mel E. Schnake and Others, ''Effects of Differences in Superior Communication Practices,'' **Journal of Business Communication** (Winter 1990), pp. 37–50.

49. Schmuck and Runkel, ''The Handbook of Organizational Development in Schools,'' pp. 128–129.

50. J. Gaines, ''Upward Communications in Industry: An Experiment,'' **Human Relations** (December 1980), pp. 929–942.

51. Dennis W. Jeffers and Nancy L. Lewis, ''A Case Study of Newspaper Employee Perceptions of Communications Variables Related to Organizational Climate, Immediate Supervisor and Top Management,'' Paper presented at the annual meeting of the Newspaper Division of the Association for Education in Journalism and Mass Communication, Washington, D.C., August, 1989.

52. **Technological Horizons in Education Journal,** 1989, pp. 4–5. The reader interested in additional information on communication technology networks should contact project administrators for the East Central Minnesota Cable Cooperative (ECMECC) at St. Cloud Technical College, the Corporation for Research and Educational Networking (CREN) at the University of South Carolina, or the Online Administrative and Student Information System (OASIS) at California Polytechnic State University.

3 Authority, Power, and Influence

Any administrator engaged in making decisions, mediating conflict, introducing change, supervising teachers, or any other administrative task or activity, should have a reasonable basis for action rather than behaving idiosyncratically or capriciously. In a bureaucratic organization such as a school district, that basis is typically called "authority."[1] It can be defined as, ". . . a right granted to a manager to make decisions within limitations, to assign duties to subordinates, and to require subordinates' conformance to expected behavior."[2] It is the authorization to get things done or accomplished.[3] Authority is, therefore, "power conferred," allowing an administrator the right to "decide, direct, or control."[4]

There are several possible, reasonable bases for an administrator's authority in a particular situation.[5] First of all, authority may be derived from a governing board or a superior within the organization. This type of authority is generally referred to as "legal authority." Secondly, an administrator may possess authority in a particular situation because administrators have traditionally possessed authority in that kind of a situation and because people continue to recognize that tradition by accepting the administrator's attempts to exercise authority.[6] For example, one major study of education found that ". . . Most teachers do what their principals ask of them because they feel that their principals have a legitimate right to make demands."[7] Thirdly, an administrator may be able to exercise authority successfully because people respect the person or the position and therefore are willing to allow their behavior to be directed, irrespective of their judgments of the merits of the directives.[8]

It should be noted that because an administrator's authority is usually believed by school boards to be either inherent in the position or associated with the assigned responsibilities, some of its specific elements and scope may not always be defined.[9] This lack of specificity can sometimes cause problems if the administrator is not supported by superiors when exercising authority or if the recipients of the authority resist. However, as long as superiors back the administrator and as long as the people who respond to the administrator's exercise of authority *believe* it is the administrator's right to exercise it, either because of the position in the organization or for some other reason, no serious problems may occur. This is true, despite the fact that the nature and limits of the authority may have never been fully defined.

Cooper addresses the myths that currently operate in regard to the assumptions and beliefs that underlie the issue of where authority for school reform resides.[10] He argues that in educational settings, there are two separate, even competing, bases of authority. Administrators base their authority on their status in their organizational hierarchy, be it as principals, central office supervisors, or district superintendents. Their expertise is derived from their position in the hierarchy and their specialized knowledge of school system operations and management.

Teachers, however, base their authority on their knowledge of the subject matter and pedagogy

Figure 3.1 Possible Sources that Grant and Limit Administrator Authority.

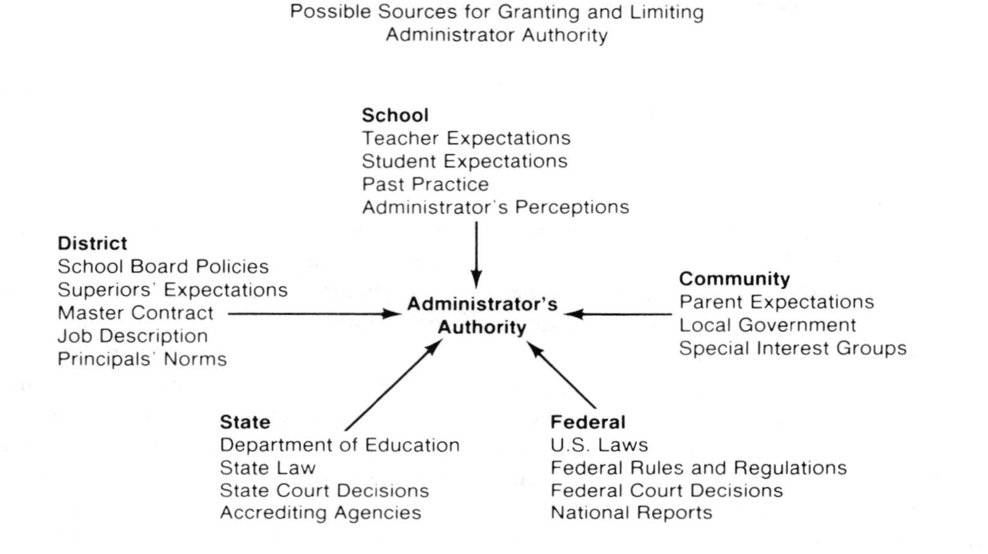

as it relates to their students. Superintendents speak generally about curriculum reform measures while teachers can explain how a particular objective worked with a special group of students. Teachers believe that they have authority and control over children and classrooms, while administrators believe that all the authority and control emanates from them, i.e. top-down control. Unfortunately, these assumptions or beliefs can constrain genuine calls for reform from parents and the community, since teachers and school leaders each believe they have proper authority. These myths impair innovations initiated by top leadership because teachers are not part of the process. A reorientation and a rethinking of the current paradigm of authority and of who controls what in our schools must occur before any meaningful reform measures can be jointly implemented by teachers and administrators, as well as by the community. This reorientation issue means that an administrator, especially one new to a school or school district, should give high priority to the identification and understanding of sources that grant and limit authority.

SOURCES THAT GRANT AND LIMIT AUTHORITY

As the previous discussion makes clear, the administrator's authority may be derived from more than one source. An important step, then, for any administrator is to ascertain the specific nature and extent of the authority to carry out the responsibilities and to take action when needed. Figure 3.1 identifies a number of possible sources that may, formally or informally, grant an administrator the authority to act and that may also place formal or informal limitations on the administrator's prerogatives to exercise authority. In other words, each of the sources identified in Figure 3.1 can potentially serve a dual function, that is, to grant authority and to restrict authority.

A school administrator can usually determine, for the most part, the specific nature and extent of authority by examining the job description, school board policies, and the district's master contract.[11] However, the prerogatives to exercise authority may also be broadened or limited by the superior's expectations,[12] state law and regulations, federal court decisions, and a number of other elements, as identified in Figure 3.1. For example, the same superintendent who grants a certain type of authority can also take it away or restrict it in some manner. The same faculty who, through their expectations, informally grant their principal the authority to take certain actions can change those expectations and remove their support.[13]

Although the number of *potential* sources of limitations presented in Figure 3.1 is large and may seem overwhelming to some readers, an administrator's initial response should be to investigate policies, regulations, expectations, and conditions in the principal's own school situation rather than *assuming* a certain pattern of limitations. (For further discussion of reference group expectations, see Gorton and Thierbach-Schneider.[14]) Some of the potential sources of limitations identified in Figure 3.1 may not be actual constraints in a particular school district.

For example, under District, in Figure 3.1, Principals' Norms are listed as a possible source of limitation to the exercise of authority. Although rarely discussed in the professional literature, a principal's peers in the school district can develop norms which may act to limit to some extent what a principal can do in school.[15] These peer norms can be especially powerful in influencing the behavior of a new or "outerdirected" principal.[16] However, it should be pointed out that it is not inevitable that a new principal will find that the norms of peers limit the exercise of authority in the school. In many school districts the norms of the principals are not well developed, nor is there much evidence that sanctions would be imposed by other principals unless the behavior in question was extreme. Some beginning principals have been assisted in gaining an understanding of peer norms, job expectations, and clarification of subtle signs and signals, by implementation of a "buddy system" or mentoring program.[17] However, the norms of the other principals in a school district do constitute a *potential* source of limitation on a principal who wishes to exercise authority in school, and therefore these norms need to be weighed as to their importance.

Another example of a potential source of limitation on a principal's exercise of authority is the principal's own perception of policies, expectations, and conditions. If an administrator *perceives* a condition as a limitation of authority, then it is a constraint, regardless of whether any other administrator in the same situation would perceive that condition to be restrictive.[18] For instance, some principals who assume a position at another school are reluctant to change any school procedures or practices that have been in existence for a long time because they believe that such changes might upset certain people. While there is nothing necessarily wrong with proceeding cautiously in a new situation, other principals who face the same circumstances would not perceive the possible negative reactions of others to change as a constraint on their authority. If they were convinced of the need for change, these principals would take whatever steps were necessary to bring about the change. The latter group of principals is not necessarily exercising authority effectively; it is simply that they don't perceive the same conditions as a constraint to their exercise of authority as do the first group of principals in our example.

A school administrator should not be intimidated or immobilized by the possibility of constraints on existing authority. However, the wise administrator will make few assumptions about having authority to act and will carefully and objectively examine the situation to determine the limits and the strengths of the various sources of authority. The administrator will also be constantly aware of a characteristic of formal authority that Blau and Scott have perceptively observed, namely, that formal authority only

". . . promotes compliance with directives and discipline, but does not encourage employees to exert effort, to accept responsibilities, or to exercise initiative."[19]

FACTORS TO CONSIDER IN EXERCISING AUTHORITY

School administrators exercise authority in a variety of ways. For example, they make decisions, promulgate rules and regulations, interpret policies, and issue directives. The purpose of exercising authority should be to bring about some desired response from others. The ideal outcome would be the acceptance of the administrator's right to exercise authority, along with willing cooperation in carrying out the administrator's expectations. Although this ideal is frequently realized in school administration, it is not always achieved.

Simon has suggested, based on earlier work by Barnard, that subordinates' characterization of the administrator's exercise of authority can range from "clearly unacceptable" to "unquestionably acceptable," with several degrees of variation in between.[20] (Wilkes and Blackbourn have devised a useful instrument for measuring the degree of acceptability of various kinds of administrative directives to teachers.[21]) Whether or not people will find the administrator's directives acceptable would appear to depend on a number of factors, including the personality of the administrator and the way the authority was exercised, as well as the personality and needs of the recipients of the directive.[22] For example, research found that teachers were more likely to accept the directives of the principal when the administrator was perceived as strong in the leadership dimensions of both consideration and initiating structure.[23]

Experience and observation would suggest, however, that most administrators at one time or another will encounter negative reactions when they attempt to exercise authority, and they will not always be able to avoid these kinds of reactions. In order for administrators to deal effectively with this problem, there must first be the recognition that negative responses to the exercise of administrative authority can take a variety of forms. In Peabody's study of an elementary school faculty, nine different types of negative responses were identified that could result from the exercise of administrative authority perceived as unreasonable.[24]

1. The teacher may consciously question the order, but accept it as binding.
2. The teachers may inform the administrator of their views and seek to be converted to the administrator's point of view, while complying with the order.
3. The teachers may discuss the situation with the administrator and try to work for change, while complying with the order.
4. The teachers may attempt to gain support for their contrary views by appealing to co-workers.
5. The teachers may go around their superior and try to gain the support of those above in the hierarchy or people from the outside.
6. The teachers may discuss the order, but ignore, evade, or try to modify it, while seeming to comply.
7. The teachers may ignore, evade, or try to modify the order without discussing it.
8. The teachers may openly reject the order.
9. The teachers may transfer or resign.

The type of negative reaction that teachers display toward the exercise of administrative authority would undoubtedly depend on many situational factors. In most circumstances, however, subordinates are unlikely to reject openly the exercise of administrative authority or resign because of it, unless the authority has been exercised in an extremely arbitrary or capricious manner. However, staff members may react to what they perceive as the unreasonable exercise of authority by responding in one or more of the first seven ways identified in Peabody's study.

When encountering a negative reaction to the exercise of authority, an administrator should first attempt to diagnose the reasons why that type of reaction is occurring. This approach may not be the initial predisposition of many administrators when they encounter a negative reaction to the exercise of their authority.[25] Instead, they may become upset or defensive and try to *impose* their authority on those reacting negatively. An administrator who attempts the latter may believe the power exists to impose authority, but, as discussion in the next section will make clear, an administrator's power is limited and should always be verified before it is used. While, to some extent, these emotions are normal and understandable, the thoughtful administrator will quickly gain control over such tendencies and will try to avoid doing anything that might exacerbate the situation. The administrator should also try to understand the reasons for a negative response to authority in order to be in a more knowledgeable position to take appropriate steps.

Also, it needs to be emphasized that the questioning or challenging of authority is not necessarily bad and can be instructive if its causes are understood. Although organizations (especially large bureaucracies) seldom encourage dissent and frequently do not tolerate it, a negative reaction to the exercise of authority may signal the inappropriate use or understanding of that authority.[26] Teachers, one of the groups that will be a recipient of the administrator's authority, frequently do not consider themselves to be subordinates or employees working for a superior, but professionals whose expertise and autonomy must be respected.[27]

The key for an administrator who encounters a negative response to authority is to try to diagnose the causes of the reaction by first conferring with the parties involved. The initial inquiry should be along the line that "perhaps there has been a misunderstanding." An effort should be made to avoid putting the other party on the defensive, and there should be an attempt made to understand the other person's frame of reference before explaining the administrator's own position. In this kind of a situation, the use of concepts from *The Administrator as a Recipient of Communication* in Chapter 2, along with concepts from Chapter 5 on *Conflict Management* will be very important.

If a negative reaction to the exercise of authority persists, the administrator will then need to make a judgment as to whether the authority was appropriately exercised.

Before making that judgment, the administrator may want to consult with superiors, examine school board policies, the master contract, or any other sources that are used as a basis for exercising authority. If the basis for the administrator's exercise of authority is sound, and if the original objective sought is still desirable *and* attainable, the administrator should proceed to insist that the authority of the administrator be obeyed.[28] No administrator should permit the reasonable exercise of legitimate authority to be ignored, evaded, or rejected. Such responses to the exercise of legitimate authority represent possible insubordination and, if permitted, could weaken the authority base of an administrator and could lead to more widespread noncompliance.

The administrator should keep written, dated documentation of the initial negative reaction to the exercise of authority and of all subsequent meetings, contacts, correspondence, and reactions between the administrator and others involved in the situation. An excellent monograph which provides further guidelines to preparing needed documentation has been published by the National Organization on Legal Problems of Education and is entitled *A Documentation System for Teacher Improvement or Termination.*[29]

The specific steps that an administrator should take to gain compliance from those who are resisting or evading the exercise of authority will undoubtedly vary according to the circumstances. When continued opposition is likely, given the results of an initial conference with the parties involved, the administrator will want to confer with superiors to obtain their ideas and support of certain courses of action. Also, the legality of proposed administrative actions and due process requirements need to be clearly understood and followed.

In most cases, unless the negative response to authority is extreme, it will be better for the administrator to begin insisting on compliance with authority gradually by conferring again with the parties involved. At this second meeting, the administrator should make sure that whoever is resisting or evading the directive fully understands the possible implications of such actions. Before the meeting is over, if the continued reaction of the other party is negative, then the administrator should explicitly state expectations verbally. If the reaction continues to be negative, then the administrator should issue a written warning to the other party that disciplinary action will be taken if compliance is not forthcoming by a certain date. Before writing this letter, the administrator should consult with superiors and obtain legal guidance. At some point, stronger negative sanctions may need to be used, including recommended disciplinary measures or even dismissal of an employee if compliance cannot be obtained. While an administrator should want people to accept the administrator's legitimate authority and carry out the directives cooperatively, in the final analysis, when people are reacting negatively, there must be compliance.

There are no doubt numerous specific reasons why people question, challenge, or resist authority, some of which were discussed in Chapter 1 on Decision Making. However, Chester Barnard indicated in his analysis of the authority problem in organizations that a person *can* and *will* accept authority when four conditions prevail: when the individual understands the order, when there is the belief that the order is consistent with the perception of the purposes of the organization, when there is the belief that the order is in the individual's own personal interest, and when the individual is mentally and physically able to comply with the order.[30]

Based on Barnard's concept of the prerequisites for compliance with authority, it would appear that administrators should keep in mind the following guidelines in issuing directives or orders:

1. In deciding on the need for a directive and in its formulation, presentation, and execution, administrators should take into consideration how the order will affect the recipients *personally,* recognizing that people are likely to question or resist directives that they feel are not in their best interest.
2. Administrators should take into consideration the strengths and limitations of those who will be expected to implement a directive. They should avoid issuing orders for which people lack the necessary motivation, skill, or training to carry out.
3. They should explain thoroughly the rationale behind each directive and its relationship to the goals of the organization. They should not assume that people understand the reasons for an order or that people will necessarily see the logic or value of an order.
4. They should leave room for modifying the original order or its method of implementation. Flexibility and a willingness to compromise when appropriate are key factors in exercising administrative authority successfully.
5. They should issue only those directives which they are relatively sure will either be obeyed or can be enforced if they are resisted. Orders which cannot be enforced in one situation weaken the administrator's authority for successfully issuing orders in other circumstances.

While some administrators and supervisors may be reluctant to exercise authority, particularly in light of the human relations and empowerment emphasis in school administration and challenges by various groups to administrative authority, it should be clear that if the administrator is to perform assigned responsibilities effectively and work with others in the improvement of the organization and the achievement of its goals, it may be necessary to utilize authority. The use of authority is an inescapable aspect of an administrator's job. The important question then, is not *whether* authority should be exercised, but *how,* and *in what circumstances*. The preceding and the following discussion should be helpful to an administrator in answering that question.

ADMINISTRATIVE POWER

Although many administrators and even some theorists use the terms *authority* and *power* interchangeably, these concepts are quite different as to their function and implications. The successful use of administrative authority is based first on the willingness of subordinates to comply with an administrator's expectations and second on the fact that the authority that is being exercised has been granted by one or more of the sources in Figure 3.1. When these two conditions are adequately met, an administrator does not need power. Power represents the ". . . capacity or potential for effecting desired results in one or more persons that would not have otherwise occurred."[31] According to this definition, administrators possess power if they can get people to do what the administrators want them to do, even when people resist or refuse to accept authority in a certain situation.

More recently, the traditional compliance model of power has competed with newer concepts of personal and collective empowerment. In regard to the latter, power is viewed as the ability to predict the consequences of one's actions in complex situations as well as the ability to maintain individual control over one's feelings and behaviors. The administrator or supervisor serves primarily as the catalyst or charismatic leader who prompts individuals to transform themselves at the same time they transform the social environment. Beaven suggests that more attention needs to be focused on those who actually change themselves, on their response to leader control, and on the phenomenon known as charismatic, transformational leadership.[32]

What types of power are available to an administrator? Several theorists have proposed paradigms that are somewhat useful in answering this question. For example, Etzioni has advanced the proposition that there are three general kinds of power: (1) coercive power (e.g., suspending an employee), (2) remunerative power (e.g., control over resources), and (3) normative power (e.g., control over prestige).[33] Parsons has identified four types of power or influence, using the terms interchangeably: (1) persuasion, (2) inducement, (3) activation of commitment (e.g., use of negative sanctions to influence another person's intentions), and (4) deterrence (e.g., negative sanctions to control a situation).[34] Furthermore, French and Raven, in what is probably the most elaborate proposed model of power, have suggested five types of social power, the strengths of which they believe will be determined by certain conditions.[35]

1. *Reward Power.* Capacity to provide rewards, such as higher salary or better assignment.

   Conditions

   a. The strength of the reward power of the administrator will increase with the magnitude of the rewards which the other person perceives can be obtained by the administrator.
   b. The strength of the reward power will depend on the actual rewards produced, not on what the administrator hopes or would like to produce.
   c. Unsuccessful attempts by the administrator to exert reward power will tend to decrease the perceived strengths of that power in the future.

2. *Coercive Power.* Capacity to provide punishment or negative consequences, such as teacher dismissal.

   Conditions

   a. The strength of the administrator's coercive power will increase with the magnitude of the punishments or costs which the other person perceives that the administrator can exercise.
   b. The strength of the coercive power will depend on the *actual* sanctions or costs which the administrator can apply, not just on hopes or possibilities.
   c. Unsuccessful attempts to exert coercive power will tend to decrease the perceived strength of that power in the future.

3. *Legitimate Power.* Defined by French and Raven in a way very similar to the definition of "legitimate authority" discussed earlier.

4. *Referent Power.* The tendency of other individuals to be attracted by and to identify closely with the administrator, e.g., the identification of teachers with the administrator.

   Conditions

   a. The greater the perceived attractiveness of the administrator by another person or group, the more likely there will be identification with the administrator.
   b. The stronger the actual identification with the administrator by another person, the greater will be the likelihood that reference power can be successfully used by the administrator.

5. *Expert Power.* Special knowledge or skill, e.g., supervision, scheduling, group dynamics.

   Conditions

   a. The strength of the expert power of the administrator will vary with the actual knowledge and skill that the administrator possesses and with the perceived expertise of the administrator.
   b. The stronger the perception by others that the administrator possesses expert power, the higher will be the group's satisfaction and evaluation of the administrator as a leader.

Table 3.1 presents examples of the five types of social power identified by French and Raven.

Paul Hersey and Walter Natemeyer have developed a Power Perception Profile instrument to assess why someone responds to another's attempts to exercise power. They expanded French and Raven's five power types into seven, adding connection power based on the perception that the supervisor has relationships with influential people inside or outside the organization and information power which is based upon the leader's possession of or access to information perceived as valuable to others. This latter power base is important to others because they need this information or want to be "in on things."[36]

A recent comparison of the Hersey-Natemeyer instrument with the "Richardson Power Profile" instrument, both of which are measures of a leader's reliance on power bases to affect followers within organizations, questions the presumption that seven discrete power bases exist. Richardson identified fewer than the seven factors (underlying perceptions of power base use in organizations) proposed by the theories of earlier studies. Apparently the power bases are not all independent or distinct but suggest, for example, that legitimate power tends to be correlated with expert power, inasmuch as these two power bases are perceived as being similar.[37]

Also, Buhler more recently writes that it is important to recognize that power is not unilateral but is generally shared and distributed. Teachers,

Table 3.1 Examples of the Use of Different Types of Power

Categories	Examples
Reward power	"I believe that you are interested in . . . Perhaps we can work something out, but before we do, you need to . . ."
Coercive power	"I find your behavior unacceptable, and if it doesn't change . . ., I will have no choice except to suspend you."
Legitimate power	"Consistent with my responsibilities as principal, I am assigning you . . ."
Referent power	"You have believed in me in the past, and I am asking you to trust me now."
Expert power	"This is an area in which I have background and experience, and therefore . . ."

for example, hold a great deal of potential power in the degree of compliance and in their willingness to comply. Buhler further believes that "most employees throughout the organization have the ability to make their boss look bad." This important political element can often be overlooked by the principal. There is also power in terms of whom teachers are aligned with and the great loyalty they have for these individuals. For example, in business when a senior executive leaves the company, a whole group generally follows. In school systems, administrators and teachers may not have the flexibility to follow their superior immediately, but the information and communication network of loyal past employees is nevertheless powerful and influential. People tend to group together in order to achieve and sustain power.[38] Particularly in educational settings, power should be used, when possible, as a shared resource.

Power sharing encourages teachers, principals, department chairs, counselors, and other staff at all levels of the school to be involved in decision making without feeling coerced or manipulated. A recent study on empowering teachers at the elementary level found personal power of the principal who incorporated referent, information, and expert subordinate perception bases highly valued by teachers. Teachers, however, resent principals who falsely see themselves as relying on personal power when, in fact, they use positional power bases such as reward, coercion, connection, and legitimate authority. Connection power, where the principal has a personal relationship with influential people inside or outside of school, could be a source of personal power as well. Yet, teachers in this same study tended to "devalue their principals' connections as being part of an old boy's network. They resented the fact that their principals with connections spent a good deal of time away from the schools."[39]

The appropriate exercise of personal power is one of the means of obtaining higher levels of teacher satisfaction and cooperation. Empowerment through the use of personal power gives teachers a sense of ownership, raises their level of self-esteem, and increases participatory decision making and communication. Other means that administrators can use for gaining cooperation would fall under the category of influence, to be discussed next.[40]

"Giving teachers greater power is a major way to make them more professional and to improve their performance."[41] Teachers should have an impact on policy decisions and work in collegial relationship, "sharing power" with administrators. Through this relationship, principals become facilitators of school goals, empowering teachers and allowing them to generate their own ideas. This, in turn, gives more dignity to the profession of teaching. As teachers become more empowered, they will have to accept the burden of responsibility. Whereas in the past teachers could "blame the administrators for problems," this blame should decline as teacher empowerment increases. However, it should be noted that, in order to empower teachers and expect them to be successful in carrying out their responsibilities, they must be educated and trained in the skills necessary for appropriate decision making.[42]

Successful shared decision making is also dependent upon the school board's willingness to empower employees. According to Mitchell, "Unless school board members are behind it, any attempt to move decision making closer to the classroom will surely fail."[43] Shared decision making requires that the school board members and the central office be committed to sharing authority and control. It is also imperative that the school board develop policies that describe the new system of management and clearly send a message to all professional and nonprofessional staff—that the board is committed to the implementation of the process. As a result of establishing these policies, teachers, noncertified staff and administrators should be aware of their level of responsibility and accountability. However, if school employees are given the opportunity to make decisions, they must be accountable for their actions.[44]

In examining the various conceptualizations of power, a question could be raised as to whether, in some cases, the concepts that the theorists are presenting should not more properly be characterized as sources or types of social *influence* rather than power. Types of "power," such as control of prestige, persuasion, and referent and reward power, seem to represent sources of influence rather than sources of, or types of, power (more will be said later about influence). It is difficult to see how these types of power could be used to force someone to comply with authority if the person was determined to resist it.

If a subordinate is determined to resist an administrator's authority, the only effective type of power may be coercive power, defined as "the capacity to force people to do something against their will."[45] However, it needs to be emphasized that most school administrators are quite limited in their possession of coercive power.[46] By and large, this kind of power is based on the backing of an administrator's superiors; it may also need to be validated by some outside agency–for example, the courts, if the legality of the use of power is challenged. To complicate matters, the basis for the use of coercive power is frequently vague and often not predictable or dependable.[47] For instance, seldom will an administrator find in school board policies or in a job description any discussion of the right to use coercive means to gain compliance from employees. This type of power is rarely made explicit and is usually, at most, implied.

On the other hand, an administrator may be able to achieve initial compliance from others or overcome resistance to the exercise of authority as a result of other people's *perception* of the administrator's coercive power.[48] However, three perceptual conditions must be present:

1. Others must perceive the administrator as possessing a certain kind of coercive power.
2. They must perceive this power as something that they definitely would like to avoid.
3. They must perceive the administrator as ready to actually use coercive power if compliance is not forthcoming.

If, for example, a teacher believed that a principal could and *would* use punishment in some way for failing to monitor the corridor when students are passing between classes, and if the teacher wanted to avoid that punishment, then the teacher would probably comply with the administrator's expectations. In this case, the perception is more important than the reality. If a subordinate *perceives* that an administrator possesses coercive power, then the subordinate will act on that perception, irrespective of whether the administrator actually possesses that power. As Wheeless and his colleagues point out ". . . People act not on the basis of the situation but on the basis of their perceptions about the situation. . . It makes no difference, for example, if the agent [administrator] making a threat has the ability to carry out that threat. If the [individual or group] being threatened perceive such an ability, the agent has power."[49]

Nevertheless, it is important for an administrator to understand that coercive power is most effective when it is not used, but when it is believed that it would be exercised and supported if compliance were not forthcoming. The more an administrator actually has to resort to the use of coercive power in order to gain compliance, the greater the possibility of exposing its limited or inadequate basis, thereby exacerbating a situation, or resulting in some other unanticipated consequence.[50] Although certain circumstances may warrant the use of coercive power, in most situations the administrator should, due to the limitations of power, utilize other means for gaining compliance and, especially, cooperation.

TYPES OF INFLUENCE

Most of the kinds of power identified in the previous section would seem to represent types of influence rather than power. Power, of course, can be and has been defined broadly by a number of theorists. Kotter aptly notes that inherent in every position in an organization is a certain degree of power, and individuals have the potential either to enhance or decrease the power of their position by the behavior they display.[51] However, when power is defined broadly, then such a definition (and sometimes the mere use of the term) can inadvertently mislead an administrator into thinking there is more capacity to bring about change than the administrator actually possesses in certain situations. Unquestionably, power and influence are closely related on a theoretical basis;[52] however, little research exists about the effects of a leader's influence-seeking behaviors on subordinate perceptions of leader effectiveness in an organizational context. Specific descriptive theory and valid empirical research on possible linkages between perceived leader behavior and attributions of power are virtually nonexistent.

Hinkin and Schriesheim[53] in a recent study found that although influence and power are closely related constructs, respondents using French and Raven's social bases of power were able to distinguish between influence behaviors and attributions of power.[54] Most importantly, Hinkin and Schriesheim discovered that subordinate perceptions of leader expert and referent power are consistently and positively related to subordinate satisfaction and preference, while the results for attributions of reward, coercive, and legitimate power have been much more variable. The use of rationality was the most commonly used influence tactic and was positively related to legitimate, expert, and referent power. Their findings certainly support the popular notion that effective administrators possess "expertise" and "charisma," that the use of rationality as an influence tactic is particularly important, and "that it should be emphasized by managers as a key influence tactic to both enhance personal power as well as provide desired organizational and subordinate outcomes."[55]

Influence, when compared to power, seems to be a more positive concept and more in line with the realities of organizational life for most school administrators. Influence can be defined as ". . . the ability of an [administrator] without recourse to force or legitimation, to affect another's behavior."[56] Influence is the shaping of decisions through "informal and nonauthoritative means."[57] It differs from authority in that (a) many people can influence a decision while only one person has final authority, (b) influence may be distributed unequally, while authority is usually distributed equally, and (c) authority is top-down management, while influence is multi-directional.[58] An administrator has influence if other individuals or groups can be persuaded to comply with the administrator's expectations, despite their ambivalence or objections. In light of the limitations of power and considering the periodic challenges to authority that most administrators will experience during their careers, it would appear that the concept of influence offers a positive and constructive alternative basis for many administrative actions.

If the administrator is to exert influence successfully, the administrator's actions must be based on some factor which will persuade people to act in accordance with the administrator's decisions or directives. Successful implementation of directives will, in large measure, be contingent upon the perception of the individual receiving the directive from the administrator.[59]

Utilizing, with minor modification, French and Raven's concepts, it would appear that administrators may be able to exert influence based on other people's identification with them (referent influence), their ability to obtain rewards (reward influence), or on their perception of administrators' expertise as educational leaders (expert influence).

Referent Influence

The identification of other individuals or groups with the administrator as a person is the basis for the referent influence of an administrator. An administrator who possesses certain qualities such as an attractive personality, a strong character, or a charismatic leadership style, may be successful in securing the cooperation of other people as a result of their identification with these characteristics.[60] Even if teachers, parents, or students question the decisions or policies set forth by an administrator, they may oblige, simply because they react positively to the personal qualities the administrator possesses.

There is considerable observational evidence that people will respond favorably to an administrator's attempt to influence them as a result of their identification with the individual. Administrators in business and government, as well as in education, have found it possible to secure the cooperation of others, in spite of objections to a particular policy or action, because of their positive feelings about the administrator. There is little doubt that the identification by others with the administrator can be a powerful basis for influencing them if the administrator possesses the requisite personal characteristics.

One problem with referent influence, however, is that research has not conclusively established the kinds of personal characteristics with which people identify positively. It appears that not all people respond the same way to particular personal characteristics. Qualities which one group may find attractive or charismatic might be perceived by other individuals or groups as undesirable. For example, ingratiation, acting friendly toward another, or flattering another, may be enjoyed by some employees, but be seen as a sign of weakness by others.[61] Consequently, there is no single pattern of personal attributes for all situations which can be recommended without qualification to the administrator. However, a study by Hoy and Kupersmith suggests that administrator ''authenticity'' could be very important.[62] In addition, a study by Johnston and Venable suggests that an administrator's style in administering personnel rules may be significantly related to the degree of loyalty that teachers feel toward the administrator.[63]

Another important limitation of referent influence is the fact that its potential is largely determined by factors over which most administrators have little or no control. By the time a person becomes an administrator, personality and leadership style are usually already developed. Therefore, if the administrator does not currently possess the kinds of personal characteristics with which people identify, the likelihood of developing them is not great. Although an administrator can often improve personal traits, the task is not an easy one, and change is frequently slow. Despite these obstacles, it would be in the best interest of any administrator to improve personal qualities and leadership style so that greater referent influence can be exercised (see Chapter 4 on *Group Leadership*).

Reward Influence

A second kind of influence which an administrator may be able to utilize in persuading people to adhere to the administrator's wishes is reward influence. This type of influence is based on the administrator's actual or perceived possession of certain rewards which can be distributed to those who comply. Examples of these rewards range from a better work schedule to greater administrative receptivity and accommodation to the recommendations and special needs of certain individuals or groups.

Unfortunately, it would appear that most administrators do not possess a great deal of influence based on rewards, since they frequently find themselves in a position where they cannot distribute to one individual or group any rewards which do not need to be distributed equally to other individuals or groups. Unlike executives in private enterprise, educational administrators can seldom selectively reward their employees according to merit or increased productivity. They may occasionally be able to offer a reward to one individual or group without having to give similar recognition to other involved individuals or groups, but this possibility does not occur often. In education, preferential treatment seems to be regarded with suspicion, and students, teachers, and parents are alert to situations in which the administrator seems to be favoring one individual or group over another.

There is also the problem that only a limited number of rewards is available to most administrators to utilize in influencing other people. School board policy, bureaucratic regulations, the nature of public control over resources, and teacher, student, and parent militancy are factors which tend to restrict the number and importance of rewards that are available to an administrator.

This does not mean that the administrator possesses no reward influence or that it should not be utilized. There are some administrators who, over the years, have been able to develop a wide variety of rewards. For example, Cusick pointed out in discussing the behavior of one principal who attempted to use reward influence, ". . . Because he administered the schedule, additional assignments, and unallocated resources, he controlled just those things that many teachers wanted in order to fill out their fields. The principal could award a department chairperson with a free period, a favorite class, a double lunch period, an honors section, or support for a new activity."[64] Teachers in the Rockefeller Foundation's Collaboratives for Humanities and Arts Teaching (CHART) program, designed to facilitate empowerment, identified additional rewards such as providing faculty business cards, establishing relationships with services from local universities, providing a paid stipend for participating in professional development programs, allowing the faculty to call the principal by a first name, and letting the faculty "get out of the building" to network with business and industry during the work day.[65]

In addition to control over resources, a school administrator has available a simple but frequently overlooked source of rewards: positive reinforcement. This can, for example, take the form of verbal and/or written appreciation to a person who volunteers for an activity, praise for a job well done, a commendation for a significant effort to improve, or some other type of reward. Although most school administrators may believe that they are already utilizing this potential source of influence sufficiently, there is evidence to the contrary.[66]

To be effective in influencing behavior, positive reinforcement must be directly linked to the specific effort or performance that warrants the reinforcement.[67] For example, the school administrator who gives praise indiscriminately or who does not clearly relate the delivery of praise to the production of a certain type of behavior is not likely to be successful in influencing others with positive reinforcement.[68] In addition, unless the kind of positive reinforcement used by a school administrator is valued by its recipient, the latter's behavior is unlikely to be influenced. Consequently, to be effective in using positive reinforcement, the school administrator needs to become knowledgeable about the reward predisposition of the people to be influenced.

An administrator perceived as someone who has influence with superiors may also be able to exert reward influence with teachers. Such influence can be manifested in at least two important ways: by securing additional resources from the district that subordinates need, and by being an effective advocate and supporter of subordinates in their interactions with the district office. This type of hierarchical influence has received some research support and represents a frequently overlooked source of rewards that an administrator may be able to generate for subordinates.[69] For two interesting studies of the techniques that people use to try to exert upward influence, see Schmidt and Kipnis[70], and Schilit and Locke.[71]

Although it is important for an administrator to make maximal use of whatever resources or reward influence that exists, it should be understood that, in many situations, the administrator's reward influence is not extensive and that there are significant constraints that may make it difficult to take advantage of this type of influence. Therefore, although an administrator should try to develop and use as many sources of rewards as possible, inasmuch as there are limitations to administrative influence based on rewards, other sources of influence will be needed as well. Glinow has written a provocative article on reward strategies which speaks to this issue.[72]

Expert Influence

Although the foregoing discussion of referent and reward influence has emphasized the personal and situational limitations of these bases for administrative action, there is one source of administrative influence which potentially would seem to offer the administrator a truly viable basis upon which to gain the cooperation of others. That source is expertise, i.e., specialized knowledge or skill.

Empirical support for the primacy of this source of administrative influence was furnished in a study by Horstein. He discovered in an investigation of 325 teachers who worked in 14 different schools in two school districts that the most important factor associated with teacher satisfaction and high evaluation of principal leadership was the principal's tendency to base attempts to influence teachers on possession of expertise, rather than on other sources of influence.[73] Administrative attempts to influence teachers based on the possession of certain rewards for compliance were not associated with high teacher satisfaction or high evaluation of the administrator's leadership. Referent identification as a source of influence was positively related to teacher satisfaction, but the relationship was not statistically significant. Horstein's research also revealed that in those situations where the administrator based behavior on legitimate authority or coercive power, the faculty was not satisfied with this individual as a principal and did not give the principal a good evaluation as a leader.

While the data from Horstein's investigation seem to suggest that an administrator can successfully influence teachers if the actions are based on expertise as a source of influence, there is other evidence that, regrettably, many administrators seem to lack expertise or are perceived by others as lacking expertise. The ability of administrators to manage a school or school district effectively and humanely has come under attack periodically through the years, and these criticisms have recently escalated with the emphasis on school accountability and on student, teacher, and parent demands for involvement in school decision making. For a further discussion on this problem, see Gorton and Thierbach-Schneider.[74]

On the other hand, research on effective schools has demonstrated that principals with expertise can exert influence in their schools and that their leadership contributions are important to the success of these schools.[75] In the area of instructional supervision, for example, Guditus and Zirkel found that, "The influence of principals depends to a considerable degree on their possession of special knowledge and skills which enable them to help teachers achieve their goals."[76] For example, principals could increase their influence on teachers by learning more about teaching and by visiting classrooms.

"Managing by walking around may give administrators an opportunity to influence faculty and staff."[77]

The effectiveness of an administrator's influence would also seem to depend on the extent to which attempts to influence others fall within the teachers' zone of acceptance. See Clear and Seager,[78] Kunz and Hoy,[79] and Johnston and Mullins[80] for further discussion of the relationship between the zone of acceptance and administrator influence. Therefore, it would appear that one of the keys for an administrator's successful exercise of influence is to assist teachers and relevant others to meet their goals and to help them relate those goals to the overall goals of the school and school district. This may require an administrator to develop greater expertise in instructional leadership, program development, student discipline, conflict resolution, working with groups, or some other type of special knowledge or skill that is needed. In many cases, an administrator may need to identify and deploy other people who possess special knowledge and skill that the administrator does not possess and would find difficult to develop. The important consideration is not who possesses the special knowledge or skill, but that it be utilized to help the people associated with the school to become more effective.

A FINAL NOTE

By the very nature of their positions in an organization, administrators will be assigned major responsibilities. In order to carry out those responsibilities successfully, authority, influence, and perhaps, in some cases, power must be exercised effectively. Appropriate understanding and use of the concepts presented in this chapter should help the administrator achieve these objectives.

Although most of the case studies, suggested learning activities, and simulations presented in Part II of the text require the appropriate use of the ideas in this chapter on authority, power, and influence, the following exercises should provide the best opportunities for testing understanding and effective use of authority, power, and influence concepts: Cases 21, 22, 27, 28, 38, 49 and the Mid-Year and End-of-the-Year In-basket exercises.

Notes

1. Max Weber, *The Theory of Social and Economic Organization*, trans. A. M. Henderson and Talcott Parsons (New York: Oxford University Press, 1947), pp. 56–57.
2. C. Resser, *Management, Functions, and Modern Concepts* (Chicago: Scott, Foresman, 1973), p. 132.
3. Douglas E. Mitchell and William G. Spady, "Authority, Power, and the Legitimization of Social Control," **Educational Administration Quarterly** (Winter 1983), p. 12.
4. Patrick Houston, "The Power Vacuum: High Anxiety," **Business Month** (June 1990), p. 34.
5. Weber, *Social and Economic Organization*, pp. 56–77.
6. Harvey Bleacher, "Why Teachers Carry Out Orders," **Education** (Spring 1985), pp. 333–336. Also, see John Lindelow and James J. Scott, "Managing Conflict" in *School Leadership Handbook for Excellence* (Clearinghouse on Educational Management, 1989), p. 350.
7. Kenneth A. Tye and Barbara B. Tye, "Teacher Isolation and School Reform," **Phi Delta Kappan** (January 1984), p. 321.
8. Daniel J. Brass, "Being in the Right Place," **Administrative Science Quarterly** (December 1984), pp. 518–539. Also, see Herbert A. Simon, *Administrative Behavior* (New York: Macmillan, 1959), p. 22; and, Carl D. Glickman, "Directive Control Behaviors," *Supervision of Instruction: A Developmental Approach*, 2nd ed. (Boston: Allyn and Bacon, 1990) pp. 162–174.
9. Joan R. Egner, "Collective Bargaining and Administrative Prerogatives," **Peabody Journal of Education** (November 1968), pp. 142–149. For a more general discussion of this problem, see Robert L. Peabody, *Organizational Authority* (New York: Atherton Press, 1964), pp. 84–89.
10. Bruce S. Cooper, "Bottom-Up Authority in School Organization. Implications for the School Administrator," **Education and Urban Society** (August 1989), pp. 380–391.
11. For an interesting analysis of the impact of the master contract, see Donald L. Robson and Marlene E. Davis, "Administrative Authority, Leadership Style, and the Master

Contract,'' **Journal of Educational Administration** (Winter 1983), pp. 5–13.

12. Kent D. Peterson, ''Mechanisms of Administrative Control over Managers in Educational Organizations,'' **Administrative Science Quarterly** (December 1984), pp. 573–597. Also, see John Lindelow and James Heynderickx, ''School-Based Management'' in *School Leadership Handbook for Excellence,* 2nd ed., an ERIC Report, Ed 309–504.

13. For examples, see the cases in this text.

14. Richard A. Gorton and Gail Thierbach-Schneider, *School Based Leadership: Challenges and Opportunities* (Dubuque, IA: Wm. C. Brown, 1991), pp. 93–101.

15. For an insightful discussion of how new administrators are socialized into their role, see William D. Greenfield, Jr., ''The Moral Socialization of School Administrators,'' **Educational Administration Quarterly** (Fall 1985), pp. 99–119; see also Mark E. Anderson, ''Training and Selecting School Leaders'' in *School Leadership: Handbook for Excellence,* 2nd ed., an ERIC report, Ed 309–504.

16. The concept of outer-directedness was first developed by David Riesman, *Lonely Crowd* (New Haven: Yale University Press, 1973).

17. Anderson, ''Training and Selecting School Leaders.''

18. For the role of perception, see Lawrence R. Wheeless et al., ''Compliance-Gaining and Power in Persuasion,'' in *Communication Yearbook 7,* ed. Robert N. Bostrom (Beverly Hills, CA: Sage, 1983), p. 120.

19. Peter M. Blau and W. Richard Scott, *Formal Organization: A Comparative Approach* (San Francisco, CA: Chandler, 1962), p. 61.

20. Simon, *Administrative Behavior,* p. 133.

21. Sam Wilkes and Jo Blackbourn, *The Design of an Instrument to Measure Zones of Indifference of Teachers to Directives Issued by Administrators,* an ERIC report, Ed 212–063.

22. Charles B. Handy, *Understanding Organizations* (New York: Pengium, 1981), pp. 119–120. Also, see Paul Hersey and Kenneth H. Blanchard, *Management of Organizational Behavior: Utilizing Human Resources,* 5th ed. (Englewood Cliffs, NJ: Prentice-Hall, 1988) p. 171, and an empirical study by M. Afzalur Rahim, ''Relationships of Leader Power to Compliance and Satisfaction with Supervision: Evidence from a National Sample of Managers,'' **Journal of Management** (April 1989) pp. 545–556.

23. Daniel W. Kunz and Wayne K. Hoy, ''Leadership Style of Principals and the Professional Zone of Acceptance of Teachers,'' **Educational Administration Quarterly** (Fall 1976), pp. 49–64; see also Ann W. Porter and Donald K. Lemon, ''How Teachers Perceive a Principal's Power,'' **Principal** (January 1988), pp. 30–32.

24. Peabody, *Organizational Authority,* pp. 107–108.

25. Charles A. O'Reilly III, and Barton A. Weitz, ''Managing Marginal Employees: The Use of Warnings and Dismissals,'' **Administrative Science Quarterly** (September 1980), pp. 467–484.

26. John D. Stanley, ''Dissent in Organizations,'' **Academy of Management Review** (January 1981), pp. 13–19. Also, see Antoinette A. Kirkwood, ''The Role of the Principal as a Manager of Conflict Resolution,'' an ERIC report, Ed 321–373.

27. Gorton and Thierbach-Schneider, *School Based Leadership: Challenges and Opportunities,* pp. 95–98.

28. Many of the ideas for the recommended steps in this section come from D. Cameron, ''The When, Why and How of Discipline,'' **Personnel Journal** (July 1984), pp. 37–39; and from O'Reilly and Weitz, ''Managing Marginal Employees,'' **Administrative Science Quarterly,** pp. 467–484. See note 25.

29. Kelly Frels and Timothy Cooper, *A Documentation System for Teacher Improvement or Termination* (Lawrence, KS: National Organization on Legal Problems of Education, 1985).

30. Chester Barnard, *The Functions of the Executive* (Cambridge: Harvard University Press, 1948), p. 165.

31. Wheeless et al., ''Compliance-Gaining and Power in Persuasion,'' *Communication Yearbook* 7.

32. Mary H. Beaven, ''Leadership, Charisma, Personality, and Power,'' Paper presented at the Annual Meeting of the National Women's Studies Association, Towson, MD., June, 1989. For further discussion on how constituents gain power, thus developing a sense of personal and collective efficacy and self-control leading to empowerment, see E. J. Langer, *The Psychology of Control* (Beverly Hills, CA: Sage, 1983); A. R. Willner, *The Spellbinders: Charismatic Political Leadership* (New Haven, CT: Yale University Press, 1984); and R. deCharms, *Personal Causation: The Internal Affective Determinants of Behavior* (New York: Academic Press, 1968).

33. A. A. Etzioni, *A Comparative Analysis of Complex Organizations* (New York: Macmillan, 1961), p. 5.

34. T. Parsons, ''On the Concept of Influence,'' **Public Opinion Quarterly** (Spring 1963), pp. 36–62.

35. John R. P. French and Bertram Raven, ''The Bases of Social Power,'' in *Studies of Social Power,* ed. Darwin Cartwright (Ann Arbor: University of Michigan Press, 1959), pp. 155–164.

36. Hersey and Walter Natemeyer, *Power Perception Profile* (Escondido, CA: Center for Leadership Studies, 1979).

37. Rita C. Richardson, ''A Comparison of Measures of Administrator Reliance on Power Bases for Influence.'' Paper presented at the Annual Meeting of the Southwest Educational Research Association, Houston, TX, January, 1989.

38. Patricia M. Buhler, ''Power and Conflict in the Workplace,'' **The American Salesman** (September 1988), pp. 3–4.

39. Jerry D. Stimson and Richard P. Appelbaum, ''Empowering Teachers: Do Principals Have the Power?,'' **Phi Delta Kappan** (December 1988), pp. 313–316.

40. Ibid.

41. E. I. Maeroff, *The Empowerment of Teachers: Overcoming the Crisis of Confidence* (New York: Teachers College Press, 1989), pp. 4 and 82–86.

42. Ibid.

43. James E. Mitchell, ''Sharing the Power,'' **American School Board Journal** (January 1990), pp. 42–43.

44. Ibid.

45. Weber, **Social and Economic Organization,** p. 152.

46. For guidelines on how to make the best use of those limitations, see Gary A. Yukl, *Leadership in Organizations* (Englewood Cliffs, NJ: Prentice-Hall, 1989), 2nd ed, pp. 56–58.

47. Richard D. Arvey, "Use of Discipline in Organization," **Journal of Applied Psychology** (August 1984), pp. 448–460.

48. Wheeless et al., "Compliance-Gaining and Power," p. 127.

49. Ibid., p. 127.

50. Rodney Muth, "Toward an Integrative Theory of Power and Educational Organizations," **Educational Administration Quarterly** (Spring 1984), pp. 25–42. For more information on the use of coercive power, see Ted J. Foster, "The Nature and Use of Coercion," Paper presented at the Annual Meeting of the Central States Speech Association (April 1988).

51. J. P. Kotter, *Power and Influence: Beyond Formal Authority* (New York: Free Press, 1985). Also, see Edward R. Lilley, "The Determinants of Organizational Power Styles," **Educational Review** (March 1989), pp. 281–293.

52. G. A. Yukl, *Leadership in Organizations,* 2nd ed. (Englewood Cliffs, New Jersey: Prentice-Hall, 1989). John S. Dean, "Principals' Leadership and School Effectiveness: A Descriptive Study of the Principals' Exercise of Authority and Influence in Effective and Ineffective Elementary Schools," Ph.D. Dissertation, Pennsylvania State University, 1990.

53. Timothy R. Hinkin and Chester A. Schriesheim, "Relationship Between Subordinate Perceptions of Supervisor Influence Tactics and Attributed Bases of Supervisory Power," **Human Relations** (March 1990), pp. 233–235.

54. French and Raven, *The Bases of Social Power.*

55. Hinkin and Schriesheim, "Relationships Between Subordinate Perceptions of Supervision Influence Tactics and Attributed Bases of Supervisory Power," pp. 233–235.

56. Muth, p. 27.

57. Sharon Conley, " 'Who's on First?' School Reform, Teacher Participation, and the Decision-Making Process," **Education and Urban Society** (August 1989), pp. 366–379.

58. Ibid.

59. Hinkin and Schriesheim, "Relationships Between Subordinate Perceptions of Supervision Influence Tactics and Attributed Bases of Supervisory Power," p. 224.

60. For a description of an interesting theory of charismatic leadership, see R. J. House, "A 1976 Theory of Charismatic Leadership," in *Leadership: The Cutting Edge,* ed. J. G. Hunt and L. L. Larson (Carbondale, IL: Southern Illinois University Press, 1977). Also, see William F. Adams and Gerald D. Bailey, "Managerial Leadership Behaviors: A Model of Choice," **Performance and Instruction** (January 1989), pp. 43–46.

61. Hinkin and Schriescheim, "Relationships Between Subordinate Perceptions of Supervision Influence Tactics and Attributed Bases of Supervisory Power," p. 226.

62. Wayne K. Hoy and William Kupersmith, "Principal Authenticity and Faculty Trust: Key Elements in Organizational Behavior," **Planning and Changing** (Summer 1984), pp. 80–88.

63. Gladys Styles Johnston and Bernice Proctor Venable, "A Study of Teacher Loyalty to the Principal: Rule Administration and Hierarchical Influence of the Principal," Paper presented at the annual meeting of the American Educational Research Association, Chicago, 1985. Also, see J. J. Blase, "Politics of Favoritism: A Qualitative Analysis of the Teacher's Perspective," **Educational Administrative Quarterly** (May 1988), pp. 152–177.

64. Philip A. Cusick, "A Study of Networks Among Professional Staff in Secondary Schools," **Educational Administration Quarterly** (Summer 1981), pp. 132–133.

65. Maeroff, pp. 19–31.

66. Gorton and Thierbach-Schneider, *School-Based Leadership: Challenges and Opportunities,* pp. 253–263.

67. Philip M. Podsakoff et al., "Situational Moderation of Leader Reward and Punishment Behavior," *Organizational Behavior and Human Performance* (August 1984), pp. 23–26. Also, see James M. Kouzes and Barry Z. Posner, "Recognize Contributions: Linking Rewards with Performance" in *The Leadership Challenge: How To Get Extraordinary Things Done in Organizations* (San Francisco: Jossey-Bass, 1990), pp. 241–258.

68. Podsakoff, pp. 27–28.

69. Johnston and Venable, "Teacher Loyalty to the Principal."

70. Stuart M. Schmidt and David Kipnis, "Managers' Pursuit of Individual and Organizational Goals," **Human Relations** (October 1985), pp. 781–794. Also, see Allan R. Cohen and David L. Bradford, "Influence Without Authority: The Use of Alliances, Reciprocity, and Exchange to Accomplish Work," **Organizational Dynamics** (Winter 1989), pp. 5–17.

71. Warren K. Schilit and Edwin A. Locke, "A Study of Upward Influence in Organizations," **Administrative Science Quarterly** (June 1982), pp. 304–316.

72. Mary Ann von Glinow, "Reward Strategies for Attracting, Evaluating and Retaining Professionals," **Human Resources Management** (Summer 1985), pp. 191–206.

73. Harvey Horstein et al., "Influence and Satisfaction in Organizations: A Replication," **Sociology of Education** (Fall 1968), pp. 380–389. For a more recent related study, see Reginald High and Charles M. Archilles, "An Analysis of Influence Gaining Behaviors of Principals in Schools of Varying Levels of Instructional Effectiveness," **Educational Administration Quarterly** (Winter 1986), pp. 111–119.

74. Gorton and Thierbach-Schneider, *School Based Leadership: Challenges and Opportunities,* pp. 319–324.

75. For an excellent review of this research, see Jo Ann Mazzarella, "The Effective High School Principal," **R and D Perspectives** (Winter 1985), pp. 1–8. Also, see Thomas Biester, *Effects of Administrative Leadership on Student Achievement* (Philadelphia: Research for Better Schools, 1984) and Lawrence F. Rossow, *The Principalship: Dimensions in Instructional Leadership* (Englewood Cliffs, NJ: 1990), pp. 34–42. For additional information, see Bill Luche, "The Principal and Supervision Elementary Principal Series No. 4," Phi Delta Kappan Educational Foundation, 1989, an ERIC report, Ed 315–914.

76. Charles W. Guditus and Perry A. Zirkel, "Bases of Supervisory Power Among Public School Principals," Paper

presented at the annual meeting of the American Educational Research Association, 1979, p. 16. Also, see T. Sergiovanni and J. H. Moore eds., ''The Leadership Needed For Quality Schooling'' in *Schooling for Tomorrow: Directing Reform to Issues That Count* (Boston: Allyn and Bacon, 1989).

77. Sharon Conley, '' 'Who's on First?' School Reform, Teacher Participation, and the Decision-Making Process,'' p. 369.

78. Delbert K. Clear and Roger Seager. ''The Legitimacy of Administrative Influence as Perceived by Selected Groups, **Educational Administration Quarterly** (Winter 1971), pp. 46–63.

79. Kunz and Hoy, ''Leadership Style of Principals and the Professional Zone of Acceptance of Teachers,''

80. Gladys Styles Johnston and Toni Mullins, ''Relationships Among Teachers' Perceptions of the Principal's Style, Teachers' Loyalty to the Principal, and Teachers' Zone of Acceptance,'' Paper presented at the annual meeting of the American Educational Research Association, 1985. Also, see Wayne K. Hoy and Bonnie Leverette Brown, ''Leadership Behavior of Principals and the Zone of Acceptance of Elementary Teachers,'' **Journal of Educational Administration** (March 1988), pp. 23–28.

4 Group Leadership

It has been said that, "The organization without effective leadership is in trouble."[1]

Most administrators recognize that providing leadership is a major expectation for their role. This aspect of their role is emphasized in the educational literature they read and at the various professional meetings they attend. But what constitutes leadership? And how does the administrator exercise leadership? In response to these questions, literally hundreds of studies have been conducted, and thousands of articles and many books have been written. While these efforts have, in many instances, provided insights into the subject of leadership, the concept remains an elusive one. In large part, this may be because leadership involves the effective utilization of *all* of the other concepts presented in this text, and it is difficult to analyze as a separate and distinct concept. Rather than reviewing in detail all that has been written on the subject of leadership, the particular ideas and concepts that seem to possess major relevance and implications for the school administrator who would like to function as an educational leader (especially in working with groups) will be described and analyzed.

DEFINITION AND NEED FOR LEADERSHIP

Leadership has been defined in a variety of ways by theorists, researchers, and practitioners.[2] Probably the most commonsensical definition of leadership was put forth by Cowley, who in the 1920's stated, "The leader is the one who succeeds in getting others to follow him."[3]

As theorists and researchers began to analyze the term "leadership," more elaborate and sophisticated definitions evolved. Stogdill, a respected authority on the subject, defined leadership as those activities engaged in by an individual or members of a group which contribute significantly to ". . . development and maintenance of role structure and goal direction, necessary for effective group performance."[4] Stogdill's definition emphasizes that leadership need not be limited to one individual, such as the school administrator, and that the focus of leadership activities should be on increasing the performance effectiveness of the group. More recently, the issue of empowerment has had an impact upon the way leadership is defined. According to Taylor and Rosenbach, "Leadership involves assisting everyone working with the organization to collectively gain control over resources for the common good."[5]

Another major contribution to the literature on leadership and one that the authors believe to hold significant implications for the educational administrator, was developed by Lipham.[6] Lipham made an important distinction between the administrator and the leader. He defined the administrator as "the individual who utilizes existing structures or procedures to achieve an organizational goal or objective."[7] He went on to say, "The administrator is concerned primarily with maintaining, rather than changing established structures, procedures, or goals."[8] Thus the administrator, according to Lipham, must be viewed as a stabilizing force.

In contrast, the *leader* as defined by Lipham, ". . . is concerned with initiating changes in established structures, procedures or goals; he is a disrupter of the existing state of affairs." Leadership, to Lipham, is "the initiation of a new structure or procedure for accomplishing organizational goals and objectives."[9] Consequently, an administrator can be a leader by attempting to introduce change, but is not a leader just because the individual occupies what has been referred to as a "leadership position." It is not the *position* that determines whether someone is a leader; it is the *nature of that individual's behavior* while occupying that position.

Conger and Kanungo also make a distinction between leader and manager, contending that motivation is the "very essence" of true leadership, coupled with the ability of leaders to build an emotional attachment with their followers. Leaders also use intuition, that is "insight, judgement, and executive ESP." The leader's behavior, according to Conger and Kanungo's research, is characterized as charismatic and visionary. One important personality trait is the leader's understanding of the need for power and the approach to its use. The leader must also have the organizational vision necessary to direct the organization into its future, and the ability to articulate this vision.[10]

However, as Lipham acknowledged, the administrator who adopts the role of leader will be unable to spend all of the time on leadership. Adequate attention must also be devoted to administering the school. There is considerable doubt whether an organization can successfully maintain itself if the administrator spends all or most of the time in initiating new procedures or goals. Nevertheless, it is equally clear that organizational improvement may suffer if the administrator spends all of the time maintaining the status quo. As Bennis aptly observes, "Managers are people who do things right; leaders are people who do the right things," and good managers successfully handle the routine, daily jobs, but seldom question whether these jobs should be done in the first place.[11] If the organization is to improve its effectiveness and reach new heights, the administrator must initiate change in procedures and organizational goals. And, if these changes achieve the desired ends, then not only has the administrator attempted to exercise leadership but also has succeeded in exercising *effective* leadership, which seems to be needed more than ever before in education.

Although the professional literature on school administration has long emphasized that one of the major responsibilities of the school administrator is that of providing leadership, this emphasis has taken on new urgency in recent years. Beginning in the 1970s with the "effective school" research[12] and continuing into the 1990s with various national and state reports recommending major changes in education,[13] the school administrator has frequently been cited as a pivotal figure in bringing about needed school reform and improvement. While some may doubt whether all, or, for that matter, many school administrators possess the necessary qualities for leadership,[14] there is general agreement that administrative leadership is needed if the schools are to improve significantly.[15] New developments in leadership theory, for example, have focused on values and beliefs frequently embedded in the mission of the school or school district,[16] on vision or "aesthetic motivation,"[17] and on the role of symbols, culture, and purpose.[18] Whether the focus is on defining a clear school purpose and mission, developing a definite set of staff expectations for improved student learning, providing an orderly school environment where serious learning can take place, or one of the other elements that school effectiveness research has identified,[19] *some* type of leadership contribution by the school administrator would seem *necessary*.

In the following sections, several theories of leadership which contain the *most* useful ideas for the school administrator will be presented, including an extensive exploration of the administrator's leadership role in working with groups. Wexley and Yukl discuss other theories of leadership not covered in this text that may be of further interest to the reader.[20]

THE BEHAVIOR OF EFFECTIVE LEADERS

One major approach to leadership examines the phenomenon in terms of the behavior of effective leaders.

In research conducted by Halpin, the behavior of aircraft commanders and school superintendents was studied, and two sets of behavior were found to be associated with effective leadership.[21] The first, *initiating structure,* refers to a leader's behavior in delineating the relationship between the leader and the members of the work group and in endeavoring to establish well-defined patterns of organization, channels of communication, and methods of procedures. The leader who assumes this leadership role will attempt to define the behavior expected from each member of the organization and will emphasize the importance of "getting the job done." In a sense, this behavior is similar to that of a *nomothetic* leader, first conceptualized by Getzels and Guba, in that work-related needs rather than the personal needs of the members of the group are emphasized.[22] The importance of this type of behavior has been documented in studies of the behavior of the principal in effective schools. For example, in one study it was observed, "[The principal] sets clear expectations for the teachers, and all staff as professionals are accountable for the results of their efforts."[23] In another study it was reported, "These [effective] principals set high academic standards."[24] In a related report on effective schools, the principal is seen framing and communicating goals, setting expectations, monitoring instructional progress, coordinating the curriculum, and supervising and evaluating the faculty.[25]

The second leadership variable identified by Halpin was a factor which was termed *consideration.* Consideration involves the expression of friendship, mutual trust, respect, and a certain warmth between the leader and the group. The administrator who assumes this leadership role will attempt to develop a positive and satisfying relationship between leader and followers and will try to promote a spirit of cooperation among the different members of the group being led. This type of leadership has also been characterized by Getzels and Guba as *idiographic* leadership, in that it stresses the personal and emotional needs of the members of the group.[26] And, as emphasized by Cohen in his review of the literature on effective schools, "Effective principals require the ability to work closely with others."[27]

Consideration behavior on the part of a leader represents an attempt to meet the maintenance needs of a group, while initiating structure can be regarded as behavior designed to help a group achieve its objectives.

Some administrators may feel that they are leaders if they *either* initiate structure *or* provide consideration. Halpin emphasizes, however, that *both* types of behavior are important.[28] That is, the leader must initiate action and get things done. But in most situations, in order to achieve these objectives successfully, the leader must meet the personal and emotional needs of people in order to secure their continuing cooperation and commitment.

For example, if an administrator emphasizes the initiation of structure in order to facilitate organizational achievement, but neglects the needs of a group for consideration, cooperation in achieving the goals of the organization may not be attained. If, on the other hand, an administrator stresses the consideration dimension, but pays insufficient attention to the initiation of structure needed to promote organizational achievement, the administrator may succeed in meeting a group's needs for maintenance but may fail to meet fully the organization's needs for achievement. Halpin's concept of leadership stresses that the administrator who wishes to be a leader must engage in *both* types of behavior (although not

Figure 4.1 Situational Variables and Leadership.

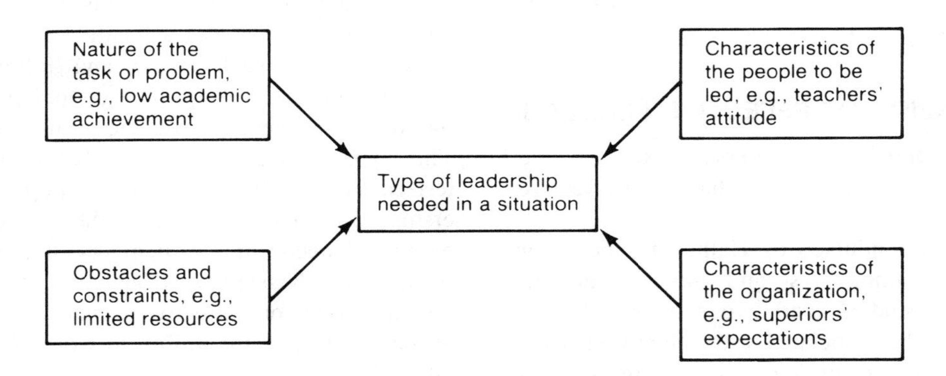

necessarily at the same time) in order to meet the achievement goals of the organization, while maintaining positive and satisfying relationships with others. This type of leadership will require the administrator to integrate the expectations of the organization with the personal needs of the people who work in that organization. This style has been referred to by Getzels and Guba as *transactional leadership*.[29]

SITUATIONAL LEADERSHIP AND THE CONTINGENCY MODEL

A second major approach to leadership emphasizes that the most important variable that should determine the leader's behavior is the nature of the situation in which the leader functions. This school of thought rejects the premise that one approach to leadership is preferable to another. Instead, the proponents of situational leadership set forth the propositions that the leadership approach employed by an individual should be relative to the situation, and that different situations call for different kinds of behavior on the part of the leader.[30] Figure 4.1 presents several major situational factors that could influence the type of leadership needed in a school or school district.[31]

As a conference on effective schools sponsored by the National Institute of Education made clear:

> There are very important contextual factors such as composition of the teaching staff, the student body, the community, the district situation, state mandates, and the principal's own past experience that seem to shape how the principals accomplish their role.[32]

While the empirical evidence is not conclusive,[33] there is considerable observational experience to support the situational theory of leadership. For example, persons who are appointed or elected as leaders in one situation may not be chosen again when circumstances change. Individuals who are successful in leading a group in a given situation may not be successful with a different group or at another time.

The importance of situational leadership can easily be observed in educational administration. The individual chosen for any specific administrative position is usually selected primarily on the basis of possessing certain personal qualities and a style of leadership which meets the needs of the situation in which the administrator will be working. School boards, for instance, do not all look for the same type of leader to fill the position of superintendent. They want an individual who they feel will provide the type of leadership to meet the unique needs of the school district. In one situation, a school board may look for a superintendent who can successfully introduce basic changes in the schools, perhaps over the strong opposition of a number of people. At another time the board may want a superintendent who can play the role of harmonizer and who can ameliorate the conflicts between the school and its constituencies. On each occasion, the school board will seek someone who possesses the unique personal qualities and leadership style for a particular situation.

However, circumstances change, and herein lies one of the fundamental problems of administration. The administrator who has been appointed for one situation on the basis of the possession of certain leadership characteristics may lack the necessary qualifications when a different set of circumstances arises. Perhaps a principal is hired because of organizational ability and a background in curriculum. For several years the principal operates a very efficient school and introduces several curricular innovations. Gradually, the principal gains recognition as an outstanding educational leader in the district. However, things begin to change during the fifth year. Racial conflicts erupt between white and nonwhite students. Teachers become more militant and demand a colleaguelike relationship with the administration. The community grows more critical of the school, and antagonism develops between teachers and parents.

Obviously, new characteristics and problems have been added to the situations in which this principal functions. The reasons for these changes are not immediately evident, but it is clear that a different set of personal qualities and a different leadership style are now required of the principal. Whether or not the administrator in this situation can meet the new requirements is undetermined. However, success as an appointed leader will greatly depend on the extent to which a principal possesses or develops the attitudes, skills, and approaches necessary to respond adequately to new circumstances.

The situational theory of leadership maintains that no particular style of leadership or personal qualities of a leader is appropriate for every situation. The theory places a high premium on the administrator's adaptability and flexibility. A major problem with this theory, however, is that many administrators are influenced in their choice of a leadership style and in the way they behave as a leader by their own personality and need disposition that tends to be rather consistent and unchanging over time and in different situations. Therefore, although the nature of the demands for leadership in education frequently change, an administrator's basic personality may not make it possible to adapt individual leadership style to a new situation. Badaracco and Ellsworth have also addressed this problem. They stress that leaders have certain personality traits that make it difficult to change styles to match the situation. They suggest leaders use their own personal philosophies of management and leadership to solve situational dilemmas or problems.[34]

One way to ameliorate this problem is for organizations and groups to select those administrators who are, or who can become, flexible and adaptable in their leadership responses to changing leadership demands. Another possibility is to select leaders who possess the type of personality characteristics and leadership style for the leadership demands of the situation, and then rotate these leaders to a new environment when the current situation changes. This approach is suggested by the "contingency model," that attempts to incorporate the factors of personality, leadership style, and the nature of the situation by focusing on the interactive dynamics of these three variables.[35] A leading theorist of this school of thought is Fred Fiedler, who has researched and written extensively on the topic.[36] The approach is termed the "contingency model" because it is based on the assumption that effective leadership is *contingent* on a compatible relationship between the administrator's personal qualities and style and the demands of the situation. (For the reader who is interested in investigating other types of contingency approaches, see Wexley and Yukl.[37])

THE GROUP DYNAMICS APPROACH

To exercise leadership, an administrator will need to try to influence the various groups that are associated with the school or school district.[38] In some of these situations, the administrator may be heading a group, such as the faculty; in other circumstances, the administrator may be acting as an advisor to a group, such as the P.T.A.; and in other contexts, the administrator may be in an adversarial relationship with a group, as for example, a community pressure group. Regardless of the nature of the group or the relationship the administrator has to the group, in order to be an effective leader, the administrator must possess knowledge and skills in utilizing group dynamics concepts. In addition, ideas discussed in other concept chapters of this text must be well understood and properly applied. While it will be impossible to provide in this chapter a comprehensive treatment of a topic on which entire books have been written, an attempt will be made to present important aspects of group dynamics that a school administrator should know.

RECOGNIZING POSSIBLE GROUP PROBLEMS

When an administrator initially becomes the head of a group, individual or group problems are seldom considered. Usually there is a task or goal to be achieved and, although the administrator may be cognizant of certain problems, there is probably a lack of awareness of most difficulties that the group may encounter. While not all groups experience problems, the administrator needs to realize that most groups encounter one or more of the following major types of difficulties.[39]

1. Lack of understanding by certain individuals as to why they are members of a group, and a consequent lack of commitment to the group.
2. Lack of understanding and/or acceptance by members of the group of the goal or task the group is supposed to address.
3. Difficulty in developing a constructive atmosphere that minimizes conflicting loyalties, competition, and individualistic needs, and promotes positive attitudes and collaborative efforts among the members of the group.
4. Difficulty in keeping people's attention and efforts focused on the task or goal to be achieved.
5. Inadequate group leadership, organization, or communication.
6. Lack of knowledge, skill, or resources on part of the members of the group.
7. Inadequate follow-through on group decisions or assignments.

Because of the involuntary nature of the membership of many groups which the administrator heads, there may be a lack of commitment on the part of certain members of a group and a lack of understanding of how or why they have become members of the group. The administrator may also experience a lack of leadership acceptance by the members of the group. As a consequence of their lack of understanding, commitment, and acceptance, certain members of the group may express apathy or hostility, or both. The administrator may also find it difficult to develop among members, the feelings of cohesiveness and collaborative effort that facilitate productivity.[40]

In most of these situations, because of bureaucratic restrictions, there may be very little the administrator can do to avoid the problems described. The administrator can, however, be more aware of the involuntary nature of the membership of most of the group, the circumstances by which the administrator became the head of the group, and the possible implications of these two factors. More effort could also be devoted to developing an understanding on the part of the members regarding the reason(s) they were included in the group and their potential contributions and roles. For example, the administrator can attempt to demonstrate the ability to lead and show an appreciation of the participation and contribution of each member of the group. These steps may not eliminate all of the problems a group could encounter, but they should be helpful in preventing many problems and ameliorating others.

In the final analysis, whether a group is ultimately successful depends as much on what happens to the group *after* it has been in operation as it does on the initial formation of the group and the way the group's head was selected.

DEVELOPING A PRODUCTIVE GROUP: INITIAL PRIORITIES—THE IMPORTANCE OF COHESIVENESS AND TRUST

An essential priority for an administrator in working with most groups, especially newly formed ones, is the development of cohesiveness and trust. Group cohesiveness is the degree to which the members of a group are attracted to the group, are willing to take personal responsibility for its tasks, and are willing to engage in cooperative actions to achieve its goals.[41] Group trust is the extent to which the members of a group feel secure with each other and are open toward each other.[42] Both factors are important contributors to the effective functioning of a group.

In order to develop a high degree of group cohesiveness, the administrator should consider several needs. First of all, the members of a group need to feel that their membership is valued and that they can make an important contribution to its effectiveness.[43] This is particularly important for the members of an involuntary group, such as an appointed faculty committee, with the administrator as the head. The members of this type of group may not necessarily have wanted to join the group and may have mixed feelings about their identity and contribution. However, it is not unusual for the members of other types of groups also to wonder about the extent to which they are valued. People generally possess needs for self-respect, affection, and recognition;[44] group interaction can either meet these needs or leave them largely unfulfilled. The administrator should try, to the extent possible, to meet these needs by showing the members of the group that their participation is necessary and valued and by encouraging group members to recognize and reward each other's contributions. It also should be emphasized that this kind of recognition and encouragement by the administrator must be conveyed periodically, rather than only occasionally, or its impact will be diminished over time.

A second major condition that will influence the cohesiveness of a group is the extent to which its members understand the goals of the group and the extent to which these goals are compatible with members' personal goals.[45] For example, a group will have a difficult time developing a very high degree of cohesiveness if members do not understand the goals of the group and/or do not agree with those goals. While the administrator who is heading a group may feel that a particular goal is essential and that group members *should* understand and accept it, the members, in fact, may neither understand nor accept the goal, and for that reason may become apathetic or hostile in response to efforts to involve them in working toward the goal. Until the administrator can develop a better understanding and acceptance of the goal on the part of the members of this group, cooperative action and progress may be limited.

A third major condition that can influence the degree of a group's cohesiveness is the extent to which the leader and members can work cooperatively between and among themselves.[46] Cooperation encourages acceptance and a feeling of "esprit de corps" and is necessary for the effective accomplishment of many tasks and goals. *It does not result automatically with the forming of a group.* The head of the group needs to help its members work cooperatively with each other. According to Johnson and Johnson, several understandings must occur in order for a group to develop cooperative interaction among its members.[47]

1. Individual members must understand the total problem or task which is to be addressed.
2. Individual members must see how each can contribute toward solving the problem or accomplishing the task.
3. Individual members must be aware of the potential contributions of the other group members and the need for coordination.
4. Individual members must understand and be sensitive to the other members' problems.
5. Individual members must be aware of and accept the need for cooperation in order to achieve the group goal.

While these five elements are important, the key to developing cooperative interaction and cohesiveness in a group, according to Johnson and Johnson, is the development and maintenance of a high level of trust among the members of the group.[48] If a group has a high level of trust, its members will more openly express their feelings, concerns, opinions, and thoughts. If the trust level is low in a group, then its members are more likely to be evasive, competitive, devious, defensive, or uncertain in their interaction with the other members. Cooperation and a positive identification with and commitment to a group are unlikely with a low level of trust among its members. For cooperative interaction and a high level of group cohesiveness to exist, there must be openness, sharing, and acceptance among the members of a group—all ingredients of a trusting relationship.[49]

The administrator has an important role to play in developing a high level of trust among the members of a group. Above all, the administrator must be trusting and cooperative, modeling such behavior if the members of the group are to behave similarly. The administrator cannot expect them to behave in a trusting manner if the administrator does not demonstrate qualities of acceptance, openness, sharing, and nondefensiveness. The administrator will also need to *emphasize* the importance of openness and acceptance among the members of the group and reward these qualities when they surface. By developing a high level of trust among the members of the group, the administrator should find it more possible to obtain cooperative action and the group should function with a higher level of cohesiveness.

Two additional conditions which can influence a group's cohesiveness are the size of the group and the similarity of background and interests of group members. In general, the larger the group, the less cohesive it is likely to be. As Tsouderos has observed, "With an increased membership there is a corresponding heterogeneity of the groups in terms of sentiments, interests, dedication to the 'cause,' etc., and a corresponding decline in a feeling of intimacy and frequency of interaction."[50] Although the administrator may not always have much discretion in deciding on the size of the group, frequently such discretion is possible. Therefore, the administrator should consider the impact of size on group cohesiveness whenever forming a group, such as a committee or task force, to address a particular problem or task.

The administrator should also consider, to the extent possible, the similarity of background and interests of individuals who might be appointed to a group. For the most part, the more the members of a group have similar backgrounds and interests, the more probable it is that they will like each other and be willing to work cooperatively together. On the other hand, in forming a group, the administrator should keep in mind that it is not always to the advantage of the group if everyone thinks the same way. Different backgrounds, experiences, and interests can generate ideas over and above those developed in situations when all the members think the same way.[51] Therefore, while the administrator should aim for a fairly high degree of similarity of background and interests on the part of the members of a group in order to develop cohesiveness, sufficient diversity to stimulate new ideas should also be provided. The administrator should not, however, provide for so much diversity in interests and thinking that it will be difficult for the members of the group to agree upon and become committed to the achievement of organizational goals.

The Importance of Group Goals

All groups need goals of one kind or another.[52] A goal is an identifiable focal point in the future toward which effort is directed. Goals are important motivators of human endeavor and can form the basis for the evaluation of individual or group performance. A group without a common goal is like a ship without a rudder; the group may not disintegrate, but its efforts will be erratic and its progress will be uncertain.

To be successful, a group needs *achievable* organizational goals that are understood and accepted by its members, goals that stimulate cooperation and effective action. For the types of groups that the school administrator heads, it would not be wise to assume that their members will understand and accept the goals intended for the group. In many situations, the administrator will discover multiple goals.[53] There will be the goal that the administrator has in mind for the group (which may or may not be understood or accepted by certain members of the group); the goal that a minority of members possess, and the personal goals that individual members of the group would like to achieve (goals that may or may not be compatible with the other goals). Just because an administrator has identified a goal for the group to achieve, there may be other goals, which can and may interfere with reaching the original goal set forth for the group. To the extent to which these multiple goals exist and conflict with each other, group cooperation and goal achievement will be impaired.

In order to arrive at a common group goal, the administrator should try to involve a group in the development of the goal; or, if involvement is not possible or desirable, then the administrator may need to try to direct or coerce the members to adopt a particular goal. There is evidence indicating that group involvement is the preferred approach. For example, Coch and French found in their classic study of overcoming resistance to change that the best way to get the members of a group to accept a new goal is for the administrator to use a process of persuasion and group involvement.[54] Their study suggests that the administrator's most effective approach to developing a common goal on the part of the members of a group is to involve the members of the group in the adoption of the goal and for the administrator to utilize influence rather than authority and/or power in working with the group. This approach will also be helpful by empowering the members of the group. On the other hand, if involvement by the members of a group in the adoption of a goal is not possible or desirable, then the administrator may need to attempt to direct or force the members to adopt a certain goal. While the latter approaches may be necessary, particularly when working with groups formed involuntarily, these more coercive approaches have some definite limitations that are described in Chapter 3—*Authority, Power, and Influence*.

In thinking about common group goals, the administrator needs to be concerned about three basic characteristics: (1) the extent to which the goal is understood, (2) the degree to which the goal is realistic, and (3) the degree to which the goal is acceptable to the members of the group.

All too frequently in education, a meeting of a group is called or a task is assigned to a group, but the ultimate goal is not clear to the members. The goal may be clear to the administrator who called the meeting or assigned the task, but the members of the group may fail to understand what they are to accomplish, and why. Goal clarity and understanding are important determinants of a group's effectiveness. If the members of a group do not clearly understand the goal of the group, their efforts are likely to be unfocused and lethargic. As Cartwright and Zander have noted, "One reason groups get bogged down and never 'get anywhere' is that they have failed to formulate acceptable operational goals."[55]

An operational goal promotes clarity, understanding, and direction to the members of a group.[56] If an administrator convenes a group meeting to discuss parental apathy, then a goal *may* exist, but it is not an operational goal because the specific outcome to be achieved from discussing parental apathy is not clear. On the other hand, if that same administrator convenes a meeting of a group to discuss parental apathy, then indicates that the purpose of the meeting is to identify at least three possible ways of reducing parental apathy (and that goal is understood by group members) then an operational goal does exist.

Groups need operational goals in order to focus efforts, give direction, and provide a basis for evaluation. In the absence of operational goals, a group is likely to flounder and become sidetracked, greatly reducing its potential for productivity.[57]

While it is desirable that the goal of a group be clear and understood, it is also necessary that the goal be a realistic one. It makes little sense for a group to adopt a goal that is not likely to be achieved or one that can be achieved too easily. A group needs a goal which is attainable, but challenging enough so that it will stimulate the members of the group to exert cooperative efforts.[58] An *attainable* group goal is desirable because its achievement can bring important dividends in terms of improved group morale and confidence; failure to achieve a group goal can result in a lowering of group morale and a loss of members' confidence in the group and/or their leader with regard to future group efforts.

Although it is preferable to avoid failure by adopting an attainable goal, the administrator should avoid the convenient approach of adopting a goal that can be so easily achieved it requires little group cooperation or effort. The accomplishment of such a goal may make the administrator or the group "look good" in the eyes of a superior but will possess little real meaning to the members of the group and may lead to an attitude of cynicism toward the adoption of future goals.

A group goal may be understandable and attainable, yet it still may not stimulate group cooperation and effort if the goal is not *acceptable* to a number of its members. Whether or not a member of a group will accept a goal will depend primarily on that member's judgment of the attainability of the goal, the possibility of deriving satisfaction from its achievement, and the degree to which the members believe costs will be incurred in the process of the group achieving the goal.[59] In essence then, for the members of a group to *voluntarily* accept a goal, they must feel that the goal is attainable and they are likely to derive more satisfaction than costs in their efforts to achieve the goal and in its final accomplishment. The word "voluntarily" is emphasized because, in a bureaucratic organization such as the school, there will be many situations where the members of a group and the administrator will need to accept a goal, whether they like it or not. This type of acceptance, however, is shallow endorsement of a goal and is unlikely to result in much commitment toward achieving it. If, on the other hand, the members of a group voluntarily accept a goal, they are more likely to possess a commitment toward achieving that goal and to invest their time and effort in cooperative group activities.

GROUP MEETINGS: THE ADMINISTRATOR'S ROLE

Most groups are scheduled for periodic meetings of one kind or another. The role of the administrator in regard to these meetings will depend on whether or not the administrator is the head of the group. As the leader, responsibility for planning and conducting the meeting and for implementing the outcomes must be assured. This does not mean that the administrator is the only one who should perform these functions. However, it is the administrator's responsibility to see to it that these functions are carried out in such a way that the meetings are productive and satisfactory to a majority of the group's members.

While most administrators may believe that their group meetings are productive and satisfactory to the members, there is some evidence that the members themselves may be perceiving these meetings differently. For example, in a survey of the principals and teachers in eleven school systems, Gorton and Herman found that most principals felt that their faculty meetings were productive and satisfactory to the faculty, whereas a majority of teachers indicated the opposite.[60] In general, teachers expressed dissatisfaction with the planning of the meetings, the nature of problem solving during the meetings, and the lack of follow-up after the meetings.

Although there is little research on the effectiveness of various school meetings, the research and analysis that exist suggest that most meetings are probably not as successful as they should be. In order to improve the success of the group meetings that an administrator may hold, a number of guidelines are offered for consideration.[61]

Planning the Meeting

An administrator should schedule only those meetings for which there is a clearly defined need—one that is, or will be, recognized by those attending the meeting.[62] Many organizations seem to subscribe to the philosophy that there should be regularly scheduled meetings. While there may be certain advantages to regular meetings and certainly a group that seldom meets is likely to experience more difficulty in maintaining cohesiveness, the administrator should review the need and purposes for holding any meeting before actually scheduling it. A basic question is, "Is this meeting really necessary?" A related question is, "Is there some other way that the problem or task under consideration could be addressed without scheduling a meeting?"

If the administrator has decided that a meeting of a group is necessary, a specific agenda should be developed. The agenda should include the purpose of the meeting, the objectives to be achieved, the topics and activities to be pursued at the meeting, time limitations (if any) on discussion of topics, responsibilities of various people during the meeting, and the date, time, and location of the meeting.[63] In developing the agenda, the administrator should be sure to solicit topics, concerns, and/or questions that the other members of the group would like to see discussed. While the administrator may be scheduling the meeting because of interest in a particular topic or problem, it is also important that the agenda reflect the concerns of the other members of the group if they are to develop an adequate sense of commitment to addressing the items on the agenda.

Once the agenda for a meeting has been developed, copies ought to be disseminated (along with related background material) to the members of the group several days prior to the meeting. One of the frequent complaints expressed about meetings is the lament that prior to the meeting, the members of the group had no idea, or only a vague one at best, about why the meeting was being scheduled and what was going to be presented. By developing and disseminating an agenda several days before the meeting, not only will the administrator be more likely to be better organized at the meeting, but also the other members of the group will have received an opportunity to give some advance thought to the problems and/or topics to be discussed. As a result, participation at the meeting is likely to be more productive.

In planning for a meeting an administrator should, in addition, give consideration to the physical arrangements in the meeting room, and to the desirability and feasibility of providing refreshments.[64] Examples of the physical arrangements of a meeting room which may warrant advance planning (depending on the purpose and activities of the meeting) would include the need for a chalkboard or flip chart, writing tools, projection screen, podium, and moveable tables or desks. In addition, while no research has ever discovered that the provision of refreshments increases the productivity of a meeting, refreshments may improve group members' satisfaction. However, unless some acceptable way can be devised for rotating the responsibility of providing refreshments, this type of accommodation may not be feasible on a regular basis.

Conducting the Meeting

Whoever is head of a group will generally be responsible for conducting meetings of the group. The question of what approach the head of a group should utilize in conducting a meeting will depend, in large part, on the purpose of the meeting. For example, if the purpose of the meeting is to utilize the insights and perceptions of the members of the group in arriving at a decision or solution to a problem, then one or more of the approaches discussed in Chapter 1, *Decision Making* (for instance, Quality Circles) should be considered; for more information on the use of Quality Circles during a meeting, see ERIC Report: Ed 238–112.

Regardless of the meeting approach an administrator uses, whoever is leading the group should begin the meeting by reviewing the agenda, clarifying the objectives to be achieved, and outlining the group process to be employed.[65] During the meeting, the group leader should encourage the appropriate participation of all members. Certain members of the group may be shy or reticent about participating and will need to be drawn out by a question such as, "How do you feel about this idea?" On the other hand, some group members may try to dominate the discussion, and it will be necessary for the group leader to redirect their participation by a comment such as, "I wonder if you would be willing to hold your thoughts for a while until I have heard from some of the others who haven't given their views yet?" In chronic cases of member domination, it may be necessary for the group leader to confer privately with the individual about this type of participation.

During the meeting, the group leader should attempt to facilitate members' participation by clarifying questions and ideas and by periodically summarizing the main points that have been made. The group leader needs to keep the group on task during the meeting but should avoid becoming so task-oriented that the members of the group become dissatisfied. In regard to these two aspects, research has identified a number of major leadership behaviors that are important to a group's productivity and satisfaction. These leadership behaviors have been characterized in different ways by different authorities,[66] but basically the behaviors fall into two broad categories: (1) task accomplishment behaviors and (2) human relations behaviors. Both are essential to the effective functioning of a group, particularly during a meeting. The task accomplishment behaviors include:[67]

1. *Initiating.* Providing orientation to the group as to goals, tasks, and roles, proposing tasks or goals, defining a problem, suggesting a procedure or ideas for solving a problem, or focusing discussion.
2. *Seeking Information or Opinion.* Asking for suggestions and ideas, requesting facts, and seeking relevant information.
3. *Giving Information or Opinion.* Presenting suggestions or ideas, providing relevant information, offering facts or observations, identifying issues and/or concerns.
4. *Clarifying and Elaborating.* Reflecting or interpreting ideas and suggestions, identifying and clarifying issues and alternatives.
5. *Reality Testing.* Challenging viewpoints or conclusions that appear to be too easily accepted; examining the practicality and workability of ideas.
6. *Diagnosing.* Investigating the causes of difficulty for members in working

effectively and in making progress toward group goals.

7. *Summarizing.* Pulling together the main ideas of a discussion, offering a synthesis or conclusion of the previous discussion.
8. *Evaluating.* Providing feedback on group performance.
9. *Implementing.* Following through on the decisions reached; monitoring and evaluating progress.

While the task-accomplishment behaviors are important to the achievement of a group's goals, a group is composed of individuals whose feelings, emotions and needs also require attention if the group is to be effective. In order to respond constructively to these aspects, the administrator and/or other members of the group should exercise certain human relations behaviors as needed. These human relations behaviors include the following:[68]

1. *Encouragement.* Being friendly, encouraging everyone to participate, demonstrating openness to the ideas and suggestions of others, giving recognition to contributions.
2. *Expressing Group Feelings.* Acknowledging feelings and mood relationships within the group which, if not recognized and dealt with constructively, may impair group effectiveness.
3. *Relieving Tension.* Easing tension when it occurs, by humor, a change of pace, or suggesting a break in group activity.
4. *Harmonizing Conflict.* Attempting to resolve disagreements constructively.
5. *Facilitating Communication and Trust.* Helping the group by being a good listener, encouraging all points of view, being empathic to the feelings of others, being open and non-defensive, and encouraging others to be so too.

In regard to the fifth human relations behavior identified above, Ross and Hendry feel that the two most important qualities that a group leader should possess are empathy and consideration.[69] And Gordon states that, "Probably the most important single function performed by the group centered leader is that of listening to the contributions of others in the group."[70]

Although some authorities may emphasize the importance of human relations behavior in working with a group, while others stress the importance of task accomplishment behavior, *both* sets of behavior are essential. A group leader who concentrates primarily on task accomplishment behavior, ignoring or neglecting the feelings, emotions, and needs of the members, will soon encounter apathy, hostility, or some other negative reaction that will impair the possibility of accomplishing a task or goal. On the other hand, if a group leader overemphasizes the human relations aspects of working with a group and does not give enough attention to providing task accomplishment behavior, the group may flounder or fail to accomplish its task or goal.

It should be emphasized that the administrator should not assume that all of the group leader functions must be performed by the leader. Other individuals in the group may be able to supplement the administrator's efforts, or, in some cases, do a better job of performing a particular leadership function than the administrator. In fact, one very important leadership contribution an administrator can make is that of identifying and encouraging other members of the group to perform leadership functions, when appropriate and possible. The significant point is the fact that the various leadership functions be performed well, not who performs them.

In recent years the issue of empowerment has dominated the research on group leadership and group dynamics. Conger and Kanungo define empowerment as, "a process of enhancing feelings of self-efficacy among organizational members through identification of conditions that foster powerlessness and through their removal by both formal organizational practices and informal techniques of providing efficacy information."[71] Conger stresses four ways in which effective leaders empower subordinates. First, they structure tasks so that staff members have success and are rewarded. Second, these leaders use verbal persuasion to convince followers that they are able to successfully complete difficult tasks. Third, effective leaders reduce tensions and build excitement and pride in the organization. Finally, good leaders model empowerment through their own behavior, in that they show that they, too, are empowered when dealing with their superiors and thereby demonstrate what self-confidence can accomplish.[72]

Lilly, on the same subject of empowerment, writes that, "power is the ability to get things done, rather than the ability to get one's way against resistance."[73] He distinguishes between distributive power and collective power. The former is adversarial and controlling, while the latter results from empowering all individuals involved. The use of collective power increases the power of all people as they reach the goals together that may have been impossible to accomplish independently. According to this author, the powerful administrator is not an independent one but an interdependent administrator. Evidence that a group is truly empowered is a situation where people feel significant because everyone is making a contribution, leaders model behavior that values the learning and competence of people in the organization, and the work is exciting. Finally, leaders who empower their employees pull them, rather than push them, to a goal by embodying the vision toward which the rest of the group strives.[74] Effective leaders are themselves empowered and seek to do the same for their staff. They are willing to take risks and encourage their subordinates to be risk takers. "Risk taking leaders do not wait for the future to occur. They create the future by actively engaging in it."[75]

Following the Meeting

After a meeting has been concluded, it is important that the minutes be distributed within a few days (or, if the group meets frequently, the minutes may be attached to the advance agenda for the next meeting). The minutes should indicate who attended and should provide a brief summary of what was discussed, a listing of the decisions that were reached, the identification of needed follow-up steps, and a designation of responsibility and deadlines for those steps.[76]

Organized follow-up activity after a meeting will often be essential. Such activity may include, for example, investigating questions that were raised at the meeting but could not be answered, appointing a committee to make recommendations on a problem that was discussed at the meeting, or drafting and distributing a memorandum outlining guidelines in regard to a topic that was raised at the meeting.

The administrator should assume primary responsibility for initiating and directing the follow-up activity after a meeting. Although decisions may have been discussed, unless the administrator takes responsibility for following up on these matters, the likelihood of anyone else doing it is not great. Perhaps, more important, the productivity and satisfaction of the group are likely to be significantly less than they should be if the administrator does not carry out this follow-up responsibility adequately.

THE ADMINISTRATOR AS A MEMBER OF A GROUP

While most of the administrator's interaction with a group will occur in situations led by the administrator, a certain amount of time will also be spent as a group member. A K–12 curriculum committee, the district administrative team, a leaderless group at an assessment center, and the bimonthly meeting of principals at the district office are all examples of groups where the administrator may function as a member, but not as the head, of a group.

Being a member of a group, rather than its head, can be a valuable learning experience for any administrator, as well as an opportunity to make a significant contribution to group effectiveness. Although it is apparently true that many of the group meetings that administrators attend are not very interesting or worthwhile,[77] the alert and perceptive administrator can use the time in these kinds of meetings to observe and study the group in order to help it function more effectively, as well as learn something about group dynamics—information that can pay dividends later when the administrator heads up the group.

As someone who has been the chairperson of many groups, the administrator should already be aware of the various kinds of leadership roles or behaviors discussed earlier in this chapter that are necessary for a group to function effectively. As a member of a group, rather than its head, the administrator should study the group to ascertain which roles are being played and which ones are not; attempt, when feasible, to adopt certain roles that are not being performed; and encourage other members of the group to adopt other roles that have not been taken.

In some situations, the group may need certain task accomplishment roles played, and the administrator can be a contributing member of the group by focusing discussion, providing relevant information, identifying and clarifying issues and alternatives, challenging viewpoints or conclusions that appear to be too easily accepted, or summarizing the main ideas of a discussion, or some other task accomplishment role. In other situations, the group may need certain human relations roles played and the administrator can be a contributing member by being friendly and encouraging others to participate, helping the members of the group to express their true feelings and concerns, helping to relieve tensions within the group, being a good listener, or performing some other human relation role.

By adopting one or more of these leadership roles, and encouraging and supporting the other members of the group to play certain roles, the administrator can make an important contribution to a group's effectiveness and is likely to derive more satisfaction from being a member of that group. One word of caution is in order, however. Since many of the task accomplishment and human relations roles are frequently thought of as leadership roles, the administrator who is a member of a group should make sure that the head of the group shares the philosophy that all leadership does not emanate from its head and that leadership can come from different members of the group. If the administrator is a member of a group where the chairperson has a more limited concept of who can exercise leadership in a group, then it may be necessary to proceed more cautiously until the situation changes.

In addition to the roles specified previously, the administrator as a member of a group can contribute to its effectiveness by manifesting the following attitudes and behaviors.

1. *Responsibility.* The contributing group member comes to meetings well prepared and accepts responsibility for group tasks and for making an effort to resolve problems. The contributing member does not wait passively for someone else to volunteer to do something, but actively seeks and accepts responsibility.
2. *Commitment.* The contributing group member is willing to commit to the achievement of the goals of the group and is willing to devote time and energy to group activities, even if this means some personal sacrifice.
3. *Cooperation.* The contributing group member attempts to cooperate with the other members of the group by sharing responsibilities, ideas, and tasks, and coordinating efforts.
4. *Open-mindedness.* The contributing group member is willing to listen to all points of view. The individual comes to meetings with an open mind and is willing to consider a broad range of issues and ideas. There is no hidden agenda or ax to grind.
5. *Flexibility.* The contributing group member is willing to have a change of mind and

behavior, if appropriate. The individual avoids rigid stands on issues and tries to adapt to the best interests of the group.

6. *Objectivity.* The contributing group member tries not to let biases color judgments of other people and their ideas. The individual attempts to keep a proper perspective and an open mind about ideas and people.

By exhibiting these six attitudes and behaviors, the administrator can make a valuable contribution as a member of a group and can help the group to improve its effectiveness.

EVALUATING THE EFFECTIVENESS OF A GROUP

Any group, if it is to be successful, should be periodically evaluated as to its effectiveness. Evaluation is useful for identifying strengths as well as areas of improvement. It can also be helpful in diagnosing the reasons why a group is not progressing the way it should.

Below are presented criteria that can be utilized to evaluate the effectiveness of a particular group.[78]

1. The goals of the group are understood and accepted by the members, and they are attainable.
2. The contribution that each member of the group is to make is understood, acceptable, and attainable.
3. Each member of the group is respected, and the contribution is valued and recognized.
4. A high level of trust exists among the members of the group and between the members and the head of the group.
5. Communication in the group is open, relevant, and helpful to the achievement of group tasks and goals.
6. Necessary resources and time are provided for the group to accomplish its tasks and goals.
7. Problems and obstacles to group effectiveness are addressed immediately and directly.
8. Progress toward group goals is monitored, and the functioning of the group is periodically evaluated.
9. The group is receiving the type of leadership necessary for operating effectively and achieving its goals.
10. The group is making reasonable progress toward the achievement of its goal(s).

More recently, Keyton and Springston have found that group effectiveness is influenced mainly by feelings of satisfaction rather than by feelings of cohesiveness. Satisfaction comes as a result of "positive feelings about group performance, recognition of the quality of the group output, positive feelings about the group work, and positive feelings for the other group members."[79]

The evaluation of the effectiveness of a group should not be limited to the administrator's own observations and conclusions. Instead, periodically all the members of the group should be involved in applying the evaluation criteria previously presented. This type of involvement by members of the group can make them more sensitive and understanding of possible obstacles or problems the group is encountering and can also result in the identification of problems or obstacles to group effectiveness unobserved by the administrator. Several useful instruments for conducting an evaluation of a group and its meetings can be found in Schmuck and Runkel's *Handbook of Organizational Development*.[80]

> Although many of the case studies, suggested learning activities, and simulations presented in Part II of the text require the appropriate use of the ideas in this chapter on group leadership, the following exercises should provide the *best* opportunities for testing understanding and effective use of group leadership concepts: Cases 32, 39, 41, 46, 54, 55, and 58.

Notes

1. Fred E. Fiedler and Martin M. Chemers, *Leadership and Effective Management* (Glenview, IL: Scott, Foresman, 1974), p. 1.

2. Bernard M. Bass and Ralph M. Stogdill, *The Handbook of Leadership: Theory, Research, and Managerial Applications,* 3rd ed. (New York: Free Press, 1990). Also, see A. G. Jago, "Leadership: Perspectives in Theory and Research," **Management Science** (March 1982), pp. 315–336; and Glenn L. Immegart, "Leadership and Leader Behavior," in *Handbook of Research on Educational Administration,* ed. Norman J. Boyan (New York: Longman, 1988), pp. 259–277.

3. W. H. Cowley, "Three Distinctions in the Study of Leaders," **Journal of Abnormal and Social Psychology** (April 1928), pp. 144–157.

4. Bernard M. Bass and Ralph M. Stogdill, *Handbook of Leadership* (New York: Free Press, 1990), p. 411. Also, see Alan Scharf, "How to Change Seven Rowdy People," **Industrial Management** (November/December 1989), pp. 20–22.

5. Robert T. Taylor and William E. Rosenbach, *Leadership Challenges for Today's Manager* (New York: Nichols Publishing, 1989), p. 207.

6. James M. Lipham, "Leadership and Administration," in *Behavioral Science and Educational Administration,* sixty-third yearbook of the National Society for the Study of Education, ed. Daniel Griffiths, (Chicago: University of Chicago Press, 1964), pp. 119–141.

7. Ibid., p. 122.

8. Ibid.

9. Ibid, Lipham. Christopher Hodgkinson denies the difference between administration and leadership, arguing for a value perspective on administration in *Educational Leadership: The Moral Art* (New York: State University of New York Press, 1991).

10. Jay A. Conger and Rabindra N. Kanugo, "The Empowerment Process Integrating Theory and Practice," *Academy of Management Review* (Boston: Harvard Business School Press, 1989), pp. 6–9.

11. Warren Bennis, "Why Leaders Can't Lead," **Training and Development Journal** (April 1989), pp. 34–39.

12. For one of the first indications that the school administrator's leadership is important, see G. Weber, *Inner-City Children Can Be Taught to Read: Four Successful Schools* (Washington, D.C.: Council for Basic Education, 1971). Also, see R. Edmonds, "Effective Schools for Urban Poor," **Educational Leadership** (October 1979), pp. 15–23; and, J. V. Greer, "Cultural Diversity and the Test of Leadership," **Exceptional Children,** (1988).

13. National Commission on Excellence in Education, *A Nation at Risk: The Imperative for Educational Reform* (Washington, D.C.: U.S. Department of Education, 1983); John Goodlad, *A Place Called School* (New York: McGraw-Hill, 1984); Theodore Sizer, *Horace's Compromise: The Dilemma of the American High School* (Boston: Houghton-Mifflin, 1984), *Time for Results: The Governors 1991 Report on Education* (Washington, D.C.: National Governors Association Center for Policy Research and Analysis, 1986) and The University Council for Educational Administration, *Leaders for America's Schools: The Report of the National Commission on Excellence in Educational Administration* (Tempe, AZ: UCEA, 1987).

14. Nancy Pitner and W. W. Charters, Jr., "Principal Influence on Teacher Behavior: Substitutes for Leadership," (Eugene, OR: Center for Educational Policy and Management, University of Oregon, 1984). Also, see Russell Gerstein et al., "The Principal as Instructional Leader, A Second Look," **Educational Leadership** (December 1982), pp. 47–50, and, W. D. Greenfield, "Moral, Social, and Technical Dimensions of the Principalship," **Peabody Journal of Education** (Summer 1986).

15. Jo Ann Mazzarella, "The Effective High School Principal: Sketches for a Portrait," **R and D Perspectives** (Winter 1985), pp. 1–8; Thomas Biester, *Effects of Administrative Leadership on Student Achievement* (Philadelphia: Research for Better Schools, 1984) and, Wilma F. Smith and Richard L. Andrews, *Instructional Leadership: How Principals Make a Difference* (Alexandria, VA: Association for Supervision and Curriculum Development, 1989).

16. Terrence E. Deal, "The Culture of Schools," in *Leadership: Examining the Elusive,* eds. Linda T. Sheive and Marian B. Schoenheit (Alexandria, VA: Association for Supervision and Curriculum Development, 1987); and, Thomas J. Sergiovanni, *Value Added Leadership: How to Get Extraordinary Performance in Schools* (New York: Harcourt, Brace, Jovanovich, 1990).

17. Warren Bennis and Burt Nanus, *Leaders: The Strategies for Taking Charge* (New York: Harper & Row, 1985).

18. Tom Peters, *Thriving on Chaos: Handbook for a Management Revolution* (New York: Alfred A. Knopf, 1987) and, James M. Kouzes and Barry Z. Posner, *The Leadership Challenge: How to Get Extraordinary Things Done in Organizations* (San Francisco: Jossey-Bass, 1989).

19. For a comprehensive review of these elements, see D. MacKenzie, "Research for School Improvement: An Appraisal of Some Recent Trends," **Educational Researcher** (April 1983), pp. 5–17.

20. Kenneth N. Wexley and Gary Yukl, *Organizational Behavior and Personnel Psychology* (Homewood, IL: Richard D. Irvin, 1984), Chap. 7. Also, see JoAnn Mazzarella and Stuart C. Smith, "Leadership Styles," in *School Leadership: Handbook for Excellence,"* an ERIC report, Ed 309–506, pp. 28–52, and Lawrence F. Rossow, *The Principalship: Dimensions in Instructional Leadership* (Englewood Cliffs, NJ: Prentice-Hall, 1991), pp. 11–22.

21. Andrew W. Halpin, *Theory and Research in Administration* (New York: Macmillan, 1966), pp. 86–130.

22. See J. W. Getzels, James Lipham, and Roald Campbell, *Educational Administration as a Social Process* (New York: Harper and Row, 1968), pp. 145–149.

23. Daniel Kunz et al., *Successful School Series,* an ERIC Report, Ed 221–640, p. 2.

24. Steven T. Bossert et al., *Making Our Schools More Effective,* an ERIC report, Ed. 249–576, p. 66.

25. Philip Hallinger et al., "Identifying the Specific Practices, Behaviors for Principals," **National Association of Secondary School Principals Bulletin** (May 1983), pp. 83–91.
26. Getzels et al., *Educational Administration.* (See note 22.)
27. In Chester E. Finn, *A Principal's Leadership in Developing the Characteristics of Excellent Schools,* an ERIC report, Ed 233–446.
28. Halpin, *Theory and Research,* p. 87. (See note 21.)
29. Getzels et al., *Educational Administration,*, pp. 145–149.
30. Gary A. Yukl, *Leadership in Organizations,* 2nd ed. (Englewood Cliffs, NJ: Prentice-Hall, 1989), p. 130.
31. The basis for this figure was developed from an analysis of Yukl's ideas, ibid., Chapters 6 and 7.
32. National Institute of Education, *Making Our Schools More Effective,* ERIC report, Ed 249–576.
33. For a critical review of this literature, see Claude L. Graeff, "The Situational Leadership Theory: A Critical View," *Academy of Management Review* (April 1983), pp. 285–291, and Nancy J. Pitner, "The Study of Administrator Effects and Effectiveness," in *Handbook of Research on Educational Administration,* ed. Norman J. Boyan (New York: Longman, 1988), pp. 99–122.
34. Joseph L. Badaracco and Richard R. Ellsworth, *Leadership and the Quest for Integrity* (Boston: Harvard Business School Press, 1989), pp. 6–9.
35. E. P. Hollander, "Style, Structure, and Setting in Organizational Leadership," **Administrative Science Quarterly** (March 1971), pp. 2–3.
36. Fred E. Fiedler and Martin M. Chemers, *Leadership and Effective Management* (Glenview, IL: Scott, Foresman, 1974), pp. 73–120. Also, for an excellent analysis of research on Fiedler's Contingency Model, see Ellen Crehan, "A Meta Analysis of Fiedler's Contingency Model of Leadership Effectiveness," Ph.D. Dissertation, University of British Columbia, 1984.
37. Wexley and Yukl, *Organizational Behavior and Personnel Psychology.* Also, see JoAnn Marzarella and Stuart C. Smith, "Leadership Styles" in *School Leadership: Handbook for Excellence,* pp. 28–52.
38. Stephen J. Knezevich, *Administration of Public Education* (New York: Harper and Row, 1984), Parts 3 and 4. Also, see Van Morris et al., *Principals in Action* (Columbus, OH: Charles E. Merrill, 1984), Chapter 3, and, a report by the National Association of Elementary School Principals, *Principals for 21st Century Schools* (1990), Chapter 5. Also, see Carl D. Glickman, *Supervision of Instruction: A Developmental Approach,* 2nd ed. (Boston: Allyn and Bacon, 1990).
39. Donelson R. Forsyth, *An Introduction to Group Dynamics* (Monterey, CA: Brooks/Cole, 1983), Pt. 4.
40. Rodney W. Napier and Matti K. Gershenfeld, *Groups: Theory and Experience* (Boston: Houghton Mifflin, 1981), pp. 78–79. See also Albert M. Koller, Jr. "Developing and Managing a Winning Team," **Management** (November/December 1989), pp. 2–31, Colin Leicester, "The Strategic Manager as Leader," **International Journal of Manpower** (April 1990), pp. 3–10.
41. Richard M. Steers, *Introduction to Organizational Behavior* (Glenview, IL: Scott, Foresman, 1984), pp. 234–235.
42. Joseph Luft, *Group Processes* (Palo Alto, CA: Mayfield, 1984), p. 27.
43. Forsyth, *Group Dynamics,* p. 350.
44. Marilyn Bates et al., *Group Leadership* (Denver: Love, 1982), Chapter 3.
45. Miriam Erez and Frederick H. Kanfer, "The Role of Goal Acceptance in Goal Setting and Task Performance," **Academy of Management Review** (July 1983), pp. 454–463.
46. For an excellent analysis of the research on the benefits of cooperation in a group, see Dean Tjosvold, "Cooperation Theory and Organizations," **Human Relations** (September 1984), 743–767.
47. David W. Johnson and Frank P. Johnson, *Joining Together: Group Theory and Group Skills* (Englewood Cliffs, NJ: Prentice-Hall, 1975), pp. 104–105.
48. Ibid., p. 246.
49. Ibid., p. 247.
50. J. Tsouderos, "Organizational Change in Terms of a Series of Selected Variables," **American Sociological Review** (April 1955), pp. 206–210.
51. Forsyth, *Group Dynamics,* pp. 349–368. Group leaders need to avoid the "groupthink" phenomenon. See Gregory Moorhead and John Montanari, "An Empirical Investigation of the Groupthink Phenomenon," **Human Relations** (May 1986), pp. 399–410.
52. Most of the ideas for this section are based on Chapter 4 of Napier and Gershenfeld, *Group Theory and Experience.*
53. Mel. E. Schnake and David S. Cochran, "Effect of Two Goal-Setting Dimensions on Perceived Intraorganizational Conflict," **Group and Organizational Studies** (June 1985), p. 169.
54. Lester Coch and John R. P. French, Jr., "Overcoming Resistance to Change," **Human Relations** (1948), pp. 512–532.
55. Darwin Cartwright and Alvin Zander, *Group Dynamics: Research and Theory* (New York: Row, Peterson, 1960), pp. 353–354.
56. Ernest Stech and Sharon A. Ratliffe, *Effective Group Communication* (Lincolnwood, IL: National Textbook, 1985), pp. 229–230.
57. Luft, *Group Processes,* p. 170. (See note 42.)
58. Schnake and Cochran, "Two Goal-Setting Dimensions," pp. 168–169.
59. Erez and Kanfer, "Role of Goal Acceptance." (See note 45.)
60. Richard A. Gorton and Chuck Herman, "Faculty Meeting," in *National Forum of Educational Administration and Supervision,* vol. 1 (1984–85), pp. 29–34.
61. These guidelines are based in part on a synthesis of ideas from Richard A. Schmuck and Philip J. Runkel. *The Handbook of Organizational Development in Schools* (Prospect, IL: Waveland Press, 1988), Chapter 4; Elizabeth Chell, *Participation and Organizations* (New York: Macmillan, 1985), Part 2; and Ernest Stech and Sharon A. Ratliffe, *Effective Group Communication,* Section 5. Also, see Larry Frase and Robert Hetzel, *School Management By*

Wandering Around (Lancaster, PA: Technomic Publishing, 1990), pp. 144–155.

62. Norman B. Sigband, "Meetings with Success," **Personnel Journal** (May 1985), p. 49. Also, see Edward R. Lilly, "Hold Productive Staff Meetings," **The School Administrator** (March 1988), pp. 47–48.

63. John Lindelow, "Making Meetings More Effective," **The Practitioner** (February 1984), pp. 4–5. Also, see Glynis J. Bean, "Don't Let a Dominator Spoil the Session for Everyone," **Marketing News** (January 1988).

64. Ibid. (Lindelow)

65. Clayton Thomas, "Group Processes," in *Encyclopedia of School Administration and Supervision,* ed., Richard A. Gorton et al. (Phoenix, AZ: Oryx Press, 1987).

66. The initial research and conceptualization in this area were developed by Kenneth D. Benne and Paul Sheats, "Functional Roles of Group Members," **Journal of Social Issues** (Spring 1948), pp. 42–47. For an excellent introduction to group facilitation skills for administrators and a framework to help managers recognize and solve group process problems, see Frances Westley and James A. Waters, "Group Facilitation Skills for Managers," **Management Education and Development** (1988), pp. 134–143.

67. Adapted and extended from Taylor McConnell, *Group Leadership for Self Realization* (New York: Petrocelli Books, 1974), pp. 149–157.

68. Ibid., pp. 144–149.

69. Murray Ross and Charles Hendry, *New Understanding of Leadership* (New York: Association Press, 1957), pp. 43–44. For a more recent discussion on additional personality traits of top executives and gifted entrepreneurs, see Warren Bennis, "Ten Traits of Dynamic Leaders," **Executive Excellence** (February, 1988).

70. Thomas Gordon, *Group Centered Leadership* (Boston: Houghton Mifflin, 1955), p. 177.

71. Jay A. Conger and Rabindra N. Kanungo, *Charismatic Leadership* (San Francisco: Jossey-Bass, 1988), pp. 3–5.

72. Jay A. Conger, *The Charismatic Leader* (San Francisco: Jossey-Bass, 1989), pp. 109–117.

73. Edward R. Lilly, "The Determinants of Organizational Power Style," **Educational Review** (1989), pp. 281–290.

74. Warren Bennis, "Why Leaders Can't Lead," **Training and Development Journal** (April 1989), pp. 34–39.

75. Barry G. Morris, "The Executive: A Pathfinder," **Organizational Dynamics** (Spring 1988), pp. 62–75.

76. Sigband, "Meetings with Success," p. 55.

77. See Gorton and Herman, "Faculty Meetings," pp. 29–34.

78. Adapted in part from Johnson and Johnson, *Joining Together,* pp. 2–5.

79. Joann Keyton and Jeff Springston, "Redefining Group Cohesiveness and Effectiveness: Replicating and Extending Within New Perspectives." Paper presented at the Annual Meeting of the Speech Communication Association, San Francisco, November, 1989, p. 16. An ERIC Report, Ed 314–776.

80. Schmuck and Runkel. *Organizational Development,* Chapter 4. Also, see Deborah L. Gladstein, "Groups in Context: A Model of Group Effectiveness," **Administrative Science Quarterly** (December 1984), pp. 499–517; and Phyllis Paolucci-Whitcomb, William E. Bright and Robert V. Carlson," Interactive Leadership: Process for Improving Planning," in *Educational Planning: Concepts, Strategies, Practices,* eds. Robert V. Carlson and Gary Awkerman (New York: Longman, 1991), pp. 295–312.

5 Conflict Management

It is understandable that an administrator should wish to avoid conflict, especially if a particular conflict could be disruptive. However, by trying to avoid all conflict, an administrator could be ignoring or suppressing significant problems or issues that need to be brought out into the open if they are to be ameliorated or resolved. Moreover, as Wexley and Yukl have emphasized, "Interpersonal and intergroup conflict occur to some extent in all organizations and are a natural part of social relationships."[1] The challenge, according to Wynn, ". . . is not to eliminate conflict but to minimize its destructive impact and make it a positive force in the organization."[2]

To meet this challenge, the administrator will need to engage in conflict management. In this chapter, conflict management will be broadly defined to indicate efforts designed to prevent, ameliorate, or resolve disagreements between and among individuals and groups; it will also include efforts by the administrator to initiate conflict. Although the concept of initiating conflict may be perceived by many readers as a radical idea, the social science literature supports the proposition that in some cases it may be necessary for an administrator to take action that may create conflict in regard to an individual or group that has become complacent or stagnant in performance.[3] More will be said about this later in the chapter.

Since many of the conflicts which arise in an organization are role conflicts, a discussion of the basic concepts of role theory will first be presented as an introduction to conflict management.

ROLE CONCEPTS

For every administrative position in an effectively managed organization, there are written job descriptions or policy statements, emanating from a governing board, that embody the formal expectations of the organization. In addition, in every organization there usually are implicit, frequently unexpressed expectations for an administrator's behavior that originate with the various individuals or groups with whom the administrator comes into contact. Together, both sets of expectations comprise a behavioral definition of the role that different individuals or groups—both formal and informal—believe the administrator *should* perform in a particular situation. As Getzels has observed, "The expectations define for the actor [administrator], whoever he may be, what he should or should not do as long as he is the incumbent of the particular role."[4] The expectations also serve as "evaluative standards applied to an incumbent in a position,"[5] and therefore can represent a powerful source of potential influence on any administrator's behavior.

However, the behavior of an administrator is also affected by personal needs in regard to the role the administrator should play. These needs become the administrator's self-expectations and may be more important than the expectations of others in determining the role to be taken in a given set of circumstances. For example, if an administrator would rather play the role of manager than instructional leader, most energies will be focused on administering an efficiently run school, despite the expectations other individuals

Figure 5.1 Major Functions that Influence an Individual's Behavior.

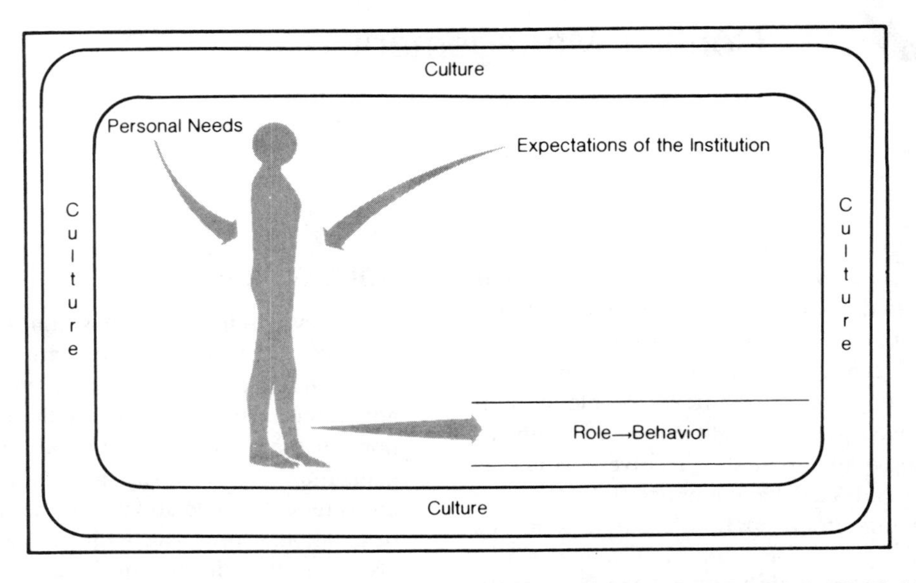

and groups have for the administrator to perform the role of instructional leader.

Figure 5.1, based on the Getzels model, illustrates major factors that can influence an individual's role behavior.[6] It shows that the institution and the individual, i.e., the administrator, are influenced in the development of their expectations and need dispositions by the larger culture. The model implies that one source of the administrator's self-expectations is underlying personal needs. It further indicates that the administrator's behavior is affected not only by personal needs, but also by the role expectations that are held by other relevant individuals and groups. Finally, the model suggests that the administrator's behavior is a result of *interaction* between personal need dispositions and the role expectations held by others associated with the institution. Based on the Getzels model, it would appear that as long as the administrator's need dispositions are compatible with the expectations of others, conflict will be minimal. However, when need dispositions and expectations clash, role conflict is likely.

INDIVIDUALS OR GROUPS WHO HOLD EXPECTATIONS

From the preceding discussion, it becomes evident that it is important for an administrator to be aware of the role expectations of others. However, no inference should be drawn that an administrator must conform to these expectations or that all people in a specific reference group will hold the same expectations. As Campbell has noted, "Only by an understanding of these expectations can the administrator anticipate the reception of specified behavior on his part. Such anticipation seems necessary if the area of acceptance is to be extended and the area of disagreement minimized. Moreover, such understandings are necessary if a program of modifying expectations is to be started."[7]

Figure 5.2 identifies the various individuals and groups whose expectations may generate conflict for the administrator.[8]

The need for the administrator to identify and to understand the role expectations of others cannot be overemphasized. Frequently the administrator's

Figure 5.2 Referents Holding Expectations for the Role of the Administrator.

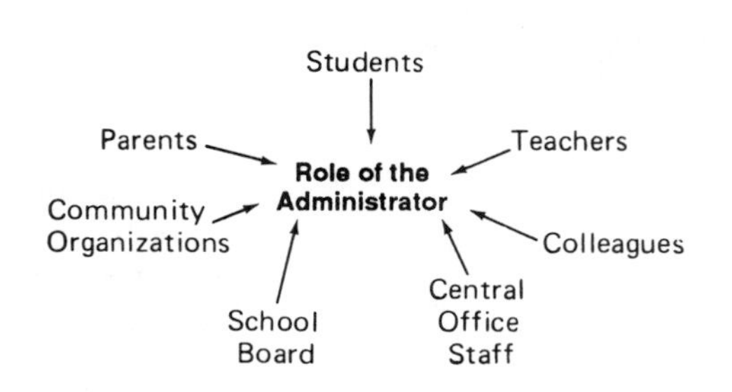

problem is deciding which individual or group expectations are the most important to ascertain. It is not inconceivable that all the individuals and groups identified in Figure 5.2 would have an opinion about the way an administrator should behave with respect to a certain issue. However, it is neither reasonable nor practical for the administrator to attempt to discover and understand the expectations of everyone in the school organization and the community. The administrator must, therefore, concentrate on developing an awareness and understanding of the expectations of those individuals or groups who may influence the administrator's effectiveness in some important regard. If expectations, as previously defined, constitute the "evaluative standards applied to an incumbent of a position,"[9] the administrator needs to learn the expectations of those individuals or groups whose evaluation may impair or enhance the administrator's effectiveness. According to Gross, role expectations can vary in *direction, clarity,* and *intensity.*[10]

Direction

The direction of the expectations for the administrator's role may range along a continuum, from complete agreement to absolute opposition. The primary factor which seems to determine the direction of an individual's or group's expectations is the nature of the situation that has created the expectations.

For instance, a decision by an administrator not to involve teachers in the consideration of a schedule change may be in complete agreement with the teachers' expectations that it is not necessary for the principal to secure faculty participation on any decision to change the school's schedule. However, in another situation, concerning a *curricular* change, a decision by the administrator not to involve teachers in discussing the change may be in direct conflict with the expectations of the faculty about the role of the administrator, because in the area of curriculum faculty expect to be involved on all matters. The critical variable, then, that will typically determine the direction of an individual's or group's expectations is the nature of the situation giving rise to their expectations.

Clarity

Another aspect of role expectations that the administrator needs to take into consideration is clarity. Since expectations are frequently unwritten and sometimes unspoken, the administrator may occasionally be unaware that a particular group holds any role expectations. For example, a principal may delegate to one assistant the responsibility for working with various student organizations in the school. In this situation the students of a particular group may expect the principal, rather than the assistant, to help them. Nevertheless, the circumstances may be such that the students are reluctant to express their feelings about the role of the principal. As a result, the principal's behavior may fail inadvertently to meet their expectations, and problems of dissatisfaction may be created.

In another context, the administrator may be aware that an individual or group possesses behavior expectations, but the specific intent of those expectations may not be clearly communicated. For instance, the school board may have expressed its expectation that educational leadership become a primary responsibility of all administrators in the district. However, in the absence of further explication of the term "educational leadership," it may be difficult for any administrator to know exactly what is expected. Does the term mean that the administrator should work to bring about basic changes in the school curriculum? Perhaps. But the administrator may later discover that educational leadership means to the board members that the administrator should try to operate a more efficient program. Unfortunately, the school board initially expressed their expectations in such general terms that their intent was unclear. Role ambiguity is a major problem in school administration, one that would be greatly alleviated by more clearly written and definitive job descriptions.[11]

Expectations that are not clearly communicated or expectations that are unexpressed represent an important source of misunderstanding between the administrator and those possessing role expectations, constituting a major problem in school administration. For an extensive review of the research on role ambiguity, see Jackson and Schuler and more recent research studies and writings by Leigh, Lucas, and Woodman.[12]

A related problem is the tendency on the part of too many administrators to perceive inaccurately the expectations of others. The potential for role conflict is already present when the expectations of an important reference group and those of the administrator are in disagreement. However, a possible role conflict can be created unnecessarily when an administrator *misperceives* the expectations of others. For example, a study by Hencley found that 72% of the superintendents in a sample inaccurately perceived the expectations of their reference groups in at least one of four ways.[13]

1. The actual expectations of the reference group and the role orientation of the superintendent were identical, but the superintendent perceived them to be different.
2. The superintendent thought that the role orientation and the expectations of others were in agreement when in reality they differed.
3. The superintendent failed to perceive a group's strong support for the role orientation.
4. The superintendent completely misjudged the reference group's opposite expectations.

It should be emphasized that Hencley's research made no attempt to examine the relationship between the superintendent's accuracy of perception and the clarity with which their reference group's expectations were expressed. But the findings of his study strongly suggest that all administrators, not just superintendents, need to exert greater effort toward improving their accuracy in perceiving the expectations of their reference groups if they want to avoid conflict. This is particularly important since studies have shown that there is a tendency to perceive the expectations of others to be closer to one's own than they really are.[14] A useful first step, then, is for the administrator to examine and, if possible, validate the assumptions held by a reference group.

Intensity

The intensity of role expectations is a third dimension identified by Gross.[15] In a given situation a group may expect that the administrator absolutely *must* act in a certain way or *perhaps* act in a certain way.

It is clearly in the best interest of the administrator to assess accurately the intensity of an individual's or group's expectations. An expectation that it is absolutely essential for the administrator to play a particular role carries markedly different implications for behavior than one which is based on the feeling that *perhaps* action on an issue should be taken.

For example, in regard to an administrator's role in initiating a program to improve student behavior, the expectation by parents that the principal should *perhaps* initiate a program is different in intensity and carries different behavioral implications than an expectation that such a program should be initiated or that it is *essential*. In the first instance, the administrator will probably feel very little pressure from the parents, and may be able to act appropriately, with no repercussions. However, if the administrator ignores the expectations of parents when they believe that a program should be started to improve student behavior, there will possibly be parental complaints, and the principal's status in the community may suffer. If the principal attempts to ignore parental expectations when parents feel that a program is *essential,* these parents may attempt to impose whatever negative sanctions or pressures they can command in order to bring about compliance by the principal.

The problem faced by most administrators in this kind of a situation is that it is usually more difficult to determine the intensity of a group's expectations than the direction of those expectations, since the former characteristic may not be made explicitly or public. This obstacle points to the need for all administrators to engage in continuous efforts to ascertain the *intensity* of the expectations of individuals and groups with whom they work.

THE NATURE OF ROLE CONFLICT

Thus far we have discussed the nature of role expectations in terms of direction, clarity, and intensity. However, role expectations can also vary in their compatibility, that is, the degree to which they are in agreement with each other. For example, in the area of student discipline, the teachers may expect the principal to play the role of a strong and strict disciplinarian while the students may feel the principal should play the role of a flexible, understanding parent. The parents may be divided in their expectations, some agreeing with the teachers and others agreeing with the students. To complicate matters further, the principal's own role orientation toward handling student discipline may not coincide with the expectations held by any of the three referent groups. Consequently, a situation may exist where there is incompatibility of expectations for the role of the principal.

Although incompatible expectations are the main cause of role conflict, a lack of agreement in role expectations is not always synonymous with—nor will it necessarily lead to—role conflict.[16] Whether role conflict actually results from incompatibility of expectations depends on how the lack of agreement is perceived. For example if an administrator perceives disagreement in role expectations, but remains certain an action should be taken, there is no role conflict so far as the administrator is concerned. If, on the other hand, the incompatibility of role expectations causes the administrator to be uncertain about which role to adopt, role conflict is present. This kind of role conflict can be termed "intra-role conflict" because it arises as a result of uncertainty within the individual.

A second type of role conflict that can create problems for the administrator occurs when other individuals or groups attempt to impose their expectations by directly challenging the role the administrator has chosen. For example, an administrator may perceive disagreement with the tenured teachers in the school in regard to the role the administrator should play in classroom supervision. The administrator may feel that it is essential to conduct classroom observations of everyone on the staff, regardless of their tenure status. The tenured teachers may feel, however, that the principal should make no attempt to supervise their classrooms.

In this particular instance, the administrator may be aware of the disagreement the tenured teachers have about the role of the principal in the classroom supervision and yet feel no uncertainty about the role to play. Therefore, there is no intra-role conflict for the principal. However, if several tenured teachers refuse to permit the administrator to visit their classrooms, their action will bring their expectations into direct conflict with the role which the administrator has chosen. This type of role conflict can be termed "extra-role conflict" because it is imposed on the administrator externally, rather then initially arising from any inner doubts.

There are, of course, other types of role conflict.[17] Since the administrator usually works with a wide variety of individuals and groups with diverse backgrounds, values, interests, and perspectives, there is apt to be conflict about the role to be taken in many situations. The conflict may result from the incompatibility of (1) the administrator's personality and the various roles to be performed, (2) the administrator's self-expectations and those of one or more individuals or groups, (3) two or more individuals' or groups' expectations for the role of the administrator, or (4) expectations of members of the same group in regard to the administrator's role. Although the role expectations of any individual or group with whom the administrator has contact may occasionally pose role conflict problems, there is evidence to suggest that students, teachers, and parents are the primary sources of role conflict for the school principal,[18] and the school board and teachers sources of role conflict for the superintendent.[19] However, it should be noted that studies have revealed a relatively high degree of agreement in expectations for the administrator's role, despite differences in school, community, and individual characteristics.[20] Therefore, it appears that, although role conflict is an inescapable aspect of educational administration, it is not the norm in most organizational situations. Nevertheless, when role conflict does occur, it can lead to serious consequences.

CONSEQUENCES OF ROLE CONFLICT

The possible consequences of role conflict are varied and, in some cases, far reaching.[21] For the individual administrator, role conflict can result in frustration, tension, stress, impaired effectiveness, disillusionment and, in some extreme cases, dismissal. For the person or group whose expectations are in conflict with the administrator's, the conflict can result in a negative attitude toward—and a negative evaluation of—the administrator. Furthermore, these negative feelings can create hostile action toward the administrator or, paradoxically, a withdrawal from any interest or involvement and a general feeling of dissatisfaction and low morale.

The point needs to be made, however, that these possible consequences of role conflict are not inevitable. Individuals and groups differ in their reactions to role conflict, as well as the extent to which they can manage or cope with role conflict. The impact of a role conflict on any particular administrator or reference group may be minor or major, depending on the nature of the role conflict, the personalities of the people involved, and the strategies or approaches these people utilize to deal with the conflicts. In the following section, we will discuss some strategies and approaches for preventing role conflict.

PREVENTION OF ROLE CONFLICT

An administrator can take several steps to *prevent* role conflict. While these steps will not prevent all role conflict, they should be helpful in reducing its incidence.[22]

An important first step in preventing role conflict is to develop comprehensive and clear job descriptions for all positions in an organization. In the absence of such descriptions, some people will be unclear as to their responsibilities and may, therefore, fail to meet the expectations of the organization, while others may initiate actions that they believe to be within their responsibility, but which go beyond the expectations of the organization. Although most administrators probably believe that the job descriptions for positions in their particular organization are already comprehensive and clear, a review of those descriptions is recommended. Such a review should include the involvement of the person who occupies the position, as well as those who hold expectations for the position, in an attempt to gain commitment to the role.

A job description, even a comprehensive and clear one, needs to be communicated periodically to all groups who may hold expectations for the person responsible for that job. Unfortunately, too many job descriptions are placed in a handbook of some kind and are seldom examined. A job description needs to be reviewed regularly (at least once a year, probably at the beginning of each year) with the occupant of the position and with those groups who are likely to hold expectations for the role. Such a review will not prevent all role conflicts, but can be helpful in preventing those that are based on some misunderstanding of a role.

A considerable amount of role conflict could be prevented by better personnel selection procedures. When a vacancy occurs, an organization needs to be clear in its expectations as to the responsibilities of the position that needs to be filled and the type of person who can best meet those expectations. Then the organization needs to initiate rigorous methods for selecting the most appropriate person for the vacancy. Although research is limited as to the most effective selection methods,[23] the techniques used in assessment centers seem to offer the most promise.[24]

Regardless of which selection techniques are used, a high priority should be given to involving, during the selection process, representatives from those groups which are most likely to hold strong expectations for the new person. For example, teachers, parents, and students can provide special insights during the selection process and, more importantly, the selection process can educate these groups as to the organization's expectations for the new person filling the vacancy.

Once a new person is employed, then the expectations of the organization may possibly need to be reviewed periodically with the administrator, and adequate opportunity should be provided for clarification of role feedback on performance. The lack of opportunity for clarification and expectations and for feedback on acceptability of role performance can cause considerable role conflict.[25] An administrator can prevent much of this type of role conflict by meeting regularly with personnel for the purpose of clarifying expectations and by offering suggestions on how job performance might be improved.

While the steps mentioned previously should be helpful in preventing role conflict, an administrator should not ignore the possibility that the administrator's own personality or behavior could be causing or exacerbating a conflict. For example, the way an administrator makes decisions, exercises authority, and treats people could provoke conflict of one kind or another. In many cases the conflict may be unavoidable and is simply part of the price the administrator will have to pay in carrying out legitimate responsibilities. On the other hand, if the administrator could have employed a less stressful, perhaps more perceptive approach to reaching the same goals, the conflict might have been preventable.

Whether an administrator's own personality or behavior is causing conflict will be difficult to ascertain, especially if it is unintentional. Most administrators probably believe that whenever conflict occurs, it is a result of other factors. However, in analyzing conflict and trying to determine how future conflict might be prevented, an administrator needs to at least examine the possibility that aspects of the administrator's personality or approach to working with people may be causing unnecessary conflict—conflict that might be prevented if certain changes are made. For example, Wall and Nolan emphasize that a feeling of inequity in group members can cause conflict between group members. According to these authors, equity theory holds that "an individual's perception of justice or fairness in a relationship is determined by the assessment of his or her outcomes and investments relative to another." Thus, a principal must be sure that subordinates perceive fairness in the amount and type of work each is responsible for and fairness in the results of this work that could be in the form of recognition, formal evaluations, and pay incentives. In equity theory research, perceived inequity is most "strongly associated with people-centered conflicts, less strongly associated with task-centered conflicts, and least strongly associated with no reported conflicts," while management conflict styles impact upon the perceived inequity in a group and avoidance management styles increase perceptions of inequity.[26]

In another study on managing conflict, Lindelow and Scott outline the types and sources of social conflicts, a prevalent occurrence in schools. They define social conflict as "conflict between individuals and conflict between groups common to the school environment." The authors identify four primary sources of social conflict within the school: communication problems, organizational structure, human factors such as personality, and limited resources. Poor communication is a major cause of conflicts. For example, teachers who do not receive regular feedback about performance may have poor morale and negative attitudes, resulting in an unwillingness to respond to administrative directives. The type of organizational structure also has a direct effect on conflicts. Schools where the administration encourages empowerment will have more frequent conflicts, although minor. Major disruptive conflicts lessen as empowerment increases. When the staff participates in decision making, the opportunity to express minor conflicts increases, but, at the same time, this prevents minor problems from snowballing into major incidents. Human factors, the third source of social conflict, cannot be eliminated by an administrator. However, they must be properly managed. Differing values or goals are one of the most important human sources of conflict. The fourth source of conflict, according to Lindelow and Scott, is competition over limited resources. For example conflict results when teachers fail to get raises they think they deserve or when the science department fails to get desired equipment. The administrator's job is to assure all groups that they have been treated fairly in resource distribution, thus preventing unnecessary conflict.[27]

CONFLICT INITIATION

Although most, if not all administrators would probably like to prevent conflict from occurring, it may be necessary in some situations for an administrator to *initiate* action that may result in a conflict with another individual or group. Usually these circumstances come about because a particular individual or group is not performing as well as expected and does not want to change. The theoretical and research literature on initiating conflict is limited. The ideas in this section are based primarily on an analysis by Robbins and on insights developed from the authors' experiences as administrators.[28]

For example, a principal has observed a teacher who is ineffective in motivating students. However, in a follow-up conference, the teacher does not perceive a problem and believes a good job of teaching is occurring. To further complicate the matter, suppose that the teacher is tenured, a leader in the union, and an individual with a very strong personality. At this point, the principal could pull back and refrain from discussing the problem that was observed in the teacher's classroom. However, if the principal is to fulfill the responsibilities of an educational leader, the problem may need to be directly presented, which *could* create a conflict with the teacher. (It should be emphasized that in this context, conflict is not inevitable; much will depend on the principal's approach in working with the teacher.) Nevertheless, the scenario that has been presented thus far suggests that total avoidance of any type of conflict between the principal and teacher may not be easy, and initiating conflict may be necessary in order to reduce the complacency of the teacher and, ultimately, to bring about improvement.

Administrators must, of course, carefully consider all of the possible ramifications before initiating conflict. The administrator will want to be reasonably sure that the problem which needs to be addressed is sufficiently serious to warrant intervention and that approaches would solve the problem without arousing conflict are tried first (see Chapter 3 on *Authority, Power, and Influence*). Also, it will be important for an administrator to delay initiating conflict with an individual or group, if possible, when the administrator is already involved in other kinds of conflicts that may drain emotions and energies. Too much conflict will impair the administrator's effectiveness. But assuming that the latter is not the case, and that an individual or group does not respond to other approaches the administrator has tried, then conflict may need to be introduced.

In initiating conflict the administrator should begin with the lowest possible profile. Anticipating and preparing for possible negative reactions will be essential. Generally, when individuals or groups are informed of a problem they do not want to address, they will become defensive. When this happens, the administrator should discuss the problem as calmly and evenly as possible. This may not be easy, since an individual or group that becomes defensive could grow antagonistic and hostile, thereby stirring the administrator's own emotions. While it is a real test of self-control to remain calm and rational in the face of a defensive reaction, the administrator should make every effort to do so, and to persist in focusing individual or group attention on the problem and its possible solution.

AN APPROACH TO CONFLICT RESOLUTION

Although research and theory are limited regarding how best to ameliorate or resolve a conflict, Gross has theorized that when an individual is faced with a role conflict, there are four pathways to resolution:

1. The individual conforms to the expectations of Group A.
2. The individual conforms to the expectations of Group B.
3. The individual performs some compromise behavior that represents an attempt to conform, in part, to both sets of expectations.
4. The individual attempts to avoid conforming to either set of expectations.[29]

A fifth alternative identified in a replication of the Gross study is the possibility of the administrator resolving conflict by actively trying to change the direction or intensity of one or both sets of expectations.[30]

If these, then, are the options available to an administrator who is faced with role conflict, which alternative should be chosen? Based on an investigation into the ways superintendents resolve their role conflicts, Gross has theorized that three conditions determine how a role conflict will be resolved:

1. The administrator's feeling about the legitimacy of each of the role expectations that are in disagreement. (Legitimacy in this context is defined as the perceived right of an individual or group to expect the administrator to play a certain role.)
2. The administrator's perception of the negative sanctions that the administrator may suffer for nonconformity to one set of expectations, as compared to another.
3. The administrator's primary orientation to either legitimacy or sanctions as a justifiable basis for resolving a role conflict.[31]

Illustrative of the application of Gross's theory of role conflict is the principal who, when faced with a conflict of expectations between teachers and students with regard to the principal's role in student discipline, decides to conform to the expectations of the teachers, because of a greater concern for their reactions. In this set of circumstances, the administrator resolves this role conflict based on the perception of the sanctions that might result from failure to conform to the expectations of the teachers. The legitimacy of the student's expectations is not a consideration for this principal.

The reader may feel that a principal should try to base resolution of role conflict on the legitimacy of each group's expectations. However, conditions can develop that will not allow the sanctions of a group to be ignored. For example, an administrator may feel the members of a group have no "right" to expect the administrator's behavior to conform to their expectations. Yet, if the group's power is such that it can disrupt or create problems within the school system, the principal may agree to adhere to their expectations in order to avoid serious difficulties that might otherwise arise. While the legitimacy of each group's expectations should be given primary consideration by an administrator in resolving a role conflict, the sanctions that a group can bring to bear for failure to fulfill expectations cannot be overlooked. An accurate understanding on the part of the administrator of *both* the legitimacy of the role expectations *and* the potency of the sanctions associated with noncompliance with those expectations is essential for the successful resolution of any role conflict.

OTHER APPROACHES TO CONFLICT MANAGEMENT

Gross's model of role conflict resolution identifies some of the basic factors that may influence an administrator in attempting to resolve a role conflict. This model does not, nor was it intended to, indicate the *best* way to resolve a role conflict.[32] Neither does it address itself to the problem of how an administrator can best resolve conflict arising between two or more individuals or groups who are associated with the school, e.g., students v. teachers, teachers v. parents, students v. parents. Since role and school conflicts seem to be associated with the job of the administrator, it would appear desirable to suggest additional possible techniques that an administrator may consider for managing role or group conflict.

Barker, Tjosvold, and Andrews, for example, describe four approaches to conflict management: cooperative, confirming, competitive, and avoiding. The cooperative approach emphasizes mutual group goals, understanding others' views, and compromising to create a mutually useful solution. The confirming approach stresses the importance of communicating mutual respect for group members' competence, while the competitive approach to conflict resolution sees conflict as a win-lose battle in which others must be persuaded or coerced into submission. Finally, avoidance occurs when people withdraw from discussing problems or smooth over differences quickly.

Results of research done by Barker et al. confirm that administrators who use a combination of cooperative and confirming approaches are much more successful in conflict management than are those using a competitive-avoidance approach. Administrators who use a cooperative approach also use a confirming approach. (Neither approach was used exclusively but always in conjunction with the other.) The authors suggest that perhaps this is because of the fact that confirmation of competence brings a feeling of security, promoting a cooperative conflict mode by allowing team members to take risks. On the other hand, administrators who use a combination of competitive and avoidance approaches to conflict management are seen as extremely ineffective. "Presumably these managers went back and forth between the two approaches, competing when they thought they could win and avoiding when they were uncertain." The authors recommend that in cases where leaders do not possess the necessary interpersonal skills to use a cooperative and confirming approach, a member of the group who has these skills should be designated to act as a "communication facilitator and group maintenance leader."[33]

While the theoretical literature on conflict management strongly recommends a contingency approach—that is, the selection of the most appropriate techniques for managing a conflict should depend on the nature of the situation[34]—there is some evidence to suggest that administrators may be more influenced by their own personalities in selecting a technique for conflict management than by any other factor.[35] For example, the authoritarian person would appear more likely to select a unilateral, power-based technique for managing a conflict, while the cooperative, people-oriented individual would seem more likely to select a joint problem-solving technique. (It should be emphasized that research on the relationship between personality and conflict management is limited, and the findings are only tentative.)

Although an administrator needs to consider individual personal needs in selecting a conflict management technique, the main factor that *should* determine selection is the nature of the conflict situation itself. As Schmuck and Runkel have emphasized, the method an administrator should select for managing a conflict ought to " . . . depend on the type of conflict, the intensity of the disagreement, the persons participating in the conflict, the seriousness of the issues for them, and the authority, resources and knowledge they possess."[36] While this approach, referred to as the "contingency method," takes into consideration an administrator's personality, it also considers other characteristics and factors in the conflict situation. For example, Utley, Richardson, and Pilkington found in their research that when administrators attempted to resolve interpersonal conflict, personality factors played less of a role than did situational or conflict target factors such as a professor, parent or friend.[37] Since the kinds of conflict situations that an administrator may encounter are likely to differ, a number of alternate techniques for managing conflict will be presented.

Power Struggle Bargaining

If the administrator is in a situation where conflict is inevitable, agreement or compromise between parties in conflict is impossible, and the achievement of the administrator's objectives in the conflict are extremely important, then the administrator is likely to engage in what is referred to by Blake and his colleagues as "power struggle bargaining."[38] In other words, the administrator will do everything possible to resolve the conflict in the administrator's favor. This includes refusing to concede the legitimacy of any aspect of the other party's position and downgrading that position. It also involves refusing to compromise any aspect of the administrator's position and rationalizing any shortcomings in that position. This type of conflict resolution is seen all too frequently during the collective bargaining process in public education.

The disadvantages of power struggle bargaining as a method of resolving conflict are that the process used can be destructive to the personal and professional relationships of those involved, and the conflict is often only temporarily and superficially resolved. Conflicts which *appear* to be resolved by power struggle bargaining frequently resurface later, perhaps in a different form, but based on the same old antagonisms which were exacerbated during the previous bargaining sessions.

The main advantage to the administrator of this type of conflict resolution is the possibility that it may result totally in the administrator's favor. However, whether this occurs or not largely depends on the accuracy of the administrator's assessment of possessing more authority, power, or influence than the other party to the conflict, so that the conflict can be resolved favorably. At best, this is a tricky assessment for anyone to make, and miscalculations can be disastrous. Power struggle bargaining may be necessary in certain situations, but the administrator should carefully examine the validity of the assumptions about the extent of authority, power and influence relative to the other party to the conflict, as well as the likelihood of compromise and the long-range effects that power struggle bargaining may exert on interpersonal relationships.

Conflict Avoidance Methods

At the opposite pole from power struggle bargaining is a set of techniques for resolving a conflict which can be characterized as "conflict avoidance" methods. Blake and his colleagues have identified four such methods: (1) withdrawal, (2) indifference, (3) isolation, and (4) "smoothing over."[39] An example of the use of withdrawal is illustrated by the administrator who, in a meeting with a superior, gets involved in an argument over a directive for the school that is felt to be not in the best interest of either students or teachers. Rather than continuing to pursue the matter, however, the administrator withdraws from the conflict and accepts the directive. In the same situation, an administrator employing the use of indifference as a method of conflict resolution would not have gotten into an argument about the matter in the first place, but would have acted as though the issue did not really matter. The administrator who utilizes isolation as a technique would have tried to avoid any circumstances of conflict with a superior. And, in the case of "smoothing over," the administrator would have accepted the directive from the superior, emphasizing the elements of agreement on the issue, rather than disagreement, and, in general, would have tried to minimize any discord between the two.

Avoidance techniques do not really resolve conflict, but rather circumvent it. They may be necessary in situations where the other party clearly possesses the authority, power, or influence to force an opponent's will, and/or when negative consequences would result from a more active or aggressive approach. Avoidance methods are typically employed when an individual or group feels somewhat powerless, apathetic, or disillusioned about the likelihood of bringing about change in the other party.

PROBLEM-SOLVING APPROACH

A third major method of conflict resolution is the problem-solving approach.[40] It is the approach which seems to be the most effective means of resolving many conflicts.[41] It is based on the assumptions that the parties to the conflict are people of worthy motives and good will, that agreement is possible, that each party has something valuable to contribute to the process of resolving the conflict, and that final resolution need not ignore basic interests of all sides.[42] Glickman suggests the following problem-solving procedures for resolving conflicts within groups:

1. Request that group members state their conflicting positions.
2. Ask that group members state their opponents' position.
3. Clarify with group members if conflict still exists.
4. Request that group members state why their viewpoints continue to be valid.
5. Ask that group members present an additional position that "synthesizes, compromises, or transcends the conflict." If none is presented, restate members' viewpoints and confirm that no resolution can be achieved.

While theorists may differ somewhat on the elements which should be included in a problem-solving approach to conflict resolution, the following steps seem most important.[43]

Early Identification

Tjosvold contends that "all organizations try to avoid social conflict,"[44] and there is observational evidence to support his contention. In general, conflict is not viewed as a desirable state of affairs, and consequently people tend to avoid it as long as they can. Although a potential or minor conflict may become worse and eventually develop into a major crisis, the attitude of many administrators seems to be, "Why kick sleeping dogs?"

While it is true that too much attention to a minor conflict may cause it to loom larger in everyone's eyes than it deserves, and by a lack of attention a problem may go away on its own, the opposite consequences can also occur, and when they do, they are likely to be more significant. By failing to identify and take appropriate action at an early stage of a potential or minor conflict, an administrator risks the very real possibility that the conflict may become worse. And by the time the administrator is forced to take action, the conflict may be very difficult to resolve. As Wynn has observed, "The most tragic instances of school conflict are usually those in which the conflict reaches the advanced stages before administrators respond to it."[45] Clearly an important first step in conflict resolution is to identify potential or minor problems at an early stage before they further deteriorate and become unmanageable.

Diagnosis and the Importance of Trust

Once an administrator has identified a conflict, the causes need to be diagnosed.[46] In other words, the reason(s) for the disagreement or dispute must be investigated, for according to Chanin and Schneer, a conflict may be caused by "incompatible goals, ideas, values, behaviors, or emotions."[47]

In diagnosing which factors are causing a conflict, it will be important, if the conflict involves the administrator, to try to avoid the natural inclination to assume that the other party is wrong. Rather, the administrator's attitude and actions should be based on the assumption that there may be merit in the expectations or positions held by others and try to understand the reasons for these feelings.

Understanding the basis for a conflict is also important for the administrator who hopes to resolve a dispute between two or more other individuals or groups. In this kind of situation, the administrator's role is that of mediator. But before an administrator can effectively mediate between two or more parties, there must be accurate and complete understanding of the way in which each side perceives the other and the way each side perceives the main issue that has created the conflict. Without accurate and complete information on these two variables, the administrator may inadvertently exacerbate a conflict rather than ameliorate it. As Wynn points out, "Perhaps 90% of all human conflict could be satisfactorily resolved if the major parties would take the time to talk and listen."[48]

In this early stage of working with the parties to a conflict, it is extremely important for the administrator to develop and maintain an attitude of acceptance and trust on the part of all concerned.[49] If an administrator is to act as a mediator (or in some related role in resolving the conflict), then the participants in the conflict need to accept that role and have trust that the administrator will act fairly and constructively. It needs to be emphasized that this trust and acceptance will not be easy to earn if the administrator is perceived as favoring one side over another or possessing a particular vested interest. Objectivity, impartiality, and good human relations skills are essential qualities for anyone attempting to gain the acceptance or trust of others.

It is also important that the administrator begin working on developing mutually positive attitudes on the part of the participants in a conflict. This obviously will not be easy. There is evidence that disputants tend to view each other in nonobjective, hostile, and emotional terms.[50] In many situations the mentality of the participants is expressed in the "them versus us" form, and the other side is viewed as the "enemy." However, the difficulty of changing the attitude of the participants to a conflict in no way negates its importance, for until the various parties to a dispute can begin to view each other in a more positive light, compromise and eventual resolution of the conflict will probably not be possible.

Since the parties to a conflict are likely to have a negative attitude toward each other, it is recommended that the administrator acting as a mediator attempt, in the early stages of trying to resolve the conflict, to meet with each side *separately* to the extent possible. If the administrator brings together the various parties to a conflict before working with them separately, they may only continue to engage in conflict provoking behavior that could make the situation worse. The mere presence of conflicting parties together at a meeting may actually serve to intensify an already emotional charged situation. By meeting with them separately in the initial stages, the administrator will have a better opportunity to begin the process of persuading each side to think and behave more rationally and to view each other more positively. Crouch and Yetton write that administrators with good conflict management skills should bring subordinates together to solve conflicts. However, those with poor conflict management skills should not try to resolve conflict by bringing subordinates together since this will only create reduced employee performance. Further, Crouch and Yetton recommend conflict management training for both managers and subordinates.[51]

In attempting to resolve a conflict, the administrator would do well to ignore the extreme rhetoric used by those involved in a dispute. People who are embroiled in a conflict are usually frustrated and are likely to become angry and immoderate in their speech or writing. Recommendations may be expressed as demands, epithets may be hurled, and ultimatums may be presented. Such extreme behavior may either be a part of a strategy to intimidate others or, as suggested earlier, it may simply be a result of frustration. Regardless of the reasons for the extreme rhetoric, the administrator should attempt to maintain an objective and professional attitude toward the disputants. This may be a difficult task, particularly if the administrator is the focus of such rhetoric. However, administrator reactions which may escalate the conflict are to be avoided.

Fact Finding

After the administrator has ascertained how the parties to a dispute view each other and the issue in question, the facts need to be validated in the situation. While it is true that the perceptions people hold represent "the facts" from their point of view, those "facts" need to be verified. There is evidence suggesting that people in conflict tend to present their side in a totally favorable light and the other side in a totally negative light.[52] They may not be doing this intentionally, and they may be very sincere in their representations. However, all too frequently, their emotions have distorted their perceptions and memory. Therefore, it is essential that the administrator attempt to validate the information from the various parties to a conflict rather than accepting the information at face value. For example, which statements by the conflicting parties rest on assumptions and which are based on evidence which is solidly grounded in reality? What are the *additional* facts which, thus far, the parties to the dispute have been unaware of or have failed to take into account?

It is at this stage that the administrator needs to recognize that although people in conflict may ultimately agree on the facts in a situation, they may, nevertheless, fail to reach accord in their *interpretations* of the facts. For instance, agreement may eventually be reached by a group of parents and the superintendent that the attitude of the school board members, rather than that of the superintendent, is currently the main barrier to initiating a proposed program of community involvement. However, the parents and the superintendent may continue to disagree about their *interpretations* of the problem. The parents may conclude that the administrator should play a more active role in trying to change the school board's attitude toward community involvement, while the superintendent, as the school board's representative, may believe the school board to be the one who should try to change the attitude of the parent group. At one level, the parents and the administrator all agree that the school board is the main barrier to achieving community involvement, but they continue to disagree about what should be done in light of this obstacle.

The goal of the administrator in fact finding should be to clarify and broaden the areas of agreement and to narrow the issues of disagreement. If the administrator is not one of the parties to the dispute, it will be easier to play the role of mediator in reaching this goal. However, if the administrator is personally involved in the disagreement, an outside resource person may be needed to be called in for assistance in mediating the conflict.

Developing an Integrative Solution

Long lasting conflict resolution seldom occurs when one party to a dispute makes all of the gain while the needs of the other party have not been accommodated in some way. It is important for the administrator to recognize that a conflict between individuals or groups will seldom be permanently resolved if some parties feel that they were the only losers in the resolution of the conflict. The administrator should, therefore, try to develop a conflict resolution in which there are no clear-cut winners or losers.

To achieve this result may require compromise on the part of everyone involved in the conflict. However, before the administrator attempts to persuade the disputants to compromise, a resolution to the conflict which would meet the needs of all sides should first be explored. This type of conflict resolution is referred to in the social science literature as an "integrative solution."[53] It involves ascertaining the needs and objectives of all parties to the conflict and trying to develop a solution in which all of the parties could meet their needs and objectives in a way that would not require the others to sacrifice their needs and objectives.

The integrative solution in most conflict situations will not be easy to achieve because it requires considerable creativity and persistence on the part of the conflict mediator and open-mindedness and flexibility on the part of all those involved in the conflict. However, it is the ideal solution and the one most likely to result in a permanent resolution of the conflict.

Developing a Basis for Compromise

In many situations the integrative solution will not be possible, and compromise on the part of one or more parties to the conflict will be necessary.

A major obstacle to developing a compromise resolution of a conflict is that the participants may feel that to compromise is to appear weak and ineffective and that compromising may reduce the chances of achieving their goals.[54] In our society, winning a victory is a more attractive result than compromise. The very term "compromise" has a mixed, or even a negative connotation, to many people. For these reasons, the administrator may encounter resistance to attempts to help both sides see the need for compromise. The approach of the administrator should be to show the participants that without compromise, their conflict is unlikely to be resolved. This won't be easy, but an attempt must be made because the alternatives of a stalemate or heightening of the conflict are likely and undesirable.

Assuming that the various parties to a dispute can be made to see that compromise is needed to resolve the conflict, an understanding also needs to be reached that it will probably be necessary for *both* sides to compromise. Typically, individuals or groups who are in conflict do not think about the need to modify their own position but assume that the other party is the one who should or must change. However, it is unlikely that either side to a dispute will change without the assurance that the other side will also agree to compromise. Since in many circumstances each side is convinced that it is right and the other side is wrong, the administrator may have difficulty in persuading those who are involved that there must be "give and take" on both sides before progress can be made in resolving the conflict. Nevertheless, the mediator must attempt to develop this understanding on the part of both sides if resolution of the conflict is to be accomplished.

Another important prerequisite to an acceptable solution to a disagreement is an understanding by both sides of the *full implications* of their own point of view, as well as the *full implications* of the other side's position. While both parties may clearly understand their own position, it is not unusual for them to fail to recognize the full ramifications of their demands or their stand on a particular issue in relation to the other party to the dispute. Frequently, by showing how one group's demands will affect the other party, the mediator will be able to make it clearer to all concerned why certain actions are unacceptable or not possible.

There is also little doubt that a major deterrent to the successful resolution of a conflict is a lack of understanding of the opposite point of view on the part of one or more sides to a dispute. Usually the parties in conflict concentrate most of their energies and attention on presenting and arguing the merits of their own position and consequently do not spend sufficient time trying to understand the way that the other side looks at the issue. A useful technique which can be employed to reveal this problem is to ask all parties to state the supporting rationale and main components of the opposition's arguments.[55] This step frequently identifies the areas of inadequate understanding and, if periodically employed with appropriate follow-up discussion, can also build the foundation of understanding that is needed for compromise and ultimate solution of the conflict. If compromise is required to resolve conflict, then certainly a better understanding of the positions and points of view of both parties is needed before that compromise can occur.

The Counterproposal

Conflicts are usually resolved on the basis of modification of the original positions taken by one or more parties to a dispute. As stated before, unless there is movement away from the original stand on an issue, toward the opposing point of view, there is little likelihood of resolving the conflict. Someone must change, but usually neither party is willing to be the first to modify its position. The perspective that the mediator needs to develop in parties to a conflict is the idea that their alternatives are not restricted to either total rejection or complete capitulation. Instead, each side should be encouraged to offer a counterproposal[56] which at least recognizes the merits of some of the opposing arguments and suggests a possible compromise that might represent a better situation for those concerned than would be true if the previous position of the other side were accepted in total.

The development of a counterproposal is a complex task. The proposal must make sufficient advancement towards incorporating the main points raised by each party so that it will command attention and study, rather than immediate rejection, and yet it cannot sacrifice the basic integrity of either point of view. Its presentation must be timed for just the right moment, lest it be rejected because the other side is not yet ready to consider a possible modification of its original position or because the other side is past the point of being willing to consider a change. The key to acceptance of a counterproposal is a recognition on the part of all involved that each side must acknowledge, to some extent, the validity of the other side's arguments if the conflict is to be resolved.

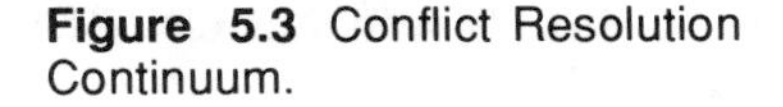
Figure 5.3 Conflict Resolution Continuum.

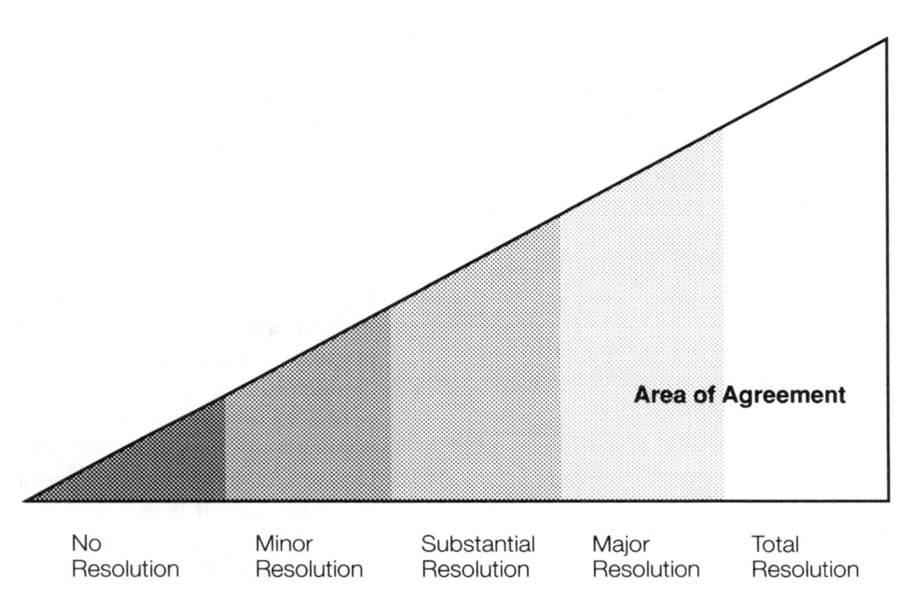

Arbitration

The administrator should recognize that some conflicts cannot always be resolved through the process of mediation and that arbitration may become necessary.[57] Arbitration means that the conflict is submitted to a third party, and both sides to the dispute agree to accept the arbitrator's judgment. The arbitrator may be a superior in the organization or may be an outside party, depending on the nature of the conflict and the surrounding circumstances. When both sides to a dispute agree to submit the issue to an arbitrator, they commit themselves to accepting and implementing the arbitrator's resolution of the conflict.

Arbitration by an outside party is a relatively new phenomenon in education, although the process of internal arbitration by a superior in the organization has been in existence for many years. The more frequent use of outside arbitration reflects a growing polarization of points of view on the part of many groups in education and a lack of success in utilizing more traditional means of resolving conflict. While arbitration is not acceptable to many because of the freedom that is relinquished in submitting to the judgment of an arbitrator and because it does not guarantee that the conflict will not erupt again, we can probably anticipate its continued use when other methods of resolving conflict fail.

EVALUATION OF CONFLICT MANAGEMENT EFFORTS

Regardless of which conflict management approach is used, it will be important for the administrator, as well as the other participants, to keep in mind that conflict cannot always be totally resolved, due to its difficult and intractable nature. Figure 5.3 illustrates the variation in possible outcomes of efforts to resolve conflict.

If an administrator cannot achieve a total resolution of a conflict, this does not mean that the administrator has failed. Conflict amelioration represents a worthwhile achievement in many situations and may be the only attainable objective under difficult circumstances. However, evaluating whether or not the conflict was totally resolved is not the only aspect of conflict management which should be assessed. In order for an administrator to determine whether the efforts to resolve a conflict have been successful, the following questions should be addressed:

1. To what extent do all parties to the conflict feel that the administrator has acted *fairly?* Evidence?
2. To what degree was the initial problem which produced the conflict ameliorated or resolved? Evidence?
3. How much time, energy, and frustration were spent during efforts to resolve the conflict? Evidence?
4. To what degree do the participants now have a more positive attitude toward each other? Evidence?
5. To what extent have the participants in the conflict developed new skills or approaches to preventing similar conflicts in the future or resolving them more effectively if they were to occur? Evidence?

Obviously, these questions will not be easy for an administrator to answer, nor should there be an attempt to address them without the involvement of the other parties to the conflict. However, by trying to answer these questions, the administration will not only be more likely to draw accurate conclusions about the success of conflict management efforts, but also to learn something during the process of evaluation that could improve future effectiveness.

FINAL OBSERVATIONS ON CONFLICT RESOLUTION

Although conflict has been studied by many scholars, there still appears to be no single, proven method or formula for preventing or resolving discord. However, based on experience and the writing of those who have examined the problem, the following observations are offered in conclusion:

1. Conflict is often inevitable in an educational organization and, to some extent, it may indicate that important changes are being proposed, considered, or implemented. A complete absence of conflict over a long period of time may suggest a stagnant organization or educational program.
2. Disruptive, continuous, or pervasive conflict is a sign that all is not well within the organization. This type of conflict is deleterious to the emotional health of those who are associated with the organization and can impede the achievement of organizational objectives if it is not successfully ameliorated or resolved. The administrator must take the initiative in identifying, diagnosing, and mediating this type of conflict.
3. Emotions are as important to consider in dealing with a conflict as are facts. Facts may change emotions, but unless there is a sufficient understanding of the way people *feel* about the issues and about the other parties involved, the conflict will probably not be resolved.
4. The "win or lose" philosophy that characterizes so much of what occurs in our society has no place in conflict resolution. All references to, or impressions of "winners and losers," or "the good guys and the bad guys" should be avoided. To the greatest extent possible, the final resolution of a conflict should advance the interests of all of the parties.

5. The process of conflict resolution should not end at the time of final resolution. Hurt feelings may still exist, and scars incurred during early stages of the conflict may still require the administrator's attention if future problems are to be prevented.
6. A sense of humor, perspective, and a belief in the innate good intentions of most people are important to the resolution of conflict. Disputes are irritating and their resolution can be a frustrating experience. The successful resolution of a conflict may depend in many situations more on the personal characteristics of the participants than on any other factor.

Administrators must be prepared to resolve conflicts. They can gain conflict management skills through internships, case studies, sensitivity training, and simulations, in addition to studying theory and research.

> Although most of the case studies, suggested learning activities, and simulations presented in Part II of the text require the appropriate use of the ideas in this chapter on conflict management, the following exercises should provide the best opportunities for testing understanding and effective use of the concepts regarding conflict management: Cases 12, 18, 19, 22, 24, 31 and the Mid-Year and End-of-the-Year In-basket Exercises.

Notes

1. Kenneth N. Wexley and Gary A. Yukl, *Organizational Behavior and Personnel Psychology* (Homewood, IL: Richard D. Irwin, 1984), p. 192.
2. Richard Wynn, *Communication: The Key to Conflict Management* (Reston, VA: National Association of Secondary School Principals, 1985), p. 1. Also, see D. W. Johnson and R. T. Johnson, *Joining Together: Group Theory and Group Skills,* 3rd ed. (Englewood Cliffs, NJ: Prentice-Hall, 1987).
3. Stephen P. Robbins, " 'Conflict Management' and 'Conflict Resolution' Are Not Synonymous Terms," **California Management Review** (Winter 1978), pp. 69–70; and Richard A. Cosier and Charles R. Schwenk, "Agreement and Thinking Alike: Ingredients for Poor Decisions," **Academy of Management Excellence** (February 1990), pp. 69–74.
4. Jacob W. Getzels, "Administration as a Social Process," in *Administrative Theory in Education,* ed. Andrew Halpin (Chicago: University of Chicago Midwest Administration Center, 1958), p. 153.
5. Neal Gross et al., *Explorations in Role Analysis: Studies of the School Superintendency Role* (New York: John Wiley, 1958), p. 58. For additional information on role expectations, see James M. Kouzes and Barry Z. Posner, *The Leadership Challenge: How to Get Extraordinary Things Done in Organizations,* (San Francisco: Jossey-Bass Publishers, 1990), pp. 15–27.
6. Numerous studies have been conducted supporting the validity of the Getzels model. These are described in detail in *Educational Administration as a Social Process: Theory Research and Practice,* Jacob W. Getzels, James M. Lipham, and Roald Campbell (New York: Harper and Row, 1968). Also, see Wilburn R. Clouse, "A Review of Educational Role Theory: A Teaching Guide for Administrative Theory," an ERIC Report, Ed 314–824, 1989.
7. Roald F. Campbell, "Situational Factors in Educational Administration," in *Administrative Behavior in Education,* ed. Roald Campbell and Russell Gregg (New York: Harper and Row, 1968), p. 264. Also, see, Lynne L. Adduci et al., "The Department Chair: Role Ambiguity and Role Strain," (Philadelphia: Research for Better Schools, Inc., 1990), an ERIC Report, Ed 321–398.
8. Larry W. Hughes and Thomas A. Robertson, "Principals and the Management of Conflict," **Planning and Changing** (Spring 1980), p. 5. Also, see Robert J. Bies, Debra L. Shapiro, and Larry L. Cummings, "Causal Accounts and Managing Organizational Conflict," **Communication Research** (August 1988), pp. 381–399.
9. Gross et al., *Exploration in Role Analysis,* p. 58.
10. Ibid., pp. 59–60.
11. Eric W. Vetter, "Coping with the Demands: Role Pressure and the School Principal," **National Association of Secondary School Principals Bulletin** (November 1976), p. 14. Also, see Lynne L. Adduci et al., "The Department Chair: Role Ambiguity and Role Strain," an ERIC report, Ed 321–398.
12. Susan E. Jackson and Randall S. Schuler, "A Meta Analysis and Conceptual Critique of Research on Role Ambiguity and Role Conflict in Work Settings," **Organizational Behavior and Human Decision Processes** (August 1985), pp. 16–78. For additional information on role ambiguity, see James H. Leigh, George H. Lucas, and Richard W. Woodman, "Effects of Perceived Organizational Factors on Role Stress—Job Attitude Relationships," **Journal of Management** (March 1988), pp. 41–58.
13. Stephen P. Hencley, "The Conflict Pattern of School Superintendents," **Administrator's Notebook** (May 1960). For a study of principals with similar kinds of problems, see Dolores Hanse, "Elementary Principals' Role Conflicts and Their Relationship to Job Effectiveness, Job Satisfaction, and Career Satisfaction." Ph.D. Dissertation, University of Utah,

1984. Also, see Daniel L. Duke, "Why Principals Consider Quitting," **Phi Delta Kappan** (December 1988), pp. 208–312.

14. Kenneth DeGood, "Can Superintendents Perceive Community Viewpoints?" **Administrator's Notebook** (November 1959), pp. 1–4.

15. Gross et al., *Explorations in Role Analysis*. p. 60.

16. Victoria Berger-Gross and Allen I. Kraut, " 'Great Expectations,' A No Conflict Explanation of Role Conflict," **Journal of Applied Psychology** (May 1984), pp. 261–271.

17. Mary van Sell et al., "Role Conflict and Role Ambiguity," **Human Relations** (January 1981), p. 44.

18. Hughes and Robertson, "Principals and the Management of Conflict."

19. Larry Cuban, "Conflict and Leadership in the Superintendency," **Phi Delta Kappan** (September 1985), pp. 28–30. Also see A. Blumberg, *The School Superintendent: Living with Conflict* (New York: Teachers College Press, 1985) and Marilyn L. Grady and Miles T. Bryant, "Critical Incidents Between Superintendents and School Administrators: Implications for Practice," an ERIC report, Ed 318–114, 1990.

20. For an extensive review of the expectations of various reference groups for the role of the administrator, see Richard A. Gorton and Gail Thierbach-Schneider, *School Based Leadership: Challenges and Opportunities* (Dubuque, IA: Wm. C. Brown, 1991), pp. 93–102. Also, see Edward G. Buffie, "The Principal and Leadership Elementary Principal Service No. 1," (Bloomington, IN: Phi Delta Kappan Educational Foundation, 1989), an ERIC Report, Ed 315–911.

21. Jackson and Schuler, "Role Ambiguity and Conflict." For more information on consequences of role conflict, see Dennis Calderwood, "Some Implications of Role Conflict and Role Ambiguity as Stressors in a Comprehensive School," **School Organization** (March 1989), pp. 311–314.

22. The ideas for this section were stimulated by a reading of the references previously identified, and from Richard A. Schmuck and Philip J. Runkel, *The Handbook of Organizational Development in Schools,* 3rd ed. (Prospects Heights, IL: Waveland Press, 1988).

23. Gorton and Thierbach-Schneider, *School Based Leadership: Challenges and Opportunities,* Chapter 7.

24. For an extensive discussion of assessment centers, see G. D. Thornton and W. C. Bigham, *Assessment Centers and Management Performance* (New York: Academic Press, 1982), and Dennis A. Jainer, "Assessment Centers in the Public Sector: A Practical Approach," in *Human Resource Management in Education* (Bristol, PA: Open University Press, 1989), pp. 171–184. Also, see Frederick M. Jablin and Vernon D. Miller, "Interviewer and Applicant Questioning Behavior in Employment Interviews," **Management Communication Quarterly** (August 1990), pp. 51–86.

25. Gorton and Thierbach-Schneider, *School Based Leadership: Challenges and Opportunities,* pp. 605–612. For an example of this problem, see Case 35, "Administrator Evaluation," in Chapter 12.

26. Victor Wall and Linda Nolan, "Small Group Conflict: A Look at Equity, Satisfaction, and Styles of Conflict Management," **Small Group Behavior** (May 1987), pp. 193, 205 and 208.

27. John Lindelow and James Scott, "Managing Conflict," *School Leadership: Handbook for Excellence,* (Eugene, OR: Clearinghouse on Educational Management, 1989), an ERIC report, Ed 309–519, pp. 339–355.

28. Robbins, " 'Conflict Management' and 'Conflict Resolution' " pp. 67–75.

29. Gross et al., *Explorations in Role Analysis,* p. 284. Also, see Kenneth A. Shaw, "Making Conflict Work for You," **New Directions for Higher Education** (Spring 1988), pp. 53–58.

30. Donald L. Sayan and W. W. Charters, Jr., "A Replication Among School Principals of the Gross Study of Role Conflict Resolution," **Educational Administration Quarterly** (Spring 1970), pp. 36–45; and Walter F. Daves and C. L. Holland, "The Structure of Conflict Behavior of Managers Assessed with Self and Subordinate Ratings," pp. 741–756. Also, see Patricia B. Link, "How to Cope with Conflict Between the People Who Work with You," **Supervision** (January 1990), pp. 7–9.

31. Gross et al., *Explorations in Role Analysis,* pp. 285–318.

32. For identification of some additional ways of resolving role conflict, see van Sell et al., "Role Conflict and Ambiguity," pp. 63–64; and John Lindelow and James J. Scott, *School Leadership: Handbook for Excellence,* Chapter 15.

33. Jeffrey Barker, Dean Tjosvold, and Robert Anderson, "Conflict Approaches of Effective and Ineffective Project Managers: A Field Study in a Matrix Organization," **Journal of Management Studies** (March 1988), pp. 167–178.

34. For related research on this point, see Ann Case, "The Role of Power in Conflict Resolution Among School Administrators." Ph.D. Dissertation, Boston University, 1984.

35. Michael N. Chanin and Joy A. Schneer. "A Study of the Relationship Between Jungian Personality Dimensions and Conflict-Handling Behavior," **Human Relations** (October 1984), pp. 863–879; Robert E. Jones and Charles S. White, "Relationships Among Personality, Conflict Resolution Styles, and Task Effectiveness," **Group and Organizational Studies** (June 1985), pp. 152–167. Also, see Walter F. Daves and C. L. Holland, "The Structure of Conflict Behavior of Managers Assessed with Self and Subordinate Ratings," **Human Relations** (August 1989), pp. 741–756.

36. Schmuck and Runkel, *Organizational Development,* p. 295.

37. Mary Utley and Deborah Richardson, "Personality and Interpersonal Conflict Management," **Personality and Individual Differences** (October 1989), pp. 287 and 293.

38. Robert R. Blake et al., *Managing Intergroup Conflict in Industry* (Houston, TX: Gulf, 1964), pp. 18–49. For a more recent discussion of these techniques, as well as the conflict avoidance and problem-solving approaches, see Wexley and Yukl, *Organizational Behavior and Personnel Psychology,* pp. 198–205, and Phillip B. DuBose and Charles D. Pringle, "Choosing a Conflict Management Technique," **Supervision** (June 1989), pp. 10–12.

39. Blake, *Managing Intergroup Conflict in Industry,* pp. 62–69.

40. Dean Tjosvold and Don W. Johnson, *Productive Conflict Management: Perspectives for Organizations* (New York: Irvington, 1983).

41. C. James Riggs, "Dimensions of Organizational Conflict," in *Communication Yearbook,* ed. Robert N. Bostrom (Beverly Hills, CA: Sage, 1983, pp. 517–531. Also, see Hughes and Robertson, "Principals and the Management of Conflict," **Planning and Changing** (Spring 1980), p. 5.

42. Dean Tjosvold, "Making Conflict Productive," **Personnel Administrator** (June 1984), pp. 121–130.

43. Carl D. Glickman, *Supervision of Instruction: A Developmental Approach,* 2nd ed., (Boston: Allyn and Bacon, 1990) pp. 378–379.

44. Dean Tjosvold, "Making Conflict Productive," pp. 121–130.

45. Richard Wynn, "Administrative Response to Conflict," **Today's Education** (February 1972), p. 32.

46. M. Afzalur Rahim, "A Strategy for Managing Conflict in Complex Organizations," **Human Relations** (January 1985), pp. 81–89.

47. Chanin and Scheer, "Personality and Conflict-Handling," p. 864.

48. Richard Wynn, "Communication: The Key to Conflict Management," **The Practitioner** (May 1985), p. 3.

49. Robert A. Rothberg, "Trust Development: The Forgotten Leadership Skill," **National Association of Secondary School Principals Bulletin** (December 1984), pp. 18–22. Also, see James M. Kouzes and Barry Z. Posner, *The Leadership Challenge: How to Get Extraordinary Things Done in Organizations,* pp. 146–160; and C. John Tarter, James R. Bliss, and Wayne K. Hoy, "School Characteristics and Faculty Trust in Secondary School," **Educational Administration Quarterly** (August 1989), pp. 294–308.

50. Wynn de Bevoise, "Conference Explores Effects of Collective Bargaining on Schools and Administrators," **R and D Perspectives** (Summer 1982), p. 5.

51. Andrew Crouch and Phillip Yetton, "Manager Behavior, Leadership Style, and Subordinate Performance: An Empirical Extension of the Vroom-Yetton Conflict Rule," **Organizational Behavior and Human Decision Process** (June 1987), pp. 282–286.

52. Renis Likert and Jane G. Likert, *New Ways of Managing Conflict* (New York: McGraw-Hill, 1976), pp. 61–62. Also, see Michael Maccoby, *Why Work* (New York: Simon and Schuster, 1988), pp. 226–227.

53. A. C. Filley, "Some Normative Issues in Conflict Management," **California Management Review** (Winter 1978), pp. 61–65. Also, see Robert R. Blake and Jane S. Mouton, *Solving Costly Organizational Conflicts* (San Francisco: Jossey-Bass, 1984); John Gray and Angela Pfeiffer, "Skills for Leaders," National Association of Secondary School Principals, an ERIC Report, Ed. 279–964, 1987, p. 62, and James M. Kounzes and Barry Z. Posner, *The Leadership Challenge: How to Get Extraordinary Things Done in Organizations,* pp. 142–145.

54. Dean Tjosvold, "Control Orientation, Nonnegotiable Demands, and Race in Conflict Between Unequal Power Persons," Paper presented at the annual meeting of the American Educational Research Association, April 1976. For more recent information on the political advantage of compromise, see Joseph L. Badaracco, Jr. and Richard R. Ellsworth, *Leadership and the Quest For Integrity* (Boston: Harvard Business School Press, 1989), pp. 29–31; and for a discussion on confrontation versus compromise, see Chapter 7 in Badaracco and Ellsworth, *Leadership and the Quest For Integrity.*

55. Malcom E. Shaw et al., *Role Playing: A Practical Manual for Group Facilitators* (San Diego: University Associates, 1980), pp. 57–58: and William M. Fox, *Effective Group Problem Solving: How To Broaden Participation, Improve Decision Making, and Increase Commitment to Action* (San Francisco: Jossey-Bass Publishers 1987), pp. 157–164.

56. Donald Livingston, "Rules of the Road: Doing Something Simple About Conflict in the Organization," **Personnel** (January/February 1977), pp. 23–29. Also, see Dan DeStephen, "Mediating Those Office Conflicts," **Management Solutions** (March 1988), pp. 5–10.

57. William W. Notz et al., "The Manager as Arbitrator: Conflicts Over Scarce Resources," in *Negotiating in Organizations,* ed. Max H. Bazerman and Roy J. Lewicki (Beverly Hills, CA: Sage, 1983), pp. 143–164. The reader is encouraged to examine other articles in the same book in order to develop *additional* background in the utilization of techniques of negotiating in situations that are outside of the management/labor bargaining setting. More information can also be found in Loraliegh Keashly, "A Comparative Analysis of Third Party Interventions in Intergroup Conflict," Ph.D. Dissertation, University of Saskatchewan (Canada), 1988.

6 Organizational Culture

Scholars have long been interested in the social factors that seem to influence individual or group behavior in an organization.[1] A classic example of this focus was the Western Electric studies in the 1930s which found that employees develop a set of implicit group norms that influence and, in some cases restrict, the levels of performance for an individual in a group.[2] Since the 1930s, there have been several studies of the types of social and professional norms that develop in a school[3] and research on effective schools has identified the culture of a school as an important effectiveness variable.[4] Therefore, to understand and ultimately enhance the organizational culture of a school or school district would appear to be an important priority for an administrator desirous of improving the morale and productivity of the people associated with the organization.

In the following sections the theory of organizational culture will be examined, especially as it relates to effective schools.

MAJOR ELEMENTS OF ORGANIZATIONAL CULTURE

What is the organizational culture of a school, and how would an administrator recognize it? According to Smircich, who synthesized a number of ideas from other theorists, "Culture is usually defined as social or normative glue that holds an organization together. It expresses the values or social ideas and beliefs that organization members come to share."[5] Brighton and Sayeed describe culture as "the social energy that drives (or fails to drive) organizations," and allows an organization "to survive the external environment and manage the internal environment."[6] It would appear, from research by Halpin, that schools differ in their cultures and that those cultures have an impact on students.

> In one school the teachers and the principal are zestful and exude confidence in what they are doing. They find pleasure in working with each other; this pleasure is transmitted to students . . . In a second school the brooding discontentment of teachers is palpable; the principal tries to hide his incompetence and lack of direction behind a cloak of authority . . . And the psychological sickness of such a faculty spills over on the students who, in their own frustration, feed back to teachers a mood of despair. A third school is marked by neither joy nor despair, but by hollow ritual . . . In a strange way the show doesn't seem "for real."[7]

Whether or not schools differ in their organizational cultures, conceptually every organizational culture seems to be composed of several elements.[8] These elements are depicted in Figure 6.1.

As Figure 6.1 indicates, an administrator's analysis of a school's organizational culture should begin with developing a good understanding of the values and ideals that the school represents.[9] The basic question that needs to be asked is, "What kinds of behavior are valued in this school, and what does the school aspire to become?" (It will be important for an administrator to distinguish between those values and ideals given only lip service by the people who are

Figure 6.1 Major Elements of Organizational Culture.

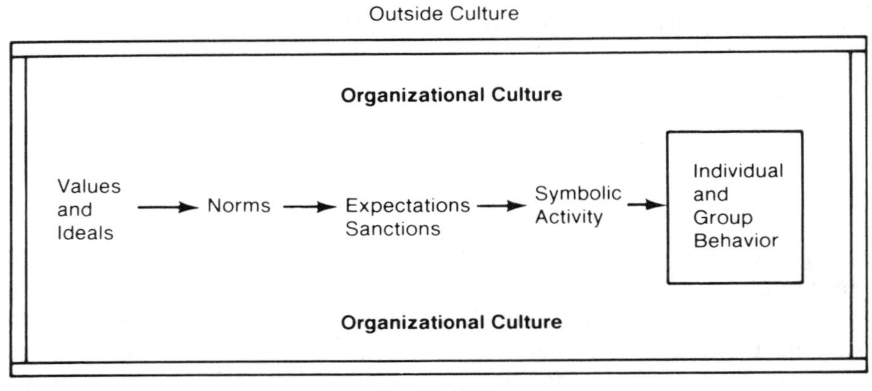

associated with the school and those on which their behavior is based.)

The values and ideals of a school may be difficult to ascertain, but they usually will be reflected in its *norms.* Norms, according to Josefowitz, are ". . . the unwritten rules stating what people should and should not do."[10] They serve the purpose of regulating and controlling behavior. An example of a desirable faculty norm would be that "teachers should share ideas about how to improve instruction."

Norms, it should be emphasized, are not values that an administrator can *impose* on a group. For example, faculty and staff come to school with personal value systems. Organizational values are then communicated to the individual through rules and processes. Shockley-Zalabak and Morley's research demonstrates that when organizational rules and personal values are congruent, an individual is more satisfied with the job and projects high estimations of organizational quality and success.[11] Consequently, as Miller points out, "Any lasting change of a school will occur only because the staff itself changes norms of expectations, appropriate role definitions, standards of accountability, and patterns of behavior."[12]

The *expectations* of an organizational culture are the norms applied to a specific situation.[13] For example, "Bob Elliott, an experienced sixth grade teacher, should be willing to share his expertise with Julie Adams, a new sixth grade teacher," is a specific expression of the faculty norm presented previously. In another situation, "Dr. Brown, the principal, should support Mr. Armstrong's attempts to discipline a student," represents an example of an expectation that is based on a faculty norm that maintains, "The principal should always support the teachers, right or wrong." While it is important for an administrator to become *aware* of the expectations of others as part of understanding the culture of the school, it must also be stressed that an administrator needs to evaluate the merits of those expectations before deciding to meet them. For example, for a school to become more effective, it may require that teachers expend effort and time beyond the normal work day, and improvement may require a focus on teaching reasoning and analytical skills, with a reduced emphasis on skills that are easier to teach.[14]

Expectations, if they are to be effective in shaping the behavior of the people associated with the school, must carry sanctions. These sanctions represent the *means* by which an organization or group tries to bring about compliance with its expectations.[15] The sanctions may be negative or positive, and they may be exercised formally or informally. They can range from a punitive action to personal recognition and reward. The extent to which an organization or group possesses significant sanctions will determine the degree to which it can maintain conformity of behavior on the part of its members.

For example, an administrator may decide to instruct teachers to hold conferences before the end of the grading period with any students who receive a *D* or *F*. In this situation the administrator is counting on the cooperation of the staff to carry out the directive. However, a majority of the faculty may feel that holding these conferences will take too much time, so they decide to ignore the administrator's directive. Unless the administrator possesses adequate monitoring procedures for detecting a lack of follow-through on the part of the faculty, the principal may never discover that the policy on teacher-student conferences is not being carried out. If their failure to comply with the instruction is discovered, the principal may not be able to do anything about it unless the administrator can persuade them of the desirability of these conferences or possesses adequate sanctions to force the teachers to adhere to the directive, despite their lack of voluntary cooperation.

It should be noted that the noncompliance of an individual or group ordinarily does not take the form of a direct challenge to the administrator. Instead, resistance is usually expressed by underachievement or lack of implementation in response to the administrator's expectations. As Harry Truman observed in recalling the problems of the presidency, the executive may say, "Do this! Do that!" and yet find, to his chagrin, that "nothing will happen."[16] Often the reason for the lack of follow-through is the conclusion by the subordinates in the hierarchy that the action desired by the administrator is either not in their best interest or not in the best interest of the institution. So they have ignored the instructions. As a result, the implementation of administrative policy is completely delayed or thwarted.

The expectations and sanctions of a school or a group associated with a school may be communicated directly, or they may be expressed indirectly through *symbolic activity*. As Morgan and his colleagues note, "Many organizations consciously attempt to create complex symbol systems which are intended to signify the desirability of engaging in rigorous patterns of rational, instrumental, and pragmatic action. Symbols [reinforce] the pursuit of excellence, achievement, aggressiveness, competitiveness, and intense commitment to organizational ends . . ."[17] An organization's symbolic activity, according to Smircich, may take different forms, including story-telling about important events, such as how an organization faced up to a particular challenge; group rituals, such as the annual banquet at which awards of recognition are presented; or organizational slogans,[18] such as "Excellence is our goal."

Symbolic activity can also be found in the behavior of an administrator. For example, the principal who would like to show support of a "Reading Break" program and encourage teachers to support the program can certainly communicate these feelings and expectations at a faculty meeting. However, if the administrator does so, and yet is never seen reading a book during the reading break and does not use negative sanctions against teachers who fail to participate in the program, this constitutes a stronger message to the faculty about the principal's attitude toward the program than any comments made at a faculty meeting. On the other hand, if the principal is regularly observed reading a book in classrooms, this nonverbal behavior is likely to send a symbolic message to teachers that will be more effective than anything that might be said at the meeting. The main impact of symbolic activity is not so much what is said as what can be inferred from the actual behavior of the people who are formal and informal leaders in an organization.

CULTURAL ELEMENTS OF AN EFFECTIVE SCHOOL

"Organizational culture and the symbols which are a part of this culture are not politically neutral but represent levels of power and control."[19] Blanch studied culture as a control mechanism. Her research indicates that four core values define school culture: 1) cooperative community/parent relationships, 2) cooperative teacher relationships, 3) student needs, and 4) principals as cultural transmitters. Her research further demonstrates that strong congruence of "group sensemaking" with school values indicates that culture is a strong control mechanism. She suggests that schools should attempt to foster consensus and that principals should act as consensus builders in the early stages of culture development which are dominated by indirect strategies. Direct strategies are diluted to minimize divisiveness, and principal/teacher sensemaking acts as a gauge of cultural controls," according to the author. Her research implies that strong cultural control impedes change, and cultural control neglects instruction, and, ultimately, achievement.[20]

Earlier studies tended to focus on the negative influence that the culture of an organization can exert on the achievement and behavior of the individuals or groups who are associated with the organization. However, researchers have recently emphasized the importance of developing and maintaining a positive organizational culture if a school is to be effective. For example, Purkey and Smith have concluded that ". . . an academically effective school is distinguished by its culture: a structure, process, and climate of values and norms that channel staff and students in the direction of successful teaching and learning."[21]

But what kind of an organizational culture best promotes successful teaching and learning? While scholars continue to pursue this question, research has produced some tentative findings which suggest a number of major elements of the culture of an effective school.[22]

An examination of Figure 6.2 shows that the organizational culture of an academically effective school includes a set of school-wide norms that stress academic effort and accomplishment. While other kinds of effort and achievement may also be important to parents and students, such as developing ethical behavior, the research on effective schools stresses that the norms of an academically effective school will give the highest priority to academic effort and achievement.[23] These latter norms may be reflected in an organization's mission statement, educational goals, or in some other documents.[24] Regardless of how the norms manifest themselves, Saphier and King underscore the point that norms should represent ". . . a clear, articulated vision of what the school stands for, a vision that embodies core values and purposes."[25]

Since organizational norms are usually expressed in the form of expectations for the members of the organizations, what are the expectations for those associated with effective schools? In general, these expectations emphasize academic effort, improvement, and accomplishment. For example, "striving for excellence" would be one important expectation in an effective school. Saphier and King illustrate this emphasis by quoting a staff member, "In this school the teachers and administrators are held accountable for high performance . . . While we [teachers and administrators] often feel under pressure to excel, we thrive on being part of a dynamic organization."[26]

A second important expectation for teachers in an effective school would be that they should adopt the attitude that all students are capable of achieving, and therefore teachers should behave accordingly. In a study of effective inner city elementary schools, Larkin found that "staff members

Figure 6.2 Major Elements of the Culture of an Effective School.

1. A clear set of school-wide norms that emphasize the values of academic effort and achievement
2. A *consistently* applied set of expectations that stress the importance of staff members striving for excellence and students performing up to their potential
3. A system of symbolic activity and sanctions that encourages and rewards effort, improvement, and accomplishment, while discouraging disorder and complacency

verbally and behaviorally expressed the belief that all of their students could achieve, regardless of socioeconomic status or past academic performance.''[27] A third expectation characteristic of an effective school culture is that the faculty members should strive to improve themselves, in part by helping each other, and in part through experimenting with different approaches. An example of this expectation, presented by Saphier and King, is, ''In this school the professional staff help each other . . . Around here we are encouraged by administrators and colleagues to experiment with new ideas and techniques because that is how teachers and schools improve . . . We are always looking for more effective ways of teaching.''[28]

A fourth major expectation which seems to be associated with the culture of an effective school is that students and teachers will be expected to behave in ways that contribute to a safe and orderly school environment.[29] As Purkey and Smith point out, ''. . . Common sense alone suggests that students cannot learn in an environment that is noisy, distracting, or unsafe.''[30] And Edmonds found that in effective schools, a safe and orderly environment was established when ''. . . all teachers take responsibility for all students, all the time, everywhere in the school.''[31] Moreover, in a study of several hundred schools, Wayson and Lasley discovered that

> Schools with well-disciplined students have developed a sense of community, marked by mutually agreed upon behavioral norms; these norms surround students with examples of subtle rewards and sanctions that encourage students to behave appropriately.[32]

While there may be other expectations associated with the culture of an effective school, it would appear that the ones described are the most important. Of course, these expectations will need to be communicated and reinforced, activities that usually occur in an effective school as a result of symbolic actions and sanctions.[33] Such symbolic activity may, for example, take the form of a school slogan on the importance of learning, a school policy which states that students who fail a subject will not be allowed to participate in extracurricular activities, or a procedure requiring all students to make up their work, irrespective of the reason for their absence. In these examples a certain symbolic message is being communicated: ''Academics are important!''

Both positive and negative sanctions will also be necessary to encourage the achievement of school expectations. While some administrators may be reluctant to use negative sanctions, such as those discussed in Chapter 3 on *Authority, Power, and Influence,* individuals or groups whose behavior is in conflict with the ideals and values that the administrator is trying to promote should not be ignored. Of course, use of positive sanctions is preferable in encouraging adherence to organizational expectations. Several researchers have found that schools that recognize student accomplishment tend to have higher

Figure 6.3 Major Factors Impacting on Organizational Culture.

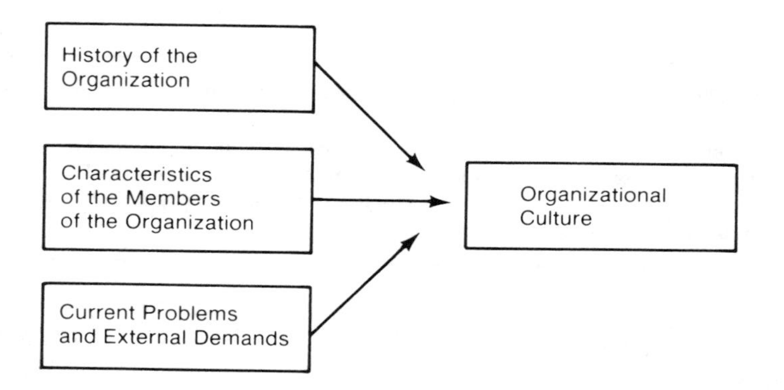

levels of achievement.[34] In addition, the recognition and support of teachers is also characteristic of the culture of an effective school. For example, in another illustration presented by Saphier and King, it was observed, "Good teaching is honored in this school and community," and, "Despite financial constraints, we have sabbaticals, summer curriculum workshops, and funds to attend professional conferences."[35]

THE ADMINISTRATOR'S ROLE

The administrator's role in regard to the organizational culture of a school is multifaceted. First of all, the administrator needs to develop and maintain an adequate understanding of the various elements of the school culture. While few new administrators are likely to operate on the assumption that they are knowledgeable about the organizational culture of the school, many experienced administrators may falsely assume that they already know about their school culture, since they have held a position in the school for several years. However, an organization's culture is not a static entity but is constantly changing and evolving.[36] Figure 6.3 shows a number of major factors that can affect the nature of the organizational culture that exists in a school.[37]

By analyzing the factors identified in Figure 6.3, an administrator can take an important step toward better understanding how the present organizational culture has developed into what it is today and how it may be changing. To help achieve this understanding, the administrator should consider using one or more of the instruments that have been designed for assessing the organizational culture of a school. Although most of these instruments have been developed for the purpose of measuring the *climate* of a school (a broader concept), the data from such an assessment would also be valuable in understanding the organizational culture. Instruments that would be useful for this objective include the Organizational Climate Description Questionnaire,[38] the Elementary School Environment Survey,[39] the Quality of School Life Questionnaire,[40] and the Effective Schools Battery Survey.[41] In addition, the National Association of Secondary School Principals has developed a climate instrument that appears to hold promise.[42] These standardized instruments measure factors common to schools and typically have a high degree of validity and reliability. However, these instruments may not address the specific areas of interest of a particular administration. Rojewiski et al., outline steps that may be used to develop an individualized, school-climate survey.[43]

Once an administrator has attained a good understanding of the organizational culture of the school, the administrator will then, and only then, be in a position to try to enhance that culture if changes are needed. While most, if not all, administrators would probably like to develop an organizational culture that is characteristic of effective schools, trying to change an organizational culture, especially a school culture, will not be easy. One problem is the fact that schools, particularly secondary schools, are often referred to as "loosely coupled" organizations,[44] that is, the authority and other bureaucratic linkages between the principal and the staff are often indirect. For example, an administrator may want teachers to emphasize more time on tasks in their classrooms and may, in fact, direct them to do so. But once the classroom doors are closed, a school administrator frequently has no adequate mechanism to enforce these wishes.

Moreover, although the discussion in this chapter, for the purpose of simplification, has referred to the organizational culture of a school as though it were a homogeneous entity, it is, in reality, more complicated than that. As Smircich has observed, "Much of the literature refers to an organizational culture, appearing to lose sight of the great likelihood that there are multiple organization subcultures, or even countercultures; competing to define the nature of situations within organizational boundaries."[45] This type of condition is particularly characteristic of secondary schools with their different departments, orientations, and needs. It is conceivable that in a secondary school, each of the departments may have its own subculture and, more important, many of the subcultures may not be compatible—and may be in conflict with—what the administrator would like to see as the overall organizational culture. And, considering that students may have their own subcultures (or, in fact, several of them),[46] which may be in conflict with the other subcultures of the school, then the complexity and the difficulty of trying to change the organizational culture of the school become apparent.[47] As Conway points out, "We are asking schools to restructure themselves and their culture, to go through an organizational learning of the most difficult type."[48]

In spite of these complexities and difficulties, an administrator may be able, to a limited extent, to shape the organizational culture of the school or school district. However, principals should remember that combining "professional management with inspirational leadership and a collectivist culture" may lead to role conflicts and confusion.[49] Based on an analysis of the social science and educational literature on organizational cultures,[50] the following suggestions are offered.

First of all, an administrator needs to be clear about which values and ideals the school should be promoting. An administrator who has no notion of what an ideal school would look like will not be able to create policies for moving in a positive direction.[51] Research by Hallinger indicates that, "Principals can influence student learning by developing a clear mission that provides an instructional focus for teachers throughout the school."[52] Unfortunately, many administrators become bogged down in the everyday duties of managing a school and have not thought through what it is that their school should aspire toward. A basic question that needs to be answered is, "What should be the primary mission and goals of this school?"[53] Obviously, the administrator should not be the only one who attempts to answer this question; teachers, students, and parents, among others, also need to be involved in order to gain deeper insights and commitment. However, the principal appears to play the major role, beyond that of parent, in developing a school climate of high expectations.[54] If an administrator is not clear about what the school should stand for and should be aspiring toward, the administrator will be in a poor position to shape the organizational culture in a different direction. As Firestone and Wilson have emphasized,

"The principal's task and challenge is to develop a clear vision of the purposes of the school that give primacy to instruction and to carry it through consistently during those countless interactions with [important others]."[55]

Once an administrator has developed a clear vision of the "purpose" of the school, particular attention must be paid to the kinds of individuals recommended as future members of the faculty and to the people appointed to important leadership positions within the school. For example, every time an administrator has an opportunity to replace a member of the faculty, the potential exists for shaping the culture.[56] Since the principal's greatest influence may well be in the power "to recruit, select, promote, and demote staff members," it may take years of this process for a principal to reshape the school's culture. Hiring and retaining teachers who especially value experimentation, for example, will certainly make innovation or change easier to facilitate for principals.[57] It is true that, in the instance of a single vacancy, there is little chance of hiring someone whose values and ideals are exactly what the administrator wants the organizational culture to reflect. However, the *cumulative* effect of selective hiring over a number of years could potentially change the culture of a school in important ways.[58] In the final analysis, it is the people associated with an organization who are the major contributors to its culture. Their values and ideals are the building blocks of the group norms that greatly influence individual and group behavior. By emphasizing certain values and ideals in the hiring process, an administrator can shape the culture of an organization over a period of time.

An administrator will also have an opportunity to shape the culture of the organization when making appointments of people to leadership positions within the organization.[59] Periodically, an administrator will need to appoint a chairperson of a committee or select someone for an important position, e.g., department head. In these situations an administrator should take care to select or appoint people who will best represent the organizational values and ideals that the administrator is trying to promote. By selecting such individuals, the administrator will not only obtain people who share a commitment to certain organizational priorities but, perhaps more importantly, will be communicating symbolically to others in the school those values and ideals which the administrator thinks are important for people to possess. The administrative act of selection or appointment can potentially carry great symbolic influence, especially if the administrator emphasizes publicly the reasons for these selections. However, according to Hallinger, these appointments also lessen the opportunity for the administrator to personally communicate key values and place greater reliance on instructional leaders to aid in fostering a positive school climate.[60]

In addition to selecting with care those individuals who will occupy important leadership positions in the school, an administrator who wishes to shape the organizational culture will need to identify and develop an appropriate relationship with the *informal leaders* of the school.[61] This is particularly true for a new principal at a school because the formal and informal leaders who are already in place form a large portion of the school's power structure. Developing a commitment from the school leaders will be crucial to the achievement of the principal's goals.[62]

An informal leader generally operates in every group. The informal leader may be the same person as the formal leader; however, whether or not that is true depends on the formal leader's personal influence with other members of the group rather than on any formal appointment by the principal. An informal leader can best be identified by examining a group's interaction patterns: The individual with whom there is the greatest interaction and communication within the group and whose opinion and judgment is most respected by the other members is the informal leader.

Obviously, in most situations it would be best for an administrator if the informal leader and the formal leader were the same person. However, that may not be the case, especially if an administrator has not exercised good judgment in selecting the formal leaders within the organization, or if there has been very limited opportunity to appoint new formal leaders, or if the informal leader's values are not consistent with those that the administrator would like to see adopted by the organization.

When the informal leader of a group is a different person from the formal leader, a potential for conflict may exist. For example, the administrator and a department chairperson may be trying to promote a certain work ethic on the part of members of a particular department. However, if the informal leader of that department is opposed to the new work ethic, then the other members of the department may develop a group norm that will influence the members to resist the proposed work ethic. This type of conflict can be detrimental to developing a cohesive, overall organizational culture.

Unfortunately, there are no easy answers to resolving this type of conflict between formal and informal leaders, although the concepts that are presented in Chapters 3 and 5 should be helpful. The administrator could, of course, attempt to influence the informal leader by using persuasion to convey the desirability of what the organization is trying to accomplish. In addition, the administrator could attempt to try to develop a rival informal leader within the group who could possibly lead the group in a direction that would be more compatible with the overall purposes of the organization. While the social science literature provides few clues as to how the administrator might accomplish this, it would appear that the key to a solution lies in identifying and nurturing some individual in the group whose personal qualities are liked and respected by colleagues, but whose values and ideals are more congruent with the administrator's. By encouraging the administrator–approved informal leader to exert leadership within the group and then rewarding such efforts, an administrator may be able to change the group norms of a subculture to make them more consistent with the overall purposes of the organizational culture.

In attempting to shape the culture of an organization, it will be important for the administrator to articulate at every opportunity those values and ideas being promoted.[63] This needs to be done in such documents as student and teacher handbooks, and at meetings with faculty, students, and parents. For example, Brookover and his colleagues suggest that in an effective school the administrator and faculty should develop a statement of purpose and beliefs that would include the following:[64]

1. The purpose of the school is to educate all students to high levels of academic performance.
2. To fulfill this purpose, the members of this school staff believe that
   a. All students should have a challenging academic program.
   b. All students should master their grade level objectives.
   c. Teachers are obligated to prepare all students to perform at mastery level on the objectives for the course.

Whether a school administrator and faculty should adopt this particular statement of purpose and beliefs, or some other, is not the issue. The important concept is that if the administrator is to shape the organizational culture of the school, a clear statement of purpose and beliefs must be formulated and communicated.

Also, while formal communication will be essential, an administrator needs to use informal and symbolic communication as well, in order to shape the future of the organization. Some researchers have discovered that informal and symbolic communication, which takes the form of stories, rituals, and slogans, can influence the culture of an organization.[65] For example, the slogan, "Academic excellence—no sweat, no gain," communicates symbolically the value that a school places on hard work. Anecdotes retold to new personnel about how students and teachers have invested extra efforts to improve themselves and to help achieve certain organizational goals symbolically emphasize the types of values and ideals that a school promotes. What a principal talks about, pays attention to, and reinforces while walking around the building or conducting school activities, will greatly influence teachers' behavior, and thus the organization's culture, according to Peterson.[66]

In addition, rituals or ceremonies that an administrator initiates and supports provide an opportunity to stress the values and ideals the administrator is trying to emphasize, while at the same time, providing an occasion for rewarding behavior exemplifying these values and ideals. For example, one high school which is attempting to promote academic excellence has established a comprehensive program of rituals and rewards for students and teachers.[67] Examples of this program include the following:

1. *Academic Superstar Recognition.* Each week the school honors a student for outstanding performance in a particular academic area by displaying on the office bulletin board a picture of the student at work.
2. *Homework Recognition.* The school honors students who have completed all of their homework assignments in all of their classes with a grade of B or better by providing them with a special certificate and a reward, e.g., tickets to a movie.
3. *Average-Raisers Recognition.* The school honors students who raise their grade point averages from the previous term by .5 on a 4.0 scale by presenting them with special certificates and rewards.
4. *Teacher of the Month Recognition.* One teacher is selected monthly by a P.T.A. committee to receive a special certificate and a night's dinner and entertainment for the teacher and a guest.

While the total program of this school is much more comprehensive than is revealed in the examples, the four illustrations are intended to give a sense of communicating symbolically the values and ideals that are important to an organization. As Iannaccone and Jamgochian point out, "When symbol and ceremony fit student perception that teachers care about their achievement and the perception of teachers that administrators place improved student performance foremost in their orientation in their jobs, then a strong and consistent school cultural consensus [will emerge]."[68]

A FINAL NOTE

An organizational culture is a complex entity, one that is constantly evolving. Unless there is a positive organizational climate and culture, it is unlikely that the necessary technical improvements that benefit students in teaching and curriculum will be implemented.[69] For example, the rapidly increasing cultural diversity of students in our schools can create serious misunderstandings among students, teachers, parents, and administrators and further diminish or erode a positive climate. Principals and staff must be able to recognize and resolve culturally-based school and community problems.[70] However, an administrator should not be intimidated by these challenges. Instead, focus should be on maintaining an accurate understanding of the culture and direction of the organization and on those factors influencing its development. The administrator can then try, with the assistance of others, to shape the culture towards desirable ends. In the process of pursuing positive results, the administrator will be involved in school improvement, the subject of the next chapter.

Although many of the case studies, suggested learning activities, and simulations presented in Part II of the text require the appropriate use of the ideas in this chapter on organizational culture, the following exercises should provide the *best* opportunities for testing understanding and effective use of the concepts about organizational culture: Cases 17, 20, 23, 35, 41, 51 and the Mid-Year and End-of-the-Year In-basket Exercises.

Notes

1. Some theorists refer to these social factors as the "climate" of an organization, e.g., Carolyn S. Anderson, "The Search for School Climate: A Review of the Research," **Review of Educational Research** (Fall 1982), pp. 368–420; others refer to the "culture" of an organization, e.g., Edgar H. Schein, "Coming to a New Awareness of Organizational Culture," **Sloan Management Review** (Winter 1984), pp. 3–16; and some writers use the two terms interchangeably, e.g., "The Culture of an Effective School," **Clearinghouse on Educational Management** (February 1984), pp. 1–4. Although it would appear that there is considerable overlap between the theories of organizational climate and organizational culture—and ideas from both will be used as appropriate—this chapter will concentrate primarily on organizational *culture,* which seems to be the most definable of the two.

2. F. J. Roethlisberger and W. J. Dickson, *Management and the Worker* (Cambridge, MA: Harvard University Press, 1938).

3. For example, see Donald Willower, *The Teacher Subculture and Curriculum Change,* an ERIC report, Ed 020–588. Also, see Mark S. Rosenbaum, "The Organizational Cultures of Two Academically Dissimilar Elementary Schools," Ed.D. Dissertation, Hofstra University, 1988.

4. Stewart C. Purkey and Marshall Smith, "Too Soon to Cheer? Synthesis of Research on Effective Schools," **Educational Leadership** (December 1982), pp. 64–69. Also, see Daniel U. Levine, "Creating Effective Schools: Findings and Implications from Research and Practice," **Phi Delta Kappan** (January 1991), pp. 389–393.

5. Linda Smircich, "Concepts of Culture and Organizational Analysis," **Administrative Science Quarterly** (September 1983), pp. 64–69.

6. Harvey J. Brighton and Lutfus Sayeed, "The Pervasiveness of Senior Management's View of the Cultural Gaps Within a Division," **Group and Organization Studies** (September 1990), pp. 266–278.

7. Andrew W. Halpin, *Theory and Research in Administration* (New York: Macmillan, 1966), p. 131.

8. This figure is based on conclusions drawn from Peter J. Frost et al., *Organizational Culture* (Beverly Hills, CA: Sage, 1985) and Meryl R. Louis, "Organizations in Culture Bearing Milieux" in *Organizational Symbolism,* ed. Louis R. Pondy et al. (Greenwich, CT: JAI Press, 1983), pp. 39–54.

9. Edgar H. Schein, "Coming to a New Awareness of Organizational Culture," **Sloan Management Review** (Winter 1984), pp. 3–16.

10. Natasha Josefowitz, *Paths to Power* (Reading, MA: Addison-Wesley, 1980), p. 56.

11. Pamela Shockley-Zalabak and Donald Dean Morley, "Adhering to Organizational Culture: What Does It Mean? Why Does It Matter?," **Group and Organization Studies** (December 1989), pp. 483–500.

12. Stephen K. Miller, "Significant Achievement Gains Using the Effective Schools Model," **Educational Leadership** (March 1985), p. 41. Also, see Cynthia Cherrey, "Understanding and Shaping Organizational Culture," **Campus Activities Programming** (April 1990), pp. 60–65 and Michael Paul Kirsch, "Organizational Culture as a Third Order Control System: A Cognitive Approach (Volumes I and II)," Ph.D. Dissertation, Michigan State University, 1988.

13. Wilbur Brookover et al., *Creating Effective Schools* (Holmes Beach, FL: Learning Publications, 1982), pp. 55–58. Also, see Lawrence C. Stedman, "The Effective Schools Formula Still Needs Changing: A Reply to Brookover," **Phi Delta Kappan** (February 1988), pp. 439–442.

14. Barbara O. Taylor and Daniel U. Levine, "Effective Schools Projects and School-Based Management," **Phi Delta Kappan** (January 1991), pp. 394–397.

15. Richard C. Wallace and Wendy D. Wallace, *Sociology* (Boston, MA: Allyn and Bacon, 1989), p. 49.

16. Richard E. Neustadt, *Presidential Power* (New York: Macmillan Publishing Company, 1964, 1980), p. 22. Also, see Barry Kampol, "Empowerment: The Institutional and Cultural Aspects for Teachers and Principals," **National Association of Secondary School Principals Bulletin** (October 1990), pp. 104–107.

17. Gareth Morgan et al., *Organizational Symbolism,* ed. Louis R. Pondy et al. (Greenwich, CT: JAI Press, 1983), p. 13.

18. Linda Smircich, "Organizations as Shared Meanings," in *Organizational Symbolism,* ed. Louis R. Pondy et al. (Greenwich, CT: JAI Press, 1983), pp. 55–65.

19. Bernard J. Reilly and Joseph A. DiAngelo, Jr., "Communication: A Cultural System of Meaning and Value," **Human Relations** (February 1990), pp. 129–140.

20. Mary Cristine Blanch, "Culture as a Control Mechanism In Schools," Ph.D. Dissertation, University of Utah, 1989.

21. Stewart C. Purkey and Marshall Smith, "Too Soon to Cheer?," p. 68.

22. This figure is based on an analysis of a large number of reports on effective schools, especially those by Brookover et al., *Creating Effecting Schools,* pp. 23–74; Jon Saphier and Matthew King, "Good Seeds in Strong Cultures," **Educational Leadership** (March 1985), pp. 67–74; Carolyn S. Anderson, "The Search for School Climate," pp. 368–420.

23. For an excellent discussion of other important school outcomes, see Stewart C. Purkey and Susan Degen, "Beyond

Effective Schools to Good Schools,'' **R and D Perspectives** (Spring 1985), pp. 1–6.

24. Brookover et al., *Creating Effective Schools,* p. 46.

25. Saphier and King, ''Good Seeds,'' p. 67.

26. Ibid., p. 68. Also, see Carolyn Carter and Jack Klotz, ''What Principals Must Know Before Assuming the Role of Instructional Leader,'' **National Association of Secondary School Principals Bulletin** (April 1990), pp. 36–41.

27. Maureen McCormack Larkin, ''Ingredients of a Successful School Effectiveness Project,'' **Educational Leadership** (March 1985), p. 33. Also, see Jeannie Oakes and Martin Lipton, *Making the Best of Schools* (New Haven, CT: Yale University Press, 1990) and Diane S. Pollard, ''Against the Odds: A Profile of Academic Achievers from the Urban Underclass,'' **Journal of Negro Education** (Summer 1990), pp. 297–308 and Ellen C. Baylor and Petra E. Snowden, ''Expanding the School's Role as Care Provider,'' **Principal** (January 1992), pp. 8–9.

28. Saphier and King, ''Good Seeds,'' p. 68. For additional information on professional development, see Mary Louise Holly and Cavens McLoughlin, *Perspectives on Teacher Professional Development* (Philadelphia: Falmer, 1989) and Daniel L. Duke, ''Setting Goals for Professional Development,'' **Educational Leadership** (May 1990), pp. 71–75. For a comparison of professional development and staff development, see D. Duke, ''Setting Goals for Professional Development,'' **Educational Leadership** (May 1990), pp. 71–75.

29. Ronald R. Edmonds, ''Programs of School Improvement: An Overview,'' **Educational Leadership** (December 1982), pp. 4–11. Also, see California State Department of Education, *Safe Schools: A Planning Guide for Action,* an ERIC report, Ed. 313–815.

30. Stewart C. Purkey and Marshall S. Smith, ''Effective Schools: A Review.'' Paper presented at a conference sponsored by the National Institute on Education, 1982, p. 41.

31. Ronald R. Edmonds, ''Programs of School Improvement.''

32. William W. Wayson and Thomas J. Lasley, ''Climates for Excellence: Schools that Foster Self Discipline,'' **Phi Delta Kappan** (February 1984), p. 419. Also, see Helen Bain et al, ''A Study of First Project Star Class-Size Research: A Study of Fifty Effective Teachers Whose Class Average Gain Scores Ranked in the Top 15% of Each of Four School Types in Project STAR,'' an ERIC report, Ed. 321–887.

33. William A. Firestone and Bruce L. Wilson, ''Using Bureaucratic and Cultural Linkages to Improve Instruction: The Principal's Contribution,'' **Educational Administration Quarterly** (Spring 1985), pp. 7–30.

34. M. Rutter et al., *Fifteen Thousand Hours: Secondary Schools and Their Effects on Children* (Cambridge, MA: Harvard University Press, 1979). Also, see E. A. Wayne, *Looking at Schools: Good, Bad, and Indifferent* (Lexington, MA: D. C. Heath, 1980). Also, see James M. Dowdle, ''Keeping Kids in School,'' **North Central Association Quarterly** (Winter 1990), pp. 470–472.

35. Saphier and King, ''Good Seeds,'' p. 68.

36. Purkey and Smith, ''Effective Schools,'' p. 43. Also, see Sofia Zamanou, ''Managing Organizational Culture,'' Ph.D. Dissertation, University of Oregon, 1988, and Terry Michael Dearstone, ''Using a Cultural Change Intervention to Improve Organizational Effectiveness: An Evaluative Case Study,'' Ed. D. Dissertation, 1989.

37. This figure is based on conclusions reached after analyzing several of the sources previously identified. However, the major source of insight was *Creating Excellence* by Craig R. Hickman and Michael A. Silva (New York: New American Library, 1986), pp. 72–78; and an article by Alan L. Wilkins and William G. Ouchi, ''Efficient Cultures: Exploring the Relationship between Culture and Organizational Performance,'' **Administrative Science Quarterly** (September 1983), pp. 468–481.

38. Andrew W. Halpin and Donald B. Croft, *The Organizational Climate of Schools* (Chicago: University of Chicago, 1963). For a recent attempt to update OCDQ, see Wayne K. Hoy and Sharon I. R. Clover, ''Elementary School Climate: A Revision of the OCDQ,'' **Educational Administration Quarterly** (Fall 1986), pp. 93–110. Also, see C. Halderson, E. A. Kelley, J. W. Keefe, and P. S. Berge, *Technical Manual* (Reston, VA: National Association of Secondary School Principals, 1989) and Betty Ann Topalosky, ''Culture and Innovation in Higher Education: A Semiotic Study,'' Ph.D. Dissertation, Ohio University, 1989.

39. R. L. Sinclair, ''Elementary School Educational Environments,'' **National Elementary Principal** (April 1970), pp. 53–58.

40. J. L. Epstein and H. J. McPortland, ''The Concept and Measurement of the Quality of School Life,'' **American Educational Research Journal** (Winter 1976), pp. 15–30.

41. Gary Gottfredson, *Assessing School Climate in Prevention Program Planning, Development and Evaluation,* an ERIC report, Ed 250–804.

42. James W. Keefe et al., ''School Climate: Clear Definitions and a Model for a Larger Setting,'' **National Association of Secondary School Principals Bulletin** (November 1985), pp. 70–77. Also, see James W. Keefe and Edgar A. Kelley, ''Comprehensive Assessment and School Improvement,'' **National Association of Secondary School Principals Bulletin** (December 1990), pp. 45–63. For an instrument to measure a principal's attitude about organizational culture, see Beverly Jean Weldon Ihinger, ''Development of an Attitude Scale for Elementary Principals About Organizational Culture and the Role of Cultural Leader,'' Ed.D. Dissertation, Texas Tech University, 1988.

43. Jay W. Rojewiski, Frederick C. Wendal, Sara McInerny, DeAnn Currin and Elizabeth Smith, ''Individualizing School-Climate Surveys,'' **The Clearing House** (January 1990), pp. 202–206.

44. Arthur Blumberg, *Supervision in Weakly Normal Systems,* an ERIC report, Ed 239–381. Also see, Earl E. Weick, ''Educational Organizations as Loosely Coupled Systems,'' **Administrative Science Quarterly** (March 1976), pp. 1–19; David Gomez and Richard Jamgochian, ''The Kinds of Behaviors Teachers Value,'' **Thrust for Educational Leadership** (September 1989), pp. 40–44 and Michael Elmer and David Wilemon, ''Organizational Culture and Project Leader Effectiveness,'' **Project Management Journal** (September 1988), pp. 54–63.

45. Smircich, ''Concepts of Culture,'' p. 346.

46. James S. Coleman, *The Adolescent Society* (New York: Free Press of Glencoe, 1961).

47. For further discussion of the problems of subcultures, see Frost et al., *Organizational Culture,* Chapters 2 and 8.

48. James A. Conway, ''A Perspective on Organizational Cultures and Organizational Belief Structures,'' **Educational Administration Quarterly** (Fall 1985), p. 9.

49. Edward Vaughan, ''The Leadership Obsession: An Addendum to Mangham's 'In Search of Competence','' **Journal of General Management** (Spring 1989), pp. 26–34.

50. Sources which were especially helpful, either for specific suggestions or for stimulating insights, were Edgar H. Schein, *Organizational Culture and Leadership* (San Francisco, CA: Jossey-Bass, 1985), Pt. 3; Brookover et al., *Creating Effective Schools; and Edgar A. Kelly, Improving School Climate* (Reston, VA: National Association of Secondary School Principals, 1980). Also, see Kery D. Kafka, ''Organizational Culture in Four High School Effectiveness Programs,'' Ph.D. Dissertation, Marquette University, 1988.

51. Richard P. DuFour, ''Clear Vision for Successful Leadership,'' **National Association of Secondary School Principals Bulletin** (April 1990).

52. Phillip Hallinger et al., ''What Makes a Difference? School Context, Principal Leadership, and Student Achievement.'' Paper presented at the Annual Meeting of the American Educational Research Association, March 1989.

53. Hickman and Silva, *Creating Excellence,* p. 64. Also, see William E. Webster, *The High Performing Educational Manager,* an ERIC report, Ed 296–470.

54. Hallinger et al., ''What Makes a Difference? School Context, Principal Leadership, and Student Achievement.''

55. William A. Firestone and Bruce L. Wilson, ''Using Bureaucratic and Cultural Linkages to Improve Instruction: The Principal's Contribution,'' **Educational Administration Quarterly** (Spring 1985), p. 22. Also, see David Gomez and Richard Jamgochian, ''The Kinds of Behaviors Teachers Value,'' pp. 40–44.

56. Gareth R. Jones, ''Psychological Orientation and the Process of Organizational Socialization,'' **Academy of Management Review** (July 1983), pp. 464–474. Also, see Mark S. Rosenbaum, ''The Organizational Cultures of Two Academically Dissimilar Elementary Schools,'' Ed.D. Dissertation, Hofstra University, 1988, and Thomas F. Casey, ''Making the Most of a Selection Interview,'' **Personnel** (September 1990), pp. 41–43.

57. Kent D. Peterson, ''Mechanisms of Culture Building and Principals' Work,'' **Education and Urban Society** (May 1988), pp. 250–261.

58. For an interesting example of how this happens in the business world, see Tom Peters and Nancy Austin, *A Passion for Excellence: The Leadership Difference* (New York: Random House, 1985), pp. 268–269.

59. Ibid., Pt. 4.

60. Phillip Hallinger, ''Developing Instructional Leadership Teams in Secondary Schools: A Framework,'' **National Association of Secondary School Principals** (May 1989), pp. 84–92.

61. Elbert W. Stewart, *Sociology* (New York: McGraw-Hill, 1981), pp. 146–147. Also, see S. J. Brown et al., ''Teachers' Powerlessness: Peer Assessments and Own Perceptions,'' **Planning and Changing** (Spring 1985), pp. 22–34, and Katherine I. Miller, ''Cultural and Role-Based Predictors of Organizational Participation and Allocation Preferences,'' **Communication Research** (December 1988) pp. 699–725.

62. Michael A. Morehead and Lawrence Lyman, ''Three Strategies for New Principals,'' **National Association of Elementary School Principals** (January 1990).

63. Maryan S. Schall, ''A Communication-Rules Approach to Organizational Culture,'' **Administrative Science Quarterly** (December 1983), pp. 557–577. Also, see Jack Blendinger and Linda T. Jones, ''Starting With Culture to Improve Your Schools,'' **School Administrator** (May 1989), pp. 22–25.

64. Brookover et al., *Creating Effective Schools,* p. 46. For a good discussion of how to develop a mission statement, see John Farley, *How to Build a Mission Statement for School Improvement* (Reston, VA: National Association of Secondary School Principals, 1986), and Joseph F. Rogus, ''Developing a Vision Statement—Some Considerations for Principals,'' **National Association of Secondary Schools Bulletin** (February 1990), pp. 6–12.

65. Peters and Austin, *A Passion for Excellence,* pp. 274–283. Also, see William A. Firestone and Bruce L. Wilson, ''Culture of School Is a Key to More Effective Instruction,'' **National Association of Secondary Schools Bulletin** (December 1984), pp. 7–11.

66. Kent D. Peterson, pp. 250–261.

67. John Childs and Jim McCoy, ''A Positive Approach to Academic Excellence,'' **National Association of Secondary School Principals Bulletin** (May 1985), pp. 64–67; Elaine Phillips, ''Developing a District-Wide Academic Awards Program,'' **Gifted Child Today** (November–December 1989), pp. 6–10 and Barry S. Roebeck, ''Transformation of a Middle School,'' **Educational Leadership** (April 1990), pp. 18–21.

68. Laurence Iannaccone and Richard Jamgochian, ''High Performing Curriculum and Instructional Leadership in the Climate of Excellence,'' **National Association of Secondary School Principals Bulletin** (May 1985), p. 31. Also, see J. Thomas Mitchell, ''In Search of Organizational Culture: A Case Study of an Excellent High School (Effective Schools),'' Ph.D. Dissertation, Pennsylvania State University, 1989.

69. G. Grant, *The World We Created at Hamilton High* (Cambridge, MA: Harvard University Press, 1988).

70. Sheldon S. Varney and Kenneth Cushner, ''Understanding Cultural Diversity Can Improve Intercultural Interactions,'' **National Association of Secondary School Principals Bulletin** (October 1990), pp. 89–94.

7 School Improvement

In education it would appear that people are seldom satisfied with the status quo.[1] As a result, various changes have been proposed through the years which have ranged from the non-graded school to competency-based education. While the success rate of different innovations has not been high, the concept that improvement in education is needed and desirable continues to hold strong appeal for many people. This concept has taken on increased importance with the recent emphasis on the need for schools to become more effective. Schools are expected not only to conserve our values and standards but also to be dynamic, reflecting the fact that the world around us is constantly changing. Therefore, schools must develop processes and techniques to facilitate effective change.[2]

The rationale for change in education seems to be based on the following premises: (1) even if the status quo is not necessarily bad, there is usually room for improvement; (2) while all change does not necessarily lead to improvement, improvement is not likely to occur without change; (3) unless we attempt change, we are not likely to know whether a proposed innovation is better than the status quo; and (4) participation in the change process can result in greater understanding and appreciation of the desirable features of the status quo and can lead to a better understanding and appreciation of, and skill in, the change process itself.

Although it is clear that proposed change holds the potential for improvement in education, an administrator would be well advised to be skeptical of those who say, "This is new and therefore good" or, conversely, "This is old and therefore better." Periodic assessment of traditional practices and careful evaluation of proposed innovations in education are essential first steps in validating the need for improvement.

PRESSURES FOR CHANGE

In recent years schools have been bombarded with proposals, research findings, and mandates for change.[3] For example, schools have been told that they need to increase student time on task, provide career ladders for teachers, introduce computer study into the curriculum, enhance their organizational culture, improve students' basic skills, increase parental involvement, improve personnel evaluation, tighten curriculum standards, develop partnerships with business, and so on. Many of these pressures for change emanate from various national reports,[4] including the designation of six national goals for public education. These goals deal with preschool education, the dropout rate, improving competency in basic skills, adult literacy, and drug-free schools.[5] Pressure from the state level has also been placed on the schools in the form of new mandates and regulations[6] including a call to completely restructure the schools.[7] In addition, in some situations, pressure for change has originated within the school district's central office.[8]

While national reports and research findings can be helpful in identifying possible areas in need of change in the schools, evaluations of change efforts during the 1960s through the 1980s raise grave doubts as to whether national prescriptions, state mandates, and school district directives can be successful in bringing about significant *and lasting* school improvements.[9] In general, studies show that past attempts to impose certain changes on the schools have not been successful, for the most part. State regulations frequently usurped the authority of teachers, principals, parents, and local communities. The regulations sought to make the curriculum "teacher-proof," when in fact, they served to make schools "learning-proof."[10] Many of the proposed changes were either not implemented at all or were modified in such a way to fit local needs that the value of the change was questionable.[11]

Although the federal and state governments can make an important contribution to school reform by publicizing the need for improvement and by providing financial and technical assistance to schools that would like to change, the history in this country of attempts to change the schools suggests that significant and lasting school improvement can seldom be prescribed, mandated, or directed by agencies or individuals outside of the school. Part of the difficulty is that, as mentioned in Chapter 6, schools are "loosely coupled organizations,"[12] that is, there are seldom explicit and direct connections or linkages between the external agents who are pressuring the schools to change and the people (in most cases, teachers) who will have to implement the changes. This makes it hard to direct and monitor adequately what is going on in the schools. Another difficulty is that many teachers and building administrators have become accustomed to pressures for change—after all, there has been a lot of change over the years—and educators realize that much proposed change is faddish in nature and that the pressure for change will likely diminish when the change agent leaves or funds are cut back.[13]

A basic implication of research on change efforts the past thirty years is that the primary leadership for bringing about school improvement must come from the organizational level of education where the change is to take effect. In most situations, that will be at the school site level, even though important contributions can be made at all levels.

NEEDED LEADERSHIP FOR CHANGE

There is little doubt that the involvement and cooperation of many people will be necessary for the successful implementation of school improvement. An administrator cannot and should not attempt to introduce and implement a proposed change single-handedly. As Joyce and his colleagues have pointed out, "Charismatic superintendents and principals can change schools, sometimes quite rapidly, by developing ad hoc executive structures; but the institutionalization of change is very difficult."[14] In order for change to occur, one "highly-motivated, goal-oriented individual must serve as the initial change agent. However, lasting change requires more than the efforts of a single individual."[15] Consequently, introducing lasting change will require the cooperation and support of a variety of people.[16] The administrator should recognize that the leadership for introducing school improvement can come from many sources and thus should try to encourage ideas and support for change throughout the school or school system.

One specific way in which an administrator can attempt to facilitate school change is to establish a school improvement committee.[17] Such a committee should be established at the district level in order to provide overall direction and coordination of school improvement efforts, and each school should also establish a school improvement committee to focus on improvement at the school site level. At the latter level, the committee should be headed by the principal and should comprise representative assistant administrators, teachers, parents, and students who are interested in school improvement and possess skills and/or insights that would be helpful in bringing about needed and successful change. For an excellent example of how students can be involved in the change process, the reader is referred to Furtwengler.[18] The school improvement committee should be charged with the responsibility for assessing the need for change, encouraging efforts to improve the school, coordinating and providing assistance to those efforts, and monitoring and evaluating progress and achievements.

In order for this type of committee to be successful, its membership should be voluntary rather than required, and each member should have something useful to offer. Once established, the committee will need adequate resources, assistance, and periodic recognition from the administrator. In some cases, inservice training for committee members may even be needed. Chapter 4 on *Group Leadership* provides further guidelines on the administrator's role in working with a group. It will also be important for the committee to be supported by the rest of the school. Every effort needs to be made to avoid the development of a perception that the committee is a behind-the-scenes, elitist group. Open meetings and frequent communications will help to eliminate or reduce this possible problem.

While the establishment of a school improvement committee represents an important organizational step toward successfully bringing about school improvement, it also needs to be recognized that the administrator, particularly the principal (if the proposed change is to be introduced at the building level), is a key figure in the implementation of an innovation. Seldom can a proposed change be successfully implemented without the understanding, support, and, frequently, the leadership of the building administrator. As Demeter observed in his study of innovation in local schools, ". . . Building principals are key figures in the innovation process. Where they are both aware of and sympathetic to an innovation, it tends to prosper. Where they are ignorant of its existence, or apathetic, if not hostile, it tends to remain outside the bloodstream of the school."[19] Reinforcing the importance of the principal to the successful implementation of any proposed change, Sarason emphasized that ". . . The principal is the crucial implementor of change. That is to say, any proposal for change that intends to alter the quality of life in the school depends primarily on the principal."[20]

Although the nature of the situation should determine the specific role an administrator should play in regard to introducing and implementing a particular change,[21] one study of principals who had successfully implemented new programs in their schools found that the principal "*was a believer,* feeling a genuine commitment to the project; an *advocate* who promoted and defended the project before a variety of audiences; *a linker* who connected the project with other parts of the system; a *resource acquirer* who obtained and allocated tangible and intangible resources for the project; *an employer* who hired project staff or assigned teachers to it; *a leader* who supplied initiative, energy, and direction; *a manager* who provided problem-solving assistance and support; *a delegator* who 'moved backstage' when teachers assumed leadership; *a supporter* who provided words of encouragement and acts of assistance; and *an information source* who gave feedback to teachers and project staff."[22]

Hall in his research found that the principal's leadership style determines the successful implementation of change. Principals in his study had three main styles: (1) the initiator; (2) the manager; and (3) the responder. The initiator's style was most successful, followed by the manager's, while the responder's style was least successful. The specific styles are described as follows:

1. Initiators - have clear goals that include implementation of innovation. They place high expectations upon the students, their staff, and themselves.
2. Managers - fall between initiators and responders. They may initiate action in support of change but also demonstrate responsive behavior.

3. Responders - rely on teachers and others to act as change agents while they proceed with administrative tasks.[23]

Hitt identifies the following ten characteristics of managers who are effective change agents:

1. They view change as a friend—see it as a challenge and an opportunity.
2. They have "power tools" and know how to use them. These "power tools" include:
   a. information (knowledge and expertise)
   b. resources (people, funds, materials, space, and time)
   c. support (from influential people at many levels)
3. They are able to deal with both the logical planning aspect of change and the psychological aspect, that is, the ability to handle the people problems associated with change.
4. They establish a climate for change through exemplary, day-to-day actions.
5. They start the change process within themselves rather than within others.
6. They do not force change but facilitate it.
7. They create their own enthusiasm.
8. They are able to let go of an old idea and experiment with alternative concepts. They are open-minded.
9. They seek out and accept criticism of their ideas.
10. They are able to get others to buy into their ideas for change.[24]

While the multifaceted role of these principals may seem a little overwhelming to many readers, especially prospective administrators, the Institute for Educational Leadership identified perhaps the most important qualities needed in school improvement efforts when it concluded, "There is no magic. All it takes is the commitment, the time, and the guts to stay with it."[25]

THE PROCESS OF CHANGE

Although it seems clear that the administrator is a pivotal figure in the change process and, in many cases, may need to be the primary change agent in introducing and implementing a proposed innovation, the administrator's effectiveness and the innovation's success are not automatic or inevitable. While many factors can influence the likelihood of successful school improvement, it is not likely to occur in a school or school district without the administrator and the school improvement committee developing an understanding of, and skill in, the process of introducing and implementing change. Kilmann identifies the following four critical stages in planning a "completely integrated program for improving organizations":

I. Ascertaining Whether the Organization Is Ready for a Successful Improvement
II. Diagnosing Problems—Using a Questionnaire
   A. Designating the barriers (problems).
   B. Designating the channels for success (opportunities).
III. Scheduling Planning Tracks
   A. Culture.
   B. Management skills.
   C. Team building.
   D. Strategy structure.
   E. Reward system.
IV. Implementing Planning Tracks
   A. Encouraging flexibility, as change is implemented in each track.
   B. Making sure employees take responsibility for the change.[26]

Although theorists on change may differ somewhat in their terminology and emphasis, most social scientists and innovators would agree that the process of introducing change should include the stages and steps listed in Figure 7.1.[27] The administrator and school improvement committee who adopt the process outlined in Figure 7.1 should greatly increase the likelihood of successfully introducing and institutionalizing a proposed change in a school

Figure 7.1 Important Stages and Steps in the Change Process.

Stage I

Conduct a Needs Assessment

A. Identify the need for change. Examine the present system to ascertain which aspects need to be improved.

B. Develop or evaluate and select a new approach or system which will replace the former method.

Stage II

Orient the Target Group to the Proposed Change

A. Create an awareness of and interest in the proposed innovation on the part of the target group, e.g., teachers.

B. Institute with the target group an examination of the strengths and weaknesses of the proposed change. Pilot-test and refine the new system prior to its introduction.

C. Identify, with the help of the target group, the commitments that will need to be made in terms of additional resources, in-service training programs, and/or building modifications.

Stage III

Decide Whether to Introduce the Proposed Change

A. Identify those who should participate in the decision.

B. Decide on the process by which the decision will be made.

C. Decide whether to proceed with the implementation of the proposed change.

Stage IV

Plan a Program of Implementation

A. Plan and carry out a program of in-service education for those involved in the proposed change.

B. Provide the resources and facilities necessary for successfully introducing the change.

C. Anticipate and attempt to resolve in advance the operational problems that may be encountered in implementing the proposed innovation.

Stage V

Implement the Proposed Innovation

Stage VI

Conduct In-Process Evaluation

A. Design and institute a system that will provide feedback on the extent to which the proposed change is accomplishing its objectives.

B. Diagnose those aspects of the program or its implementation that need improvement.

Figure 7.1 *—Continued.*

Stage VII

Refine and Institutionalize the Innovation

A. Modify the innovation and, if necessary, provide additional orientation, training, resources, facilities, etc.

B. Gain the acceptance of the innovation (if it is successful) as a regular and permanent part of the total educational program in the school or school district.

and school district. The process recommended is a rational one, although it is recognized that what actually occurs does not always follow rational lines. It begins with the identification of the need for change and ends with the integration of the proposed innovation into the routine of the school. Throughout the process, there is an emphasis on decision making, planning, organizing, diagnosing and evaluating—the very skills which are central to administration.

In the remaining sections of this chapter, each of the stages in the change process found in Figure 7.1 will be further analyzed and discussed.

Initial Considerations

The first stage in the process of change may well be the most important one. If the administrator, with the cooperation of relevant others, does not periodically evaluate the current program, activities, and practices in the school and school district, the administrator is unlikely to be aware of, or be sensitive to, the need for change. Worse yet, the administrator may react defensively to external pressures for change and attempt to defend a status quo that has not been examined carefully. Therefore, an effective administrator will have in operation a needs assessment plan providing objective information about the strengths and weaknesses of the various educational programs and activities. Such an assessment plan will be essential for identifying and validating the need for change, and it will also be helpful to others in developing an understanding of the need for change. An excellent description of how to develop such a plan is presented by Kaufman and Stone.[28]

Once the need for change has been established, the administrator, in cooperation with relevant others, should attempt to develop, or evaluate and select from various alternatives, a new approach or system that would replace or modify the current program or practice. This will not be an easy task. Administrators are faced with what must seem at times to be a virtual barrage of proposals for changing the school program. The challenge for the school practitioner is to select those innovations which show potential for significantly improving education in the school. Unfortunately, this is easier said than done. The main problem is finding an innovation that has been systematically developed on the basis of theory and research, with subsequent experimental testing and refinement before dissemination to the schools. Research and development centers and regional laboratories are a source for information on innovations. Also, the local school district may need to establish contact with its state department of public instruction to ascertain its participation in the U.S. Office of Education's National Diffusion Network. Since many of the innovations to be considered are not ''proven'' products in any sense of the term, the administrator will need to evaluate carefully the strengths and limitations of each proposed change before seeking its adoption in the school or school district.

In conducting an evaluation of a *proposed* innovation, the administrator and the School

Improvement Committee should attempt to seek answers to the following basic questions:

1. What are the objectives of the proposed change or innovation? What is it supposed to accomplish?
2. Are the objectives of the proposed innovation sufficiently relevant to the particular need for improvement in the local school or school district? How do we know this?
3. How will the proposed innovation accomplish its objectives? What is the evidence that the proposed innovation will accomplish its objectives, and how adequate is that evidence?
4. How difficult will it be for people to understand and accept the proposed innovation?
5. To what extent do people have the skills to implement the proposed innovation? If skills are lacking, how easily can these skills be acquired?
6. What are the financial costs of implementing the proposed innovation? Are there sufficient resources for implementing the proposed change?
7. How will we know, if we implement the proposed innovation, that it has accomplished its objectives?
8. In general, what are the advantages and disadvantages of implementing the proposed change?

As mentioned earlier, evaluating a proposed innovation is seldom an easy task. However, it is an essential activity for the administrator who wishes to avoid introducing an innovation that may not only be inappropriate for the needs of the school or school district but, if not successful, may also result in disillusionment and cynicism about future efforts to innovate.

Important Reference Groups

For most proposed changes, it will be important for the change agent to develop understanding, commitment, and possibly new skills on the part of those individuals or groups who will be affected by a school innovation. Generally, the groups who will be most affected by a school innovation will include the faculty, the students, the parents, the school board, the administrator's superiors, and the state department of public instruction.

These six groups represent, in most circumstances, the greatest sources of potential support for, or resistance to, a proposed change.[29] However, the administrator who wishes to play the role of the change agent needs to recognize that the acceptance and effectiveness of the proposed innovation may also be enhanced or impeded by the attitudes and actions of other individuals and groups associated with the school district: the personnel of other schools in the district, social and civic organizations within the community, visitors to the school, and the news media.[30] Because each of these groups is part of the informal communication network that exists within a school district or community, it is essential that the change agent identify the potential of these groups for support or resistance, and take these factors into consideration in introducing an innovation. As Baldridge and Deal have perceptively noted in regard to the external environment of the school (that includes not only local community but also the state and national scenes), "The environment is a major impetus for change, for new environmental demands are an initial source of new ideas, new procedures and new activities. Not only is change promoted by the environment, but changes made internally must also be supported by environmental connections."[31]

Perhaps the most important group to consider in the establishment of the need for change, and in the selection and introduction of a proposed innovation, is the faculty. If the faculty of a school or school district does not understand a proposed innovation, or lacks the skill for participating effectively in its implementation, the likelihood of the innovation's successful implementation is slight. This is particularly true of an innovation that is to be implemented in the classroom. Therefore, the administrator should make every effort to be sure that the faculty or its representatives are involved in each step of the change process, that they understand thoroughly the different facets of the proposed innovation, and that they are provided with adequate opportunity to acquire the skills necessary to implement the change.

Adoption of the Innovation

According to Havelock, an individual (or group) in the process of adopting an innovation goes through the following six stages:[32]

1. *Awareness Stage* The individual is exposed to an innovation and becomes aware of it, although not necessarily knowledgeable about it or possessing a strong interest in finding out more about it.
2. *Interest Stage* The individual is developing an interest in finding out more about the innovation and is beginning to develop some possible negative and positive attitudes toward it.
3. *Mental Stage* The individual is now actively evaluating the innovation as to how it might be implemented and is also seeking the assessment of the innovation from respected people.
4. *Trial Stage* The individual actually attempts to implement the innovation on a pilot basis to see if it will work.
5. *Adoption Stage* The individual adopts the innovation and implements it fully.
6. *Integration Stage* The individual internalizes the innovation in such a way that it becomes a routine part of the person's behavior or situation.

It should be emphasized that an individual or group will not always go through all six stages. Possibly at the end of the Mental or Trial Stage the proposed innovation will be rejected. What Havelock's concept of stages of adoption indicates is that adoption is a more complicated process than perhaps is realized. For example, the implementation of an innovation from a leadership perspective occurs in four different stages, according to Sergiovanni. In the first stage, **initiation,** the leader and the follower have independent, but organizationally related, objectives. Sergiovanni refers to this stage in leadership as "bartering." Stage two, **uncertainty,** is a time to muddle through. The leadership is "building." In the third stage, **transformation,** there is a breakthrough as the goals of leaders and followers are shared. The leaders and followers are bonded together in a moral commitment. In the fourth stage, **routinization,** improvements are turned into routines so that they become second nature. Leadership is "banking."[33]

Adequate orientation to the innovation, it would appear, is a key factor to successfully proceeding through Havelock's first three stages of adoption. In attempting to orient the faculty to the proposed innovation, the administrator needs to be aware of the typical concerns teachers have about innovations. According to a model developed at the Research and Development Center at the University of Texas, teachers go through several stages of concern.[34] Initially, their concerns seem to focus on how the proposed innovation, if it is implemented, will affect them *personally.* If these self concerns can be ameliorated or eliminated, then the teachers' questions are likely to reflect concern about how to perform the tasks associated with the innovation. And, finally, if the task-related concerns can be resolved, then the teachers' concerns will center on how the innovation will affect students.

Research at the R and D Center at the University of Texas subsequently supported the validity of the concept of stages of concern.[35] This research found that it was possible, using an instrument based on the concept of stages of concern, to predict with better than 90% accuracy those teachers who eventually used an innovation and those who did not. While the concept and instrument have not been validated with other groups who might also have concerns about an innovation, e.g., students and parents, it does appear logical that the administrator consider adapting the instrument for use with these groups as well.

During the process of addressing concerns, the administrator's role should not be one of "selling" or "advocating" an innovation. Such an approach will impair the administrator's objectivity and sensitivity to people's concerns. Instead, the administrator should be trying to develop an understanding of the innovation and people's concerns about it. To accomplish these objectives, the administrator needs to create a climate or atmosphere conducive to objectivity, trust, and confidence. Research by a number of individuals and groups suggests that to create this type of atmosphere, the change agent will need to be perceived by the teachers as someone who:

1. Is not trying to "foist" a change on them or manipulate them into making a change.
2. Is a good communicator who not only understands a particular innovation but also knows how to explain it clearly.
3. Respects teachers and encourages them to voice their concerns.
4. Listens carefully when concerns or objections surface and takes action to try to ameliorate those concerns and objectives.
5. Practices the perspective that successful change requires the cooperation and contribution of everyone.
6. Has skills for helping to facilitate the proposed change.[36]

Resistance to Change

Resistance to change exists in all organizations, be they public or private. Bowsher classified seven types of resisters to change in the following manner:

1. "Positive" resister—the person who agrees with all the new programs but never does anything about them.
2. "Unique" resister—although the changes may be good for other areas of the organization, they are never right for this individual's department.
3. "Let me be last" resister—will not say change is wrong, but uses the strategy of trying to be last to implement change, hoping all new ideas will die out before his or her department must institute a new program.
4. "We need more time to study" resister.
5. "States rights" resister—resists any new program from headquarters, stressing that only local programs will be effective.
6. "Cost justifier" resister—prior to any changes, everything must be cost justified.
7. "Incremental change" resister—the most difficult to win over to a new system. New approaches are tried only if they have everything the old system had.[37]

In every situation involving change, there will operate certain restraining, as well as facilitating, forces.[38] The facilitating forces—those conditions that make it easier to introduce a particular innovation—will probably be obvious to the administrator. They include such factors as outside pressures for change and the administrator's own convictions about the need for change. On the other hand, the restraining forces—those conditions that will make it difficult to introduce the innovation—may not be so obvious. However, their symptoms are usually manifested in people's concerns or expressions of resistance to a proposed change. One should assume that change will often be resisted, since experience and research both indicate that resistance to change is not unusual.[39] Sample verbal reactions to proposed change that suggest resistance are presented on the next page.

"Everything is going all right, so why change?"
"People aren't ready for change."
"Has anyone else tried this?"
"It won't work in this school."
"We've never done it before."
"We're not ready for that."
"We're doing all right without it."
"It's too radical a change."
"We don't have enough time to do it."
"It's too complicated."

These comments suggest concern as well as possible resistance to proposed change and should not be dismissed lightly. The worst thing the administrator can do is to dismiss resistance without examining its merits or to react defensively when opposition to change is expressed. Instead, the administrator should view the expression of resistance or concern as a warning sign that needs to be taken seriously and attempt to better understand and diagnose the motivation and reasoning behind such expressions. In so doing, the administrator needs to be aware that resistance to change may be based on one or more of the following restraining factors:

Habit. Habit is the tendency of people to behave in the same way that they have always behaved, and the familiar becomes a form of security. Proposed change challenges this security, and the challenge is frequently met with resistance.[40]

The Bureaucratic Structure of the School District. The school district as a bureaucratic institution emphasizes the maintenance of order, rationality, and continuity. Uniformity of educational programs and procedures among the schools of the district seems to be valued, whereas diversity does not. Attempts by individual schools to introduce new programs or procedures are sometimes viewed with suspicion. Because of these attitudes and the hierarchical structure of the district, proposed change may be diluted before it is finally approved, or it may be rejected because it threatens the stability of the institution.[41] However, recent research suggests that the bureaucratic structure of a school district can, depending on its nature and on how it is used, facilitate the process of change rather than restrict it.[42]

The Lack of Incentive. Change can be a difficult and frustrating experience for the individuals or groups involved. Although the administrator may be personally convinced of the benefits that will accrue if a proposed change is adopted, the administrator can seldom guarantee those benefits or offer incentives (monetary or otherwise) to persuade others to adopt the innovation.[43] As a result, the administrator is dependent upon the ability to influence others to adopt a proposed change that may have high personal costs in terms of time and frustration and no immediate gain.

The Nature of the Proposed Change. Innovations can vary according to complexity, financial cost, compatibility with the other phases of the school's operation, ease of communicability, and time and energy needed to make the change.[44] Some innovations, because of these factors, are more difficult to introduce into a school system than other proposed changes. As Baldridge and Deal note, "Many plans fail because they simply are not viable in terms of what the organization can afford."[45] Therefore, the characteristics of the innovation itself may constitute a major obstacle or problem in securing its adoption.

Teacher and Community Norms. Teacher and community norms can act as significant barriers to innovating in the schools. For example, there is evidence that teacher norms support autonomy and do not encourage interaction and exchange of new ideas among colleagues.[46] As a result, efforts by the administrator to bring about change in a teacher's role or methods may be viewed as a challenge to that teacher's professional autonomy. Research has further revealed that community groups may feel threatened by change because of its implications for upsetting the stability of the power relations within the community.[47] Both sets of norms—teacher and community—can act as powerful sources of resistance to the administrator who is trying to introduce a particular innovation.

Lack of Understanding. People may resist a proposed change because they don't possess an adequate or accurate understanding of it. Their deficiency may be caused by a failure on their part to pay close attention at the time that the proposed change was explained, or, on the other hand, information about the change may have been poorly or inaccurately communicated. In any respect, a lack of understanding of a proposed change can act as a significant deterrent in its successful implementation.[48]

A Difference of Opinion. A proposed change may be resisted because of an honest difference of opinion about whether it is needed or whether it will accomplish all that its proponents claim. The difference in opinion may be based on conflicting philosophies and values of education in regard to teaching and learning, or it may result from variant assessments of how much improvement would actually occur if the proposed change were implemented.

A Lack of Skill. A proposed change may be resisted by an individual or group who will be required to perform new skills and roles. The change from traditional roles and skills to new ones is viewed as an unsettling experience by many people. Therefore, any innovation requiring new skills or roles on the part of the participants should be accompanied by an inservice program that will enable these people to develop the new skills or roles.[49]

Resistance to change is a complex phenomenon, and the administrator should spend a considerable amount of time in diagnosing its source(s) before drawing any conclusions about how it might best be reduced. In many situations there will be more than one reason for resistance to change, and the administrator should assess the validity of each of the possible factors identified previously. By accurately diagnosing the reasons for resistance, the administrator will be in a better position to ameliorate it and smooth the way for successful implementation of a proposed improvement. A useful approach for diagnosing whether or not a school is ready for change has been developed by McCalley.[50]

Of course, one recommended means for dealing with the possibility of resistance to change is to introduce an innovation in such a manner as to avoid or minimize the likelihood of resistance. Some generalizations by Goodwin Watson developed from a review of the research and theoretical literature on resistance to change that may be useful to the school administrator are:[51]

1. Resistance will be less if administrators and other participants feel that the project is their own—not one devised and operated by outsiders.
2. Resistance will be less if the project innovation clearly has wholehearted support from top officials of the system.
3. Resistance will be less if the participants see the change as reducing, rather than increasing, their present burdens.
4. Resistance will be less if the project is in accord with values already acknowledged by participants.
5. Resistance will be less if the program offers the kind of new experience that interests participants.
6. Resistance will be less if participants feel their autonomy and security are not threatened.
7. Resistance will be less if participants have joined in diagnostic efforts leading them to

agree on what the basic problem is and its importance.

8. Resistance will be less if the project is adopted by consensual group decision.
9. Resistance will be reduced if proponents are able to empathize with opponents; to recognize valid objections; and to take steps to relieve unnecessary fears.
10. Resistance will be reduced if it is recognized that innovations are likely to be misunderstood and misinterpreted, and if provision is made for feedback of perceptions of the project and for further clarification of need.
11. Resistance will be reduced if participants experience acceptance, support, trust, and confidence in their relations with one another.
12. Resistance will be reduced if the project is kept open to revision and reconsideration—if experience indicates that changes will be desirable.

While it may be difficult, if not impossible, to meet all of these conditions in every situation, the administrator and the school improvement committee should take Watson's guidelines into consideration in planning a school improvement.

FACILITATING THE INTRODUCTION OF CHANGE

Although it has been felt by many administrators that the crucial, if not the sole problem in the successful introduction of an innovation, was to overcome the initial resistance of the individuals and/or groups whose behavior and attitude were going to be affected by a change, this belief has now been challenged. Gross and his associates, for example, found that despite an initially favorable predisposition by those who were going to be especially affected by a certain change in a school, the proposed innovation ultimately met with failure.[52]

Based on teacher interviews, questionnaires, and daily field observations, Gross and his colleagues identified four factors that seemed to account for the innovation's lack of success, all possessing implications for the educator who is concerned about the successful implementation of a proposed change.

1. Although the faculty had received orientation about the innovation prior to its introduction, six months after the innovation had finally been initiated, most teachers still did not seem to understand what was involved in their new role.

   Implication. The administrator should not assume that one or two explanations of an innovation will be adequate. Rather, the administrator must continuously secure feedback and provide clarification to those who will be affected by the change.

2. The teachers seemed to lack the knowledge and skills necessary for performing their new role. When they encountered problems as a result of these inadequacies, teacher resistance to the innovation developed.

   Implication. Behavioral and attitudinal change is complex and difficult to achieve. The job of the administrator is to identify clearly and precisely those skills and understandings needed by the people affected by the innovation and to provide the training necessary to acquire them. Teachers, for example, need continual assistance in adopting a new role.

3. The teachers' role in the new program was designed on the assumption that much of the student learning would result from contact between the students, who were using highly motivating, self-instructional materials. Unfortunately, the materials were in short supply and apparently not sufficiently motivating and self-instructing.

Implication. If the success of an innovation depends on materials which possess special characteristics, e.g., highly motivating, self-instructing, it is the responsibility of the administrator to see that such materials are available in sufficient quantity.

4. Other aspects of the school program, such as grading and developing the school schedule were not changed to facilitate the adoption of the new teacher role.

   Implication. A change in one aspect of the school program may affect and be affected by other aspects of the program and may necessitate further change.

The research conducted by Gross would appear to suggest two conclusions about proposed change: (1) that it will not always be initially resisted; and (2) that an innovation may ultimately fail, despite its preliminary acceptance, if the people involved have not been provided with adequate role orientation, training, materials, and other prerequisites.[53]

In a related review of the literature on the implementation of change, Kritek found that, in addition to the factors identified by Gross, attempts to innovate failed because of goals that were too vague and ambitious, minimal planning to operationalize the innovation and to integrate it into the school, resources that were too limited, and the failure to anticipate adequately, and deal constructively with, the developments that occurred after the innovation was implemented.[54]

Several implications are suggested by Kritek's review of the literature on the implementation of change. First of all, it will be important for the administrator who is thinking about introducing change to define the objectives of the innovation clearly and realistically. Full and accurate communication to those who could be affected by the proposed change is essential.

To avoid the problem of excessively ambitious goals, it may be necessary to consider introducing the innovation on a pilot project basis rather than to the entire school or school district.[55] A pilot project represents a scaled-down version of the originally proposed change. The proposed innovation might be reduced in terms of size, length of operation, or number of participants involved. For example, rather than introducing a new, schoolwide language arts curriculum, the change could be implemented on a pilot basis at only one grade level. Or, perhaps, rather than implementing a curricular change at one grade level, several *units* of the curriculum could be introduced by all of the teachers in the school during the first semester of the school year. And, of course, other variations of the pilot project approach are also possible.

The pilot project approach to introducing change has several distinct advantages. It can be conducted with a smaller number of participants and can involve those who would be more willing to try out new ideas. If the pilot project is successful, its results may favorably influence other people who initially resisted the proposed change. It can also be useful in identifying and addressing defects or weaknesses in the originally proposed innovation that may not have been obvious before implementation. And, finally, a pilot project may prove useful in demonstrating that a proposed change will not work, either because of a defect in the concept of the proposed change, or because local conditions make it impossible to implement fully.

The pilot project is no panacea for introducing change, but it may avoid the problem of overly ambitious objectives for an innovation and, for that reason alone, should be considered by the administrator.

After planning for the introduction of an innovation, the administrator should attempt to ascertain whether or not it was planned carefully enough and in sufficient detail. Many innovations seem to fail because there was not a well-conceived **plan** for implementing the innovation. Planning is concerned primarily with the question of how an objective is to be achieved or a decision implemented.[56] In a situation involving the planned implementation of an innovation, the following types of questions need to be answered:

1. What kinds of activities or actions must occur in order to introduce the innovation?
2. What kinds of resources—personnel, facilities, supplies—must be obtained to introduce the innovation?
3. What kinds of problems and possible consequences might the introduction of the innovation generate? How should these problems and consequences be dealt with?
4. How should activities be sequenced to best advantage and resources most efficiently coordinated in order to introduce the innovation?
5. What kind of time schedule should be followed in implementing the plan of action?

In an oversimplified sense, the administrator who engages in the planning process is attempting to answer the question, "Who does what, with whom, and over what period of time in order to implement the innovation?"

In summary, a well-conceived plan for implementing an innovation will go far toward avoiding the problems referred to by Gross and Kritek and will increase the possibility that the innovation will be successfully implemented.

POST-IMPLEMENTATION PROBLEMS

Although the evidence is somewhat mixed, there is considerable indication that many innovations that are implemented are later abandoned or drastically modified. There are many possible reasons for the failure of an innovation, most of which have been discussed in the previous two sections of this chapter. Certainly any innovation attempt where the objectives and operational activities are not well understood, where the implementation is not well planned, and where implementation is attempted, despite the opposition of significant members of relevant reference groups, carries with it the seeds of self-destruction. However, even if these negative factors can be avoided, some innovations still encounter problems after they are implemented, problems that can lead to their demise.[57]

One of these problems is that the individuals who are responsible for implementing the innovation may eventually become "burned out." Implementing change frequently requires a high level of energy expenditure. There may be new roles to be learned, long hours to be invested, and often anxiety and frustration are associated with the implementation of an innovation. Introducing change is usually hard work and, typically, there are few external rewards for the participants. The morale in a school implementing an innovation frequently vacillates from high to low, without much stability.

If not ameliorated, over a period of time these conditions will negatively influence the attitude of the participants toward the innovation and will impair their effectiveness. However, the administrator who is sensitive to conditions in the school will provide timely assistance and rewards to those individuals who need them, and the problem of the participants becoming "burned out" can be prevented or reduced.

Coping with problems is very important for successful change. According to Miles and Louis, "Good problem coping (dealing with problems, actively and with some depth) is the single biggest determinant of program success." The authors suggest that problems should be solved structurally. For example, if teachers complain about being overloaded, a proper solution would be to allow shared planning or to give added technical assistance rather than just asking teachers to persevere or to be more dedicated. Problems should be located and seen as "natural, even helpful occurrences, without blaming anyone, arousing defensiveness, or implying a predetermined solution."[58]

Two frequently unanticipated problems which can occur after an innovation has been implemented are a "bad press" and the reduction of resources and support by the district administration or external agency that is funding the innovation. Negative newspaper or television reports on an innovation can do immeasurable damage to the image of the innovation and can significantly affect the spirit of the participants and the attitudes of those who are judging the merits of the innovation. It matters little whether the press or television reports are accurate or not—media coverage usually has the appearance of validity.

A major problem with press coverage of an innovation is that generally the press will want to report on the innovation soon after it has been implemented, even though at that stage the school is still discovering and trying to iron out the "bugs" in the innovation. Consequently, the media spotlight is on the innovation early and tends to focus on the problems it is encountering, resulting in a "bad press." There is no easy answer to this problem, given the nature of the press and the process of introducing change. The media are generally more interested in problems because they are newsworthy, and the period just after the innovation has been implemented is frequently the time when many problems arise. The administrator can, however, attempt to develop a positive relationship with the news reporters in the community and try to develop an understanding on their part (**before** the innovation is introduced) about types of problems which are likely to occur because of the innovation's novelty as well as the school's contingency plans for dealing with those problems.

Another possible post-implementation problem is the gradual reduction in resources and moral support provided by the central office of the district or an outside funding agency. A school which is attempting to innovate will frequently need a higher level of resources and support than one that is not. Over a period of time, the central office may encounter budgeting pressures, as well as criticism from the other schools in the district for better treatment of the innovative school. Or, if the innovative school is funded by an external agency, that source of funding may be gradually reduced or terminated and the school district may not make up the difference. And if the innovative school has received a bad press and/or has encountered some problems after the innovation has been implemented, the principal may find that the moral support of the central administration may be lacking when it is most needed.

Fortunately, most of the circumstances described in this section can be avoided, or at least reduced, if the administrator anticipates them and takes corrective action before the problems become major. The difficulties essentially are a result of events going less smoothly after the innovation has been implemented than had been anticipated when people were planning for its introduction. In these situations some of the famous "Murphy's Laws" are operating: "Most things are more complicated than they initially appear to be," and "Most things take longer than originally anticipated."

Problems are a normal occurrence, since the planning process—even under the best of conditions—always involves assumptions, some of which may turn out to be untenable. However, problems need not significantly influence the fate of an innovation if the administrator becomes aware of them at an early stage before they develop into a crisis, and if the administrator takes quick action to remedy the situation. Catching problems early requires the initiation of a formative evaluation system that will alert the administrator to incipient problems and good leadership skills on the part of the administrator are necessary for quick action in a crisis.

FORMATIVE AND SUMMATIVE EVALUATION

If the administrator is to be aware of problems associated with the implementation of an innovation before these problems become major crises, arrangements need to be made for the initiation of some type of formative evaluation. A formative evaluation represents an assessment of an innovation's strengths and areas in need of improvement before a conclusion or decision is

Figure 7.2 Formative Evaluation Survey.

FEEDBACK ON THE IMPLEMENTATION OF THE COMPUTER LITERACY PROGRAM

Instructions: Please check (X) below as to whether you are a teacher or student, and then give your reactions on the remainder of the form. You need not sign your name on this form unless you so desire.

Teacher ______________________ Grade Level ______________________

Student ______________________ Grade Level ______________________

1. What do you see as the main problems which need immediate action? Please be as specific as possible, and if you have ideas about resolving these problems, so indicate.

   Main problems ____

   Possible solutions ____

2. What do you see as the main advantage(s) of the computer literacy program so far? ____

3. Is there any special help or assistance that you need? ________________

____

____

Signature (optional)

reached on its success.[59] Formative evaluation is diagnostic in nature since it is searching for aspects of the innovation, or the implementation plan, that are in need of improvement.

This type of evaluation is very important in the early stages of implementing an innovation because it is during this period that unanticipated problems are likely to arise and immediate corrective action may be needed in order to avoid exacerbating the problems. For ease of understanding, an example of a relatively simple formative evaluation survey used by one school is presented in Figure 7.2.

A formative evaluation can range from simple to complex in the nature of its data gathering format and analysis, but the important consideration is that it provides the administrator with useful information on the progress and problems of the innovation and/or the plan for implementation. This type of evaluation should not, however, be used by the administrator, or anyone else for that matter, for making decisions about whether or not the innovation is a success and should be continued or discontinued. **After** the innovation has been given a reasonable amount of time to prove itself, then a decision should be considered in regard to continuing or discontinuing the innovation, and, at that point, the administrator will need to make arrangements for the initiation of what is referred to as **summative** evaluation.

A summative evaluation, as applied to the assessment of an innovation, represents an attempt to ascertain whether or not the innovation is adequately meeting school or school district objectives and whether or not the advantages of the innovation sufficiently outweigh the disadvantages.[60] Summative evaluation usually necessitates the collection of data, but it also frequently involves subjective judgments on what the data mean. Examples of some different kinds of summative evaluations include the following.[61]

1. Comparison of **student behavior** before and after the innovation has been implemented.
2. Comparison of **student achievement** before and after the innovation has been implemented.
3. Comparison of **student attitudes** before and after the innovation has been implemented.
4. Comparison of **teacher attitudes** toward the innovation before and after the change.
5. Comparison of **parent attitudes** toward the innovation before and after the change.
6. **Effectiveness of the plan** for introducing the innovation.
7. Extent of **disruption** of other activities because of the change.
8. Amount of **additional costs** as a result of implementing and operating the innovation.

The methods one uses to conduct summative evaluation should depend on three factors: (1) what is to be evaluated, (2) what information is needed, and (3) what method is most appropriate and most accessible to provide the desired information. Possible evaluation methods range from questionnaires and interviews to content analysis and standardized tests.[62] There is no perfect method! All too frequently administrators reject or are critical of an evaluation method without offering a better alternative; as a result, no evaluation is ever performed. Instead, administrators should select the best possible alternative from the evaluation methods that are available and appropriate for assessing the innovation.

Ultimately, administrators cannot avoid the evaluation of an innovation. If arrangements are not made to see that a sound assessment is carried out, then other people, including parents and members of the community, will make their own evaluation, using their own criteria and methods.

A FINAL NOTE

In most situations, change is inevitable. An administrator can watch it occur, can resist it, or can help guide and direct it. By utilizing the concepts presented in this chapter, the administrator should be able to make an effective contribution by responding constructively to the need for improvement in education.

> Although many of the case studies, suggested learning activities, and simulations presented in Part II require the appropriate use of the ideas in this chapter on school improvement, Cases 50–58 in Chapter 15 should provide the best opportunities for testing understanding and effective use of the concepts concerning the change process.

Notes

1. This conclusion is supported by the findings of various Gallup polls reported in the **Phi Delta Kappan** over the years. Also, see Larry Cuban, "Reforming Again, Again, and Again," **Educational Leadership** (January 1990), pp. 3–12, and Stanley M. Elam and Alex M. Gallup, "The 21st Annual Gallup Poll of the Public's Attitudes Toward the Public Schools," **Phi Delta Kappan** (September 1989), pp. 42–54.

2. Bruce Bowers, "Initiating Change in Schools," **National Association of Elementary School Principals** (April 1990), p. 1, and Daniel U. Levine, "Creating Effective Schools: Findings and Implications From Research and Practice," **Phi Delta Kappan** (January 1991), pp. 389–393.

3. Excellent critiques of this literature are found in Harry A. Passow, *Reforming Schools in the 1980s: A Critical Review of the National Reports* (New York: Institute for Urban and Minority Education, Teachers College, 1984), Marilyn Clayton, *Improving Our Schools: 33 Studies That Inform Local Action* (Newton, MA: Educational Development Center, 1985), and John O'Neill, "Piecing Together the Restructuring Puzzle," **Educational Leadership** (April 1990) pp. 4–10.

4. For example, The National Commission on Excellence in Education, *A Nation at Risk: The Imperative*

for Educational Reform (Washington, DC: U.S. Department of Education, 1983), Paul E. Peterson, *Making the Grade: Report of the Twentieth Century Fund Task Force on Elementary and Secondary Education Policy* (New York: Twentieth Century Fund, 1983), *Time for Results: The Governors' 1991 Report on Education* (Washington, DC: National Governors' Association, 1986), *Leaders for America's Schools: The Report of the National Commission on Excellence in Educational Administration* (Arizona: The University Council for Educational Administration, 1987), *Tomorrow's Teachers: A Report of the Holmes Group* (New York, 1986), *An Imperiled Generation: Saving Urban Schools* (Princeton, NJ: Carnegie Foundation for the Advancement of Teaching, 1988), and *America 2000: An Education Strategy* (Washington, DC: U.S. Department of Education, 1991).

5. **Phi Delta Kappan** (December 1990). The entire issue dealt with these national goals.

6. Chris Pipho, "Quantity vs. Quality: States Aim to Improve Teaching and Teachers," **Phi Delta Kappan** (January 1986), pp. 333–334, and Terry Peterson, "Measuring Up: Questions and Answers About State Roles in Educational Accountability," U.S. Department of Education (November 1988), pp. 1–8.

7. Linda Darling Hammond, "Achieving Our Goals: Superficial or Structural Reforms?," **Phi Delta Kappan** (December 1990), pp. 287–294, and Mary Anne Raywid, "The Evolving Effort to Improve Schools: Pseudo-Reform, Incremental Reform, and Restructuring," **Phi Delta Kappan** (October 1990), pp. 139–143.

8. Deborah Meier, "Getting Tough in the Schools," **Dissent** (Winter 1984), pp. 61–70.

9. John De Santis and David Cohen, "The Lawn Party," in *The Dynamics of Organizational Change in Education,* ed. J. Victor Baldridge and Terrence Deal (Berkeley, CA: McCutchan, 1983), pp. 114–126. Also, see chapter by Terrence Deal and Samuel Nutt on "Planned Change in Rural School District" in the same book. For an excellent example of how states may be able to contribute effectively to school improvement, see Beverly Anderson and Allan Odden, "State Initiatives Can Foster School Improvement," **Phi Delta Kappan** (April 1986), pp. 578–581; also, see pp. 582–596 in the same issue, and Terrence E. Deal, "Reframing Reform," **Educational Leadership** (May 1990), pp. 6–12.

10. Mary Hartwood Futrell, "Mission Not Accomplished: Education Reform in Retrospect," **Phi Delta Kappan** (September 1989), pp. 10–14.

11. De Santis and Cohen, p. 114. Also, see John I. Goodlad and M. Francis Klein, *Looking Behind the Classroom Door* (Worthington, OH: Charles E. Jones, 1970).

12. Karl Weick, "Educational Organizations as Loosely Coupled Systems," in *The Dynamics of Organizational Change in Education,* ed. J. Victor Baldridge and Terrence Deal (Berkeley, CA: McCutchan, 1983), pp. 35–37. Also, see Larry Cuban, "Reforming Again, Again, and Again," **Educational Leadership** (January 1990), pp. 3–12.

13. Frances C. Fowler, "Why Reforms Go Awry," **Education Week** (November, 1985), pp. 17, 24.

14. Bruce R. Joyce et al., *The Structure of School Improvement* (New York: Longman, 1983), p. 71.

15. Bruce Bowers, "Initiating Change in Schools," **National Association of Elementary School Principals** (April 1990), p. 1.

16. Michael Fullan, *Implementing Educational Change,* an ERIC report, Ed 221–540, and "Staff Development, Innovation, and Institutional Development," *Changing School Culture Through Staff Development* (Alexandria, VA: ASCD, 1990), pp. 3–25. Also, see Pat L. Cox, "Complementary Roles in Successful Change," **Educational Leadership** (November 1983), pp. 10–13; and David F. Salisbury, "Major Issues in the Design of New Educational Systems," an ERIC report, Ed 321–403, pp. 1–9.

17. Joyce et al., *Structure of School Improvement,* Chapter 6. Also, see Herbert Klausmier, *A Process Guide for School Improvement* (Lanham, MD: University Press of America, 1985).

18. Willis J. Furtwengler, "Implementation Strategies for a School Effectiveness Program," **Phi Delta Kappan** (December 1985), pp. 262–265; Murry H. Dalziel and Stephen C. Schoonover, *Changing Ways* (New York: Amacom, 1988), pp. 21, 58–63, 146.

19. Lee Demeter, "Accelerating the Local Use of Improved Educational Practices in School Systems," Ph.D. Dissertation, Columbia University, Teacher College, 1951. Also, see Gene F. Hall, "The Principal as Leader of the Change Facilitating Team," **Journal of Research and Development in Education** (Fall 1988), pp. 49–59, and William D. Hitt, *The Leader-Manager,* (Columbus, OH: Battelle Press, 1988), pp. 17–38, 21, 24–27.

20. Seymour B. Sarason, *The Culture of the School and the Problem of Change* (Boston, MA: Allyn and Bacon, 1982), p. 148; Grant W. Simpson, "Elements of School Culture That Sustain Innovation," **Educational Leadership** (May 1990), pp. 34–37; and, Connie Golman and Cindy O'Shea, "A Culture for Change," **Educational Leadership** (May 1990), pp. 41–43.

21. Gene Hall et al., "Effects of Three Principal Styles on School Improvement," **Educational Leadership** (February 1984), pp. 22–29; and Murry H. Dalziel and Stephen C. Schoonover, *Changing Ways* (New York: Amacom, 1988), p. 59. Also, see France R. Westley, "The Eye of the Needle: Cultural and Personal Transformation in a Traditional Organization," **Human Relations** (March 1990), p. 273.

22. Spencer H. Wyant, *Of Projects and Principals* (Reston, VA: Association of Teacher Education, 1980). For additional discussion of the administrator's role or style, see Hall et al., "Three Principal Styles," and Richard I. Arends, "The Meaning of Administrative Support," **Educational Administration Quarterly** (Fall 1982), pp. 79–92. Also, see Jane M. Howell and Christopher A. Higgins, "Champions of Change: Identifying, Understanding, and Supporting Champions of Technological Innovations," **Organizational Dynamics** (Summer 1990), pp. 40–46; and Kent D. Peterson, "Mechanisms of Culture Building and Principal's Work," **Educational and Urban Society** (May 1988), pp. 250–261.

23. Gene F. Hall, "The Principal as Leader of the Change Facilitating Team," **Journal of Research and Development in Education** (Fall 1988) pp. 49–59.

24. Hitt, *The Leader-Manager,* p. 22.

25. Institute for Educational Leadership, *What Makes for an Effective School?* (Washington DC: George Washington University, 1980), p. 102.

26. Ralph H. Kilmann, "A Completely Integrated Program for Creating and Maintaining Organizational Success," **Organizational Dynamics** (Summer 1989), pp. 5–19.

27. The recommended process of introducing change is not based on any particular source, but instead represents the conclusions of the author after analyzing various research reports on change.

28. Roger Kaufman and B. Stone, *Planning for Organizational Success: A Practical Guide* (New York: John Wiley, 1983); and, Robert V. Carlson and Gary Awkerman, Editors, *Educational Planning* (New York: Longman, 1991), pp. 241–246.

29. David Crandall and Susan Loucks, *A Roadmap for School Improvement: Executive Summary of the Study of Dissemination Efforts Supporting School Improvement,* an ERIC report, Ed 240–722.

30. Leslie W. Kindred et al., *The School and Community Relations* (Englewood Cliffs, NJ: Prentice-Hall, 1989), Chapter 8. Also, see Tom R. Vickery, "ODDM: A Workable Model for Total School Improvement," **Educational Leadership** (April 1990), pp. 67–70.

31. J. Victor Baldridge and Terrence E. Deal, *Managing Change in Educational Organizations* (Berkeley, CA: McCutchan, 1975), p. 16; Sharon Conley, " 'Who's On First?' School Reform Teacher Participation, and the Decision-Making Process," **Education and Urban Society** (August 1989), pp. 366–379; and Richard F. Elmore, "Early Experience in Restructuring Schools, Voices from the Field" an ERIC report, Ed 306–634, 1988, pp. 5–6.

32. Ronald G. Havelock, Janet C. Huber, and Shaindel Zimmerman, *A Guide to Innovation in Education* (Ann Arbor, MI: University of Michigan Center for Research on the Utilization of Scientific Knowledge, 1970).

33. Thomas J. Sergiovanni," Adding Value to Leadership Gets Extraordinary Results," **Educational Leadership** (May 1990), pp. 23–27.

34. William L. Rutherford, "An Investigation of How Teachers' Concerns Influence Innovation Adoption," Paper presented at the annual meeting of the American Educational Research Association, 1977, p. 4. Also, see David Salisbury, "Major Issues in the Design of New Educational Systems," an ERIC report, Ed 321–403, pp. 1–9.

35. Ibid, William L. Rutherford, p. 26.

36. For example, see Susan S. McCoy and Geralyn Shreve, "Principals—Why Are Some More Successful Than Others in Implementing Change?" **National Association of Secondary School Principals Bulletin** (September 1983), pp. 96–103, and Sauita Kumari and Kamah Dwivedo, "Effect of Organizational Climate in Attitude Toward Change—A Comparative Study," **Social Science International** (June–July 1988), pp. 9–14.

37. Jack E. Bowsher, *Educating America, Lessons Learned in the Nation's Corporations* (New York: Wiley & Sons, 1989), pp. 144–146, 170.

38. Kurt Lewin, "Group Decision and Social Change," in *Readings in Social Psychology,* ed. G. E. Swanson et al. (New York: Holt, Rinehart, and Winston, 1952), pp. 463–473; and Ralph Killman, "A Completely Integrated Program for Creating and Mainstreaming Organizational Success," p. 9.

39. Stuart M. Klein and R. Richard Ritti, *Understanding Organizational Behavior* (Boston: Kent, 1984), pp. 569–572.

40. Myron Lieberman, "Why Reform Was 'Dead on Arrival,' " **Education Week** (29 January 1986), p. 20, and Michael Beer and Elise Walton, "Developing the Competitive Organization," **American Psychologist** (February 1990), pp. 40–46, 157–158.

41. Max G. Abbott, "Hierarchical Impediments to Innovation in Educational Organizations," in *Change Perspectives in Educational Administration,* ed. Max G. Abbott and John T. Lovell (Auburn, AL: Auburn University School of Education, 1965), pp. 40–53. Also, see Joseph Raiche et al., "School Improvement," an ERIC report, Ed 239–396, and Thomas W. Rhoades and Phyllis H. Sunshine, "History and Politics in State Accountability Reform," an ERIC report, Ed 321–347, 1990, pp. 1–23.

42. M. Fullan, *The Meaning of Educational Change* (New York: Teachers College Press, 1991).

43. Robert E. Blum, "Pitfalls in Implementing Secondary School Improvements," Paper presented at a conference sponsored by the Center for Educational Policy and Management, University of Oregon, October 1983. For an example of the use of incentives to facilitate change, see Dale Mann, "The Impact of Impact II," **Phi Delta Kappan** (May 1982), pp. 612–614.

44. David L. Clark et al., "Effective Schools and School Improvement: A Comparative Analysis of Two Lines of Inquiry," **Educational Administration Quarterly** (Summer 1984), pp. 56–58.

45. Baldridge and Deal, *Managing Change,* p. 18.

46. J. E. Deal and L. D. Cellotti, "How Much Influence Do (and Can) Educational Administrators Have on Classrooms?" **Phi Delta Kappan** (March 1980), pp. 471–473. For ideas on how to address the problem of teacher norms, see H. Dickson Corbett, "To Make an Omelet, You've Got to Break the Egg Crate," **Educational Leadership** (November 1982), pp. 34–35, and Mary E. Dietz, "On the Road to Change," **Instructor** (April 1990), p. 36.

47. Fullan, *Meaning of Educational Change,* p. 194. For ways of addressing community norms, see Thomas Popkewitz., *The Myth of Educational Reform* (Madison, WI: University of Wisconsin Press, 1983).

48. J. Stanislao and B. C. Stanislao, "Dealing with Resistance to Change," **Business Horizons** (July–August 1983), pp. 74–78. Also, see Mathew B. Miles, and Karen Seashore Louis, "Mustering the Will and Skill for Change," **Educational Leadership** (May 1990), pp. 37–61.

49. For further guidelines on this aspect, see Joyce et al., *Structure of School Improvement,* Chapters 9 and 10; and Leonard Allen, "A Model for Creating Effective Change," **Directions** (February 1990), pp. 1–2.

50. John McCalley, *Diagnosing a School's Readiness for Change,* an ERIC report, Ed 188–310. Also, see Yoram Zeira and Joyce Avedisian, "Organizational Planned Change: Assessing the Chances for Success," **Organizational Dynamics** (Spring 1989), pp. 31–45.

51. Goodwin Watson, "Resistance to Change," in *Concepts for Social Change,* ed. author (Washington, DC: National Training Laboratories, 1966), pp. 22–23, and Kenneth K. Tewel, "Restructuring Urban High Schools," **The Clearing House** (October 1989), pp. 73–77.

52. Neal Gross et al., "An Attempt to Implement a Major Educational Innovation; A Sociological Inquiry," Paper presented at the Center for Research and Development in Educational Differences, Harvard University, 1968, and Robert E. Herriott and Neal Gross, eds., *The Dynamics of Planned Educational Change* (Berkeley, CA: McCutchan, 1979).

53. Also, see Ralph Parish and Richard Arends, "Why Innovative Programs Are Discontinued," **Educational Leadership** (January 1983), pp. 62–65.

54. William J. Kritek, "Lesson from the Literature on Implementation," **Educational Administration Quarterly** (Fall 1976), pp. 86–102; and see Jack P. Krueger and Ralph Parish, "We're Making the Same Mistakes," **Planning and Changing** (Fall 1982), pp. 131–138.

55. Richard A. Gorton and Gail Thierbach-Schneider, *"School-Based Leadership: Challenges and Opportunities,"* 3rd ed. (Dubuque, IA: Wm. C. Brown, 1991), pp. 376–378.

56. W. E. Webster, "Operating the Planning Process in Schools," **Planning and Changing** (Summer 1985), pp. 82–87.

57. The discussion in this section is based on the authors' experience and observation, coupled with an analysis of a number of studies already mentioned and those by John Daresh, *Factors Supporting or Inhibiting Innovative Practice in Senior High Schools,* an ERIC report, Ed 206–285.

58. Mathew B. Miles and Karen Seashore Louis, pp. 37–61.

59. Harriet Talmage, "Evaluation of Programs," in *Encyclopedia of Educational Research,* ed. Harold E. Mitzel (New York: Free Press, 1982), p. 603. Also, see Roland Kimball, "Program Evaluation for School Improvement: Cultivating Excellence—A Curriculum for Excellence in School Administration," **New Hampshire School Administrators Association** (June 1989), p. 7.

60. Talwage, "Evaluation of Programs," p. 603.

61. Adaptation and extension of factors identified by Joseph A. Kreskey, "A Critical Review of Procedures and Organizing for Curriculum Improvement in High Schools," Ed.D. Dissertation, New York University, 1967, p. 635. An excellent discussion of additional variables and designs for evaluating a variety of types of programs can be found in Bruce Joyce and Beverly Shower, "Evaluating Staff Development Programs," *Student Achievement Through Staff Development* (New York: Longman, 1988), pp. 111–129.

62. Gerald R. Adams and Jay Schvaneveldt, *Understanding Research Methods* (New York: Longman, 1985), Section 4, and Blaine R. Worthen and James R. Sanders, *Educational Evaluation* (New York: Longman, 1987).

Part

CASE STUDIES AND SIMULATIONS

Clinical Materials and Learning Experiences for School Administrators and Supervisors

8 Introduction to Clinical Materials and Learning Experiences

Many readers, if not most, will have difficulty in fully understanding and, more importantly, utilizing *effectively* the types of concepts presented in Part 1 of the text without some practice in actually applying the ideas. Therefore, the remainder of the book presents a large number of representative case studies, suggested learning activities, and in-basket exercises which have been designed to help the reader become more skilled in using the various concepts discussed in Part 1 of the text.[1] Since many readers may not be familiar with case study analysis, in-basket experiences, role-playing or other kinds of clinical experiences,[2] the following sections of this chapter will discuss these approaches, identifying possible problems, and offering strategies for preventing and resolving problems that may develop.

THE NATURE OF CASE STUDIES

Case studies have been used for training programs for a long time, with a wide variety of content and formats.[3] Although it is hoped that the case studies in this text will provide interesting reading, their primary purpose is to stimulate individual and group involvement in situations requiring the application of the concepts in Part 1. The majority of the cases emphasize critical problems in educational administration and supervision and are organized around particular themes: problems encountered by a new administrator, student problems, administrator-staff relationships, school-community relations, administrative role and organizational problems, racial and drug issues, and problems of change.[4] While most of the problems focus on the principalship, certain cases are devoted to problems associated with other administrative and supervisory positions, such as the superintendent and the central office supervisor.

In most of the cases, the characters depicted are either creating problems through their own actions or are being confronted with problems resulting from the behavior of others. This stress on school problems merely reflects the orientation of the text; the reader should not draw the implication that administrators and others associated with the schools are *always* creating or facing problems. Nor should the reader assume that the individuals described in the cases are typical of all administrators, supervisors, teachers, parents, or students. Although it should be obvious, it perhaps needs to be pointed out that not all teachers cause problems, not all students are troublesome, and not all administrators behave the way the administrators act in these cases. However, it is the *problem* dimension of human behavior in school administration, rather than the routine duties, that should be studied, and it is this aspect toward which preparation and inservice training programs need to direct most of their attention if prospective and experienced administrators and supervisors are to be equipped with the skills required for the 90's and beyond.

An examination of the cases will reveal that most of them are limited as to contextual information, e.g., nature of community and school district; and other details that the reader might desire for the resolution of a problem may be missing. This approach of limiting the available information has been taken for two reasons: 1) It allows for a much larger number of cases to be presented in the text, and 2) It provides the instructor or group leader with an excellent opportunity to tailor a case to specific local circumstances by supplementing the case with pertinent details, e.g., urban vs. suburban setting, elementary student body vs. secondary, etc.

It should also be noted that the cases in the text are open-ended. While the attempted resolution of subsidiary problems is sometimes described, the administrator in each case is generally left with the need to resolve a major conflict or dilemma. It is recognized that some individuals have mixed feelings about this type of a case study, and there is little doubt that an unresolved problem or conflict will demand more thought and effort from the student and the instructor. But the construction of the cases was based on the premise that the student would derive greater benefit from cases that require a resolution to the problems identified than from cases presenting a ready-made solution.

The case study approach may be unfamiliar to the reader; therefore, a sample case is included at this point, followed by a discussion of the role of the student regarding each of the suggested learning activities and the problems that may be experienced with respect to this kind of learning.

Sample Case Study:
WHO DECIDES THE NATURE OF INSTRUCTION?

Bill Taylor had been teaching in his present school district for almost two months, and he was very pleased with his new situation. Last spring, when he had been interviewed by the principal, Bill had been deliberately vague in responding to questions about his philosophy of teaching for fear that he might not be hired for the position, which carried quite an advancement in salary. He had previously taught for four years in a smaller school district where the community was very conservative and no teachers were permitted to teach anything that might be considered controversial. Apparently, though, Bill had nothing to worry about here. He had not experienced any difficulty thus far, and his colleagues seemed to be fairly liberal.

His approach to teaching was to stimulate discussion and debate on the issues and problems of society, both past and present, and he frequently played the role of "devil's advocate" in order to bring out different points of view. He felt that, in general, the social studies text at his students' grade level took a rather uncritical view of history and contemporary affairs, and that it tended to whitewash many of America's problems and past blunders. For example, the text contained none of the revisionist historians' ideas about American history. The book also failed to treat in any depth the current problems facing American society or any of the solutions which had been proposed by so-called "radical" groups.

Bill believed that an examination of current problems provided good motivation for students in a study of the relevance of history, and that every point of view—no matter how extreme—should be presented to students. Thus far, he had limited himself to the material in the text, but on Wednesday he planned to introduce a unit on conflict that would focus on some of the controversies surrounding the country's foreign policy, problems of the poor, and civil rights. He was determined to challenge his students' values and, if possible, to develop a more critical attitude on their part toward the hypocrisy in America. He realized that this might mean taking some rather radical positions on the problems and issues of the day, but he believed that the role of the teacher should be to influence his students' thoughts and values. He saw no great advantage in remaining neutral, considering the state of affairs in society, and he questioned whether it was possible for any teacher to remain completely objective in teaching.

On Wednesday the teacher's classroom was visited by the principal as a part of the routine visitation program for new staff. During the class period the principal became very concerned about what he believed were significant departures from the regular district curriculum in social studies. The principal felt that there was too much emphasis on current affairs and on what was wrong with America. He was also bothered by Bill Taylor's style of teaching, which seemed deliberately designed to challenge the students' beliefs and to make them question their values. The principal realized that the teacher was probably trying to stimulate student thought and discussion, but there seemed to be too much challenging going on and not enough time spent teaching social studies.

At the end of the class period, the principal considered expressing his concerns to the teacher but decided that it was not the proper time or place to discuss the matter. Teachers were touchy these days about anyone trying to question what they were teaching, and the faculty in this school had always hung together when any of its members were criticized. He decided that he would need to give more careful consideration to how he should approach Bill.

Although the principal had the teacher on his mind for several days, other problems arose which demanded more immediate attention. The next week, however, the principal received an angry complaint from Mr. Riley, the commander of a local veterans' organization, who demanded an investigation into the matter of what Bill Taylor was teaching his students. Mr. Riley's daughter had reported that the teacher was very critical of the government and had cast scorn on the expression of patriotism.

The principal told Mr. Riley that the matter would be investigated, but the parent did not appear to be satisfied with that promise. "I'll call you again on Friday to see what steps you've taken to correct this deplorable situation," he said. Then he added, "You should be aware that there are others in the community who are also concerned about this situation and who will not sit back and allow our children's attitudes toward our country to be poisoned by malcontents teaching in our schools!" And Mr. Riley hung up.

SUGGESTED LEARNING ACTIVITIES

Analyze the Case

1. What should the principal have done to discover the teacher's philosophy and methods of teaching before hiring him?
2. What is your evaluation of the strengths and weaknesses of the teacher's point of view and approach to teaching?
3. What factors may be affecting the principal's judgments about the acceptability of the teacher's approach?
4. What steps should the principal take to investigate community reaction and attitudes in regard to Mr. Bill Taylor?

Discuss the Larger Issues

1. To what extent should a teacher's philosophy and approach to teaching play a determining role in deciding whether or not he/she is hired for a position in a district?
2. What proportion of the school's curriculum should be devoted to the study of controversial issues, problems, and points of view?
3. What should be the role of the teacher in presenting controversial issues, problems, and points of view?
4. To what extent should community opposition determine the school's evaluation of the merits of a teacher's approach to teaching?

Be a Problem Solver

Assume that you are the principal in this case and you have been contacted by the commander of the local veterans' organization who is disturbed about the approach to social studies used by a teacher in your school. The caller has implied that if nothing is done to correct the situation, there will be trouble. How will you handle the problem? What assumptions are you making? Utilize administrative and social science concepts from Part 1 of the text in the planning and implementation of your approach to dealing with the problem described in the case study.

Test Your Solution

In order to test your proposed plan of action for dealing with the problem presented at the end of this case, you and the class should create and role-play one or more of the following interactions:

1. A meeting between the principal and the teacher.
2. A telephone call to the principal from a parent who is very pleased with the new teacher.
3. A second telephone call from Mr. Riley to the principal.

Investigate Further

1. What interview procedures and application forms are utilized by your district to ascertain the degree of effectiveness of a prospective teacher's teaching philosophy and approach?
2. What is your district's policy on teaching controversial issues?
3. How do the curriculum guides in your district treat subject content? Are the guides suggestive or prescriptive?

UTILIZING THE SUGGESTED LEARNING ACTIVITIES

"Analyze the Case"

In reading through a case study, the reader should attempt to utilize relevant concepts from Part 1 of the text rather than merely react to the events described.

The initial questions for the reader who is analyzing a case should be: 1) What seem(s) to be the main problem(s)? and 2) What conceptual tools from Part 1 of the text would be most helpful in addressing the situation? In almost all the case studies, better use of decision-making and communication concepts would have been helpful in preventing a problem's occurrence or in resolving a problem that has developed. Better understanding and use of concepts of authority, power, influence, and conflict management would be helpful in many case studies. And, of course, an in-depth analysis of a number of the case studies would call for use of concepts relating to organizational culture and introducing change.

Each case in this book describes a problem situation in educational administration or supervision. As the student reads a case, it will be important to examine carefully the sequence of events, the attitudes of the participants, and their reactions to the various circumstances. Also, note that certain intermediate decisions or actions by the administrator often determine the direction or ultimate severity, of a problem.

For example, the principal in the sample case apparently failed to elicit information about the teacher's philosophy and methods until after the teacher had been hired. Many readers find it easy to criticize the administrator's failure in this regard. However, it is incumbent upon the readers to demonstrate how *they* would have obtained a candid response from an applicant who was deliberately trying to avoid revealing his true attitudes.

An important consideration in analyzing any case is the student's perception of the problem nature of the case. As Halpin has observed, administrators' perception of the problem determines their behavior.[5] If, for example, the reader decides in regard to the sample case that the teacher's philosophy and style of teaching are acceptable, then the problem will lie in coping with the complaint from within the community. On the other hand, if the teacher's philosophy and style are perceived by the reader as undesirable, then the problem will center upon changing them.

Questions presented at the end of each case are designed to initiate the student's analysis of problem aspects of the case. These questions are illustrative of the kinds of analyses that should be undertaken and are meant to stimulate other questions, as well, by members of the group or their leader. As a result of careful analysis and discussion, the student of administration should develop a better appreciation for the complexity of administration and should gain ideas about handling similar situations.

"Discuss the Larger Issues"

The cases which have been selected for this text are intended to help the prospective administrator become more sensitive to the vital issues of education in the 90's and beyond. There is already considerable evidence that school administration in this decade will be affected significantly by issues of professional empowerment, parental and community involvement, restructuring education, student diversity, and race and drug problems.[6] It is therefore imperative that the reader become more aware of these forces and issues.

Today's administrator must decide, for example, whether there is a need for parental choice in determining the school for their children; whether teachers should be given greater professional autonomy and less supervision; whether innovation is needed and, if so, what kind; and whether the school should play a role in promoting racial integration and drug control. The administrator must also determine the role that students, parents, and teachers should play in each of the problem areas described in Part 2 of the text. For instance, it is important to examine one's own attitudes and formulate a position on student misbehavior, teacher militancy, and parental censorship. These are not easy issues to resolve, and, in most cases, there will probably be considerable disagreement about how they should be handled. However, the difficult and controversial nature of the issues should serve only to emphasize to the student of administration the importance of working out and critically examining the merits of a position on each of these crucial areas.

One of the potentially valuable aspects of *group* discussion of the issues presented is the opportunity for each participant to hear contrasting points of view expressed. It is, therefore, extremely important for every individual to feel free to offer opinions that may contradict or conflict with those of the instructor or other members of the group. By hearing and analyzing various perceptions of a particular problem, the student will develop a greater awareness of the fact that different people perceive situations in different ways. Also, new ideas or information may be acquired that could cause a participant to modify a particular point of view.

Sometimes participants in a group discussion hesitate to express their opinion for fear that it will be challenged by other members of the group or by the group leader. This is an understandable, but unfortunate attitude. The student of administration needs evaluative feedback from the rest of the group in order to enhance the process of gaining problem-solving and decision-making skills. This feedback will not be available unless each member of the group assumes a personal responsibility for evaluating and reacting to the comments, ideas, or recommendations offered for discussion.

"Be a Problem Solver"

The central task of administration is problem solving. Analyzing the different aspects of a case and discussing some of its overriding issues are important preliminary activities. However, the crucial test for students of administration is whether they can effectively come to grips with the main problem that is left unresolved at the end of each case. The basic question posed for the reader is: "If you were the administrator in these circumstances and were faced with the problem described at the end of the case, what would you *do*?"

To answer this question, the student will need to utilize the concepts described in Chapters 1 through 7 and will, of course, need to analyze the particular circumstances presented in the case itself. However, in addition to these activities, students should attempt to:

1. Define the nature of the problem.
2. Evaluate the seriousness of the problem.
3. Determine the extent to which some kind of action is immediately required.
4. Identify and assess the various alternative courses of action.
5. Decide on a particular course of action.
6. Develop a plan to implement the decision.

Pretesting of case materials and the related learning activities revealed that some students have difficulty with steps 5 and 6. These students generally spend a considerable amount of time on steps 1, 2, 3, and 4, but seem reluctant to commit themselves to a course of action for dealing with the problem and tend to gloss over the need to develop any *plan* to implement their decision, once it is made. Problem solving, however, usually requires administrative *action* in addition to analysis and discussion. Therefore, the student who engages in the learning activity entitled, "Be a Problem Solver," must indicate what should be *done* about the problem, as opposed to merely discussing the nature of the problem and the various available alternatives.

"Test Your Solution"

In the real world of the school administrator, the action taken in solving a problem usually triggers a response: the solution is either rejected, accepted partially, or completely accepted. As a result, the original problem may be exacerbated, unchanged, greatly ameliorated, or completely resolved. In any event, in actual practice, the administrator *does* discover the effectiveness of a proposed solution.

In completing the learning activity called, "Be a Problem Solver," many students of administration appear to think that they have successfully resolved the problem in a case if a solution can be developed that seems reasonable and meets with the approval of the other members of the group. However, in the process of developing a possible solution, the student often makes certain assumptions about people, events or plans. Therefore, in actuality, the key to the success of any proposed solution to a problem usually lies in the tenability of those assumptions (which are almost always necessary and may prove dangerous only if the student is unaware that they underlie a proposed solution) as well as the general merits of the proposed solution. It is for this reason that the student is asked to simulate some of the situations which *could* occur during the attempted resolution of a particular problem.

Therefore, the learning activities recommended under "Test Your Solution" encourage the student and the other members of the group to create and role-play one or more of several situations that could arise during the process of implementing a proposed solution to a problem.[7] The situations presented at the end of each case are only briefly described, and there is generally little indication of the specific direction which the participants or the events might take.

One suggestion which is made in regard to the sample case study directs the reader and the other members of the group to create and to role-play a meeting between the principal and the teacher. No explanation is provided to tell why this meeting should be initiated or what might be the attitude of the principal or the teacher during the meeting. These matters are left for the group to specify. The setting, purpose of the meeting, and the attitudes and objectives of the participants can, therefore, be varied in a number of ways to test a particular solution against possible contingencies.

In other circumstances, clues are presented suggesting the type of situation that ought to be created by the class in order to test the solution(s). For example, the two other activities described under "Test Your Solution," following the sample case, suggest that the class create and role-play a telephone call to the principal from a parent, who is pleased with the new teacher, and a follow-up telephone call to the principal from the commander of the veterans' organization, who objects strenuously to the teacher's approach. In both instances the group is provided with a general idea about the type of situation that needs to be created. However, the role-players involved may still need to be briefed by the group leader on the actions or reactions they should express.

It is worth noting that the utilization of videotape equipment in conjunction with the role-playing activities can be extremely helpful.[8] Viewing a videotape of the interactions that transpire during a simulation session will enable the members of the class to identify strengths, analyze the mistakes which are made, and focus on areas for improvement.

Without a doubt, the effectiveness of simulation and role-playing activities depends on the students' commitment to self-improvement. First, each member of the group must be interested in testing a proposed solution. If participants are hesitant or fearful of testing their ideas, it is unlikely that simulation and role-playing situations will be successful. It is essential that all students be open and receptive to testing their ideas if there is to be professional growth.

Secondly, each member of the group must be willing to become actively involved in playing the role of the individuals identified in the recommended activities. In certain situations these roles may be assigned, while in other circumstances the members of the group will need to volunteer to play a particular role. In either instance, it is vitally important that each member of the group internalize the role being assumed. This requires an awareness and recognition of all the limitations and potential that characterize the situation. It literally requires that the student consciously try to *become* the administrator in that situation.

It is equally important that the individuals playing roles other than that of the administrator internalize the appropriate characteristics and attitudes. Playing the role of a parent or newspaper reporter will seem unfamiliar or difficult to some students. It will require careful consideration of how a person in that role would behave toward or feel about another individual or a particular issue. The role-player will need to take on the attributes or personal characteristics which are suggested. This is no easy task, but the success of simulation and role-playing activities depends heavily on the credibility of the roles played.

Classroom experience with simulation has shown that as students gain familiarity with role playing, they begin to enjoy and look forward to the mental stimulation and learning opportunities that it provides.

"Investigate Further"

Most of the learning activities have been designed to involve the reader or members of the group in the case itself. However, associated with each case are issues and problems that may carry implications for education and administration in the school district where the reader is currently employed. Therefore, as follow-up activities (or as preparation for discussing a particular case), several questions are presented for students to investigate with reference to their local district. These questions frequently focus on the areas of school board policy, state law, administrative procedures, or the opinion of various individuals or reference groups within the district or at the building level.

For example, after the sample case under the heading, "Investigate Further," the reader is asked about the district's policy on teaching controversial issues. Experience shows that students are frequently uninformed about their own district's policies on this and other matters. An important learning exercise for the student, then, is to investigate the local school situation in regard to the issues and problems presented in the cases.

Case Studies: ANTICIPATED PROBLEMS

The student should recognize by now that the case study approach requires a great deal of hard work and effort, and that it may at times prove to be frustrating. The purpose of the remainder of this section is to present possible problems that students may experience in responding to a case and to offer suggestions for ameliorating these problems or, at least, placing them in proper perspective. It should be emphasized that it is not inevitable that a student will experience any of these problems. However, in the senior author's 22 years of utilizing the case study method, the following student problems have periodically occurred.

"There Isn't Enough Information." After perusing a case, the student may complain that insufficient information has been provided about the situation or problem.

Since no case can ever provide more than a partial representation of reality, a certain amount of ambiguity is inevitable and frequently is intentional. Each case has been constructed loosely enough to be adapted to different learning environments.

Because "real life" problems are seldom clearly defined or neatly packaged, the student of administration should recognize that in an actual crisis or conflict, rarely will there be readily available all the facts and information that could possibly shed light on a matter and facilitate decisionmaking. In the class situation, however, the individual who is bothered by a case that, seems to provide insufficient information or facts for analysis and resolution can choose either to work with the facts provided or to request the instructor to "complete" the case by introducing additional facts and information as new variables.

For example, the sample case does not provide a description of the school system or community, nor does it specify the grade level at which the teacher is employed. These factors may or may not play a role in the nature of the administrator's response to the problem described in the case. However if the group feels that these facts are especially important, the class can experiment with filling in different descriptions of the school district, type of community, and grade level, to see whether and how these variables would make a difference.

"This Couldn't Ever Happen to Me." More experienced students sometimes take the position that a problem, issue, or conflict described in a case would never have arisen in their school or school system because things are done differently there. For example, the teacher in the sample case was deliberately vague in responding to questions about his philosophy of education, and apparently the principal who interviewed him had not discerned the teacher's true attitude toward teaching. In dealing with this case, certain students might contend that the situation couldn't have happened in their district or that, if *they* had been interviewing the teacher, he would not have been hired in the first place.

It is entirely possible that the particular circumstances presented in the cases would be unlikely to take place in some schools or districts. It is easier, of course, to reach this conclusion when one is evaluating a situation that has already taken place, has resulted from someone else's error. However, almost all administrators make errors in judgment at some time which in retrospect may seem very obvious. Nevertheless, they are faced with the unhappy consequences of that judgment and must proceed to deal with the problem at hand. Perceptive administrators also recognize that problems occasionally develop as a result of action that at the time seemed rather innocuous. Since it is unlikely that students of administration will improve their problem-solving skills by saying, "This couldn't ever happen to me," it is incumbent upon these students, to assume that such a situation could, indeed, have occurred, and to proceed to address themselves to the task of solving the resultant problem described in the case.

"I'm Not Sure That I Like This Type of Learning." Case analysis and subsequent role-playing activities place weighty and frequently unfamiliar responsibilities on the shoulders of the learner. Many students are accustomed to attending classes or meetings and doing little more than

listening or taking notes on someone else's ideas. Since they are not often required to participate actively in the process of learning, students may initially react with ambivalence or apprehension to requests for their active participation. Consequently, they may withdraw and fail to take part in group discussion or to volunteer for the role-playing activities because they would prefer that the instructor or group leader assume the primary responsibility for what transpires.

In order for students to progress in the development of their problem-solving skills, it is essential for them to become actively involved in those activities which engage them in the process of problem solving. Student participation in case analysis, group discussion, and role-playing is fundamental to the improvement of problem-solving skills.

"I Am Reluctant to Question or Challenge Others." Group discussion of a case requires relatively free interaction among all members of the group. Unfortunately, a few barriers must be surmounted before this goal can be achieved.

Occasionally a group may encounter an initial barrier represented by a dominating instructor or group leader who restricts group discussions to the degree that most of the interaction is between the instructor and one or two students. However, in situations where the case study approach is utilized, the main obstacle is more typically the reluctance of the participants in the group to challenge each other's points of view. For example, when one member of a group presents an idea, the other members may react in only a limited way, or not at all. This occurs either because they are concentrating on what *they* are going to say next to the group leader or because they are reluctant to react to the comments expressed previously.

The lack of response from the other members of the discussion group to an individual's contribution is obviously a major barrier to the group's reaching the best possible solution to the problem or conflict under consideration. It is only through interaction among the members of the group that such a goal can be accomplished. Students who simply sit quietly without reacting are not contributing to their own growth or to that of the group as a whole. Therefore, each student needs to respond to the other members of the group by raising questions or reacting to ideas or proposals that have been expressed. A free exchange of ideas and thoughts among all members of a group is required in order for each individual and the total group to progress and to determine the best solution to a problem.

"What Did He Say?" Too frequently the participants in a discussion pay insufficient attention to what others have said and then inadvertently repeat or ignore preceding comments or observations. Sometimes they aren't listening to the speaker at all because they are concentrating on what they are going to say next or they are thinking about something else.

Paying attention, naturally, involves listening carefully to what the speaker has to say. Furthermore, it requires *thinking* about what has been said. It is entirely possible for a person to *hear* what has been said without the message registering. Parents accuse their children of letting conversation "go in one ear and out the other," but often adults may be inattentive.

The person who is really paying attention must not only listen to what the speaker is saying but must also evaluate the content and implications of the comments. Such a process involves mentally asking, "What is the speaker really saying? Is it true? What assumptions have been made? Does the speaker have all the facts? Does it make sense? What implications should be considered if what was said is true?"

"What About This Solution?" Students will occasionally attempt to ignore or distort the nature of the information presented in the case or will fabricate additional "facts" that will allow the problem to be resolved more easily. For instance, an individual may try to resolve the problem described in the sample case by ignoring the statement that "the faculty in this school had always hung together when any of its members

were criticized." Obviously, any realistic solution to the problem must take into consideration this important fact about the teachers in the school.

In order to provide another easy solution to the problem in the case, some students may fabricate the "fact" that the school board has a policy specifically prohibiting the teacher's actions, and then these students may suggest that the principal merely order the teacher to adhere to school board policy. Of course, the case itself does not indicate that the school board has any policy whatever on this matter. But even if such a policy were in existence, it is doubtful whether the problem could be that easily resolved, given the characteristics of the teacher described in the case.

Most thoughtful administrators recognize that problem solving is seldom an easy task. Therefore, the person who wants to gain experience and further develop skill in dealing with problems will avoid the easy way out and will concentrate on working with the realities presented in the case.

"There Doesn't Seem to Be Any Solution to This One!" Individuals and groups whose experience with the case study approach and with problem solving in general is rather limited may initially feel, after reading a case, that the problem described is irresolvable. It is true that most of the cases in this book represent difficult and complex problems which call for skills and attitudes that are not immediately or easily acquired. At the same time, however, it should be stated that many of the problems described are no more involved or frustrating than those which today's school administrators face on a regular basis.

Although easier problems could have been selected, it is questionable whether the student of administration would profit greatly from being "spoon-fed" more simplistic problems or situations. It should also be recognized that few problems in real life have a single, easy, or perfect solution. Fortunately, most issues or problems can be eventually resolved if the student is willing to exert sufficient initiative, imagination, perseverance and hard thinking.

THE NATURE OF IN-BASKET EXERCISES AND PRIORITY SETTING

Each of the case studies, as discussed previously, provides an opportunity for the reader to focus on a particular situation. Usually only one problem is initially apparent, although complications may be discerned by further analysis.

The in-basket exercises, on the other hand, provide a different kind of learning opportunity where the reader can analyze problem situations in school administration and supervision, applying the concepts presented in Chapters 1–7. Rather than facing only one task to accomplish or one problem to address, as in the case studies, the in-basket exercises present a large number of representative problems and situations.[9] Although the typical administrator or supervisor may not *often* be confronted with a large number of problems within a short time frame, such circumstances do arise in actuality, so prospective administrators and supervisors need to gain experience in responding effectively to myriad problems of varying complexity in a time-critical setting.

The scope of the problems presented and the limited time frame within which to address them stress the importance of setting priorities. Few administrators have the luxury of dealing with a single problem at a time or taking as much time as they would like in order to resolve a situation. Problems and assigned tasks frequently arrive in bunches, and an administrator must decide what should be addressed first, second, and so forth. Therefore, it is essential for a prospective administrator to develop skills in establishing priorities.

At this point the reader may be asking, "But *how* do I establish priorities?" While there is probably no best way to establish priorities that will be effective for every situation, the following guidelines extracted from a review of the literature and interviews with successful administrators

Figure 8.1 Priority Designation.

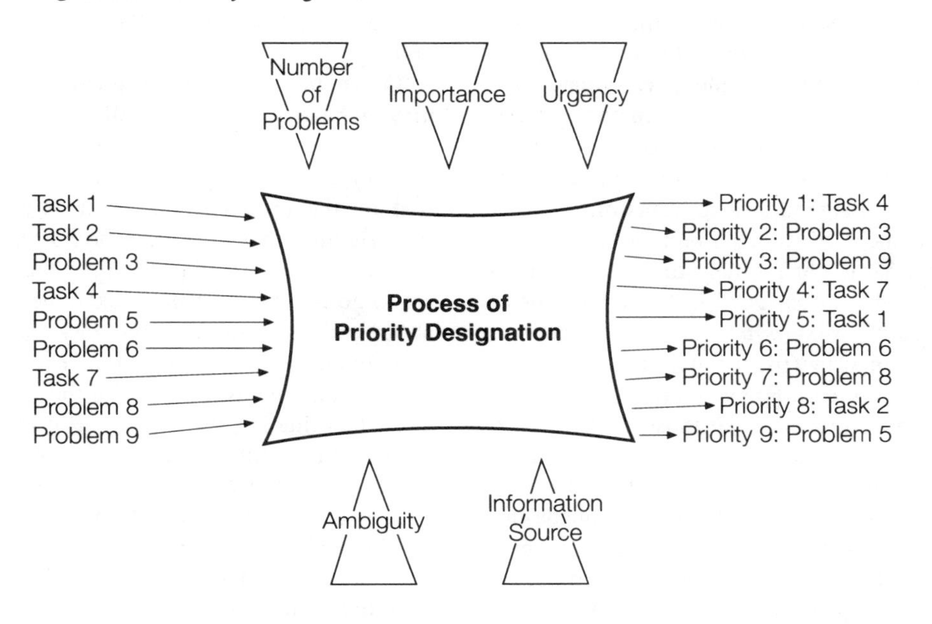

have been designed to help the readers of this text to improve their priority-setting skills.[10]

GUIDELINES FOR PRIORITY SETTING

For effective priority setting, the reader needs to examine a number of factors that may influence the level of a priority that should be assigned to any particular problem or task (within a larger set of problems or tasks to be addressed or accomplished). Those factors are identified in Figure 8.1.

As Figure 8.1 shows, effective priority setting involves the consideration of a variety of factors in determining the level of priority for each problem or task in a group of problems and tasks confronting the administrator. Since the various factors identified in Figure 8.1 are not self-explanatory, the following section will be devoted to a discussion of their application.

The first factor the reader needs to consider in priority setting within a group of problems and tasks is the *number* of problems and tasks for which priorities must be established. In other words, how many problems and/or assigned tasks require an administrative response? If an administrator faces only two of three problems or assigned tasks for which priorities must be established, then priority setting may not be as important, and the administrator may be able to take more time in the process than if there are many problems and tasks that must be addressed.

In general, a fairly useful guideline is, "The more problems and/or assigned tasks that call for an administrative response, the more *decisive* the administrator needs to be in evaluating the other factors identified in Figure 8.1 and in deciding the priority of each problem and assigned task." Effective participation in the in-basket exercises presented in this book will require the reader's *decisiveness* because of the large number of problems and assigned tasks represented.

However, taking into consideration the number of problems and assigned tasks that need to be prioritized is not the only factor that must be considered in effective priority setting. The reader also needs to consider the *importance* of each problem or assigned task. But the reader may wonder, "How does one *determine* importance?" Although some people may equate *importance* with *urgency*—another factor to be discussed—the authors offer a different perspective on *importance.* We evaluate the importance of a problem or assigned task in terms of the possible consequences of an incorrect or ineffective decision on a particular problem or assigned task.

Those problems or assigned tasks that are most likely to result in *significant negative* consequences if an incorrect decision is made regarding their solution or implementation should be assigned a higher priority than those problems or tasks that are most likely to result in few, if any, negative consequences for the administrator (in the event that an incorrect decision is made in trying to address them). The more serious the potential consequences of an incorrect administrative action on a problem or assigned task, the higher the priority that should be given to that problem or task. Giving a problem or task a higher priority generally means that it will receive *more attention sooner* than a lower priority problem or task. Obviously, those problems or tasks with the greatest potentially negative consequences in the aftermath of an incorrect decision demand more immediate and more extensive attention than other kinds of problems and tasks which carry fewer potentially damaging consequences.

The *urgency* of each problem and assigned task is, perhaps, the factor with which most readers are more familiar in priority setting. The urgency of a problem or assigned task is defined in this discussion as its explicit or implicit deadline for being addressed.

Many assigned tasks or problems are presented with a specific deadline. For example, the superintendent may request a particular report from all principals by a certain date. Or, a parent's letter about a certain problem that a son is experiencing with a teacher may request a response from the principal by a particular date. Or, a telephone message from a newspaper reporter may request that the principal respond to the call within the hour.

Other problems or assigned tasks, however, may not carry explicit deadlines, but a deadline may be *implicit* in the message to the administrator. For example, a teacher may request some action by the principal "as soon as possible." Or the principal may receive a bomb threat message which does not mention the time that the bomb is set to go off. Each of these examples of messages about problems or assigned tasks communicates an explicit or implicit deadline. The more explicit the deadline, the easier will be the administrator's task of evaluating its urgency. But in some cases, such as the bomb threat, the *nature* of the problem will influence the evaluation of its urgency, even if the deadline for action is unstated.

The difficulty that many administrators experience with considering the urgency of a problem or assigned task is that they fail to recognize that the deadline communicated represents someone *else's* expectation. Whether that expectation should be met will depend on the *administrator's* consideration of other factors associated with the task or problem such as its importance or ambiguity.

For instance, suppose the administrator receives a message at 8:55 A.M. that requests a return telephone call to a tennis partner by 9 A.M. The message seems urgent, given the deadline for returning the call. However, the administrator may know that it is not an *important* deadline, based on the personality of the tennis partner and the history of their association. Suppose, further, that the administrator has been given other messages with later or less explicit deadlines but which are potentially more important, such as a bomb threat. The point is that the urgency of a message needs to be compared with the pressing needs of other messages that need to be addressed, and that urgency should not be the *sole* factor to be considered in determining the priority of a particular problem or assigned task.

The *ambiguity* of a problem or task is another factor which a prospective administrator should learn to consider in establishing priorities. Two types of ambiguity may characterize a problem: first, the content of a message, and second, the nature of a problem or task to be addressed.

Some messages' content will be more ambiguous than others. The individual communicating the message may deliberately have chosen to be cryptic in the expression of a problem, or the communication may be unintentionally vague or lacking in detail needed to evaluate its priority. On the other hand, even if the description of a problem or assigned task is clear, the characteristics of the problem or assigned task may be highly complex, making it difficult for an administrator to determine how best to proceed.

As an example, the superintendent may want each principal to prepare a report on how the school could raise its student test scores by 10 percent. The message seems clear enough, and if the superintendent stated that she wanted the report in a month, then the urgency of the matter could also be evaluated. Certainly the fact that the request is coming from the superintendent suggests the *importance* of addressing the request successfully. But a major question that remains is, "What would be involved in the preparation of such a report that would meet the superintendent's expectation and goal?" In this case, the nature and scope of the superintendent's requests is ambiguous because the extent and time commitment of the activity is not readily discernible.

Administrators frequently must deal with problems and tasks that differ in their ambiguity. In general, the more ambiguous a problem or assigned task, the higher the priority that should be assigned. However, as with any other factor, ambiguity should never be the only consideration. All of the factors in Figure 8.1 should be evaluated for every problem and assigned task before determining each one's priority. Obviously, the judgment that will be reached during this process will weigh certain factors more heavily than others. However, the reader should avoid any tendency to focus on only one, or even two factors, while ignoring the others.

The last factor shown in Figure 8.1 on the lower right is one rarely, if ever, mentioned in the professional literature. Nevertheless, in priority setting it is important to ascertain the potential information value of the person communicating a message about a certain problem or task in terms of that individual as an *information source*. It is possible that a certain messenger is knowledgeable about only one particular problem or task; on the other hand, if the message sender is also likely to be knowledgeable about some other problem facing the administrator, or about some of the individuals involved in other problem situations, then the problem or task that this messenger has presented should be given a higher priority than would otherwise be true. By giving that problem a higher priority, it is likely that the administrator will be contacting this particular message sender earlier and, by so doing, will not only be resolving that problem but may also obtain some potentially valuable information about some other significant problems or individuals.

Key information sources in the school are likely to be such people as assistant principals, secretaries, department chairs, and custodians, as well as informal leaders (see Chapter 6). Therefore, even when these information sources present problems which do not intrinsically warrant a high priority, the administrator may increase the priority ranking because of the messenger's potential for offering additional information that could contribute to a better understanding of *other* problems.

Although it may seem to the reader that setting priorities is a very complex and time consuming process, additional experience with the process will increase proficiency and reveal shortcuts. Learning the skill of priority setting is hardly different than learning any other skill, such as learning how to drive. Given an effective procedure for developing the skill, all that remains are practice and experience, and before long, the application of the skill becomes

Table 8.1 Priority Worksheet

High Priority Items	Moderate Priority Items	Low Priority Items
1	5	2
3	7	6
4	8	10
9	11	13
18	12	15
14	16	20
	17	
	19	

automatic, and the time required is reduced significantly. One of the purposes of the in-basket exercises in this book is to give prospective administrators an opportunity to practice and gain experience with setting priorities.

As readers prioritize the various problems and tasks that are included in an in-basket exercise, they are advised to assign one of three levels of priority: high, moderate, or low. A sample worksheet has been designed to facilitate the assignment of priorities. The form, as shown in Table 8.1, has already been completed, based on a hypothetical set of problems and tasks in order to provide the reader with a better idea of how the form is to be used.

In examining an in-basket exercise, the reader will note that each of the items has been numbered to make it easier in a class situation to direct attention to a particular problem. The assigned numbers also facilitate the use of a priority worksheet, obviating any need to write out a description or title for each in-basket item.

It should also be emphasized that the number of items which should be assigned high, moderate, or low priority in any given in-basket exercise will depend on many factors, including the time of year and the kind of school being administered. The profile in Table 8.1 is, therefore, only a hypothetical one and it is not intended to be illustrative of any typical set of circumstances.

IN-BASKET PROBLEM SOLVING

The in-basket exercises provide a different kind of an opportunity for the reader to analyze problem situations in school administration and supervision, and to apply the concepts presented in Chapters 1–7. The problems presented in these exercises differ from the case studies not so much in their nature or severity as in the amount of information provided. The paucity of information available in the messages underscores the importance of the first step in decision making, namely, attempting to define more precisely the nature of the problem or situation. (It should be emphasized that the reader will also need to utilize other relevant concepts presented in Chapters 1–7 in solving the problems described in the in-basket material, but the nature of the in-basket items makes *essential* the reader's attention to problem definition, the all important first step in any decision making.)

The crucial questions that the reader needs to be asking while first addressing an in-basket problem are, "What do I know and what *don't* I know about this situation?" and "How, or from whom, could I obtain more information in order to define more accurately the nature of this problem?"

Figure 8.2 illustrates the process involved in defining more precisely the nature of a problem and shows how this process leads to the next step of problem solving: the generation of alternatives.

To help the reader gain a better understanding of *how* the process in Figure 8.2 can be applied

Figure 8.2 Problem Definition Process.

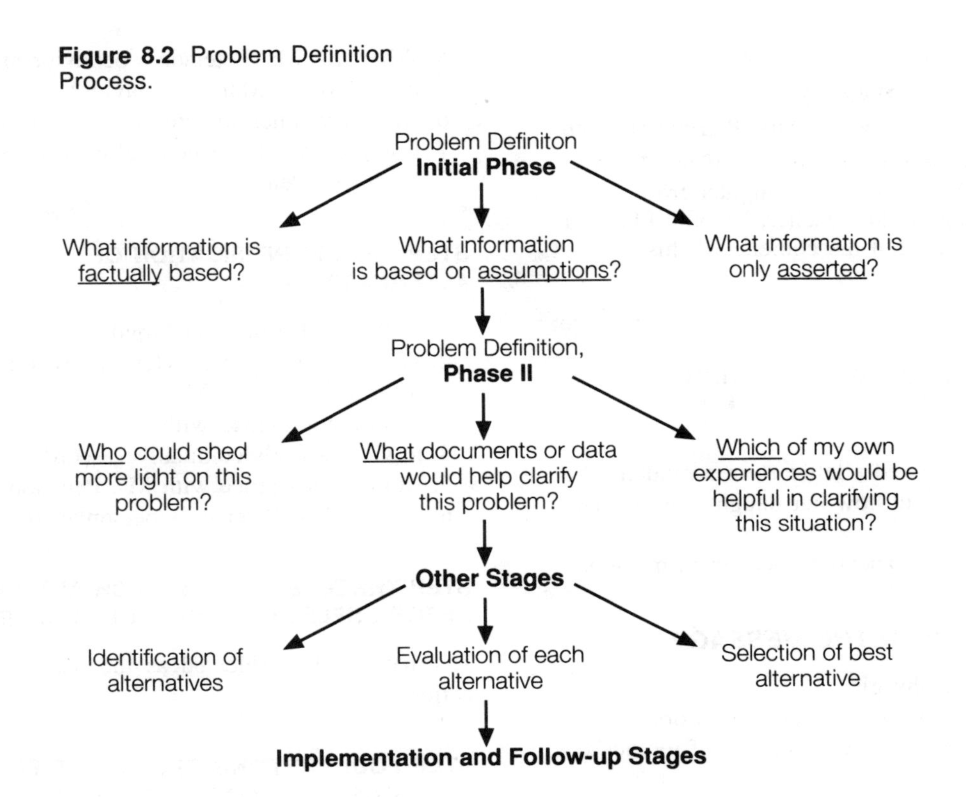

to a set of circumstances, a sample in-basket item is presented below, followed by a step-by-step application of the concept of problem definition and other concepts that would be relevant to resolving this particular problem.

Sample In-Basket Item #1

Dear Dr. Brown:

I am instructing my daughter, Mary, not to report to the girls' physical education classes anymore, until some changes are made.

Mary, as you know (or maybe you don't know), is a shy girl. She doesn't like taking off her clothes in front of other people, and I can't say that I blame her. However, Ms. Peterson, the physical education teacher, has forced my daughter to disrobe in front of the other girls as part of compulsory shower regulations. I have told Mary to inform the teacher that Mary will take her bath at home, and therefore does not need to take a shower at school, but the teacher has rejected this alternative.

I personally have some concerns about Ms. Peterson. My daughter has reported, and I have heard other stories, that Ms. Peterson watches the girls while they are undressing and that she actually *touches* the girls to make sure that they are wet and have taken a shower.

I don't know how you feel about these matters, but Mary is my responsibility, and I am not going to permit her to be exposed to this type of treatment. I have instructed her to report to the school library during gym period until some basic changes are made.

I expect to hear from you soon.

Sincerely,

(signed) Mrs. Patricia Herman

P.S. Due to the sensitive nature of this letter and my desire to save my daughter from recriminations by the teacher, I would like you to keep confidential the contents of this communication.

STEP ONE: PROBLEM DEFINITION

FACTS

1. I have received a letter from a mother who is upset about how her daughter is treated in P.E.
2. The mother expects to hear from me soon.

ASSERTIONS IN THE MESSAGE

1. Mary is a shy girl.
2. Teacher has forced Mary to disrobe.
3. Student has informed teacher of mother's feelings.
4. Teacher has rejected mother's alternative.
5. Teacher has touched students to see if they have taken showers, as alleged by mother.
6. Student is now going to library rather than P.E. class.

QUESTIONS

1. Has the mother actually instructed her daughter to avoid reporting to P.E., and, if so, is the daughter following those instructions?
2. What exactly did the daughter tell the mother?
3. What are the sources for the ''other stories'' the mother refers to?
4. What are the P.E. Department's regulations about taking showers? Are they consistent with school board policy?
5. What was Ms. Peterson's behavior in the locker room? Mary's behavior?
6. Are there other students involved in this?
7. Has this ever happened before with Mary? With Ms. Peterson?

STEP TWO: IDENTIFICATION OF ALTERNATIVES

1. Call Mrs. Herman on Monday.
2. Write a letter to Mrs. Herman, seeking more information.
3. Hold a conference with Mary.
4. Review Mary's cumulative record.
5. Hold a conference with Ms. Peterson.
6. Review Ms. Peterson's personnel file.

STEP THREE: EVALUATE EACH ALTERNATIVE BEFORE SELECTING MOST DESIRABLE ONE

Alternative #1 is selected as the main course of action.

STEP FOUR: SETTING OBJECTIVES FOR THE COURSE OF ACTION SELECTED

1. Get Mrs. Herman to view you as someone who will investigate thoroughly and do what is best for the student.
2. Obtain answers to the first three questions identified under ''Questions.''

STEP FIVE: DESCRIPTION OF PROPOSED IMPLEMENTATION

Call the mother and thank her for bringing this matter to your attention. Indicate that you will take appropriate action, but before you can act, you will need some additional information from her. Then ask the mother the questions identified above. Also, ask her if this has been a problem for Mary in the past and, if so, what approach was taken with the problem? Close the telephone conversation by again thanking her for bringing the problem to your attention and providing the additional information. Assure her that you will be continuing to investigate the matter so you can get back to her in the next day or so.

STEP SIX: IDENTIFICATION OF FOLLOW-UP STEPS

1. Review Mary's cumulative record.
2. Review Ms. Peterson's personnel file.
3. Contact physical education supervisor, if one is available.
4. Schedule conference with Mary and Ms. Peterson, separately.

As illustrated by Figure 8.2 and the hypothetical administrator's response to the mother's letter to Dr. Brown, essential steps in problem definition include identifying basic facts, differentiating between facts and assertions, and asking perceptive questions. Any administrator who does not competently define a problem is unlikely to be successful in ultimately resolving the problem.

To facilitate the reader's acquisition of the skill of problem definition, as well as the skill of applying other relevant concepts in Chapters 1–7, it is recommended that the reader write or type out an analysis of the first in-basket exercise, much like the hypothetical analysis presented on the previous page. After gaining experience and proficiency with analyzing the various concepts, then the reader can use a more abbreviated approach. An example of an abbreviated approach will be presented next, in response to a different, sample in-basket item.

Sample In-Basket Item #2

MEMO

TO: Dr. Brown

FROM: Alice Kelly, Supervisor

You were busy when I got ready to leave the school on Wednesday so I thought I would write you a memorandum.

I have been very concerned about the disciplinary methods of Mr. Hardnose (a member of your faculty). I have observed him using corporal punishment to discipline students and, as you know, the school board has a policy prohibiting its use.

Also, I think you should know that Mr. Hardnose may have a drinking problem. The class I last observed was right after lunch, and I thought I detected alcohol on his breath. I know that he is going through a divorce, but somehow he has to get hold of himself.

I haven't said anything about any of this to Mr. Hardnose because it didn't seem to be affecting his teaching, and I felt that you were in a better position to handle it. Obviously, something is going to have to be done.

Sample Analysis

The memo from Alice Kelly asserts problems about the teacher's behavior that, if true, are very serious. However, more information is needed. What kind of corporal punishment was observed? How frequently? How long has all of this been going on? How many students were involved? And what were the reactions of the students, those who were observing the alleged corporal punishment, as well as those who were punished? Also, why wasn't all of this reported to the assistant principal? Regarding the alleged drinking problem, how recently did this class meet when Alice Kelly "detected alcohol on the teacher's breath"? What does she mean, she "detected" it? Does she have any other evidence that the teacher has "a drinking problem"? Is the teacher actually going through a divorce? If so, does it have any relationship to the alleged drinking problem? What is the school board's policy on drinking, particularly during the noon hour, if the staff is off-campus? (Identification and assessment of alternatives and selection of best alternative have not been written out in this abbreviated approach.)

SAMPLE MAIN ACTION

I would write a memo to Alice Kelly.

MEMO

TO: Alice Kelly, Supervisor

FROM: Dr. Brown

Thank you for bringing to my attention your concerns about Mr. Hardnose. These are indeed serious matters. In order to take appropriate action, I will need some additional information about the nature of the corporal punishment, its frequency, etc., and the circumstances associated with your observation of Mr. Hardnose's class after lunch. Therefore, I would appreciate it if you would schedule an appointment with me, through my secretary, as soon as possible this week.

Again, I appreciate your note bringing this to my attention. I look forward to meeting with you.

SAMPLE FOLLOW-UP STEPS

1. Review personnel file of Mr. Hardnose.
2. Review school board's policy on corporal punishment and on drinking.
3. Schedule a classroom observation of Mr. Hardnose after lunch.
4. Eventually schedule a conference with Mr. Hardnose—if Alice Kelly's allegations are valid. (Confer with superior before meeting with Mr. Hardnose.)

Once the reader becomes proficient in applying the concepts in Chapters 1–7, it will not usually be necessary to *write* out the analysis and all of the other steps previously described. In fact, in a crisis situation (such as a student's threatening a teacher with a knife) the administrator obviously wouldn't be able to take time to write it up even though it might be desirable. However, in those circumstances that do not involve an immediate crisis, but which possess potentially long-range, serious consequences, the administrator should attempt to write out the analysis of the problem and a proposed plan of action, time permitting. Frequently the act of putting ideas on paper helps to clarify them and to assess considerations that may have initially only *appeared* to be sound in the conceptual process. (Further consideration of one's own written thoughts often may reveal gaps in logic, errors, or lead to additional insights.)

Although the overall discussion of ways to respond effectively to the in-basket exercises has been designed to be helpful to the readers, the authors recognize that, initially at least, the process and analysis of problem solving may be somewhat overwhelming and may even temporarily complicate matters. However, pilot testing of the guidelines on priority setting and the suggestions on problem solving has shown that after readers gain some practical experience in applying them, these recommendations prove to be very helpful. The key for the reader is to be persistent and patient in applying the process. As in developing most other skills, the initial stages may be difficult, but with continued practice, things get easier.

A FINAL NOTE

In the following chapters a large number of case studies, suggested learning activities, and in-basket exercise problems are presented. Although there are more materials and activities than any reader or group is likely to complete, the variety represented should provide a sufficient opportunity to gain experience in applying the concepts presented in Chapters 1 to 8 *and* to gain additional insight into the reality of school administration and supervision.

It should be noted that at the end of each concept chapter in Part I of this text, specific case studies and in-basket exercises are identified that can be used to best advantage for applying the ideas in that chapter. Table 8.2, on the following pages, shows how each of the case studies and in-basket exercises relate to other aspects of school administration and supervision.

Table 8.2 Analysis of the Cases, According to Level, Type of Position, and Area of Administration

	Level		Position				Area of Administration							
Case #	Elementary	Secondary	Principal	Asst. Prin.	Supt. or Asst. Supt.	Supervisor	Staff Pers.	Comm. Rel.	Pupil Pers.	Curriculum	School Org.	Inter-Org. Relations	Finance	Supervision
Beginning Challenges														
1	X	X	X	X	*	*	*					*		*
2	X	X	X	*	*		X	X	*					*
3	X	X	X	*	*		X	X	X	*	X	*	*	X
4	*	X	*	X	*		X	X	X	*	X	X	*	X
5	*	X	*	X	*		X		X		X			X
6	*	X	*	X	*		X		X					X
7	X	X	X	*			X	*	*					X
Student Problems														
8	X	X	X	*	*		*	X	X					X
9	X	X	*	X			X	*	X					X
10	X	X	X				*	X	X					
11	*	X	X	*			X	*	X					
12	X	X	*	X			X	*	X					X
13		X	X	*	X	X	X	X	X	*	*	*	*	X
14	*	X	X	*	*		X	*	X	*				X
15	X	X	X	X			X	*	X	*				
Administrator-Staff Relations														
16	X	X	X	*			X							X
17	X	X	X	*			X							X
18	X	X	X	*			X							X
19	X	X	X	*			X	X						X
20	X	X	X	*		*	X		*		X	*		X
21	X	X	X	*	X		X				X	X	*	X
22	X	X	X	*	*	*	X		*		*			X
23	X	X	X	*	X	*	X	X	*	*	X	*	X	X
School-Community Relations														
24	*	X	X	*	X		X	X	X	X				X
25	X	X	X	X				X						
26	X	X	X		*		*	X						
27	X	X	X		*		X	X	*	*			X	
28	X	X	X	*	X	*	X	X	*	*		X		
29	X	X	X	*	*		*	X	*	*		*		
30	X	X	X	X	*		X	X	X					X
31	*	X	X		X		X	X	X	X				X
32	X	X	X		X		*	X	*	*		X	X	

Table 8.2 —*Continued.*

Case #	Level		Position				Area of Administration							
	Elementary	Secondary	Principal	Asst. Prin.	Supt. or Asst. Supt.	Supervisor	Staff Pers.	Comm. Rel.	Pupil Pers.	Curriculum	School Org.	Inter-Org. Relations	Finance	Supervision
Role and Organizational Problems														
33	X	X	X	X	*	*	X	X	X	X	X	X		X
34	X	X	X	X	*	*	X	X	X	X	X	X		X
35	X	X	X			X	X		X	X	X			X
36	X	X	X		X			X				X		X
37	*	X	X	X	*						X			X
38	X	X	X			X	X				X	X		X
39				X		X			X			X		
40	X	X	X		X					X				X
Race & Drug Issues														
41	X	X	X	*	*		X	*	*	X	X			X
42	X	X	X		X		X	X	X	*		X		X
43	X	X	X	*	X		*	X	*	X		X		X
44	X	X	X	X	X		X	X	X	*		X	*	X
45	X	X	X		*		X	X	X	X				X
46	*	X	X	X	*		X	X	X	*				X
47	*	X	X	*	X		X	X	X	X				X
48	*	X	X	*	X		X	X	X			X		X
49	*	X	X				X	X	X	*	X			X
Problems of Change														
50	X	X	X	X		*	X	X	*	*	X			X
51	X	X	X	*	X	*	X	X	X	X	X		*	*
52	X	X	X	*	X	*	X	X	X	X	X	*	*	*
53	X	X	X	*	X	X	X		*		X	X		X
54	X	X	X	*	X	X	X			*	X			X
55	X	X	X				X			*				X
56	X	X	X				X			*				X
57	X	X	X	*	X		X	X	*	*		X		X
58	X	X	X		X		X	*	X	X				X

X Major Emphasis or Implications
* Indirect Emphasis or Implications

Notes

1. For additional sources of clinical materials and learning experiences, readers should contact the University Council for Educational Administration at Tempe, Arizona, and examine the following publications: Carl R. Asbaugh and Katherine L. Kasten, *Educational Leadership: Case Studies for Reflective Practice* (New York: Longman, 1991), and "Simulations and Games," an ERIC Bibliography, Ed 288–877.

2. The reader who is interested in considering further discussion of these topics should see Sandford F. Borins, "Simulation, The Case Method and Case Studies: Their Role in Public Management Teaching and Research," *Canadian Public Administration* (Summer, 1990), pp. 214–228; George Thornton and Jeannette N. Cleveland, "Developing Management Talent through Simulation," *American Psychologist* (February, 1990), pp. 51–58; Gwendoline Williams, "The Case Method: An Approach to Teaching and Learning in Educational Administration," an ERIC Report, Ed 270–136.

3. Thomas Ellis, "Training Principals: Research Roundup," an ERIC Report, Ed 301–855. Also see the following for a discussion of the limitations of the case study approach: Careth Smith, "The Use and Effectiveness of the Case Study Method in Management Education," *Management Education and Development* (Spring, 1987).

4. Periodic surveys, interviews, and observations of beginning and experienced administrators and supervisors by the senior author provide strong support for the kinds of cases presented in Part II of the text.

5. Andrew Halpin, "A Paradigm for Research on Administrative Behavior," *Administrative Behavior in Education,* ed. Roald F. Campbell and Russell T. Gregg (New York: Harper and Row Publishers, 1957), pp. 166–167.

6. See references at the end of each of the following chapters.

7. For further information on the value of role playing and suggestions for structuring it effectively, see Vicki Kenan and Cynthia Benison, "Roleplay Simulations for Employee Selection," *Public Personnel Management* (Spring, 1988), pp. 1–8.

8. Scott A. Amo and Teri G. Mills, "An Advanced Staff Development Program for Administrators," an ERIC Report, Ed 280–223.

9. For an early use of the in-basket approach in assessing school administrators' performance, see John K. Hemphill et al., *Administrative Performance and Personality* (New York: Columbia University, Bureau of Publication, 1962).

10. For additional discussion of the importance of and guidelines for setting priorities, see Phoebe Spinard, "The Inbasket: Real World Teaching for a Real World Task," *Journal of Business and Technical Communication* (January 1989), pp. 89–99.

9 Beginning Challenges

Beginning a new job can be a challenging experience. Whether you are a neophyte starting your first year as an administrator or an experienced administrator who has obtained a different position in another school or school district, there are certain adjustments to be made and problems to be faced that may be caused or complicated by your unfamiliarity with the new circumstances.

The case studies and related exercises presented in this chapter represent the kinds of problems and issues that can surface when you seek, and then assume, an administrative position in a new situation.

The first case presents some of the challenges involved in seeking and preparing for a first job interview in school administration. The next case describes some of the frustrations and considerations involved in obtaining an entry position in school administration, moving to a different city, planning for the beginning of a new school year, and starting to develop relationships with other people at the school. Following this case are two in-basket exercises, one involving a new principal, the other a new assistant principal. Both in-basket exercises place the reader in a new administrator's position at the beginning of the school year and include a large number of representative problems and issues that could confront any school administrator who takes a new position in different circumstances. (Chapter 13 presents two additional in-basket exercises, involving the same new principal, with mid-year problems and with end-of-the-year problems.)

After the in-basket exercises, the reader will find two case studies that focus on female administrators, including an assistant principal. For most individuals who obtain an entry position in school administration, that position will be an assistant principalship, especially if it is in a secondary school. In addition, in the last decade, the number of women entering the field of school administration has seen a significant increase. Therefore, a major emphasis on the assistant principalship and on female administrators seems appropriate in this chapter on *Beginning Challenges*. (However, it should be noted that the problems experienced in these two case studies could, for the most part, be faced by any beginning administrator.)

The final case study describes a common problem for many administrators, experienced as well as novice, that of time management. By analyzing the behavior of the administrator in this case study, discussing the larger issues, addressing the problems identified in "Be a Problem Solver," testing the solutions that are reached, and further investigating related matters, the reader should gain insights on how to become a more perceptive and competent manager of time.

It should be emphasized that most, if not all, of the problems and issues presented in the case studies and in-basket exercises require considerable analysis, discussion, and problem solving. Therefore, appropriate utilization of the ideas contained in Part 1 (and in Chapter 8) and participation in the suggested learning activities at the end of each case study will be important.

BACKGROUND READING

For the reader who would like to develop further background and understanding of the problems and issues presented in this chapter, the following list is provided:

John C. Daresh and Marsha A. Playko, "Mentor Programs," *NASSP Bulletin* (September 1990), 73–77.

Melvin W. Donaho and John L. Meyer, *How to Get the Job You Want: A Guide to Resumes, Interviews, and Job-Hunting Strategies,* Englewood Cliffs, NJ: Prentice-Hall, 1990.

Richard A. Gorton and Gail Thierbach-Schneider, "Part VI, Career Considerations" in *School-Based Leadership: Challenges and Opportunities,* 3rd ed. Dubuque, IA: Wm. C. Brown Publishers, 1991, 573–629.

Catherine Marshall et al., "The Assistant Principalship," *NASSP Bulletin* (January 1992), 80–88.

Thomas J. Quirk, "The Art of Time Management," *Training: The Magazine of Human Resources Development* (January 1989), 59–61.

Stuart C. Smith and Philip K. Piele, *School Leadership, Handbook for Excellence,* 2nd ed. Eugene, OR: ERIC Clearinghouse on Educational Management, 1989, chapters 4 and 14.

Kathryn S. Whitaker and Kenneth Lane, "What Is 'A Woman's Place' in Educational Administration?" *The School Administrator,* reprinted in *Education Digest* (November 1990), 12–15.

1
PREPARING FOR THE JOB SEARCH

It was now February, and Wes Johnson was in the final semester of completing his administrator preparation program. He wouldn't be certified as an administrator until after the present semester, but he wanted to get started with his plans for seeking employment.

It had been seven years since Wes had last sought a new job, so he was a little fuzzy about all of the elements in the process. However, he knew that he probably needed to begin a new placement file and should get some recommendations for it. He didn't know whether he should also prepare a resumé, but he decided that he probably should.

Other ideas that he had been exploring in his own mind were whether to direct that his placement file be sent only to those school districts where the University Placement Office informed him that vacancies existed or whether to send a copy of his resumé to other school districts where he wanted to work, but where there were no current vacancies. (That way, he thought, he would be in on the ground floor with the latter group of school districts if an administrative vacancy did occur.)

Tomorrow, Wes decided, he would begin his work on the resumé and then initiate steps to develop his placement file.

PART II

Sarah Santee was disappointed with the way her job search for an administrator vacancy was progressing. It was already June, and thus far, she had not obtained any job interviews at all. She couldn't figure out why no one had contacted her.

Sarah had been a teacher for six years, had completed her administrator preparation program last December with excellent grades, and had also received very good recommendations for her placement file, regarding her potential as a future administrator. (She had established an "open" file with the Placement Office, so she knew the content of the recommendations.)

What was going on, she wondered? She had been tempted to call or write some of the school districts that had sent her letters of rejection to ask them why she hadn't even been given an interview. (Typically, the rejections letters were very general and not especially instructive.) But she decided not to follow up, for fear that the school districts might think she was being too aggressive.

On Tuesday of the next week, however, Sarah received a letter from the people in one of the school districts where she had recently applied, inviting her to contact them to schedule a job interview. Sarah was elated, although the school district was located in another part of the state, with which she was not too familiar.

Sarah called the school district immediately and set up an interview for the following week. She had about ten days to get ready for the interview. The question now was, what should she be doing during those ten days to prepare herself?

SUGGESTED LEARNING ACTIVITIES

Analyze the Case

1. What is your evaluation of Wes Johnson's decision making and planning? What assumptions does he seem to be making?
2. What might be some possible reasons why Sarah Santee has not been getting any job interviews until now? Is there anything she may be doing or not doing that has hampered her in securing interviews?
3. What are the advantages and disadvantages of Sarah Santee's attitude toward seeking more informative responses from school districts regarding the reasons for her rejection?

Discuss the Larger Issues

1. To what extent does a university department or college have the responsibility for helping the students prepare a placement file and prepare for job interviews?
2. What should be the role of an individual university adviser in helping the advisees to find a job?
3. What are the advantages and disadvantages of "open file" recommendations?
4. What is the responsibility of school districts to help applicants to better understand why they were not selected for interviews and/or the job itself?
5. To what degree are there ethical considerations that should be observed in the preparation of placement files? A resumé? Conducting a job interview?

Be a Problem Solver

Assume that you are Wes Johnson and then Sarah Santee. What decisions need to be made and steps taken in order for you to be successful? (For Wes, the initial objective is to obtain job interviews; for Sarah, it is getting the job.) Utilize relevant concepts from Part I of the text.

Test Your Solution

To test your thinking about the problems on the previous page, you and the class should create and role-play one of the following situations:

1. Prepare a resumé and have the class and/or instructor critique it.
2. Discuss the kinds of people you should contact to ask for recommendations and have the class and/or instructor critique your choices.
3. Simulate a job interview. Videotape it and have the class and the instructor critique it.

Investigate Further

1. Investigate the extent of services offered by your university placement office regarding the preparation of a placement file and resumé and approaches to interviewing.
2. Consult with your university adviser about possible steps you need to take in order to secure an administrative position in education.
3. Interview your administrative superior(s) in your present school district to ascertain what advice they might offer you in seeking an administrative vacancy.
4. Ascertain what books your library might have available on preparing resumés and job interviewing.

2
FROM TEACHER TO ADMINISTRATOR

This was his first job as a principal. He had been a teacher for several years and had obtained his master's degree in educational administration the preceding summer. Last spring he had looked around for a position in administration, but nothing seemed to be available for someone with no previous administrative experience.

During the summer he had gradually accepted the idea of another year of teaching, but in mid-August he had received a call from the superintendent of a small school district who was looking for a building principal. The former principal had just resigned to take a job in a larger school system, and since classes were scheduled to begin in two weeks, the superintendent was anxious to hire someone to fill the vacancy. Within a few days, after several telephone conversations and a personal interview, the superintendent had offered him the job.

Although the offer had been rather flattering, he had experienced mixed emotions about accepting it. It had bothered him a little to think about requesting a release from his own school district so late in the year, although he had been fairly sure that there would be no problem in obtaining it. He had also had reservations about working in such a small school system and community. Still, he had realized that a person had to start somewhere, and this job would at least provide him with experience. So, with that thought in mind, he had accepted the position.

His decision had precipitated the need for numerous other decisions within the next week and a half. Such matters as putting his home up for sale and locating suitable housing for his family in the new community had to be taken care of, and before he knew it, the time which he had hoped to spend learning about the educational program of the district and planning for the opening of school had almost dwindled away.

Now, with only two days left before the faculty was to return for their annual fall workshop, the principal began to panic a little. He still hadn't come to a decision about which items should be covered during the two-day teacher workshop, and he was beginning to become concerned about how the teachers would react to him as their new principal. Several of them had stopped by, the previous day, but it was difficult to tell how they felt about him. He suspected that he was younger than many of the faculty members, and he had misgivings about how the older and more experienced teachers might perceive him.

He had also started to experience some uncertainty about how well the students and their parents were going to accept him. Although he had always gotten along all right with both groups while he was a teacher, he wasn't sure that they would respond to him the same way now that he was a principal.

He wondered whether he was really ready for all the responsibilities that a principal had to handle. He recalled that in the past he had never been especially awed by the principal's duties but, from this new perspective, things seemed to look a lot different.

SUGGESTED LEARNING ACTIVITIES

Analyze the Case

1. What additional questions or reservations might the new principal have raised about resigning from his teaching position in mid-August? What is your evaluation of the thought process that the principal went through prior to accepting the new position?
2. If the principal had taken sufficient time, what specific aspects of the educational program of the district should he have investigated, and what plans should he have made for the teacher workshop and the opening of school?
3. Assess the validity of the concerns expressed by the principal with respect to gaining the acceptance of the faculty, the students, and the parents.

Discuss the Larger Issues

1. What are the ethical considerations with regard to requesting a release from a present contract to accept a better position somewhere else?
2. How important is it for an administrator to be "accepted" by the faculty, student body, and the parents? What are the advantages and disadvantages of such acceptance?

Be a Problem Solver

The principal of the school has no administrative experience and is concerned about the fast-approaching teachers' inservice workshop and about establishing good relationships with teachers, students, and parents. If you were the principal, what would you do? What assumptions would you make? Utilize administrative and social science concepts from Part I of the text in planning and implementing your approach.

Test Your Solution

To test your proposed plan of action, you and the class should create and role-play one or more of the following situations:

1. The principal as he begins the first day of the two-day workshop.
2. The principal in his first formal meeting with the student body.
3. The principal at the first P.T.A. meeting.

Investigate Further

1. What does research suggest are the expectations that teachers hold for the behavior of the principal?
2. What do new principals believe to be the most difficult aspects of the first year as an administrator?

3

THE NEW PRINCIPAL (IN-BASKET ACTIVITIES)

BACKGROUND

You are Dr. Brown. You were approved by the School Board on August 11 to succeed Mr. Sanders as principal of Kennedy School. However, due to a death in your family, you were unable to report to Kennedy School until the weekend of August 22–23. You have arrived at the school on Saturday morning to look at your mail and start organizing things.

> Specific information about the context of this situation, including a description of the school, the district, and the community, has not been provided in order that these details might be varied, depending on the composition of the class or group and the objectives of the instructor. Information of this nature may be provided by the instructor, to the extent needed and at an appropriate time.

INSTRUCTIONS

1. You will be given 90 minutes to read and take action on all of the in-basket items presented following the instructions. You are not expected merely to *describe* what you would do, but to *do* it. For example, if you decide to write a letter, then compose the letter. If you decide to telephone a person or see someone for a conference, then outline your objectives, as well as the main points or questions that you would present. (Utilize relevant concepts from Part I of the text in your responses.)
2. Each of the in-basket items requires a separate action which you should present on another sheet of paper, adding the identification number in the upper left-hand corner of the in-basket item. Although the in-basket items are numbered, you may deal

with them in whatever sequence you prefer; however, you should indicate on your response sheet the priority number which you have assigned to each item: 1 = high priority, 2 = moderate priority, and 3 = low priority.

3. Proceed to address the in-basket items.

In-Basket Item #1

August 19

Dear Dr. Brown:

I am writing you to request a meeting to establish a Parent Council for the school. I was a member of the P.T.A. that folded a couple of years ago because of a lack of leadership from the principal. What we need now is a new parent group with more responsibility and more enlightened leadership from the principal than we have received in the past. As someone with an advanced degree, I am sure you support parent involvement in education.

I look forward to working with you.

Sincerely,
Peggy Kim
Parent

In-Basket Item #2

Telephone Message

For	Dr. Brown
From	Tom Roberts (*State Journal*)
Time	9:30 A.M., August 14

Please call back. The newspaper would like to do a feature on you as the new principal, and I need to set up a time for interviewing you and some of the teachers and students.

In-Basket Item #3

Dr. Brown, I hope that things are going to be better this year on the first day of school than last year. Last year I had to begin classes without enough textbooks and some important supplies like chalk didn't arrive until Friday of the first week. I know you are new and you have a lot on your mind, but teachers think it is important that classes run smoothly on the first day of school. Hopefully with your help we can get off to a better beginning.

Pattie Quinn

In-Basket Item #4

Dear Dr. Brown:

First of all, welcome to Kennedy School. From all I have heard, you should bring some much needed leadership to the school.

The reason I am writing you (I tried to get in to see you but your secretary said you weren't seeing anyone for awhile) is that I would like you to emphasize at the first meeting with the teachers the importance of consistently enforcing the discipline rules, especially the rules on students being on time to class with appropriate materials to work with (you know, like pencils and paper—that kind of stuff) and the gum-chewing rule. The last two years things have been deteriorating and last spring was a mess—too much teacher inconsistency. I don't like to complain about my colleagues, but something's got to be done before the kids take over the school. What this school needs is a real crackdown. I have heard that you're the type that is prepared to "bite the bullet" and in my judgment that time has definitely arrived.

Sincerely,
Bill Stone

In-Basket Item #5

August 17

Dear Dr. Brown:

The purpose of this letter is to request your approval to conduct a study on the impact of new leadership at the school site level. The study would employ ethnographic methods—essentially, shadowing and interviews—of your first six months on the job. I am trying to ascertain the kind of impact a new principal can have on a school. Having a doctorate yourself, I am sure you value research and can appreciate the need for someone like myself—a doctoral student—to complete my dissertation.

Thank you in advance for your interest and cooperation. I look forward to hearing from you.

Sincerely,

Bob Turtle

Doctoral Student

In-Basket Item #6

July 17

MEMO

TO: Principals

FROM: Assistant Superintendent

All principals should remind teachers at the first faculty meeting before school begins this year that *all* teachers will be evaluated, using the new Teacher Accountability Evaluation form that the school board approved last year. Also, principals should emphasize at this first meeting that teachers need to be more careful in using their sick leave days, as there were apparent abuses last year.

In-Basket Item #7

Dear Dr. Brown:

I would like to have a *confidential* conference with you to discuss an urgent matter in regard to another staff member. I have been reluctant to say anything until now, but I feel this is something you would want to know. I must, however, have your written commitment that you will keep all of this *strictly confidential,* including the fact that I would be telling you this. I really don't want to be involved or implicated in any way.

Hazel Smith

In-Basket Item #8

August 20

Dear Dr. Brown:

You don't know me, but I have been a substitute teacher in this school from time to time for the last several years. I don't like to complain because I am really not that kind of person and, besides, I really like the school. But I feel there are a few things that you should know about, and maybe some improvements will result. They didn't with Mr. Sanders, but I have heard that you are a real "take charge" person, and certainly there are some things about this school that need to be improved. I don't think this is the time and place to go into all of the various problems, but there is one thing that I would hope could be changed immediately, and that is the lack of lesson plans that substitute teachers encounter when they come to school. Rarely have I found (and I am not alone in this regard) an up-to-date lesson plan from a teacher who is absent for that day. And frequently I can't find any lesson plan at all. A substitute teacher's job is tough enough, but without a decent lesson plan, it is terrible.

As a parent with children in this district, I certainly have to wonder about the quality of planning by teachers and since Mr. Sanders didn't take any action, one also wonders whether administrators really care or are willing to take a tough stand with teachers. I hope that with new leadership at the school something can be done about this deplorable situation.

Sincerely,
(Mrs.) Ruth White

In-Basket Item #9

Dr. Brown—

We may have to shut off the water for a short time during the first week of school to repair the main boiler. I know this is a bad time to be shutting off the water, and we hope it won't be necessary. Sam and me are trying to get the thing fixed ourselves, but we got a call in to that guy upstate who fixes them if we can't get it done. He can't get here until the week after the laber day weekend and even then he don't know which day it will be. I am trying to get him to come at night but he don't promise nothing. I'll get back to you if anything changes.

Al
Head Custodian

In-Basket Item #10

Dear Dr. Brown:

I hope this year is going to be different. At least with a new principal there is hope.

I live near the school, and for several years now, I have had trouble with students vandalizing my flowers. I have complained to the principal before, but Mr. Sanders only said he ''would look into it'' but nothing was ever done. I hope this year SOMETHING WILL BE DONE. Maybe you could say something to the students at the first assembly program or maybe over the PA system. I know something's got to be done this year or I am going to the school board. It's not right. I am a taxpayer who pays for these schools and I don't even have any kids. I want something done!

Alice Snap

In-Basket Item #11

August 1

MEMO

TO: All Principals

FROM: The Superintendent

Please clear your calendars for Monday afternoon of the second week of school for a meeting in my conference room to discuss how we can improve student achievement test scores for each of your schools. Bring your ideas!

In-Basket Item #12

July 20

Dear Mr. Sanders:

I am president of the Council on Children's Problems, and we would like to present an assembly program to your students this fall on child abuse. As you know, child abuse is a very pervasive problem, and all of us must do everything that we can to prevent this kind of problem from happening to any child, regardless of age and regardless of who the abuser is. Our assembly program is a very stimulating one with ''hands-on'' experiences (no pun intended).

I look forward to hearing from you as to when it would be possible to present our program.

Sincerely,
Ted Allen, President
Council on Children's Problems

In-Basket Item #13

Dr. Brown—

You might want to give some thought to what you are going to do with the teachers during the preschool in-service day. Mr. Sanders sort of "played it by ear" but maybe you have something specific in mind. I know the faculty will be interested in hearing your views at the first meeting. (Also, do you want to send any message to parents?)

Peg Albright
[principal's secretary]

In-Basket Item #14

Mr. Sanders:

I will need to leave school a little early each Monday this fall (10 minutes after dismissal) to get to my university class. I know you will understand since you are working on your advanced degree, too. Plus, I always stay late on other nights anyway, and other teachers have left early in the past.

Mary Eager
Teacher

In-Basket Item #15

Aug. 17

Dear Dr. Brown,

We tried to get an appointment to see you but your secretary said you were going to be too busy to see people until you got your feet on the ground.

Anyway, we would like to use this letter to formally recommend that you eliminate hall passes for this coming school year. Hall passes are demeaning to students and reflect a lack of trust on the part of the faculty and administration toward students.

We recognize that there are a few students who can't be trusted and they probably do need hall passes. But why should the rest of us be penalized for the few?

We have been told that you graduated with a doctor's degree from one of the leading universities. We would hope that you would bring a more enlightened view of students to this school. Let's all start out fresh this year by trusting one another. Are you willing to take the first step? We have!

Sincerely,

Jack Staker

Camilla Black

Bill Elliot

STUDENT COUNCIL REPRESENTATIVES

In-Basket Item #16

Dr. Brown,

I hope that you can do something this coming year about the litter in the hallways and in the cafetteeria during lunch. Maybe, you could say something to the teachers during your first meeting with them. The last few years, things have really gotten out of hand. We need a crackdown—by everybuddy!

Sam Clean
Custodian

In-Basket Item #17

July 15

Dear Mr. Sanders:

Jim and Alice won't be in school for the opening day because our family will not be returning to town from our cottage until September 5. I am sure you will understand.

Sincerely,
(Mrs.) Patricia Rosehips

In-Basket Item #18

August 18

Dear Dr. Brown:

I am writing this letter to request permission for my children to be absent from school next March 15 to April 15 in order to be with me while I am attending an international law conference in the Union of South Africa.

I am sure you recognize the cultural and educational benefits of such a trip. In addition, since I am a single parent and there is no one with whom I could leave my children, there is a practical aspect of my request. Furthermore, the trip will provide a nice change of pace for them, since they tend to get easily bored around that time of the year.

Sincerely,
Thomas Steele
Attorney at Law

In-Basket Item #19

MEMO

August 12

TO: Dr. Brown

FROM: Tim Parker, Assistant Principal

Just a short note to congratulate you on being chosen as new principal of our school. As you can probably imagine, I would have been happier if the school board had chosen me, but I guess those are the breaks. After 12 years as assistant principal, they must figure that's all I'm good for. Anyway, good luck.

4

THE NEW ASSISTANT PRINCIPAL (IN-BASKET ACTIVITIES)

BACKGROUND

You are Dr. Chris Allen. You were previously a teacher for a number of years, and during that time you obtained a doctorate in curriculum and instruction. You intended to be a central office supervisor. But when Mr. Reeves, assistant principal in another school in the district, suddenly resigned in the third week of school, you were asked to take over and you agreed to take the assistant principalship post. After only four days on the job, you had to be away from school on Friday, October 1, because of illness in your family. It is now Saturday morning, October 2, and you have returned to school to check on your mail and telephone messages.

> Specific details about the context of this situation, including a description of the school, the district, and the community, have not been provided in order that such data might be varied, according to the objectives of the instructor and the composition of the class or group. Information of this nature may be provided by the instructor, to the extent needed and at an appropriate time.

Instructions

1. You will be given 90 minutes to read and take action on *all* of the items presented following the instructions. You are not expected merely to *describe* what you would do, but to *do* it. For example, if you decide to telephone a person or see someone for a conference, then outline your objectives, as well as the main points or questions that you would present. (Utilize relevant concepts from Part I of the text in your responses.)

2. You may respond to the in-basket items in whatever sequence you prefer. However, you should first read *all* of them, *quickly*. As you do so, indicate on a separate piece of paper in one of three columns whether a particular in-basket item represents a "High Priority" situation (1), a "Moderate Priority" situation (2) or a "Low Priority" situation (3).
3. Each of the in-basket items requires a separate action, which you should present on another sheet of paper, adding the identification number in the upper left-hand corner of the in-basket item. If you understand all of the instructions up to this point, you may begin now or when your instructor so indicates.

In-Basket Item #1

September 26

Dear Dr. Allen:

I know this is short notice but your predecessor, Mr. Reeves, had promised to give a talk to the PTA at its meeting on October 12, and I am hoping that you are willing to take his place. The topic is, "The Parent's Role in Helping Students to Build Self-Discipline," but if you don't feel comfortable with that, maybe some related topic could be selected. I know the parents will all be eager to meet you and hear your ideas. Please let me know as soon as possible.

Mrs. Trudy Spellman
P.T.A. President

In-Basket Item #2

Dr. Allen, I don't normally complain about *anything* but I am getting sick and tired of putting up with the noise and fooling around that goes on in Janet Webster's class. As you know, her classroom is next door to mine, and she had discipline problems last year. But because she was new, I didn't say anything to her or to anyone else. However, this year—even with different students—it is all starting in again, and I have concluded that she just doesn't know how to handle kids. I have mentioned the noise to her a couple of times already this year, but it doesn't seem to have any lasting effect. I request that you stop in and get this situation squared away before something major erupts. It has already had a negative effect on my own class.

Rocky Bell

In-Basket Item #3

Sept. 29

MEMO
TO: All Assistant and Vice-Principals
FROM: Assistant Superintendent

Since you are the ones who administratively deal most directly with drop-outs and children at risk, I am inviting you to a meeting at the Central Office, Room 1131, on October 5, to discuss this problem. Please bring ideas about how we might deal more effectively with the students.

In-Basket Item #4

Telephone Message

FROM: Mr. Yaeger
TIME: 9:00 A.M. Friday

Yesterday after school two students kicked a soccer ball into his yard and smashed right through his roses getting the ball. Please return his call as soon as possible.

In-Basket Item #5

MEMO

TO: Chris Allen

FROM: Dave

Late last spring the superintendent directed all of us principals to come up with criteria and a process for evaluating their assistant/vice-principals. I got really busy with a number of things at school during this last summer and didn't get to this task. Now the superintendent wants us to submit something by October 5.

Chris, I know this is short notice, but could you give me your ideas on possible criteria and the process by October 3? I would like to involve you in this since it will be your evaluation, and I will definitely appreciate your ideas about the evaluation criteria and process. One of my ideas is that we would provide for some teacher participation in the process, but I would like your own ideas.

In-Basket Item #6

Dr. Allen: Friday was a relatively quiet day, fortunately. But we did get some referrals from a few teachers, and they will need some action on Monday. I've stapled them to this memo.

Nan Wing

Secretary

Eastside School
Referral Form

Date: October
Student's Name: Stanley Bauer
Teacher: Maria Gomez

Problem: Stanley was wearing a button on his shirt that said "Question Authority." I told him to take it off, but he refused, so I'm sending him to your office to be disciplined.

Eastside School
Referral Form

Date: Oct. 1
Student's Name: John Chang and Kevin Dortch
Teacher: Brad Lee

Problem: John and Kevin got into a fight during the noon hour. John got his nose broken (at least I think it was broken) and had to be sent to the doctor. I told them both that you would be wanting to speak to them first thing Monday morning.

Eastside School
Referral Form

Date: Oct. 1
Student's Name: Betty Burmeister
Teacher: Kay Seritoma

Problem: Betty was fooling around in the classroom and refused to settle down. I didn't know what to do with her, and she was disrupting the class. So I thought maybe you could perform some kind of miracle with her. (This kid is a loser.)

Eastside School
Referral Form

Date: Oct. 1
Student's Name: George Edgar
Teacher's Name: Mary Wynn, Librarian

Problem: Last May George Edgar was supposed to pay his library fine of $35.00 before taking his final exams. (He ruined an art book.) He said that he would take care of it but never did, and the teachers felt sorry for him and let him take his exams anyway. This year I have excluded him from the library, but he still hasn't paid me. I think he should be suspended until he pays what he owes.

the student lives in my neighborhood, and I think the situation has gotten pretty bad. Somebody has to help this girl, but I can't.

Mrs. Rachel Sprechter

In-Basket Item #7

Dear Dr. Allen:

This Thursday my teacher Mr. Bell made me stand for 45 minutes in class because I didn't get my homework done on time and because he said I talked back to him. I thought about talking to you Thursday after school, but my foot hurt so much (I have flat feet and have trouble with my feet) that I had to go see the doctor. Then I told my mother Thursday night, and she said I should tell you, but when I went to your office on Friday they said you were gone. Anyway, I don't think what Mr. Bell did was right and besides making my foot worse, it embarrassed me in front of all the other people in the class. I don't know what you can do but something ought to be done.

Marilyn Pick

In-Basket Item #8

Telephone Message

TO: Dr. Allen

FROM: Detective Stevens

He says the police heard a rumor that a group of your students is planning a big party on Saturday, when one of the student's parents are gone. Please call him as soon as possible at 392–9782.

In-Basket Item #9

Dear Mr. Reeves:

This is probably none of my business since I don't have any kids at school anymore, but I thought you ought to know that one of your students is being sexually abused by her stepfather. Don't ask me how I know because I won't tell you, since I really don't want to get involved. The only thing I will tell you is that

In-Basket Item #10

Telephone Message

FOR: Chris Allen

FROM: Scoop Jackson, *Herald Express*

TIME: 3 P.M. Friday

Please call him as soon as possible. He has been assigned a feature on the drug problem in our schools, and he'd like to interview you on Monday.

In-Basket Item #11

Telephone Message

TO: Dr. Allen

FROM: Mrs. Stuart

TIME: Friday, 9:14 A.M.

Mrs. Stuart's son was kept after school for detention on Thursday by his math teacher, Mary Colbert, causing him to miss his ophthalmologist appointment. Please call her Monday morning as early as possible at 354–2298. She says it takes nearly four weeks to get in to see this doctor, and she may have to pay for the missed appointment.

In-Basket Item #12

Dear Dr. Allen:

I don't know whether I should be telling you this or not—probably not—but I can't handle it by myself anymore. One of my friends (I wish I could tell you her name, but she made me promise not to breathe a word of any of this to anyone!) is being sexually harassed by her teacher, Mr. Wiley. She was too ashamed to give me many details, but she is very upset, and I am afraid that she will commit suicide or something. Please talk to him but don't use my name!

Betsy Meadows

In-Basket Item #13

Dear Dr. Allen:

Congratulations on your new appointment. By way of introducing myself and several of my staff, I would like to invite you and your spouse to a small gathering at my home on October 5 for hors d'oeuvres, etc., followed by a special event treat which I am sure all will enjoy and remember forever. Please rest assured that no business conversations will be permitted, and the emphasis will be on getting acquainted and enjoying ourselves. Directions to my home can be secured when you RSVP at 377–4040.

Nick Strokely, Representative
Banner Yearbooks

P.S. I wonder if you've had an opportunity to meet my daughter, Joy, who is a student at your school.

In-Basket Item #14

Dr. Allen, I wanted to let you know that when I substituted for Ken Clark on Friday, he didn't leave any lesson plans. Also, he didn't answer his phone when I tried to reach him. Needless to say, this made teaching his class very difficult. An inexperienced sub would have faced an impossible situation! It would be unfortunate if this would occur again.

Toni Wolff

In-Basket Item #15

Dear Mr. Reeves:

I hope you can help my son. He is being harassed by some other boys on the school bus when he rides to and from school. Apparently, they don't like the fact that he is reading his Bible, and they make remarks about him and about our religion.

I have already tried contacting the boys' parents. While only one of them was completely uncooperative (she told me my son shouldn't even be reading the Bible on a school bus), the other parents don't seem to have much control over their children.

My son doesn't bother anyone, and I would like you to intervene and get this harassing to stop. We're supposed to have freedom of religion in this country.

Mrs. Marilyn Smith

In-Basket Item #16

Dr. Allen:

It looks like we got a problem already this year with drugs. I found some drug parfernalia on the floor in the boys locker room which somebody dropped by mistake. I haven't told anybody else about this, except my wife which may have been a mistake. I don't know how you want to handle it. I don't have any idea about who may have had the stuff.

Lew Armstrong, Custodian

In-Basket Item #17

Telephone Message

FOR: Dr. Allen

FROM: Mrs. Alice Pick

TIME: 11:30 A.M. Friday

Please call her early Monday morning.

In-Basket Item #18

Dr. Allen, I don't think you know me (no reason why you should know all students), but I and several of my friends want to establish a club called Christians for New World Order, and we want to meet every Wednesday after school. I don't know whether we need a sponsor or not, but Mrs. Webster, our English teacher, said she would do it. We should like to meet this coming Wednesday, so if there is no problem, would you please sign us a room. You are welcome (in fact encouraged) to attend our meetings.

Sue Clemens

5
WHY DOES A WOMAN NEED TO ACT LIKE A MAN?

She was beginning the second semester of her first year in the principalship at Doolittle School. Her predecessor had apparently been a strong disciplinarian and well respected by the faculty. He had left for a job as assistant superintendent in a different state. She had been hired, according to the superintendent, because the school board wanted someone at Doolittle School who was the change agent type with excellent interpersonal skills, and her recommendations indicated that she would fit the bill.

She had a Specialists's Degree in school administration and supervision from a major university. She had developed a strong concentration in curriculum and instruction within her degree program and had achieved high grades. She was a small person, but possessed a lot of drive and energy. She was considered to have a warm and accepting personality and to believe in the basic goodness of people.

Although she had approached the beginning of the school year with great enthusiasm, things had not gone particularly well during the first semester. The faculty was an older group who, for the most part, placed a high priority on strict student discipline and the absolute backing of the principal. She wasn't opposed to student discipline, but she felt that the school needed to develop some alternatives to simply punishing students. She also felt that the teachers needed to spend more time with those students who were misbehaving in class to try to diagnose why the students were acting out, instead of simply referring the students to the assistant principal. Most teachers, however, resisted this approach, and she had heard rumors that they felt she wasn't "tough enough."

Al Kicker ("Big Al," as he was called by the teachers), the assistant principal, was another problem. He had applied for the principal's vacancy at Doolittle School and had been passed over. She knew he was unhappy about that, although he had never talked to her about his disappointment. But the main problem was that he just couldn't seem to accept her as the principal of the school. True, he was polite and respectful of her with his, "Yes, ma'am" and "No, ma'am" and "If that's what you really want, ma'am," but he never opened up with her. He treated her more like a woman on a pedestal than a capable professional who was his superior. Also, he was himself a very strict disciplinarian who encouraged teachers to send misbehaving students to him ("to get straightened out") rather than trying to get the teachers to first work with problem students on their own. She sensed that the teachers liked Al better than her and that they looked to him for leadership more than to her.

Although she wasn't sure what to do about her assistant principal, she was most troubled by her lack of acceptance by the other principals in the school district. The male principals were older, much more experienced, and, apparently with only one exception, quite conservative in their philosophy of education and their attitudes toward teachers and students. They had sort of a "them versus us" mentality, and they espoused a strict, rigid approach toward student discipline. As a group, they seemed aloof and appeared to her to have a "you still need to prove yourself to us" attitude toward her.

She had initially thought that her lack of acceptance by the male principals was due to the fact that she was a woman (and she continued to believe that many of them, if not most, were sexist). But since the other female principals seemed to get along with the male principals all right, she had concluded that her lack of acceptance was because she was new and really did need to prove herself. She wasn't sure how to do this or even whether she should need to prove herself to the male principals. Thus far, she hadn't figured out how to handle this problem.

Complicating the matter was the fact that the other female principals seemed to be acting differently toward her. Initially they had appeared friendly to her, but during the first semester they had gradually become more reserved. As she reflected more about this development, it seemed to her that the other female principals were more like the male principals in their attitudes and behavior than they were like her. Whereas she was a warm, open, trusting kind of person, the other women seemed to be more abrasive and circumspect. It was almost as though the other female principals felt that they had to be tough and "out-macho" the male principals. She wondered whether that was the kind of personality and approach they had when they joined the school district, or if they had changed in response to conditions and expectations that existed within the district.

She wasn't sure what she was going to do about her numerous problems, but she felt herself being pulled in various directions. Maybe she would have to become tougher in order to survive. But, if that was required, would she be willing to pay the price? She still believed that it should be possible for a woman who is warm, open, trusting, and holding progressive ideas to succeed, but she certainly hadn't figured out what her strategy should be for the second semester. One thing she did know was that she still believed in herself. She wouldn't give up easily.

SUGGESTED LEARNING ACTIVITIES

Analyze the Case

1. Should the new principal have taken steps during and after the hiring process to become better informed about some of the conditions she experienced later? If so, what might those steps have been?
2. If you were the new principal in the case study, what additional information would you want to know before attempting to solve the problems identified, and how would you go about obtaining that information? Explain why the additional information you seek is necessary in order to ameliorate the problems.
3. To what degree do you think the new principal has brought on some of her own problems, and to what extent do you think she is overreacting to some of the problems?

Discuss the Larger Issues

1. Is there a certain kind of personality or set of attributes that a school administrator is expected to possess in order to be successful?
2. Are women administrators expected to meet an essentially masculine set of expectations, i.e, "Be strong, be tough"? To what extent are expectations for female or, for that matter, male administrators related to research on administrator or leadership effectiveness?
3. To what extent should an individual administrator attempt to resist, modify, or even reject expectations of others when they are not compatible with the administrator's own administrative style or educational vision?

Be a Problem Solver

Assume that you are the new principal at Doolittle School. Outline the steps you would try to take to resolve each of the problems identified in the case study. Utilize administrative and social science concepts from Part I of the text in planning and implementing your problem-solving approach.

Test Your Solution

To test your proposed plan of action for dealing with the circumstances described in the case study, you and your colleagues should create and role-play one or more of the following situations:

1. A faculty meeting to discuss philosophy and procedures for handling student discipline.
2. A conference between the new principal and the assistant principal.
3. A meeting or conference between the new principal and one or more of the male or female principals.

Investigate Further

1. Investigate the literature on problems that administrators face in becoming socialized into a new situation.
2. Interview one or more female administrators to determine the extent to which they encountered an acceptance problem because of their sex.
3. Investigate the extent to which there exists within your school or district any support groups to help new administrators with initial problems adjusting to a new job setting.

6
GIMME THAT OLD TIME DISCIPLINE

Shirley Nolan had been appointed vice principal only a week before classes were to begin in the fall. She had been certified as a school administrator for the last two years, but had been unable to find a job, so she had continued teaching.

Her opportunity to become a vice principal had occurred when the previous vice principal had left education at the last moment to become a salesman for an insurance company. The school district hadn't had much time to fill the vacancy, so they had called Shirley, interviewed her, and then informed her that she had the job if she wanted it—all on the same day. She wasn't prepared for events to move that fast, but despite some misgivings about facing the challenge of becoming a new administrator (in addition to relocating to a different school), she had accepted the district's offer. She felt that she had a certain advantage in her new position, inasmuch as she would still be working for the same school district.

Her first two days on the job consisted of attending the various district and building meetings that occur just before fall classes begin. She had, of course, spent some time with the principal, who seemed nice but whose philosophy of discipline was much different from her own. She had first recognized this during the job interview but had decided to "tell them what they wanted" in order to get the job. The principal believed in strict discipline and strong punitive consequences for misbehavior, while her own approach was more one of trying to understand what was causing the misbehavior and attempting to counsel with the student in order to improve the behavior. She had been successful with this approach as a classroom teacher, and she knew of no reason why it wouldn't work in her new role as vice principal. Still, she didn't argue with the principal about their differences when they had met, in the hope that maybe over time he would "soften up" a little and, if she were effective with her approach, might gradually change his mind.

Unfortunately, most of the faculty members she met also seemed to be from the old school of student discipline and appeared to subscribe fully to the principal's views. Shirley was pleased that some of the younger teachers were more attuned to her approach to student discipline, but one of her problems was that the school had this very rigid set of discipline rules:

FOLSUM SCHOOL'S STUDENT DISCIPLINE CODE

Introduction

Everyone needs discipline: athletes need discipline, executives need discipline, soldiers need discipline.

Rules are developed and promulgated in order to facilitate and promote discipline. Without rules, there would be no discipline.

The following rules have been developed in order to achieve the discipline necessary for the orderly environment that is required for effective teaching and learning. By following these rules, you will become a good school citizen, develop better self-discipline, and become a more effective learner. You will also help us create a positive atmosphere needed for a quality educational program. Although the rules may seem to you to be a little strict, they are really for your own good and for the best welfare of the greatest number of students in the school.

Obey the rules. Be a good citizen. Be a positive example for others.

Behavioral Guidelines

1. All students will come to school prepared for class, appropriately dressed and with necessary materials and equipment.
2. Students will be on time for school and for class. Punctuality is very important at Folsum School.
3. Student fighting or fooling around will not be tolerated anywhere in the school, on the school grounds, or coming or going from school.
4. Smoking or use of drugs will not be tolerated and will result in immediate suspension or recommendation for expulsion, depending on the nature of the offense.
5. Acts of vandalism will be punished by suspension or expulsion, depending on the seriousness of the offense.
6. Students are not allowed to chew gum in class or to eat candy or other food in or out of class, except during the lunch period in the cafeteria.
7. The use of profanity will not be tolerated in this school and may subject a student to suspension or other appropriate action.
8. Disrespect for teachers will not be permitted, and appropriate action will be taken if it occurs.
9. Students are not allowed to run or fool around in the hallways.
10. Any student action that interferes with teaching, learning, the rights of others, or the smooth operation of the school will receive disciplinary punishment.

After looking over the Student Discipline Code again, Shirley considered what, if anything, she could or should do to try and change the rules. She had been told by one of the older teachers that the present code had been in existence for about seven years and, as far as that teacher was concerned, had worked very well. However, for Shirley, the code was at odds with her philosophy and approach to student discipline. The question was, "What could or should she do in light of all the various circumstances in this school?"

SUGGESTED LEARNING ACTIVITIES

Analyze the Case

1. Given the circumstances that the new vice principal had faced at the time she was offered the job at Folsum, should she have taken it? Why or why not?
2. If you had been Shirley Nolan, would you have acted any differently in your meetings with the principal?
3. Analyze and evaluate the Folsum School Student Discipline Code, using concepts from communication theory and recommendations from authorities on school discipline.

Discuss the Larger Issues

1. To what extent should a person seeking a position "tell them what they want" in order to get a job? What ethical problems might be involved? Is this approach to getting a job ever justified and, if so, under what sort of circumstances?

2. What is the ultimate objective of a student discipline code, and what type of a code is likely to achieve that objective?
3. What should be the role of punishment in disciplining students? What does research say about its effectiveness?
4. To what degree should students and parents be involved in the development or revision of a student discipline code?

Be a Problem Solver

Assume that you are the vice principal in this case study. Outline objectives and plans for responding to the various circumstances with which the vice principal is faced. Utilize appropriate administrative or social science concepts from Part I of the text in planning and implementing your approach.

Test Your Solution

To test your proposed plans for dealing with the circumstances described in the case study, you and the class should create and role-play one or more of the following interactions:

1. A follow-up conference between you and the principal to discuss the Student Discipline Code.
2. A teacher referral to the vice principal about a student who persists in sucking on lozenges in class.
3. The first meeting of a special committee, composed of representative students, teachers, parents, and the vice principal, whose charge is to make recommendations on what changes, if any, are needed in the Student Discipline Code.

Investigate Further

1. Determine what criteria and methods are used to evaluate your school's student discipline code and how often evaluation occurs.
2. Ascertain the extent to which your school's discipline code is understood and accepted by teachers, parents, and students.
3. Evaluate the student discipline code in your own school, using concepts from communication theory and recommendations from authorities on student discipline.

7
IS BEING BUSY NECESSARILY PRODUCTIVE?

Driving to school, Steve Fuller slowed reluctantly for a traffic light. As he waited for the signal to change, the new principal of Franklin School speculated idly about what the day might bring. It seemed that he was always busy, regardless of how a day started out.

Today, for example, he didn't have any conferences or meetings scheduled until later in the afternoon, to the best of his memory. However, he was certain that something would come along to dominate the morning. He had hoped to get into some classrooms and do some supervision, but he hadn't mentioned anything to the teachers yet, in case something were to come up to prevent him from accomplishing that task.

Finally, the green light appeared, and Steve accelerated the car to compensate for lost moments. By 7:55 he pulled into the school parking lot at his usual time, parked the car and entered the school. His secretary had arrived some time earlier, and after five minutes of chitchat with her, the principal was interrupted by a teacher who wanted to talk about the faculty party that was to occur in about two weeks. The conversation lasted until 8:25, at which time the teacher had to leave for a class that began at 8:30 A.M.

At 8:40 Steve Fuller was sitting in his office deciding what he should do next, when he remembered that he had hoped to do some classroom supervision that morning. But, as he started to leave, his secretary intercepted him, asking whether they could talk now about revising some of the office procedures. Since there was a lull in her work schedule, it seemed to her like a good time to discuss the matter. The principal momentarily experienced some mixed feelings, but he didn't reveal them to his secretary. Instead, he smiled and said that he would be happy to discuss those matters with her.

At 9:20 the principal and his secretary were still talking (although they had been interrupted by two telephone calls to the principal), when the secretary brought to the attention of the principal his scheduled conference with a parent, Mrs. Channing, at 9:30. The principal was mildly surprised, as he had anticipated that the parent conference was to be held in the afternoon. He thought to himself that the classroom observation would have to wait until after the parent conference.

At 9:45 Mrs. Channing finally appeared for her conference with the principal. Mr. Fuller was a little frustrated because he had expected her to arrive at 9:30, and he hadn't been able to get much done except to talk with a student who had dropped by the office.

However, he concealed his frustration and tried to be as friendly and helpful to Mrs. Channing as possible. The parent wanted to talk with him about her son's discipline difficulties in school, but it quickly became clear that she should have talked to the assistant principal or the counselor instead, each of whom could have been more helpful to her. Unfortunately, when he asked his secretary to contact one of them, neither was free at that time.

As the conference with the parent dragged on and on, the principal became more and more frustrated. Finally, at 10:40, the parent concluded her conference with the principal and thanked him for his help. The principal thought to himself that he really hadn't been very helpful, but he was happy that he was finally rid of the parent.

Since it was now 10:45 A.M., the principal decided that he needed a coffee break, and he left his office to go down to the faculty room. After he had poured his coffee, he decided to sit in the back of the faculty room where he hoped to be somewhat alone, and perhaps clear his head from the parent conference. However, almost immediately, a couple of teachers came over and initiated a discussion about last Sunday's pro football game. The principal had hoped for some privacy, but he was reluctant to turn away the two teachers and besides, he really liked football. So the conversation continued, and before he knew it, it was 11:15 A.M.

Excusing himself, the principal left the faculty room and returned to his office. While sorting through some papers on his desk, a teacher stopped by and asked if he was busy. The principal thought to himself that he really wasn't busy yet, but there were some things that he knew should be done. On the other hand, at this point, he hadn't started anything specific, and since he had told his faculty that he had an open-door policy and they could see him anytime he wasn't busy, he indicated to the teacher that he would be happy to see her.

The principal's conference with the teacher was about the possibility of the school or the district's purchase of a television set for her classroom so that she could begin to teach students to become more critical consumers of television. The conference lasted until 11:45, when the principal had to excuse himself to go to lunch with the P.T.A. president.

After returning from lunch, Mr. Fuller answered several telephone messages on his desk, and attempted to open and process his mail. This took about 40 minutes, until it was nearly 1:45 P.M. At that point, his secretary came in to remind him of the meeting that he had to attend at the district office at 2:30. The principal had temporarily forgotten about the meeting, although he knew that there was some type of meeting that he was supposed to attend later in the afternoon. He thanked his secretary for reminding him and decided that he'd better prepare to leave, as it would take about 30 minutes to drive downtown to the district office.

At 4:00 the district office meeting concluded. Mr. Fuller decided against returning to the school and instead proceeded home. It had been a boring meeting and, in general, a frustrating day. He felt he had been busy all day but wondered what he had really accomplished. He knew there was something important that he meant to do that he hadn't accomplished, but he couldn't remember anymore what it had been. He thought to himself that he needed a drink, and that perhaps tomorrow would bring a more satisfying and productive day.

SUGGESTED LEARNING ACTIVITIES

Analyze the Case

1. What planning steps might the principal have taken before he arrived at work that would have improved his productivity?
2. Analyze the different activities in which the principal engaged during the day and suggest how he might have handled things more efficiently.

Discuss the Larger Issues

1. To what extent should an administrator be concerned about how efficiently he uses his time?
2. What costs are there to not being well organized or efficient?
3. What costs are there to being *too* organized and efficient?
4. Why are some administrators more productive than others? Do they have more time, or is it due to other factors?

Be a Problem Solver

Assume that you are the supervisor of the principal in this case. How would you approach the principal to help him use his time more productively? Utilize administrative and social science concepts from Part I of the text in planning and implementing your approach.

Test Your Solution

To test your proposed approach to dealing with the circumstances presented in this case, you and your colleagues should create and role-play one or more of the following situations:

1. A conference between the principal and his supervisor.
2. The development of a plan for implementing the supervisor's suggestions.

Investigate Further

1. To what extent are the problems experienced by the principal in the case similar to the problems experienced by the administrators in your district? What seems to be causing the problems?
2. What kinds of assistance are being given to the administrators in your district to deal with these problems?

10 Student Problems

Many student problems are as old as formal schooling itself. For example, student truancy, vandalism, cheating, smoking, profanity, talking back to teachers, and other similar kinds of problems have confronted most administrators at one time or another over the years. And although student strikes, assaults of teachers, and other more extreme behavior may seem to be of recent origin, one historical record reported that in 1837 over 300 schools in Massachusetts alone were broken up by rebellious students. Still, the limited data that are available suggest that student misbehavior has become a more serious problem in recent years and has been the subject of considerable public concern.

While disruptive student behavior certainly merits the attention of administrators and the general public, there are other kinds of student problems that may not be so obvious to the school and the public because they cause little, if any, immediate difficulty, but they are nevertheless worthy of consideration. Examples would be the student who is doing average work in school but who is under a great deal of pressure to perform better in order to meet parental expectations and the overachieving student who seems anxious much of the time. These kinds of students may have problems which, if not addressed by someone at the school, could result in extreme behavior, such as suicide or drug abuse. There are also those students who don't react in such a life-threatening manner, but simply drop out of school. The point is that administrators should not limit their attention to only the more obvious student misbehavior; early diagnosis of more subtle symptoms of student problems is also necessary.

Why students experience problems or cause the school difficulty is, of course, a complex question that must be approached on an individual basis, as well as at a class or school level. Certainly, there are a number of theories, and these may be pursued in the list of readings provided at the end of this introduction. Also, the reader will need to examine and utilize the administrative and social science concepts presented in Part I of the text. There are no easy, ready-made answers to student problems, but an accurate understanding and appropriate utilization of these concepts are prerequisite to effective action.

Finally, it needs to be emphasized that not all students experience problems or cause the school difficulty, and what may be a problem for one student or school may not be a problem for another student or school. However, it seems clear that dealing with student problems of one kind or another will continue to be a major aspect of the school administrator's responsibilities and, for that reason, representative case studies are presented for study and analysis.

BACKGROUND READING

For the reader who would like to develop further background and understanding of the problems and issues presented in this chapter, the following list of readings is provided:

Michael Aytes, "Student Press Fosters Responsibility," *Educational Leadership* (November 1991), 71–72.
William E. Davis and Edward J. McCaul, *At Risk Children and Youth: A Crisis in Our Schools and Society,* Orono, ME: University of Maine, 1990.
Melissa Etlin, "Preventing Teen Suicide: Programs That Work," *NEA Today* (May–June 1990), 6.
Robert F. Kronick and Charles H. Hargis, *Drop-Outs: Who Drops Out and Why—And the Recommended Action,* Springfield, IL: Charles Thomas Publishers, 1990.
Robert Major, *Discipline: The Most Important Subject We Teach,* Lanham, MD: University Press of America, Inc., 1990.
Laurence F. Rossow and Janice A. Hiniger, *Students and the Law,* Bloomington, IN: Phi Delta Kappa, 1991.

8
SCHOOL YARD DANGERS

The dark skies were just beginning to lighten as the principal drove into the school's parking lot. He had decided to arrive at work early so he could catch up on some paperwork that had piled up on his desk, and he was looking forward to a quiet time of concentration, without teacher or student interruptions.

Approaching the back door of the school, he was surprised to see seven or eight students standing around in that area. Having made a special effort to arrive early himself, he wondered briefly how early these students must have left home that morning, and why.

He greeted the students and unlocked the door, aware that they were watching him, hopeful that he might allow them into the building. "Sorry," he said, with a regretful smile. "No students are allowed inside until the bell rings at 8:15." As an afterthought, he asked, "What are you kids doing here so early in the morning, anyway?"

There was little response from the students. One of the girls gave him a half-smile, and others turned away. Not wanting to put them on the defensive, he didn't persist, but commented, "You really shouldn't get here so early. Get a little more sleep tomorrow morning, and try not to show up until 8:15."

The door closed behind him, locking automatically, and he groped his way down the dark corridor to flip the light switch on the wall, then headed toward his office. Inside, he checked the answering machine and then settled himself at his desk to sort through the paperwork.

An hour later he heard his office door open, and his secretary's voice called out, "Are you here already, Mr. Lasky?" She poked her head around the corner and gave him a smile. "What an early-bird today! Trying to catch up after yesterday's busy schedule?"

He made an affirmative noise, finishing one of the forms he was completing for the state, and turned to her. "Martha, I noticed there were a number of students out behind the school when I arrived. Is today a special day or something, that they couldn't wait to get here?"

Martha snorted. "Special? Hardly! Those are just kids whose parents drop them off on the way to work in the morning, and they hang around the doors, waiting to get into the school. I don't know what time you arrived, but there are usually 20 or more by the time I get here at 7:45. By the time we unlock the doors at 8:15, forty or fifty kids will come streaming in. And every year the number seems to grow. I guess it's because there are a lot of working mothers and they don't like to leave the kids at home alone. They must think it's safer at school."

Phil Lasky was a little uncomfortable at the thought. "But it was just getting light when I drove in this morning. Those kids must have been dropped off pretty early."

"I expect so," Martha agreed, hanging up her coat and turning on the computers.

Off and on during the day Phil Lasky would be reminded of the little group of students who had been outside the school that morning, and he marveled at how things had changed since *he* went to school. He remembered sleeping as late as possible until his mother called him. Then he'd smell the aroma of eggs and bacon, and sleepily stumble down the stairs, plunking himself in front of the table to be served. At the time it had seemed like the natural order of things, but obviously times had changed.

In the interoffice mail that arrived in the afternoon, he pulled out an envelope from the superintendent, to give it immediate attention. As he read the memo, the timeliness of the message really hit home.

TO: All Principals
FROM: Harvey Richards, Superintendent

It has been brought to my attention that we need to take purposeful steps to deal with a problem of student safety. Many students are arriving at school in the early morning while it is still dark, dropped off by parents on their way to work.

While we can appreciate the motivation and reasoning behind this practice, it is not in students' best interest to be left unattended at a deserted school an hour or more before adults arrive. Parents apparently have the mistaken idea that their students will be supervised, no matter how early they arrive at school.

Obviously, the school is incurring undesirable liability in this situation. We need to develop a policy that addresses not only the school's liability for students before and after the formal school day, but preferably a program to deal with the need for student supervision, which is evident at almost all schools.

Within the next week I would like you to (a) assess the situation at your own school, documenting the time at which students first arrive, and a general time-graph of the numbers involved, and (b) develop some ideas to deal with the problem. It goes without saying that the alternatives you identify cannot further strain our already tight budget, nor do I think it realistic to look at parents as a source of volunteers, inasmuch as the ones who are employed will not be available, and the ones who aren't will want to stay home to supervise their own children. Also, remember anything involving teacher supervision would have to go to the bargaining table.

This is a sticky issue, but we need to address it as expeditiously as possible.

That evening at the dinner table Phil mentioned the problem to his wife. "I was really appalled to see those kids at school this morning while it was still *dark,*" he commented. Then he noticed a strained expression on her face. "What's wrong? Is there something I should know?"

She rose from the table, and he watched questioningly as she went to the kitchen counter and returned with the newspaper. "Apparently, you haven't seen the evening headlines yet," she said, thrusting the paper into his hands.

A headline read, "Middle School Student Sexually Assaulted," and the story related how a girl had been accosted in the early morning as she approached the playground of a city school.

Phil's first thought was that the incident described could easily have occurred at *his* school. His next thought was that he was living on borrowed time. Things were going to heat up—fast.

SUGGESTED LEARNING ACTIVITIES

Analyze the Case

1. Which concepts from Part I of this text would have been helpful in preventing or ameliorating the problem of student safety before and after regular school hours?
2. Why was Phil Lasky caught off-guard by this problem?

3. How might Mr. Lasky best assess the *extent* of need for supervisory activities and/or personnel before and after school?
4. How do you think Phil Lasky would have responded to learning about students arriving early in the morning if he had not received the letter from the superintendent?

Discuss the Larger Issues

1. The problem of unsupervised children appears to be one consequence of changing demographic and economic patterns in this country. What should be the role of the school, if any, in responding to this problem? What should be the role of the community?
2. Evaluate the role of the news media in identifying areas for improvement in education. Is the influence basically positive or negative?
3. To what extent should funding for extended hours of student supervision at school come from parent fees or from local taxes? Should state funds be provided?

Be a Problem Solver

Assume that you are Phil Lasky. In light of potential danger to unattended children at school in the early morning hours, how would you

1. address the immediate problem at your school?
2. respond to the superintendent's request for recommendations for a long-term resolution of the problem?

Test Your Solution

To test your proposed plan of action for dealing with the problem presented in the case, you and the class should create and role-play one or more of the following interactions:

1. A telephone call from a local television reporter who plans to do some videotaping at your school one day this week, early in the morning, and wants to interview you briefly regarding student safety before and after the school day.
2. A telephone call from the PTA president, communicating concerns expressed to her by neighbors and friends after seeing the newspaper article on the student's assault.
3. A meeting of the district administrative team with the superintendent to review recommendations and select a course of action for ensuring student safety before and after normal school hours.

Investigate Further

1. How does your school assure student safety for students who may arrive early in the morning?
2. What is your district's *written* policy regarding students who come to school early or who are not picked up by parents until 5 or 6 P.M.?
3. Does your district sponsor an after-school program for students who have no home supervision?
4. What is the school's legal liability for students who arrive on the premises before school hours and/or stay late in the afternoon?

9
WHO IS REALLY DISABLED?

Mr. Hill had finished his lunch break and was heading back to his classroom when he heard loud voices in the boys' restroom. He started to enter the restroom when several boys dashed out through the doorway, almost knocking him down. Before he had a chance to recover, the boys were gone and he had not been able to get a good look at them.

Now, however, Mr. Hill thought that he heard sobbing inside the restroom. He opened the door, looked around, and spotted a boy huddled in the corner with his face down. Mr. Hill didn't recognize him immediately, but when he asked the student whether he was all right, the boy looked up and the teacher identified him. Although the teacher didn't know the student very well, he remembered that his name was Ted Robertson, and that he was one of the handicapped kids that the school was attempting to mainstream in his classroom. Mr. Hill's impression was that Ted was a quiet student, never bothered anyone, and seemed like a good kid.

Mr. Hill noticed that Ted's shirt had been torn and his nose was bleeding. He told Ted to tuck in his shirt, quit crying, and dry his face. The teacher then tried to question the boy about what had just happened in the restroom, but the student couldn't or wouldn't respond to the questions. Mr. Hill knew that classes would begin momentarily and that he didn't have much time to spend, so he took Ted to the administration offices, in hopes that Mr. Denison, the vice-principal, might be able to extract more information about the incident.

After the teacher had apprised Mr. Denison about the situation and had left, the vice-principal indicated to Ted that he should sit down. Glancing across the desk at the student, Mr. Denison wondered what kind of kid Ted was. The vice-principal had never had any direct contact with the boy before, and as far as he knew, Ted was a nice boy, not like some of the other handicapped kids who were always in trouble for one thing or another.

Mr. Denison attempted to question Ted about what had happened in the restroom, but the student twisted his hands nervously and wouldn't respond. Finally, Ted blurted out, "Three boys beat me up for not giving them my lunch money. Yesterday they said they would protect me from the other kids if I would give them my lunch money, beginning today. I wasn't sure what to do, but I was scared about the way students have been treating me and some of the other handicapped kids. We've been sworn at, jostled in the halls, even spit on."

"Still," Ted continued, more slowly, "I didn't feel that I could afford to give up my lunch money for 'protection,' and, besides, I wasn't at all sure that those three guys who promised to protect me would really follow through. But when I refused to give them the money today, they knocked me around."

Mr. Denison felt himself becoming upset as he listened to Ted, wondering why the boy had not reported these incidents earlier. When Ted finished talking, the vice-principal asked, "Have you mentioned any of this previously to your teachers? Why haven't you reported these incidents to the administration?" Ted merely shrugged his shoulders and then shook his head slowly.

The vice-principal considered what his next step should be. Although he never expressed his true feelings about the handicapped students, he had had doubts from the outset about whether they really belonged in the same classes with normal students. It would not have been his decision to mainstream them, but obviously it was up to him to eliminate the type of harassment that was taking place. It appeared that some heads needed to be cracked!

SUGGESTED LEARNING ACTIVITIES

Analyze the Case

1. What is your assessment of the teacher's behavior in responding to the situation outside the boy's restroom?
2. What is your evaluation of the vice-principal's attitude toward handicapped students and Ted Robertson in particular?
3. What administrative or social science concepts did the vice-principal not utilize which might have been helpful during the conference with Ted Robertson?
4. If you had been the vice-principal, what, if anything, would you have done differently during the conference with the handicapped student?

Discuss the Larger Issues

1. To what extent should the school be concerned about the way students treat each

other, particularly the handicapped students? What can the school do about this problem?
2. What is the school or district's responsibility to provide orientation for students, parents, teachers, and administrators and inservice training for the latter two groups on the subject of handicapped students? What should be the nature of this orientation and inservice training?

Be a Problem Solver

Assume that you are the vice-principal in this school and a teacher has referred Ted Robertson to you. How would you handle the situation? What sort of follow-up activities would you institute after the conference? What administrative and social science concepts would you utilize in your approach to this situation?

Test Your Solution

In order to test your proposed plan of action for dealing with the problems presented in the case, you and your colleagues should create and role-play one or more of the following situations:

1. A continuation of the conference with Ted Robertson.
2. A telephone call from Mrs. Robertson.
3. A conference with one of the boys who allegedly beat up Ted Robertson.
4. A faculty meeting that focuses on the handicapped student.

Investigate Further

1. What percent of the students in your school are handicapped students?
2. What is the attitude of the other students, the teachers, and the administration toward the handicapped students? What is the attitude of the handicapped students toward school?
3. What is your school or school district doing to provide for the needs of the handicapped? What is your assessment of these efforts, and what else needs to be done?

10
THE UNDERACHIEVER

The principal was busy filling out evaluation forms for nontenured teachers when his secretary interrupted him. She explained that Mrs. Buckley was in the outer office and wanted to talk with him about her son, Randy.

For a moment, the principal hesitated. He still had a stack of forms to complete and submit within several days, and this was the morning when he had hoped to accomplish the bulk of the task. He wished that Mrs. Buckley had first telephoned to make an appointment. Still, now that she was here, he knew that he would have to see her anyway, so he nodded to his secretary.

As Mrs. Buckley entered his office and sat down, she apologized for bothering him and explained that she was very concerned about her son. She felt that Randy was an intelligent boy, but his grades were considerably lower than what she thought that he could achieve. His older sisters had always done well in school and received good marks. Sometimes she felt that he just wasn't putting out enough effort, but she had tried everything that she could think of to improve his performance and had not seen any noticeable effect. She had tried offering rewards for good grades and she had tried taking away privileges until there was improvement, but nothing worked.

She was particularly concerned because Randy's lack of achievement in school was causing conflict within the family. His father, who was becoming more and more impatient with the boy, attributed the problem to laziness on the part of his son. There was currently so much tension between the two that it was upsetting others in the family. Mr. Buckley was an insurance executive and often needed to make business trips that took him away from home for several days at a time. But he maintained a strong interest in the school performance of all his children, and he expected his wife to make sure that their educations were proceeding smoothly.

She knew that Randy was probably sick of her constant nagging about doing his best, and it was impairing her own relationship with him. Still, she shared her husband's philosophy that everyone should always try hard, no matter in what endeavor. Randy's father was a hard worker; he had put himself through college and achieved a high position in his firm by always giving a great deal of himself. It didn't seem right that Randy should be allowed to drift along if he were capable of doing better. Certainly, when Randy became an adult, that kind of an attitude wouldn't get him very far.

The principal had listened to the mother pour out her concerns, and when she seemed finished, he asked to be excused for a moment to secure Randy's cumulative record. He stepped into the outer office and located the boy's folder, which shown that he had an IQ of 118, but that his first semester's grades had consisted of two D's in English and math and four C's. Glancing over previous years, the principal noted that Randy's grades had been mixed: several D's in English and math, but mostly C's.

The data in the cumulative record offered little else in the way of clues to Randy Buckley's underachievement. The principal knew that the mother wanted some help with the problem and that she expected him to be the expert and provide the answer. It would be nice if it were that easy.

SUGGESTED LEARNING ACTIVITIES

Analyze the Case

1. What other questions might the principal have asked to bring out the nature of the causes for Randy's underachievement?
2. What other sources of information might the principal consult to shed light on the problem?
3. At what stage, if any, would it be appropriate to draw the boy or his father into the conference?
4. On the basis of the information provided in the case, what do you think are the main reasons for Randy's underachievement?

Discuss the Larger Issues

1. To what extent is the school responsible for student underachievement?
2. To what degree should the school be held accountable for student underachievement?
3. What should be the role of the school in regard to dealing with the problem of student underachievement?

Be a Problem Solver

As the principal in this case, what steps would you take and/or what advice would you give to Mrs. Buckley?

Test Your Solution

In order to test your proposed plan of action for dealing with the problem presented at the end of the case, you and the class should create and role-play one or more of the following situations:

1. A continuation of the conference between Mrs. Buckley and the principal.
2. A conference between the principal and Randy's teacher(s).
3. A subsequent conference between the principal and Mr. Buckley, scheduled by the latter.
4. A meeting between the principal, the parents, Randy, and his teacher(s).

Investigate Further

1. What are the criteria for determining underachievement in your school?

2. What do the following groups in your school or school district believe to be the main reasons for student underachievement?
   a. Students.
   b. Parents.
   c. Teachers.
   d. Administration.
   e. Guidance counselors.
3. What programs does your school have for dealing with the problem of student underachievement?

11
WHAT SHOULD BE THE ROLE OF THE STUDENT NEWSPAPER?

It had been two weeks since the first issue of the Riverside student newspaper, "The Sword," had been published. Although the tempers in the guidance department had now cooled, the principal sensed that the emotional vibrations generated by the paper's attack on the counselors had still not completely subsided.

The principal himself had been rather upset about the article—a strong indictment of the guidance department for its alleged lack of interest and concern with the non-college bound students. However, since the principal felt that the facts and observations made in the news story were essentially true, he didn't think that he should censor or criticize the student editors—in spite of strong pressures from the counselors that he do so. When they came to him complaining about the newspaper article, he conceded that the students should have used more tact and diplomacy, but the counselors were not easily mollified, and it was clear that they were going to be unhappy for some time.

Although the school newspaper had become more and more outspoken in recent times, it had never before attacked any department or made editorial comment about educational or professional matters. In the past, "The Sword" had primarily confined itself to reporting on social activities, athletics, student personalities, clubs, or specific subjects in the curriculum. It had occasionally included articles on abortion, militarism in America, and other social issues, but in general, the principal had been pleased with the content. He felt fortunate that "The Sword" was not like some of those school papers—particulary of the underground variety—that spent all of their time on either social issues or attacks on the school itself.

In fact, the principal could recall only one other article that might have been considered critical, and in that instance, the criticism had been directed toward the school prom. At the time he hadn't been very happy about it, but he had overlooked the article, hoping that there would not be a recurrence.

This year, though, it appeared that the principal might face a troublesome situation if the first issue of the student newspaper was any harbinger of things to come. The editorial board was now composed of students who were bright and very independent, and they would not be easy to deal with. The principal had already decided—contrary to the recommendations of his assistant principal and the guidance department—that he would ignore the tenor of the first edition. He preferred to avoid a conflict with the student editors and the journalism advisor, all of whom had strong feelings about adult interference. He also hoped that things would settle down and the paper would become more occupied with student-oriented activities. Now, as he thought about that decision, the principal hoped fervently that it had been the right one.

On Friday the second issue of "The Sword" was distributed in classes during the last five minutes of the school day. Normally the teachers looked over the paper before passing it out to the students, but this Friday there was no such opportunity, since the paper arrived late. Immediately after the papers were handed out, the dismissal bell rang and the students flocked out of the classrooms, reading and chattering on the way to their lockers. With few exceptions, the teachers

Editorial

Although it is early in the year, we are already beginning to develop serious doubts about the commitment of this school to its students. Why is it so difficult to find teachers immediately after school for a conference and nearly impossible to locate a teacher or counselor *after* four o'clock? Why is it so difficult to secure advisors or chaperones for some of the extra-curricular activities which take place after four o'clock?

We believe that we have the answers to these questions. It is because the majority of the faculty, on any given day, is down at the faculty room having coffee within five minutes after the dismissal bell rings. It is also because at four o'clock sharp, the faculty in this school, with few exceptions, go scurrying out to their cars to leave—as though somehow their responsibilities and the needs of their students end promptly at four.

We recognize that, according to teachers' contracts, they are legally obliged to stay at school only one-half hour after all classes are dismissed. But what about their professional obligation and their commitment to being available to students?

Are teachers, counselors, and librarians *only* clock-watchers, or are they really—as they frequently claim—professionals? The term "professional" means to us that they should be readily available to the people who really need them—and *not* just on their own terms.

The question we would like to pose for our faculty is this: are you prepared to become professionals and give yourselves totally to students, or will you continue to function only on an "8:00 to 3:30" basis, to the detriment of education in this school?

headed down to the faculty room for their after-school cup of coffee.

As several of the teachers in the faculty room began to read "The Sword," one of them swore and directed the attention of the others in the room to the student editorial on the paper's second page.

As the teacher finished reading the editorial aloud, there was considerable muttering and complaining from the other people in the room. Everyone was upset about the paper's criticism, although a few teachers silently conceded to themselves that its main thrust was accurate. Someone suggested that the administration should immediately take disciplinary action against the student editor and the newspaper staff, and most of those in the room seemed to agree that such a step would be the least that should be done. A counselor proposed that in the future all editorials and newspaper articles should be screened by a faculty committee prior to publication. The counselor's suggestion was viewed by a few faculty members as representing censorship and an extra burden on the faculty, but many of the teachers felt that the administration, or someone else with authority, should pass judgment on the contents of the newspaper before it was approved for publication. Obviously no one had carefully examined the current issue in advance.

Finally the guidance director volunteered to go see the principal and apprise him of how most of the faculty felt about the student newspaper. No one could predict how the principal would respond to the editorial, but the teachers were hopeful that he would be as concerned as they were. As one of them put it, "First the guidance department and now the teachers. The next attack could easily be on the administration!"

SUGGESTED LEARNING ACTIVITIES

Analyze the Case

1. What is your assessment of the concept held by the principal about the role of the student newspaper in this school?
2. If you had been the principal in this situation, how would you have responded differently, if at all, from the way that the principal in this case did to the counselor's complaint about the article in the student newspaper criticizing the guidance department?
3. At what point would you have taken action to either change the role of the student newspaper or prepare the other members of the school community for a more critical paper? What is the specific nature of the action which you think should have been taken?
4. Assume that the editorial on page two of the second issue of "The Sword" contained charges which were accurate.
   (a) Do you think that the student paper has a right to print this kind of an editorial?
   (b) What action, if any, do you think the principal should take in regard to the conditions described in the editorial?

Discuss the Larger Issues

1. What should be the role of the student newspaper in the school? Should it be permitted to criticize and expose groups and/or individuals associated with the school? What might be the ramifications of such criticism? Where should the line be drawn on what may be printed in the student newspaper?
2. Who should determine what is published in the student newspaper? What role, if any, should the administration play? The faculty advisor to the newspaper? The faculty as a group? The students?
3. What is the best way to ensure that the policies and procedures established for the operation of the newspaper, whatever they may be, are followed by all concerned?

Be a Problem Solver

In this case the criticism of the student newspaper has offended the faculty. They have decided to send a representative to the principal to inform him of their feelings and persuade him to take action to prevent future articles of this nature from being printed. If you were the principal, how would you handle this situation?

Test Your Solution

In order to assess the strengths or weaknesses of your proposed solution, you and your class should create and role-play one or more of the following situations:

1. A conference between the guidance director and the principal.
2. A conference between the principal and the newspaper advisor.
3. A meeting between the principal and the student editorial board.
4. Any other situation which would provide feedback on the strengths or weaknesses of your proposed solution.

Investigate Further

1. What are the *legal* rights and obligations of the student newspaper in your school?

2. What is the school board and administration policy in your district on what the student newspaper can or cannot print?
3. If the editorial presented in this case appeared in the student newspaper at your school, and the observations of the student editor(s) were true, how would the following groups react:
   (a) Teachers?
   (b) Administrators?
   (c) Central office?
   (d) Parents?

12
A COMPLEX DISCIPLINE PROBLEM

After the vice-principal concluded his telephone conversation with Mrs. Richardson about her daughter Cindy's attendance problems, he started to leave his office to go down to the faculty room for coffee. As he went out the door, he felt a surge of irritation as he confronted Billy Cunningham, no stranger to the vice-principal's premises. The boy explained that Mrs. Blackman had kicked him out of class. Should he wait in the outer office?

The vice-principal had really been looking forward to a few moments of relaxation in the faculty lounge and didn't feel in the mood for talking with Billy Cunningham, but as he weighed the alternatives, he decided that he might as well take care of the boy now.

Frowning, the vice-principal directed Billy toward the inner office and sighed as he remembered his earlier contacts with the student. Billy had been sent to the vice-principal's office a number of times in the past and on at least two other occasions this semester, usually for attendance and disciplinary reasons. The boy was frequently absent or tardy, and he had been sent to the office previously by Mrs. Blackman for talking back to her.

Billy did poorly in school and his grades were usually low. His family had limited education and both of his parents worked. They had been called to the school for conferences several times, and although they seemed interested in their son's welfare, they were apparently unable to exercise any control over him.

The vice-principal knew that he hadn't been very successful in working with Billy in the past, and he wondered what kind of luck he would have this time. Obviously, it wasn't going to be easy to square this kid away.

In response to the vice-principal's questioning, Billy explained with a shrug that Mrs. Blackman had always "had it in" for him. Today, when he was trying to find out an assignment from someone, she had chewed him out for fooling around in class. He had tried to establish his innocence, but the teacher became angry, accused him of back talk, and told him to get out.

The vice-principal listened carefully to the student's explanation and tried to pin down or expose inconsistencies, but Billy stuck to his story. Recognizing that it would be necessary to talk with Mrs. Blackman, the vice-principal told Billy to wait in the outer office for a few minutes while he went to see the teacher.

When the vice-principal knocked on the door to Mrs. Blackman's classroom, she responded as though she had been expecting him. They discussed the incident in the hallway, and Mrs. Blackman related that Billy had been persistently inattentive and was distracting other students. When she had directed him to quit bothering the people sitting around him and to start paying attention to what was going on in class, he started to argue with her, claiming that he hadn't done anything wrong and that she was always picking on him. She had told Billy that she would be glad to discuss it with him later, but he had continued to argue, so she finally just sent him to the office.

The vice-principal was momentarily stymied. The two stories were obviously in conflict. He decided not to mention the discrepancies to the teacher, but told her that he would talk to Billy.

Walking back down the corridor to the office, he tried to evaluate what he had heard. Although he leaned towards accepting Mrs. Blackman's version of what had happened, he couldn't be sure. The vice-principal had occasionally heard parents complain that Mrs. Blackman was too strict and rigid in her expectations for student behavior. It was possible that Billy, annoying as he might be, was simply unfortunate in drawing the teacher's ire, without actually being responsible for disrupting the class. However, in light of the student's previous record, the vice-principal was hesitant to reject the teacher's explanation of what had happened in the classroom.

But even if the teacher was right, the vice-principal knew that he would have trouble improving Billy's behavior. The vice-principal had not experienced much success in the past in working with Billy, and he certainly didn't have any ideas now about how to proceed with the boy.

SUGGESTED LEARNING ACTIVITIES

Analyze the Case

1. What personal and situational factors may be responsible for Billy's performance in school?
2. In what way, if any, would you have handled the conference with Billy Cunningham differently?
3. What aspects of the vice-principal's attitude toward both the student and the teacher may unconsciously influence his resolution of the discrepancies between the two stories and his final action in regard to either the student or the teacher?

Discuss the Larger Issues

1. To what extent is the school and its program responsible for student discipline problems?
2. What should be the role of the following individuals and groups in regard to preventing and dealing constructively with student discipline problems?
   a. The vice-principal.
   b. The principal.
   c. The teachers.
   d. The student body.
   e. Parents.
3. To what degree are current practices for preventing and dealing with student discipline problems effective? How could improvement be best achieved?

Be a Problem Solver

The vice-principal is faced with the fact that the story the student related to him and the story that the teacher told him are in conflict. He also still has Billy Cunningham in his office. If you were the vice-principal in this situation, what would you do? What assumptions are you making? Utilize appropriate administrative and social science concepts from Part I of the text in planning and implementing your approach.

Test Your Solution

To test your proposed plan of action for dealing with the problem presented at the end of the case, you and the class should create and role-play one or more of the following interactions:

1. A conference between the vice-principal and Billy Cunningham.
2. A conference between the vice-principal, Billy Cunningham, and Mrs. Blackman.

Investigate Further

1. What innovative approaches to preventing and dealing constructively with student discipline problems have been developed during the last several years?
2. What is the school board policy in your district for preventing and dealing constructively with student discipline problems?
3. What is the role of the following individuals or groups in your school or school district with regard to student discipline problems?
   a. The vice-principal.
   b. The principal.
   c. The teachers.
   d. The student body.
   e. Parents.

13

THE DROP-OUT PROBLEM (SIMULATION EXERCISE) BACKGROUND AND INSTRUCTIONS

You are to assume that the coordinator of research in your district has completed a study showing that the school district has a significant student drop-out problem. The school board has directed the building administrators and supervisors (of which you are one) to address the problem. In order to accomplish this objective, you (and the rest of the class) need to

1. Ask those questions of the coordinator of research (the instructor or group leader will play this role) that will elicit information shedding light on the nature of the problem.
2. Develop a set of recommendations for ameliorating the drop-out problem.
3. Present those recommendations in a simulation where several class members play the role of the superintendent's cabinet receiving your report.

Note to instructor or group leader: Since one of the main purposes of this exercise is to provide students with practice in asking relevant, incisive questions, no information is provided in the text about this district's drop-out problem, other than it is a significant one. The instructor may assume whatever characteristics of the problem he or she feels would be likely, given the background of students in the class.

14

STUDENT CAN'T TAKE PRESSURE ANY LONGER

Miss Edwards looked up from the paper she was correcting, scanning the room for what seemed like the umpteenth time, carefully looking for any unusual behavior as her students worked on their test. She supposed that she was being unnecessarily vigilant, but she knew that this test was very important to the students, and she felt that with so much riding on it, there might be efforts by some students to cheat.

The examination the students were laboring over was an end-of-the-year competency test to ascertain whether they had mastered certain skills deemed appropriate for that grade level. The school district had moved to competency testing recently because of a feeling shared by most administrators and teachers, as well as a large segment of the community, that students were not achieving as well as they should, and that there needed to be a tightening of standards. The district policy now required that students who did not achieve a certain level on the end-of-the-year competency test would be retained in the same grade for another year, unless they could pass the exam during summer school.

Most students had little reaction to the testing program, perhaps resigned to its inevitability, but a small group of students had vigorously protested the policy of keeping students back for a year. Their protests, however, were to no avail. The school board and administration had felt that something had to be done to improve academic standards.

As Miss Edwards tried to concentrate again on correcting her papers, she remembered how quiet the classroom had grown on the day she had announced the date of the examination and the subject matter that the test would cover. She had asked whether anyone had any questions about the examination, but no one had said anything. At the time, she was puzzled by their lack of responsiveness, but she knew today from the students' expressions that they were nervous about the test. She supposed that she would be worried too, if she were in a similar situation, and thanked her lucky stars that she wasn't.

Miss Edwards looked up from her papers and again scanned the room, checking on her students. As she looked around, she suddenly noticed that Tim Brown appeared to be looking at the answer sheet of the student to his left. She couldn't be certain, but it seemed as though Tim Brown was cheating. She knew that if she got up from her desk and walked around, her students would be alerted that she was looking for something unusual, so she remained at her desk and pretended to continue correcting papers. However, as she worked on her papers, she continued to view Tim. There seemed to be little question that the boy was cheating.

At the end of the examination period Miss Edwards asked Tim Brown to remain in the room, and she proceeded to compare his answers with those of the boy seated to his left. There could be no doubt: with only two exceptions, the answer sheets were identical. Obviously, Tim had copied most of his answers. However, when she confronted him with the evidence, he refused to admit his guilt.

Sensing that she would not be able to extract a confession, Miss Edwards told Tim that he would have to see the principal.

A short time later, Miss Edwards and Tim entered the principal's office, where Miss Edwards proceeded to explain to Mr. Matthews what had transpired. When Tim maintained only silence in response to the teacher's report, Mr. Matthews decided to interrogate the boy.

"Well, Tim, it appears as though you were caught in the act, weren't you?"

"No, I didn't do it."

"Then why were your answers almost exactly the same as the ones on the other answer sheet?"

"I don't know."

"You realize that if you don't tell us the truth, something very serious will happen to you. We already know that you cheated. You were observed copying someone else's answers, and we have evidence that you were cheating. If you lie to me, then you're committing another serious offense. Perhaps we need to give your parents a call about this matter."

Tim didn't say anything for a few moments, but then a tear escaped his downcast eyes. In a shaky voice he finally conceded that he may have cheated, but only because a number of the other students in the class were also cheating. Several students had managed to obtain a copy of the answer key and had been using it during the test.

The principal had heard a rumor just that morning that a teacher's answer key had been stolen, but the rumor had seemed farfetched, and no one on the staff had reported such a loss. Now he tried to press Tim Brown for more information.

"Who are these other students?"

Silence.

"You'd better tell me, because you know I'm going to find out sooner or later."

Silence.

Since Tim did not appear inclined to be cooperative, and it was nearly the end of the day, the principal told the boy that over the weekend he had better decide to come up with the names of the other students who had been cheating. Tim was also instructed to bring his parents to the principal's office when he returned to school on Monday. Mr. Matthews concluded the conference by saying that, as things stood now, Tim would probably be given a failing grade on the end-of-the-year competency test, although that decision *might* be changed if Tim would agree to identify the students who had the answer key.

Tim's expression was strained as he left the principal's office, and Miss Edwards could tell that he was shaken. She felt sorry for him because she knew from a previous conference with his parents that he would be in deep trouble when they found out about the matter. They were achievement-oriented people who set high standards for Tim. He generally worked very hard to meet those expectations, but because his ability was only average, his efforts were frequently disappointing to his parents. Tim's latest behavior would surely contribute further to their frustration.

After Tim had left, the principal questioned Miss Edwards a little about her perception of the other students who were taking the examination, but there wasn't much help she could give. Mr. Matthews instructed her to meet with him the first thing on Monday morning so they could map out a strategy for getting at the problem.

Perhaps before then, Tim would reveal the names of other students who had been cheating.

Miss Edwards left the principal's office and went to the faculty room for a cup of coffee. There she discussed what had happened with a colleague, Mrs. Bailey. Mrs. Bailey was not particularly surprised by the behavior of Tim or the other students and even contended that it was perfectly understandable, given the importance placed on passing the competency test. She felt that students were subjected to too much pressure by the testing program and by the policy of retaining students in the same grade if they did not do well on the end-of-the-year examination. "Besides," she observed, "a lot of people in our society cheat. I'm not condoning what Tim did, but look at the people who cheat on their income tax, pad their expense accounts, exceed posted speed limits, or cheat in other ways. For that matter, think about how many teachers "cheat" on their daily school arrival and departure times, or take "sick days" when they're just tired of coming to school. I wonder what kind of models we adults are providing for kids like Tim."

Miss Edwards disagreed with Mrs. Bailey, told her so, and then walked out of the faculty room feeling distressed. She was not looking forward to the weekend or the following Monday morning.

On Sunday there was a brief item in the city newspaper.

> Tim Brown, son of Dr. and Mrs. Lester Brown, 8415 Newcastle Road, was found unconscious in the basement of his home on Saturday. Nearby was found an empty bottle of amphetamines. He was rushed to City Hospital where his stomach was pumped, and he is now in satisfactory condition. A handwritten note found in the basement suggested a possible suicide attempt.

SUGGESTED LEARNING ACTIVITIES

Analyze the Case

1. What, if anything, should the teacher have done differently when she observed Tim Brown cheating?
2. Evaluate the principal's approach to Tim Brown. What administrative and/or social science concepts does he appear to be employing? Not employing?
3. What is your assessment of the arguments advanced by Mrs. Bailey?

Discuss the Larger Issues

1. Why do some students cheat and other students not cheat?
2. What can the school do about preventing student cheating? What should it do when it apprehends student cheaters?
3. What kinds of factors contribute to student suicides? What can the school do about these factors?

Be a Problem Solver

Assume that you are the principal in this case and you have just finished reading the newspaper article about Tim Brown. What would be your approach to dealing with this situation and the other problems mentioned in the case study? Utilize administrative and social science concepts from Part I of the text in the planning and implementation of your approach.

Test Your Solution

To test your proposed plan for dealing with the problems presented in this case, you and your colleagues should create and role-play one or more of the following situations:

1. A meeting between the principal and Tim Brown's parents.
2. A conference between the principal and Miss Edwards.
3. A conference between the principal, Miss Edwards, and Tim Brown.

Investigate Further

1. What is the attitude of students, teachers, administrators, and parents at your school toward student cheating?

2. How widespread is student cheating at your school? How reliable and valid are the data about the extent of cheating?
3. Ascertain your school or district's policy toward student cheating.
4. How significant a problem is student suicide in your school? How reliable and valid are the data about this problem? What, if anything, is the school doing about the possibility of student suicides?

15
AN ISSUE OF MORALS AND PRIORITIES

Eisenhower School had recently adopted a "language code" for its students. The principal, Mr. Goodfine, was a new administrator who had become increasingly concerned about the "gutter" language which a number of students were using. He recognized that many people in the society, particularly in certain subcultures, used that kind of language, but he felt the school had a responsibility to teach students to speak appropriately, and he wasn't going to permit the use of certain words in his school.

When the principal first mentioned the new language code at the faculty meeting, several of the teachers pressured him to identify specific words to which he objected. But he refused to let himself get boxed in on that point. He explained to the faculty that he believed the language code should not actually repeat the words that everyone knew were bad, but instead should be a simple statement of policy that would read:

> Any word of expression that a teacher or administrator feels is inappropriate for use in a school setting is prohibited. This includes, but is not limited to, profanity, obscenity, and language which tends to cast aspersions on someone's race, religion, or sex. First offense violations shall result in a conference with the administration; repeated violations could lead to suspension.

The school counselor was flabbergasted when she first heard the news about the language code policy. Obviously, some of the students used language which *she* wouldn't use, at least not in school, but she doubted whether a new language code was the answer. She also felt that it was a case of misdirected priorities.

The counselor believed, even though she had experienced trouble in convincing the principal, that the most serious problem facing the school was sexual promiscuity on the part of an increasing number of students. Girls and boys were both reaching puberty earlier than in the past and, as a result of this factor and a general lack of sex education in many homes, the number of pregnancies had increased greatly, along with abortions and other kinds of sexual problems.

She had tried to bring this situation to the attention of the principal, but he had taken the position that this was not a school problem. She found the principal's attitude medieval, but she didn't know what could be done about the matter. Perhaps she would talk with the vice-principal and see if he had any ideas.

SUGGESTED LEARNING ACTIVITIES

Analyze the Case

1. What factors did the principal seem to consider in deciding on the language code policy? Were there any factors that he apparently did not consider that could carry implications for the eventual success of the language code?
2. Analyze the language code, using concepts and principles of communication. What are its strengths and limitations? Could the message be strengthened in any way, and if so, how?
3. What kinds of values and priorities are reflected in the attitude of the principal toward the language problem versus his attitude toward the situation brought to his attention by the counselor? What are the

possible implications and ramifications of these values and priorities?

Discuss the Larger Issues

1. Should an administrator of a school attempt to establish the *moral* climate of the school? What factors may need to be considered?
2. To what extent should the school be concerned about the type of language students use? What, if anything, should the school do about the matter?
3. Can the school legally and effectively prohibit certain types of language usage? What factors might influence the school's effectiveness in this effort?
4. What is the role of the school in dealing with the types of problems reported by the counselor to the principal?

Be a Problem Solver

Assume that you are the vice-principal or the principal in this school. What kinds of situations and problems are you possibly going to be facing before too long? What do you propose to do about those matters? What administrative and/or social science concepts should you be considering and utilizing in your role as problem solver?

Test Your Solution

In order to test our plan of action for dealing with the problem(s) presented in the case, you and your colleagues should create and role-play one or more of the following situations:

1. A conference between the counselor and the vice-principal.
2. A discipline hearing involving a student who called another student "bitch." (The student was referred to the assistant principal by a teacher.)
3. A telephone call from a parent who objects to the language code policy.
4. A rumor that one of the students is pregnant and is planning an abortion, passed on to the principal by another mother.

Investigate Further

1. What is your school's or district's formal or informal policy on student language? Is the policy enforced? How successful is it?
2. To what extent is your school experiencing problems similar to those referred to by the counselor in the case? How reliable and valid is the information the school possesses about these problems?
3. What is your school doing about the types of problems referred to by the counselor in the case? What is the attitude of the administration, faculty, parents, and the student body toward these problems?

11 ADMINISTRATOR-STAFF RELATIONSHIPS

Although the overall relationship between school administrators and their staffs has historically passed through periods of tranquility and crisis, the advent of collective bargaining and teacher militancy in the 1960s complicated that relationship and made it increasingly difficult. Prior to collective bargaining, the relationship between many school administrators and their staffs was often paternalistic. In most situations the administrator had a choice of whether or not to consider teachers' grievances, consult with them about work assignments, or involve them in school decision making, and all too often—at least, according to teachers' perceptions—the administrator chose not to do so.

The advent of collective bargaining and teacher militancy markedly changed the nature of the relationship between the administrator and the staff. The introduction of collective bargaining and the resultant master contract have meant that in most situations, an administrator must consider teacher grievances and must consult with teachers regarding working conditions and other matters affecting their welfare.

It should be emphasized that collective bargaining and the master contract have neither eliminated the authority of the administrator nor removed the person in that position as head of the school or school district. However, administrators need to recognize that they can no longer act unilaterally on decisions which may affect teachers' welfare without encountering difficulty; they will now, in most situations, need to administer the school with the assistance of faculty input and consultation.

Although in recent years most school administrators have adapted to the new realities of working with a professional staff, even those administrators with good intentions and a collaborative leadership style may occasionally run into difficulty with a teacher or staff member who, for whatever the reason, sees things differently from the administrator.

The cases presented on the following pages do not represent typical teachers, faculties, or administrators. The vast majority of school personnel are friendly, dedicated, hardworking, and competent people. However, these types of individuals are not the ones likely to cause problems; they don't provide the kind of case study material that gives the reader the best opportunity to use the concepts in Part I of the text and become an effective problem solver. Consequently, the case studies presented in this chapter are problem-oriented. Although the problems may not be "typical," they do represent realistic situations which could confront any administrator. And, with regard to the first case on teacher selection, most administrators will need to carry out this task at one time or another in their careers.

BACKGROUND READING

For the reader who would like to develop further background and understanding of the problems and issues presented in this chapter, a list of readings is provided below:

Joseph Blase and Peggy C. Kirby, *Bringing Out the Best in Teachers: What Effective Principals Do,* Newbury Park, CA: Corwin Press, 1991.
James S. Cangelosi, *Evaluating Classroom Instruction,* White Plains, NY: Longman, 1991.
Larry Frase (Ed.), *Teacher Compensation and Motivation,* Lancaster, PA: Technomic Publishing Company, 1992.
Richard A. Gorton and Gail Thierbach-Schneider, "Staff Recruitment, Selection, Induction," and "Administrator/Staff Relations" in *School-Based Leadership: Challenges and Opportunities,* 3rd ed., Dubuque, IA: Wm. C. Brown Publishers, 1991, 188–216, 244–282.
Susan M. Johnson, *Teachers at Work: Achieving Success in Our Schools,* (New York: Basic Books, 1990).
Sheila Moran, "Schools and the Beginning Teacher," *Phi Delta Kappan* (November, 1991), 210–213.

16
TEACHER SELECTION

It was late spring, and the principal was reviewing with a central office supervisor the applications received for a teaching position to be available at Silver Spring School in the fall. The position had opened after Brent Thomas, a teacher who had been at the school for three years, had decided to move out of the state and had returned unsigned the contract that had been offered to him for the following year.

Silver Spring School served a rather heterogeneous student clientele, characterized by a wide range of student backgrounds, interests, and ability and achievement levels. The school was experimenting with team teaching, and since Mr. Thomas was a member of one of the teams, the principal was particularly sorry to see him leave. He felt that it was very important that a good replacement be secured.

After looking over a number of applicants' placement papers, the principal and the central office supervisor had narrowed their choice to two candidates: Mr. James Timm and Ms. Sylvia Goldstein. Each candidate's folder contained an application form providing general background information and, in addition, a set of recommendations.

Background Information on Mr. Timm

Mr. James Timm was 28 years old, married, and the father of two children. He had attended a state university and had graduated with a B.A. He had completed six hours of course work beyond his bachelor's degree. There was no transcript, but his grade point average was listed at 3.0. His application form stated that his hobbies were hunting, fishing, golfing, and his family. He had taught for five years in another school district. Two rating forms were in Mr. Timm's folder, one completed by his principal and the other one by a colleague.

Background Information on Ms. Goldstein

Ms. Sylvia Goldstein's application stated that she was 25 years old and single. She had attended a private college and had graduated with a B.A. She had taught for two years and had nearly completed all of the requirements for a master's degree in her subject field. Her undergraduate grade point average had been 3.7, and her graduate grade point average was 3.6. Reading was the only hobby that she had listed.

Two rating forms were also in Ms. Goldstein's folder, one completed by her principal and the other by an assistant superintendent.

After the principal of Silver Spring School and the central office supervisor had re-examined all the data on Mr. Timm and Ms. Goldstein, there were still a number of issues about each candidate that needed to be clarified. Before that could be accomplished, however, the two candidates

question was ''Which of the two should be interviewed first?'' Once that was decided, the administrators would have to give some thought to the areas that were most important to explore further with each candidate, as well as some thought to the interview techniques and questions that should be employed to secure the kinds of information necessary for reaching a final decision with respect to filling the vacancy.

With those points in mind, the principal and the central office supervisor continued their discussion and scrutiny of the candidates' papers.

UNIVERSITY PLACEMENT SERVICE

Please give your evaluation of MR. JAMES TIMM who has registered with our teacher placement service. All information will be kept in strict confidence.

Check one of the five categories for each of the items	Poor			Below Average			Average			Above Average			Excellent		
1. Teaching techniques									X						
2. Relationships with students									X						
3. Relationships with teachers												X			
4. Relationships with parents											X				
5. Relationships with administration											X				
6. Character									X						
7. Health												X			
8. Professional attitude									X						
9. Discipline								X							
10. Skill in motivation								X							
11. Personality									X						
12. Knowledge of subject									X						
13. Promptness and thoroughness												X			
14. Appearance												X			
15. Tactfulness										X					
16. Self-control									X						
17. Loyalty										X					
18. Outlook on life (enthusiasm)												X			
19. Overall Rating											X				

20. General Comments. Please elaborate on your impression of the applicant, indicating his/her general strengths and weaknesses.

Mr. Timm has been with us for five years. We know of his desire to teach elsewhere and we respect his wishes. We appreciate what he has done for us the past five years, and we hate to lose him.

Signature *Harold Brown* Position: Principal

UNIVERSITY PLACEMENT SERVICE

Please give your evaluation of MR. JAMES TIMM who has registered with our teacher placement service. All information will be kept in strict confidence.

Check one of the five categories for each of the items	Poor			Below Average			Average			Above Average			Excellent		
1. Teaching techniques												X			
2. Relationships with students												X			
3. Relationships with teachers															X
4. Relationships with parents												X			
5. Relationships with administration												X			
6. Character													X		
7. Health												X			
8. Professional attitude													X		
9. Discipline												X			
10. Skill in motivation												X			
11. Personality												X			
12. Knowledge of subject															X
13. Promptness and thoroughness													X		
14. Appearance												X			
15. Tactfulness												X			
16. Self-control												X			
17. Loyalty													X		
18. Outlook on life (enthusiasm)													X		
19. Overall Rating													X		

20. General Comments. Please elaborate on your impression of the applicant, indicating his/her general strengths and weaknesses.

A very fine teacher.

Signature *Bob Peters* Position: Fellow Teacher

UNIVERSITY PLACEMENT SERVICE

Please give your evaluation of MS. SYLVIA GOLDSTEIN who has registered with our teacher placement service. All information will be kept in strict confidence.

Check one of the five categories for each of the items	Poor			Below Average			Average			Above Average			Excellent		
1. Teaching techniques														X	
2. Relationships with students												X			
3. Relationships with teachers										X					
4. Relationships with parents								X							
5. Relationships with administration								X							
6. Character											X				
7. Health													X		
8. Professional attitude									X						
9. Discipline														X	
10. Skill in motivation														X	
11. Personality									X						
12. Knowledge of subject														X	
13. Promptness and thoroughness									X						
14. Appearance										X					
15. Tactfulness							X								
16. Self-control							X								
17. Loyalty									X						
18. Outlook on life (enthusiasm)										X					
19. Overall Rating										X					

20. General Comments. Please elaborate on your impression of the applicant, indicating his/her general strengths and weaknesses.

No comment.

Signature *Merle Robbins* Position: Principal

UNIVERSITY PLACEMENT SERVICE

Please give your evaluation of MS. SYLVIA GOLDSTEIN who has registered with our teacher placement service. All information will be kept in strict confidence.

Check one of the five categories for each of the items	Poor			Below Average			Average			Above Average			Excellent		
1. Teaching techniques														X	
2. Relationships with students													X		
3. Relationships with teachers													X		
4. Relationships with parents											X				
5. Relationships with administration								X							
6. Character											X				
7. Health												X			
8. Professional attitude										X					
9. Discipline														X	
10. Skill in motivation														X	
11. Personality										X					
12. Knowledge of subject														X	
13. Promptness and thoroughness														X	
14. Appearance									X						
15. Tactfulness								X							
16. Self-control								X							
17. Loyalty														X	
18. Outlook on life (enthusiasm)														X	
19. Overall Rating												X			

20. General Comments. Please elaborate on your impression of the applicant, indicating his/her general strengths and weaknesses.

Sylvia is an excellent teacher. She has had some difficulty because she doesn't "suffer fools" easily. However, I would sure hate to lose her!

Signature Bruce Thompto Position: Ass't Superintendent

SUGGESTED LEARNING ACTIVITIES

(The nature of the vacancy in this case is intentionally left for the reader to specify, e.g., grade level, subject, etc.)

Analyze the Case

1. On the basis of the information provided in the case, what do you see as the main strengths and limitations of each candidate?
2. Why might the principal and the central office supervisor disagree in their evaluations of the candidates or on the criteria that should be applied in the selection of a teacher to fill the vacancy?
3. What are the areas that you think should be explored further with Mr. Timm and Ms. Goldstein in an interview?

Discuss the Larger Issues

1. What are the strengths and limitations of the kinds of information (e.g., rating scales, application forms, etc.) that are typically included in the papers of applicants for a vacancy?
2. What are the main elements of the criteria which an administrator should use in selecting a teacher? What should these criteria be based on? Which aspects of the criteria should receive top priority?
3. Why is it difficult to be completely objective in the process of selecting a teacher? What factors may interfere with the objectivity of the process?
4. Who should be involved in the recruitment, selection, and assignment of teachers, and what role should each individual or group play?

Be a Problem Solver

A vacancy exists at Silver Spring School, and the field of applicants has been narrowed to two candidates. If you were the principal or the central office supervisor, which candidate would you invite for the first interview, and what interview techniques and questions would you employ with each candidate to secure the kinds of information needed in order to make a good decision with regard to selecting one of the applicants?

Test Your Solution

To test your proposed plan of action for dealing with the problem described previously, you and the class should create and role-play one or more of the following situations:

1. Continue the discussion between the principal and the central office supervisor, focusing on the identification of interview techniques and questions which will be used in the interviews with both candidates.
2. Carry out interviews between the principal, the central office supervisor, and each candidate.

Investigate Further

1. What are the procedures utilized by your school district in the recruitment, selection, and assignment of teachers?
2. What criteria are used by your district in the selection of teachers? What are the criteria based on?
3. How does your district ascertain whether its current program of teacher recruitment, selection, and assignment is effective?

17
PROBLEMS OF A BEGINNING TEACHER

As he walked from the parking lot to the school building, the principal of Mitchell School noticed Mrs. Carter, the nurse, who was heading in the same direction. She smiled and waited for him, and they discussed the weather as they entered the building. Then, as the principal started to enter his office, Mrs. Carter followed him, asking whether he might have time after school to talk with her about a problem. He nodded and suggested that they could take a few minutes to talk before school started, but Mrs. Carter declined, saying that she would rather wait until after school when there would be more time.

After the nurse left the principal's office, he wondered to himself what the nature of her problem might be. She had been serving as school nurse at Mitchell School for six or seven years, and usually spent two or three days each week in the building, checking on absences, screening the students for visual and hearing defects, and so forth. Whatever her difficulty was, he hoped that it wasn't too serious.

At 3:30 that afternoon, Mrs. Carter entered the principal's office. He greeted her and tried to put her at ease; but when he asked how he could help her, she hesitated. Finally, she explained that she would like to talk with him in confidence about Miss Hiller, the new math teacher who had just graduated last spring from college and had begun teaching at Mitchell School this fall.

From a recent conversation with Miss Hiller, Mrs. Carter had learned that the new teacher was becoming very discouraged and disillusioned. For example, she had admitted that she didn't seem to know how to motivate her students, and said that they didn't appear to be very interested in what she was teaching. They were often inattentive, and Miss Hiller was worried not only about their failure to learn what she was presenting, but about her own inability to develop a good, positive relationship with them. She was rather shy and quiet by nature, but it bothered her that the students didn't seem to like her.

Mrs. Carter went on to say that Miss Hiller had confided that she was also experiencing problems with discipline. The students just didn't seem to respond to her attempts to keep order in the classroom. The noise level was usually high, and there were two boys, in particular, who were about ready to drive her "up the walls."

Finally, and perhaps most shattering to the new teacher's morale, was Miss Hiller's feeling that the other teachers on the staff did not accept her. Most of the teachers had taught at the school in previous years and had already established relationships with one another. The faculty was divided into cliques, and Mrs. Carter knew for a fact that it was difficult for any newcomer to gain acceptance. She had personally experienced trouble along that line, but she was older and more self-possessed, so she hadn't let their reaction bother her. Besides, she was only at Mitchell School part-time anyway. However, she could see how the situation would be difficult for a shy, sensitive girl like Miss Hiller, who didn't have much self-confidence.

The principal was troubled to hear about the new teacher's problems and inwardly blamed himself for not being more perceptive about her difficulties. Still, she had always seemed rather aloof to him, and he had assumed that she was quite self-sufficient. He asked Mrs. Carter whether Miss Hiller had asked anyone for help. Why hadn't the teacher herself come to him with her problems?

Mrs. Carter believed that Miss Hiller's reluctance to seek help could be attributed to her shyness and to the fact that the teacher probably didn't want to admit that she was having difficulties. It was only by chance that Mrs. Carter had found out anything. She had gone into Miss Hiller's classroom to discuss a student's health problem and had discovered the teacher sitting at her desk, crying. The nurse had encouraged her to talk about her problems; otherwise the teacher would never have opened up to her. In fact, Mrs. Carter was sure that Miss Hiller would be horrified to know that the principal had even been told about the situation.

The only reason Mrs. Carter had finally decided to relate the incident to the principal was her conviction that she felt Miss Hiller desperately needed help. Since Mrs. Carter was just a nurse and not really a member of the faculty, she didn't feel adequate to provide advice or assistance. But surely there must be something that the principal could do before that poor young girl completely lost hope in her future as a teacher!

SUGGESTED LEARNING ACTIVITIES

Analyze the Case

1. What circumstances and psychological factors will make it particularly difficult for the principal to discuss Miss Hiller's problems with her?
2. What situational barriers will need to be overcome before Miss Hiller can feel more accepted in the school?
3. Why will the nurse's friendship with Miss Hiller probably be of little help in integrating the teacher into the social structure of the school?
4. How can the principal best ascertain to a greater extent the teacher's classroom problems without upsetting her?

Discuss the Larger Issues

1. What should be the role of the principal in helping the beginning teacher to become accepted in the school and in the community?
2. What type of inservice procedures should be designed to help the inexperienced teacher resolve classroom problems successfully?

Be a Problem Solver

The school nurse has just related to the principal, in confidence, the difficulties being experienced by a new, inexperienced teacher. Recognizing that Miss Hiller is an extremely shy, sensitive person, what would you do, if you were principal, to help resolve her problem? Utilize appropriate administrative and social science concepts in planning and implementing your approach.

Test Your Solution

In order to test your proposed plan of action for dealing with the problem presented at the end of the case, you and your class should create and role-play one or more of the following situations:

1. A continuation of the conference between the principal and the nurse.
2. A conference between the principal and Miss Hiller.
3. A faculty meeting.

Investigate Further

1. What procedures, formal or informal, does your school have that facilitate the acceptance of new teachers by students and other teachers?
2. What do the new teachers in your school believe to be the most difficult aspects of being in a first-year teaching situation?

18
WHO NEEDS LESSON PLANS?

The principal was disturbed. This was the second time this quarter that Bill Robertson had failed to turn in his lesson plans to the school office. Last year Bill had occasionally neglected to hand in his written plans, but the principal had chalked it up to forgetfulness. Now a pattern of negligence appeared to be developing, and the principal decided he'd better call the matter to the teacher's attention.

The following day the principal stopped Bill in the hall and asked whether he was experiencing any problems in submitting his lesson plans. To the principal's amazement, Bill offered neither excuse nor apology, but launched immediately into an attack on the rationale behind lesson plans. The teacher made it quite clear that he did not believe in behavioral objectives, he already knew what he planned to do without writing it down, he found writing lesson plans to be a time-consuming activity, and nothing ever seemed to be done with them.

Bill conceded that perhaps a written lesson plan could be of help to a substitute teacher, but he complained that the quality of substitutes in the district was so poor that they either couldn't or wouldn't follow the plans anyway. He also argued that a daily or even a weekly lesson plan placed a straitjacket on a teacher and restricted classroom activities from arising spontaneously in response to the needs of the students. Bill contended that lesson plans make it difficult, if not impossible, to develop a more creative approach to teaching.

The principal was taken aback by the severity of Bill's denunciation of lesson plans and decided that the hallway was not the place to pursue the issue. He told Bill that he didn't have time to discuss the matter further and that the teacher should stop in at the office after school for a conference.

Later the principal sat at his desk, examining the lesson plan form that he himself had designed only last year.

Daily Lesson Plan

Name ________ Subject ________ Date _____

1. *Objectives*	(Specify in behavioral terms what you and the students are trying to achieve.)
2. *Plan of Action*	(Specify how you are going to achieve your objectives; include proposed teaching methods, materials, and audio-visual aids.)
3. *Evaluation*	(State the means by which you are going to ascertain the extent to which you and the students have achieved or have made progress toward your goals.)

The longer the principal studied the form, the less rational seemed Bill's objections. The principal believed that many of the problems in education stemmed from the fact that too few teachers took the time to think through what they were trying to achieve, other than covering the next five pages. If a teacher could not specify the type of behavior which would indicate that his students had actually learned a concept or skill, then how could he be sure whether any learning had really taken place?

It seemed to the principal that writing lesson plans consisted of no more than organizing logically one's thoughts on paper as to *what* should be achieved, *how* it should be achieved, and how to tell *whether* it had been achieved. He was aware that written lesson plans had never been very popular with teachers, but he had seldom encountered overt resistance and, over the years, teachers had submitted them on a regular basis. It was true that thorough planning was time-consuming, particularly for individuals who had trouble organizing their thoughts in a systematic manner. But it wasn't the writing that took so much time; rather it was the hard work that a teacher had to invest in the construction of a good lesson. Nevertheless, the principal believed that this was not an adequate reason to discard the requirement of lesson plans.

He also felt that Bill's characterization of lesson plans as a "straightjacket" was greatly exaggerated. There was no school requirement binding a teacher to the fulfillment of the daily plan. The principal wondered whether the spontaneous teaching and learning that Bill had referred to might, in some instances, only reflect last-minute, "seat of the pants" planning. As far as the principal could tell from his own observations, spontaneity did not guarantee quality in teaching.

However, Bill's contention that lesson plans were not used by the office was one point that bothered the principal. The procedure was established that teachers would submit a copy of their plans each Monday to the principal's office. From time to time, he looked through the lesson plans, and he had occasionally scheduled a meeting with a teacher for the specific purpose of discussing some aspects of a class procedure or project. But for the most part, the principal had to agree that there wasn't much done with the teachers' plans. The principal could see, as he thought more about the situation, that this was one dimension of the lesson plan program that was in need of improvement. However, he rejected the idea that this need for improvement constituted a sufficient or reasonable excuse for Bill Robertson's failure to submit his lesson plans.

The principal did not look forward to another meeting with Bill on the subject of lesson plans. Bill was not an easy person to talk to on any matter. He was a tough, argumentative teacher who had become rather critical of administrators in the last few years. He had led the fight for a stronger teachers' organization in the district and was now the teacher representative for the building—not the kind of person that an administrator would want to antagonize. And yet the principal realized that he could not ignore Bill's lack of cooperation. There was a good possibility that the teacher was using this method to challenge the whole idea of required written lesson plans and if he were successful, it wouldn't be long before others would be following his example.

But how should Bill be approached, the principal wondered, and what if the teacher should flatly refuse to comply? Bill was popular among the faculty, and it was likely that many of the other teachers would back him if any kind of confrontation developed. Would it be possible to avoid a clash and yet preserve the planning process necessary for quality teaching? As far as the principal could see, it was an issue that could not be avoided.

SUGGESTED LEARNING ACTIVITIES

Analyze the Case

1. What is your evaluation of the steps taken by the principal in regard to Bill Robertson? How would you have acted differently?
2. What is your assessment of the teacher's objections to written lesson plans? What factors may be influencing the principal's objectivity in assessing Bill's reaction to lesson planning?
3. What do you feel are the main strengths and weaknesses of the lesson plan form which the principal designed? What is your evaluation of the arguments he sets forth for lesson planning?

Discuss the Larger Issues

1. Should written lesson plans be required? Should they be daily, weekly, monthly?
2. How should lesson plans be used?
3. What responsibilities do administrators and supervisors have for improving the effectiveness and value of teacher prepared lesson plans?

Be a Problem Solver

The principal has scheduled a meeting with Bill Robertson after school to discuss the teacher's failure to submit lesson plans. Knowing the circumstances described in the case, how would you—if you were the principal—handle the teacher?

Test Your Solution

In order to test your proposed plan of action for dealing with the problem presented at the end of the case, you and your class should create and role-play one or more of the following situations:

1. A conference between the principal and Bill Robertson.
2. A faculty meeting requested by the teachers.
3. Any other situation that might provide feedback on strengths and weaknesses of your proposed situation.

Investigate Further

1. What is the lesson plan format and policy in your district?
2. What use is made of lesson plans in your district?
3. How do the following groups in your district feel about required lesson plans?
   a. Building principals?
   b. Department heads?
   c. Teachers?
   d. Central office administration?

19
CONFLICT OVER TEACHER CITIZENSHIP RIGHTS

As the telephone rang at 6 A.M. interrupting his sleep, the superintendent groped for the receiver, longing for the luxury of an unlisted number. Still half-asleep, he answered the phone, only to be startled by a barrage of questions from a reporter calling for a local T.V. station. What did the superintendent think about the disturbance over the welfare budget cuts that had broken up the county supervisors' meeting last night at the courthouse? Was he personally opposed to the action that had been taken by the supervisors?

Rather irritably, the superintendent pointed out that the welfare department did not fall within the jurisdiction of the superintendent of schools and suggested that the reporter direct his questions to the head of the welfare department.

But the reporter persisted. Didn't the superintendent have anything to say about Sara Conklin, the teacher at Lincoln School, who had participated in the demonstration and had to be forcibly removed from the meeting?

"Not at this time," the superintendent replied curtly, hanging up the phone. A teacher involved in a violent demonstration? Well, he could expect a lot of telephone calls this morning at the office.

By the time he arrived at his office an hour later, the morning newspaper had been delivered. As he read the lengthy front page account of the disturbance, he wondered how long it would take before he would begin to hear from the conservative element of the community demanding that Ms. Conklin be fired. He decided that he'd better call her principal.

The principal at Lincoln School had already heard the news on the radio about the courthouse disruption involving Sara Conklin, and he agreed with the superintendent that it would be a good idea to relieve her of all teaching responsibilities until further notice. If Ms. Conklin returned to her classroom that morning and her classes proceeded smoothly, the school might have a more difficult time taking further action, should it prove necessary to do so because of community complaints about her out-of-school activities. The superintendent also suggested that the principal talk with Ms. Conklin if she came to school and, on the basis of that discussion, prepare a recommendation that could be considered by the superintendent and several of the school board members when they conferred informally the next day.

When Ms. Conklin arrived at Lincoln School shortly before classes began that morning, the principal immediately called her into his office. He informed her that she had been identified on several radio and television news reports as one of the protestors who had participated in the disturbance at the courthouse the preceding evening. He further mentioned that she had been described as a teacher at Lincoln School, which would cause a lot of parents to wonder about the example she was setting for her students. He indicated that he seriously questioned whether participation in a demonstration or protest—particularly one in which the participants had to be forcibly removed from the meeting—was an appropriate activity for a professional teacher. Was there any rational explanation that she could offer for her behavior last night?

The teacher appeared tired, but sparks blazed in her eyes as she exclaimed, "Why in the world should I have to give *you* any explanation about my personal, out-of-school activities? As long as I carry out my responsibilities here at school, you have absolutely no basis for criticizing me! Whatever I do during the rest of my time is *my* business and nobody else's."

The principal started to reply, but Miss Conklin plunged on in a sudden torrent of emotion. "You talk about setting an example for kids. Well, I happen to believe that a teacher has the responsibility to set an example in ways other than showing the traditional virtues of promptness and neatness. I happen to think that it's important to try to teach more than just what's written between the covers of a book. I want to show these kids that there are certain things in life that are important enough to go all out for, to lay your job on the line for. Or maybe even your career! But it seems to me that all *you* can think about is how this minor episode might reflect unfavorably on the school or on you, personally. Are you afraid that people might think you don't have your teachers completely under control? If I had my way, *more* of the teachers in this school would be taking a hard look at the significant issues facing society and doing something about them. Didn't you ever hear that all that is needed for evil to flourish is for good men to do nothing?''

The principal waited until the teacher paused to take a breath, and then he countered with his own views. ''I'm not questioning your motivation, Sara, but there are certainly more proper channels for changing society: legal action, persuasion, political power. Other teachers in this district have equally strong convictions about improving conditions for the poor, but they don't go around getting themselves forcibly ejected from meetings! Instead, they write letters to their representatives and to the communications media, trying to peacefully influence public opinion. They participate in voluntary programs to try to clean up the city and to help kids read. Surely, you can't believe that protests and demonstrations are the only means of ameliorating society's problems!''

The principal concluded by saying that he did not believe teachers should engage in any activity that might reflect adversely on the school where they taught, or on their image as professional educators. Further, he told Ms. Conklin that, although he had not yet determined what his final recommendation to the superintendent would be, he had decided that she was to be relieved temporarily of her teaching responsibilities until further notice.

Ms. Conklin was obviously trying to control herself, but when she spoke, her voice quivered with anger as she expressed her total disagreement with the principal's position. It seemed to her that teachers still had certain rights as private citizens, including the right to engage in public demonstrations. She wasn't going to spend the rest of her life writing letters to public employees while people lived in poverty!

Finally, beginning to cry from frustration, the teacher started for the door but turned back to say, ''This isn't the last you've heard from me on this issue! I haven't broken any laws, and no charges have been filed against me. The only thing I may be guilty of is being thrown out of a public meeting.'' Before the principal could respond, Sara Conklin hurried out of his office, slamming the door angrily behind her.

After she left, the principal found that he was experiencing difficulty regaining his emotional stability. He had been upset by the teacher's reaction. But now he had to think carefully. What should he recommend to the superintendent? If she were disciplined, there would probably be an outcry from many of the students or their parents and from some of the faculty members who approved her motives and identified with what they perceived as her courage. Ms. Conklin was not yet tenured, but the teaching association might back her in her stand, and it was possible that the local civil liberties union would defend her also.

On the other hand, if she were to resume her teaching responsibilities without any further action taken by the administration, there would surely be complaints from several important sectors of the community. It was hard to know what to do about Sara Conklin.

SUGGESTED LEARNING ACTIVITIES

Analyze the Case

1. If you had been the superintendent, how might you have responded differently to the reporter calling from a local television station? Why do you suppose the superintendent did not want to talk to the reporter at that time about the teacher who had participated in the demonstration?

2. What factors appear to be significant in influencing the decision by the administration to relieve Ms. Conklin of her teaching responsibilities? What options, other than relieving her of her teaching duties, should have been explored?
3. What is your assessment of the position taken by Sara Conklin during her conference with the principal? What is your evaluation of the position taken by the principal during the conference?
4. In what way, if any, would you have proceeded differently during the conference if you were the principal?

Discuss the Larger Issues

1. In relation to the issue presented in this case, what rights should a teacher be able to exercise as a private citizen? Are there any rights that teachers should voluntarily relinquish, in view of their status in the community and relationship with young people?
2. At what point would a teacher's out-of-school activities impair effectiveness as a teacher? What criteria should be used in making this judgment? What evidence should be used in determining whether the criteria have been met? Who should be involved in making such a decision?
3. What procedures of due process should be followed by the administration regarding problems similar to the one presented in this case?

Be a Problem Solver

The superintendent has requested that the principal submit a recommendation on the disposition of the problem involving Sara Conklin. Ms. Conklin had indicated to the principal that, "This isn't the last you've heard from me on this issue!" If you were the principal in this set of circumstances, what would you do?

Test Your Solution

In order to test your proposed action for dealing with the problem presented at the end of the case, you and the class should create and role-play one or more of the following situations:

1. A meeting between the principal and the superintendent, to go over the principal's recommendation.
2. A telephone call from the president of a local group of conservatives.
3. A telephone call from the president of the civil liberties union, who indicates that he is representing Ms. Conklin in her protest against being relieved of her teaching duties.

Investigate Further

1. What is the policy (written or unwritten) in your school district regarding the out-of-school activities of teachers?
2. What laws or court decisions in your state would have a bearing on the main issues in this case?
3. What would be the attitude of the following groups in your district toward the out-of-school activities of the teacher and the response of the administration?
   a. The school board?
   b. The teacher association?
   c. The executive committee of the parent organization?
   d. The administrators?

20
FACULTY DISSATISFACTION AND LOW MORALE

Entering the faculty workroom, Mary Beth Williams crossed the room to a table where Alice Spencer was correcting papers, spread out before her in organized confusion.

"At it again, I see," Mary Beth greeted the other teacher.

"It never ends, does it?" Alice responded. "And I have a meeting right after school, besides.

I hope I can finish these, because there's another stack on my desk that I have to take home tonight.''

''You're on that Lesson Plan Committee, aren't you?'' Mary Beth said, sitting down across the table. ''How's that going, anyway?''

''About as well as you might expect. I mean, really, what good is this committee going to do anyway? It's the *principal's* committee—he's the one who thinks there needs to be a change in the lesson plan format. As far as I can make out, none of the teachers see any need to change it at all, except maybe Bill Challenge, who wants to eliminate lesson plans altogether. Boy, you should have seen the principal's face when Bill brought up that idea! I mean, Mr. Hizway has previously been making this big statement about how the teachers on this committee need to participate more and get involved, and how receptive he was to hearing our ideas on the subject when, bam! Bill Challenge brings up this suggestion to eliminate lesson plans completely—although I don't think he meant to eliminate planning. I thought Mr. Hizway was going to have a stroke. He got very red in the face and then quickly said that Bill's ideas weren't worth discussing and immediately changed the subject.''

''Really? You mean,'' Mary Beth asked incredulously, ''he just cut Bill off and didn't even permit discussion of the idea?''

''Exactly. Cut him off *cold,*'' Alice replied, sorting through the papers to find her gradebook.

''Well, how did Bill react?''

''Needless to say, he wasn't happy about it, but when the principal cuts you off that way, it doesn't do much good to object.''

''Wow, I bet that didn't help his problems any,'' Mary Beth observed.

''What problems?''

''Well, I don't know if I should say anything, Alice. . . .''

Alice turned back to her gradebook, entering the scores from the papers. ''It's okay, I understand.''

''I don't think it's really confidential. . . . Anyway, Bill's wife and I are pretty good friends, and I know she's worried about him. Apparently he's been under a lot of pressure this year. For one thing, he has that different teaching assignment that he was given, and it's always hard to do *one* new preparation, let alone your whole teaching load. And then he has more problem students assigned to him this year. You know, Alice, Bill has never had discipline problems before, but he really does this year, and it bothers him a lot. And his wife is concerned that he may also be going through some kind of midlife crisis, both personally and professionally. She doesn't elaborate on the personal bit, but she has said that he's expressed uncertainty as to whether he is even the same teacher he once was and whether he has the same capabilities he once possessed.''

''Bill Challenge? Mary Beth, you can't be serious. He's always seemed to me to be an excellent teacher, always so confident.''

''I guess he's not feeling so confident these days.''

''Really!'' Alice sat back, reflecting on Mary Beth's disclosures. ''You'd never know it from his behavior on the Lesson Plan Committee. He's *very* outspoken at the meetings.''

''That may just be the pressure building up and then exploding,'' Mary Beth speculated. ''Lord knows, there's enough going on in this school to upset anybody! And Bill has always been such a perfectionist anyway.''

''I suppose that's true. I know that serving on this committee for lesson plan revision has to be as frustrating for him as it is for me. I mean, this committee is going *nowhere*. I've been here eight years now, and this is just like so many committees that I've served on at the district level—the administrator already has his mind made up when he establishes the committee, so all he really wants—at least this is how it seems—is for us to endorse his thinking, and then he can say that he provided for teacher involvement and input. Sometimes I feel like saying, 'Just tell us what you want, and we'll say it, and then everybody can go home.' What difference does it make, anyway, what the teachers do on this lesson plan committee? The principal never even does anything with the lesson plans. I can't tell that substitute teachers use them very much and, quite frankly, I don't follow them all that strictly myself—not that I'm against planning, of course."

"Sure. I know what you mean," Mary Beth agreed. "And even if a committee comes up with some good ideas, the administrator rejects them on the spot if they don't agree with what he wants to do. Or else we just don't ever hear anymore about them. Doesn't it seem sort of dumb for Mr. Hizway to always be asking us for our ideas if his mind is already made up about things? Or if he's going to ignore our recommendations anyway?"

Alice nodded. "Definitely. I just think a lot of these committees and meetings, particularly faculty meetings, are a waste of time. They hardly ever deal with teachers' needs."

"That's for sure. You want more coffee, Alice?"

She shook her head, now engrossed with their discussion. "You know, Mary Beth, I don't know how you feel about this, but I think a lot of teachers are just getting fed up with their situation at this school. Here we are, getting larger classes, being assigned to more committees, and always being asked to do more with less. And yet, really, what appreciation do we get? Look at our salaries! Compared with my expenses, I tell you, I'm going backwards! And I don't think most parents really *care* anymore about their kids or about teachers. I sure don't see much appreciation from the administration for the job we're doing. It really seems to me that, at best, we're taken for granted, and at worst, we're being exploited!"

"Absolutely. The administration is more concerned with public relations and raising students' achievement test scores. I think a lot of teachers are just plain burned out. I know I am, too."

"Well, Mary Beth, burned out or not, I've got to get back to my room and put some things on the board before next period begins. You know, I've been working on these papers like mad, and I still haven't finished recording all the grades."

"You're right. I've got to get back to my room, too. I have a student coming in for some extra help before class begins."

Later that month the Lesson Plan Committee presented its report to the faculty at an after-school meeting. The principal explained the report, which proposed a more elaborate lesson plan format, requiring more details of teacher planning. When he asked for reactions to the proposed plan, no one responded. Waiting a moment or two for comments, the principal finally indicated that the changes would go into effect the next fall.

During the summer, however, the principal of the school left for an administrative position in another district. The new principal who was hired for the school had not previously worked in the district, so she didn't know too much about the students and faculty. However, she felt optimistic about her new assignment and looked forward to the challenges and opportunities for leadership in the school. She would be starting the next day, and she was to begin the morning with a meeting with two of her teachers who had requested to see her, one named Mary Beth Williams and the other Alice Spencer. With only three weeks to go before classes began, the principal was delighted to have an opportunity to meet with some of her faculty.

SUGGESTED LEARNING ACTIVITIES

Analyze the Case

1. Analyze the conversation between Mary Beth Williams and Alice Spencer, using concepts from Chapter 2 on communication.
2. Analyze the conversation between Mary Beth Williams and Alice Spencer in regard to its implications for faculty morale.

3. What is your assessment of the possible reasons for the lack of faculty reactions to the proposed lesson plan format changes? If you had been the principal, what would you have done at this point in the meeting?

Discuss the Larger Issues

1. What responsibility—if any—does an administrator have for becoming aware of the personal problems that members of the faculty are experiencing? If he or she has such responsibility, what would be the best approach to becoming more aware of personal problems?
2. If an administrator becomes aware of certain personal problems that a member of the faculty is experiencing, what steps—if any—should be taken?
3. Why are teachers frequently frustrated by committee work? What can an administrator do to prevent or ameliorate that frustration?

Be a Problem Solver

Assume that you are the new principal of this school and that Mary Beth Williams and Alice Spencer had ''filled you in'' on the status of faculty morale in the school. How would you approach this situation? What assumptions are you making? Utilize social science and administrative concepts from Part I of the text in planning and implementing your approach.

Test Your Solution

To test your proposed approach to the problems described in this case study, you and the class or group should create and role-play one or more of the following situations:

1. A conference between the new principal and Mary Beth Williams and Alice Spencer. Assume that they are initially a little reluctant to talk about the problems of the school and that you will need to draw them out.
2. Preparation of a response to a memorandum from the superintendent asking all principals to make a strong statement to their teachers about the importance of not abusing sick leave and about the importance of volunteering for district committees.
3. A faculty meeting.
4. A conference between the new principal and Bill Challenge.

Investigate Further

1. What is your school district's policy *and* practice with regard to developing high faculty morale and satisfaction?
2. What does the educational literature suggest about programs and/or approaches for developing and sustaining high faculty morale?

21
TEACHER FILES A GRIEVANCE

Eileen Turner was looking forward to taking some guidance courses during the coming summer. She felt that the courses would help her in her teaching and would prepare her for the day when she might decide to get out of teaching and become a school counselor.

She had decided that she was going to make a determined effort that morning to see the principal. The school's master contract stipulated that a teacher must submit a form which the principal was to use to indicate to the teacher his approval of courses which could be applied toward meeting the district's professional development requirement and the salary schedule. Eileen had submitted the appropriate form a month earlier, but she had as yet received no response from the principal. She had already tried several times last week to see him, but his secretary always said that he was busy. Today Eileen was going to see him . . . one way or another.

Later in the morning, as Eileen was on her way to the principal's office, she encountered him in the hallway. She asked him if she could see him for just a few minutes in his office.

The principal responded that he wouldn't be able to return to his office, since he was on his way to see the assistant principal. Unfortunately, he wouldn't have time to see her in the afternoon, either, because he had to leave the building to attend some meetings. However, he would take a moment to talk with her in the hallway if it was something that could be taken care of easily.

Feeling that she had better capitalize on whatever opportunity was available, the teacher proceeded to explain that she wanted to take some guidance courses during the summer, and had requested earlier that he approve them for professional development and salary schedule purposes. When the principal seemed puzzled and hesitant, the teacher reviewed for him her reasons for wanting to take the courses, namely, that they would help her to improve as a teacher and would also prepare her for a counseling job, should a vacancy ever develop at the school.

As the principal listened to the teacher explain the reasons for her request, he suddenly remembered having come across the form that she had submitted and recalled his ambivalence about the matter. He didn't really like the idea of discussing the situation in the hallway, and he was already late for his conference with the assistant principal. In fact, he would be busy all afternoon. He supposed that he could tell Mrs. Turner that he would see her tomorrow to discuss the matter, but he wasn't sure he wanted to see her then, either. He had reservations about whether the guidance courses would really help the teacher that much and, even if they would, he wasn't certain that he wanted her as a counselor on the staff. Still, he didn't know whether he felt strongly enough to reject her request, and at this moment he hadn't figured out what to tell the teacher. Also, he remembered that he had approved related courses for other teachers in the past. He needed more time to think.

The principal told Mrs. Turner that he needed more time to consider her request before he could approve it. However, she pressed the principal further for some kind of an indication of his feelings about the request. "Can you tell me whether you have any particular or strong objections to my taking these courses?"

"Well, I . . . I guess that . . . I don't . . . have any ah ah ah. . . ."

"Is it all right to take these courses, then, this summer?"

"Well, I suppose that . . . that it . . . might not hurt . . . but . . . but I would really like to talk to you again about this matter. I just don't have the time right now. I'm late for my meeting with the assistant principal." Already edging away from Mrs. Turner as he was speaking, the principal turned and hurried down the corridor.

As the teacher watched the principal walk away, she felt rather pleased with what she had accomplished. True, the principal had not been enthusiastic about her request, but he seemed to have given it his tentative approval.

By the end of the week, however, Eileen Turner still had not heard from the principal. Since she needed to send in her summer school registration by the Tuesday of the following week, she decided to write the principal a brief reminder.

> Dear Mr. Peters:
>
> As I am sure you remember, we discussed my request to take some guidance courses this summer in order to meet the district's professional development and salary schedule requirements. Tuesday of next week is the last day that I can send in my registration for summer school. Unless I hear from you by then to the contrary, I will assume that—on the basis of our earlier conversation—it is all right to send in my registration materials for the guidance courses.
>
> Sincerely,
> Eileen Turner

The following Tuesday passed without any response from the principal, so the teacher sent in her summer school registration materials to the university. Nothing was mentioned by either the principal or the teacher about the matter during the rest of the school year.

In the summer the teacher attended classes at the university and took nine credit hours of guidance courses.

In September Eileen Turner attempted to apply the summer school credits toward meeting the district's professional development requirement and the salary schedule. Her application was rejected by the district office because she had not obtained prior approval of her summer school plans by the principal of the school. When she went to her principal to secure help in appealing the rejection, he refused to help her and took the position that he had never really given her his approval.

Later in the day, the teacher filed a grievance against the principal. Her position was that, although the principal had not formally approved her request, he had never formally rejected it either, despite the fact that he had had an opportunity to do so for over a month. In addition, the teacher felt that since the principal had given her request verbal approval in the hallway and had never responded to her follow-up letter, she was more than justified in believing that she had his approval, particularly since he had approved such courses for other teachers in the past.

The following day a grievance conference was scheduled for the principal, the teacher, and the union representative, and was to take place on Friday at 3:30 P.M.

SUGGESTED LEARNING ACTIVITIES

Analyze the Case

1. What alternatives should the principal have considered in deciding whether or not to talk with Eileen Turner in the corridor? How feasible are those alternatives?
2. Evaluate the conversation held between the principal and Mrs. Turner, utilizing concepts of communication and school administration. In your judgment, did the principal agree to the teacher's request during the conversation?
3. What should the principal have done upon receiving the letter from the teacher? Why did he appear to take no action?

Discuss the Larger Issues

1. What sorts of conditions or circumstances can lead to teacher grievances?
2. How can an administrator's behavior sometimes contribute to a teacher grievance?
3. What can and should an administrator do to *prevent* the conditions that lead to teacher grievances?

Be a Problem Solver

Assume that you are the principal of the school. How will you handle the grievance conference? Or, assume that you are the principal's central office supervisor, and the principal's attempted resolution of the grievance is being appealed by the teacher. How will you handle the appeal? Utilize administrative and social science concepts from Part I of the text in planning and implementing your problem-solving approach to dealing with these situations.

Test Your Solution

To test your proposed approach to dealing with the circumstances described above, you and your colleagues should create and role-play one or more of the following situations:

1. A grievance conference between the principal, the teacher, and the building representative for the teachers' union.
2. A conference between the principal, the principal's superior, the teacher, and a representative for the teachers' union.

Investigate Further

1. What circumstances are grievable in your district?
2. What are the grievance procedures in your school district?

3. What is the attitude of teachers in your school toward the principal's handling of teacher grievances?

22
TEACHER REACTS NEGATIVELY TO PERSONNEL EVALUATION

The deadline for submitting teacher evaluations was nearing, and the principal had stayed after school to write up the results of class visitations made that day. He was pleased that in the past he had hired a fairly good group of teachers. However, there was one notable exception: Mrs. Stevens. He had visited her classroom several times, and it was evident that she was having difficulty. The students didn't appear to be sufficiently involved in learning; most seemed disinterested in the classroom proceedings, and many of them hardly bothered going through the motions of responding when the teacher called on them. There was no doubt that Mrs. Stevens was intelligent and had an excellent background in her subject matter, but she just didn't seem to know how to motivate her students. Perhaps as a result, she was also experiencing difficulty with pupil control.

The principal had noticed each time before entering the teacher's classroom that there was an unusual amount of noise coming from inside. Students were apparently talking at will, and there seemed to be considerable movement. Of course, as soon as he entered the room, things would settle down. But even then the principal observed that the students showed little respect for their teacher. Not that they openly defied her—it was just that she seemed to exert little influence on them.

On Thursday of that week he held a post visitation conference with Mrs. Stevens. He found her to be irritable, hostile to suggestions, and difficult to communicate with. When he tried to subtly suggest that she might try to involve her students more, as there seemed to be a problem in motivating her students, the teacher reacted very defensively.

She countered that she did try to motivate the students by involving them in informal discussion and said it wasn't her fault if the students clammed up every time the principal came into the room! Besides, she retorted, there was no conclusive research that would prove classroom achievement depended on student involvement. The principal was discouraged by the teacher's intractability and finally brought the meeting to an end with no progress having been made in eliciting from Mrs. Stevens any admission of inadequacy in her teaching. As he later reflected on the conference, he wondered whether it would really be worth the effort to continue working with her. Finally he decided he'd better visit her classroom once more before submitting his evaluation to his superior and the recommendation about whether she should be rehired.

The following Monday he again visited Mrs. Stevens' class. There was little noticeable improvement in the class situation, and Mrs. Stevens seemed to be encountering her usual problems in carrying on class discussion. There was too much teacher lecturing, and student participation was limited to rote recitation.

The principal knew he ought to say something to the teacher at the end of the period, but since he couldn't think of anything positive, he left without comment. He had now decided that he would recommend Mrs. Stevens' contract not be renewed for the following year. There would, no doubt, be some unpleasantness in informing her of this decision, but a favorable recommendation from him at this time would grant tenure to the teacher. Once that happened, the principal would be stuck with her, and he was determined to avoid that kind of catastrophe.

That afternoon he painstakingly completed the teacher evaluation form, noting Mrs. Stevens' inadequacies and concluding with a recommendation that her contract not be renewed. Then he put a note in the teacher's mailbox indicating that he would like to see her after school the following

Teacher Evaluation Form			
	Below Average	**Average**	**Above Average**
Personality	X		
Relationship with Others			
Students		X	
Parents		X	
Fellow Teachers		X	
Administrators		X	
Professional Interest and Attitudes	X (not responsive to supervision)		
Teaching Ability	X (great difficulty in motivating students)		
Discipline			X (some problems in class management)

The teacher's contract for next year is to be ______ renewed

__X__ not renewed

day in order to review his evaluation of her before forwarding it to the superintendent's office.

At the scheduled time the following afternoon the teacher and the principal met for the conference. She pointedly ignored his attempts to put her at ease, so he handed her the rating form and asked her to look it over.

The teacher looked at the rating form briefly and threw it back on the principal's desk, denouncing the evaluation as inaccurate and unfair. She exclaimed that she did not deserve the low ratings and she was a much better teacher than the principal had indicated. Perhaps she had not done her best when he was in her classroom, but this was as much his fault as hers. The presence of anyone in the back of the room always upset her and also affected the behavior of her students.

"Besides," the teacher went on, "what basis do you have for telling me what's wrong with my teaching! You've never taught my classes. You say that I need to motivate my students by involving them to a greater degree, but they are already involved as much as they can be. It's easy to say 'involve them more,' but you haven't ever offered any practical ideas on how to do it and neither has my supervisor. As far as I'm concerned, the supervision I've received has not been helpful at all. How can you say that I haven't been responsive to supervision? I haven't received any real supervision yet!"

At that point the teacher stood up and walked to the door. "What you decide to do with this form is up to you. But I want you to know that I don't intend to take this kind of rating without a fight. It's not a fair evaluation, and if I do have problems, I certainly haven't received any help from you. It's the supervision in this school that has failed, not me. I'll take that issue to court, if necessary!"

SUGGESTED LEARNING ACTIVITIES

Analyze the Case

1. What factors may be influencing the behavior of Mrs. Stevens and her class while the principal is conducting his classroom observations?
2. What factors seem to be influencing the conclusions drawn by the principal, based on his classroom observations of Mrs. Stevens? What other kinds of conclusions could be drawn?
3. Why did the principal's first conference with Mrs. Stevens seem to go poorly? How would you have handled the situation differently? What assumptions are you making?

4. What are the strengths and weaknesses of the particular teacher evaluation form used in this case?
5. What is your evaluation of the principal's rationale for not recommending renewal of Mrs. Stevens' contract? Considering the circumstances, what would you have done?
6. In what way would you have approached the second conference with Mrs. Stevens differently?

Discuss the Larger Issues

1. What do you think is the likelihood that a teacher will be unaffected by a supervisor's presence in the classroom, and that the supervisor will observe her as she typically behaves?
2. What, if anything, can be done by a supervisor to obtain an accurate impression of how a teacher usually acts in a classroom situation?
3. What teacher characteristics and behaviors, if any, are *known* to be associated with teacher effectiveness, and should be observable to a supervisor during class observation?
4. What are the responsibilities of a principal for helping a teacher to become more effective?

Be a Problem Solver

The teacher has accused the principal in this case of failing to provide her with adequate supervision, and she has threatened to take the issue to court if the district fails to rehire her. As the principal in the situation, what would be your response to the accusation and the threat?

Test Your Solution

In order to test your proposed plan of action for dealing with the problem presented at the end of the case, you and your class should create and role-play one or more of the following situations:

1. Continue the conference between the principal and the teacher.
2. Conduct a meeting between the building representative for the teachers and the principal.
3. Have the teacher's attorney call the principal on the telephone.
4. Have the superintendent call the principal.
5. Role-play any other situation that would provide feedback on the strengths and weaknesses of your proposed solution.

Investigate Further

1. What are the characteristics and format of the teacher evaluation form used in your district?
2. What is the school board and administrative policy in your district in regard to classroom visitation, and teacher supervision and evaluation?
3. Determine whether there are state laws or court decisions that would have a bearing on whether the teacher in this case could be legally dismissed in your district.

23
FACULTY SLOWDOWN

CITY COUNCIL CUTS SCHOOL DISTRICT'S BUDGET

Class Sizes Will Have to Go Up, Says Superintendent

The headlines in the local paper highlighted the problem for the Skyline School District. The super- intendent and the school board had tried valiantly to keep the budget down this year, recognizing that the city fathers were determined to hold the line against any tax increase. However, the attempt to economize had failed to overcome the costs of inflation, building modifications, and higher salaries negotiated by teachers earlier in the year.

Ultimately there had been no alternative for the school district except to submit an increased school budget. But in the face of a threatened taxpayers' revolt, the city council had felt that it had no choice except to cut the budget. After the council meeting, the superintendent was quoted in the newspaper as saying that because of the budget cuts, the district would probably have to lay off teachers and that as a result, class sizes would be larger in the fall.

The following Monday, acting on the recommendation of the superintendent, the school board voted to eliminate several major items in the budget, including salaries for several teachers who were to be notified that they were no longer needed.

Several days later the newspaper printed an open letter from the local teachers' association to the superintendent of schools:

> We, the teachers, are appalled by the recent action taken by the city council and share your concern about its effects on the educational program of our school district. However, we deplore your recommendation and the school board's action to cut the budget and to lay off teachers.
>
> As you have publicly admitted, the result will be increased class sizes. We recognize that the city, in effect, forced you into this untenable position. But the teachers of this district want to make it perfectly clear that we may have no alternative other than to cut back on professional services. We feel that the teacher-pupil ratio is already too high and, if it is increased, teachers will find it impossible to carry out many of the activities which contribute to quality education.
>
> The teachers of this district should not and cannot be expected to provide the same level of professional services in the future that would be possible if class sizes were lower. It is impossible to say at this time exactly which services may be affected, but unwieldy class sizes will inevitably curtail the teachers' ability to conduct courses as they would like.

Surprisingly, the public's reaction to the teachers' letter was minimal.

During the next month the superintendent made several attempts to ascertain the precise nature of the implications in the letter. However, the representatives of the teachers' association refused to elaborate, indicating only that several possibilities were being considered.

The following September school opened smoothly, in spite of the increased number of students. Classes were larger and teacher complaints were heard, but there was no evidence of a cutback in teacher services. By the end of the second week classes were proceeding as usual, and the central administration and school board began to relax, unaware that a problem was starting to develop at Jefferson School.

On Tuesday a parent called the principal to report that her son's teacher was not correcting all of the written work which the students had been assigned. The parent had previously complained to the teacher but had received no satisfaction. The teacher had said that as a result of the heavier work load created by larger classes, it would be impossible to correct all the written work and that less would be assigned during the year. The parent had not wanted to become involved in an argument with the teacher, but now wanted to know what the school was going to do about the problem. The principal replied that he would talk to the teacher and "try to straighten things out!"

After school he met with the teacher, Mr. Sullivan, and related the parent's complaint to him. When the principal asked whether the allegation was true, the teacher admitted it at once. He took the position that his heavier work load had made it impossible for him to do the job that he wanted to, and added that he was not alone in this regard. All of the teachers had decided that their larger classes prevented them from maintaining their usual professional standards. The administration should understand that this was not a condition for which the teachers were responsible, and they deplored its effects. But correcting homework was a tremendously time-consuming task and, with the additional students, there was really no other choice than to assign less written work and to spot-check the completed assignments.

The principal thought to himself that at one time he would have been flabbergasted by such an attitude. Now he merely wondered wearily, whatever had happened to the dedicated teacher who placed the education of his students and their needs before his own. The principal recognized the additional burden that larger classes placed on a teacher's work load, but what could a principal—or, for that matter, the superintendent—do about that now? The city council had already established the amount to be spent by the schools, and everyone would simply have to work a little harder. It was unfortunate, but the problem wouldn't be solved by people refusing to meet the challenge!

The principal decided that in his present frame of mind, it would be better not to say anything at the moment to the teacher. Moreover, he wasn't sure about the extent of his own authority in the event that Mr. Sullivan should adamantly refuse to correct any additional papers. So he told the teacher that he was disappointed with his attitude and that the issue would have to be referred to the central office.

After Mr. Sullivan left, the principal called the superintendent and informed him of the recent developments. The superintendent seemed upset and was quite critical of the teachers. He pointed out that if they had not been so insistent on higher salaries this year, the district probably could have afforded to hire more teachers, and class size would not have become a problem. He was not sure, at this point, what the principal should do—particularly if the teachers should flatly refuse to carry out aspects of their normal teaching assignment. He would have to return a call to the principal later.

By the end of the week the principal still had not heard from the superintendent. However, in Friday's afternoon mail a letter arrived from the superintendent which said:

I am sorry to be so long in responding, but the problem at your school has caused us a great deal of concern. Your situation has been discussed informally with members of the school board, and we at the central office have concluded that the teachers in your school are engaged in an unprofessional and unethical slowdown which can in no way be justified by the current class sizes.

However, to be quite frank, we are uncertain about the legal remedies available to the school district if your teachers do not desist from their present course of action. Nevertheless, we would encourage you to exercise whatever influence and leadership you can exert on these teachers to make them "see the light." It should be emphasized that your efforts in this regard are particularly important. We have heard that if the teachers at your school are successful, the practice of cutting back on assigning and correcting student work may spread to other schools. All of us must do everything we can to prevent that from happening.

In closing, may I just suggest that you exercise great care not to stir up the teachers. They are very unhappy about the higher class sizes as well as some of the other effects of budget cuts which were necessary. If they become greatly exacerbated, they could stage a walkout. Obviously, we don't want that to happen either!

Do the best you can and keep us posted on developments.

Sincerely,
Malcom Lewis
Superintendent of Schools

SUGGESTED LEARNING ACTIVITIES

Analyze the Case

1. What action, if any, should have been taken by the school administration when the local teachers' association publicly criticized the administration and the school board?
2. What is your evaluation of the position taken by Mr. Sullivan in his conference with the principal? In what way would you have acted differently, if you had been the principal, during the conference with Mr. Sullivan? What assumptions are you making?

3. What might be some of the reasons why the superintendent responded in the way he did to the principal's request for assistance?

Discuss the Larger Issues

1. Should a teachers' association—or an individual teacher, counselor, or administrator—take a public stand which may be critical of certain actions by the administration and the school board?
2. Under what set of circumstances, if any, is a work slowdown a legitimate tactic by an individual school employee or a teachers' organization?
3. Administratively, who should have the primary responsibility for solving the main problem described in this case? Why?

Be a Problem Solver

The superintendent has encouraged the principal to exercise his influence on the teachers to make them "see the light" but not to "stir them up." If *you* were the principal, how would you handle this situation? Outline the steps you would take and the people you would involve. Utilize appropriate administrative and social science concepts from Part I of the text in planning and implementing your approach.

Test Your Solution

To test your proposed plan of action for dealing with the problem presented at the end of this case, you and the class should create and role-play one or more of the following interactions:

1. A telephone call between the principal and the parent who previously called.
2. Another meeting between the principal and Mr. Sullivan.
3. A telephone call to the principal from a newspaper reporter.

Investigate Further

1. What is the school board policy in your district in regard to how much written work a teacher *must* assign and correct?
2. What is the policy of your local teachers' association and that of the state and national teachers' associations on how much written work a teacher must assign and correct?
3. What written statements and documents could you produce which could be used in court to support the position of the teachers or that of the administration on the issue of homework practices?

12 School-Community Relations

The primary purpose of education in most societies is to perpetuate the culture and to prepare the students for productive adult roles. In the United States, the control over this aspect of acculturation has historically been vested by the state in local boards of education which are usually elected by their respective communities.

While the dominant orientation of many communities seems to be toward maintaining the status quo, there are educators who have introduced new ideas, materials, and approaches to learning which they feel will make the school more relevant to the needs of students and the larger society. These educators—teachers and administrators—believe that the primary purpose of the school is to stimulate students to become more independent, to think for themselves, and to assess their own values as well as those of the community. In the process of introducing change, they have, in many instances, challenged the norms of the local community or groups within the community, and conflict between the community and the school has frequently resulted.

Although professional challenges to community norms represent one major source of potential school-community conflict, community challenges to professional norms have also tended to lead to friction between the school and its constituencies. In recent years many parents and community groups have grown increasingly dissatisfied with the effectiveness of school programs, achievements, and personnel. These individuals and groups reject the concept that the school board should have sole responsibility for the development of school policy and that other professionals in the school should be accountable only to each other and to the board of education. Such parents and community groups desire more meaningful involvement in the establishment and modification of school policies and in the evaluation of the extent to which the school and its personnel are meeting their responsibilities. These expectations represent a direct challenge to the professional norms of many educators and constitute a major source of school-community conflict.

It should be noted that, in spite of the emphasis in the educational literature on the desire of citizens to become more involved in school affairs, experience would suggest that, paradoxically, administrators may encounter considerable apathy as well as interest if they try to increase community involvement in the schools. An inescapable conclusion is the view that the task of maintaining and improving school-community relations is a challenging and sometimes frustrating one, and relating with the news media is a part of this challenge.

Most of the cases presented in this section illustrate the two main factors responsible for school-community conflict: professional challenges to the norms of the community and community challenges to the professional norms of the school. In addition, cases are included which focus on parental apathy, school public relations, and on the recurring financial crisis in the schools. All the cases represent serious problems which, if not constructively addressed, could result in the deterioration of school-community relations.

BACKGROUND READING

For the reader who would like to develop further background and understanding of the problems and issues presented in this chapter, the following list of readings is provided.

A New Look at Empowerment: How Educators and Communities Can Empower Each Other, Arlington, VA: American Association of School Administrators, 1990.

Don Davies, "Schools Reaching Out: Family, School, and Community Partnerships for Student Success," *Phi Delta Kappan* (January 1991), 376–382.

Richard A. Gorton and Gail Thierbach-Schneider, Part V. "The School and the Community," *School-Based Leadership: Challenges and Opportunities,* 3rd ed., Dubuque, IA: Wm. C. Brown Publishers, 1991, 511–570.

Institute for Responsive Education, "Success for All Children through School-Family-Community Partnerships, *Equity and Choice* (Winter 1990), 21–25.

Susan McAllister Swap, "Parent Involvement and Success for All Children: What We Know Now." An ERIC Report Ed 321–907.

William W. Wayson et al., *Handbook for Developing Public Confidence in Schools,* Bloomington, IN: *Phi Delta Kappan,* 1990.

24
CURRICULUM UNIT UPSETS PARENTS

Placards and shouts greeted visitors to the city council meeting: "Clean up Morgan River!" "Vote funds for anti-pollution and beautification!" For the past two hours students had been marching with their pickets near the entrance to City Hall, and now they moved inside the building as the meeting of the city council began.

The students, about two dozen of them, were from Morgan Falls School. They had come to protest the council's recent deletion of funds from the budget, funds that had earlier been tentatively allotted for a clean-up and beautification project for the river that flowed near the city.

The young people had carried on a local campaign for several months, stressing the potential of the river for recreation and scenic enjoyment. The local newspaper had supported their idea and had even printed pictures which were found in the files, showing families swimming and boating in Morgan River forty years ago.

Although the students had managed to raise $975 through their efforts, the cost of the project to clean up the river far exceeded that sum. When they took the idea to the city council, the aldermen had initially responded favorably to their plans and included a large allocation in the proposed budget. Recently, however, a tight financial situation had developed, and at their last meeting the members of the city council had eliminated the item.

As the mayor called for order, the student chants grew louder. Furious with what he felt was a deliberate disruption of the meeting, the mayor directed the guards to clear the building of all students. In the next moments bedlam broke out. Placards were thrown, there was much screaming and yelling, and finally several of the students had to be literally dragged from the building.

That night the late TV news carried a filmed report of the disruption at City Hall, followed by an editorial which was quite critical of the students' tactics.

The next morning the school buzzed about the incident. Were the students justified in their use of such tactics? Should the school punish those who had actually been involved? There was considerable difference of opinion on these issues, and tempers flared more than once during the many informal discussions that took place in various parts of the building.

At 1:00 P.M. the principal received a call from someone identifying herself as Mrs. Thompson. Was the principal aware that her son's teacher was actually *instructing* students in approaches to overthrowing the government, and that most of the students involved in the previous night's disruption were in that teacher's class?

The principal assured Mrs. Thompson that he was quite certain no one at his school was advocating that students overthrow anything. Yes, it was possible that some of the students at last night's meeting were from the same class, but he doubted whether that teacher could be held responsible for the students' actions. Well, he would check into the matter and call her back if there appeared to be a problem.

After school that day, the principal called to his office the teacher whom Mrs. Thompson had identified. The principal informed the teacher that a call had been received from a parent who complained that her son and others were being taught radical methods of changing society. Was this true?

The teacher responded by explaining that the whole question of how to achieve social change was a major issue with young people, since there were many pressing problems needing solutions. It seemed to the teacher that the topic of how to deal with those problems and how to overcome resistance to change was important for students to learn about, so this year he had introduced a special unit on strategies for bringing about change. Obviously, many methods had been discussed with students, including tactics of confrontation and disruption. However, at no time had violent or extreme approaches been recommended as superior to peaceful means. Students had been told, though, that in some situations when everything else had failed, radical methods might represent their only viable recourse. Nevertheless, he had tried to emphasize to his class that his personal philosophy was that the critical point in a situation was a question of judgment and the individual's conscience. Each person would have to make that determination for oneself and live with the consequences.

After the teacher finished his explanation, the principal didn't comment for a few moments. Then he said that he would have to talk with the teacher's subject matter supervisor before he could make a decision on what should be done about the situation.

The following morning the principal didn't have a chance to see the district supervisor, but he continued to receive telephone calls from parents complaining about the students. Evidently, the news was out that a unit which included the study of both violent and nonviolent means of bringing about change was being presented at Morgan Falls School, and that some of the young people who had been involved in the disruption at City Hall were from the class where the unit was being taught. The parents were very upset, and the principal was a little at a loss as to what to say to them.

At 10:15 the superintendent also called to inquire about the situation, and although he appeared concerned about the lack of a decision from the principal on the problem, he refrained from giving any directive that the unit be abandoned. He did say that his wife had mentioned that the whole matter was a primary topic of conversation where she worked. People generally seemed to be attributing the incident at the city council meeting to the school's unit on bringing about change. It appeared that a major controversy might be shaping up.

The superintendent concluded the conversation by saying that, while he could appreciate the students' and teacher's convictions about the role of the school, they might have to reconsider their position on the issue if the community strongly objected. Until that time, however, the superintendent wanted the principal to know that he would support the school 100 percent.

After the principal put down the phone, he thought about what the superintendent had told him. It was clear that at least a certain segment of the public (how large, he couldn't be sure) was quite disturbed. In addition, there was now a measure of doubt in his own mind about whether the superintendent would support him and the teacher if the community outcry should reach the school board in the form of an organized protest against the school's curriculum. There was little question that it was imperative to get together with the department head.

Just then the phone rang again. It was the president of the school's parent group, who had been deluged with calls all day from parents wanting a special meeting to air their complaints about the school's unit on change processes. The president suspected that it might be a rather heated meeting, and there was a good possibility that the press would attend, and perhaps even several school board members. Should he go ahead and schedule the meeting?

The principal didn't say anything immediately. He was thinking. The opposition has organized themselves more rapidly than he had anticipated, and a strategy for dealing with the problem was badly needed.

He informed the president of the parents' group that he would call him back in an hour.

As the principal put down the phone, he thought to himself that, regardless of what he did, he was going to make somebody very unhappy.

SUGGESTED LEARNING ACTIVITIES

Analyze the Case

1. What, if anything, should or could the principal have done to prevent the student demonstration from ever taking place?
2. What action do you feel the principal should have taken in regard to the particular students who had disrupted the city council meeting?
3. What assumptions is the principal making in his response to the comments of
   a. Mrs. Thompson?
   b. The teacher?

   How tenable are those assumptions?
4. What is your evaluation of the superintendent's comments? What are their implications?

Discuss the Larger Issues

1. What is the responsibility of the school for preparing students to adjust to and/or change society and its institutions?
2. What should be the attitude of the school toward students who go into the larger society to carry out techniques of change they have learned in school?
3. Do teachers have a right to discuss issues in class that may violate the customs or mores of the community? Or does the community have the right to determine the content of their children's education?

Attempt to Be a Problem Solver

A large number of people are urging that an open meeting be held to discuss a recent community disturbance and its relationship to what has been taught by a social studies teacher. How should the situation be handled?

Test Your Solution

In order to test your proposed plan of action for dealing with the problem presented at the end of this case, you and your colleagues should create and role-play one or more of the following situations:

1. A conference between the principal and the department head
2. A conference between the social studies teacher, his supervisor, and the principal
3. The telephone call between the principal and the president of the school's parents' group
4. A general meeting among the principal, the supervisor, and the parents
5. Another phone call to the principal from the superintendent

Investigate Further

1. What is the extent to which a teacher is legally liable for acts carried out by students in his/her class, acts that they have previously discussed in that teacher's class? What is the principal's or department head's liability for what their teachers teach?
2. What is the policy in your district in regard to the teaching of controversial issues?
3. May a teacher in your state be legally dismissed for teaching content which is strongly opposed by the community?

25
PARENTAL APATHY

Mrs. Rose was a new assistant principal at John F. Kennedy School. She had just finished her final course work during the summer and had been looking forward to her new job. Now, four months after being on the job, she wasn't sure about some aspects of the situation.

In summer school she had taken a course on school-community relations and had come away from the course convinced of the need for a comprehensive program of school-community relations, and with some ideas and considerable enthusiasm for getting something started. Certainly, it appeared, after only two months on the job, that her own school had a very limited program of contact or involvement with the parents and the larger community. For example, there was no P.T.A. or parents' organization, and there was no parent newsletter sent home on a regular basis. There were also no advisory committees operating, although apparently there had been some parents' groups at one time or another.

She had talked to her principal about her concerns and ideas, but she hadn't received much encouragement from him. The principal had taken the position that everything was going fine at the school and the parents were better off left alone. He had informed her that he had felt differently when he first started in administration, but he had encountered a lot of parental apathy. Not many parents showed up for meetings, and when he had tried to solicit parent volunteers to work in the cafeteria, he had received a very poor response. The principal wasn't sure that parents really wanted to get involved, and if the school tried too hard to get them involved, that effort might just get them stirred up about something and they might be harder to handle.

The principal had also asserted that he was in direct contact with the community and that he felt, on the basis of the telephone calls he received and the parents he saw who came in for conferences, that he could sense the pulse of the community. His sense of the community was that people really didn't want to be involved and they expected the educators to do the work.

Mrs. Rose had been dismayed by the principal's comments, but while she didn't agree with his assessment of the situation, she had decided at that moment not to say anything.

However, later in another conference with the principal, she had again brought up the need for *some* type of parent involvement. To her surprise, the principal agreed, although with some ambivalence, to schedule a meeting to see if parents would even be interested in getting involved. However, he had made it clear that he wasn't going to approve of any type of P.T.A. He might go along with the idea of a parents' advisory group, but nothing more.

On Friday, an announcement was distributed to the students in their classrooms at the end of the day and they were asked to give the announcement to their parents. It read:

> AN INVITATION TO PARENTS
> There will be a special meeting at the school a week from this coming Monday at 7:30 P.M., on parent involvement. If you are interested and can attend, please come to the auditorium by 7:30.

The night of the meeting eight parents showed up. In the back of the auditorium the principal and Mrs. Rose were discussing whether to go ahead with the meeting, in light of the low attendance. The principal was not in favor of proceeding with the meeting, given the poor turnout and the probable nonrepresentativeness of those who were present. He turned to Mrs. Rose, the assistant principal, for her views.

SUGGESTED LEARNING ACTIVITIES

Analyze the Case

1. What is your assessment of the attitude initially expressed by the principal about school-community relations? How typical is that attitude?
2. What, if anything, would you have done differently in the first conference with the principal if you had been the vice-principal? How might the amount of your experience in the position and your gender influence your response?
3. Evaluate the parents' invitation presented at the end of the case, utilizing concepts of communication and school/community relations. Hypothesize as to why only eight parents attended the meeting.

Discuss the Larger Issues

1. What should be the main objective of school/community relations? What should be the role of the school, and what should be the role of the community?
2. What are the implications of a limited program of parental involvement?
3. What factors contribute to parents' apathy? What factors contribute to parental and community involvement, confidence, trust, and support of the school?

Be a Problem Solver

Assume that you are the vice-principal of this school. Considering the circumstances described in this case, how do you propose to handle the situation? Utilize appropriate administrative and social science concepts from Part I of the text in planning and implementing your approach.

Test Your Solution

To test your proposed plan for dealing with the problems described in the case, you and your colleagues should create and role-play one or more of the following situations:

1. The meeting on parental involvement attended by the eight parents and the principal and vice-principal.
2. A conference between the principal and the vice-principal.
3. A new communication from the school to the parents.

Investigate Further

1. Ascertain the nature and scope of your school's community relations program.
2. What is the evidence of the effectiveness of your school's community relations program? What is the attitude of faculty, parents, and administrators toward the program?
3. What is the role of the administration, faculty, and parents in your school or district in developing and maintaining good school-community relations?

26

WANTED: A PLAN FOR IMPROVING PARENTAL AND COMMUNITY INVOLVEMENT

Elaine Black had been away from her school for three days, attending a national principals' convention. Although the convention had been enjoyable, both as a respite from the demands of her job and the several useful sessions at the convention, she was anxious to return to her school. Since she was in only her second year as principal, she didn't feel totally secure about being gone from the building for an extended length of time. Besides, she knew that the work would just pile up during her absence. Therefore, upon returning she had decided to go to her office early in the morning and get a head start by sorting through her mail.

As Elaine started examining the mail, she noticed an envelope from the superintendent, marked "Important." Tearing open the envelope, she removed a memorandum and began reading it.

MEMO

TO: All School Principals
FROM: The Superintendent of Schools

As most of you know from your reading of the research on effective schools, parental and community involvement is an important component of an effective school. The members of the school board have been discussing this aspect informally for several months and last night formally adopted a motion which mandates that all school principals develop a plan for improving school-community relations for their school and for increasing parental and nonparental involvement.

The district administration has been asked by the school board to develop an overall plan for the district, but each principal is to develop a plan for his or her own school. This plan should specify improvement objectives, proposed ways or approaches to bring about improvement, and possible problems that will need to be overcome, as well as strategies for dealing with these problems. The plan can be in outline form, but should provide enough detail so as to make the plan clear.

Although I apologize for any pressure this may put on you, I am scheduling a principals' meeting for two weeks from the date you should have received this memorandum for the purpose of having several of you present your plan to the superintendent's cabinet. The school board is pushing hard to get these plans initiated as soon as possible, and this meeting with me and my cabinet should, in addition to giving some impetus for the development of these plans, provide an opportunity for some sharing of ideas prior to finalizing your plans. I will contact you a day or two prior to the meeting to see if you are ready to present your plan. It should be emphasized that whether or not you are asked to present your plan, you should have organized your plan by the date of the meeting.

Elaine sat back and drew a deep breath. A knot had been developing in her stomach as she had read the superintendent's memo. Two weeks wasn't much time, and she wasn't looking forward to making any presentation to the superintendent's cabinet. On the other hand, she certainly wanted to be prepared in case he called on her for a presentation, and there was always room for improvement for school-community relations at her school.

Very little parental participation was taking place at her school except for a parent-teacher conference program during American Education Week, and that was not especially well attended. She had given some thought to initiating more parental or community involvement during her first year, but she had been so busy just getting her feet on the ground and learning about her new job and school that, before she knew it, the first year was over. Besides, it seemed as though the teachers, for the most part, were not keen on parental involvement. It was true that now she was in her second year, she should have been doing more in the area of school-community relations, but she hadn't really given it a high priority, and, as a consequence, nothing had been done. Perhaps, she thought to herself, the school board's action and the superintendent's memo were blessings in disguise.

SUGGESTED LEARNING ACTIVITIES

Analyze the Case

1. Assess the superintendent's memo, using concepts from Chapter 2 on Communication.
2. Evaluate the principal's reactions to the superintendent's memo. What would be your reaction if you were a principal in this school district?

3. What immediate steps should be taken by the principal after carefully reading the superintendent's memo?

Discuss the Larger Issues

1. Should the superintendent and the school board have solicited the input of the building principals in regard to whether there was a need to improve school-community relations? What other perceptions should have been sought?
2. What criteria and methods should be used to ascertain whether there is a need to improve school-community relations? What criteria and methods should be employed to evaluate the adequacy of a proposed improvement plan and its eventual implementation?
3. What *role* should teachers, parents, and other members of the community play in developing and implementing a plan for improving school-community relations?

Be a Problem Solver

Assume that you are one of the principals who has received the superintendent's memo and that the circumstances in regard to school-community relations in your school are similar to those described for Elaine Black's school. Prepare a response to the superintendent's memo. Utilize appropriate administrative and social science concepts from Part I of the text in developing the plan and (if requested to present your plan) in your presentation of the plan you have developed.

Test Your Solution

To test your proposed plan for improving school-community relations for your school, you and your colleagues should create and role-play one or more of the following situations:

1. An initial meeting between the principal and a committee appointed by the principal to help develop the plan.
2. A meeting at which the principal and the planning committee decide on the adequacy of a plan that a subcommittee has developed.
3. A meeting of the superintendent's cabinet at which you, as principal, present your school's plan.

Investigate Further

1. Examine the educational literature on school-community relations to identify elements that should be included in a comprehensive, effective program of school-community relations. What is the role of the principal and the superintendent in developing these elements?
2. Ascertain what *criteria* and *methods* are used to monitor the effectiveness of school and district programs of school-community relations in your school and school district.
3. Determine which schools in your district have effective programs of school-community relations. What factors contribute to their effectiveness?

27
A NEW ROLE FOR THE PARENTS' ORGANIZATION

The principal was concerned about the newly formed parents' organization. He had experienced mixed feelings about the group ever since last spring when they had decided to discontinue their affiliation with the national P.T.A. and to function as an independent organization. He personally felt that the P.T.A. had been a positive force in education, and he had always known that he could count on its support. He wasn't sure about the new organization.

When the newly formed parents' group had elected officers the previous spring, there had been considerable discussion about "parent participation" and "community involvement." The principal had had difficulty in assessing the rhetoric he had heard at the meeting because there didn't seem to be anything specific that parents were unhappy about other than their own alleged lack of involvement. Their attitude had puzzled him since he had always tried diligently to give his P.T.A. an important role in the school program. For example, under his administration, the P.T.A. had taken a greater part in the planning of the annual parents/staff picnic, had initiated parent-teacher conferences, and had helped in promoting a bond referendum for an addition to the building.

Although the principal didn't feel that the P.T.A. or the parents should actually be involved in school decision making or the development of instructional or curricular policies, he did believe that they had an important role to play in supporting the school program: he only hoped that he could get the new group to accept this role.

On Thursday the principal met in his office with the representatives of the new parents' organization. He had scheduled the meeting in order to discuss the annual back-to-school night program that he had planned.

After the usual exchange of amenities, the principal proceeded to review the way in which the back-to-school night had been presented in the past and finally concluded by asking for the parents' reactions. He didn't have long to wait.

The president of the parents' group, a young attorney, responded that the officers, having already discussed the traditional program, had decided that a change was needed. Back-to-school nights in the past had done little more than familiarize parents with their children's schedules and, in many instances, had confused parents rather than helped them to understand the educational process.

This year, he said, the parents wanted to find out what was really going on in the classrooms. Specifically, they wanted the school to sponsor a series of back-to-school meetings focusing on one or two subjects each evening of the week and also teacher-parent conferences during American Education Week. Parents would be free to participate in any or all of the meetings, while the teachers would be responsible for making individual presentations on their respective evenings, as well as being available on the remaining evenings for parent-teacher conferences.

At that point the principal attempted to raise a question, but the president ignored him and continued speaking. Beyond a new back-to-school night program, he stressed, the parents' organization wanted to become more involved in the decision and policy making processes of the school. Parents had an important stake in the quality of education offered to the students and felt that they had something to contribute. In fact, parents believed that they should become equal partners with the school in deciding what was best for the children. He and the other parents recognized that the school board set the broad policies for the district, but they were convinced that the local parents' organization needed to play a greater role in developing and deciding on policies affecting their particular school.

The president went on to explain that the officers had met the preceding week and had established parents' committees on discipline, teacher performance, curriculum and total school evaluation, which would meet regularly during the school year. The committees planned to observe conditions in the school, collect data from students, parents, and teachers, and issue policy statements on the need for change. All the parents were hopeful that they could work cooperatively with the administration of the school and that they could count on the principal's support.

The parents' proposal for greater involvement took the principal by surprise. He wondered why he hadn't been informed about the meeting the parents had held to establish those committees. Wouldn't the new committees end up interfering with the normal operations of the school? Surely the parents must recognize that he was in favor of appropriate parental involvement and participation in school affairs. However, as principal, he was the one who would be held accountable if anything went wrong, and therefore, he must be the one to decide policy. Why couldn't these parents understand that and be satisfied with the role they had played in the past?

Regardless of his personal feelings about the situation, however, the principal recognized that he needed to respond to the parents in a way which would meet their concerns. The problem was how to accomplish this without upsetting the educational program of the school.

SUGGESTED LEARNING ACTIVITIES

Analyze the Case

1. Why do you suppose that the principal in this case feels the way he does about what the role of the P.T.A. should be?
2. How do you size up the leadership of the parents' organization?
3. What questions do you feel the parents' recommendations raise? What are the merits of their recommendations? What personal and situational factors may be influencing your evaluation of the proposal?
4. What barriers would have to be overcome before the parents' recommendations could be implemented by the school?

Discuss the Larger Issues

1. What do you feel should be the role of the P.T.A. or other parent groups in helping to improve education in the school?
2. What might be the reason(s) why P.T.A.'s or other parent organizations are unwilling to play the limited role proposed by some administrators?
3. What should be the role of the principal in regard to the P.T.A. or parent organization? What should be the role of the faculty in relation to the P.T.A. or parent organization?

Be a Problem Solver

The officers of a new parent organization have presented to the principal a rather extensive proposal for a different back-to-school night and for increased involvement in school affairs. As the principal in that situation, what would you do? What are the available alternatives? Utilize appropriate administrative and social science concepts in planning and implementing your approach.

Test Your Solution

In order to test your plan of action for dealing with the problem presented at the end of the case, you and the class should create and role-play one or more of the following situations:

1. Continuation of the meeting between the officers and the principal.
2. A faculty meeting during which the principal explains the parents' proposals.
3. A conference between the principal and the building representative for the teachers.

Investigate Further

1. What is the role of the P.T.A. or parent organization at your school?
2. How do the principal, teachers, and the parents at your school feel about the current role of the P.T.A.?
3. To what extent would certain school board policies restrict increased involvement by parents (or a parent organization) in your district?
4. Are there any legal constraints on the role that can be played by a P.T.A. or parent organization in your state?

28

HOW MUCH SHOULD PARENTS BE TOLD?

There was no longer any doubt. This was going to be a sticky issue! For some time now, the superintendent had heard rumors that the South Side Parents' Advisory Council was organizing a protest against the district's policy of denying public access to IQ and achievement test results. This morning he had received a letter from the group which revealed the nature of their concern. The communication was addressed, "An Open

Letter to the Superintendent of Schools and Members of the Board of Education from the South Side Parents' Council.'' He read the letter again, slowly:

We believe that the purpose of the school system should be to educate our children. At the present time we have no *satisfactory* way of knowing whether that goal is being effectively accomplished. Our contacts with the school and with other parents raise grave doubts about whether the needs of our children are being met.

As a parent council, however, we lack the kind of information that would either confirm or alleviate our concern. We have asked our principal to provide us with the school's IQ and achievement test scores, but he has rejected our request because of "Board Policy." We therefore seek to have that policy changed, so that our parent council can be provided with student IQ and achievement test scores showing:

(1) how our school compares with the other schools in the district, in terms of potential for learning (IQ) and actual accomplishment (achievement test scores), and

(2) how teachers in the same subject area and grade level in our school compare to one another in terms of capitalizing on the potential learning ability of our children.

There is much talk in education today about accountability. We believe that the school, in general, and each teacher, in particular, should be held accountable to the *parents* for making the most effective utilization of every child's potential for learning and growth. In order to evaluate and ascertain whether that objective is being met, the Parent Council, which represents the South Side community, needs student IQ and achievement test results for every class and for the total school.

In conclusion, we would like to point out that the information which we seek is in the public domain. The schools are public institutions and, therefore, have no right to maintain secret records. We do not ask for the identification of individual student names, but rather the individual and class scores and averages for *each* teacher and for the total school, with data on how these scores compare with results in other situations. No teacher or administrator who is doing a good job need fear public disclosure of this information. It is time for everyone in our community—including the policy makers—to become more concerned about whether the children of our school and of this school district are receiving the kind of quality education that they need and deserve.

The superintendent sighed and put the letter down on his desk. It had been less than two years ago that he had urged the School Board to establish parent advisory councils as a means of promoting greater community participation and involvement in the schools, particularly at the building level. The councils were designed to play strictly an advisory role to the principal and staff. But several of the groups had not been satisfied with limiting their role to that function, and many of the principals had mixed feelings about the whole idea of parent involvement in the school. It was interesting to note that the South Side parents' group had changed their title, removing the word ''advisory'' altogether; they now referred to themselves as the ''Parent Council.'' Judging from their letter, they planned to do more than just render advice!

The superintendent decided that this was an issue which needed to be dealt with carefully. He knew that the president of the School Board would probably be calling him later in the day for his tentative reactions to the letter. The superintendent wanted to be prepared. Whatever was decided in regard to the South Side group's request would not only carry implications for the other schools' treatment of test results, but also might set a precedent for the future exercise of power by other parents' advisory councils. This would be an important decision, one which should be thoroughly discussed by all concerned.

He called his secretary into the office and asked her to arrange a meeting at 1:30 that afternoon with his administrative council and all the building principals. She was not to inform them of the nature of the meeting.

At 1:30 the superintendent began the meeting promptly by reading the letter from the South Side Parent Council. Then he asked for reactions to the group's request for test information, indicating that he wanted to hear the other administrators' ideas before he made any comments of his own. No one said anything at first, but finally the assistant superintendent spoke up. It seemed to him that the South Side parents had overstepped their bounds. They were not a school board, but only an advisory group, and were not authorized to receive test information. Beyond that, the school district had a long-standing policy of denying public access to test results.

At that point the superintendent emphasized that the South Side Parent Council was recommending a *change* in board policy and that their request for test information could not be turned down simply because it violated current policy. The issue was, what *should* be the policy?

For the next two hours the different aspects of the issue were discussed, and tempers grew short as the arguments became heated. Most of the principals opposed the release of test information that would permit comparison among schools. They felt the test scores could be misinterpreted, were not always reliable or valid, and that the tests could not possibly reflect the many intangible outcomes of education which the school promoted and fostered. However, several principals took the position that the tests, while not perfect, were perhaps the best available method for evaluating the schools' performance. If a particular test was not reliable or valid for a school, then another test should be secured. And although it was true that the achievement tests did not measure all of the schools' outcome, that limitation should not be used as an argument against allowing the public to evaluate the measurable aspects of the program.

"How about the parents' request that test information be released about classes of the individual teachers?" the assistant superintendent asked.

On this point there was general agreement. Almost no one felt that it would be a good idea to release either IQ or achievement test scores for individual teachers' classes, particularly if that procedure would allow parents to make comparisons among teachers. The consensus was that parents would use this information only to try to evaluate their children's teachers, and this could stir up trouble. Besides, parents were not qualified to evaluate teachers. This was the responsibility of the school system.

"Then how can parents assure themselves that an individual teacher is doing a good job?" the guidance director inquired.

"They can ask us!" one of the principals immediately responded, and the rest nodded in agreement. "The principal is accountable for what goes on in the building, and if a teacher isn't doing a good job, then it's the responsibility of the building administrator to take action. Of course, this can't be done on the basis of some emotional complaint or personal animosity—there has to be *evidence* that the teacher is not doing a good job. The teachers' associations and the courts can make it tough to get rid of teachers these days, particularly if they're on tenure."

It was growing late and the superintendent thought it was time to bring the meeting to a close. He indicated that it was his impression that, with perhaps a few exceptions, the administrators were opposed to any change of board policy in regard to disclosing test results. He personally agreed with that opinion and felt that the school board was the only group which represented the public and which should have access to IQ and achievement test information. Test scores could easily be misinterpreted if they fell into the wrong hands, and they should not be used for comparing individual schools anyway—certainly not for evaluating the teachers within a school! In essence then, this would be his recommendation to the School Board.

That evening Mr. Wilcox, the President of the School Board, called the superintendent. Mr. Wilcox was concerned about the letter from the South Side parent group and wanted to know how the superintendent felt about the request.

The superintendent described his meeting with the administrative cabinet and the building principals and said that the administration's recommendation would be to leave the board policy unchanged. A full report detailing the reasons for this position, as well as a proposal for a more structured role for the parental advisory councils, would be sent to all board members before the next meeting.

Mr. Wilcox sounded relieved and agreed that this was probably the best way to handle the situation. He was not, however, looking forward to the next board meeting.

The remainder of that week passed without incident. First semester grades had been distributed, and the schools were closed for the semester break. The city paper carried a brief news item on the parents' request for a change in board policy, but the letter to the superintendent and board members was not printed, nor did the paper take an editorial stand on the issue.

The following Monday evening the school board held its regular meeting. It was customary for the board to allocate the first fifteen minutes for receiving communications and questions from the floor. The superintendent had anticipated that a representative from the South Side Parents' Council might be present and had advised Mr. Wilcox to expect some type of a statement.

As the meeting was opened for questions and comments, a man jumped to his feet and requested recognition. He said he knew that the school board had received a letter from the South Side Parents' Council, and that they would be interested in some additional information which had recently come to light. Would the board permit him to read a brief statement?

Mr. Wilcox looked at the superintendent, but receiving no clear sign as to how to proceed, he indicated that the man should go ahead with his statement.

The gentleman in the audience cleared his throat and then began to read from a rather crumpled piece of paper. "Last week the South Side Parents' Council sent a letter to the superintendent and the school board requesting a change in board policy in releasing IQ and achievement test results to the public. This weekend the Council surveyed the South Side parents to ascertain the distribution of grades given by teachers for the first semester. Two facts were revealed as a result of our investigation: first, a large number of the students at South Side School, over 40 percent, received D's or F's; second, two teachers in particular failed about one-third of their students. These facts have dramatized the need for and have strengthened our determination to secure IQ and achievement test results for each teacher's classes and for the total school. What is needed is an accounting of who is failing—our kids or the school. We will not be satisfied with anything less!"

As the speaker sat down, the superintendent looked over at the president of the school board and then out into the audience where the executive secretary of the teachers' association sat. The secretary's face was livid; the school board president seemed worried. There was a murmur of voices from the audience.

All eyes were now looking expectantly at the superintendent.

SUGGESTED LEARNING ACTIVITIES

Analyze the Case

1. What action, if any, do you think the superintendent should have taken when he *first* began to hear "rumblings" about and from the South Side Parents' Advisory Group? What should he have done after receiving the letter from the parents?
2. What is your assessment of the different arguments which were advanced for and against the parents' proposal during the superintendent's meeting with the administrators? What are some of the less obvious factors which may (even unconsciously) be affecting the thinking of the administrators about this proposal?

3. In what ways would you have behaved differently from the superintendent during the administrators' meeting or during the week prior to the school board meeting?

Discuss the Larger Issues

1. What do you think should be the role of parent advisory groups, e.g., Parents' Council, P.T.A., in the school system? Under what set of circumstances can parent advisory groups become quite powerful? How much power should they have? What aspects of the school's program should legitimately come under their review?
2. Should each school or "cluster" of schools have their own school board, in addition to the city school board? What are the advantages and disadvantages of decentralized school boards?
3. Should the results from standardized tests be used to evaluate a school's program? An individual teacher? Can or should test results remain confidential within the school system? What are the advantages and disadvantages?
4. How can parents and the larger community be assured that the school is doing a good job? Why are some people unwilling to accept the district's or the principal's word that the school is meeting the needs of their children? How can this situation be corrected?

Be a Problem Solver

It would appear at the end of this case that everyone is waiting for the superintendent to make the next move. If *you* were the superintendent, what would you do to solve the immediate problem? The long-range problem?

Test Your Solution

In order to test your plan of action for dealing with the problem presented at the end of the case, you and the class should create and role-play one or more of the following situations:

1. The school board meeting, continued.
2. A meeting between the superintendent, the principal, and the South Side Parent Council.
3. Any other situation that would provide feedback on the strengths and weaknesses of your proposed solution.

Investigate Further

1. Are there any legal constructs in your state which would restrict the public disclosure of IQ and achievement test information?
2. What is your school board's policy on public disclosure of IQ and achievement test results?
3. What would be the opinion of your superintendent, school principal, parents, and teachers on public disclosure of IQ and achievement test results?

29
ADMINISTRATOR-PRESS RELATIONS

Bill Image, principal of Roseview School, was feeling frustrated. He had been trying to get in touch with a reporter, Miss Hardin, at the local newspaper but after several weeks had not been successful. He had first written the reporter a letter inviting her and a photographer to attend and write a story on next month's school assembly program honoring the students who had achieved perfect attendance during the first semester, 10% of the student body. However, since the reporter had not responded, he telephoned her several times, but she always seemed to be out of the office on assignment and never returned his phone messages.

The principal was initially surprised by Miss Hardin's lack of responsiveness and later became annoyed by it. He could perhaps understand her behavior if he were frequently calling her to cover school news and had worn out his welcome. But in the two years he had been principal of Roseview School, he had only phoned her once before, on some minor matter, and even then she hadn't called back. In fact, he had never actually met the lady, although he had seen her a number of times at school board meetings that he had attended. He had thought at the time that Miss Hardin seemed young, rather aggressive, and brash. Pretty, he conceded, but in a hard sort of way. Still, the reporter appeared to be bright, and the thought had occurred to him that he would really need to be on his toes in dealing with her, or she might draw something out of him that would be better kept out of the newspapers. He felt that the papers tended to exaggerate and sensationalize things, anyway. Why couldn't they concentrate on reporting more of the goods things that were happening in the schools, like this upcoming assembly program?

The principal decided to try one more time to reach the reporter and, to his amazement, after only one ring of the phone, she was on the line.

''Hello, Sylvia Hardin speaking. What can I do for you?''

The principal cleared his throat. ''Uh, this is Bill Image, Miss Hardin. As you probably know, I'm the principal at Roseview School, and—''

''Who?''

''It's Mr. Image,'' he repeated. ''Principal at Roseview School.''

''Oh, yes. And what is it that I can help you with?''

''Well, as you probably remember, I wrote to you two weeks ago and invited you to an assembly program we're holding to honor 10% of the students with perfect attendance for the first semester of the year.''

Hearing no response at the other end, he moved on quickly. ''I know you've been busy, since you didn't answer my letter or phone calls, but could you find the time to cover this assembly program?''

''Yes, I have been very busy, but I apologize for not returning your calls,'' the reporter acknowledged. ''I guess I've been avoiding the need to respond to your invitation, but now that we're talking about the matter, I must tell you, quite honestly, that I don't think your assembly program is very newsworthy.''

The principal was taken aback. ''Why not?''

''Because it just isn't that unusual,'' Miss Hardin explained. ''Oh, I know that it's nice to recognize the kids who have had perfect attendance. In fact, if you would send me their names, I'd try to get them mentioned in a future issue of the paper. However—''

The principal interrupted. ''But here is an opportunity for the press to show the community some of the *good* things that are happening in the schools, and I personally feel that there are a *lot* of good things happening at Roseview School that deserve publicity and that would improve people's perceptions of the school.''

Miss Hardin sighed audibly. ''Really, Mr. Image, I don't care much about 'people's perceptions' of the school, but for the sake of discussion, what *are* these so-called 'good things'?''

Put on the spot, the principal hesitated, trying to think of some activities that this reporter would be impressed with. ''Well, just recently we had our first semester's honor roll, and . . . and . . . well, there's some fantastic stuff being done in our art classes. This teacher has so much enthusiasm, she just keeps all the kids going. And . . . and . . .''

The reporter interrupted. ''That all sounds very worthwhile, but I'm not sure that it's *newsworthy*. Anyway, I am sorry, but I have an appointment I need to keep. Perhaps we could talk more later, if you would like. But for now, I must be on my way. It's been nice talking with you.''

After the reporter had hung up the phone, the principal slammed down his receiver, frustrated and somewhat angered by his conversation with the reporter. Why hadn't she answered his call when he initially telephoned her? And what did she mean, expressing skepticism about whether the school's assembly program and the art program were worthwhile. If perfect attendance for these kids wasn't worthwhile, then what *was*? He decided that it was futile to continue to get Miss Hardin to cover next month's assembly program.

In fact, it was probably useless to talk with her anymore, since they obviously had such different points of view on what was worthwhile. His only hope was that maybe she would get transferred, or married, or *something*.

For the next eight weeks Bill Image was busy with various aspects of developing the next year's class schedule and proposed budget, as well as a variety of other kinds of tasks and problems that occupy a principal's time during the late winter—early spring months. In March the students took their competency tests, and by mid-May the results for Roseview School were returned to the principal.

As Bill Image sat in his office, looking at the competency test results, he was initially surprised and then worried about the large number of students who had not passed the examination. At least it seemed to the principal that a larger number of students had failed than in previous years. It looked as if there was going to be a sizeable number of students who would have to attend summer school this year, and if they still couldn't pass the competency test, they would have to be retained in the same grade for another year.

The principal decided that he would present the overall results to the faculty before giving the bad news to individual students and parents, so that the teachers could help cushion the blow for the failing students. Next Monday's regularly scheduled faculty meeting seemed to the principal like a good time to present the test results to the teachers.

On the Tuesday following Monday's faculty meeting, the principal came back to his office after going out for lunch. On his desk he discovered a phone message from Miss Hardin, the local reporter. He asked his secretary if she knew the nature of the call, but she indicated that the reporter had declined to comment, saying only that it was urgent.

The principal thought to himself that he wasn't aware of anything that was urgent—at least from his vantage point—and he had some other activities that he needed to pursue that afternoon. Besides, he wasn't sure that he *wanted* to talk with Miss Hardin, considering his last experience with her. He acknowledged to himself that he would probably have to talk with her sooner or later, but it would have to be later, when he might feel more like talking to a reporter.

Pushing the phone message into his coat pocket, the principal informed his secretary that he was going to be working on the final details of next year's class schedule in a small, unused room in a different part of the building, and he didn't want to be disturbed for *any* reason.

The rest of the afternoon the principal worked on the next year's class schedule. When he returned to his office, he found several additional phone messages from Miss Hardin (all marked "Urgent") and one telephone message from a gym equipment salesman who was responding to a letter from the principal. He knew that he should call Miss Hardin, but instead he added her recent phone messages to the one already in his pocket and then telephoned the gym equipment salesman instead. After a very pleasant conversation, which lasted longer than the principal had anticipated and resulted in a scheduled conference at the school with the salesman on Friday, the principal went home.

That night, about seven o'clock, the principal answered his phone. It was the reporter.

"Hello, this is Sylvia Hardin. Why haven't you answered my phone messages? I told your secretary that it was urgent that I talk with you."

The principal immediately felt a surge of irritation, which turned to apprehension after hearing the reporter speak. "Well, I . . . uh . . . well, I . . . uh . . . was really *busy* this afternoon and uh . . . I, ah, planned to call you right away when I got to school tomorrow."

"I can't wait until tomorrow," the reporter responded angrily. "I need some information *now*. I have heard from a reliable source that a large number of students at Roseview School flunked their competency tests. Is that true?"

The principal hesitated. "Well, I, ah, I wouldn't necessarily say it was real large . . . but

. . . anyway, I can't really discuss those test results because the test results of those students are, ah, *confidential* information."

"What is confidential about them?" persisted the reporter.

"They are confidential," the principal explained, "because . . . that is . . . ah . . . ah . . . *personal* information about a student that would be violating his privacy to discuss."

"But I'm not asking you to tell me the test scores of *individual* students," the reporter shouted in an exasperated voice, "but only how many of them failed."

The principal thought for a moment and then replied, "Well, ah, I don't see where that information will do anybody any good." His voice became stronger and more authoritative. "Besides, these test scores are a very complex matter, and I believe that unless someone has a really good understanding of all the complexities involved, they really wouldn't know how to put them to proper use."

"What complexities?" queried the reporter.

"Well, ah . . ." the principal's voice began to falter, "ah, that's something that is a little hard to talk about on the phone. Ah, I really don't appreciate . . ." the principal's voice picked up strength again, "receiving a call like this at my home. Please call me tomorrow at school if you *really* need to talk to me further," the principal closed, and hung up the phone.

The rest of the evening the principal fretted as he wondered whether he had handled the call from the reporter in the right way, and he worried about what he would do if she called him the next morning. *What* was he going to do?

Early Wednesday morning the local newspaper was distributed to the community. In the second section was an article by Sylvia Hardin about the competency testing program. The article followed a heading that announced, "Principal Refuses to Answer Questions about Test Scores; Doesn't Think Information Would 'Do Anybody Any Good'."

When Mr. Image arrived at school, his secretary gave him two telephone messages for calls that had already come in. One was from the superintendent of schools; the other came from a reporter for a local television station who wanted to visit the school that morning to interview the principal. Both callers had asked that the principal return their calls as soon as possible.

SUGGESTED LEARNING ACTIVITIES

Analyze the Case

1. Are there any steps that the principal should have taken to become acquainted with the reporter *before* calling her about school news?
2. Evaluate the telephone dialogue between the principal and the reporter when he first talks with her. How would you have handled this conversation differently if you had been the principal? What should have been your goal(s) during this telephone conversation?
3. Assess the principal's decision-making behavior in regard to the way he handled the competency test results and the phone messages he received on Tuesday, following the faculty meeting on Monday.
4. Evaluate the Tuesday evening telephone dialogue between the principal and the reporter. How would you have handled this conversation differently if you had been the principal? What should have been your goal(s) during the conversation?

Discuss the Larger Issues

1. What type of relationship should an administrator (principal or superintendent) try to develop with the press? How should an administrator go about developing that relationship? *Be specific.*
2. What should be the role of teachers and other adults working at the school in school-press relations?

3. What should be a school's or district's policy on disseminating and releasing information to the press? On providing access by the press to the school building and its occupants?
4. What is the responsibility of the school district and news organizations to provide inservice education to their personnel on how to function more effectively with each other?

Be a Problem Solver

Assume that you are the principal of this school (it is recognized that you probably would not have gotten into this much trouble). How would you respond to the circumstances that have developed, especially those at the end of the case study? Utilize appropriate administrative and social science concepts from Part I of the text in planning and implementing your approach.

Test Your Solution

To test your proposed plan for resolving the problems described in the case study, you and your colleagues should create and role-play one or more of the following situations:

1. Set up a simulation involving you as a principal making a telephone call to a reporter for the purpose of asking the latter to cover some aspect of the school program.
2. Set up a simulation involving you as a principal receiving a call from a reporter who wants to ask you some questions about your school's competency test results. Set up another simulation in which a reporter leaves a telephone message at the school that he wants to talk to you about a "possible *teacher* drug problem" at the school.
3. Handle a request from a TV reporter who has submitted a request to come to the school during the noon hour to interview students on what they think about the competency testing program.

Investigate Further

1. Examine the educational literature to identify elements that should be included in a *policy* on school-press relations and on the role of the administrator in dealing with the press.
2. Ascertain and evaluate the nature of your school district's or school's policy on school-press relations.
3. Identify the role of the principal in your school district in regard to press relations.
4. Determine what inservice education is provided to administrators in your school district to help them with their role in school-press relations. Evaluate the adequacy of that inservice education and propose improvements.

30
PUBLIC RELATIONS: WHAT'S REALLY IMPORTANT?

As the principal had anticipated, the first month of school had been hectic. But now that October had arrived, he decided that it would be a good time to send a letter home to parents, offering his impressions of the beginning weeks of the school year.

He believed that school communication to the home was an essential public relations technique, and it was important for community support that parents be kept informed of all the good things that were happening. He further felt that the news media tended to be too critical of education and that he had a responsibility to see that the parents received the true story about what was happening at school.

For the next 20 minutes he thought about and wrote the letter that he wanted to send home to the parents. The message read:

> Dear Parents:
> As you know, we are now in the second month of the school year and we are off to a tremendously fine beginning. Although there were a few minor

problems the first day—which, of course, could be expected—everything has been proceeding smoothly, and we expect a truly excellent year. We have an outstanding staff and, we believe, a truly exciting curriculum representing a wide diversity of enriching experiences for students with varying interests and aspirations. This year we have initiated several new educational thrusts which should offer a more multifaceted, individualized program for your children. I hope to have more to report to you later on these new educational ventures.

I know that this coming year will be filled with countless new challenges for your children and we are gratified to offer them so many learning opportunities. We have had your continuing support and trust in the past, and we hope that we can continue to receive it in the future.

In closing, I would like to emphasize that my door is always open to you if you have a question or concern. I believe that this is a school about which you can truly be proud, and I would welcome the opportunity to talk with you at any time.

Sincerely,
Dr. William Kendall

The letter to the parents looked fine to the principal. He instructed his secretary to have it typed and to make sufficient copies for distribution to the students at the end of the school day so that they could take it home to their parents.

During the time the principal had been working on his letter to the parents, a visitor had come to the school. The visitor, who supervised student teachers from the university, had not been to the school previously, and therefore mistakenly entered through the back of the building. Since he was early for his appointment with the student teacher, he decided to wait in the principal's office. However, because it was not immediately clear how to get to the principal's office, he asked a couple of students, who merely giggled and shrugged their shoulders. Fortunately, the very next person he asked was a teacher who directed him to the principal's office on the other side of the building.

As he proceeded toward the office, the supervisor couldn't help noticing how littered and messy the corridors appeared. He also noticed that the people in the halls—both students and teachers—didn't seem to pay much attention to him. They weren't exactly unfriendly, but they just seemed to ignore him.

When the supervisor reached the principal's office, he took a seat in what appeared to be a general administrative office and reception area. He was going to tell anyone who asked that he was just waiting for his appointment with the student teacher, but no one asked.

As the supervisor sat in the reception area, he observed the school secretaries at work. One of them answered the phone: "Lakeview School. What is it you want? No, he isn't here now. I don't know where he is. He probably will be back before very long." The supervisor watched the same secretary take another telephone call: "Lakeview School. What is it you want? No, he is in conference right now. I am not sure when he will be done; can I have him call you? You will call some other time? All right."

During the last telephone conversation the supervisor noticed that a student had approached the counter and was waiting for someone to acknowledge him. At the end of the telephone conversation, the vice-principal walked into the reception area and stood beside the student at the counter. When the secretary greeted the vice-principal and asked if she could help him, the vice-principal responded that the student had been there first. But before the student could say anything, the secretary said sharply, "Administrators always come first—students can be taken care of later," and she proceeded to wait on the vice-principal, who apparently agreed. The supervisor looked at the student for some reaction but the student seemed resigned to the matter.

For the next ten minutes the supervisor continued to observe the secretaries at work and was struck by their casual, almost indifferent attitude toward the people who came into the reception area, particularly students. The supervisor wondered whether or not he should say anything to the principal, but decided not to pursue the matter. He remembered from talking previously to the student teacher at the university that she had felt that the principal was very ego-involved with his school and seemed to have the attitude that everything was perfect at Lakeview. It didn't appear that it would do any good to talk to the principal. Still, it seemed that *something* should be done.

EPILOGUE

Shortly after the first of the year, the principal, Dr. Kendall, suffered a heart attack and had to take a medical leave for the remainder of the school year. The vice-principal of the school was appointed by the school district to be acting principal, and one of the teachers who had completed a master's degree in school administration was appointed acting assistant principal.

In the latter part of January the university supervisor who had visited the school earlier in the year was meeting for a conference with one of his student teachers at Lakeview. As long as he was at the school, he decided that he might as well drop in on the acting principal and share some of his observations about the school. Perhaps the acting principal would be more interested in improving conditions.

SUGGESTED LEARNING ACTIVITIES

Analyze the Case

1. What is your assessment of the principal's conception of public relations?
2. Evaluate the principal's letter to the parents, utilizing concepts and principles of communication and public relations.
3. What kinds of factors may be negatively affecting the public relations of this school? How likely is it that the principal is aware of the factors? Why, or why not?

Discuss the Larger Issues

1. What should be the main purpose and emphasis in a school's public relations program?
2. How can the administration, faculty, students, and parents best contribute to these purposes?
3. When does public relations become public manipulation? And by what criteria and methods should the public relations program of a school or district be evaluated?

Be a Problem Solver

Assume that you became the principal of this school in the middle of the year, and the kinds of circumstances described in the case came to your attention. What would be your approach to dealing with this matter? Utilize appropriate administrative and social science concepts from Part I of the text in planning and implementing your approach.

Test Your Solution

To test your proposed plan for dealing with the problems described in the case, you and your colleagues should create and role-play one or more of the following situations.

1. A faculty meeting.
2. A meeting with the secretaries.
3. A letter to parents.

Investigate Further

1. What is the concept of public relations and its purpose held by the administration, teachers, students, and parents in your school or school district?
2. Describe the public relations program, including the role of the administrator and faculty, in your school or school district. How is this program evaluated?
3. How effective is the public relations program in your school or school district? How reliable and valid are the data upon which judgments of effectiveness are made?

31
CENSORSHIP? OR PARENTS' RIGHTS?

Something was obviously wrong with Barb Smith, a student in the fifth period class. The teacher had noticed that the usually talkative girl was very quiet this week and had hardly participated in group discussion. The class had been studying Claude Brown's *Manchild in the Promised Land,* and the teacher wondered momentarily whether Barb's reticence might be related to the book they were reading. However, he dismissed the possibility as he remembered the girl's initial enthusiasm when the class had chosen the book from several alternatives presented. Nevertheless, he decided that he should schedule a conference to see what was bothering her.

After school he discovered that his first premonition had been correct. Barb informed him that she personally liked the book and agreed with what the teacher had said about the need to better understand the racial problem. But when her father examined the novel, he had exploded and had refused to let her finish it. He had further forbidden her to participate in any class discussions or to complete any assignments. Her father planned to get in touch with the school, but meanwhile he wanted her to be assigned another book.

The teacher tried to explore with Barb her father's objections, but the girl seemed embarrassed to discuss the matter further. She would only say that her father felt that it was a "dirty book" and not something that a girl should be allowed to read. The teacher wanted to question Barb further, but he could see that she was becoming upset. So he told her not to worry about the situation, and indicated that he would try to work something out.

Early the next morning the teacher met with the principal and presented the problem. The principal's initial reaction was one of concern, but he admitted that he was unfamiliar with the book and could not recall why it had been originally selected.

The teacher explained that this particular novel was being used because it depicted social conditions existing for minority groups in many parts of the country. The teacher had requested and received approval from Mr. Collins, his department head, to teach on an experimental basis a book on racial relations to one section of students. Hopefully, through class discussion and study of *Manchild in the Promised Land,* students would develop a better appreciation of some of the problems and attitudes of black Americans. In addition, the book had literary merit and was written by a recognized black author. The teacher concluded by saying that he felt that both black and white students should be exposed to this kind of writing and thought.

At that point the principal brought up the main objection by Barb's father. Was it a "dirty book"? The teacher vehemently rejected such a characterization and went on to strongly defend Brown's work as being exceptionally worthwhile.

Finally the principal broke in on the teacher's somewhat lengthy and emotional defense of the book, pointing out that no one was questioning its literary merits. The issue was whether a school should—or even could—force a student to read a book which her parents strongly opposed. Besides, the principal went on to say, there was no reason why another book couldn't be provided since only one student was involved.

The teacher could hardly believe what he had heard and inwardly felt that the principal was taking the parents' side. But not wishing to antagonize his superior, he reluctantly agreed to provide the student with an alternate assignment.

That evening the principal received two calls from parents who wanted him to know that an undesirable book had been made required reading for their children. Both callers were very outspoken in demanding different assignments for their children and were critical of the principal for approving *Manchild in the Promised Land* for school use. They warned him that many other parents were also upset. The principal tried to discover the basis for their concern, but only one of the parents would comment, and she alluded to the fact that there were several sexual scenes in the book. She indicated that a number of parents were calling each other, and that the matter had become an important issue in the community, even among parents whose children were not in that class.

The principal felt very uncomfortable during both telephone conversations since he still had not read the book. Although quite reluctant to permit different student assignments without first talking to the teacher, he finally conceded that the school would provide alternatives to the selection currently being studied. After finishing the telephone conversations, he made a mental note to talk to the teacher in the morning and to definitely get his hands on that book! Could it be as bad as those parents were suggesting?

First thing the next day the principal secured a copy of the book. As he read the novel, he did not feel that it was a "dirty book," but he could see why some parents might be bothered. He decided he'd better send a note to the teacher describing the complaints he had received last night and the decision he had made to provide alternate assignments for two more students. He would be sure to emphasize that, although future consideration might result in withdrawing the book from class study, its use for present class purposes was still approved.

The teacher received the principal's message that afternoon and read it with mixed feelings. He, too, had received calls from parents outraged about the book who had demanded its elimination from the curriculum. But he had responded negatively to their demands and was irritated that the principal had approved alternate assignments without first consulting him. He was concerned about what the principal might do if the objections grew or if a formal protest was made to the school board. He doubted whether the principal could stand up under that kind of pressure.

On the other hand, the teacher was glad that the book would not be immediately withdrawn from his course. It was entirely possible that if the school "held its ground," the book would ultimately gain greater acceptance. Just this morning several students had mentioned in class that their parents approved the book as a relevant and timely choice for student discussion. One boy said that his father felt that it was about time that the school began to deal with the vital issues facing the nation.

In the meantime though, the teacher was faced with the problem of making different class assignments for two additional students. What should he do about them? He decided that he would seek the advice of Mr. Collins, his department head.

At that moment the principal was reading a copy of a letter that had been delivered to his office, although it was addressed to the superintendent and the school board. Apparently a copy had also been sent to the newspaper. The letter, signed by thirty-three individuals, read:

> We, the undersigned, take extreme exception to the teaching of Claude Brown's *Manchild in the Promised Land* at Whitecliff School. The book presents some of the worst aspects of our society and does nothing to show students the more positive characteristics of our great American culture.
>
> It is clear from only a cursory reading of the novel that its author is a troublemaker who is trying to promote feelings of anxiety and guilt on the part of the white people about the blacks' problems.
>
> In addition, we strongly object to the school's approval of a book that uses such foul language and which depicts sexual activities in detail. We demand that this book be immediately eliminated from the school curriculum and from the required reading of any student at the school. It is time that someone in a position of authority take a strong stand in support of those parents who want the school to become more responsible to the moral climate of our community.

The principal slammed the letter on top of his desk. It was obvious that the problem was getting out of hand. *No* book was worth this much conflict or unfavorable publicity. He would simply withdraw the book. After all, the class had only been studying it on an experimental basis, and clearly the experiment had failed; the community was not ready for this type of material. He decided to inform Mr. Collins, the department head, about his decision, and together they would explain to the teacher why it was not possible at this time to continue the study of the book.

Just then the principal's secretary said that Mr. Collins wanted to talk with him for a few minutes. After Mr. Collins came into the office, the principal began to fill him in on the situation. While the principal was speaking, the department head waited quietly with a very serious and determined expression on his face. When the principal finished explaining his position, Mr. Collins indicated that he had previously spoken with the teacher, and they had both decided against providing alternatives for the three students whose parents had objected to the original selection.

The department head further informed the principal that the entire department believed that the school, and particularly the administration, should take a very strong stand in support of the study of *Manchild in the Promised Land*. The department felt that the school should not allow a minority of parents to dictate to the teachers the books that could or could not be read in class. It seemed inevitable that once the minority had succeeded in imposing their will on the school, no teacher would be immune from their attacks. To withdraw the book now would be tantamount to surrendering to the minority, and his department had no intention of capitulating. "The real question," Mr. Collins said, "is who is running the school?" And with that parting shot, the department head walked out.

The principal sat down slowly. It looked like he had a real school-community conflict on his hands.

SUGGESTED LEARNING ACTIVITIES

Analyze the Case

1. What might account for the fact that the principal had not previously read the book in question and could not recall why it had been originally selected?
2. What is your reaction to the reasons given by the teacher for studying *Manchild in the Promised Land?*
3. What is your evaluation of the principal's actions in the following situations?
   a. His conference with the teacher
   b. His telephone conversations with the two parents
   c. His memo to the teacher
   d. His decision to withdraw the book
4. What is your assessment of the position taken by the English Department on the issue of using *Manchild in the Promised Land?*
5. What are some of the factors that add to the complexity and difficulty of resolving the problems in this case?

Discuss the Larger Issues

1. To what extent should a teacher be influenced in the selection of class materials by the fact that they may conceivably disturb a number of parents? Under what set of circumstances (if any) should a school concede to parent or community objections?
2. What role should parents and the larger community play in book selection or approval? What role should the faculty play? The principal? The central office? What criteria should determine the nature and extent of the responsibilities of each of these groups or individuals in book selection or approval? Who should have the final responsibility for approving a book for classroom or library use if there is objection to the selection?
3. What should be included in a school policy statement covering the circumstances

described in this case? Who should be involved in developing the statement? What difficulties might be encountered in applying such a policy to problems of the nature described in this case?

Be a Problem Solver

Assume that you are the principal and you are faced with a situation entailing apparently growing parental objection to a book and potential faculty-community and faculty-administration conflict. What should be done to resolve these problems? What alternatives are available to you and what factors will you need to take into consideration in solving the problems? Utilize appropriate administrative and social science concepts from Part I of the text in planning and implementing your approach.

Test Your Solution

To test your proposed plan of action for dealing with the problems presented at the end of the case, you and the class should create and role-play one or more of the following situations:

1. A telephone call to the principal from the superintendent, who reports that board members have received complaints about the book and would like to know what the principal is going to do about it.
2. Another meeting between the principal and the teacher involved.
3. A telephone call from a reporter for a national press dispatch who has gotten wind of the controversy and wants to know the details.
4. A telephone call from an officer of the state civil liberties union who has been contacted by a parent who fears that censorship may take place.

Investigate Further

1. What is your school's or district's written policy on teaching controversial literature?
2. What legal precedents have been set in cases in which a parent has sought to remove a book from the curriculum or the library?
3. How do administrators and teachers in your district feel about the right of parents to decide whether or not their children should be taught controversial material?

32

FINANCIAL CRISIS!

The superintendent shuddered as he looked again at the sheets of figures spread across his desk. This was going to be a tough year financially for the school district. The mayor and several city council members had already publicly made a stand to hold the line on taxes. But flying in the face of that commitment were the cold facts: proposed building operating costs were up, reflecting previously delayed expenditures, and the state legislature had reduced state aid. A higher school budget seemed inescapable.

He thought back to previous years. The costs of education had been rising for some time, but in the past the P.T.A. and other community groups had always campaigned for the budget while putting pressure on city hall for more money toward education. Now everyone seemed concerned about rising taxes, and there was not much outward support for the school.

It seemed to the superintendent that people these days were more critical and demanding of education, and yet were unwilling to provide the necessary funds. He realized that part of the problem was the way in which education was financed, but what could *he* do about that?

During the development of the budget the superintendent had instructed his staff and all the principals to cut proposed expenditures wherever possible and to recommend only items which a school absolutely needed. He had told them that the goal was to achieve a "bare bones" budget. He knew that anything not absolutely essential for next year would eventually be cut by either the school board of the city council.

The superintendent remembered that the principals had complained about his instructions. He could understand their feelings, since there was only so much that a principal could cut from the teachers' requests. However, he had been disappointed to hear through the "grapevine" that they felt he was sacrificing quality in education for economy. Well, maybe they were right. But what do you do when you are faced with a fiscal crisis and an adamant city council? Do you fight? Do you compromise? Do you work for fiscal independence? While the latter was a potentially viable alternative, it would certainly not solve the immediate problem. It was easy for the principals to talk—they didn't have the responsibility. Still, the superintendent knew that the principals had their troubles too, and they had to contend with their faculties when budget items were cut. There didn't seem to be any easy way out. He only hoped that next week's board meeting wouldn't go too badly.

The following Monday the school board met to consider the budget. Represented at the special meeting were several taxpayers' groups and others who opposed raising the mill rate. There didn't seem to be anyone in the audience who in the past had been a "friend of the schools."

As the meeting began, the questions started to flow. Why were teachers' salaries so high? Why not raise class sizes in order to save money? Why was so much money spent on athletics? Why should items for teachers' professional improvement be paid by the public? Why couldn't a citizens' committee be established to examine more closely the rationale behind each budget item?

These were difficult questions for the superintendent and his staff to answer. For example, they were unable to *prove* that raising class sizes would impair teacher effectiveness, although a logical case could be presented in that regard. But this year people simply were not satisfied with "explanations"—they wanted *evidence.* It wasn't so much that they were against education. Rather, they were determined to hold the line against any tax increase; a reduced school budget was necessary to achieve that end. Although the superintendent and the school board were sympathetic, they felt that to cut the budget further would result in significant damage to the overall school program.

As the last speaker finally finished at 11:30 P.M., the president of the board asked for a formal motion on the budget. It had been a long evening, full of heated and sometimes hostile discussion. The superintendent was hopeful, however, that the school board would pass the budget as proposed. He had involved the members of the board in the budget process from the beginning, and they had considered every item.

The board approved the budget, 5 to 2, and the superintendent felt a momentary relief until he remembered the city council meeting scheduled to be held in two weeks. The budget would have to be sent to the council immediately for their consideration.

During the next week the newspaper and the radio carried several editorials criticizing the school budget, particularly class sizes and the number of classes teachers taught. Letters to the editor also reflected concern about the tax money spent on athletics and other extracurricular activities. The major problem seemed to be that people were tired of raising taxes; they were not going to stand for another hike. Taxes were already at an all-time high, and the proposed school budget would raise the rate by 2.34 mills.

Worried by the widespread community opposition to the budget, the superintendent arranged to speak to various P.T.A.'s and civic organizations. In these talks he repeatedly emphasized that the proposed budget represented essential items for the education of the children in the community, and that further cuts would mean a curtailment in services. Although the audiences seemed to understand the rationale behind the budget, they continued to return to the point that property owners could not afford higher taxes.

By the time the city council met on Monday, it was clear that a confrontation was inevitable. Long-suffering taxpayers, eager to express themselves, filled the council chambers. Speaker after speaker elaborated on the tax squeeze and denounced the "frills" of education. Throughout the evening there were only sparsely sprinkled statements from citizens who favored meeting the schools' needs.

Finally at 10:30 a formal motion was introduced to cut the school budget by 10%. After an hour of discussion, the president of the council called for a vote on the motion. The superintendent held his breath as the results were announced: the motion carried, 9 to 5; the school budget was cut 10%. The school board was to determine where the specific cuts would be made.

Afterwards, completely disheartened by the action of the city council, the superintendent and his staff met for a brief time with the members of the school board. There would be a number of difficult decisions to be made. Educational priorities would have to be re-examined and undoubtedly some services would have to be curtailed. Where should the cuts take place? What was really essential to keep in the budget? The future of education in the district was at stake.

SUGGESTED LEARNING ACTIVITIES

Analyze the Case

1. Why do the superintendent and the building principals look at the budget in different ways? How can this difference in perception be narrowed?
2. How would you assess the superintendent's preparation for the school board meeting on the budget? Were the questions asked at the meeting inquiries for which the superintendent should have possessed definitive answers? Why or why not?
3. What additional steps could the superintendent have taken before the city council meeting to cope with the growing resistance of the community to the budget?

Discuss the Larger Issues

1. In what ways is the school at least partially responsible for the deterioration or reduction of support by groups that have traditionally supported it? What can schools do to maintain the support of important community groups in the face of rising school costs?
2. What do you feel is the "answer" to the financial problems faced by the schools? What problems or barriers would have to be overcome before any solution to the schools' financial problems could be successfully implemented?
3. What can administrators, teachers, and parents do individually or collectively to bring about change in the way education is presently financed?

Be a Problem Solver

Assume that you are the superintendent and you must decide with your board how to cut the school budget by 10%. You have already eliminated every possible item that was not basic to the students' education. Now something essential will have to be curtailed or eliminated. How do you propose to solve this problem? Utilize appropriate administrative and social science concepts from Part I of the text in planning and implementing your approach.

Test Your Solution

To test your proposed plan of action for dealing with the problem presented at the end of the case, you and the class should create and role-play one or more of the following situations:

1. A call to the superintendent from a local reporter.
2. A call from the representative of the local teachers' organization.
3. A call from a parent who has heard that you may eliminate a program in which her daughter is enrolled for the following year.

4. A meeting between the superintendent and the principals to cut the budget further.

Investigate Further

1. What type of public relations procedures have proved effective in averting community resistance to greater school expenditures?
2. What steps would be necessary in your state for a school board to obtain fiscal autonomy? What would be the advantages and disadvantages of such a move? From what individuals or groups would you be likely to obtain support? Resistance?
3. What legal changes can be made to reduce the burden of school taxes on local property owners?

13 Role and Organizational Problems

A major activity in this chapter consists of the in-basket exercises entitled "Middle-of-the-Year Problems and Priorities," and "End-of-the-Year Problems and Priorities." In these exercises the reader is asked to play the role of principal and assume the same characteristics of the school, school district, and community that were assumed for "The New Principal" in-basket exercise presented in Chapter 9.

This second set of in-basket items arises during the middle of the year and the last month of the school year, and the principal is presented with a wide variety of problems and issues in the form of memos, telephone messages, notes, and so forth. Addressing these problems and issues effectively will require the appropriate use of many of the concepts presented in the first eight chapters of the book.

Also included in this chapter are a number of case studies that focus on problems of role and organizational conflict. Since there are, of course, many different kinds of problems associated with role and organizational conflict, only a sampling of such problems is possible in this chapter. However, the case studies which are presented should give the reader exposure to a number of representative problem situations that could develop during a career as an administrator or supervisor. By responding to the situations described in the case studies, on the basis of careful analysis and appropriate utilization of the concepts in Part I of the book, the reader should develop increased effectiveness in preventing or dealing with problems of this nature.

BACKGROUND READING

For the reader who would like to develop further background and understanding of the problems and issues presented in this chapter, the following list of readings is suggested:

Mark E. Anderson, "Evaluating Principals: Strategies to Assess their Performance," ERIC document no. Ed 306–672.

Miles T. Bryant and Marilyn L. Grady, "Where Boards Cross the Line," *American School Board Journal* (October, 1990), 20–21.

Ronald G. Corwin and Kathryn M. Borman, "School as Workplace: Structural Constraints on Administrators" in *Handbook of Research on Educational Administration,* ed. Norman J. Boyan (New York: Longman, 1988), pp. 209–238.

The Equal Access Act and the Public Schools, (Arlington, VA: American Association of School Administrators, 1991).

Richard A. Gorton and Gail Thierbach-Schneider, "The School Administrator's Role, Expectations, and Social Factors" in *School-Based Leadership: Challenges and Opportunities,* 3rd ed. (Dubuque, IA: Wm. C. Brown Publishers, 1991), pp. 84–117.

Stuart C. Smith and Philip K. Piele, *School Leadership: Handbook for Excellence,* 2nd. ed. (Eugene, OR: Eric Clearinghouse on Educational Management, 1989), Chapter 12.

33
PRINCIPAL'S MID-YEAR PROBLEMS AND PRIORITIES (IN-BASKET ACTIVITIES)

Background

You are Dr. Brown, and you are in your first year as principal of Kennedy School.

It is the first week in December, and you have gone to the school on Saturday morning to check your mail and telephone messages, having been out of town since Wednesday evening participating in an accreditation evaluation of another school.

You are to assume the same characteristics of the social context of this situation, including the nature of the school, the district, and the community, as were assumed in responding to the in-basket items in Chapter 9. Any other additional information will be provided by the instructor or group leader, as appropriate.

Instructions

1. You will be given 90 minutes to read and take action on *all* of the items presented following the instructions. You are not expected merely to *describe* what you would do, but to *do* it. For example, if you decide to telephone a person or see someone for a conference, then outline your objectives, as well as the main points or questions that you would present. (Utilize relevant concepts from Part I of the text in your responses.)
2. You may respond to the in-basket items in whatever sequence you prefer. However, you should first read *all* of them, *quickly*. As you do so, indicate on a separate piece of paper in one of three columns whether a particular in-basket item represents a ''High Priority'' situation (1), a ''Moderate Priority'' situation (2) or a ''Low Priority'' situation (3).
3. Each of the in-basket items requires a separate action, which you should present on another sheet of paper, adding the identification number in the upper left-hand corner of the in-basket item. If you understand all of the instructions up to this point, you may begin now or when your instructor so indicates.

In-Basket Item #1

Confidential Note

Dr. Brown:

You were busy, and I have tried unsuccessfully several times to get in to see you, so I am writing you this note.

As you know, I am a conscientious member of this faculty, and I believe in change and innovation and all that ''good stuff.'' However, I am getting tired of Bob Love's kids coming in to my classroom all excited, some of them holding hands and others hugging each other. It takes me an extra 5–10 minutes just to get them settled down again whenever he has those kids doing certain exercises. I know Bob has introduced this unit on human relations and nonverbal communication, and I suppose it is a good unit. But he gets the kids all worked up.

Is there anything you can do about this problem? Please don't use my name because I don't want to get in trouble with Bob. Also, as you know, he is very popular with the students and most of the faculty.

Kay Stern

In-Basket Item #2

MEMO

TO: Dr. Brown

FROM: Tim Parker

I have been thinking for some time about this idea and finally decided that I would propose it to you. As you know, we are presently developing an individualized education program (IEP) for handicapped or disabled students of one kind or another. What I would like to propose is that the teachers develop an IEP for each nonhandicapped student who is a chronic or serious discipline problem.

These students are just as much in need of an IEP as the handicapped students, and it would probably do more to improve their discipline behavior than anything that I could do out of my office. I know this would require the cooperation of the teachers, but I believe that with your leadership the idea can be sold to the faculty. Let me know what you think.

In-Basket Item #3

November 29

Dear Dr. Brown:

My purpose in writing this letter is to register a formal complaint about the fact that I am being left out of my daughter Valerie's education. As you may or may not know, I am divorced from Valerie's mother who, in a travesty of justice, was given custody of our daughter. At the present time the decision about custodianship is being appealed. In the meantime, I am also challenging the visitation access to my daughter provided by her mother.

All of the preceding is by way of background. My specific complaints with the school are that I am not being informed by the school of my daughter's grades, nor am I being invited to parent-teacher conferences when they are held. Dr. Brown, I want you to know that I love my daughter dearly, and I know she loves me. I continue to be very interested in her education, and I would like you to rectify the present situation regarding communication about Valerie's grades and providing for participation in parent-teacher conferences.

I look forward to your positive action at the earliest possible date.

Sincerely,
Anthony Springfield

In-Basket Item #4

MEMO

TO: Dr. Brown
FROM: Pat Concern, Counselor

Dr. Brown, I have been giving a lot of thought to this, and I feel we need some sort of a *faculty* inservice on AIDS and other sexually transmitted diseases, and ways of preventing them. I know in the health classes we try to address these problems for students, but we have never done anything for faculty. I don't know for sure that there is any specific need, but I have heard rumors, which of course I would *never* repeat. Anyway, I think we should do something in this area, and I know someone who would do a good job in presenting the inservice. Can I contact him?

In-Basket Item #5

Dr. Brown, while you were gone, something happened that I thought you should know about. On Friday Mary Eager wore a button on her dress which says, "Sexism is a social disease." I didn't say anything to her but I did overhear some students talking about it. What do you think we ought to do?

Tim Parker

In-Basket Item #6

MEMO

TO: Dr. Brown
FROM: Cathy Collins

As president of the Teachers' Association, I tend to be in close contact with the various concerns expressed by the faculty, not only in our building, but in the district at large. The latest issue to surface is administrator evaluation. What many (if not most) of the teachers seem to want is the opportunity to evaluate or offer feedback to the administrators on their performance. At this stage I don't believe there is any consensus on what form the evaluation of administrators would take, but it seems there is agreement that something should be done.

Therefore, I have been asked to request that you add to the agenda for the next faculty meeting the topic of faculty evaluation of the administrators.

In-Basket Item #7

Telephone Message

FOR: Dr. Brown
FROM: Al Wood, Channel 12
TIME: 12:15, Friday

Please call as soon as possible, at 332-8562. I want to do a feature on at-risk students, and I have already obtained their parents' permission.

In-Basket Item #8

November 28

Dear Dr. Brown:

This is not an easy note to send you, and I wish I didn't have to, but I think you should know that one of your teachers, Mr. King, has AIDS. The reason I know this is that I have dated Mr. King and I recently was tested and found to have been infected with AIDS. I have confronted Mr. King about this situation, but he doesn't want to talk about it. I am concerned that he may infect someone else at the school. I am writing this anonymously because I don't want any trouble. But I thought you should know about Mr. King.

A Concerned Parent

In-Basket Item #9

Dr. Brown, I am afraid that we are going to have a problem on Monday. While you were gone, the clocks and the bell system got screwed up. The clocks aren't all on the same time, and the bells aren't ringing at the right time. This all happened Friday afternoon, and me and Sam tried to get it fixed but nothing seemed to work. So I called the company late Friday to ask them to come in and fix it, but they said they couldn't send anyone until sometime Monday. I guess we will have to make the best of it until then.

Al, Head Custodian

In-Basket Item #10

Dr. Brown—

You may or may not know of me, but I teach a course on the principalship at the University. I have heard many positive things about you and your school, and I would like you to talk to my class next semester sometime on the topic of "Instructional Leadership."

Please let me know as soon as possible which week might be most convenient for you. My class meets on Wednesday evenings from 6:30 to 9:30 P.M.

Sincerely
Thomas Sloan, Ph.D.
Professor, Educational Leadership

In-Basket Item #11

Dr. Brown, something happened on Friday that I thought you should know about. Candy Williams fainted in the faculty lounge and Mr. Parker gave her mouth-to-mouth resuscitation to relieve her. I don't know much about it because I wasn't there. But I heard via the grapevine that Candy was embarrassed by the incident, and that Wendy Stack tried to pull Mr. Parker away from Candy before he had finished reviving her. This is all probably very innocent. However, I thought you ought to know about the situation, just in case.

Peg Albright
Secretary

In-Basket Item #12

TO: All Principals
FROM: Superintendent Ramirez

I have just come from a conference with a group of parents who are concerned about improving school-home communications. One of their recommendations, which I strongly endorse and am directing you to implement beginning with a faculty meeting, is that teachers take the initiative to schedule a conference with any parents whose child is in danger of failing a course during any particular marking period.

The conference should be held in sufficient time before grades are given so that the student would have a reasonable amount of time to improve the grade. I believe this procedure will greatly alleviate the concern of a number of parents who presently don't find out if their children are failing until grades are sent home.

In-Basket Item #13

Dr. Brown, while you were away on Friday, 3 kids showed up (2 boys and a girl, who said they weren't related) who wanted to enroll here. I questioned them a bit because they looked really pathetic, with ratty-looking clothes and were generally unkempt. I found out that they are homeless, although they all apparently live in two old cars that are located within our school boundaries. I didn't know what to do, so I told them to come back before school begins on Monday, and you would meet with them.

Peg Albright

In-Basket Item #14

Dr. Brown

I don't know whether I should tell you this or not, and Al wasn't sure either. But I talked to my wife and she says that I should, before something gets real messy. Anyway, late Wednesday after the students and faculty had long left the building I found a used condom in the faculty lounge. I didn't know what to do with it for sure, but I saved it in case you wanted it for evidence or something. Al thinks it's two faculty members but he really don't know anything. Please let me know as soon as possible what to do because I would like to get rid of it.

Sam Clean, Custodian

In-Basket Item #15

November 30

MEMO

TO: Principals
FROM: Assistant Superintendent Fong

In the last meeting of the superintendent's cabinet it was decided that this year the guidance counselors should be evaluated more formally and consistently. Since the district does not currently utilize a standard counselor evaluation instrument, we need to develop something defensible and useful. Please submit your ideas within two weeks on what should be included in such an evaluation instrument, the steps that ought to be followed in the evaluation process, who should be involved in the process, etc. Once I have all of your ideas, I will try to put together a model evaluation instrument and process for counselors and get your reactions to it before formal adoption by the district.

In-Basket Item #16

November 26

Dear Dr. Brown:

As you know, there is considerable discussion these days about abortion and use of contraceptives. Students are exposed almost daily to these ideas, and I know in the district's own health classes these kinds of topics are explored.

What my group would like to do is to present the pro-life point of view. Specifically, we would like to present a program at a future PTA meeting and at a future student assembly this year. Parents and students alike need to receive positive information about the wonderful miracle that God has bestowed upon us all.

Dr. Brown, our group is offering some excellent films that can be shown, and we have an array of outstanding speakers for this purpose. We would like to schedule something in January. Please let me know as soon as possible what specific dates might be available.

Alice Darling, President
Council for the Beauty of Life

In-Basket Item #17

Dear Dr. Brown:

The Student Council members have been discussing informally two ideas that we would like you to react to. First, although we are sure that the cafeteria staff works hard, the food is terrible. Therefore, we would like you to see if McDonald's couldn't be used as either a substitute or as some additional choice we could have for our lunch.

Second, we would like to be able to listen to some of our own music during the noon hour while we are eating. We did a little poll, and almost everyone likes rap music. And since you really have to listen to the words to get the most out of it, the cafeteria would be a lot quieter. Please let us know what you think of our ideas.

Sincerely,
Jack Staker
Sandy Elliot
Student Council Reps

In-Basket Item #18

Telephone Message

FROM: Betty Spokes
TIME: Friday, 3 P.M.

Betty Spokes called about her daughter Valerie. Her ex-husband has been picking up Valerie after school, and she wants Valerie to take the bus instead.

In-Basket Item #19

November 26

Dear Mr. Brown:

I would like to know what is going on in Mr. Love's classroom. My son comes home from school and complains because in Mr. Love's class the students are supposed to hug each other and to do other things with their faces. My son says that this is some sort of a human relations unit, but he doesn't like it and from what I have heard about it, I don't like it either.

It seems to me that the school has enough to do with just teaching the basics without getting into all of this other stuff. Mr. Clark and I feel that we do just fine in teaching our son all the human relations he needs, and we definitely don't like the idea of the school requiring him to hug someone from a different background if he doesn't want to.

I expect some sort of action on this matter and look forward to a response from you—*soon*.

Bea Clark

34

PRINCIPAL'S END-OF-THE-YEAR PROBLEMS AND PRIORITIES (IN-BASKET ACTIVITIES)

Background

You are Dr. Brown, and it is your first year as principal of Kennedy School.

It is May 10, and you have gone to the school on a Saturday morning to check over your mail and telephone messages, having been out of town since Wednesday evening, attending a conference on instructional leadership.

You are to assume the same characteristics of the social context of this situation, including the nature of the school, the district, and the community, as were assumed in responding to the in-basket items in Chapter 9. Any other additional information will be provided by the instructor or group leader, as appropriate.

Instructions

1. You will be given 90 minutes to read and take action on *all* of the in-basket items presented following the instructions. You are not expected merely to *describe* what you would do, but to *do* it. For example, if you decide to write a letter, then compose the letter. If you decide to telephone a person or see someone for a conference, then outline your objectives, as well as the main points or questions that you would present. (Utilize relevant concepts from Part I of the text in your responses.)
2. Each of the in-basket items requires a separate action, which you should present on another sheet of paper, adding the identification number in the upper left-hand corner of the in-basket item. You may deal with the in-basket items in whatever sequence you prefer; however, you should indicate on your response sheet the priority 1 = high priority, 2 = moderate priority, and 3 = low priority.
3. Proceed to the in-basket items.

In-Basket Item #1

MEMO

May 9

TO: Dr. Brown
FROM: Mary Eager

Dr. Brown, I have applied for summer school curriculum work and, although I haven't been turned down yet, I feel that the district is dragging its feet.

As you know, my proposal is to work on developing a peace studies component in our curriculum. I would appreciate it if you would write a letter or something to get them moving in the district office. I don't know what their problem is!

In-Basket Item #2

MEMO

May 6

TO: All Principals and Supervisors
FROM: Superintendent

The school board has expressed interest again in the concepts of career ladders and merit pay. What I would like each of you to do is to develop some recommendations for establishing an effective and feasible merit pay program and a career ladders program for teachers. I know these ideas are controversial, but put your ideas in memorandum form and send them to me as soon as possible. Consult with whomever you would like. However, the school board would like to get some initial input on this before the end of the school year.

In-Basket Item #3

Telephone Message

FOR: Dr. Brown
FROM: Tom Roberts (State Journal)
TIME: 12:05 P.M., Thursday

Please call him back today. He wants to set up an ''in-depth interview'' with you about your experiences during this first year.

In-Basket Item #4

May 5

Dear Dr. Brown:

As you may know, my son Randy has not been achieving up to his potential this year. We think we know now that the reason is that he has an unusual reading problem. We are considering having someone at the school work with him this summer, or sending him to a private learning center that has recently opened in the community. What do you think? Do you have anyone on your staff that you could recommend? What do you think of this private learning center? I think it is called Horizons Unlimited.

Sincerely,
Mrs. Eddie Grover

In-Basket Item #5

Dr. Brown, you may not be aware of this, but Mr. Sanders, the previous principal, always put out a memo toward the end of the year, identifying for teachers the various things they needed to do before they left school on the final day. Also, he usually made a little speech at the last faculty meeting of the year, commenting about the type of year it was and projecting some goals for the school for the following year. I don't know whether you want to continue these practices, but I thought you should be aware of them.

Peg Albright
Secretary

In-Basket Item #6

May 4

Dear Dr. Brown:

I tried to call you several times last week, but your secretary always said you were busy. Therefore, I decided to write you. I am a single, working parent with a child in your school. It has seemed to me that the faculty in this school need to be made more sensitive about the fact that there are a lot of us, and that because of our circumstances, it is not as easy for us to become involved in school as when there are two parents and one of the parents is not working. I am not sure what the answer is to this, but I would like your help in setting up a single-parent school organization or support group. I also think the school needs to set up some type of a program for ''latchkey'' students, of which my son is one. Would you be willing to help me? I know there are a lot of people like me out here.

Sincerely,
Nancy Drive

In-Basket Item #7

May 9

Dr. Brown, I just received a call from my husband, and he is being transferred to another location out of state. He will have to leave in two weeks and, of course, he wants me to go with him. I really hate to leave my job, and I would like to stay at least until the end of the school year, but when I mentioned this to him, he didn't seem too receptive. I don't know what to do. Do you have any advice?

Peg Albright
Secretary

In-Basket Item #8

Dr. Brown, I don't know what you want to do about it, but a student told me that Mary Eager is distributing the enclosed leaflet. I would think that a union rep would know better than this. I thought you would want to handle this.

Tim Parker
Assistant Principal

> A Message to the Children and
> Young People of the World
>
> All of you know the name Hiroshima, and you remember what it means . . . nuclear holocaust. Today we are drawing ever closer to an even greater holocaust because of the actions or inaction of political ''leaders.'' If the world is to be saved, then young people need to show leadership. Join the Crusade to Stop Nuclear Warfare. Send your ideas and contributions to Young People for a Peaceful America, Colgate Building, Suite 317, Washington, D.C. 20036.

In-Basket Item #9

Dr. Brown, do you have any problem with my taking my classes outside if the weather is nice? The kids begin to get restless this time of the year.

Hazel Smith
Language Arts Teacher

In-Basket Item #10

MEMO

May 9

TO: Dr. Brown
FROM: Wendy Stack, Teacher

The purpose of this memorandum is to register a formal complaint against Mr. Parker, our assistant principal. This man has sexually harassed me on various occasions, and I want it to stop. He has made remarks about my bust, and he has placed his hands on my buttocks numerous times. He has also propositioned me, twice. I know I am a new teacher, but I don't think I should have to take this kind of abuse! I have also heard that he has done similar things with some of the other young female teachers. Please help me.

In-Basket Item #11

Dr. Brown, it's probably none of my business but I think faculty morale is pretty low right now. I don't know why exactly, but many of the teachers seem to lack spirit. I'm not sure what can be done about the situation, but I thought you ought to know about it.

Pat Concerned
Counselor

In-Basket Item #12

Doctor Brown — Monday is not gonna be a day you will forget. Sometime that a.m. a BOMB is gonna go off and you better get those kids out of there before it happens.

This ain't no prank or nothing.

COMMITTEE FOR A STRONGER AMERICA

In-Basket Item #13

Dr. Brown,

I know you are busy but I think we got a problem on our hands. Some of these kids are starting to use smokeless tobacco in school and it is staining the floors and some of the fixtures where they spit. I heard that even Bill Stone is using the stuff. I mean if teachers can use it what can we expect of the kids. Anyway I think something's got to be done about it before it spreads.

Sam Clean

In-Basket Item #14

May 5

Dear Dr. Brown:

Our organization, The Pro-Nuclear Energy Group, would like to make a presentation at one of your assembly programs. Our organization is made up of power companies in the area that attempt to provide safe and economically efficient energy for the people. We feel that, as a result of various television programs and newspaper reports, the young people are receiving an inaccurate impression about nuclear energy and its advantages. What is needed is a more balanced report, and we would intend to do that in our presentation at your school.

Please consider our request, since we are taxpayers too, and we want to work cooperatively with the school.

We look forward to hearing from you at your earliest convenience.

Sincerely,
(Signed) Bud Strong
President

In-Basket Item #15

Dr. Brown—

I am not sure what I should do about this referral. As you probably know, Bill Morris (the student) is the son of one of the school board members. I have never gotten along with the old man too well (we were on rival teams when we were in high school) so I would appreciate it if you would handle this one.

Tim Parker

KENNEDY SCHOOL

Student Discipline Referral Form

Date Thursday

Student's Name Bill Morris

Teacher Jack Armstrong

Problem: Kid keeps fooling around and is disrespectful to me. I am sick and tired of this kid and I don't want him back in class until he shapes up.

In-Basket Item #16

May 6

Dear Dr. Brown:

For some time now, I have been wanting to bring something to your attention, but my daughter has not wanted me to contact you about the matter. However, I feel now that I must say something, whether my daughter wants me to or not.

You are probably not aware of this, but one of your teachers, a Miss Spencer, is dating a high school student and from what I hear, things have progressed pretty far if you know what I mean. I think this kind of a situation sets a poor example for students, and it makes it difficult for those of us parents who are trying to set a moral tone in our own families. I know you will want to take a strong stand on this. The talk around town is that this boy already has Miss Spencer in trouble if you know what I mean and that she is considering an abortion.

Obviously, Miss Spencer should not be allowed to continue in her position.

Sincerely,
(Mrs.) Roberta Little

In-Basket Item #17

Telephone Message

FOR: Dr. Brown
FROM: Mr. Morris
TIME: 9:00 A.M., Friday
Please call as soon as possible.
332-9698

In-Basket Item #18

May 5

Dear Dr. Brown,

I would like to register formally my objection to the way my daughter has been abused in physical education classes. Because she was supposedly "fooling around in class" (whatever that means) she has been required several times by Mr. Jack Armstrong to do push-ups. Now, my daughter tells me she wasn't fooling around, and even if she was, it seems to me that there must be a more educationally sound way of dealing with this matter than requiring students to do push-ups!

My daughter is not a physically strong person, and when she can't do the push-ups, everyone in the class—including the teacher—laughs at her. This causes her to cry and it embarrasses her in front of the entire class.

I want something done about this matter immediately, or I am going to pursue it with the proper authorities.

Sincerely,
Priscilla Block

cc: President of the School Board
Superintendent of Schools

---

35 PRINCIPAL'S DILEMMA

Scowling, the supervisor turned the pages of the report on her desk. It was her first opportunity this week to examine the departmental summary of teacher grades for the quarter, and she was appalled by the large number of D's and F's that had been assigned. She had tried to persuade the teachers before school opened in the fall that grading standards would have to become more flexible, due to the different nature of the student body, now composed of a large proportion of minority and economically disadvantaged students. Apparently she had convinced very few of them.

It seemed unlikely that additional attempts to persuade the teachers would prove to be any more productive, but it was obvious to the supervisor that she could not sit by and allow the current grading practices to continue.

After lengthy consideration, she finally decided that the solution to the grading problem might lie in a new program of increased teacher-student conferences. If each teacher in the department were required to hold at least one conference during the first six weeks of every quarter with each potential D or F student, it seemed probable that grading practices would improve. Teachers would develop a better understanding of the special learning problems of their students while the students would receive remedial assistance which should enable them to improve their classroom performance. The supervisor was confident that a program of teacher-student conferences would improve the grading situation in the department immensely.

The following Monday she met after school with the members of the department and distributed a statement to them. It read:

New Department Policy on Teacher-Student Conferences

1. Beginning with this nine-week session and continuing thereafter, each teacher will confer some time during the first six weeks of the quarter with every student who might conceivably receive a D or F grade at the end of the quarter.
2. The teacher should schedule at least one conference with potential D students and at least two conferences with potential F students.
3. The teacher should encourage D and F students to schedule the conferences themselves. However, if a particular student has not scheduled a conference by the beginning of the fifth week, it is the responsibility of the teacher to take the initiative in scheduling the conference. If the student refuses to come to the scheduled conferences, the teacher is not required to schedule additional meetings, but should continue to be receptive to helping the student.
4. Teachers are encouraged to go beyond the minimum number of conferences indicated above. Also, it is assumed that teachers will continue to hold conferences *after* the first six weeks of each quarter, and that conferences with A, B, and C students will be scheduled whenever appropriate throughout the quarter.

After distributing the policy statement to the teachers, the supervisor explained her belief that students should not be assigned a D or F grade until after the teacher had attempted to work with them individually to improve their performance. The supervisor went on to say that she realized that individual conferences would be time-consuming and probably would have to take place during the teachers' ''free'' periods, or before or after school. Nevertheless, she felt strongly that no student should be assigned an F or D grade without a prior attempt by the teacher to ascertain the student's problems and to provide specific remedial assistance to correct them. If the student failed to respond to the teacher's efforts, then the student would be held accountable. However, the initial responsibility would be the teacher's.

After the supervisor finished, she invited teacher reactions, but no one said anything until finally one of them asked whether the conferences were recommended or required. The supervisor responded that teacher-student conferences were in the teachers' best interest as well as the students'. She added that she hoped the teachers would agree, and that it would not be necessary to formally require the conferences.

Although the supervisor continued to encourage the teachers to express their feelings, no other questions or comments came forth. Recognizing finally that it was useless to persist, she terminated the meeting, emphasizing her expectations that the new program of student-teacher conferences would begin that week.

The next morning before school began, a delegation of teachers from the department appeared at the principal's office. They were disturbed about the new policy on teacher-student conferences, and it was obvious to the principal that they had met previously as a group to discuss the situation at length. Now they wanted the principal to tell them whether their supervisor could actually require them to hold student conferences and, if so, where they were going to get the time.

They informed the principal that the entire department opposed the new policy and did not plan to carry it out. They indicated that they did not object to the teacher-student conferences, but they felt that it was the students' business, not the teachers' responsibility, to schedule conferences. If the individual teacher found time to schedule conferences and there were not too many of them, fine. But the matter should be left to the professional judgment of each teacher.

The principal was faced with a dilemma. He believed that, in theory, it was the teachers' responsibility to confer with the D and F students on an individual basis before assigning nine-week grades. However, he wasn't sure that teachers should be *required* to hold such conferences. Still, he didn't want to undermine the position of the supervisor, and he realized that if the conferences were not required, some teachers would fail to hold them. He tried to quickly weigh the consequences of a decision either way, realizing that the teachers were waiting for his response.

SUGGESTED LEARNING ACTIVITIES

Analyze the Case

1. What alternatives, in addition to the program of teacher-student conferences, should have been considered by the supervisor in response to the apparent grading problems in the department?
2. What is your assessment of the supervisor's strategy for introducing change? How would you have proceeded differently? What assumptions are you making?
3. What is your evaluation of the teachers' position on the issue of teacher-student conferences?

Discuss the Larger Issues

1. What steps do you think a school should take in order to adapt its total educational program to the type of student population described in the case?
2. What is the role of the principal in bringing about the changes identified in response to Question 1? The role of the supervisor? Other individuals or groups within or outside the school?
3. What should be the nature and scope of a supervisor's authority over the teachers in the department?
4. What position should the principal take in a conflict between a supervisor and the teachers in the department? What should be the role of the principal in resolving the conflict?

Be a Problem Solver

As principal, you have been approached by a delegation of teachers who are asking, essentially, that you overrule the decision of their supervisor. What should you do? What preliminary steps might be necessary?

Test Your Solution

In order to test your proposed plan for action for dealing with the problem presented at the end of the case, you and your class should create and role-play one or more of the following situations:

1. A conference between the supervisor and the principal.
2. A meeting of the entire department which you have been asked to attend by the supervisor.
3. A telephone call from the representative of a delegation of parents who want to schedule a meeting with you, the principal, to discuss the consistently low grades that their sons and daughters received at the end of the last quarter.

Investigate Further

1. How is the role of supervisor defined by your district, in terms of actual authority? By your school? How specifically is the policy spelled out?
2. How would the majority of teachers in your department react to the idea of requiring teachers to hold conferences with students who may receive low grades?

36
PRINCIPAL'S PERSONAL CONDUCT RESULTS IN POSSIBLE SUSPENSION

Superintendent Donald Barry was in the middle of a staff meeting on a hot August morning when he was called out of the room by his secretary. She indicated that a reporter from the newspaper was telephoning him about a school principal who had apparently gotten himself in some trouble. Dr. Barry was somewhat irritated by the fact that his secretary had called him out of the meeting, but when he was informed that the reporter had said it was urgent and in the best interest of the school district for the call to be completed, he hurried to the telephone to talk with the reporter.

The reporter immediately asked the superintendent if he was aware that Mr. Robert Curtis, principal at Westlawn School, had been charged by the police with shoplifting at a neighborhood supermarket.

Dr. Barry was stunned and didn't respond immediately to the reporter's question. Finally, he responded that he had not been aware of the situation and would need to look into the matter. But the reporter persisted in his questioning of the superintendent, focussing on the question of how Dr. Barry felt about the principal's conduct and what the district was going to do about the principal's behavior. The superintendent, however, refused any further comment and terminated the conversation.

Shortly after talking to the reporter, the superintendent placed a call to the police. As a result of the call he was able to confirm the reporter's story that the police had indeed charged Bob Curtis with shoplifting at Shop-and-Save Supermarket. According to the complaint that had been filed, he had surreptitiously tried to remove three sirloin steaks from the store premises without having first paid for them. Upon apprehension by store officials, Mr. Curtis had initially denied any wrongdoing, but when the merchandise was found on his person, he had explained that he had left his wallet at home and intended to pay for the steaks later. Although Mr. Curtis had not been detained by police, they were continuing to investigate.

After the telephone call to the police, Dr. Barry sat in his office, uncertain of what to do next. He knew that Bob Curtis was one of his better principals and was someone who could be counted on to do a job right. He was also very popular with students and parents. The superintendent was perplexed about why Bob would even consider taking something from a store without having paid for it. His salary was certainly adequate to permit such a small luxury.

The superintendent didn't know what his next step should be, but obviously he had a serious problem on his hands.

SUGGESTED LEARNING ACTIVITIES

Analyze the Case

1. Could the superintendent have better handled the telephone conversation with the reporter? If so, how?
2. Is there any additional information that the superintendent should have attempted to obtain from the police?
3. What additional calls and/or contact should the superintendent make before he determines what to do about Mr. Curtis?

Discuss the Larger Issues

1. To what extent should the out-of-school behavior of an administrator be of concern to the employer?
2. What rights does the accused have in situations like the one in this case, and what should be the role of the employer in protecting those rights?
3. To what degree should the attitude of students and parents toward an administrator's alleged or real misdeeds be considered by an employer in deciding what to do about the administrator?
4. What action should an employer take if it has been validated that an administrator has committed an indiscreet act or has broken the law?

Be a Problem Solver

Assume that you are the superintendent in this case. What would be your approach to dealing with the circumstances that have developed? Utilize administrative and social science concepts in planning and implementing your approach.

Test Your Solution

In order to test your proposed plan of action, you and your colleagues should create and role-play one or more of the following situations:

1. A conference between Superintendent Barry and Mr. Curtis.
2. Another telephone call from the reporter to the superintendent.
3. A call from a parent who has read a newspaper item about Mr. Curtis.

Investigate Further

1. Ascertain whether or not your district has a policy on procedures to be followed when an administrator gets involved in a police action.
2. Has a situation similar to the one described in the case ever happened in your school or school district? If so, how was it handled?

37
INTRA-ORGANIZATIONAL ROLE CONFLICT

The vice-principal had made up his mind to improve the guidance program. Two years ago in a reorganization of administrative tasks within the building, the principal had given him the responsibility of administering the entire pupil personnel program, including student attendance, discipline, and counseling and guidance. Prior to that time, the guidance department had functioned more or less autonomously. But in an effort to provide better coordination between guidance, attendance, and discipline, the principal had decided to appoint the vice-principal to be in charge of all these programs.

At first the vice-principal had made no attempt to supervise the counselors. He was by no means sure that he would be able to assume the responsibility without offending the guidance director who previously had been assigned this function. But after observing the guidance program for some time, he gradually became convinced that a number of changes were needed. Counselors seemed to be spending too much time with staff conferences, telephone calls, and out-of-building meetings.

The vice-principal had also noticed that all of the contacts between counselors and students were limited to individual conferences. Since each counselor in the school was assigned approximately 400 students, the vice-principal did not see how the guidance program could meet the needs of *all* students through individual conferences. There simply were not enough hours in the day or enough counselors to provide that kind of service. The vice-principal was not opposed to individual counseling, but he believed that some type of a group counseling or guidance activity was also necessary.

The problem was that he was uncertain about how to approach the counselors with proposed changes for their work schedule and program. He thought about calling a meeting to inform the counselors about his observations, but he decided against that step. He didn't feel that he was well enough accepted yet by the counselors to meet with them face-to-face in a meeting to discuss ways of restructuring their job. There must be a better alternative.

He then considered the possibility of discussing his concerns with the guidance director. However, in the months since the vice-principal had been appointed head of the entire student personnel program, their relationship had been strained. The guidance director had been sensitive about the administrative reorganization and the requirement to report to the vice-principal. In spite of attempts by the latter to maintain good rapport, the guidance director had not responded positively. Their conferences were often nonproductive, and in recent weeks the two ceased to meet on a regular basis and conferred only in time of crisis. Although the vice-principal was convinced that there existed a real need for improving the guidance program, he doubted whether a conference with the guidance director would help matters much.

Finally he decided to write a memorandum to all of the counselors. In this way the vice-principal hoped to bypass the guidance director, who seemed unlikely to assume any leadership in bringing about the change needed for improvement. The vice-principal decided not to refer directly in the memo to the inefficiencies he had observed, but rather he would try to persuade the counselors of the advantages of developing a group guidance program and keeping a counseling log. The log would provide a better picture of the counselors' activities and would also be useful in helping the vice-principal and the principal to interpret the guidance program to teachers and the general public.

The next Monday, after securing the principal's approval, the vice-principal sent the following memo to all of the counselors:

> I am sure that you would agree that the Guidance Department offers one of the most important programs in the school. Like any good program, however, the basis for its success rests on continuous improvement.
>
> At the present time the administration needs additional information to give us a more complete picture of the guidance program and the various counselor activities.
>
> Therefore, I would like you to maintain a daily counselor log or record for the next month which would *briefly* describe your activities during each class period. This information will be of great value in identifying areas needing improvement and in pointing out strengths of the program to teachers, school board, the general public, etc.
>
> I would also like the counselors to initiate a group guidance or counseling course. As you know, the present counselor load is nearly 400 students, so it is difficult—if not impossible—to see each individual. Through the utilization of group counseling and guidance, as well as individual conferences, you will be better able to have contact with more of your students than is possible under the present arrangement.
>
> Please let me know within two weeks your reactions to the two proposals described above. My sole objective is to improve the Guidance Program. I hope that you share that goal and will respond favorably.

During the rest of the week the vice-principal was particularly observant of the counselors' attitude toward him, but he was unable to detect any significant difference. Still, he was uneasy and began to develop second thoughts about the memo he had sent to them, although he was certain that he could have accomplished little through a direct meeting with the counselors or the guidance director.

On Friday morning he found in his mailbox a memo from the guidance director. It read:

> The counselors appreciate your interest in the counseling program and have given considerable thought to your suggestions for improvement. However, we feel that it would be impractical to maintain a counselor log, since this would take valuable time—already in short supply—away from our counseling.
>
> In regard to the group guidance course, we feel that, although we could *perhaps* see more students, our role might be confused with that of a teacher. We have strong reservations about whether such a course would constitute 'counseling' as we know it.
>
> We are pleased that you believe the counseling program to be one of the more important programs in the school. We feel that our primary needs for improvement at this time are for additional clerical help and a reduced counselor-student ratio. We know that you are interested in continuing to provide a quality counseling and guidance program, and we seek your leadership and support in meeting our needs.

SUGGESTED LEARNING ACTIVITIES

Analyze the Case

1. What are the strengths and weaknesses of the principal's plan of placing the pupil personnel department under the supervision of the vice-principal?
2. What role, if any, does the factor of "specialized expertise" play in the vice-principal's reluctance to supervise the guidance department, or in the guidance director's reaction to the vice-principal?
3. What are the merits of the vice-principal's plan for improving the guidance program? Limitations?
4. What assumptions did the vice-principal make in selecting his strategy for introducing change? What alternatives do you feel that he failed to consider?
5. What concepts or generalizations about the process of conflict management, introducing change, and the reasons for resistance to change did the vice-principal seem to ignore or utilize badly?

Discuss the Larger Issues

1. How should the Guidance, Attendance, and Discipline Programs be organized so that they can make the optimal contribution to the educational objectives of the school?
2. Should the Guidance Program be evaluated? If so, by what criteria? By whom?
3. How should administrators, who are generalists, deal with the problem of supervising counselors, who are specialists in one particular aspect of the total educational process?

Be a Problem Solver

The vice-principal has received a memo from the guidance director which, in essence, seems to reject the ideas of the vice-principal for improving the guidance department. If you were the vice-principal in that situation, what plans and steps would you take? What problems would you anticipate?

Test Your Solution

In order to test your plan of action for dealing with the problem presented at the end of the case, you and the class should create and role-play one or more of the following situations:

1. A conference between the vice-principal and the guidance director.
2. A meeting between the vice-principal and the guidance department.

3. Any other situation that would provide feedback on the strengths and weaknesses of your proposed solution.

Investigate Further

1. What is the role of the counselor in your school district? The guidance director?
2. Who in your district is responsible for supervising counselors and for introducing improvements in the guidance program? Is this responsibility spelled out or only assumed?
3. How would the counselors in your school respond to the vice-principal's ideas for improvement?

38
SUPERVISOR-PRINCIPAL RELATIONSHIP

The central office supervisor was supposed to visit Hillcrest School in the afternoon, in response to a teachers's request for assistance with a classroom problem. But as he sat in his office an hour before he was scheduled to arrive at the school, he was torn between the knowledge that a definite appointment had been established and his feelings of ambivalence about the school.

With respect to the faculty at Hillcrest, he felt that he had developed rather good rapport with the teachers he supervised, and they had called on him frequently for assistance with their instructional plans or difficulties. The problem was that Mr. Sawyer, the principal of the school, seemed to regard him with suspicion. Last fall the supervisor had visited Hillcrest, and Mr. Sawyer had stopped him in the hall and had asked him to check in at the principal's office in the future so that the principal would know when the supervisor was in the building. Reluctantly, the supervisor had complied with the principal's request.

Several months later, during one of the supervisor's subsequent visits to the school, Mr. Sawyer had implied that it would be a good idea for the supervisor to make a full report each time, on whom he had seen when he was in the building, what he had accomplished, etc. However, since the principal had not specifically required such a report, the supervisor had chosen to ignore the suggestion—not because he minded writing the report, although he didn't relish additional bureaucratic requirements, but because he was afraid that the teachers would no longer feel free to seek his assistance if they knew that he was relating to the administration the substance of their conferences with him.

The supervisor was aware of the fact that he had considerably reduced the number of visits that he typically made to Hillcrest, primarily because he wanted to avoid any conflict with the principal. This kind of compromising was unpleasant to the supervisor because he felt that he was letting the teachers down by being available less frequently. But certain kinds of instructional assistance necessitated a classroom visitation, and that was the reason that he had agreed to visit the school today.

The supervisor knew that the principal regarded himself as the instructional leader of the school and that he probably felt threatened by the strong relationship which the supervisor had been able to build with the teachers at Hillcrest. However, while the principal's attitude was perhaps understandable, his defensiveness had made it very difficult for the supervisor to work openly and freely with the teachers. The supervisor was troubled by the principal's reaction to him, but at this stage he was at a loss as to how matters could be improved.

SUGGESTED LEARNING ACTIVITIES

Analyze the Case

1. Assess the appropriateness of the principal's requests or suggestions to the supervisor and the supervisor's attitude toward and response to the principal.
2. What might be some of the less obvious reasons for the behavior of the principal and the central office supervisor?

Discuss the Larger Issues

1. What should be the responsibility of a principal and central office supervisors with respect to working with teachers and improving instruction? What should be the relationship between the two levels of supervision?
2. Whose responsibility is it to specify the appropriate relationship between central office supervision and the principal? Whose responsibility is it to resolve conflicts between the two levels of supervision?

Be a Problem Solver

The supervisor in the case is concerned about his strained relationship with the principal of Hillcrest School. He does not want to alienate the principal, but he does not believe that the request to report his activities in the school is in the best interest of his own relationships with the teachers. If you were the supervisor, what would you do? Utilize appropriate administrative and social science concepts from Part I of the text in planning and implementing your approach.

Test Your Solution

To test your proposed plan of action, you and the class should create and role-play one or more of the following situations:

1. A confrontation between the supervisor and the principal.
2. A conference between the principal, the supervisor, and the superintendent.

Investigate Further

1. What is the school board policy in your school district, regarding the working relationship between the principal and the central office supervisors?
2. What administrative policy or guidelines have been formulated in your district to prevent or to handle the kind of problem presented in this case?
3. What is the attitude of your building principal and the majority of the supervisors in the central office about the current relationship that exists in your district between principals and central office supervisors?

39

THE SUPERINTENDENT AND THE NEW SCHOOL BOARD MEMBERS

It was late in the spring, and as the superintendent thought about the recent school board election, he felt uneasy. The two incumbents had been unseated, and the composition of the school board would be changed significantly.

The superintendent had given little thought to the school board election prior to the day that the voters had cast their ballots. He had assumed that since both incumbents had been excellent board members, they would be reelected with little or no difficulty. It had been quite a shock when he had learned that neither of them had won, but had been replaced by candidates with little background or contact with the schools.

One of the newly elected board members was a man named George Thompson, an accountant, whose election flyers had described him as "a taxpayer determined to hold the line on school spending." The superintendent had heard Thompson present his views at a pre-election candidates' forum and had not been very favorably impressed by the man's abrasive manner and suspicious attitude toward the schools. Apparently it was going to be hard to develop good rapport with Mr. Thompson.

Complicating the matter was Mr. Thompson's relationship with one of the building principals in the district. During the recent candidates' forum, Mr. Thompson had made comments and had drawn conclusions about an alleged surplus in the school budget, citing a building principal as the source for his information. In response to Mr. Thompson's statements, the superintendent had been forced to concede that, in a sense, there was a surplus in the budget but that it had already been earmarked for other purposes, so a surplus really no longer existed.

It bothered the superintendent that Mr. Thompson and the building principal, who were next-door neighbors, had apparently been discussing school business with regard to a matter that the superintendent felt should have remained within the school "family." The superintendent was concerned about the behavior of the principal, as well as Mr. Thompson, and could foresee major problems if they continued to carry on the same relationship after Mr. Thompson assumed his new role as a board member. However, at the moment, the superintendent wasn't sure how to proceed with either of the two men.

The second newly elected member of the school board was Mr. Harvey Sutton, who managed a gas station. Mr. Sutton hadn't said much during the campaign, but his few public statements suggested that the new board member didn't know very much about schools. He seemed friendly enough, but the superintendent was doubtful whether Mr. Sutton was going to make a very strong contribution to the school board unless considerable orientation was provided. The problem was how best to orient him to his role as a school board member and to education in general.

The superintendent was deeply concerned about the possible implications of the election of the two new school board members in terms of the board's continued support of his plans for the school district. He had already initiated a number of changes in the educational program of the school district during the past two years, and thus far the board had always supported him, although some of the votes had been rather close. He still had plans for instituting a new sex education program and for remodeling some of the older buildings in the district. He hoped that steps could be taken to gain the cooperation of the two new members of the board as he attempted to move ahead with his plans.

SUGGESTED LEARNING ACTIVITIES

Analyze the Case

1. Based on the information presented in the case, what can you infer about the superintendent's values? What aspects of the superintendent's personality may make it difficult for him to develop a good relationship with each of the new board members?
2. How would you evaluate the superintendent's attitude toward Mr. Thompson, particularly with regard to the latter's relationship with the building principal?
3. What factors may the superintendent be failing to take into consideration in his assessment of Mr. Thompson and Mr. Sutton?

Discuss the Larger Issues

1. What role, if any, should a superintendent take with reference to the election of school board candidates?
2. What methods and prerequisites should be established for the election of school board members?
3. What should be the position of any administrator or teacher in the school system with respect to discussing school affairs with school board members or candidates?

Be a Problem Solver

The superintendent is bothered about the relationship between one of his newly elected board members and one of his building principals. He is also concerned about his own future relationship with the new board members and about orienting them to their role on the board and to education in general. If you were the superintendent, what would you do in this situation? Utilize appropriate administrative and social science concepts from Part I of the text in planning and implementing your approach.

Test Your Solution

To test your proposed plan of action for dealing with the problems presented at the end of the case, you and the class should create and role-play one or more of the following interactions:

1. A conference between the superintendent and the principal identified in the case.
2. A conference between the superintendent and either of the new board members, or both.

Investigate Further

1. What guidelines or established procedures exist in your school district for the campaigning and election of school board members?
2. What problems do the following individuals or groups in your school district see in the election of school board members?
   a. The superintendent
   b. The teachers
   c. Your building principal
   d. A sampling of parents

40
ADMINISTRATOR EVALUATION

In the second year of her first position as an assistant principal, Betty Daniels was generally happy with her job. She remembered how pleased she had been when she was selected from among all of the candidates for the position. However, there was one nagging concern: she didn't know whether her administrative superiors were satisfied with her performance.

During her first year she thought that she had done a good job, but she had received very little feedback during the year from the principal and central office supervisor, other than an occasional, "How's everything going?" and, "Hang in there." When she was sent her contract for the second year, she had received what she felt was a very small salary increase. She had thought at the time that perhaps she should request a formal evaluation from her principal and the central office supervisor and a discussion of her salary for the second year. But she had decided against that course of action. She was still fairly new on the job and a little uncertain of her relationships with her administrative superiors, and she didn't want them to think she was too aggressive.

Now, however, it was her second year, and in another month contracts would be sent to all the administrators. She knew from conversations with a friend of hers in another school district that other districts did provide their administrators with a formal evaluation every year, so administrator evaluations were not unheard of. On the other hand, she wasn't sure she wanted the same type of evaluation system that her friend had encountered, a quasi-MBO approach in which the building administrators had very little input into the development of the evaluation procedures and criteria and the central office "suggested" the objectives the administrators should be trying to achieve. Still, she felt that she had to find out where she stood with her own district, so she decided to write a letter to her central office supervisor.

> Dear Dr. Abboleanee:
>
> As you know, I am in my second year as an assistant principal. Although I think I have done a pretty good job so far, I would appreciate some feedback from my superiors. What I would really like is a formal evaluation from you and my principal, Dr. Lee. I feel that the kind of evaluation I am suggesting would help me to see any possible need for professional improvement. It is also the type of thing that other administrators in the district would probably appreciate. Since more and more districts are moving to, or are already using, formal evaluation criteria and procedures for their administrators, I hope that you will respond positively to my request.

A month passed, and Betty Daniels still had not received any reply to her letter. She had been tempted several times to go in to see her principal about the matter, but she had taken no action, assuming that she would receive *something* from the central office supervisor.

On Friday, contracts were received by all administrators. In the envelope containing Betty Daniels' contract was a short letter from Dr. Abboleanee, which read:

> Dear Miss Daniels:
>
> In response to your earlier letter, I have conferred with your principal, Dr. Lee, and we have decided that your two main areas in need of improvement are student discipline and your relationships with some of the staff. In regard to the first area, we feel you need to be firmer with students. In regard to the second area, we feel that it would be helpful if you would make a greater effort to integrate yourself with the total faculty, rather than segregating yourself so much with the female teachers.
>
> Dr. Lee and I both feel that in your first two years you have shown promise, and you are obviously a bright and hard-working woman. However, continual improvement is definitely needed in the areas indicated.

Betty Daniels was stunned by Dr. Abboleanee's letter, and when she looked at her contract and noticed her salary for next year reflected only a small increase, she became very disturbed. Her principal had hinted a couple of times that he might have handled certain discipline cases differently than she had, but he had never informed her that he wanted her to be firmer on discipline. And what did *firmer* mean? As far as her relationships with the other teachers, no one had ever said anything to her before about them. She supposed that she interacted more with the female teachers than the males, but that was not unusual in the school since the male teachers seemed to segregate themselves. Certainly the principal himself appeared to interact more with the male teachers than the female teachers. "Besides," she thought, "what difference does it make anyway?"

The assistant principal wasn't sure what her next move should be. She wondered what overall criteria the district had used in evaluating her and whether the criteria were the same that were used in evaluating the other administrators. Or was she perhaps the only administrator evaluated this year? She had a lot of questions about the whole evaluation procedure used in this district, but she wasn't certain how to proceed in this kind of situation.

SUGGESTED LEARNING ACTIVITIES

Analyze the Case

1. What do you think Betty Daniels should have done when she received her contract for the second year?
2. What is your assessment of Betty Daniels' approach to obtaining evaluative feedback on her performance?
3. What is your assessment of Dr Abboleanee's response to Betty Daniels' request for evaluation feedback on her performance?

Discuss the Larger Issues

1. Should administrators, especially new ones, be provided with a formal evaluation of their performance each year?
2. What kinds of criteria and procedures should be utilized in administrator evaluation?
3. To what extent should the individuals being evaluated be involved in the development of criteria and procedures which are to be used in evaluating their performance?

Be a Problem Solver

Assume that you are the assistant principal in this case. What should you do to respond to the circumstances which are confronting you? Utilize administrative and social science concepts from

Part I of the text in planning and implementing your approach.

Test Your Solution

To test your proposed plan for dealing with the circumstances described in the case, you and your colleagues should create and role-play one or more of the following situations:

1. A conference between the assistant principal and Dr. Lee.
2. A conference between the assistant principal and Dr. Abboleanee.
3. A conference between the assistant principal and the executive secretary of the local or state administrators' association.

Investigate Further

1. What evaluation criteria and procedures are employed in your district for the evaluation of administrators?
2. To what extent do the administrators being evaluated in your district have a role in the development of the evaluation criteria and procedures?
3. What is the attitude of the individuals being evaluated toward the fairness and usefulness of the evaluation criteria and procedures?

14 Race and Drug Issues

What the school's role should be in regard to the social problems affecting our country has periodically been a subject of great debate. Although some people seem to feel that the school should be insulated from society's turmoils and conflicts, others argue that the school represents a microcosm of society and should play an active role in trying to resolve or ameliorate its problems.

In practice, the school has never completely adopted either point of view. While the school has found it impossible to remain detached from the major controversies of the day, there is considerable evidence that administrators and teachers have been reluctant to assume a leadership role in helping to resolve the problems facing the larger society. In too many instances, the school has acted only when its participation in the matter has been forced by another social agency, such as the courts in the segregation issue, or after a particular problem has begun to affect the school directly, as in the case of the drug problem. Because the race and drug issues continue to be two of the most significant problems facing our society today, and since educational leadership can make a major contribution to their amelioration, several representative case studies are presented in this chapter for analysis and discussion.

BACKGROUND READING

For the reader who would like to develop further background and understanding of the problems and issues presented in this chapter, a list of readings is provided.

Carl A. Grant, ''Desegregation, Racial Attitudes and Intergroup Contact: A Discussion of Change,'' *Phi Delta Kappan* (September, 1990), 25–32.

Richard A. Hawley, ''The Bumpy Road to Drug-Free Schools,'' *Phi Delta Kappan* (December, 1990), 310–314.

Nitza Hidalgo et al., *Facing Racism in Education,* (Boston: Harvard Educational Review, 1990).

Christine E. Sleeter, ''Staff Development for Desegregated Schooling,'' *Phi Delta Kappan* (September, 1990), 33–40.

The Drug Free School: What School Executives Can Do. (Arlington, VA: National School Public Relations), 1991.

Joyce M. Tobias, *Schools and Drugs: A Handbook for Parents and Educators,* 2nd rev. ed. (Annandale, VA: Panda Press, 1989).

41
CAN TOTAL SCHOOL INTEGRATION BE ACHIEVED?

It was his first year in Capital City and his first position as a principal. The former principal had left to complete work on his doctorate, but during the last two years of his administration, the school had been integrated and the student body was currently composed of about 75% white and 25% nonwhite. At one time the faculty had been predominantly white, but several minority teachers had been hired and others had transferred to the school as a result of the district's desegregation plan. Apparently there had been considerable opposition to the district's initial attempts to integrate the schools, but now the atmosphere was relatively calm, and most people seemed to accept—or at least be resigned to—the changes that had been made.

The new principal had been very busy during the first few weeks of the school year. He had been involved with learning the schedule, becoming acquainted with students, teachers, and other people in the district, familiarizing himself with the program of studies, and dealing with the day-to-day routine and minor crises which are a part of the job of the building principal.

Although he was reasonably well satisfied with his new situation, there were two aspects which troubled him. In spite of the fact that the school, including the faculty, had been integrated, there was very little social interaction between white and nonwhite teachers. As a rule, they did not mingle in the faculty room nor did they sit together at faculty meetings or during the noon hour. While the principal had not detected any actual antagonism or hostility, it was apparent that the two groups of teachers were not associating with each other.

He had talked to his assistant principal about the matter, but his assistant didn't feel that any significant problem existed and took the position that, even if it did, there wasn't much that could be done about it; people couldn't be *forced* to associate with each other.

The new principal was not ready to accept his assistant principal's assessment of the situation, but at the moment he didn't have any ideas on how to improve relations between the white and nonwhite teachers. Besides, there was another problem that was possibly even more fundamental to quality education in an integrated school.

The principal had noticed, in the process of becoming familiar with the program of studies in the school, that the curriculum seemed to give inadequate attention and emphasis to nonwhite history and culture. Although the former principal had apparently tried to stimulate some interest in offering a course focusing on the culture and history of minority groups in the United States, no one on the faculty had been willing to develop an outline of study. As a result, the present social studies program was still very traditional.

The same type of situation existed in the language arts curriculum which devoted little attention to nonwhite writers. While the principal was in favor of students learning about recognized white U.S. and European writers, nevertheless he believed that there should be a better balance in the curriculum, and that there was a great deal of worthwhile nonwhite literature to which all students should be exposed. Certainly the minority students needed this kind of relevant education in order to develop a better self-identity and a deeper understanding of their culture and history. And, perhaps even more importantly, the white students needed a multiracial education if they were ever going to learn to appreciate the nonwhite culture and develop a more positive attitude toward relating and interacting with nonwhite people.

The principal realized that there would be problems in trying to achieve a truly integrated faculty and multiracial curriculum. There would no doubt be resistance from teachers of both backgrounds who really did not want to associate with each other and who questioned the need for a multicultural curriculum or who doubted the school district's commitment to this approach. There was also likely to be the feeling on the part of many white parents that minority group studies were either not necessary or not desirable.

However, the principal was deeply committed to the ideal of an integrated society and believed that it was the school's responsibility to play a major role in contributing to that end. It was true that he was new and a little uncertain about how to proceed, but he had been taught that the principalship was a leadership position, and he intended to face up to the challenges in his school.

SUGGESTED LEARNING ACTIVITIES

Analyze the Case

1. What might be some of the more subtle reasons why the white and nonwhite teachers were not associating with each other? How could you ascertain the actual reasons for their lack of interaction?
2. What is your evaluation of the vice-principal's assessment of the racial situation in the school? What might be some of the reasons why he doesn't view things the same way the principal does?
3. From what sources is there likely to be opposition to the goals of the principal in the case? What might be some of the possibly less obvious reasons why people may oppose the principal?

Discuss the Larger Issues

1. What should be the school's objective in regard to the nature of interracial relations within the faculty? What role should the principal play in attempting to achieve that objective? The superintendent or other central office personnel?
2. What kind of a curriculum should a school offer or develop for an integrated student body? A desegregated student body? Should there be any differences, and if so, why?

Be a Problem Solver

If you were the principal in the situation described in this case, what would you do? What are the alternatives? Utilize appropriate administrative and social science concepts from Part I of the text in planning and implementing your approach.

Test Your Solution

To test your proposed plan of action for dealing with the problems presented at the end of this case, you and the class should create and role-play one or more of the following situations:

1. A meeting between the principal and the faculty.
2. A meeting between the principal and the nonwhite or the white teachers.

Investigate Further

1. Regardless of the racial composition of your student body, to what extent does the curriculum in your school promote a positive attitude toward the different racial and ethnic groups in our country?
2. What is the attitude of your superintendent, principal, department heads, and faculty toward investigating ways in which the curriculum in your school and school district can do an even better job of fostering and promoting a positive attitude among the different races and ethnic groups?
3. What barriers and obstacles would have to be overcome in your district before a more multiracial faculty and curriculum could be achieved?

42
MINORITY PARENTS ARE DISSATISFIED WITH INTEGRATION

Most people felt that the Fairmount School District had made tremendous strides in desegregating the schools. There were no longer any "segregated schools," in the traditional sense of the term. School boundary lines had been redrawn, a busing program had been initiated, a number of teachers representing minority races had been hired, and a multicultural studies curriculum had been introduced.

True, most of these changes had been brought about through court actions or by local pressure groups. But now the school board and all of the administrators were genuinely proud of what had been accomplished. In fact, Fairmount was recognized throughout the state for its progress in school integration, and a national news magazine had even carried an article describing the school district's program for dealing with this major social problem.

Unknown to the administrators, however, a group of parents representing various minority groups in the city had quietly organized and for several months had been meeting in homes to discuss the racial situation in the schools. They had initially been hopeful that, as a result of integration, conditions were really going to be different and that their children were going to receive a better education.

However, many of them were developing grave doubts about the efficacy of the district's integration policies. They readily conceded that there were no longer any completely segregated schools and that many of their children had been placed in previously all white schools. But the parents still questioned whether the schools were actually integrated when most of the minority race students were in separate classes from the whites and when all of the nonwhite teachers in the school had been assigned to predominantly minority classes.

Some parents believed that the segregated classes were a result of deliberate attempts by the school administration to practice segregation, but others felt that the composition of the classes was a consequence of the district's ability grouping program. Students were assigned to groups on the basis of certain IQ, achievement, and teacher rating factors, and minority children had, for the most part, ended up in the same classes. There were a few minority children in upper ability classes, but not many.

To make matters worse, the few minority teachers in the school had been assigned to low ability classes, meaning that minority children received little or no instruction from white teachers. While the latter practice was just a secondary issue with many people, it only served to heighten the convictions of minority race parents that a segregated system had been created within the schools and that their children were really no better off than when they had been attending separate schools.

As a parent complained during a rather heated meeting in December, "If one of the major purposes of integration is for the different races to learn how to understand and get along with each other, is this purpose served by desegregating the schools, yet segregating the classes and teaching assignments?"

The answer given by all of the parents was a resounding, "No!"

"Well, then, what shall we do about it?" someone asked.

That was indeed the question. Toward the end of the meeting it was finally decided that a letter be written to the superintendent of schools, protesting the system of ability grouping and the assignment of nonwhite teachers to predominantly minority classes. A statement was drafted the same evening and was approved by all in attendance. Copies of the letter were also to be sent to the members of the school board, all building principals, the city newspaper, and local broadcasting stations.

On December 23 the letter was mailed. It read:

Contrary to public impressions, the attempt to integrate Fairmount School District has failed dismally. Although, as a result of busing, there are no longer any segregated schools, the classes and educational activities within these schools remain segregated. *Perhaps* this is not the result of willful segregation policies. However, due to the district's ability grouping program and the practice of assigning minority teachers to nonwhite classes, the effect is the same.

We therefore demand the end to all ability grouping in the schools and an immediate discontinuation of the practice of assigning minority teachers to predominantly minority classes. Minority race students should be randomly placed in the same classes as the white students. We recognize that this will increase the ability range of the classes and may make teaching more challenging. However, if people from different races are ever going to learn to live cooperatively, their children must begin to share daily experiences together in the schools.

If heterogeneous classes create problems of instruction, it is the responsibility of the school administration to provide help for the teachers. No one said that integration would be easy! The first step is to quit kidding ourselves that it can be accomplished merely by busing and get down to the business of really helping people to better understand and get along with each other.

The Committee for Truly Integrated Schools

SUGGESTED LEARNING ACTIVITIES

Analyze the Case

1. What might be some of the reasons why the administrators in this case were unaware that a group of parents representing various minority groups in the city had been meeting for several months over the racial situation in the schools?
2. What is your evaluation of the criteria used in this school district to ability-group students? How would you change the criteria, if at all?
3. What is your assessment of the contents of the letter to the superintendent? What does it tell you about the expectations of the group? What does it tell you about the group's perception of the school system? What does it tell you about the kind of group with which the administration will be dealing?

Discuss the Larger Issues

1. Should ability grouping be abandoned if it results in de facto segregation in the classes, even though its elimination might make teaching more difficult?
2. Should the district attempt to hire teachers representing minority races, in proportion to the percent of the minority students in the schools? What are the advantages and disadvantages of this kind of a policy?
3. What is the responsibility of each person associated with the school—teacher, administrator, student, parent—for helping students from different cultural backgrounds to learn how to understand and to get along better with each other?

Be a Problem Solver

A group of minority teachers has sent a letter to the superintendent of schools, with copies to the members of the school board, building principals, the city newspaper, and the broadcasting stations, demanding "the end to all ability grouping in the schools and the immediate discontinuation of the practice of assigning nonwhite teachers to predominantly nonwhite classes." What would you do now, if you were the

a. superintendent?
b. principal?
c. a teacher or counselor who read the letter in the paper?

What would your strategy be, and with whom would you meet? Utilize appropriate administrative and social science concepts from Part I in planning and implementing your approach.

Test Your Solution

In order to test your proposed plan of action for dealing with the problem presented at the end of this case, you and the class should create and role-play one or more of the following situations:

1. A telephone call between the superintendent and the president of the school board about the letter.
2. A telephone call from a newspaper reporter to the superintendent.
3. A meeting between the superintendent and the building principals about the letter.
4. A meeting between the superintendent and the parent organization.

Investigate Further

What percent of students in your school and your district are from minority groups?

43
WE WANT NEIGHBORHOOD SCHOOLS, TOO!

The Busline School District was proud of its record of desegregating its schools in the last two decades. Although in the past almost all of its schools had been either totally white or totally nonwhite, now in most schools there was a good racial balance.

Of course, to achieve these results the school district had found it necessary to initiate a massive program of busing students. Unfortunately, most of the students who were bused were minority students, primarily because they were the students who had been attending old, run-down schools, and because most white students did not want to leave their neighborhood schools to be bused into parts of the city where minority students lived.

Although there had been complaints during the past few years about the busing program and its "unfairness," no major resistance had ever developed. Now, however, a letter to the editor in the morning newspaper indicated that things might be about to change.

BUSING UNFAIR!
WE WANT NEIGHBORHOOD SCHOOLS, TOO!

We believe the time has arrived for the school district to provide minority students with "neighborhood schools." Over the years we have participated in the school district's attempts to desegregate the schools because we believed that such participation would lead to a better education. Our children have gotten up early in order to ride a bus (which was frequently late!) long distances to outlying schools where students and faculty often either ignored us or seemed to resent our presence. In our judgment, the quality of education at the end of the bus trip has not been significantly better for our children, and we reject the notion that our children need to sit next to white children in order to learn.

We have long been troubled by the double standard the school district has used in its busing and desegregation policies. Most of the students who ride the bus are minorities. This has resulted in part because of school board decisions to close a number of inner-city schools, and in part because participation of the white children to help desegregate the schools is voluntary and few of *them* want to travel by bus long distances to a different school. Nor do our children!

We believe that minority children are capable of learning with their own, and by so doing will help restore a sense of the history and culture of their community that busing has negatively affected. Therefore, we demand that the school board and superintendent change their desegregation, busing, and building policies so that minority children can attend their own neighborhood schools. We know the changes will not be easy, but we are no longer willing to accept the status quo. We demand justice, equality, and quality in education. If we do not receive them, we will be forced to take appropriate action.

(Signed) Parents United for Neighborhood
Schools and Quality Education

Following the letter to the editor was a news item indicating that the superintendent of schools had declined to comment, but that he had scheduled separate meetings of his cabinet and the building principals to consider the implications of the statement from the Parents United for Neighborhood Schools and Quality Education.

SUGGESTED LEARNING ACTIVITIES

Analyze the Case

1. What is your evaluation of the busing policies of the school district?
2. What should school officials have done about complaints about the busing program, even though major resistance was not apparent?
3. Evaluate the letter to the editor, using concepts from Chapter 2 on communication.

Discuss the Larger Issues

1. What criteria should be used in determining which students should be bused in a program of desegregating the schools? What standards of fairness should be used?
2. To what extent should busing be voluntary?
3. What should school districts do to prepare students, parents, teachers, and administrators for the busing part of a desegregation program and for any adjustments that may need to be made for students and others in the new school situation?

Be a Problem Solver

Assume that you are a principal in the school district described in the case and that several of those who signed the letter to the editor are parents of children in your school. What steps will you take to prepare for the meeting with the superintendent, and what will be your position on the letter and your role at the meeting? Utilize appropriate administrative and social science concepts from Part I of the text in planning and implementing your approach.

Test Your Solution

To test your proposed overall approach to responding to these circumstances, you and your colleagues should create and role-play one or more of the following situations:

1. A meeting between you and the parents of children at your school who signed the letter to the editor.
2. A meeting of the principals with the superintendent.

Investigate Further

1. Examine the educational literature on desegregation and busing and identify those conditions or factors that contribute to effective programs.
2. Ascertain and evaluate the effectiveness of your school district's desegregation and busing programs.
3. Determine what criteria and methods your school district uses to evaluate the effectiveness of its desegregation and busing programs. What improvements in criteria and methods are needed?

44
METROPOLITAN INTEGRATION

The State Legislature, finally acting in response to the resegregation of city schools, had enacted a law requiring metropolitan integration between large city school districts and the adjacent suburban school districts. The statute required the busing of minority students to the suburbs for their education and the busing of white students to the large city school systems. The exact number of students to be bused and the procedure for selection were defined in a rather complicated formula that took into consideration a number of factors. However, its main purpose was to integrate suburban schools to a much greater extent and to increase the number of white students attending city schools. The integration program, mandated by the legislature in February, was to begin in September, now only two months away.

Bob Edwards, vice-principal at Pleasant View School in a suburban district, felt ambivalent about the metropolitan integration. He really didn't think that busing was the answer to racial problems, and he wasn't looking forward to dealing with some of the discipline problems from the city school system. On the other hand, he felt that the white students in his school probably needed more exposure to minority students, and since metropolitan integration was now the law, he felt that it was important to do as good a job with the integration program as possible.

Edwards was concerned, however, about his school's lack of planning and inservice preparation for the minority students. With the beginning of classes only two months away, nothing much had been done yet to get ready for the minority students. But when he had tried to discuss his concerns with the principal, they had been minimized. The principal's philosophy was that "students were students," and to make any special provisions for the minority transfer students would only serve to single them out and put the spotlight on them. The principal felt that it was better not to "make any big deal" about the transfer students, and then they would be more likely to fit in, just like any other students.

The vice-principal was still concerned, though, because of the negative attitudes of a number of students, teachers, and parents at Pleasant View and because of the very real adjustment problems that the minority transfer students were likely to encounter, due to differences in the cultural background and life style. But in light of the principal's stated philosophy, Edwards felt that his hands were tied.

SUGGESTED LEARNING ACTIVITIES

Analyze the Case

1. What is your assessment of the vice-principal's thoughts regarding metropolitan integration? Are there any factors that he is not taking into consideration that may be important?
2. Assume for the moment that the vice-principal's perception of the principal's position on the minority transfer students is accurate. What is your assessment of the principal's position? What assumptions is he making?

Discuss the Larger Issues

1. What are the pros and cons of metropolitan integration?
2. To what extent should educators attempt to promote metropolitan integration as a remedy to racial problems, as contrasted with waiting for a court or a state legislature to require it?
3. What is the role of the school and, in particular, the school administration in planning for and implementing a program of metropolitan integration? What specific activities should be carried out?

Be a Problem Solver

Assume that you are the vice-principal in the case. How could you respond constructively to the problems presented? Utilize administrative and social science concepts and principles in planning and implementing your problem-solving approach.

Test Your Solution

In order to test your proposed plan of action for dealing with the circumstances described in the case, you and your colleagues should create and role-play one or more of the following situations:

1. A second conference between Mr. Edwards and his principal regarding the minority transfer students.
2. A faculty meeting where the principal has asked you to plan and present inservice for the faculty in reference to the new minority transfer students.

Investigate Further

1. To what extent is there metropolitan integration in your area?
2. What is the attitude of administrators, teachers, parents, and students toward metropolitan integration?
3. Where metropolitan integration exists, what kinds of problems appear to be associated with it and what approaches seem to be effective in dealing with these problems?

45
DO (SHOULD?) WE TREAT THEM ALL ALIKE?

"What's that display you're putting up, Mrs. Johnson?"

The art teacher continued to arrange the art objects representing African-American culture in the display case. "Black History Month is beginning," she explained, "and this display case features some of the best artwork from the African-American students in the school."

There was silence as a group of students gathered, watching their teacher arranging the hall display case. Then someone said, "We just finished a week's study on Martin Luther King in social studies classes and now we have to go through Black History Month besides?"

"Yeah, when is *Asian* History Month, anyway?"

Mrs. Johnson was holding straight pins between her lips as she was putting up the lettering for the display, and she merely shrugged her shoulders, having no answer. Then, standing back from the display case to survey the total effect, she smiled with satisfaction. It looked pretty good. However, looking around at the students' long faces, she realized that they were feeling left out. Realistically, she knew, the ethnic heritages they represented might never be recognized in a formal way at the school: Filipino, Lithuanian, Vietnamese, Hispanic.

"Just because your nationality isn't in the display case this month doesn't mean it's not important," she assured the students. "We're really lucky at Harrison School to have such a variety of nationalities, and each one of you brings something special to the school."

Having gathered together her materials, Mrs. Johnson started walking toward the Faculty Room. The students went their own ways, except for Sue Kan, who followed her. "Really, Mrs. Johnson, I know that black culture is important in this country and that Martin Luther King did a lot for equal rights. But people don't seem to recognize that Asians have been here a long time, too. And a lot of *them* came under difficult circumstances, too, like the ones who put in all the railroads in the West.

And now the black kids even have a club just for them, while the rest of us with different backgrounds seem to be almost invisible! Except that ev-erybody calls us Asians 'curve-breakers' and they seem to resent us. Haven't you noticed what a problem it's getting to be, Mrs. Johnson? Why can't we all just be treated alike? Why do black students seem to get all the attention and special assemblies, while the rest of us have to work, work, work for everything we get?"

The art teacher stopped in her tracks. What could she say to Sue, a student she knew to be a high achiever and a good school citizen? She decided to acknowledge Sue's discomfort and go from there. "It sounds like you're feeling very left out, Sue, and I'm sorry about that because you do work very hard, I know."

"Well, nobody likes a complainer, but I just get tired of the same thing year after year: Martin Luther King, black history assemblies—you'd think that a school could teach that a *lot* of other national backgrounds have also contributed to the building of this country. And now there's this African-American Club. Why does the principal allow it?"

"Sue, I think maybe we ought to ask the principal about that. Let's go to the office and see if we can set up a meeting for today."

Sue's face brightened as they walked together to the principal's office.

SUGGESTED LEARNING ACTIVITIES

Analyze the Case

1. Would you have responded any differently from Mrs. Johnson to the murmurings of the students watching her put up the display? If so, how?
2. Based on the facts presented in the case, do you agree or disagree with the students' contention that the school was giving disproportionate recognition to a single ethnic group?
3. Assess the likelihood that the principal of Harrison School is aware of the dissatisfaction expressed by students who are not black.

Discuss the Larger Issues

1. What are the advantages and disadvantages of setting aside ''special'' days or weeks to recognize a particular ethnic group in our culture?
2. Should members of a particular ethnic group be allowed by a school to have their own support group, sponsored by a sympathetic faculty member?
3. How far should a school go in making efforts to recognize the contributions of various ethnicities and cultures represented in the student body? In the larger society where the students may eventually interact?

Be a Problem Solver

Assume that you are the principal at Harrison School. How would you respond to Sue Kan's concerns? Also, how would you respond if students from other ethnic backgrounds expressed similar concerns? Utilize relevant concepts from Part I of the text in preparing and implementing your responses.

Test Your Solution

To test your proposed plan for responding to the problem described in the case study, you and your colleagues should create and role-play one or more of the following situations:

1. A meeting between the principal and Sue Kan, or with a student representative from a different ethnic group.
2. A call from a parent who complains that focusing so much attention on blacks is unfair because ''Blacks have made few significant contributions, compared to white people.''
3. A message from a local newspaper reporter who wants to know what special events are taking place during Black History Month so the paper can run a special feature.

Investigate Further

1. Determine what methods your school uses to ascertain the problems experienced in school by students from minority ethnic backgrounds.
2. Identify and interview a leader or representative in each of the ethnic groups represented in your school community. Inquire about how that person believes one's culture should be recognized in the school.
3. Anticipate how activities that recognize ethnic contributions may impact on students who may have little information on their own ethnicity, i.e., due to adoption or other reasons.
4. Pursue readings or take a course on cultural diversity.

46
STUDENT DRUG PROBLEM AT WASHINGTON SCHOOL

The faculty members congregating in the teachers' lounge before school were upset about last night's newspaper article on the outbreak of another drug problem at Washington School. Rumors had previously been circulating for some time about drugs sold in the school restrooms and cafeteria, but until now no one seemed to have any actual evidence that this was indeed taking place—although one couldn't be sure from the newspaper story.

DRUG PROBLEM AT WASHINGTON SCHOOL

Rumors continue to fly at Washington School about a recurring drug problem. While facts are difficult to ascertain, the problem seems to have started again on a very limited basis last spring and has grown, until now drug use is said to be rampant among students at the school.

> It has been alleged that a variety of drugs, including crack, marijuana, and amphetamines, are being sold in the cafeteria during the noon hour. They are also reportedly being sold and used in school restrooms.
>
> Although some differences of opinion have been expressed by students, faculty, and parents on the extent of the problem, the general feeling is that steps must be taken immediately to curb this dangerous situation.
>
> The administration of the school has voiced concern and has the matter under surveillance, but had indicated that there is "no evidence that a serious problem does, in fact, exist."

As school started that morning, classes buzzed with conversation about the newspaper article, and teachers experienced difficulty in beginning the day's lesson. When several of them finally decided to allow discussion about the issue, students spent an entire class period talking about the article and the purported problem.

In the meantime, the principal and his assistants were meeting to discuss the situation, as they had done on numerous other occasions. When rumors of drug use on school premises had first started to circulate again last spring, the administration had tried to track down each story, but to no avail. No one would volunteer any information about the actual sale or use of drugs, and the administration had not been successful in catching anyone in the act.

After school had opened in the fall, the administration had tried to increase the surveillance of restrooms and the cafeteria, but encountered certain difficulties. Girls' restrooms, in particular, had always constituted a problem, even in trying to catch cigarette smokers. The custodial matron had been told to check the restrooms periodically as she moved from area to area in her work, but this had not proved to be very effective. Either the matron did not check often enough, or she wasn't sharp enough to outwit the girls. There was also some indication that she didn't relish this additional task.

The major hindrance in surveillance, of course, was the practical impossibility for the administration to be everywhere; there were too many restrooms and too many other administrative responsibilities to carry out. Still, it was obvious that *something* had to be done. The central office had indicated concern, and several members of the school board had expressed displeasure about the unfavorable publicity. There had been some mention of assigning faculty members to cafeteria and restroom patrol duty, but the principal had rejected this idea because of the continuing lack of clear-cut evidence that drugs were indeed being sold. He was also aware that the faculty might resist or reject such an assignment. But what should be done? None of the alternatives seemed very desirable.

The following week the local newspaper printed an editorial aimed at the drug problem. It was somewhat critical of the school administration because of its unsuccessful efforts to identify and cope with the situation, and it highlighted the growing concern of parents in the community.

Not unexpectedly, the principal received a telephone call the next morning from his immediate superior conveying the central office staff's feeling that the situation was getting out of hand and that corrective measures must be taken. No concrete suggestions were offered, however, other than assigning teachers to patrol the halls and restrooms.

At ten o'clock the principal called another meeting with his assistants. There was unanimous recognition that the situation demanded action but few ideas on how to proceed. An assistant principal finally suggested that students might be able to help with the problem. Perhaps representatives from the student government or some other student group could help in the cafeteria during the noon hour and could check restrooms during their free periods.

Was it a good idea? The principal wasn't sure. Perhaps students would be willing to help, but in an actual situation would they inform on their peers? More important, was this a proper use of students? And what if someone were hurt?

After weighing the potential advantages and disadvantages, the use of students was rejected and the possibility of assigning teachers was again brought up for discussion. The principal was still concerned about assigning the faculty to patrol duty. And yet, he was conscious of the fact that his present program of surveillance was being criticized by the community because no one had been caught selling or using drugs at the school. The principal had an uneasy feeling about whether patrol duty represented an appropriate use of professional personnel and whether it would be accepted by the faculty. Unfortunately, no other alternatives were presented, so the principal reluctantly decided to utilize faculty assistance to cope with the problem.

At 2 P.M. that day a memo was placed in the faculty mailboxes announcing a meeting after school, and at 4:00 P.M. the teachers filed into the room. The principal began immediately to explain the situation thoroughly, and after 20 minutes, concluded by pointing out the limited alternatives available to the administration. Then he distributed the faculty assignments to cafeteria and restroom patrol duty, which were set up on a rotating basis so that everyone would be participating for the same length of time, not more than twice a week or a total of 60 minutes.

Although no one said anything directly or asked any questions during the principal's presentation, there were many side glances and low murmurs between faculty members. However, when he invited the teachers to ask questions after they had received their assignments, there was a dead silence. Uncertain about the meaning of the faculty's reaction, the principal tried to elaborate on his earlier remarks about the need to deal with the drug problem but found himself only repeating much of what he had already said. He therefore concluded the meeting by offering to meet later in his office with anyone who wished to ask questions or to discuss the matter further. No one ever showed up.

There was, however, considerable discussion in teachers' offices, the faculty room, and on the way home from school that day. Some teachers perceived the duty with distaste, but felt that the administration had no choice but to assign the faculty to help out with the problem. Others felt that the problem was strictly administrative in nature and that teachers should not be involved.

The discussion continued the next morning in the faculty room and elsewhere in the school over the merits of assigning teachers to cafeteria and restroom duty. Although there were some who felt that this extra duty might violate a provision of their contract dealing with the assignment of teachers, particularly during the noon hour, the assignments thus far had been made in such a way that no one lost out on a lunch period.

The major issue finally seemed to boil down to whether this was something that a professional teacher should do (although there were a few faculty members who simply didn't want to be bothered with an extra responsibility). *Should* a teacher be required to participate in, or become involved with, this type of activity? Wasn't surveillance really an area that the administration should handle, or perhaps, even the police?

Counselors, who also had been placed on the duty roster, were particularly concerned. What would this do to their rapport with the students? How could they expect students who might be bothered about drugs or even users of drugs to come to counselors to discuss their problems if counselors were viewed as "arms of the administration"? Wouldn't their effectiveness be impaired?

The following Monday the schedule of faculty patrols began. After a week and a half, the administration began to hear via the grapevine that some teachers and counselors were less than thorough in "making the rounds," and that others were not carrying out their duties at all. It was not known how widespread this was, but if at all prevalent, some action would be called for by the administration or the situation would soon deteriorate.

The principal was in a quandary. Since the faculty patrol had been initiated, parental and community complaints had died down, and the central office and school board seemed generally pleased with the improvement. Still, no one had been caught selling or using drugs, and now it appeared that an incipient faculty-administration confrontation might be brewing. What should he do? What *could* he do? Sometimes he wondered why he had gone into administration.

SUGGESTED LEARNING ACTIVITIES

Analyze the Case

1. What is your reaction to the newspaper story? To what extent do you feel that it is a "good" article? What would you do if you disagreed with the article or with the editorial which followed later in the case?
2. From the information presented in this case, do you feel that there is a drug problem at Washington School? What is the basis for your opinion? Would you take no further action if you felt that drugs were not being used or sold at the school itself?
3. What alternatives for coping with the alleged drug problem were available to the administration? What pressures and constraints were operating in the situation which made decision making difficult for the principal? Do you think that the administration should have tried the idea of using students to help with solving the drug problem? What assumptions are you making?
4. What are your feelings about the way the faculty meeting was handled? How would you have conducted this meeting differently?

Discuss the Larger Issues

1. Should a teacher take class time to discuss something like the school's alleged drug problem, even though the topic may be controversial and the discussion could be embarrassing to the administration? If so, under what set of circumstances would such action be clearly *inappropriate?* What kind of a school policy should be developed to cover this type of situation?
2. To what extent is coping with a drug problem the responsibility of everyone in the school, or only the administration? What is the professional responsibility of a teacher or counselor in regard to coping with a possible drug problem in the school?

Be a Problem Solver

At the end of this case, the principal is faced with an incipient faculty revolt and the possibility that the drug problem still had not really been solved. If you were the principal, how would you handle the situation? What factors may limit your flexibility in arriving at a solution?

Test Your Solution

In order to test your proposed plan of action for dealing with the problems presented in this case, you and the class should create and role-play one or more of the following situations:

1. A conference between the principal and those faculty members who are not carrying out their patrol duties.
2. A meeting between the principal and the faculty.
3. A telephone call to the principal from the superintendent.
4. A meeting with the student council, which is protesting the faculty's patrolling of the restrooms.
5. A telephone call to the principal from the newspaper.

Investigate Further

1. What is the possibility that drugs are being sold or used in your school? How would you ascertain that a problem exists?
2. What is your school board's policy on drugs in the school? To what extent are there problems in enforcing the policy?
3. What program does your school have for detecting student use or selling of drugs on school premises?

47

DO EXTREME TIMES CALL FOR RADICAL ACTION?
(A LEADERLESS GROUP ACTIVITY)

In November the superintendent of schools sent the following memorandum to all administrators and supervisors:

As you know, the drug problem in our schools has worsened, and the school board and community are very concerned. In the last few weeks several ideas have been projected, to which the school board and I would like your reaction. I acknowledge that these items are controversial, but extreme times may call for radical action. In any case, I would like you to consider the following proposals and give me your most thoughtful analyses and recommendations. Also, I would like your own ideas on what we should do to address the problem if you judge any of the following ideas to be undesirable or not feasible.

1. Students would periodically be randomly searched for drugs prior to entering the school corridors.

2. In those schools with the most serious drug problem, trained dogs would be used to sniff lockers, and when needed, used in classrooms to detect drugs.

3. All students participating in athletics would be subject to random drug testing.

4. Any student who is suspected of using drugs would be required to undergo drug testing.

5. Any student caught using any kind of illegal drugs on the school grounds or at a school activity would be expelled. Present policy expels only drug sellers or chronic users.

6. Any student found to have known about (but failed to inform the proper authorities about) another student's engaging in the sale of drugs at the school would be suspended.

Although there would be financial considerations to many of these proposals, at this point I want you to consider them solely on their merit, without regard to expense. Just give me your best thinking on the proposals themselves.

INSTRUCTIONS

1. Either the instructor will distribute further information about the nature and extent of the drug problem in the school district, or the members of the group will discuss these aspects and reach agreement on them prior to preparing a response to the superintendent's memo. As another alternative, it may be desirable to assume different scenarios regarding the nature and extent of the drug problem in order to see whether and how this would affect the type of response given to the superintendent.

2. Once the drug problem is further defined by the instructor and/or the group, one or more of the following activities should be pursued:
   a. The group should attempt to reach consensus on a response to the superintendent's request.
   b. Each individual should prepare a written response.
   c. Members of the group should prepare for an oral presentation to the superintendent's cabinet. Each person who is not involved in making the presentation should assume the role of a member of the superintendent's cabinet.

48
POSSIBLE TEACHER DRUG PROBLEM

"Well, this certainly looks interesting!" chirped the principal's secretary as she handed him a note which read:

> Detective Denny called while you were gone. He would like you to return his call at your earliest convenience. Says it is *quite* important.

For some reason the principal always experienced a feeling of uncertainty in responding to a call from the police. He never knew when they might come across something that would reflect adversely on the school. Also, students and parents sometimes reacted negatively to a police investigation, and the central office and the school board could be counted on to be upset if something unfavorable was printed in the newspaper. On the other hand, perhaps it was just a routine call. Still . . . . The principal dialed the station number, hoping for the best and fearing the worst.

Detective Denny answered the call and indicated that his department needed some information on Paul Allen, a teacher at Franklin School. Surprised that the inquiry was in regard to a member of his staff rather than a student, all the principal could say at first was that Mr. Allen was new this year. He hastened to add that, although there had been little opportunity to become closely acquainted with Allen, he seemed to be competent as a teacher. His strong feature was his rapport with the students. Unfortunately, he seemed to have experienced difficulty in being accepted by the faculty, particularly the older teachers, probably because of his youthful dress and manners and his attempts to experiment with different teaching materials and methods. He was very popular with the students, though, and the principal considered him personally likeable.

Detective Denny responded that something had come up about Mr. Allen which could not be discussed over the phone and that the principal should expect someone from the station to arrive at the school in about an hour to review the situation.

After his conversation with Detective Denny, the principal tried to tackle the items on his desk, but he had a difficult time keeping his mind on the job. He conjured up young Allen's face and tried to recall what he *really* knew about him. He thought back to the job interview last spring. There had been numerous applicants for the vacancy, but they were mostly women, and the principal had wanted to hire a man for the position. Allen had appeared to be personable, had studied at a large university, and had really made a good impression upon both the principal and the vice-principal, Mr. Schmidt. The principal considered calling Schmidt in now to ask further about Allen, but rejected the idea, at least until he learned more about the problem. Schmidt had occasionally let things slip in the past that should have been kept confidential, and there was no sense in possibly stirring him up.

The principal tried to recall which teachers Allen usually associated with, but he was completely at a loss. Paul typically didn't sit in the teachers' dining room, but ate with the students in the cafeteria. The principal had thought this a little strange and had wondered whether it was due to the beginning teacher's preference for young people or a tendency on the part of the older staff members to exclude him. It was hard to tell.

At two o'clock sharp Detective Denny was ushered into the principal's office. After a brief exchange of amenities, Detective Denny immediately brought up the item of concern. It seemed that, in the process of breaking up a noisy teenage party after Friday night's basketball game, police had stumbled onto some evidence that drugs had been in use. Eighteen young people were arrested, most of whom were later determined to be students at Franklin School. During their interrogation at the station, one boy finally admitted his guilt, but indicated that he was not alone, and that in addition to the other students, a teacher had been at the party earlier—a Mr. Allen.

The officers had tried to confirm the story by questioning the other students, about half of whom were girls, but with no success. The other students had refused to admit to using drugs themselves and had denied that any teacher had been at the party. Now Detective Denny wanted to know the principal's assessment of Paul Allen. Was he the type who might use drugs?

Despite the fact that the principal had prepared himself for the worst, he was concerned. Thoughts ran haphazardly through his mind. . . . A member of his own faculty involved? Was it true? What could he say? If it was true, what might this mean for the school? The investigator was still waiting expectantly for his reply, and the principal tried to collect his thoughts. He explained again that Mr. Allen was new on the staff and was not well-known. Yes, it was possible that the teacher could have participated in such a party, but the principal hoped that this was not the case. It was hard to believe that a teacher as bright and likeable as Mr. Allen would allow himself to become mixed up in something like this!

At that moment the investigator dropped the next bombshell: the student informer had reported that Mr. Allen was a regular user of drugs. Did the principal have any information about this or the possibility of other teachers on his staff who might be using or even selling drugs?

The principal was floored, particularly by the investigator's last question. Other teachers on *his* staff using or selling drugs? "My God!" thought the principal. "Is this possible?"

The principal at this stage didn't know what to say. He indicated that he had no information on the problem, but would, of course, cooperate in any way he could with the police.

Investigator Denny stated that he would like to meet with Mr. Allen and the principal immediately after the dismissal of school. The principal agreed to make the necessary arrangements and the conference ended.

At 3:30 Mr. Allen arrived at the principal's office. There was no detectable emotion on his face when the police investigator was introduced. Under questioning by the detective, he freely admitted attending the student party after the basketball game. He had chaperoned a student bus to the game and had been invited by several students to an after-game party. At the time he had been uncertain about accepting the invitation, but it all seemed innocent enough. This was his first year at the school and he had not made many friends, even in the community. He liked young people and enjoyed being around them. No, he hadn't particularly considered any negative ramifications about going to the party. Surely the day had passed when school districts could exercise control over a teacher's social life!

Neither the principal nor Detective Denny responded to the teacher's comments, but the investigator continued to raise questions about the party. "Did anything unusual take place during the course of the evening? Did anything go on that was perhaps questionable? One of the students has already mentioned drugs being used at the party. Do you know anything about that?"

Allen replied that the party had been a little noisy, but it was not wild. He had seen no one using drugs, but, of course, he had left early.

At that point the investigator confronted Allen with the student's allegation that the teacher himself was at the party, had smoked marijuana, and, in fact, according to the student, was a regular user of hard drugs. What did Allen have to say about that?

Allen was silent for a few moments as he apparently tried to organize his thoughts, but he finally stated that he would have no further comment until he could talk to his lawyer. However, he was not guilty, he said, and with that he walked out of the principal's office.

The principal nodded mutely as Detective Denny explained that further investigation would be necessary and that the police would keep in touch with the principal as new information became available. After the detective left the office, the principal wondered whether he should call his superior at the central office. He considered the possibility of waiting until the next day, hoping that things might die down a little, but eventually concluded that it would be better to call the central office immediately, in case the news leaked out from another source.

The assistant superintendent was upset by the principal's report and was uncertain about what should be done. He decided that he would have to call the principal back. He did so within half an hour, relaying the news that the story about the student drug party and the teacher's alleged presence had been aired over the radio and would probably appear in the morning paper. There was a possibility that the students would eventually have to be suspended and the teacher temporarily relieved of his duties, although there was considerable difference of opinion about this in the central office. No doubt the principal's recommendation in this regard would carry a great deal of weight. The assistant superintendent concluded by saying that the principal would be contacted by someone from the central office before school the next morning.

The assistant superintendent's prediction that the story would soon appear in the newspaper turned out to be accurate. The morning edition described the circumstances of the drug party and mentioned that Mr. Allen was alleged to be present. The article stated that several parents and at least one school board member who had been contacted felt that the students should be suspended and that possibly the teacher should be fired.

Wanting some time to think things out, the principal went to his office early that morning. But he soon began to receive telephone calls from parents who were appalled that such an incident could involve a teacher from their children's school and who wanted to know what was going to be done. The principal indicated that he was looking into the matter.

He also received calls from radio and television newsmen who wanted to set up an interview, and from a student who said that his classmates were circulating a petition backing the retention of Mr. Allen and proclaiming his innocence in the whole affair.

No one from the central office had called the principal by 8 A.M., and he found their number to be continually busy. The one time that he stepped momentarily out of his office, he was informed by Mr. Schmidt that Mr. Allen was in school and that many of the teachers were upset about the entire situation.

It appeared that a rather serious problem was quickly developing. The principal hoped that a major altercation could be avoided.

SUGGESTED LEARNING ACTIVITIES

Analyze the Case

1. Is the difficulty in becoming accepted by the faculty, experienced by Mr. Allen, unusual or is it typically a problem of a beginning teacher? To what extent do you feel that such an experience *may* have contributed to some of his other problems with which this case deals? What would you have done *if you were the principal* to help Mr. Allen be better accepted by the faculty? What assumptions are you making in answering these last two questions?
2. Are the reactions of the principal and the assistant superintendent to the news of student and teacher involvement with drugs atypical, or are they perfectly reasonable ones? On what basis can such a judgment be made? Would you have felt differently? What actions would you have taken that were different from those taken by the principal or the assistant superintendent upon *first* learning about the drug problem?
3. Do you feel that the teacher is innocent of the drug charge? What evidence is presented in the case study, one way or the other? If you feel that additional evidence is needed, what would constitute that evidence and how would you secure it?

Discuss the Larger Issues

1. Should the school have any control or concern over the activities of students and teachers *outside* of school? Under what circumstances can and should the school show concern or take action in regard to something that a student or teacher has done outside of school? How serious must the offense be? What criteria should be used? Would the same criteria be applied in other occupations or aspects of life?
2. What should be the relationship between the school and the police in matters involving the investigation of possible law violations by students or teachers? Should the principal in a situation like this arrange the questioning of a teacher or student by the police on school premises during school hours? What rights, if any, should a teacher or student have in regard to questioning by the police during school hours? What role should the principal play in protecting these rights?

Be a Problem Solver

At the end of the case the principal faces a number of rapidly developing events. If you were the principal, how would you handle the situation?

Test Your Solution

In order to test your plan of action for dealing with the problems presented at the end of the case, you and the class should create and role-play one or more of the following situations:

1. A meeting between the principal and the faculty.
2. A meeting between the principal and the students circulating the petition.
3. A telephone call from the assistant superintendent to the principal.
4. A telephone call from radio or television newsmen to the principal.
5. A meeting between the principal and a parent who walked into the office demanding to see the principal.

Investigate Further

1. What is the school board policy in your district on cooperating with police officials concerning a problem involving students or school personnel?
2. What are the local, state, federal, or constitutional laws which would govern a school's involvement in a problem like the one described in this case?
3. What do the following people think should be done if a problem like the one described in the case should occur in your school?
   a. The principal
   b. The building representative
   c. Teachers in general
   d. The assistant superintendent or superintendent

49
A DIFFERENT KIND OF "DRUG" PROBLEM

School had been in session for approximately two months, and it appeared that Madison School was off to a good beginning. It was true that for the last several years there had been a drug problem at the school, but that was now almost under control. During that period of time, however, the school had undergone considerable turmoil. Parents had been upset, the administration had had difficulty in coping with the situation, and the school had received a great deal of unfavorable publicity. Therefore, everyone was relieved that the drug problem had been successfully dealt with and pleased that no other issues had yet developed this school year.

At the weekly meeting of the school counselors, however, a problem was discussed which appeared to possess grave implications. Steve Williams, one of the counselors, reported that a rather popular student had come to see him about a personal problem which upset her greatly. She said that she had been going steady for some time, and her boyfriend had begun to make sexual advances. She had rejected his advances thus far, on moral grounds and from a fear of possible pregnancy, but now she was weakening. She further confided that her boyfriend had offered to provide her with "the pill," which he said he could secure from a source in the school. But she wanted the counselor's advice. Should she take the pill? Was it wrong for her to have sexual relations with someone she loved?

The questions posed by the girl had created several dilemmas for the counselor. At the time he had wondered what his position should be on the matter. Does a counselor have the right to influence a student about what the counselor believes is morally wrong?

Unable to resolve this inner conflict, the counselor had encouraged the girl to talk about her problem. However, when she had asked him point-blank what she should do, he had tried to hedge and finally had suggested that perhaps she should discuss the problem with her minister or her parents. At that point, the girl had walked out.

Now as Steve related the incident to his colleagues, he expressed concern about his own behavior. Had he acted appropriately during the conference? Should he have informed the principal of the possibility that someone was selling the pill in the school?

The discussion at the counselors' meeting quickly warmed up as they argued about Steve's actions and whether the administration should be informed about the possibility that birth control pills were being sold on school premises. Most of those at the meeting seemed to agree that it was not really the role of the counselor to respond to the moral question presented by the girl, but others felt that a position of neutrality offered her no assistance at a time when a word from a trusted adult might have guided her in the right direction. On the issue of whether the administration should be advised that the pill was being sold in the school, the counselors were almost equally divided, although the guidance director felt very strongly that the principal should be alerted.

After the meeting, the counselor, Steve Williams, took time to sort out his feelings. In some respects he was sorry that he had brought the problem to the attention of his colleagues. He had received no real help or ideas from them on how he might have better handled the situation, and he didn't know what he would do if the problem arose again. He was glad of one thing, though, and that was that he had not revealed to the other counselors the name of the girl or any other names she had mentioned in connection with the pill. He had now decided not to inform the administration about what the girl had confided to him.

Two days later, however, Steve Williams was called into the principal's office. The principal had been informed by the guidance director of the possibility that the pill was being sold in school and that Steve might have some information that could shed light on the situation. Rumors were circulating in the school that the pill was being peddled, and the principal had received several calls from concerned parents. What did Steve know about the circumstances surrounding the problem?

This was a difficult situation for both the counselor and the principal. The counselor respected the principal and enjoyed working at the school, but felt a loyalty to the girl who had placed her trust in him. He was *not* going to tell the principal what she had related to him.

The principal, on the other hand, wanted to "nip this thing in the bud" before the situation grew out of hand. He liked Steve and was aware of the confidentiality issue, but felt that the general welfare of the school transcended that issue. He was determined to get to the bottom of things!

SUGGESTED LEARNING ACTIVITIES

Analyze the Case

1. What do you think the counselor should have done in the conference with the student who was seeking advice? What assumptions are you making?
2. What are the advantages and disadvantages of the counselor trying to obtain help from the guidance department? To whom would you have gone for assistance if you had been the counselor?
3. What are some of the social and personal factors that are influencing the principal and the counselor as they face each other in the situation at the end of the case?

Discuss the Larger Issues

1. Should a school counselor discuss with a student personal problems like the ones identified in this case? Why or why not?
2. To what extent should a counselor working in a school setting have the right to classify information obtained from a client as confidential? Are there limits to this right? If so, what are they?

Be a Problem Solver

In the situation described at the end of the case, both the principal and the counselor have stated their views. If you were either the counselor or the principal, what would be your next step? What would be your course of action if the other person didn't change his position?

Test Your Solution

In order to test your proposed plan of action for dealing with the problem presented at the end of the case, you and the class should create and role-play one or more of the following situations:

1. The conference between the principal and the counselor.
2. A meeting between the principal, the counselor, and the teachers' association representative.
3. A meeting between the principal and the guidance department.
4. A call to the principal, inquiring about a rumor of the ''pill'' being sold at the school.

Investigate Further

1. How do the counselors in your school feel about the situation described in this case? What might be the reactions of the principal?
2. What is the school board policy in your district on what the school counselor should do if students tell him that they (or others) are using or selling drugs in school?
3. What is the law in your state on the confidentiality issue in this case?

15 Problems of Change

In recent years, educators have been bombarded with various proposals for improving education, most of which would require major changes in the schools. While the topic of introducing change has generally been written about in glowing terms, it needs to be recognized that various problems and issues are frequently associated with the process. Proposed change challenges the status quo and tends to be threatening to a number of people. An attempt to implement a certain change can also be disruptive to school routine and debilitating to the people adversely affected by it. The extent to which each or all of these negative consequences occur will depend in large part on the effectiveness of the administrator in planning for and implementing a particular innovation. Therefore, it is important that the reader examine carefully the ideas in Part I, especially Chapter 7, before addressing any of the cases in this chapter.

The case studies presented on the following pages provide the reader with an opportunity to apply the concepts learned from reading Part I. The cases focus on various problems and issues that an educator may encounter in trying to bring about change. Although most of the cases center on difficulties which can occur in the process of introducing a change, attention is also given to problems of institutionalizing a change. The innovations described could be proposed at either the elementary or secondary level, and an attempt has been made to identify different levels and kinds of administrators and supervisors in the role of change agent.

BACKGROUND READING

The reader who would like to develop further background and understanding of the problems and issues associated with introducing and implementing change in the schools should see Chapter 7 in this book and pursue the following readings.

Sharon C. Conley and Samuel B. Bacharach, ''From School-Site Management to Participatory School-Site Management,'' *Phi Delta Kappan* (March 1990), 539–544.

Robert Gilchrist, *Effective Schools: Three Case Studies of Excellence* (Bloomington, IN: National Education Service, 1989).

Bruce Joyce and Beverly Showers, ''Improving Inservice Training: The Message of Research,'' *Educational Leadership* (February 1990), 379–385.

Daniel U. Levin, ''Creating Effective Schools: Findings and Implications from Research and Practice,'' *Phi Delta Kappan* (January 1991), 389–393.

Mary Anne Raywid, ''Contrasting Strategies for Restructuring Schools: Site-Based Management and Choice,'' *Equity and Choice* (Winter 1990), 26–28.

Stuart C. Smith and Philip K. Piele, *School Leadership: Handbook for Excellence*, 2nd ed. (Eugene, OR: ERIC Clearinghouse on Educational Management, 1989), Chapters 5, 6, and 7.

50
TEACHER TRIES TO INDIVIDUALIZE INSTRUCTION

The teacher was excited about trying some of the new techniques for individualizing instruction that he had learned during the summer. He had waited until things had settled down in the fall, but it was now the third week of school and he was ready to begin experimenting with his classes.

Basically, he wanted to redesign and reschedule his classes so that he could spend more time working with individual students and small groups. He also hoped to release students from class to work on independent study projects of their own choosing. He had given considerable thought to the means by which all of this might be accomplished, and with the help of his summer school professor, he had come up with a plan of action.

He would separate each of his classes into two groups and would send half of the students to the library where they would be free to work on independent study projects, while he met with the remaining students for small group discussion or individual conferences. The following day he would reverse the procedure, so the students who had previously been engaged in class discussion would go to the library for independent study, while those who had previously been in the library would meet with him.

On the third day in the cycle he would bring the two small groups of students together for a regular class meeting that would be designed to discuss and synthesize what had been learned independently. By varying the size of the group and the nature of the teaching and learning activities, he hoped to individualize his own program to a much greater extent and, perhaps, set an example that might stimulate other teachers to diversify their methods of instruction.

The following morning he initiated the new program by explaining its rationale to the students and discussing with them their responsibilities, in and out of class. An out-of-class permit was written for the group going to the library, explaining for the benefit of anyone who might stop them in the hallway or in the library that the students had been excused from the teacher's class in order to work on independent study projects. The teacher had not felt it necessary to contact the librarian in advance since there were usually few students in the library, and the students' out-of-class permit made it clear that their activity had the approval of their teacher.

After half the students left for the library, the teacher rearranged the chairs in the room with the help of the remaining students and introduced the discussion topic. Almost immediately he sensed that the creation of a small group had brought about a change in atmosphere. Student discussion became livelier and more spontaneous, and there was greater participation from those students who, in the past, had seemed reluctant to take part in class activities. The teacher was delighted.

Suddenly, however, the classroom door opened and in walked the students who were supposed to be studying in the library. They claimed that the librarian had refused them admittance because her approval for the project had not been secured in advance. She had also informed them that the library was not a place for students who did not know specifically what they wanted to do, and that before coming to the library again, each student should identify in advance the area he wanted to investigate and obtain the teacher's approval.

The students reported that the librarian seemed annoyed by the prospect of other groups from the teacher's classroom coming to the library during that day—and on succeeding days.

The teacher tried to calm the students, many of whom seemed irritated and upset. He told them that he would attempt to straighten out matters with the librarian, but in the meantime the entire class would have to proceed as they had in the past.

At the end of the afternoon, he sought out the assistant principal for advice. It was only the second year at the school for the teacher, and he certainly didn't want to get into a conflict with the librarian. All he wanted to do was to try something different in an effort to improve his classroom instruction.

Unfortunately, his conference with the assistant principal was not very reassuring. The assistant principal did not feel that the librarian would ever be very cooperative or receptive to the idea of students using the library on a regular basis during class time—occasionally, perhaps, but not regularly. He doubted whether it would do much good to talk to the librarian, but he encouraged the teacher to continue experimenting with new approaches to teaching, whenever possible, and not to give up hope. It was apparent to the teacher, however, that the assistant principal had little inclination to become involved in helping to bring about the desired changes.

Nevertheless, the teacher was determined not to give up. He wasn't sure at the moment what his next step should be, but he certainly wasn't going to scuttle the idea of individualizing instruction in his classroom. Perhaps he should see the principal for assistance.

At that moment, the principal was in his office talking on the telephone to a parent who had called to ask how the school expected his son to get a good education if one of the boy's teachers was going to allow him to spend half his time out of class, working on whatever he chose.

It was the second time that day that the teacher's name had been mentioned to the principal. Earlier, several members of the faculty had complained about the noise in the halls caused by students going to and from the teacher's classroom after passing time. The principal decided he would have to find out what was causing all the trouble.

SUGGESTED LEARNING ACTIVITIES

Analyze the Case

1. Why did the teacher run into difficulty in this school in trying to introduce new techniques for individualizing instruction? What might be some of the reasons why the teacher incorrectly made certain assumptions, and, in other instances, did not pursue other sources of help in trying to implement his new approach?
2. What is your evaluation of the role played by the librarian? By the assistant principal? What might be some of the reasons why each of them responded the way they did? What implications do their responses have for how the principal handled the overall problem in the case?
3. Considering the type of innovation the teacher wanted to initiate, how might he have proceeded differently? What assumptions are you making?

Discuss the Larger Issues

1. What should be the role of the teacher in initiating change?
2. What institutional conditions act as a deterrent to teacher-initiated change?
3. Should there be a school policy on teacher innovations? If so, what should constitute the main elements of the policy?
4. What should be the role of the principal or other administrators in regard to teacher initiated innovation?

Be a Problem Solver

Several teachers and one parent have complained to the principal about the teacher and his innovation. If you were the principal in that situation, what would be your reactions? What action, if any, would you take to deal with the situation?

Test Your Solution

In order to test your proposed plan of action for dealing with the problem presented at the end of the case, you and the class should create and role-play one or more of the following situations:

1. A conference between the principal and the teacher.

2. A conference among the principal, the teacher, the librarian, and the assistant principal.
3. A telephone call to the principal from another parent complaining about the teacher and his innovation.

Investigate Further

1. What is the written policy in your school on teacher-initiated innovations? What is the feeling of your principal, central office supervisor, and assistant principal about teacher-initiated innovations?
2. To what extent are funds available in your district and school for implementing teacher-initiated innovations?
3. In your district and school, what barriers or obstacles would a teacher or principal have to overcome in order to initiate any program of individualized instruction?

51

EFFECTIVE SCHOOLS: HOW DO WE GET THERE FROM HERE? (A GROUP ACTIVITY)

Background

A new superintendent, Maria Rodriguez, has been selected by Ambition School District. A recent Ph.D. graduate from a major research university in a different state, she is a nationally recognized educational leader. The school board has informed her that her most important assignment is to bring about significant educational reform by creating effective schools for *all* students, not only for the academically oriented ones.

Dr. Rodriguez believes that if she is to be successful in meeting the school board's expectations, she first needs to ascertain the leadership capabilities of the school principals. To make that determination, she asks each principal in the district to propose, in a 3 to 5 page report, a plan outlining how the principal would develop an effective school. The superintendent indicates in her request that, although it will be impossible for the school district to fund all of the plans the first year, she wants each principal to develop a proposal, and those plans which cannot be funded initially will receive consideration in the future. To help the superintendent select the most deserving proposals, she will ask a committee of principals to review them and recommend to the central office the top three in rank order.

Instructions

1. Members of the class are to assume that they are the principal of the school in which they are currently employed, and that their school is a part of Ambition School District.
2. Each member of the class should prepare the proposal requested by the superintendent, identifying the name of their school and their own name at the beginning and conclusion of the proposal, respectively. The proposal should utilize the concepts in Chapters 6 and 7. Anyone who is not already knowledgeable about the research on effective schools should review this research since the superintendent *is* knowledgeable and expects her principals to be so, also.
3. Copies of each proposal should be supplied for each member of the class and distributed when requested.
4. Each class member should assume appointment by the superintendent to the committee that has responsibility for reviewing the various proposals and selecting the top three. Once the copies of the proposals have been disseminated and read, the members of the committee should attempt in group discussion to persuade the others of the merits of their own proposal for creating an effective school. The final goal of the group, however, should be to reach consensus regarding the three best proposals. The decisions of the committee

should be prepared in writing, with reasons for the final selections.

5. The role of the instructor during the group activity should be that of a resource person and observer during the initial stages, and during the critique of the activity should be that of an evaluator. The time allocated for the activity may range from 45 to 90 minutes, depending on the size of the group and the objectives of the instructor. Evaluation of student performance during group discussion should be based on the use of concepts in Chapters 4, 6, and 7.

52
SCHOOL-BASED MANAGEMENT

The Elmtree School District had been experimenting with school-based management for several years. Most of the schools in the district had implemented school-based management in varying degrees, and overall the evidence seemed to indicate that this was an innovation worth continuing.

On Friday, May 10, the following memorandum reached Steve Works, principal of 64th Street School:

MEMO

TO: Steve Works
FROM: Adrian Han, Superintendent
SUBJECT: School-Based Management

Steve, I know that this has not been an easy year for you as a new principal with a faculty that has not been especially receptive to change. However, since 64th Street School is one of the few schools that hasn't volunteered to participate in school-based management (this is certainly not a criticism of you, as you are new to the school), I would like to see your school move forward in that direction next year.
Therefore, please attempt to develop a school-based management plan that your school could implement next fall, and submit your plan to me in three weeks so that we will have time to discuss it and get it approved by the end of this school year.

Steve read the superintendent's memo a second time, placed it on his desk, and stared out the window of his office for a few moments. His first thought was that this would not be an easy assignment. He had talked informally with most of his faculty during the year to assess their attitudes toward school-based management, and they seemed to be divided among three different viewpoints. About a third of them were adamantly opposed to the idea on the basis that it sounded like more work than they could handle, another third seemed interested in the prospect, and the remainder were apathetic.

As Steve thought more about his situation, he grew a little depressed. Finally, he decided that, like it or not, he was obviously going to need to develop some plan of action. The initial questions were how should he get started, and whom should he involve?

PART II

In another school in Elmtree School District Shirley Verano, principal of Advanced School, was reading a memorandum she had received from the superintendent of schools.

MEMO

TO: Shirley Verano
FROM: Adrian Han, Superintendent
SUBJECT: The Next Stage in School-Based Management

Shirley, I have been pleased with your school's efforts in experimenting with school-based management during the past several years. So far, your school's efforts to involve teachers, parents and even students, on some occasions, in decision making about budget questions, school discipline policy, and scheduling problems have paid dividends, from all indications.

In my judgment your school should be ready to move into some new areas using school-based management. Specifically, what I would like you to do is to prepare a plan for expanding school-based management at Advanced School to include the following additional areas: staff and administrator evaluation and curriculum planning. Of course, I recognize that these are potentially controversial matters, but I would like to see at least one school in our district tackle these problems, and I have assessed Advanced School as most likely to succeed in this endeavor. Please submit your plan to me in three weeks.

SUGGESTED LEARNING ACTIVITIES

Analyze the Case

1. Evaluate each of the memoranda, using concepts from Chapter 2, especially regarding the administrator as a recipient of communication.
2. What concepts from Chapter 7 should each of the principals utilize in preparing a response? *How* should these concepts be utilized?
3. How do the assignments from the superintendent and the situation of each principal differ as to expectations and possible problems?

Discuss the Larger Issues

1. What are the advantages and disadvantages of school-based management?
2. What individuals and/or groups are likely to be impacted by the introduction/expansion of school-based management? Which individuals and/or groups are likely to oppose school-based management, and why?
3. What criteria and methods should be used to evaluate the effectiveness of school-based management?

Be a Problem Solver

Assume first that you are in Steve Works' situation; later, assume that you are in Shirley Verano's circumstances. Prepare an outline of a proposed school-based management plan, including a description of *how* you would go about introducing, instituting, and evaluating the change. Utilize appropriate concepts from Part I of the text in preparing your responses.

Test Your Solution

To test the adequacy of your response to the superintendent, you and your colleagues should create and role-play one or more of the following situations:

1. A faculty meeting during which you, as principal, present your ideas and plans for change. (Other members of the class should simulate different reactions to the principal's presentation.)
2. A meeting between you, as principal, and the superintendent's cabinet, during which you present your ideas and plans for change. (Other members of the class should simulate various reactions to the principal's presentation.)

Investigate Further

1. Examine the educational literature on school-based management.
2. Ascertain what plans, if any, your school district is considering for the introduction or expansion of school-based management.
3. Talk with people associated with schools that have experimented with school-based management. Visit these schools, if possible.

53
RESTRUCTURING STAFF EVALUATION AND SUPERVISION

For the first time in several years the superintendent was looking forward to teacher negotiations. The teachers in the district generally seemed contented with their welfare, and there currently appeared to be no major problem or crisis for their association to use as a bargaining lever. Of course, there were always a few who would never be completely satisfied, and the superintendent anticipated that there would continue to be demands for higher salaries and other fringe benefits. But the superintendent felt on top of things for a change and was confident that he and the board could handle whatever the teachers would come up with.

The following Monday he and the negotiating team that represented the school board met with the bargaining team from the teacher association. After the initial exchange of pleasantries, the teachers presented their demands for the coming year. As the superintendent listened to the list of items being read, he was pleased with the accuracy of his predictions . . . until the chairman of the teachers' negotiating team started reading the last demand: "Teachers will no longer be observed, supervised, or evaluated by administrators. All supervision, including classroom visitation and working with teachers to improve their instruction and the curriculum, will be carried out at the secondary level by the department heads and at the elementary level by master teachers released for that purpose. All teacher evaluation will be conducted by a special committee of teachers elected by and from the faculty in each building. This committee will evaluate only those non-tenured teachers about whom there is some question in regard to whether their contracts should be renewed for the following year or whether they should receive tenure. No other teachers will be formally evaluated.

"The administration and the school board may decide to review and reverse a decision by the Teacher Evaluation Committee that a teacher's contract not be renewed. In such a situation, the administration and the school board will assume full responsibility for the future actions of the teacher. However, under no circumstances may the administration dismiss a teacher whom the Teacher Evaluation Committee has determined to be professionally competent. Such a dismissal would constitute a violation of the master teacher contract and would be subject to further action by the Association."

The superintendent barely managed to retain his composure. He had never encountered such a blatant demand before. What were the teachers thinking? Could they be serious?

He decided not to make any comment until he had an opportunity to talk privately with the chairman of the teacher's bargaining committee. Instead, he presented a number of other items about which the administration and the school board were concerned. There was no immediate reaction from the teachers, so he suggested that both groups take some time to study each others' proposals and meet again in two weeks. That recommendation seemed agreeable to everyone, so a date was set for the next meeting.

As the various participants moved out of the room, the superintendent asked the head of the teachers' committee to stay a few minutes longer to talk informally about one of the teachers' demands. The superintendent explained that he was puzzled by the association's proposal that all administrators be removed from teacher supervision and evaluation. What was the basis for this recommendation and were the teachers really serious about pushing it?

The teacher representative responded that the association was indeed serious about the supervision proposal. The teachers did not believe that most administrators were competent to supervise or to evaluate them. Perhaps in the past, when teachers were not as well trained and when teaching methods and curriculum were rather standard, administrators could effectively supervise and evaluate teachers. But now teaching methods and curriculum were becoming diverse and very specialized. Today's teachers were better educated in their subject fields and simply did not feel that administrators had the background or the training to help them to improve. In fact, teachers found administrator's suggestions to be neither relevant nor helpful. Furthermore, the teachers felt that they should not be evaluated by people who were no longer involved with the act of teaching as their primary function in the school.

The representative went on to say that the teachers believed personnel evaluation to be a professional task. In the other professions, evaluation was conducted by one's peers. For example, in medicine, the hospital administrator didn't evaluate doctors—they were evaluated by each other. And in education, teachers' own colleagues were the people most qualified to supervise and evaluate them (not nonteaching administrators!), and the association was prepared to battle all the way for that principle.

The superintendent didn't know what to think about the position that the association had taken, but it was clear that the teachers were dead serious about their newest demand. He told the teacher representative that he appreciated knowing more about the teachers' feelings but that he couldn't comment at the present time on the merits of their proposal. He assured the representative that all of the teachers' recommendations would receive careful study and consideration, and that the board's negotiating team would be ready with some reactions of their own at the next meeting.

After the teacher representative left, the superintendent sat in his office and reflected on the situation. He had mixed feelings about the association's proposal on supervision and evaluation. In a way he agreed with many of the points that the teacher representative had made. Perhaps there did need to be a change toward giving teachers more responsibility in this area. However, he wondered how the other administrators and the school board would react to this rather extreme proposal. It was certain that many of the principals would reject the idea, and he doubted whether the school board would be in favor of acceding to the demand.

The superintendent had two weeks before the next meeting with the teachers. What position should he take on the matter? What strategy should he employ with the teachers' negotiation team? With the other administrators in the district? The school board? He had his work cut out for him, but the first task was to come to a decision in his own mind about what was best for education in the district.

SUGGESTED LEARNING ACTIVITIES

Analyze the Case

1. What factors prevented the superintendent from anticipating the nature of the new teacher demands?
2. What is your assessment of the strengths and weaknesses of the proposal on teacher supervision and evaluation?
3. What assumptions is the teacher representative making in his explanation of why the teachers want a new system of supervision and evaluation?
4. What is your evaluation of the superintendent's reaction and follow-up actions to the proposal advanced by the chairman of the teachers' negotiating team? If you were the superintendent in that situation, how would you have behaved differently?

Discuss the Larger Issues

1. What are some of the reasons why teachers may be dissatisfied with the present system of teacher supervision and evaluation?
2. How can the current system of teacher supervision and evaluation be improved so that it will be perceived more positively by teachers?
3. What should be the role of the following individuals or groups in the process of teacher supervision and evaluation?

(a) Central office supervisors
(b) The principal
(c) Department heads or special learning coordinators
(d) The faculty
(e) Students
(f) Parents

Be Problem Solver

The superintendent agrees with many of the points that the teacher representative has made, but doubts whether the other administrators and the school board would be in favor of the teachers' position. He will be meeting with the teachers again in two weeks. If *you* were the superintendent, how would you proceed and with whom would you talk during the weeks before the next meeting with the teachers?

Test Your Solution

In order to test your proposed plan of action for dealing with the problem presented at the end of this case, you and your class should create and role-play one or more of the following situations:

1. A meeting between the superintendent and the building principals.
2. An informal, closed-door session between the superintendent and the school board.
3. The next meeting between the teacher bargaining committee and the school board's bargaining committee.
4. Any other situation that might provide feedback on the strengths and weaknesses of your proposed plan of action.

Investigate Further

1. What is the school board and administrative policy in your district on *who* is responsible for supervision and *how* the supervision will be conducted?
2. To what extent are teachers dissatisfied with their supervision and evaluation?
3. How would the following groups react to the teacher association demands as presented in this case if the same demands were made in your district?
   (a) School principals
   (b) Central office supervisors
   (c) Department heads
   (d) Superintendent
   (e) Elementary teachers, junior high teachers, high school teachers
   (f) School board
   (g) Parents

54

CHANGING THE ROLE OF THE BUILDING PRINCIPAL

The assistant superintendent was convinced of the need for administrative reorganization at the building level. He had concluded, based on his previous experience as a principal, recent professional reading, and a review of the current status of the instructional and curricular program in the schools, that the role of the building principal should be changed.

In the opinion of the assistant superintendent, the building principal was no longer the instructional and curricular leader of his school—if he had ever been. These days teachers were better trained and were specialists in their subject fields. The principal, on the other hand, was a generalist with intensive preparation on the undergraduate college level in only one subject field. In graduate school principals had specialized in administration, but, as a rule, had taken only one course in supervision and curriculum. Consequently, they were not really knowledgeable about the content and methodologies of the various disciplines, nor did they have the time to keep up with the many changes that were taking place. As a result, many teachers, particularly experienced ones, did not recognize or accept the principal's judgments in matters of instruction and curriculum, and most principals seemed reluctant to approach experienced teachers with suggestions for improvement. Therefore, there was a decided lack of instructional and curricular leadership in the schools, and the assistant superintendent believed that it was his job to correct the situation.

That afternoon he met with the superintendent and proposed that the emphasis in the role of the principal be changed from instructional leader to professional manager, formally recognizing the role that most principals were performing anyway. Although their job descriptions still assumed that they were educational leaders in their schools, in reality the principals were generally more concerned and occupied with maintaining the on-going program in their buildings.

What was needed, the assistant superintendent suggested, was a realization on the part of the principals that they could no longer function effectively as instructional leaders and that it was necessary for them to concentrate on improving their managerial skills. Principals should recognize that they were middle management. In many ways, their position was similar to that of hospital administrators who worked with professionals, e.g., doctors, who were more specialized in their knowledge and skills than the administrator.

At that point the superintendent indicated that he agreed, but he wanted to know who would provide the instructional and curricular leadership in the schools if the principal's role were changed.

The assistant superintendent had anticipated that such a question would be raised and showed the superintendent a proposal he had worked out.

RECOMMENDED ADMINISTRATIVE REORGANIZATION

1. The role of the principal would become that of professional manager; instructional and curricular supervision and leadership would be delegated to other individuals within the school. Inservice programs would be planned and instituted to assist the principals in becoming better acquainted with and skilled in the use of techniques and procedures of middle management, e.g., PERT, PPBS.
2. At the secondary level the department heads would provide the instructional and curricular leadership for the teachers within their departments, coordinated by the assistant principal for instructional services. Each department head would be granted two additional periods of released time to carry out his or her responsibilities.
3. At the elementary level each school would be staffed with grade level coordinators who would teach part-time and work with teachers the remainder of the time to improve instruction and curriculum.
4. Central office supervisors would offer additional supervisory service to both levels.

The superintendent liked the proposal, and he said so. He was particularly impressed with the idea of capitalizing to a greater extent on the expertise which already existed within the teaching ranks. He knew that the program would be more costly, and that he might find it difficult to persuade the school board to buy the plan, but he also recognized that significant steps had to be taken to improve the present situation. Of course, the proposed changes would first have to be sold to the principals, which would not be easy, and the actual implementation of the reorganization would have to wait until the next budget year. But he gave the assistant superintendent the green light to begin laying groundwork with the building principals.

The assistant superintendent was delighted by his superior's response, and immediately after the conference, he told his secretary to set up a meeting on Friday with all the building principals. At that time he would present his plan for administrative reorganization and try to persuade the principals that a change in their role would be in their own best interests.

On Friday morning he distributed to the assembled group of principals a copy of his proposal, which had since been amplified with supporting rationale, although not changed in basic concept. For the next fifteen minutes he discussed his observations on the present role of the principal and the need for change. Then he paused and asked the principals for their reactions. He didn't have long to wait.

One principal after another objected to the proposed plan of administrative reorganization. No one spoke in favor of the idea. In fact, they were unanimously opposed to relinquishing the role of the principal as instructional and curricular leader of the school. They protested that this was the role that they had been trained for and that this was the role that their professional associations expected them to assume. Perhaps it was true that they were not subject matter experts, but, they argued, it was not absolutely necessary to be an expert in order to work with teachers in the improvement of instruction and curriculum. They felt that the main problem was that principals were too bogged down with administrative detail and didn't have the time to function the way they would like—as educational leaders. They were *not* managers, they were *educators,* and they rejected the analogy offered by the assistant superintendent comparing them to hospital administrators.

It was obvious to the assistant superintendent that he had stirred up a hornet's nest. As the principals waited for his reaction to their opposition, he wondered what his next move should be.

SUGGESTED LEARNING ACTIVITIES

Analyze the Case

1. What is your analysis and evaluation of the observations made by the assistant superintendent in regard to the role of the building principal?
2. What do you see as the strengths and limitations of the assistant superintendent's plan for administrative reorganization?
3. What is your assessment of the assistant superintendent's strategy for introducing change? What are some of the reasons why he encountered resistance?
4. What assumptions or errors in logic might the principals be making in their defense of the role of the principal as an instructional leader?

Discuss the Larger Issues

1. Specifically, what do you feel should be the role of the principal with respect to improving instruction and curriculum in the school?
2. What barriers or handicaps must a principal overcome in order to make a real contribution as an instructional or curricular leader?
3. How can the principal best utilize the other sources of expertise within the school, the school district, or the community for the improvement of instruction and curriculum?

Be a Problem Solver

The initial reactions of the principals to the assistant superintendent's proposal to change their role were negative. If you were the assistant superintendent in that situation, what would be your next step? What would be your long-range objective *and* strategy? Utilize appropriate administrative and social science concepts from Part I of the text in planning and implementing your approach.

Test Your Solution

To test your proposed plan of action for dealing with the problem presented at the end of this case, you and the class should create and role-play one or more of the following situations:

1. A continuation of the meeting between the assistant superintendent and the principals.
2. A conference between the assistant superintendent and the superintendent.

Investigate Further

1. How is the role of the principal defined in your district? What are the principal's responsibilities for instructional leadership? What system of evaluation exists for

ascertaining whether the principal is, in fact, effectively carrying out leadership responsibilities?
2. How would the principals in your district feel about a change in their roles similar to that proposed in this case? How would the teachers react? The department heads?

55

INSERVICE OR DISSERVICE EDUCATION? PART I

The principal had been staring at the wall in his office for the past five minutes. He was trying to think about topics and guest speakers for the two days of inservice education the faculty was supposed to receive this year. One inservice day was to occur on Friday, the second week in November, and the other day to be set aside for inservice education was also a Friday during the third week in April.

The problem was that it was now the latter part of October, and he had just begun to think about the need to plan something for the first inservice day. He knew that he probably should have initiated his planning early in the fall, but he had been busy with a number of other activities and the time had slipped by. Still, he figured that he had plenty of time to plan something worthwhile as long as he could line up that professor he knew, who often gave talks about lesson planning.

The principal felt that lesson planning was a major deficiency on the part of many of his teachers, as evidenced by the lesson plans they submitted to his office, and that the morning of the first inservice should focus on this topic. The afternoon could be devoted to opportunities for teachers to practice the development of model lesson plans and, later in the day, several of the better lesson plans might be presented to the entire faculty.

Having completed his planning for the first inservice day, the principal decided that he needed a break before planning for the second one, so he left his office to go to the faculty room for a cup of coffee.

SUGGESTED LEARNING ACTIVITIES

Analyze the Case

1. What is your evaluation of the reason the principal gave for not planning earlier in the year for inservice education?
2. What is your assessment of the principal's planning for the first inservice day? What assumptions is he making? What unanticipated consequences might he encounter?

Discuss the Larger Issues

1. To what extent is there a need for teacher inservice education today? Why does the need exist?
2. Who should be involved in planning an inservice program and why should they be involved? What are the advantages and disadvantages of involving others?
3. What criteria and processes should be utilized in planning for and evaluating inservice?

Be a Problem Solver

Assume that the principal in this case study proceeds with the first inservice day. Based on your answer to the second question of Analyze the Case, how would you, as the principal in this situation, address the problems that you anticipate will occur during and after the inservice program?

Test Your Solution

To test the approach you developed to deal with the problems you anticipate will arise during and after the first inservice program, you and your colleagues should create and role-play one or more of the following situations:

1. A faculty meeting where the principal announces his plans for the November inservice meeting for teachers and asks whether there are any questions or reactions?
2. Reluctance or refusal by those members of the faculty whom the principal approaches in the afternoon of the inservice program with a request to present to the rest of the faculty the lesson plans that were developed.

Investigate Further

1. How are plans for inservice education developed in your school or school district?
2. To what extent are inservice programs evaluated in your school or school district? What criteria and procedures are employed?
3. What is the attitude of administrators and teachers toward inservice education in your school or school district?

56

INSERVICE OR DISSERVICE EDUCATION? PART II

It was the last day in February, and the principal had set aside a block of time in the afternoon to plan for an inservice day in April. He felt that as a result of his teachers' negative reactions to and poor participation during the November inservice program, he had learned *his* lesson about the importance of adequate planning and teacher involvement. It was essential that he allow himself more advance time to plan for the next inservice program and that he conduct some sort of needs assessment of the teachers so the program would be relevant for them.

After instructing his secretary that he did not want to be interrupted "for any reason" during the next two hours, the principal entered his office after lunch to work on plans for the April inservice program. As the principal reflected on the planning that needed to take place, it seemed to him that the first priority was to construct some type of instrument to assess the perceived needs of his teachers. If he could find out what they were interested in or needed, then he could design an inservice program tailored to those interests or needs.

For the next hour and a half the principal worked at his desk, attempting to develop a needs assessment instrument for his teachers. His basic approach was to jot down a number of needs that he believed his teachers felt—or, at least, *should* feel—and he added to that list a number of topics about which he thought teachers *might* be interested. He then organized the list into a survey format and added instructions for the teachers to follow in responding. Before giving the survey to his secretary to be typed and distributed to the faculty, he decided that he should look it over one more time.

INSERVICE NEEDS SURVEY

February 28

Dear Teacher:

To plan inservice programs which more closely meet your needs and which have a greater chance for practical application, it is necessary for me to know your interests and needs.

Listed are nearly 30 possible inservice activities. These have been categorized (rather roughly in some cases) into four major groupings. Please consider the items in each category and put a mark (X) opposite those in which you have a definite interest or need. *Please check no more than the number allotted for each category.*

It is very important that these be completed and returned to me no later than March 4. Please put your name on the form.

Sincerely,
Ed Bain, Principal

INSERVICE INTEREST ASSESSMENT

Name: ______________________________ *Date:* ______________________________

Category 1—You As a Person

Check Only 2:

________ Stress Management
________ Time Management
________ Career Alternatives for Teachers
________ Physical Fitness and Wellness
________ Personal Investments for Educators
________ Other (Describe)____________________

Category 2—For Professional Background

Check Only 3:

________ Identifying Creativity
________ Learning Styles
________ Use of Student Records
________ Writing Meaningful Comments
________ Structuring a Parent Conference
________ Evaluating Teaching Resources
________ Human Growth and Development
________ Increasing School/Home Cooperation
________ Other (Describe) ____________________

Category 3—Improving Your Classroom Skills

Check Only 4:

________ Teaching Gifted/Talented
________ Classroom Motivation Strategies
________ Classroom Discipline Strategies
________ Making Interesting Lessons
________ Interpreting Tests
________ Time on Task
________ Creative Bulletin Boards and Posters
________ Computer-Assisted Instruction
________ Computerized Gradebooks
________ Constructing Good Tests
________ Using Drama to Teach
________ Other (Describe)____________________

Category 4—Child Development and Adjustment

Check Only 2:

_________ Improving Students' Self-Images
_________ Conferencing
_________ Brain Growth in Children
_________ Sensible Approaches to Individualization
_________ Support Services for You and Your Students (Special Education/Guidance)
_________ Alternative Family Styles (Single Parent, etc.)
_________ Other (Describe) ______________________

Satisfied that the instructions were clear and the topics important, the principal gave the needs assessment questionnaire to his secretary to be typed and distributed, then returned to his office to plan some of the other aspects of the inservice program. He didn't feel that he could begin selecting speakers for the program because he didn't know yet how the results of the needs assessment would turn out. However, one piece of planning that he could work on immediately was the development of an evaluation for assessing the effectiveness of the inservice program. After the last inservice meeting, he had neglected to conduct a formal evaluation, and although he was able to conclude from the lack of participation during that day and the subsequent negative comments he had heard about the program through the grapevine that the program had not been a total success, he wanted to conduct a more systematic and formal evaluation next time. So he worked for the next half hour on a draft of a possible evaluation form. When finished, he looked over the form to see if he had overlooked any aspect.

The principal felt satisfied with the evaluation form he had designed and believed that it should provide him with useful feedback on the effectiveness of the inservice program in April. However, one addition needed to be made. He needed to specify in the instructions a deadline for returning the completed form. He thought a couple of days ought to give the teachers sufficient time to think through their answers to the questions. If he allowed more time, some of the teachers would only misplace, lose, or forget about the form.

As the principal left his office to take the evaluation form to his secretary for typing, he felt pleased with himself. It had indeed been a productive two hours of planning, with the development of a needs assessment form as well as an evaluation form. He recognized that there were some other aspects of planning for the inservice day that remained to be accomplished—such as lining up the speakers—but he still had plenty of time to work on that after collecting the needs assessment. *Now* seemed like a good time to take a well-deserved coffee break.

SUGGESTED LEARNING ACTIVITIES

Analyze the Case

1. Analyze the principal's planning and decision making *process* in developing a needs assessment instrument for his teachers. What would you have done differently?

EVALUATION OF INSERVICE PROGRAM

Instructions:

Teachers need not identify themselves in completing the form. Its primary purpose is to give me some feedback on what you saw as the strengths and weaknesses of the activities scheduled for the inservice day. Please provide information that is as complete as possible, and then return the form to my secretary.

1. What did you think of the speakers?

Morning session	*Afternoon session*
________ Superior	________ Superior
________ Adequate	________ Adequate
________ Unsatisfactory	________ Unsatisfactory

2. How useful did you feel the handouts were?

Morning session	*Afternoon session*
________ Very useful	________ Very useful
________ Useful	________ Useful
________ Not useful	________ Not useful

3. To what extent were you satisfied with your involvement during the inservice program?

Morning session	*Afternoon session*
________ Very satisfied	________ Very satisfied
________ Satisfied	________ Satisfied
________ Not satisfied	________ Not satisfied

4. Was the time allocated to each session adequate?

Morning session	*Afternoon session*
________ Very adequate	________ Very adequate
________ Adequate	________ Adequate
________ Not adequate	________ Not adequate

5. Do you feel you learned very much from the inservice?

Morning session	*Afternoon session*
________ A great deal	________ A great deal
________ To some extent	________ To some extent
________ Not at all	________ Not at all

Thank you!

2. Evaluate the inservice needs survey that the principal developed. What are its strengths and weaknesses? What modifications would you recommend?
3. Analyze the principal's planning and decision making *process* in developing an evaluation procedure and form for assessing the effectiveness of the inservice program. What would you have done differently?
4. What do you see as strengths and weaknesses of the inservice evaluation procedure and form that the principal has designed? What modifications would you recommend?

Discuss the Larger Issues

1. Are teachers' interests the same thing as teachers' needs? Who decides, and by what criteria?
2. To what extent should an inservice program for teachers focus on teachers' needs as compared to organizational needs?
3. To what degree should the evaluation of an inservice program focus on whether the participants actually acquired whatever knowledge or skill that the program was designed to deliver? How would this type of evaluation be carried out?

Be a Problem Solver

Assume that you are an administrator or supervisor who has the responsibility for planning and evaluating two days of inservice education during the year. How would you proceed? Utilize administrative and social science concepts from Part I of the text in developing your approaches.

Test Your Solutions

To test the approach you developed in response to "Be a Problem Solver," you and your colleagues should create and, if appropriate, role-play one or more of the following situations:

1. Write a report to the superintendent, describing your plans for the two days of inservice, including the method you used for developing those plans.
2. Present your plans to the faculty, including an evaluation procedure or form.

Investigate Further

1. Examine the educational literature for recommendations regarding how you should plan for and evaluate an inservice program.
2. Interview appropriate personnel in the state department of education and/or universities for their recommendations for planning and evaluating an inservice program.

57
SCHOOL CHOICE

In March the State Legislature passed a law that would allow parents to send their school-aged children to any school of their choice in the fall, within or outside the school district where the family resided. Included in the legislation was authorization for a transportation and tuition voucher, based on a rather complicated formula that took into consideration the distance traveled and the financial well-being of the family.

There had been considerable opposition to the school choice bill while it worked its way through the legislative process. Nevertheless, once it was approved, most educators accepted the need to plan for its impact. One of the problems, however, was that few people—even the so-called "experts"—were very certain or specific on what the precise nature or extent of the impact would be. However, one implication that almost everyone agreed on was that the schools would need to compete for students on a much greater scale than had been true in the past.

Katie Hernandez, principal of Cesar Chavez School, had been sitting in her office for the last hour on a Saturday morning in the first week of May, trying without much success to jot down some ideas about getting her school ready for the implementation of school choice. This was a new task for her, and she wasn't sure about everything that needed to be done. One thing she did know, however, was that she had to put together some plan and implement it, or she might wind up with the school less than half full in September.

SUGGESTED LEARNING ACTIVITIES

Analyze the Case

1. What kind of plan is needed under these circumstances? What elements should be included in the plan?
2. Whom, if anyone, should the principal consult or involve in the development of her plan? Is there a particular planning process that should be followed?
3. Identify the concepts from Part I of the text that would be helpful to take into consideration while developing and implementing the plan.

Discuss the Larger Issues

1. What are the variations that the school choice approach might take? Identify the advantages and disadvantages of those variations.
2. Which individuals and groups are likely to favor a school choice approach, and which are likely to oppose it? To what extent is support or opposition based on the merits of school choice, as opposed to other factors?
3. What are the short-range and long-range implications of school choice? What should be the response by those educators who do not favor it?
4. What criteria and methods should be used to evaluate the effectiveness of school choice?

Be a Problem Solver

Assume that you are the principal of this school. Agree upon any additional details you will need in order to address the implementation of the school choice legislation in the school administered by Katie Hernandez. Prepare a plan for dealing with the school choice situation.

Test Your Solution

To test your plan of action, you and the class should create and role-play one or more of the following situations:

1. A call from a local reporter who would like to learn the details of your proposed plan.
2. A presentation to the faculty of a rough draft of your plan (Simulate different reactions to the plan being presented.)
3. A presentation to the P.T.A. of your plan.

Investigate Further

1. Examine the educational literature on various school choice approaches.
2. Ascertain the type of school choice legislation, actual or proposed, in your state.
3. Determine what plans, if any, have been made in your school district to respond to school choice possibilities.
4. Investigate school choice plans and/or approaches by other school districts and states.

58

SCHOOL DISTRICT CHIPS AWAY AT COMPUTER EDUCATION PROBLEMS

The superintendent had just finished reading her copy of *School Tech News*. In the latest issue, questions were raised about how schools were incorporating the study of computers into the curriculum. These questions reflected concerns that the superintendent had developed recently about the use of computers in her own district. She hadn't expressed her concerns to anyone yet because she wasn't sure she was right. But now, after reading *School Tech News*, she decided to call a meeting of the district's principals and supervisors to address the issue.

The following Friday, the meeting was held at the district office. The superintendent had decided to begin the meeting by giving some background, expressing concern, and then asking the principals and supervisors to think about the problem and send her their recommendations.

After clearing her throat the superintendent began the meeting by stating her views.

"In recent years the school district has introduced computers into elementary school curriculum, and at the high school level several courses are now offered in computer programming. In addition, our schools are now using data processing more in the area of attendance and are using the computers to help with student scheduling. Still, I am not sure that we are making maximum, or even in some instances appropriate, use of the computer.

"For example, we study keyboarding, LOGO, and the history of the computer at the elementary schools. Is this the best way to introduce computers to children? I should also mention that I have heard that a number of elementary teachers still don't feel competent in teaching the use of computers and don't like taking time away from the other subjects.

"At the high school, I see computers and computer programming being utilized primarily by math and business education teachers, but what about the rest of the teachers and curriculum? And should we be placing such emphasis on teaching high school students how to program?

"I don't have answers to these questions, but I believe strongly that the school district *needs* answers. Therefore, I would like each of you to think about how computer education and utilization could best be improved in your building or subject area, and then forward your recommendations to me by the end of next week.

"Are there any questions?"

To the superintendent's surprise, no one responded with a question. So she proceeded to the next item on the agenda.

SUGGESTED LEARNING ACTIVITIES

Analyze the Case

1. What would be your assessment of the process used by the superintendent to identify the need for change? What would you have done if you had been the superintendent in similar circumstances?
2. Assuming the superintendent is correct in her assumption about the need for change, what alternatives other than calling a meeting could she have pursued?
3. Assuming that calling a meeting was the best way to proceed in this case, how would you have planned and conducted the meeting differently?

Discuss the Larger Issues

1. How important is it for schools to incorporate computer education into their programs?
2. What is the most appropriate way for schools to introduce computer education?
3. What criteria and process should schools use to determine the extent to which their use of computers is effective?
4. To what degree should all teachers and administrators become literate *and* competent in the use of computers?

Be a Problem Solver

The superintendent of schools in the case study has expressed her concerns about computer education and the use of computers in the schools. As a principal or supervisor in this district, how would you respond to the superintendent's concerns?

Test Your Solution

To test your plan of action for dealing with the problems presented at the end of the case, you and the class should create and role-play one or more of the following situations:

1. Continuation of the meeting at the point when the superintendent asks, "Are there any questions?"
2. A faculty meeting where you present the superintendent's concerns and then discuss the matter.
3. A meeting of the superintendent's cabinet where you present your recommendation on how to improve the use of computers in the school.

Investigate Further

1. Examine the educational literature for recommendations on the best use of computers; try to identify a description of exemplary programs.
2. Ascertain how computers are being used in your own school and district. How is their use being evaluated? By what criteria?
3. Review any concept chapter presented earlier in the book that would help you improve your skills for addressing the problems in this case, e.g., Chapter 7.

Index

ALL STIRRED UP

JULIA AITKEN
ELIZABETH BAIRD
LAURA BUCKLEY
ARVINDA CHAUHAN
SUSAN CONNOLLY
NETTIE CRONISH
MARILYN BENTZ CROWLEY
CHRISTINE CUSHING
REGAN DALEY
CYNTHIA DAVID
NAOMI DUGUID
HEATHER EPP
MADELEINE GREEY
GAIL HALL
BARB HOLLAND
KAREN JULL
ANNE LINDSAY
JENNIFER LOW
BARBARA-JO McINTOSH
JAN MAIN
DANA McCAULEY
JOAN MOORE
ANTOINETTE PASSALACQUA
DAPHNA RABINOVITCH
ROSE REISMAN
ETTIE SHUKEN
MAIRLYN SMITH
BONNIE STERN
ANITA STEWART
LILI SULLIVAN
THERESE TAYLOR
HEATHER TRIM
LUCY WAVERMAN
. . . and many more . . .

ALL STIRRED UP

OVER 150 OF THE BEST RECIPES FROM THE WOMEN'S CULINARY NETWORK

EDITED BY LAURA BUCKLEY
& MADELEINE GREEY

RANDOM
HOUSE
CANADA

 Published in 2003 by Random House Canada, a division of Random House of Canada Limited. Distributed in Canada by Random House of Canada Limited.

www.randomhouse.ca

National Library of Canada Cataloguing in Publication

All stirred up : over 150 of the best recipes from the Women's Culinary Network / Laura Buckley and Madeleine Greey, co-editors.

ISBN 0–679–31155–6

1. Cookery. I. Greey, Madeleine, date— . II. Buckley, Laura

TX714.A46 2003 641.5 C2002–905604–7

Design by Carol Moskot
Typeset by Leah Springate
Printed in Canada

10 9 8 7 6 5 4 3 2 1

INTRODUCTION

IT SEEMS a long time ago that Marilyn Bentz Crowley, Heather Epp, Elaina Asselin and I were preparing lunch for 300 at King Ranch Spa north of Toronto while drinking organic coffee. That was 1990, and our days working together were numbered, for the spa was soon to close. First came the pink slips, then Marilyn's idea: why say goodbye when we could form a culinary network? And thus "the WCN" was created and our objective was made clear: to meet and work with other women in the food industry in a mutually supportive and goal-oriented environment. Our common purpose was to share professional experience, knowledge and information that could expand our horizons. Besides all those lofty aspirations, we really just wanted a professional excuse to get together and have some fun!

Thirteen years later, we've grown from a core of four to 250 members spanning the industry: chefs, food consultants, dietitians, cooking teachers, cookbook authors, food writers, business owners, students, home economists, product developers—the list goes on. Naturally, we attract women just entering the food industry and eager to make contacts, but it's our strong core of experienced and successful professionals that has helped make this network thrive. Our goal is to lend support to anyone—newbie or veteran—and we believe the WCN fills a real niche in the growing food world, giving us all a venue to celebrate each other's efforts, ambitions and successes.

Our meetings, which occur bi-monthly from September to June, are increasingly popular. We've met at private homes, hotels, commercial kitchens, retail stores and soup kitchens. The meetings accommodate both socializing and career enrichment. Many good connections have been made over wine and menu sampling, tea sipping and potlucking. Our panels and presentations offer a welcome mix of information and inspiration, prompting lots of discussion.

The backbone of our organization is our newsletter, *Women's Culinary Network News* published five times a year and edited by Therese Taylor. Each issue contains a riveting member profile, juicy member updates (in the appropriately titled Hot Flashes section) and information about past and future meetings. Our membership directory is an essential black book for anyone in the industry; many members keep it right next to their phone or computer.

As a founding member and current chair of the WCN, I can't help but marvel at our fantastic growth. Over the years, many of us have become close friends, sharing a rich camaraderie that leaves room for both professional and personal connections.

With such a strong and diverse membership, it was only a matter of time before we wrote our own cookbook. *All Stirred Up* is a perfect title for what we do and who we are. If we can't cook, who can? Enormous thanks go to Ron Fiorelli and the International Olive Oil Council for their belief in this project and the generous financial contribution that made it a reality.

I feel honoured and very happy to be part of this tremendous organization. It is a guiding force in the culinary community of Toronto—and who knows, maybe in the near future all across Canada!

Nettie Cronish
Chair, Women's Culinary Network

LIQUID GOLD

COOKS WORLDWIDE begin the everyday chore of meal planning and preparation by searching through their pantry and refrigerator for inspiration. In Canada, we have an abundance of food products to choose from, yet one staple ingredient shows up in the kitchens of sophisticated cooks time and time again: olive oil. It is simply outstanding in taste and style, offering ease of use and storage. And as studies increasingly reveal, olive oil is good for you.

Even Harvard University has realized olive oil's benefits. In a recent study of two groups of people eager for weight loss, one group received the standard 20 per cent fat-reduced diet while the other group received a calorie-matched diet, the difference being that it was rich in monounsaturated fats via olive oil. Those on the olive oil–enriched diet lost nearly twice as much weight! [*Elle* magazine, September 2001] But this is not news to the people of the Mediterranean, who are among the heaviest users of olive oil—a crucial component of the celebrated Mediterranean diet. Mediterraneans do not suffer from the same degree of obesity, cancer, bone and heart problems as North Americans, and are renowned for their vitality and long lives. Olive oil has been linked to a reduction of rates of breast cancer, positive effects on bone calcification and a lowering of the harmful form of cholesterol in the blood while leaving the beneficial cholesterol intact. [*Chatelaine* magazine, May 1995] It has potential in the prevention and control of diabetes and in warding off the effects of aging. ["Olive Oil, Quality of Life," International Olive Oil Council]. Health-inducing lycopene in tomatoes is more readily absorbed when paired with olive oil. Lycopene—a powerful antioxidant—is linked to the prevention of prostate, cervical and digestive system cancers. And garlic, long revered as another potent antioxidant and mainstay of alternative medicine, is the perfect flavour complement for both olive oil and tomatoes. Here is an age-old winner—not only does olive oil taste terrific, it is healthy, too.

The finest olive oil is extra-virgin, obtained from the first cold pressing of olives. It is fruity and very flavourful and often has a slight greenish hue or, some would argue, a yellow to golden colour. As there are wine tastings, so there are olive oil tastings, at which nuances are savoured, appreciated and evaluated. Everyday olive oil is a golden blend of more refined olive oils obtained after the first pressing, with a touch of extra-virgin oil added for fuller flavour. Also commonly available is light olive oil, which is not lighter in calories but in taste. Light olive oil is a refined blend that provides all the same health benefits. Many cooks turn to light olive oil when a rich olive taste is not desirable, such as in sweet baking.

Look at your family cooking and meals with a critical eye. Do they reflect your taste and lifestyle and provide optimum health benefits in a delicious, unobtrusive way? Or are they so eminently predictable and reliant on takeout or packages that it is getting you down? Common among all Mediterranean families is the regular consumption of grains, vegetables, fruit, fish and olive oil and the use of fresh herbs and aromatics such as onions and garlic. Due to limited resources for expensive cooking fuel and meat, their home-style cooking is often "fast food." Adding variety to your home cooking and baking with olive oil can be simple: keep a stoneware jug near your stove filled with everyday olive oil to use for sautéing; offer a small shallow dish of extra-virgin olive oil to accompany a great loaf of bread; or use light olive oil when the package or recipe calls for vegetable oil.

Of all vegetable oils olive oil is the richest in monounsaturated fat and contains vitamin E, beta-carotene, alpha-linolenic acid (an omega-3 fatty acid) and other antioxidants. These antioxidants are abundant in fresh fruit and vegetables—and olive oil is pressed from olives, which are, botanically speaking, a fresh fruit.

The talented chefs and food professionals of the Women's Culinary Network know that creating an outstanding meal is easy when the plans include olive oil, so this book was a natural fit with the International Olive Oil Council. Olive oil has cast a golden glow across the pages of *All Stirred Up*—from simple vinaigrettes drizzled over crisp salad greens, to the rich flavours of a wild mushroom and onion tart or spice-infused Moroccan tagine, to the sweet reverie of a slice of lemon fig cake. Settle down for a pleasurable read as you meander through these favourite recipes gathered by our members. Great food is about creative cooking, family dinners, suppers with friends and sophisticated entertaining. But it is also about taste sensations, eye appeal and good health. What better way to achieve these delights in your home than with olive oil?

Marilyn Bentz Crowley

RECIPE ASSUMPTIONS

Butter is salted, unless specified otherwise.
Lemon and lime juices are always freshly squeezed.
Freshly ground black pepper is used.
Eggs are large.
All milk and yogurt is 2%, unless specified otherwise.
Oven is preheated.

ACKNOWLEDGEMENTS

All Stirred Up has been a collaborative project from the get-go. For years, the network talked about and flirted with a cookbook idea, but it was only through the determined, never-give-up efforts of WCN chair and driving force Nettie Cronish that the book became a reality. It was Nettie's persuasive powers that won over Sarah Davies at Random House Canada, who signed us up for the project, kick-started our team and made sure the process was in full swing. Tanya Trafford, senior editor, also at Random House Canada, took over the helm and skillfully guided this book to completion. And let's not forget Julia Armstrong, copyeditor extraordinaire.

The book's contributors, all 66 of them, have graciously offered up so many delicious culinary secrets for this book. We want to thank each one of them for patiently responding to our endless e-mails, voice mails and letters.

Menu authors include Julia Aitken, Elizabeth Baird, Laura Buckley, Arvinda Chauhan, Susan Connolly, Nettie Cronish, Marilyn Crowley, Christine Cushing, Regan Daley, Cynthia David, Naomi Duguid, Heather Epp, Madeleine Greey, Gail Hall, Barb Holland, Karen Jull, Anne Lindsay, Jennifer Low, Barbara-jo McIntosh, Jan Main, Dana McCauley, Joan Moore, Antoinette Passalacqua, Daphna Rabinovitch, Rose Reisman, Ettie Shuken, Mairlyn Smith, Bonnie Stern, Anita Stewart, Lili Sullivan, Therese Taylor, Heather Trim and Lucy Waverman.

Single recipe contributors include Barbara Ackerman, Karen Bekker, Wendy Blackwood, Charmaine Broughton, Debbie Diament, Kate Dowhan, Janice Friis, Norene Gilletz, Mary Lou Harrison, Linda Haynes, Miriam Katz, Jenny Koniuk, Florence Kwok, Jane Langdon, Joanne Leese, Nancy Lewis, Lenore Locken, Kasia Luckevich, Trish Magwood, Debbie Murray, Kim Rabe, Irene Richards, Marsha Rosen, Dufflet Rosenberg, Sudha Sajan, Barbara Selley, Adell Shneer, Pamela Steel, Susan Thompson, Wendy Trusler, Gillian Tsintziras, Michelle Vig and Kathy Wazana.

All the recipes in this cookbook have been professionally tested. It was a huge task, but we rose to the challenge! Foremost thanks go to Lesleigh Landry for coordinating the bulk of our testing. She led a team of women, many of whom volunteered hours of help, to make sure all of these recipes were in tip-top shape. Thanks to Mary Lou Morgan and Akemi Kobayashi of Foodshare Toronto for the use of their Toronto Kitchen Incubator. And thanks to the President's Choice team for the use of their test kitchen facility. Thanks go to Marilyn Bentz Crowley, Naomi Duguid, Joanne Leese, Joan Moore, Ettie Shuken and Heather Trim for going the extra yard, and to Ritva Aalto, Teresa Black, Dawn Bone, Charmaine Broughton-Dunn, Susan Cohen, Juanita Costa, Mary Rose Cowan, Johanne Lamoureux, Debbie Diament, Riki Dixon, Heather Epp, Galit Gafny, Voula Halliday, Karen Jull, Jenny Koniuk, Rita Kramme, Lenore Locken, Pat Morris, Monika Reuter, Mairlyn Smith, Michelle Sukul-Chan,

Gillian Tsintziras and Michelle Vig. We had a lot of fun together, didn't we?

Thanks also to Ahmed Touzani, Executive Director of the International Olive Oil Council, and Ron Fiorelli.

The mouthwatering, full-colour photography gracing these pages was made possible by the superb efforts of photographer Robert Wigington and food stylist Carol Dudar. The gorgeous design of the book is thanks to Carol Moskot and Scott Richardson, and the black and white photography interspersed throughout was shot by Curtis Lantinga and Donald Nausbaum.

And, finally, co-editors Laura Buckley and Madeleine Greey want to thank their families for putting up with the insanity that is book publishing and for all the hard work contributed by so many individuals featured in *All Stirred Up.*

CONTENTS

JULIA AITKEN

JULIA AITKEN HAS BEEN A FOOD WRITER FOR 25 YEARS. HER WORK HAS APPEARED IN PUBLICATIONS IN BOTH CANADA AND THE UNITED KINGDOM, AND SHE IS CURRENTLY THE FOOD EDITOR OF *ELM STREET*, *OWL CANADIAN FAMILY* AND *EXPRESSIONS* MAGAZINES. JULIA'S FIRST COOKBOOK, *QUICK AND EASY BAKING* (GROSVENOR HOUSE PRESS) APPEARED IN 1986. SINCE THEN SHE HAS EDITED AND/OR CONTRIBUTED TO MANY OTHER COOKBOOKS. IN 1996, SHE CO-AUTHORED, ALONG WITH ANITA STEWART, *THE ONTARIO HARVEST COOKBOOK* (MACMILLAN CANADA), AND HER LATEST BOOK IS *JULIA AITKEN'S EASY ENTERTAINING* (ROBERT ROSE, 1999).

I GUESS it all started with the conger eel. My mother was an imaginative cook, and with four young mouths to feed, plus Dad and herself, she'd try anything once—as long as it was cheap. On that day in the '60s, no one else in our village seemed to want the conger eel on the fishmonger's slab, so she toted it home and pored through her extensive cookbook collection looking for "ways with conger eel." As the rest of my family dubiously pushed it round their plates, I ate every scrap of my conger eel portion, thinking it a huge adventure. I realized then that food could be exciting, interesting and more than just fuel. And the adventure continues.

There is no finer way to spend time than by sharing good food with friends. Gathering people around a table to share a meal, to drink wine and to talk—really talk—is one of the things I enjoy most about my life. Cooking for other people gives me so much pleasure; I feel like a charlatan when dinner guests commend me on the food, not least because I believe cheating is a big part of entertaining. Since there are no food police and Martha Stewart doesn't know where I live, I prefer to serve simple food that doesn't take a day and a half to prepare.

That love of socializing over food finds another outlet with my membership in the Women's Culinary Network. What better organization to belong to than one that combines professional networking with good food, good wine and good company!

A SPRING FLING

• WATERMELON AND FETA WITH MINT •
• ROSEMARY ROAST CHICKEN THIGHS WITH FENNEL AND ASPARAGUS •
• LEMON CHIVE COUSCOUS •
• WARM STRAWBERRY SLICES •

WATERMELON AND FETA WITH MINT

Sometimes the simplest of combinations is the best, and this unusual pairing of salty feta cheese with sweet watermelon is sensational. For best results, use the finest-quality extra-virgin olive oil you can find.

12 watermelon triangles, rind removed (6 inches wide at rind side x ½ inch thick)
¾ cup crumbled feta cheese (about 4 oz)
3 tbsp extra-virgin olive oil
24 small fresh mint leaves
Pepper

Arrange 3 slices of watermelon, slightly overlapping, on each of 4 salad plates.

Sprinkle feta cheese evenly over watermelon; drizzle evenly with olive oil. Scatter mint leaves over salads; grind pepper to taste over each. Serve immediately.

MAKES 4 SERVINGS.

ROSEMARY ROAST CHICKEN THIGHS WITH FENNEL AND ASPARAGUS

It takes just a couple of minutes to prep the vegetables for this easy one-dish main course. I like to use air-chilled chicken thighs since they're juicier and more flavourful than water-chilled. When serving, make sure each person gets a clove of garlic to squeeze out of its skin and mix with the rest of the vegetables.

1 bulb fennel (about 1 lb)
1 red onion, cut into 8 wedges
4 large cloves garlic, unpeeled
2 stalks (each 8 inches) fresh rosemary
2 bay leaves
¾ tsp each salt and pepper
8 skin-on bone-in chicken thighs, trimmed of excess fat (2 to 2½ lb)
2 tbsp olive oil
1 lb asparagus
2 cups cherry tomatoes (1 pint)
Fresh rosemary sprigs

Trim fennel and cut in half lengthwise; cut crosswise into ½-inch slices. Spread in a large shallow roasting pan along with onion, garlic, rosemary and bay leaves. Sprinkle with ¼ tsp each of the salt and pepper. Place chicken thighs, skin side up, on top of vegetables. Drizzle thighs with oil; sprinkle with ¼ tsp each of the salt and pepper. Roast in 450°F oven for 30 minutes.

Meanwhile, trim asparagus by snapping tough ends where they break naturally. Move any browned vegetables in roasting pan to centre of pan and less browned ones to edge. Scatter cherry tomatoes over vegetables; arrange asparagus among chicken thighs. Sprinkle remaining salt and pepper over tomatoes and asparagus. Roast for 10 to 15 minutes or until all vegetables are tender and juices run clear when thickest thigh is pierced.

With tongs, transfer chicken to warm serving platter; garnish with rosemary. With tongs, remove asparagus, arranging it around edge of second warm platter. Transfer remaining vegetables from roasting pan with slotted spoon; arrange in centre of asparagus platter, discarding rosemary and bay leaves. If you wish, skim off and discard any fat from juices in roasting pan, then pour into small bowl to drizzle over chicken and vegetables at the table. Serve immediately.

MAKES 4 SERVINGS.

LEMON CHIVE COUSCOUS

You can vary the flavourings in this easy side dish according to what you have available— good combinations are orange and mint, or lime and coriander.

2¼ cups water
¼ cup lemon juice
¼ cup butter
¾ tsp salt
2 cups couscous
⅓ cup snipped fresh chives
1 tsp grated lemon zest
¼ tsp pepper

In medium saucepan, stir together water, lemon juice, butter and salt. Bring to boil over high heat, swirling saucepan to melt butter. Stir, then add couscous. Stir briefly; cover saucepan and remove from heat. Let stand for 5 minutes. With fork, stir in chives, lemon zest and pepper; fluff couscous. Spoon into warm serving dish and serve immediately.

MAKES 4 SERVINGS.

WARM STRAWBERRY SLICES

Think of this dessert as an instant strawberry tart—it has all the taste but none of the fuss.

- 2 cups hulled sliced strawberries
- 1 tbsp granulated sugar
- 4 slices (¾ inch thick) pound cake
- ¼ cup butter, melted
- ¼ cup redcurrant jelly
- Sour cream, whipped cream or vanilla ice cream

In medium bowl, stir together strawberry slices and sugar; let stand for 20 minutes or until juices run.

Brush both sides of cake slices with melted butter, reserving any remaining butter. Place slices in single layer on foil-lined baking sheet. Stir jelly to soften slightly; spread evenly over each slice.

Spoon strawberries and their juices over jellied side of pound cake; drizzle with any remaining butter. Bake in 400°F oven for about 10 minutes or until edges of cake are golden and strawberries are softened.

With spatula, transfer 1 slice to each of 4 dessert plates; top with dollop of sour cream or whipped cream, or scoop vanilla ice cream alongside. Serve immediately.

MAKES 4 SERVINGS.

JANE LANGDON

JANE LANGDON IS THE OWNER AND PRINCIPAL INSTRUCTOR AT THE WINE COUNTRY COOKING SCHOOL, A RECREATIONAL COOKING SCHOOL AT STREWN WINERY IN NIAGARA-ON-THE-LAKE, ONTARIO. A FORMER FOOD EDITOR, JANE COMBINES A CAREER IN PUBLIC RELATIONS WITH HER LOVE OF FOOD AND WINE. THE WINE COUNTRY COOKING SCHOOL OFFERS HANDS-ON CLASSES THAT FOCUS ON FOOD AND WINE AND ON THE USE OF LOCAL, SEASONAL INGREDIENTS.

CROSTINI WITH OVEN-ROASTED TOMATOES AND GOAT CHEESE

Roasting intensifies the flavour of tomatoes, which, for this appetizer, are brushed with a garlic basil oil before roasting. You can prepare the tomatoes when they are in season, then freeze and enjoy later.

- 1 baguette
- 12 plum tomatoes
- 2 tbsp olive oil
- 1 tbsp chopped fresh basil
- 1 clove garlic, minced
- Salt and pepper
- 1 clove garlic
- 4 oz goat cheese

Slice baguette diagonally into 24 slices. Line baking sheet with foil. Cut tomatoes in half lengthwise and remove core and seeds. Place, cut side up, on greased foil-lined baking sheet.

In small bowl, combine 1 tbsp of the olive oil, basil and garlic; spoon a little over each tomato half. Season with salt and pepper. Bake in 350°F oven for 1 to 1¼ hours or until tomatoes have caramelized around edges; watch carefully during last 15 minutes of baking to ensure tomatoes do not burn. Remove from oven and let cool for 5 minutes.

Brush baguette slices with remaining olive oil. Cut garlic clove in half and rub over each slice. Broil slices on baking sheet for 30 seconds or until golden.

Spread goat cheese over each baguette slice; top with tomato half.

MAKES 12 SERVINGS (2 PIECES EACH).

ELIZABETH BAIRD

ELIZABETH BAIRD IS THE FOOD EDITOR OF *CANADIAN LIVING* MAGAZINE AND CO-HOST OF "CANADIAN LIVING COOKS" ON FOOD NETWORK CANADA. OVER THE PAST DECADE, ELIZABETH HAS SUPERVISED AND EDITED MOST OF THE *CANADIAN LIVING* COOKBOOKS, INCLUDING *THE COMPLETE CANADIAN LIVING COOKBOOK* (RANDOM HOUSE CANADA, 2001). ELIZABETH WRITES A WEEKLY FOOD COLUMN FOR *THE TORONTO SUN*.

WHEN I THINK of being in the food business, I can't help but think of the people and places that have provided the inspiration. There's the good-cook mom and food-immersed country-based matriarchy she belonged to; an always appreciative father who was a pioneer at cooking over the coals in the '50s and who liked nothing better than a dawn visit to the market for bushels of "Spies"; a proper home ec teacher, Miss Findlay, every Stratford girl's mentor for tea biscuits, peach crisp and party sandwiches; then Helen Gougeon, whose cookbook *Good Food* and recipe for Bride's Pastry earned me a reputation as a pie maker; a year in France ogling pastries, smelling fresh cherries and cutting into real Alpine meadow cheeses; and in London, England during the '60s, discovering Elizabeth David and Robert Carrier and realizing that I was happiest when cooking; publisher and dinner party guest James Lorimer, who thought there should be a celebration of Canadian home cooking, the result being *Classic Canadian Cooking*, and my entrée into food writing. And Canada—where you can buy any ingredient in the world.

Whenever I attend a Women's Culinary Network meeting, I am overwhelmed by the way food has become the life and a living for its members. Whether a woman is an author, television cook, pastry chef, personal chef, corporate chef, shelter chef, recipe creator or tester, product developer, restaurateur, home economist, dietitian, teacher or editor, food is a passion and an ongoing curiosity, publicly and professionally shared.

A QUARTET OF PRESERVES

• SEVILLE ORANGE MARMALADE •
• FOUR-FRUIT SUMMER JAM •
• PICKLED ONIONS WITH HORSERADISH •
• SALSA •

SEVILLE ORANGE MARMALADE

As far as marmalades are concerned, the bitter Seville orange makes the finest and clearest, producing an assertive citrus taste that stands up to all the sugar needed for setting. This marmalade is a bracing morning eye-opener, perfect on whole-grain toast or freshly baked biscuits, a.k.a. scones.

8 Seville oranges (4 lb)
2 large lemons
15 cups granulated sugar

With vegetable brush, scrub oranges and lemons well under water. Cut out stem and blossom ends and any blemishes. Cut in half crosswise; squeeze out juice, dislodging all seeds. Strain juice through plastic sieve into large, wide, heavy-bottomed saucepan.

Place seeds and any membranes squeezed out with juice onto double thickness of 8-inch square of fine cheesecloth. Bring up sides; tie with cotton string, enclosing loosely. Add to pot.

On cutting board and with sharp chef's knife, cut orange and lemon halves crosswise into very thin strips. Add to pot. Pour in 16 cups cold water; bring to simmer, uncovered, over medium heat. Reduce heat to low and barely simmer, stirring often and pressing seed bag frequently, for 2½ to 3 hours. (By that time, the peel must be so soft it turns to mush when pressed between thumb and index finger.)

Remove seed bag; firmly squeeze juices back into pan. Mixture should measure 15 cups. If more, continue simmering; if less, add water. Divide into 3 batches of 5 cups each.

In clean pot, stir together 5 cups of the sugar with 1 batch of peel; bring to boil over high heat, stirring often. Boil, stirring constantly for 8 to 12 minutes or until clear, thickened and set (see "Setting Point," below).

Pour into prepared 1-cup canning jars, leaving ¼-inch headspace. Seal with prepared discs and bands. Process in boiling water canner for 10 minutes (See "Canning Basics," page 8). Repeat with remaining sugar and batches of peel.

MAKES ABOUT EIGHTEEN 1-CUP JARS.

VARIATIONS:

Ginger Orange Marmalade: Use jars of preserved ginger, which comes preserved in a thick syrup and can be found in most grocery stores. Stir ¼ cup slivered drained ginger into each batch of marmalade after boiling for 5 minutes.

Whisky Orange Marmalade: Stir 2 tbsp blended Scotch whisky into each batch of marmalade when it has reached setting point.

FOUR-FRUIT SUMMER JAM

Here's a ruby red jewel-toned preserve to make in mid-July when currants, berries and cherries are all in season. Or, since all the fruit freezes well, make it on a cold winter afternoon and fill the kitchen with the heady perfume of summer.

1½ cups hulled strawberries (12 oz)
1½ cups raspberries (12 oz)
2½ cups crushed stemmed redcurrants (1 lb)
1½ cups halved pitted sour cherries (12 oz)
3½ cups granulated sugar

Pour strawberries and raspberries into large, wide, heavy-bottomed saucepan. With potato masher, crush berries thoroughly. Mix in currants and cherries. Bring to boil over medium-high heat, stirring constantly. Reduce heat to medium-low and simmer, stirring occasionally, for 15 minutes.

Remove pan from heat. Stir in sugar in thin steady stream. Place over high heat and return to boil. Boil, stirring, for about 12 minutes or until setting point is reached (See "Setting Point," below).

Remove from heat; skim off foam. Pour into prepared 1-cup canning jars, leaving ¼-inch headspace. Seal with prepared discs and bands. Process in boiling water canner for 5 minutes (see "Canning Basics," page 8).

MAKES ABOUT FIVE 1-CUP JARS.

SETTING POINT: *Before boiling each batch of marmalade or jam, chill 2 plates in freezer. As time suggested in the recipe nears, remove preserve from heat and drop about ½ tsp onto one of the plates and let cool. Tilt plate; the surface of a set preserve will wrinkle when pushed with fork. If marmalade or jam is still too liquid, return to heat and continue boiling. Return plate to freezer. Repeat test every few minutes, using coldest plate, until sample wrinkles satisfactorily.*

PICKLED ONIONS WITH HORSERADISH

Whether you slip one of these tiny pearls into a cocktail or drain and arrange a jarful on an antipasto platter, there's no mistaking that these are a special preserve, and worth every minute it takes to peel the pesky little onions. The best time of the year to pickle onions is during the September harvest. Feel free to use diminutive yellow or red onions instead of the silverskins.

8 cups small silverskin onions (about 3½ lb)
½ cup coarse pickling salt
3 small hot peppers
6 small bay leaves
4 cups white wine vinegar
1 cup granulated sugar
2 tbsp yellow mustard seeds
4 tsp grated horseradish

Place onions in heatproof bowl that holds them comfortably. Cover with boiling water and let stand for 2 minutes to loosen skins. Drain and refresh in cold water; drain and peel. Return to bowl; sprinkle with salt. Pour in enough cold water to cover; stir well. Cover lightly and let stand in cool place for 12 hours. Drain and rinse well.

Pack into 6 prepared 1-cup canning jars, leaving 1½-inch headspace. Cut hot peppers in half lengthwise; slide 1 pepper half and 1 bay leaf down side of each jar.

In large non-reactive saucepan, stir together vinegar, sugar, mustard seeds and horseradish; bring to boil over high heat. Reduce heat and simmer for 5 minutes. Return to boil quickly and pour over onions, leaving

½-inch headspace at top of each jar. Seal with prepared discs and bands. Process for 10 minutes in boiling water canner (see "Canning Basics," below).

MAKES ABOUT SIX 1-CUP JARS.

SALSA

The phone in the Canadian Living Test Kitchen rings off the hook every tomato season when cooks are ready to make their year's supply of salsa but have lost their recipe. You can make this salsa peppier by including the seeds and membranes from the jalapeño peppers, or for a volcanic version, replace them with ultra-hot Scotch bonnet or habanero peppers.

6 large jalapeño peppers (about 8 oz)
8 cups coarsely chopped peeled ripe tomatoes (about 4 lb)
3 cups chopped fresh Anaheim, cubanelle or banana peppers (about 3 lb)
2 cups diced onions
2 cups cider vinegar
1 each sweet red and yellow pepper, diced
4 large garlic cloves, minced
1 can (5½ oz/156 mL) tomato paste
2 tbsp granulated sugar
1 tbsp pickling salt
2 tsp sweet Hungarian paprika
1 tsp crumbled dried oregano
¼ cup minced fresh coriander

On cutting board and wearing rubber gloves, cut jalapeño peppers in half. Cut out membranes and remove seeds. Chop flesh finely to make 1 cup.

In large heavy-bottomed saucepan, stir together jalapeños, tomatoes, Anaheim peppers, onions, vinegar, sweet peppers, garlic, tomato paste, sugar, salt, paprika and oregano; bring to boil, stirring often. Reduce heat to medium-low and simmer, stirring often, for 1 hour or until thickened enough for 1 tbsp salsa to slide slowly down plate. Stir in coriander; simmer for 5 minutes.

Pour into prepared 1-cup canning jars, leaving ½-inch headspace. Seal with prepared discs and bands. Process in boiling water canner for 20 minutes (see "Canning Basics," below).

MAKES ABOUT ELEVEN 1-CUP JARS.

TIP: *To peel tomatoes, cut a shallow "X" across the bottom of each. Place stem end down in heatproof bowl. Cover with boiling water and let stand for 30 to 60 seconds or until tomato skins loosen. Drain, cool in cold water and peel.*

CANNING BASICS:

- Always use perfect, uncracked, unchipped canning jars, often sold as Mason jars. Wash in hot sudsy water; rinse and air-dry.
- Use new lid discs. Five minutes before filling jars, immerse discs in hot water to soften sealing compound.
- Jars processed in a boiling water canner for less than 10 minutes need to be sterilized. To do so, fill boiling water canner about two-thirds full of hot water. Place jars on rack and lower jars into hot water, letting them fill. Add wide-mouthed metal funnel and ½ cup metal measure for filling jars. Cover and bring to boil; boil for 10 minutes, timing so jars are ready at same time as preserves. Lift rack and let rest on edge of canner.
- Boil a kettle of water, ready to add to canner when filled jars are lowered for processing.
- Use funnel and metal measure for ladling preserves into jars. Remove air bubbles by sliding a clean spatula between glass and food, pressing food lightly. If jar rims get sticky, wipe with damp paper towel.

• Leave headspace recommended in each recipe. Place prepared disc on jar; screw on bands firmly without forcing.

• As jars are filled and sealed, place on canner rack; lower rack. Avoiding jars, pour in enough boiling water to come 1 inch above top of jars. Bring back to vigorous boil and start to time processing.

• Use canner tongs to remove jars from canner and place on racks to cool for 24 hours. Check that discs have snapped down; refrigerate any jars whose lids have not snapped into concave position and use within three weeks.

• Wipe and label jars; store in cool, dark and dry place.

MIRIAM KATZ

MIRIAM KATZ HAS COURTED A PASSION FOR FOOD SINCE SHE WAS 13. WITH A BACKGROUND IN NUTRITION, SHE HAS BEEN IN THE FOOD INDUSTRY FOR MANY YEARS. HER INVOLVEMENT RANGES FROM VOLUNTEERING AT TORONTO'S MOUNT SINAI HOSPITAL KITCHEN TO WORKING IN PRODUCT DEVELOPMENT FOR LOBLAWS. MIRIAM CURRENTLY WORKS AS A FOODSERVICES SPECIALIST AT NESTLÉ CANADA INC., DEVELOPING MENUS, PRODUCT CONCEPTS AND RECIPES, RESEARCHING AND ANALYZING MARKETPLACE TRENDS AND CONDUCTING SENSORY PANELS.

ORANGE GINGER BABY BACK PORK RIBS

These tantalizing ribs can be served as an appetizer or as a main dish over rice, with stir-fried Chinese greens. To serve as an appetizer, ask the butcher to split them into 1½- to 2-inch racks.

2 lb pork baby back ribs
2 tbsp vegetable oil
⅓ cup thinly sliced green onions
2 tsp thinly sliced fresh ginger
2 tsp thinly sliced garlic

ORANGE GINGER SAUCE:

1½ cups orange juice
¼ cup Seville orange marmalade
¼ cup light soy sauce
1 tbsp minced fresh ginger
1 tbsp minced garlic
1 tbsp lime juice
2 tsp honey
¼ tsp hot pepper flakes

With sharp knife or kitchen scissors, cut ribs near bone into individual pieces.

In large heavy saucepan, heat oil over medium-high heat; cook green onions, ginger and garlic for 1 minute. Arrange ribs evenly over bottom of saucepan and cook for about 2 minutes per side or until browned. Transfer ribs to plate. Drain excess fat from pan. Set aside.

ORANGE GINGER SAUCE: In small bowl, whisk together orange juice, marmalade, soy sauce, ginger, garlic, lime juice, honey and hot pepper flakes.

Place saucepan used to cook ribs over medium-high heat; add Orange Ginger Sauce, stirring to scrape pan juices from bottom. Add ribs and bring to boil. Reduce heat to medium-low, cover and simmer for 1 hour, turning halfway through cooking time. Remove lid during last 15 minutes of cooking so that sauce becomes thick and syrupy; stir often to ensure sauce coats ribs evenly.

MAKES 6 SERVINGS.

FOOD STYLIST

If you aren't in the food industry, chances are you haven't got a clue what a food stylist does. Even those of us who cook every day for a living might be surprised to discover the contents of a food stylist's toolbox. Glycerine? That makes a glass of something cold (beer, cola, iced tea) sweat the way it should. Tweezers? Just the thing to place a fleck of chopped parsley or a sliver of red pepper atop a teetering tower of food architecture. Tampon? When filled with water and heated in a microwave oven, these super-absorbent contraptions produce just the right amount of steam required for that fresh-from-the-oven television illusion.

Food stylists work in many mediums, making food look pretty for magazines, newspapers, cookbooks, television and food events like cookbook launches or parties. Generally speaking, their most demanding (and inedible) work is done for print and TV advertising, where food may have to fly, spin, steam or look frozen despite the demands of strong lighting and/or gravity. That's when the stylist's gear, like wire, tape, Silly Putty, pins and glue, are in highest demand.

Television cooking shows or magazine articles require styling that is more realistic, but it still has to look perfect! That's why food stylists are pro shoppers, knowing where to snag gorgeous food, in any season, at any time of day. It's a job that many stylists would say relies more on art and engineering than on food science or even taste (some claim to be horrid cooks). While some culinary programs now offer food styling courses, many of the WCN's stylists learned their trade the old-fashioned way and apprenticed with an expert. As food captivates more of the media's attention every year, this trade is constantly meeting new challenges. Many pros (most are freelance in the WCN) say that they have to be flexible, resilient and adaptable, while possessing that intrinsic "good eye" that knows just what the camera lens wants to behold.

M.G.

LAURA BUCKLEY

LAURA BUCKLEY IS A CHEF AND FOOD CONSULTANT. SHE TRAINED AT THE STRATFORD CHEFS SCHOOL AND HAS WORKED IN THE KITCHENS OF JUMP, AVALON AND MILDRED PIERCE. SHE ALSO RAN A CATERING COMPANY IN TORONTO, CALLED EATS OF EDEN. SHE HAS DEVELOPED AND TESTED RECIPES FOR SEVERAL PUBLICATIONS AND COOKBOOKS AND WAS A COPY EDITOR AT *CANADIAN LIVING* MAGAZINE. SHE IS CURRENTLY THE COORDINATOR OF UPSTAIRS AT LOBLAWS COOKING SCHOOL IN MARKHAM, ONTARIO.

FOR ME, food is so much more than something to fill my tummy. It is about family, friends and feeding the soul. I want to know where ingredients come from. That's why I'm a big supporter of eating locally grown, in-season foods. I look forward to rising early on weekends and going to my local farmers' market to pick out some really great produce and chat with the farmers. When I entertain, I go to the market to be inspired by what looks the best that day, and from there, I decide on the menu. That shopping trip inevitably becomes part of the evening's conversation with my dinner guests.

I am a member of the International Slow Food Movement (www.slowfood.com). It is an organization that was created in Italy in 1989 as a backlash to the opening of the first McDonald's Restaurant in Rome. It aims to celebrate the pleasures of the table, as well as safeguard and promote culinary traditions and indigenous foods. In our frenzied modern lives, we forget the importance of sitting down with family and friends to enjoy our food. But in order to preserve our food from the effects of industrialization and standardization of taste, we must take time to think about where our food comes from and how it is prepared.

I believe that one of the best ways to get to know someone is to share a meal. Perhaps that's why our best Women's Culinary Network meetings are our potluck dinners.

BRUNCH WITH FLAIR

• MAPLE-CARAMELIZED BACON •
• BERRY-STUFFED FRENCH TOAST •
• PERFECTLY POACHED EGGS ON WINTER GREENS WITH CITRUS VINAIGRETTE •
• GINGERED HOT CHOCOLATE •

MAPLE-CARAMELIZED BACON

This is a perfect buffet dish because the bacon tastes even better at room temperature.

¾ cup packed brown sugar
½ cup maple syrup
1 lb bacon

In bowl, stir together brown sugar and maple syrup. Dip bacon strips into sugar mixture and coat well; place on broiler pan or rack set over rimmed baking sheet. Bake in 400°F oven for 10 minutes; turn and bake for another 8 to 10 minutes or until bacon is dark golden brown and crisp. Transfer to rack to cool. Serve at room temperature.

MAKES 6 SERVINGS.

BERRY-STUFFED FRENCH TOAST

Enjoy a new twist on the ubiquitous brunch favourite. Keep the finished toasts warm, piled up on a baking sheet in a 150°F oven until ready to serve. If there's any leftover berry filling, put it in a bowl and serve with the toasts.

BERRY FILLING:

2 cups wild blueberries (fresh or frozen)
2 cups raspberries (fresh or frozen)
½ cup granulated sugar
1 tsp grated lemon zest
4 tsp cornstarch

FRENCH TOAST:

6 eggs
2 cups milk
1 tbsp granulated sugar
2 tsp vanilla
¼ cup (approx) butter
12 slices egg bread (challah or brioche)
3 tbsp icing sugar

BERRY FILLING: In saucepan over medium heat, combine blueberries, raspberries, sugar and lemon zest; cook for about 5 minutes or until sugar is dissolved and berries have released some of their juice. In small bowl, blend cornstarch with 1 tbsp of juice from berries; stir into berry mixture. Increase heat to high and cook, stirring, for about 5 minutes or until thickened. Remove from heat and set aside.

FRENCH TOAST: In large bowl, whisk together eggs, milk, sugar and vanilla; set aside.

In large skillet over medium heat, melt 1 tbsp of the butter. Dip bread 1 slice at a time, into egg mixture, pressing down and letting soak for 10 seconds; turn and press again for 10 seconds. Lift out, letting excess mixture drip back into bowl.

Fry soaked bread slices, 2 at a time, for 3 minutes; turn 1 piece over and evenly spread golden brown side with 2 heaping tbsp of the berry filling. Flip second slice, cooked side down, onto filling to form sandwich; press firmly with back of spatula. Continue frying for 3 minutes; turn sandwich over and fry for 3 minutes longer or until golden brown on both sides. Repeat with remaining bread slices, adding more butter to skillet as needed.

Place stuffed toast on plate and dust with icing sugar.

MAKES 6 SERVINGS.

PERFECTLY POACHED EGGS ON WINTER GREENS WITH CITRUS VINAIGRETTE

Use the freshest eggs possible. If the egg is too old, the white will completely detach from the yolk when poaching.

6 eggs
1 tbsp white vinegar

Fill large, deep saucepan or skillet with about 3 inches water. Add vinegar and bring to boil. Crack eggs into individual ramekins or custard cups; slip gently into boiling water. Reduce heat to simmer and poach eggs for about 4 minutes or until yolk is firm but slightly runny in centre. Remove eggs with slotted spoon and submerge in bowl of cold water; refrigerate, uncovered, until needed or for up to 3 days. To reheat, place in barely simmering water for about 2 minutes or until heated through.

WINTER GREENS WITH CITRUS VINAIGRETTE:

8 cups mixed winter greens (such as arugula, curly endive, baby kale, radicchio, watercress, baby spinach, etc.)
2 tbsp lemon juice
1 tbsp orange juice
⅓ cup extra-virgin olive oil
1 tsp each salt and pepper

Wash and dry greens and place in large bowl. In small bowl, whisk together lemon juice, orange juice, oil, salt and pepper. Toss greens with dressing; transfer to large serving platter. To serve, reheat eggs and place on top of greens.

MAKES 6 SERVINGS.

GINGERED HOT CHOCOLATE

Ginger and chocolate are a match made in heaven. But if you're a purist, just leave out the ginger. The mixture reheats well, so make this the night before to save time in the morning.

6 cups milk
2 tbsp grated fresh ginger
12 oz chopped bittersweet or semisweet chocolate
½ cup whipping cream, whipped
Finely chopped crystallized ginger

In saucepan, combine milk and ginger. Heat to scalding (bubbles form around edge of pan); remove from heat and let stand for 20 minutes. Using fine-mesh sieve, strain milk into clean saucepan.

Stir in chocolate and cook, stirring over medium-high heat, until chocolate is melted. Pour into mugs. Top with whipped cream and crystallized ginger.

MAKES 6 SERVINGS.

WENDY TRUSLER

WENDY TRUSLER HAS BEEN CATERING SINCE 1986, SERVING A DIVERSE CLIENTELE—FROM TORONTO COCKTAIL PARTY AND CORPORATE GATHERINGS, TO ECO-TOURISTS IN ANTARCTICA, HUNGRY NORTHERN ONTARIO TREE PLANTERS, AND AUSTRALIAN SEA KAYAKERS. WENDY CURRENTLY FOCUSES ON FOOD STYLING, WORKING ON MOVIE SETS, THE "CANADIAN LIVING COOKS" TELEVISION SHOW AND SPECIAL EVENTS FOR YTV.

CINNAMON BUNS

For smaller, bite-size buns, roll out dough into a longer, narrower 24- x 8-inch rectangle, spread with filling, roll, then cut into 24 equal pieces; top and let rise. Bake for 10 to 15 minutes or until golden. These buns are especially good with your morning coffee. Let them rise in your refrigerator overnight and bake them for breakfast.

¼ cup granulated sugar
½ cup warm water
1 pkg active dry yeast (or 1 tbsp)
⅔ cup water
⅓ cup quick-cooking rolled oats
1 cup hot water

⅔ cup skim milk powder
¼ cup honey
2 tbsp butter
1½ tsp salt
2 cups whole wheat flour
3½ cups all-purpose flour (approx)

FILLING:

1½ cups butter, softened
1½ cups packed brown sugar
1¼ cups quick-cooking rolled oats
¼ cup poppy seeds
2 tbsp cinnamon
¼ cup all-purpose flour

In small bowl, dissolve ½ tsp of the sugar in warm water. Sprinkle in yeast. Let stand for about 10 minutes or until frothy.

In small saucepan over medium-high heat, bring ⅔ cup water to boil. Stir in oats; reduce heat and cook, stirring often, for about 5 minutes or until very thick. Remove from heat and place in large bowl. Whisk in hot water, skim milk powder, honey, butter, salt and remaining sugar until smooth and butter has melted. Let cool slightly.

Add yeast mixture to cooled oatmeal mixture. Using wooden spoon, stir in whole wheat flour and 2½ cups of the all-purpose flour. Gradually stir in enough of the remaining flour to make soft but slightly sticky dough.

Turn out dough onto lightly floured surface; knead for 10 minutes or until smooth and elastic, adding enough of remaining flour as necessary to keep it from sticking. Place in greased bowl, turning to grease all over. Cover with clean towel and let rise in draft-free place until doubled in bulk, about 1½ hours.

FILLING: In medium bowl, beat together butter and brown sugar. Stir in 1 cup of the oats, poppy seeds and cinnamon. Set aside 1 cup of the mixture.

Punch down dough. Turn out onto lightly floured surface; roll out into 18- x 14-inch rectangle, letting dough rest often to allow for stretching. Spread filling evenly over dough, leaving ½-inch border at one long edge. Starting at opposite long edge, roll up into cylinder, pinching seam to seal. Using serrated knife, cut into 12 equal pieces. Place, cut sides down, in greased 13- x 9-inch baking dish.

Stir remaining oats and flour into reserved filling until mixture is crumbly. Spoon over buns. Cover with clean towel and let rise for 30 minutes or until plump.

Bake in centre of 350°F oven for 20 to 30 minutes or until golden and tops sound hollow when tapped.

MAKES 12 BUNS.

ARVINDA CHAUHAN

ARVINDA CHAUHAN OWNS AND OPERATES HEALTHY GOURMET INDIAN COOKING SCHOOL AND ALSO TEACHES AT T-SPOT AND GREAT COOKS IN TORONTO. SHE HAS CONDUCTED COOKING DEMOS AT THE ANNUAL GOOD FOOD FESTIVAL IN TORONTO, 34TH WORLD VEGETARIAN CONGRESS, TORONTO VEGETARIAN ASSOCIATION AND CANADIAN NATIONAL EXHIBITION. ARVINDA OFTEN COOKS FOR TELEVISION AND HAS APPEARED ON CFTO-TV, CITYTV, ON-TV AND LIFE NETWORK.

EVERYONE WHO comes to my house is welcomed into my kitchen and offered a warm, fragrant cup of chai, along with steamy, hot pakoras. In the true spirit of Indian hospitality, you never let a guest leave hungry.

From the tender age of seven, my interest in cooking grew. I watched my grandmother and aunts roll chapatis and grind masala spice mixtures in a heavy mortar and pestle. They taught me authentic methods of cooking, and my passion evolved.

In the '90s, I started up my cooking school just when exotic food was exploding in popularity. But Indian cuisine had become stereotyped as overspiced, greasy and laborious to prepare. I wanted to break down those misconceptions and introduce Indian cuisine as gourmet, healthy and spiced according to your own taste. These four recipes reflect that philosophy.

A VEGETARIAN FEAST FROM INDIA

•STUFFED POTATO CUTLETS WITH SPICED PEAS AND CORIANDER AND MINT CHUTNEY •

• BABY EGGPLANTS FILLED WITH SWEET-AND-SOUR PEANUT COCONUT MASALA •

• FRAGRANT SAFFRON AND CASHEW BASMATI RICE PULLAO •

• KULFI: PISTACHIO CARDAMOM ICE CREAM WITH FRESH MANGO PURÉE •

STUFFED POTATO CUTLETS WITH SPICED PEAS, AND CORIANDER AND MINT CHUTNEY

I like to use a fluffy potato like Yukon Gold or russet to ensure the patty stays together and can be moulded easily. These potato cutlets are great as an appetizer and can be served hot or cold.

1 cup frozen peas
3 tbsp vegetable oil
1 green chili pepper, finely chopped
1 tsp each ground cumin and coriander
½ tsp salt
2 tbsp chopped fresh coriander leaves
½ tsp lemon juice
½ tsp garam masala (see recipe, page 16)
2 lb potatoes, boiled, peeled and mashed
1 egg, lightly beaten
1 cup bread crumbs
Coriander and Mint Chutney (recipe follows)

In food processor, coarsely grind frozen peas. In skillet, heat 2 tsp of the oil over medium heat; cook peas, green chili pepper, cumin, ground coriander and salt, stirring, for 3 to 4 minutes or until peas are tender. Stir in fresh coriander, lemon juice and garam masala. Set aside.

For each cutlet, form ⅓ cup of the mashed potatoes into patty in palm of hand. Place 1 tbsp of the pea mixture on top and mould potato around filling to enclose. Dip cutlet in beaten egg, then coat in bread crumbs. Continue with remaining potatoes and filling.

In large skillet, heat remaining oil over medium heat; fry potato cutlets for 3 to 5 minutes per side or until golden brown. Serve with Coriander and Mint Chutney.

MAKES 6 SERVINGS.

CORIANDER AND MINT CHUTNEY

Serve this easy, fresh chutney with stuffed potato cutlets or such Indian snacks as pakoras or samosas. You could even drizzle it over a grilled chicken breast or salmon steak.

2 green chili peppers
1 apple, peeled and chopped

1 medium tomato, chopped
1 clove garlic, minced
1 cup chopped fresh coriander leaves
¼ cup fresh mint leaves
1 tsp lemon juice
½ tsp salt
½ tsp whole cumin seeds

In blender, mix together green chili peppers, apple, tomato, garlic, coriander, mint, lemon juice, salt and cumin seeds on medium speed until smooth. Serve with potato cutlets.

MAKES ¾ CUP.

BABY EGGPLANTS FILLED WITH SWEET-AND-SOUR PEANUT COCONUT MASALA

Masala is a catch-all term in Indian cuisine referring to a dry or wet paste spice mixture—even a sauce. I like to serve these flavour-packed eggplants as a main course with Indian flatbread or basmati rice. Choose baby Asian eggplants for this recipe.

1 onion, finely chopped (about 1 cup)
1 medium tomato, finely chopped
1 tsp each ground cumin and coriander
½ tsp cayenne pepper
½ tsp salt
½ tsp granulated sugar
½ tsp Garam Masala (recipe follows)
¼ tsp turmeric
2 tbsp finely chopped unsalted peanuts
2 tbsp unsweetened flaked coconut
2 tbsp finely chopped fresh coriander leaves
½ tsp lemon juice
8 baby Asian eggplants, with stems (about 1¼ lb)
2 tbsp vegetable oil

In small bowl, stir together onion, tomato, cumin, ground coriander, cayenne pepper, salt, sugar, Garam Masala and turmeric. Add peanuts, coconut, fresh coriander and lemon juice; mix until well combined. Set aside.

Using paring knife, make a cut down the length of each eggplant from stem to tip without cutting the whole way through. Stuff tomato mixture into each eggplant, pressing to close as best you can. (It will not close completely.)

In large frying pan, heat oil over medium-low heat. Place eggplant, stuffing side up, in pan; cook, covered for 15 minutes. Turn eggplants on their sides (some filling will spill out); cook for 5 to 10 minutes longer or until very tender.

MAKES 4 SERVINGS.

GARAM MASALA

Every household in India has its own special blend of Garam Masala made according to a family recipe perfected throughout the generations. Keep your cardamom pods whole, since the peel adds fibre to the dish as well as aroma.

2 tbsp green cardamom pods
1 whole nutmeg, coarsely chopped
6 sticks cinnamon
2 tbsp whole cloves
2 tbsp black peppercorns
2 tbsp whole coriander seeds
1 tsp cumin seeds
2 tbsp fennel seeds

Place all ingredients on a baking sheet and roast in 250°F oven for 10 minutes or until fragrant. Transfer to clean coffee grinder and grind finely. Store in an airtight container in a dark, cool place.

MAKES ABOUT 1 CUP.

FRAGRANT SAFFRON AND CASHEW BASMATI RICE PULLAO

Known as pilaf in other parts of the world, this rice dish adds pizzazz to the meal. If you don't have any cashews on hand, substitute pistachios.

1 cup basmati rice
½ tsp saffron threads
1 tbsp vegetable oil
½ tsp whole cumin seeds
5 bay leaves
½ cup raw whole cashews
½ tsp salt
1 tbsp chopped fresh coriander leaves
½ tsp Garam Masala (see recipe, page 16)

Wash rice gently in 4 or 5 changes of water. In medium bowl, soak rice in enough water to cover for 10 to 15 minutes. Wash again in a few changes of water; drain and set aside. In small bowl, soak saffron in ¼ cup of warm water. Set aside.

In medium skillet, heat oil over medium-high heat; cook cumin seeds, bay leaves and cashews, stirring for 3 to 4 minutes or until nuts are slightly browned. Stir in rice and salt, mixing well to coat with oil. Add 1½ cups of water to pan; bring to boil. Cover and cook for 20 to 25 minutes or until water is absorbed.

Remove from heat and stir in saffron. Cover and let stand for 5 minutes. Transfer to serving dish and garnish with coriander leaves and Garam Masala.

MAKES 4 SERVINGS.

KULFI: PISTACHIO CARDAMOM ICE CREAM WITH FRESH MANGO PURÉE

Kulfi is Indian ice cream, redolent with sweet spices and nuts. Look for traditional kulfi metal cone sets in any well-stocked East Indian store.

1½ cups evaporated milk
1 cup half-and-half cream
½ cup granulated sugar
¼ cup finely chopped almonds
¼ cup finely chopped pistachios
½ tsp vanilla or rose water
¼ tsp ground cardamom
7 saffron threads
1 ripe mango, thinly sliced
Mint leaves

In bowl, whisk together evaporated milk, cream, sugar, almonds, pistachios, vanilla, cardamom and saffron; pour into ice cube tray, kulfi or Popsicle moulds. Freeze for about 5 hours or until hard.

Purée mango in blender until smooth. To serve, unmould kulfi onto serving platter or individual plates. Drizzle with mango purée and garnish with mint leaves.

MAKES 4 SERVINGS.

SUDHA SAJAN

AS THE ELDEST DAUGHTER OF AN EAST INDIAN FAMILY LIVING IN SINGAPORE, I GREW UP IN THE KITCHEN HELPING MY MOTHER. I ALSO ACCOMPANIED MY FATHER ON HIS WEEKLY TRIPS TO THE FISH AND POULTRY MARKETS, LEARNING AT HIS SIDE HOW TO CLEAN, CUT AND PREPARE MEATS, POULTRY AND FISH. I'VE BEEN COOKING SERIOUSLY FOR FAMILY AND FRIENDS FOR 25 YEARS NOW AND LOVE EVERY MINUTE OF IT.

CURRIED CHICKPEAS WITH COCONUT FLAKES

This dish can be made a day in advance, which allows the flavours to infuse. Serve over basmati rice (see recipe, page 118) or with warm pita, naan or other flatbread. You'll find Madras curry powder in large supermarkets, fine food shops or East Indian stores.

2 tbsp vegetable oil
½ tsp black mustard seeds
½ cup chopped onion
1 tbsp finely chopped garlic
1 tsp finely chopped fresh ginger
1 tsp Madras curry powder
1 medium Yukon Gold potato, peeled and cubed
½ cup diced tomato
2 tsp salt
¼ cup water
2 cups canned chickpeas, drained and rinsed
1 tbsp chopped fresh coriander
1 tbsp sweetened flaked coconut

In large saucepan, heat oil over high heat; cook mustard seeds, stirring constantly, for 2 minutes or until popping and fragrant. Add onions, garlic and ginger; reduce heat to medium and cook, stirring occasionally, for 6 to 8 minutes or until softened. Add curry powder, stirring to completely coat onion mixture; cook for 1 minute. Add potatoes, tomato and salt; increase heat to high and cook, stirring constantly, for 2 minutes. Pour in water; reduce heat to medium-low, cover and simmer for 10 minutes. Add chickpeas; cook for 10 minutes or until potatoes are tender and chickpeas are softened. Check after 10 minutes and add a little water if mixture looks dry. Stir in most of the coriander and coconut, reserving some for garnish; cook for 2 minutes. Serve garnished with reserved coriander and coconut.

MAKES 4 SERVINGS.

SUSAN CONNOLLY

SUSAN CONNOLLY LIVES IN OTTAWA, WHERE SHE IS A CHEF BY TRADE, ADVOCATE FOR ORGANIC FARMERS AND OCCASIONAL COOKING INSTRUCTOR ABOUT TOWN. SHE RECENTLY SERVED AS CHAIR OF THE ONTARIO CHAPTER OF CUISINE CANADA AND WAS ON THE ORGANIZING COMMITTEE FOR THE NATIONAL CONFERENCE NORTHERN BOUNTY V. SUCCESSFULLY ESTABLISHING FEAST OF FIELDS IN OTTAWA WAS A PROUD ACCOMPLISHMENT FOR SUSAN.

AS TIME goes on, I realize the most important things in life are the simplest. By using quality ingredients in easy preparations, one can usually be guaranteed a good end product. Fine food is as essential to me as breathing clean air and drinking good water. Buying and eating fresh, locally and seasonally produced food is the starting point for all my cooking.

I started my career as a professional chef 25 years ago in a hotel kitchen, gradually moving through restaurants, institutions, and ending up in my own catering retail operation. Five years ago, I sold that business and now concentrate my efforts on logistical support for my family: an entrepreneurial husband and two young girls who swim competitively. I keep my sanity by bicycling hard and fast.

A desire to share my passion for food with other foodies in the nation's capital led me to found the Women's Culinary Network of Ottawa in 1995 with Sheila Whyte.

My current interest is to provide food that maximizes energy, endurance and strength for athletic performance. Maintaining good flavour is a necessary part of the equation. These recipes reflect that philosophy.

FEEDING THE ATHLETIC FAMILY

• MEDITERRANEAN-FLAVOURED LENTILS AND RICE •
• ROASTED TOMATO AND GARLIC SOUP •
• ENERGY SQUARED SNACKING CAKE •
• VITALITY SMOOTHIE •

MEDITERRANEAN-FLAVOURED LENTILS AND RICE

I like to use French dupuy *lentils for this dish. They are small, brown lentils available in specialty food stores and some supermarkets. Serve this dish hot or at room temperature, as a side with grilled meat or on its own as a vegetarian main course. You can store it in the refrigerator for 2 to 3 days.*

1 cup dried French *dupuy* or green lentils (or 1 can, 19 oz/540 mL)
1 cup long-grain brown rice
Salt and pepper
2 roasted sweet red peppers, thinly sliced
4 to 6 green onions, thinly sliced diagonally (about ½ cup)
8 dried apricots, thinly sliced (about ½ cup)
¾ cup coarsely chopped fresh parsley
¼ cup coarsely chopped fresh mint
1 tbsp finely grated lemon zest
¼ cup lemon juice
¼ cup olive oil
¼ cup balsamic vinegar
1 tsp honey
½ tsp ground cumin
½ tsp cinnamon
¼ tsp ground ginger
⅛ tsp cayenne pepper
¼ cup toasted pine nuts (optional)

In large pot of boiling salted water, cook dried lentils and rice for 30 to 40 minutes or until tender. Drain well; transfer to large bowl and season to taste with salt and pepper. (If using canned lentils, rinse, drain and add to cooked rice.) Stir in red peppers, onion, apricots, parsley and mint.

In small bowl, whisk together lemon zest, lemon juice, oil, balsamic vinegar, honey, cumin, cinnamon, ginger and cayenne; toss with lentil mixture. Taste and adjust seasoning. Garnish with toasted pine nuts (if using).

MAKES 6 SERVINGS.

ROASTED TOMATO AND GARLIC SOUP

I use Ontario greenhouse tomatoes for this soup when local field tomatoes are out of season. Garnish this simple and tasty soup with store-bought, fresh stuffed pasta for an inexpensive family dinner or with garlic sautéed shrimp for a first course.

4 large ripe tomatoes (about 2 lb)
2 large onions (about 1 lb)
3 large heads garlic
2 tbsp olive oil
½ tsp each dried thyme, rosemary and basil
½ tsp fennel seeds
Salt
4 cups chicken stock
1 tbsp balsamic vinegar
Pepper

Cut tomatoes into quarters and remove seeds. Cut onions into large wedges; separate cloves of garlic. Place all vegetables on foil-lined baking sheet. In small bowl, whisk together oil, thyme, rosemary, basil, fennel and ½ tsp salt; pour over vegetables. Roast on bottom rack of 450°F oven for 1 hour or until tender and slightly charred. Let cool slightly; remove tomato skins and squeeze garlic from skins. Place in large heavy saucepan along with any accumulated juices; add stock and bring to boil. Reduce heat and simmer for 5 minutes.

Using immersion blender or blender, purée until smooth. Pass through strainer for smoother consistency if desired. Return to medium-low heat and stir in vinegar. Cook for 5 minutes. Season to taste with salt and pepper. If desired, thin with more water.

MAKES 6 SERVINGS.

GARLIC SAUTÉED SHRIMP

Prepare this elegant yet very simple garnish right before you serve the soup. Cooking time is no more than 2 minutes. Place soup into heated soup bowls and place shrimp in centre.

2 tsp extra-virgin olive oil
1 lb large shrimp, peeled and deveined
2 tsp chopped garlic
1 tbsp balsamic vinegar
1 tbsp chopped fresh parsley

In large heavy skillet, heat oil over high heat just until smoking; cook shrimp and garlic, stirring, for 2 minutes or just until pink. Stir in balsamic vinegar and parsley. Remove from heat.

MAKES 6 SERVINGS.

ENERGY SQUARED SNACKING CAKE

Lots of energy-providing nutrition is packed into every mouthful of this easy, snacking cake. Pack in school lunches, bring along for car trips to and from sports activities or pop it into your purse for munching on the way to work. The cake is best prepared one day in advance. You'll find soy protein powder in bulk and health food stores.

1 cup white grape juice concentrate
½ cup dried cranberries, halved if large
1 tsp finely grated orange zest
¼ cup vegetable oil
2 eggs, lightly beaten
1½ cups quick-cooking rolled oats
¾ cup packed brown sugar

½ cup wheat germ
½ cup all-purpose flour
¼ cup soy protein powder
1 tsp cinnamon
1 tsp baking soda
¼ tsp salt
½ cup chocolate chips (optional)

In small bowl, combine grape juice concentrate, cranberries and orange zest; set aside to soak.

In small bowl, stir together oil and eggs. In large bowl, combine oats, brown sugar, wheat germ, flour, protein powder, cinnamon, baking soda and salt. Stir in chocolate chips (if using). Pour oil mixture over dry ingredients along with cranberry mixture; stir until just blended. Pour into lightly greased 13- x 9-inch baking dish. Bake in 375°F oven for 30 minutes or until lightly browned and cake tester inserted in centre comes out clean. Let cool completely. Cut into squares. Store tightly covered.

MAKES 24 PIECES.

VITALITY SMOOTHIE

Pre- and post-event hydration is essential, yet it's often difficult to persuade children to drink the amounts needed. This smoothie provides water, protein and easily absorbable sugars in a tasty, they'll-come-back-for-more package. The ripeness of the fruit is important to maximize the vitamin and sugar content of the smoothie.

2 cups fresh or frozen chopped ripe fruit mixture such as strawberries, bananas, pineapple, mango, peaches, raspberries, blueberries
1 cup orange or other fruit juice
½ cup fruit-flavoured or plain low-fat yogurt
4 to 5 ice cubes (if none of the fruits have been frozen or if you want a more slushy texture)

In blender, combine fruit, juice, yogurt, and ice (if using); purée until smooth. Pour into glasses.

MAKES 2 SERVINGS.

KAREN BEKKER

KAREN BEKKER WAS BORN IN SOUTH AFRICA AND EMIGRATED TO CANADA IN 1995. KAREN HAS A LOVE OF LANGUAGES, CULTURES AND HISTORY, AND A PASSION FOR EXPLORING REGIONAL CUISINES OF THE WORLD. SHE BALANCES HER JOB AS FINANCIAL CONTROLLER FOR THE HORIZON LEGACY GROUP WITH FREELANCE CULINARY CONSULTING AND INSTRUCTION THROUGH HER COMPANY, NORTHERN EPICURE.

RED RIVER CHEDDAR WALNUT MUFFINS

The Red River Valley in Manitoba is famous for its Red River cereal, comprised of cracked wheat, rye and whole flax. This is a rugged recipe, as untamed and wild as the ingredients and the method, which includes toasting the grain in foaming butter. The taste is earthy, nutty and savoury.

¼ cup unsalted butter
¾ cup Red River Cereal
1¼ cups milk

¼ cup maple syrup
1 tsp kosher or sea salt
1½ cups all-purpose, unbleached flour
4 tsp baking powder
2 eggs
½ cup whole walnuts (1½ oz), medium ground in a nut grinder (not a food processor)
1 cup shredded old Canadian Cheddar cheese

In heavy saucepan, heat butter over medium heat until foamy; cook cereal, stirring constantly, for 2 minutes or until slightly fragrant. Add 1 cup of the milk, maple syrup and salt, stirring to combine; bring to boil. Reduce heat and boil gently for 2 minutes, stirring occasionally. Remove from heat, cover and set aside for 3 minutes.

In small bowl, stir together flour and baking powder. Lightly beat eggs with remaining milk and stir into warm cereal. Add flour mixture and stir until roughly incorporated. Stir in walnuts and Cheddar without overmixing. Spoon batter into greased muffin tins, filling to top. Bake in centre of 400°F oven for 20 minutes or until brown and firm to the touch. Serve warm.

MAKES 12 MUFFINS.

NETTIE CRONISH

NETTIE CRONISH IS A NATURAL FOODS CHEF, COOKING TEACHER AND COOKBOOK AUTHOR. HER BOOKS INCLUDE *NETTIE'S VEGETARIAN KITCHEN* (SECOND STORY PRESS, 1996), *NEW VEGETARIAN BASICS* (RANDOM HOUSE CANADA, 1999) AND *BEING VEGETARIAN IN CANADA* (PRENTICE HALL, 2000). SHE TEACHES AT THE BIG CARROT NATURAL FOOD STORE, LOBLAWS AND THE LCBO, AND IS CHAIR OF THE WOMEN'S CULINARY NETWORK.

SHOPPING FOR FOOD is never a one-stop endeavour for me. When I need organic produce, I go to Karma Co-op, where I've been a member for 25 years. When it's time to buy beans, grains, cases of soy milk, juice and maple syrup, I put in an order with my food buying club, called Hen's Teeth; we're a collection of four families that have been buying natural foods for 11 years from the Ontario Natural Food Co-op catalogue.

And when I'm looking for ethnic ingredients that give flavour and soul to my food, I travel to Kensington Market in the heart of Toronto to ferret out pomegranate molasses, tamarind and chili paste, yard-long beans and kaffir lime leaves.

Because I teach cooking courses at health food stores and supermarkets, I browse their aisles just as an explorer discovers a new land, searching out what's new, convenient and delicious. As I grow older and busier, there's less time to cook from scratch, and I've had to find a balance between the clock and the purist within me.

With this menu, I've provided a delicious vegetarian meal that can be prepared in under an hour. You'll need to shop at a health food store for many of the ingredients.

A VEGETARIAN REPAST, NATURALLY

• WHITE KIDNEY BEAN AND CHOCOLATE CHILI •
• WARM KALE SALAD WITH LIME, GARLIC AND SPICY PUMPKIN SEEDS •
• PENNE WITH OLIVES, CAPERS, SUN-DRIED TOMATOES AND CHICKPEAS •
• TEMPEH FRENCH FRIES •

WHITE KIDNEY BEAN AND CHOCOLATE CHILI

I love the taste of this spicy, rich white bean chili. While they don't use chocolate chips in a traditional Mexican mole (a classic stew using Mexican chocolate or unsweetened cocoa), I like this modern North American touch for all the flavour it adds.

¼ cup olive oil
3 cloves garlic, minced
1 large red onion, chopped
8 oz frozen tofu, thawed and crumbled*
1 each sweet red, yellow and green pepper, thinly sliced
2 stalks celery, chopped
1 tsp ground cumin
2 bay leaves
2 dried ancho or chipotle peppers, toasted and ground **
1 stick (2 inches) cinnamon
1 can (28 oz/796 mL) crushed tomatoes
1 can (19 oz/540 mL) white kidney beans, drained and rinsed
2 tsp soy sauce
2 tbsp semisweet chocolate chips
¼ cup chopped fresh coriander

In wok or large skillet, heat oil over medium-high heat; cook garlic and onion for 8 to 10 minutes or until lightly browned. Add tofu, peppers, celery, cumin, bay leaves, dried hot peppers and cinnamon stick. Reduce heat to low and cook, stirring occasionally, for 10 minutes. Increase heat to medium-high; add tomatoes, kidney beans and soy sauce; bring to boil. Stir in chocolate chips and simmer for 15 minutes. Garnish with coriander.

MAKES 4 SERVINGS.

** Frozen tofu must be thawed before using. Remove any wrapping and place tofu in a deep bowl, covered with boiling water, for 10 minutes. Remove and squeeze tofu like a sponge, pressing out as much water as you can, then crumble.*
*** To prepare ground ancho or chipotle peppers: Toast peppers in a hot dry pan for 1 minute per side, let cool. Remove and grind in a spice or coffee grinder.*

WARM KALE SALAD WITH LIME, GARLIC AND SPICY PUMPKIN SEEDS

Kale is a nutritional superstar that tastes great with flavour boosters like lime, soy sauce and crunchy pumpkin seeds. Besides, the lime juice helps to preserve its vibrant green colour.

2 lb kale (about 2 bunches)
¼ cup extra-virgin olive oil
3 cloves garlic, minced
2 tbsp soy sauce
1 tbsp lime juice
Spicy Pumpkin Seeds (recipe follows)

Trim hard stems from kale leaves; wash thoroughly. In large pot of boiling salted water, cook kale, uncovered, for 3 minutes or until tender and bright green; drain and chill under cold water; drain again and pat dry. Chop coarsely; set aside.

In large skillet, heat oil over medium heat; cook garlic for 30 seconds. Stir in soy sauce. Add kale; cook for 3 to 5 minutes or until hot. Stir in lime juice. Serve garnished with Spicy Pumpkin Seeds.

MAKES 4 SERVINGS.

SPICY PUMPKIN SEEDS

1 cup shelled pumpkin seeds
1 tsp olive oil
½ tsp cayenne pepper
½ tsp sea salt
⅛ tsp pepper

In bowl, toss together pumpkin seeds, oil, cayenne, salt and pepper; spread on baking sheet and toast in 400°F oven for 10 to 12 minutes or until fragrant.

PENNE WITH OLIVES, CAPERS, SUN-DRIED TOMATOES AND CHICKPEAS

I'm a big believer in looking in the fridge and cupboard, seeing what ingredients need to be used up and combining them in a delicious, useful way. This dairy-free salad transports well and is delicious hot or cold. You can leave out the chickpeas if you like.

1 cup dry-packed sun-dried tomatoes
2 tbsp olive oil
3 cloves garlic, minced
¼ tsp fennel seeds
½ cup large black olives
¼ cup capers
2 tsp balsamic vinegar
⅛ tsp each salt and pepper
1 can (19 oz/540 mL) chickpeas, drained and rinsed (optional)
3 cups penne pasta
1 tbsp extra-virgin olive oil
½ cup finely chopped fresh parsley
½ cup toasted pine nuts

Cover sun-dried tomatoes with 1½ cups boiling water; let soften for 15 minutes. Drain, reserving soaking liquid. Chop coarsely and set aside.

In large skillet, heat olive oil over medium heat; cook garlic for about 1 minute or until just starting to brown. Stir in fennel seeds. Add sun-dried tomatoes and reserved liquid, olives, capers, balsamic vinegar, salt and pepper. Stir in chickpeas (if using). Stir to combine; remove from heat.

Meanwhile, in large pot of boiling salted water, cook pasta for 8 to 12 minutes until tender but firm. Drain and add to skillet along with extra-virgin olive oil and half of the parsley; toss to coat. Garnish with remaining parsley and pine nuts.

MAKES 4 SERVINGS.

TEMPEH FRENCH FRIES

My kids have grown up thinking french fries are made from tempeh, not potatoes! Tempeh is a high-protein soy food made by fermenting crushed soybeans with a bacterial culture. Sold frozen, it must be cooked before eaten. You'll find palm sugar in Asian stores.

2 medium leeks, well rinsed and coarsely chopped
2 cloves garlic, peeled
1 dried hot red pepper, seeded
¼ tsp chopped fresh ginger
½ cup olive oil
8 oz tempeh, sliced into matchsticks (1½ x ¼ x ¼ inch)
2 tbsp dried tamarind or tamarind paste*
1 tbsp palm or brown sugar
¼ tsp salt

In food processor, purée leeks, garlic, hot pepper, ginger and 2 tbsp water until smooth; set aside.

In skillet, heat ⅓ cup of the oil over medium-high heat. Add tempeh and stir-fry for 5 minutes or until tempeh turns reddish brown and is crisp. Using slotted spoon, remove tempeh and drain on clean dish towel or paper towel.

Add remaining oil to skillet along with leek mixture and tamarind paste; stir-fry over medium heat for 5 minutes or until most of the moisture has evaporated. Stir in sugar and salt. Add fried tempeh; cook for 3 to 5 minutes or until coated and heated through.

MAKES 4 SERVINGS.

** Tamarind is available in dried blocks or, less commonly, as a bottled paste in some large supermarkets, fine food stores and Asian stores. If you can't find the bottled paste, simply make your own from dried tamarind: soak 2 heaping tbsp of dried tamarind in ¼ cup hot water for 15 minutes, then press through a sieve, reserving paste and discarding pits.*

ADELL SHNEER

ADELL SHNEER GREW UP IN EDMONTON, SPENDING MUCH OF HER CHILDHOOD IN HER FAMILY'S RESTAURANTS: TEDDY'S AND CAROUSEL. ADELL DEVELOPED A PASSION FOR GOOD FOOD AND QUALITY INGREDIENTS AT HER GRANDMOTHER'S SIDE. SHE IS CURRENTLY A FREELANCE RECIPE TESTER FOR *TODAY'S PARENT* AND *CANADIAN LIVING* MAGAZINES AND RESIDENT BAKER AT DISH COOKING STUDIO IN TORONTO.

GINGER WHITE CHOCOLATE BISCOTTI

These spicy biscotti are delicious anytime, but they make a particularly welcome holiday gift. Fill canisters or Mason jars for your favourite friends and they'll be hoping you remember them every year. To make these extra special, try adding 1 cup macadamia nuts.

3 eggs
½ cup granulated sugar
½ cup packed light brown sugar
¼ cup vegetable oil
⅓ cup fancy molasses
1 tsp vanilla
2½ cups all-purpose flour
2 tbsp ground ginger
1 tsp baking soda
1 tsp cinnamon
½ tsp salt
¼ tsp ground cloves
8 oz good-quality white chocolate, chopped

In bowl, beat eggs with granulated sugar until light and fluffy. Add brown sugar and continue beating. Add oil in thin stream, then molasses and vanilla. In another bowl, whisk together flour, ginger, baking soda, cinnamon, salt and cloves; add to egg mixture, stirring just until combined. Stir in chocolate. Refrigerate dough for 1 hour or until firm.

Form dough into 4 equal rolls, 12 inches long. Place about 4 inches apart on parchment paper–lined or greased baking sheets. Flatten each roll until about 3 inches wide, leaving top slightly rounded.

Bake in centre of 325°F oven for 30 minutes or until firm and tops are golden. Let cool on pan on rack for 10 minutes. Transfer to cutting board; with serrated knife, cut into ¾-inch thick slices. Place biscotti, cut side down, on baking sheets. Return to 300°F oven; bake, turning once, for 15 minutes per side or until dry and crisp. Let cool on rack. Store in airtight container.

MAKES ABOUT 44 BISCOTTI.

MARILYN BENTZ CROWLEY

AFTER NEARLY A DECADE AS A PROFESSIONAL CHEF, MARILYN BENTZ CROWLEY BEGAN FREELANCING AS A FOOD STYLIST, EDITOR AND RECIPE TESTER. THAT LED TO A SIX-YEAR STINT AT *CHATELAINE* MAGAZINE AS ASSOCIATE FOOD EDITOR. MARILYN IS ONE OF TWO STILL-ACTIVE FOUNDING MEMBERS OF THE WOMEN'S CULINARY NETWORK. SHE IS CO-AUTHOR, WITH JOAN MACKIE, OF *THE BEST SOUP COOKBOOK* (ROBERT ROSE, 2000).

MY GRANDMOTHER Bertha King Bentz was a gifted cook, able to devise a recipe from recalled tastes. When visiting, she played canasta with my sister and me—and cooked. It was the mid-'50s and together we created such exotic food as pizza and enchiladas.

Now a chef trained in à la minute cooking, I continue to appreciate creative food, especially that which is served the instant after being cooked. However, since the perfect dinner hostess must orchestrate seemingly effortless entertaining, I've designed a sophisticated yet easy to master menu. I learned from author Joan Mackie to do virtually everything ahead, from the decorating and setting of the table to chilling beverages and preparing food—and sometimes even with reheating in mind!

The epiphany to form the Women's Culinary Network came to me while making endless waffles on the breakfast line at the now defunct King Ranch Spa, located just north of Toronto. Many of the chefs had become friends and were departing for other kitchen experiences. The WCN was our opportunity to keep in touch, and we have. An early meeting totalled three people, and now, a dozen years later, we plan on more than a hundred at each. From the original five founding members, the WCN has grown to more than 200. The secret of the organization is the willingness of the members to volunteer many hours ensuring that every meeting is fun, with plenty of time for socializing.

FRESH SPRINGTIME SUPPER

• MIXED GREEN SALAD WITH SEARED PEARS, TOASTED PINE NUTS AND CHÈVRE •

• SALMON FILLET WITH CRISPY HERB CRUST •

• OVEN NEW POTATOES WITH LEMON AND OREGANO •

• MAPLE CRÈME CARAMEL •

MIXED GREEN SALAD WITH SEARED PEARS, TOASTED PINE NUTS AND CHÈVRE

At Toronto's venerable Scaramouche Restaurant, I enjoyed a salad somewhat like this. The secret to this salad's success is the sautéed pears—an uncommon but delicious idea. Use a full 2 tbsp of vinegar if you prefer a tart dressing.

- 2 ripe but firm pears
- 1 tbsp butter
- 8 to 10 cups mixed salad greens (preferably including arugula or frisée)
- ¼ cup olive oil
- 1 to 2 tbsp balsamic vinegar
- ¼ tsp salt
- ⅛ tsp each pepper and granulated sugar
- ¼ cup toasted pine nuts (or coarsely chopped hazelnuts or slivered almonds)
- 2 oz (60g) goat cheese, crumbled

Peel, quarter and core pears; thinly slice each lengthwise. In skillet, heat butter over medium heat; cook pears for 8 to 10 minutes, turning once, or until golden and softened. Transfer to plate. (Can be wrapped tightly and refrigerated for up to 1 day.)

Wash and dry greens; cover and refrigerate until serving. Whisk oil with vinegar, salt, pepper and sugar; cover and set aside.

When ready to serve, toss greens with dressing; divide among chilled plates. Arrange pear slices over top; sprinkle with pine nuts and crumbled goat cheese. Serve immediately.

MAKES 6 SERVINGS.

SALMON FILLET WITH CRISPY HERB CRUST

Credit for this recipe must go to chef Nicholas Loshak of Nick of Thyme Catering and owner of Casablanca Bed and Breakfast in Kingston, Ontario. Have the fishmonger remove the bones and skin from the salmon. Allow about 5 to 6 oz of salmon per person.

- 1 side salmon (about 2½ lb), skin and bones removed
- ½ baguette or Italian loaf
- ½ cup lightly packed mixed fresh herbs (such as basil, thyme and oregano)
- 2 tbsp olive oil
- ¼ tsp salt
- ⅛ tsp pepper

Line bottom and sides of baking sheet with foil; coat with cooking spray or grease lightly with oil. Lay salmon on pan, brown fatty side down. Cut bread into chunks and place in food processor; whirl to make about 3 cups crumbs. Add herbs all at once; when finely chopped, add oil, salt and pepper. Whirl until forms moist crumb mixture that can be packed with fingers.

Using hands, firmly pat crumb mixture onto salmon surface, covering completely. Cover and refrigerate until needed. (Can be covered with plastic wrap, with frozen cold packs on top, and placed in bottom of refrigerator for up to 1 day. Fish stays fresher when really cold.)

When potatoes are almost done, unwrap chilled salmon and cook in 425°F oven for 15 to 18 minutes or until flakes easily with fork. Cut into portions; lift off foil and place fish on warm plates.

MAKES 6 SERVINGS.

OVEN NEW POTATOES WITH LEMON AND OREGANO

Here are Greek-style potatoes that are flavourful, brown and crisp with olive oil. The stock used adds great flavour.

8 medium new potatoes (unpeeled)
1 lemon
2 tbsp olive oil
½ cup chicken stock
2 tsp finely chopped fresh oregano (or 1 tsp dried)
½ tsp salt

Wash potatoes. Over piece of waxed paper and using small knife or zester, zest lemon into long, thin shreds, with little or no white pith. Squeeze 1 tbsp lemon juice; set aside.

Cut potatoes into halves or thirds and place on metal baking sheet; pour oil over top and stir until coated. Stir in stock, lemon juice, oregano and salt. Roast, uncovered, in 425°F oven, stirring often, for 45 minutes or until stock has evaporated and potatoes are browned and crisp. When almost done, place fish in oven to roast or, if necessary, remove potatoes from oven and keep warm while roasting fish. To serve, scatter lemon zest over potatoes.

MAKES 6 SERVINGS.

MAPLE CRÈME CARAMEL

This was a favourite dessert among King Ranch Spa guests. It is much lower in fat (only 7 g per serving) than usual crème caramel and has such outstanding taste and texture that the higher-fat versions are not nearly as good. Leftovers are great for breakfast! Garnish with fresh fruit such as berries or blood orange slices.

1¾ cups granulated sugar
⅓ cup water
6 eggs
3 cups whole milk
¼ cup pure maple syrup
2 tsp vanilla
½ tsp salt
Boiling water

In small, heavy-bottomed saucepan, bring 1¼ cups of the sugar and water to boil over medium-high heat; cook, without stirring, for about 8 minutes or until golden-coloured caramel syrup forms. (Watch carefully because caramel burns quickly.) Immediately pour some into each of 8 ungreased 6-oz custard cups. Carefully swirl hot caramel about halfway up sides of each cup. Place cups in roasting pan or divide between 2 smaller pans with high sides.

In large bowl, whisk eggs with milk, remaining sugar, maple syrup, vanilla and salt until well blended. Pour through fine strainer into caramel-lined cups, filling almost to top. Pull centre rack partially out of oven and set pan on rack.

Carefully pour boiling water between filled cups to come about 1 inch up side of pan. Slide rack back into oven; bake at 350°F for 35 minutes or until knife inserted near edge of one of the custards comes out clean. Using tongs, remove each custard cup to rack; let cool. Cover each with plastic wrap and refrigerate at least 24 hours or for up to 4 days. To serve, use fingers to pull away custard edge from cup; invert onto dessert plates, scraping out any caramel adhering to cup.

MAKES 8 SERVINGS.

KIM RABE

KIM RABE IS THE CHEF-OWNER OF ZEAL ENTERPRISES-PERSONAL CHEF SERVICE. KIM SOLVES THE "WHAT'S FOR DINNER?" DILEMMA BY PROVIDING MENU PLANNING, GROCERY SHOPPING AND THE PREPARATION OF MEALS IN CLIENTS' HOMES. HER SPECIALTIES ARE LOW-FAT, HEALTHY COOKING INCORPORATING SPECIALTY DIETS AND INTERNATIONAL CUISINE. KIM ALSO TEACHES COOKING CLASSES AT LOBLAWS AND REID'S INDEPENDENT IN PORT PERRY.

CURRIED LENTIL SOUP

This soup is easy to prepare as a delicious first course or a main meal with a fresh salad and crusty loaf of bread. This soup freezes well (for up to two months). Thaw in refrigerator and reheat over medium-low heat, stirring occasionally.

2 tbsp olive oil
1 onion, chopped
2 stalks celery, chopped
1 carrot, chopped
3 cloves garlic, minced
1 tbsp curry powder
1 tbsp tomato paste
5 cups vegetable stock
5 cups water
2 cups red lentils
2 bay leaves
Salt and pepper

In large saucepan, heat oil over medium heat; cook onion, celery, carrot and garlic for about 5 minutes or until onion is softened. Stir in curry powder; cook for 1 minute. Stir in tomato paste. Add stock, water, lentils and bay leaves; bring to boil. Reduce heat to low, cover and simmer for about 15 minutes or until lentils are softened and creamy. Season to taste with salt and pepper. Discard bay leaves before serving.

MAKES 6 SERVINGS.

CHRISTINE CUSHING

CHRISTINE CUSHING'S CULINARY TRAINING INCLUDES TORONTO'S GEORGE BROWN'S CULINARY ARTS PROGRAM AND THE PARIS-BASED ÉCOLE DE CUISINE LA VARENNE. SHE HAS WORKED IN SUCH TORONTO RESTAURANTS AS TRUFFLES (IN THE FOUR SEASONS) AND SCARAMOUCHE. HER FIRST STEP INTO TV WAS HOSTING "DISH IT OUT." SHE NOW HOSTS "CHRISTINE CUSHING LIVE," A ONE-HOUR LIVE COOKING SHOW ON THE FOOD NETWORK CANADA. CHRISTINE HAS AUTHORED TWO COOKBOOKS: *DISH IT OUT* (PENGUIN, 2000) AND *FEARLESS IN THE KITCHEN* (PENGUIN, 2002).

FOR AS LONG as I can remember, I have loved to cook. My mom's favourite story about me is that I asked for a plastic oven at age two. I dragged chairs up to the counter when I was six years old to make cakes for my brother and never wanted to leave the kitchen. Despite these obvious signs, I chose to follow a more practical academic path as a linguist. A couple of years of sitting in a classroom analyzing dictionaries and pronunciation cured me of that urge!

I ditched those pristine University of Toronto classrooms and entered the hot-and-heavy kitchens of

George Brown College and, later, La Varenne in Paris. Ultimately, it was that trip to France that changed the way I viewed food. Since then, I have simplified my cooking style but am still inspired to cook great food without all the formality. My path in the kitchen is driven by passion, curiosity, ethnic diversity and an insatiable desire to create.

The WCN has been very instrumental in my career, including the period when I worked at King Ranch Spa with many of the founding members. What was once just a circle of friends getting together has flourished into a professional support system.

PLEASURES OF PROVENCE

• ZUCCHINI WITH CHERRY TOMATOES AND THYME •
• PROVENÇAL ROAST LEG OF LAMB •
• FOUCASSE •
• LEMON FIG CAKE WITH LAVENDER HONEY GLAZE •

ZUCCHINI WITH CHERRY TOMATOES AND THYME

When cherry tomatoes are not in season, for a quick substitute, use canned plum tomatoes.

¼ cup extra-virgin olive oil
4 zucchini, sliced diagonally ¼ inch thick
1½ tsp salt
½ tsp pepper
2 large shallots, finely chopped
3 cloves garlic, chopped
2 tbsp chopped fresh thyme
2 cups cherry tomatoes, halved
2 bay leaves

In large skillet, heat 2 tbsp of the oil over high heat. Lay as much zucchini as will fit in skillet in single layer and cook for 2 minutes per side or until lightly browned; sprinkle with salt and pepper. Transfer to plate and repeat until all zucchini is cooked.

In medium saucepan, heat remaining olive oil over medium heat; cook shallots for 3 minutes or until slightly softened. Add garlic and cook for 1 minute or just until softened. Add tomatoes and bay leaves; reduce heat to medium-low. Simmer, stirring often, for 15 minutes or until tomatoes are softened. Add zucchini slices and thyme; cover and simmer for 3 to 5 minutes or until zucchini has absorbed sauce but still holds shape. Remove bay leaves. Taste and adjust seasoning.

MAKES 6 TO 8 SERVINGS.

PROVENÇAL ROAST LEG OF LAMB

This recipe is a true testament to how simplicity rules in Provence. You can always substitute a combination of rosemary, thyme, lavender and marjoram if you can't locate herbes de Provence, but they are readily available in most large supermarkets and fine food stores.

¼ cup olive oil
3 tbsp Dijon mustard
3 tbsp herbes de Provence
4 cloves garlic, chopped
Juice of ½ lemon
½ tsp pepper
1 leg of lamb (3½ lb)

In food processor, purée oil, mustard, herbes de Provence, garlic, lemon juice and pepper until smooth.

Rub lamb liberally with mixture and transfer to large roasting pan. Roast in 400°F oven for 20 minutes; reduce heat to 350°F and roast for 50 to 60 minutes longer or until meat thermometer inserted in centre registers 150°F for medium-rare, or to desired doneness. Transfer to platter and tent with foil; let stand for 15 minutes before carving.

MAKES 8 TO 10 SERVINGS.

FOUGASSE

This beautiful, leaf-shaped flatbread is an old favourite in Provence. If you are in a hurry, just shape it into an oval or square flatbread instead.

1 tsp granulated sugar
1½ cups lukewarm water
1 pkg active dry yeast (or 1 tbsp)
2¼ cups all-purpose flour
½ cup whole wheat flour
1½ tsp salt
¼ cup olive oil (approx)
1 tsp fresh rosemary leaves
½ tsp coarse sea salt
Pepper (optional)

In medium bowl, dissolve sugar in lukewarm water; whisk in yeast. Let stand for 5 minutes or until slightly foamy.

IF WORKING WITH STAND MIXER: Place all-purpose and whole wheat flours and salt in bowl of mixer. Add yeast mixture and knead with dough hook for 2 minutes at medium-low speed. Add 2 tbsp of the oil and knead for 1 minute. Turn out dough onto lightly floured surface and knead for a moment to get feel for dough.

IF WORKING BY HAND: Add 1 cup of the all-purpose flour and all the whole wheat flour to yeast mixture; stir until smooth. Sprinkle with salt and stir. Stir in 2 tbsp oil. Add 1 cup of the remaining all-purpose flour and stir to combine. Sprinkle work surface with remaining all-purpose flour. Turn out dough and knead for about 5 minutes, incorporating flour as necessary to prevent dough from sticking, until dough is smooth and elastic.

Place dough in greased bowl, turning to grease all over. Cover with plastic wrap and let rise for 1½ to 2 hours or until doubled in volume. Pull dough away from sides of bowl to deflate it; cover and let rise again for 30 minutes.

Line baking sheet with parchment paper, or grease with olive oil. Turn out dough onto pan; using your hands, flatten into teardrop shape 16 to 18 inches long and about 10 inches wide.

The classic fougasse is slashed in a veined leaf pattern: one central line with angled "veins" radiating from it. Position dough with wider base toward you and tapered end pointing away. With sharp serrated knife, cut 3 vertical slashes down centre of dough, each about 4 inches long, leaving 1-inch gap at either end of bread and 1-inch gap between each slash to resemble the centre stalk of leaf. Using fingers, pull open slashes.

On either side of each slash, and radiating upward away from it, cut 2 or 3 parallel diagonal slashes (like veins of leaf). Open slashes with fingers so they stay open as bread expands during baking.

Brush bread with about 1 tbsp olive oil; sprinkle with rosemary, salt and pepper (if using). Cover loosely and let rest for 30 minutes.

Bake on upper middle rack of 425°F oven for 18 to 20 minutes or until golden. Transfer to rack and let cool for 10 minutes before serving.

MAKES 1 LOAF.

LEMON FIG CAKE WITH LAVENDER HONEY GLAZE

This cake screams Provence! In a bind, use any kind of honey instead of lavender honey.

6 dried figs
2 cups cake-and-pastry flour, sifted
1 tsp each baking soda and baking powder
¼ tsp salt
¼ tsp each ground anise and cardamom
1¼ cups granulated sugar
½ cup buttermilk
¼ cup milk
¼ cup orange juice
⅓ cup olive oil
3 eggs, separated
2 tbsp lemon juice
1 tsp vanilla
Grated zest of 2 lemons

LAVENDER HONEY GLAZE:

⅓ cup lavender honey
⅓ cup water
Juice of ½ lemon
Zest of 1 lemon

Trim tops off figs and soak in boiling water for 10 minutes or until softened. Drain and set aside.

In medium bowl, sift together flour, baking soda, baking powder, salt, anise and cardamom. Stir in 1 cup of the sugar.

In food processor, combine figs, buttermilk, milk, orange juice, oil, egg yolks, lemon juice and vanilla; pulse until smooth. Add flour mixture, pulsing several times. Scrape down sides and process again for 30 seconds or until mixture is smooth. Transfer to medium bowl; stir in lemon zest.

In clean stainless steel bowl, beat egg whites on high speed until soft peaks form. Gradually add remaining sugar and beat until glossy peaks form. Fold whites gently but thoroughly into batter.

Brush 9-inch Bundt pan or mini Bundt pans with melted butter and sprinkle with flour. Pour in batter. Bake in 350°F oven for 20 to 25 minutes or until golden and cake tester comes out clean. Let cool in pan on rack for 15 minutes. Remove from pan; let cool completely on rack.

LAVENDER HONEY GLAZE: In small saucepan, combine honey, water, lemon juice and zest; bring to boil. Remove from heat and brush over cooled cakes.

MAKES 10 SERVINGS.

MICHELE VIG

MICHELE VIG HAS TURNED HER OBSESSION WITH FOOD INTO A SECOND CAREER. SHE STUDIED COOKING AT LIAISON COLLEGE OF CULINARY ARTS AND GEORGE BROWN COLLEGE IN TORONTO. HER COOKING CAREER HAS INCLUDED WORKING AS SOUS CHEF AT SEVERAL TORONTO RESTAURANTS, CATERING, AND TEACHING AT VARIOUS COOKING SCHOOLS.

CHICKEN AND FETTUCINE WITH PESTO PERNOD CREAM SAUCE

This is a great dish for entertaining—full of creamy indulgence yet simple to prepare.

1½ lb boneless skinless chicken breasts
1½ cups whipping cream
3 tbsp basil pesto
2 tbsp Pernod
2 tbsp freshly grated Parmesan cheese
Salt and pepper
8 oz fresh spinach fettucine
8 oz fresh egg fettucine

On greased grill over direct medium heat, grill chicken for about 6 minutes per side or until no longer pink inside. Slice across the grain into ¼-inch thick pieces. Cover and keep warm.

In small saucepan over medium heat, bring cream just to boil. Reduce heat and simmer until reduced by one-quarter or until thickened slightly. Stir in pesto, Pernod and Parmesan. Season to taste with salt and pepper.

Meanwhile, in large pot of boiling salted water, cook pasta for 5 minutes or until tender but firm; drain. Divide pasta among 4 plates. Spoon sauce over pasta and fan chicken slices on top.

MAKES 4 SERVINGS.

REGAN DALEY

REGAN DALEY IS A FREELANCE WRITER AND FORMER PASTRY CHEF WHOSE WORK HAS APPEARED IN *PRESIDENT'S CHOICE MAGAZINE, TORONTO LIFE, CANADIAN LIVING, CHATELAINE, THE TORONTO STAR* AND *FINE COOKING*. HER FIRST BOOK, *IN THE SWEET KITCHEN*, WAS PUBLISHED BY RANDOM HOUSE CANADA IN 2000, AND RECENTLY WON THE INTERNATIONAL ASSOCIATION OF CULINARY PROFESSIONALS AWARDS FOR BEST BOOK IN THE DESSERTS AND OTHER BAKING CATEGORY, AND THE BEST OVERALL COOKBOOK OF THE YEAR.

FOOD, AT ITS BEST, is a celebration of bounty and life and pleasure. This is most true when it is at its simplest: made with fresh, seasonal ingredients, prepared with thoughtfulness and integrity, and enjoyed slowly. I have been both a home cook and a professional chef, and I still believe it is possible for anyone to prepare the best meal, the best dish, in the world.

I am not an architect chef, just someone who is passionate about the magic in feeding body and soul. And for me, there is instant warmth, comfort and celebration in sweet things. After all, cake pretty much always means something good, even if it's just that there's cake!

We are a nation of sweets lovers. And fortunately for us, the land herself provides an enormously varied harvest: ravishing fruit, world-renowned wines, and a legacy of knowledge and recipes from generations of grandmothers and other ancestors from all over the world. Likewise, the Women's Culinary Network is itself a celebration of this abundance—a gathering of generous, like-minded women who believe passionately that making food and feeding people are among the highest priorities, and the deepest pleasures.

It's a toss-up as to which is more inspiring to me: my local farmers' market or my memories of my grandmothers' baking. The recipes that follow are a happy marriage of both.

FOUR SWEET ENDINGS

• WILDFLOWER HONEY ICE CREAM •
• CARAMELIZED PEACHES WITH SWEET WINE SABAYON •
• TARTINE D'ÉRABLE •
• WILD BLUEBERRY CRUMBLE •

WILDFLOWER HONEY ICE CREAM

This richly flavoured ice cream is wonderful on its own but also makes an exceptionally good accompaniment to many other desserts. It can be made with any good, flavourful honey.

½ cup plus 2 tbsp wildflower or other flavourful honey
2 cups light cream
6 egg yolks
1 cup whipping cream

In large, heavy saucepan, combine honey and cream. Bring just to boil; as soon as bubbles break on surface, remove pan from heat and let stand for 5 minutes.

In large bowl, lightly whisk egg yolks just to combine. Place damp kitchen towel around base of bowl to secure; gradually whisk in hot cream mixture.

Wash out saucepan, but don't dry it (this will help prevent scorching). Return custard to pan; cook over medium heat, stirring constantly with wooden spoon, for 7 to 10 minutes or until finger drawn across the back of spoon leaves clean trail. Immediately remove from heat; strain though fine-mesh sieve into bowl. Stir in whipping cream.

Press piece of plastic wrap directly onto surface of custard to prevent it from forming a skin. Poke a few holes in plastic with sharp knife to allow steam to escape. Refrigerate until very cold, at least 4 hours but preferably overnight.

Freeze in an ice cream maker following manufacturer's instructions. Transfer softly frozen ice cream to shallow freezer-proof dish; freeze until firm. Serve within 4 days.

MAKES ABOUT 4 CUPS.

CARAMELIZED PEACHES WITH SWEET WINE SABAYON

This dessert is sexy and so simple. If you can, do use icewine for the sabayon, but a lovely Canadian late-harvest Vidal or Riesling would be wonderful, too.

¼ cup butter
¾ cup granulated sugar
5 or 6 large ripe peaches (peeled if desired), pitted and cut into ½-inch pieces

SABAYON:

6 egg yolks
½ cup granulated sugar
½ cup icewine, or other late-harvest sweet white wine

In large heavy skillet or saucepan, melt butter over medium-high heat until foaming. Add sugar, stirring constantly until melted and begins to turn colour (mixture may separate slightly—it *will* homogenize again!). Watch closely and stir slowly until mixture comes together and is about the colour of toffee. Immediately slide peaches into caramel (stand back to avoid any splatters). Allow peaches to settle, then stir gently until golden and well coated. Spoon into individual serving dishes (preferably heatproof glass) and set aside.

SABAYON: In large stainless steel bowl, whisk egg yolks with sugar; whisk in wine. Set bowl over saucepan of barely simmering water (do not let water boil). Whisk constantly until mixture is light, foamy and tripled in volume. Spoon sabayon over caramelized peaches and serve immediately.

MAKES 6 SERVINGS.

TARTINE D'ÉRABLE

This gloriously messy French-Canadian dessert (also called tartine d'antan *and* tranche à l'érable) *is so simple it barely needs a recipe. Think of it as a traditional, homey, wildly addictive variation on cinnamon toast. Maple sugar blocks are sold (usually in ½-lb portions) at specialty grocers' or farmers' markets that sell maple products.*

6 thick slices very fresh homemade-style white or whole-grain bread
1 block maple sugar (or 12 tbsp granulated maple sugar)
1 cup whipped cream

Wrap bread slices in foil; heat in 330°F oven for 5 to 10 minutes or just until warm.

Place 1 slice on each of 6 large dessert plates. Grate block sugar generously over each slice, or sprinkle each with 1½ to 2 tbsp granulated maple sugar. Spoon cream over top and serve immediately.

MAKES 6 SERVINGS.

WILD BLUEBERRY CRUMBLE

Crunchy, dark and sweet, this crumble is not a bad breakfast either. In a pinch, cultivated blueberries can work, too.

TOPPING:

¾ cup all-purpose flour
¾ cup old-fashioned rolled oats
¾ cup packed dark brown sugar
¾ cup cold unsalted butter, cut into small pieces

FILLING:

¾ cup granulated sugar
6 tbsp cornstarch
¼ tsp ground cinnamon
6 cups wild blueberries
2 tsp lemon juice

In bowl, combine flour, oats and brown sugar. Using pastry cutter or 2 knives, cut in butter until largest pieces are about the size of oats. Using fingers, rub mixture until a crumbly dough forms; cover and refrigerate until needed. (Can be refrigerated for up to 2 days.)

In large bowl, combine granulated sugar, cornstarch and cinnamon. Add berries and lemon juice; toss gently to coat. Spread fruit mixture evenly in greased, shallow 10-cup baking dish (preferably ceramic). Crumble oat mixture evenly over fruit.

Place dish on foil- or parchment paper–lined baking sheet. Bake in 375°F oven for 35 to 45 minutes for shallow dish, 45 to 50 minutes for deeper casserole, or until topping is crisp and golden and filling is bubbling through cracks. Let stand for 15 minutes before serving. Serve warm or at room temperature.

MAKES 6 TO 8 SERVINGS.

TRISH MAGWOOD

TRISH MAGWOOD IS A GRADUATE OF NEW YORK'S PETER KUMP'S COOKING SCHOOL AND OWNS AND OPERATES DISH COOKING STUDIO IN TORONTO. ALL UNDER ONE ROOF, DISH INCLUDES A CAFÉ, FULL-SERVICE CATERING COMPANY, COOKING SCHOOL AND STORE. FOR MORE INFORMATION, CHECK OUT WWW.DISHCOOKINGSTUDIO.COM

FROZEN LEMON SOUFFLÉ

This is an elegant make-ahead dessert, perfect for entertaining. Make it up to one week ahead, removing from freezer 20 minutes before serving. I like to decorate slices with candied lilacs, edible flowers or seasonal fresh berries and serve with an icewine.

1 pkg (8 oz/250 g) vanilla wafers
½ cup butter, melted
4 eggs, separated
½ cup lemon juice
1 cup granulated sugar
2 tbsp grated lemon zest
⅛ tsp cream of tartar
⅛ tsp salt
1½ cups whipping cream

Grind vanilla wafers in food processor until fine crumbs. Stir in melted butter until combined. Press mixture onto bottom of 9-inch springform pan.

In large bowl, whisk together egg yolks, lemon juice, ¼ cup of the sugar and lemon zest. In stainless steel bowl, beat egg whites until light and foamy. Add cream of tartar and salt; beat until soft peaks form. Gradually beat in remaining sugar until stiff peaks form.

In another bowl, beat whipping cream. Fold egg whites into egg yolk mixture, alternating with whipped cream, just until combined. Do not overmix.

Spoon mixture into prepared pan, gently smoothing top. Freeze for at least 8 hours or until firm.

MAKES 10 TO 12 SERVINGS.

CYNTHIA DAVID

CYNTHIA DAVID HOLDS A JOURNALISM DEGREE FROM RYERSON UNIVERSITY AND A CULINARY DIPLOMA FROM GEORGE BROWN COLLEGE, BOTH IN TORONTO. SHE SPENT NINE YEARS AS A NEWSPAPER FOOD EDITOR. HER ARTICLES HAVE APPEARED IN MAJOR MAGAZINES AND NEWSPAPERS, INCLUDING *CANADIAN LIVING, FOOD & DRINK, STYLE AT HOME, NATIONAL POST* AND *THE GLOBE AND MAIL.* IN 1997, SHE WAS INDUCTED AS A FELLOW INTO THE ONTARIO HOSTELRY INSTITUTE. IN 1999, SHE WAS NOMINATED FOR A NATIONAL MAGAZINE AWARD.

PERHAPS IT WAS my Lebanese grandmother who inspired my passion for food. I can still see her removing football-shaped loaves of bread from the hot oven, which soon collapsed into tender flat discs. Other days, we tiptoed around her apartment so we wouldn't disturb the bowl of setting yogurt swaddled in towels.

Aunt Pat continued my education, taking me to a serious seafood restaurant in Toronto with my best friend, Carolyn. I was so overwhelmed by the experience I could hardly speak, while Carolyn, who later became a teacher, chatted away the entire evening. I never dreamed that one day I'd be peeling potatoes in a one-star restaurant in the Loire, or making dumplings in Beijing with colleagues to celebrate the Chinese New Year.

Since then, I have plucked frozen icewine grapes from Ontario vineyards, watched the cranberry harvest on a tiny island off Cape Breton and caught salmon in a northern B.C. river. But it is the people I have met on my journey who I remember best, and whose stories I love to share. These recipes honour Canada's pork producers, whose product is prized the world over.

THE OTHER WHITE MEAT

• ASIAN WRAPS •
• HERB-ROASTED PORK LOIN •
• GINGER PORK CHOPS •
• SPICY SAUSAGE SUPPER •

ASIAN WRAPS

This easy wrap is a hit at parties because it packs an incredible amount of taste even though there are just a few ingredients. Prepare the filling up to a day in advance and recruit friends to help you roll. Look for rice paper wrappers and Thai basil in Asian stores. You will also want to find a dip for these wraps—either bottled peanut sauce (also called satay sauce) or Asian hot sauce.

12 oz ground pork
1 tbsp grated fresh ginger
¼ tsp pepper
½ cup hoisin sauce
4 green onions, chopped
25 rice paper wrappers (6-inch diameter)
25 large Thai (or regular) basil leaves

In skillet over medium-high heat, cook pork, ginger and pepper for 5 minutes or until no pink remains in pork. Pour off fat. Stir in hoisin sauce and green onions. Let cool.

Immerse 1 rice paper wrapper in bowl of hot water for about 30 seconds or until just softened. On cutting board covered with clean tea towel, lay wrapper flat. Place basil leaf about one third of the way up from bottom of wrapper. Top with 1 tbsp of the pork mixture.

Fold bottom of rice paper over filling; fold in sides and roll up as tightly as possible. Cover with damp cloth as you work so wrappers don't dry out. Repeat with remaining wrappers and filling.

Arrange in single layer in airtight container and cover with damp paper towels. Serve within 3 hours.

MAKES 25 WRAPS.

HERB-ROASTED PORK LOIN

When you don't feel like chopping fresh herbs, wrap a small sage leaf around each garlic piece before you insert it in the roast. If your roast is tied, simply insert rosemary sprigs between meat and string. Crush fennel using a mortar and pestle or enclose in a plastic bag and crush with a rolling pin.

- 3 lb pork loin rib roast
- 4 cloves garlic, halved
- 3 tbsp finely chopped fresh rosemary (or 1 tbsp dried)
- 2 tbsp finely chopped fresh sage (or 1 tsp dried)
- 2 tsp crushed fennel seeds
- 1 tsp salt
- ½ tsp pepper
- 1 tbsp olive oil
- ¼ cup dry white wine
- 1 cup chicken stock
- Salt and pepper

Make 8 small slits in roast; push garlic half into each. In small bowl, combine rosemary, sage, fennel, salt and pepper. Rub oil over roast; press herbs evenly on meat.

Place roast on rack over shallow pan. Roast in 325°F oven for 1½ hours or until thermometer inserted in centre reads 150°F to 155°F. Transfer to cutting board and tent with foil; let stand for 15 minutes before carving.

Drain fat from roasting pan; place pan on stove and add wine. Bring to boil over high heat, scraping up any brown bits. Add stock and cook until reduced by half. Season to taste with salt and pepper.

MAKES 6 TO 8 SERVINGS.

GINGER PORK CHOPS

This ginger-spiked fall dish comes together quickly, so have all the ingredients prepared and on hand before you start cooking. Because pork is very lean, it's important not to overcook it. A hint of pink is a good thing!

- 1 to 2 tbsp vegetable oil
- 4 boneless centre-cut pork chops
- Salt and pepper
- 3 tbsp cider vinegar
- 2 tbsp granulated sugar
- ⅔ cup dry white wine
- ⅔ cup chicken stock
- 1 firm ripe pear, peeled, cored and cut into 8 wedges
- 1 piece (2 inches) ginger, peeled and cut into thin strips
- 4 green onions, cut into ½-inch lengths
- 2 tsp cornstarch, dissolved in 2 tsp water

In large skillet, heat oil over medium high; cook pork chops for 3 minutes per side or until well browned. Sprinkle both sides with salt and pepper. Transfer to plate; cover and keep warm.

Add vinegar and sugar to hot skillet; stir to dissolve sugar. Cook for 1 minute or until mixture turns dark amber. Pour in wine and stock; cook, stirring, for 30 seconds to dissolve caramel. Add pear and ginger; cook, uncovered, for 3 minutes, turning pears occasionally. Add green onions; cook for 2 minutes or until pears are tender. Whisk in cornstarch mixture. Reduce heat to medium-low; return pork to skillet. Simmer gently for 1 minute or until pork is heated through.

MAKES 4 SERVINGS.

SPICY SAUSAGE SUPPER

Good-quality sausages are highly underrated. They're so full of flavour, you hardly need to add any other ingredients for a great-tasting dish. This simple, speedy pasta is high in fibre and an excellent source of iron.

12 oz hot or sweet Italian sausages
1 can (28 oz/796 mL) tomatoes
1 tbsp tomato paste
1 tsp fennel seeds, crushed
8 oz mushrooms, quartered
2 zucchini
4 cups penne or rigatoni pasta
¼ cup freshly grated Parmesan cheese

Remove casings from sausages; crumble meat into large nonstick skillet. Cook over medium-high heat, stirring occasionally, for about 5 minutes or until browned. Drain fat from pan.

Add tomatoes, tomato paste and fennel, breaking up tomatoes with spoon. Add mushrooms; bring to boil. Reduce heat to medium and simmer for 10 minutes. Meanwhile, cut zucchini in half lengthwise; slice thinly crosswise. Add to pan; cook for 5 minutes or until tender.

Meanwhile, in large pot of boiling salted water, cook pasta for 8 to 10 minutes or until tender but firm. Drain well and return to pot. Add sauce; toss to coat. Serve sprinkled with Parmesan cheese.

MAKES 4 SERVINGS.

JOANNE LEESE

JOANNE LEESE TRAINED AS PASTRY CHEF AT SAN FRANCISCO'S RENOWNED TANTE MARIE COOKING SCHOOL. SHE HAS BAKED IN SOME OF TORONTO'S MOST CRITICALLY ACCLAIMED RESTAURANTS AND IS NOW A FREELANCE FOOD CONSULTANT AND COOKING SCHOOL COORDINATOR FOR THE LIQUOR CONTROL BOARD OF ONTARIO'S (LCBO'S) COOKING SCHOOL. JOANNE ENJOYS TEACHING AS WELL AS RECIPE DEVELOPMENT AND TESTING.

MOCHA PRALINE TORTE

The meringues for this torte can be made in advance and stored in an airtight container for a few days, or you can freeze them. The torte should be assembled on the day it is served. When serving, use a large, wet, serrated knife, rinsing under hot water after each slice.

8 egg whites (at room temperature)
1 tsp lemon juice
½ tsp salt
2 cups granulated sugar
½ tsp vanilla

PRALINE:

½ cup granulated sugar
¾ cup whole unblanched almonds

MOCHA FILLING:

3 cups whipping cream
¼ cup icing sugar
½ cup Tia Maria or other coffee liqueur
1 tbsp instant coffee dissolved in 1 tbsp warm water
3 oz semisweet chocolate, coarsely chopped

Line 2 baking sheets with parchment paper. Using an 8-inch round cake pan as guide, draw 2 circles on each sheet of paper.

In bowl, beat egg whites, lemon juice and salt until soft peaks form. Gradually beat in sugar, a little at a time, until stiff and shiny but not dry. Beat in vanilla.

With spatula, spread meringue evenly over circles on baking sheets. Bake in 225°F oven for 2½ hours or until crisp and firm. Let cool.

PRALINE: In small, heavy saucepan over medium heat, combine sugar and almonds, stirring occasionally, until sugar melts and starts to turn golden brown. Immediately pour mixture onto greased baking sheet; let cool and harden. When cool, process in blender or food processor until finely ground.

MOCHA FILLING: In bowl, whip cream until thickened; add sugar and beat until stiff. Fold in liqueur and coffee.

Place 1 meringue on serving platter or tray; spread with one-quarter of the filling. Sprinkle with one-quarter of the chocolate and 2 tbsp of the praline. Repeat with remaining meringues, filling, chocolate and praline. Refrigerate for at least 2 hours before serving.

MAKES 10 SERVINGS.

NAOMI DUGUID

TRAVELLER, COOK, PHOTOGRAPHER AND WRITER NAOMI DUGUID WORKS WITH JEFFREY ALFORD. THEIR INTEREST IS IN UNDERSTANDING AND APPRECIATING DAILY HOME-COOKED FOODS AND THE CULTURAL CONTEXT OF FOODS. THEIR AWARD-WINNING COOKBOOK *HOT SOUR SALTY SWEET: A CULINARY JOURNEY THROUGH SOUTHEAST ASIA* (RANDOM HOUSE CANADA, 2000) EXPLORES THE CUISINES OF THE MEKONG REGION WITH RECIPES, STORIES AND COLOUR PHOTOGRAPHS. THEIR EARLIER BOOKS ARE *FLATBREADS AND FLAVORS: A BAKER'S ATLAS* (1995) AND *SEDUCTIONS OF RICE* (1998).

SOMEHOW TRAVEL and being out in the world always seemed more interesting than a "serious" job. So whenever possible, I headed away—sometimes for short trips, other times for longer immersions. Eventually, through what feels like wonderful good luck, I ended up piecing together, with my partner, Jeffrey, a life structured around food and travel, as well as family. We've been working and travelling together for over 16 years now, but the chance to be out in the world, tasting and smelling the texture of life in other places, still feels rare and precious.

As a foreigner, however well intended and attentive, I know I can never do more than scratch the surface of another place or culture. With food, though, I can transmit my appreciation of places and people. These recipes are all from mainland southeast Asia—from Laos and southern Yunnan and Thailand and Vietnam. It's probably my favourite part of the world, as a traveller and as an eater.

SOJOURN INTO SOUTHEAST ASIAN

• CHICKEN SOUP WITH TOFU CUBES •
• YARD-LONGS WITH TOMATO •
• SHAN ROASTED EGGPLANT •
• SPICY FISH CURRY WITH COCONUT MILK •

CHICKEN SOUP WITH TOFU CUBES

This easy Chinese-Vietnamese soup has a delicate flavour and is very attractive as part of a rice-based meal. Clear, mild soups like this are meant to be sipped throughout the meal. Trim the fat from the pork and save it to use in the Fish Curry.

4 oz boneless pork shoulder or butt, trimmed of fat
3 tbsp Thai or Vietnamese fish sauce
Pepper
Pinch granulated sugar
8 cups mild homemade or store-bought chicken stock
Salt
8 to 10 oz tofu, cut into ½-inch cubes
2 to 3 green onions, finely chopped
¼ cup fresh coriander leaves

An hour before you wish to serve the soup, slice pork as thinly as possible across the grain; cut slices into 1-inch lengths.

In small bowl, mix together pork, 1 tbsp of the fish sauce, generous grinding of pepper, and sugar. Cover and let stand for 30 minutes.

In large saucepan over medium-high heat, bring stock to boil; add pork slices, reduce heat to medium and simmer for 5 minutes or until cooked through. Stir in remaining fish sauce. Taste and add salt if desired. Just before serving, add tofu cubes and simmer for 3 to 5 minutes or until heated through.

In each serving bowl, place several pork slices, some tofu cubes and a sprinkling of green onion; ladle broth over top. Sprinkle with coriander leaves and serve immediately. Pass remaining green onion and coriander in a small dish so guests can add to soup as they wish.

MAKES 4 TO 6 SERVINGS.

NOTE: *This soup is traditionally served over rice as a more substantial meal-in-one soup: Allow ½ cup or more cooked rice per person. Place rice in each bowl, then pour soup over top, distributing tofu and pork among the bowls.*

YARD-LONGS WITH TOMATO

Yard-long beans aren't a yard long, but about 18 inches in length and slender. They're sold in bundles in Chinese and southeast Asian shops and in Indian grocery stores. Look for firm and crunchy—not soft and wrinkled—beans, though slightly tired beans will stir-fry well. Green beans can be substituted for yard-long beans, though there will a difference in flavour and texture. Begin cooking about seven minutes before you want to serve the meal. Have all your ingredients prepared and at hand.

2 tbsp peanut or vegetable oil
2 tbsp minced garlic
3 green onions, trimmed, smashed flat with the side of a cleaver and cut into 1-inch lengths

¾ lb yard-long beans or fresh green beans, trimmed and cut into 1½-inch lengths
3 large ripe tomatoes, cut into wedges
1 tbsp Thai or Vietnamese fish sauce
1 tbsp soy sauce
½ tsp granulated sugar
½ cup water or stock
Pepper
Fresh coriander leaves

In heavy skillet or wok, heat oil over medium-high heat. Tilt skillet to coat surface with oil; add garlic and stir-fry for 1 minute. Add green onions; stir-fry for 30 seconds. Add beans; continue stir-frying for about 2 minutes or until beans start to turn bright green. Stir in tomatoes, fish sauce, soy sauce and sugar. Add water and bring to boil; cook 2 to 4 minutes or until beans are just tender.

Serve on plate or in very shallow wide bowl; sprinkle with pepper and garnish with coriander.

MAKES 4 TO 6 SERVINGS, WITH RICE.

NOTE: *For a vegetarian version, substitute 1 tsp salt for the fish sauce.*

SHAN ROASTED EGGPLANT

This innovative vegetable dish from the Shan people of northern Thailand and Burma, called makeua tam *(literally "pounded eggplant"), is a seductive combination of roasted or grilled eggplant and fresh flavours. Traditionally, it includes egg, which gives extra substance and creaminess, but we think it's good with or without the egg. We also tend to use more hot peppers than the one called for here (which gives a gentle, smooth heat), so prepare according to taste. Leftovers are very good quickly fried in a little oil with some chopped tomato.*

4 Asian eggplants (about 8 inches long)
1 dried red Thai hot pepper (or more to taste)
½ tsp salt (or to taste)
½ cup coarsely chopped shallots
½ cup coarsely chopped fresh mint
1 to 2 tbsp vegetable oil
1 or 2 cloves garlic, minced
1 hard-cooked egg, finely chopped (optional)

Prick eggplants with fork and place on baking sheet. Bake in upper third of 450°F oven for 30 to 45 minutes or until thoroughly brown and softened. Alternatively, place pricked eggplants on grill over medium heat; cover and cook, turning to expose all sides to heat, until thoroughly browned and softened. Set aside until cool enough to handle.

Meanwhile, heat cast-iron or heavy skillet over high heat; cook hot pepper just until it puffs, about 1 minute. Remove from heat, trim off stem and mince; set aside. In same skillet, dry-cook shallots turning occasionally, for about 6 minutes or until blackened on all sides.

Using mortar and pestle, grind shallots, hot peppers and salt into paste; set aside. Alternatively, place in blender and chop, adding a little warm water if neccessary to help make paste. Transfer to bowl and set aside.

Peel away and discard eggplant skins and stems. Transfer eggplant to mortar and pound, blending into other ingredients. Alternatively, add eggplant to paste in bowl and use fork to blend together. Stir in half of the mint.

In heavy skillet or wok, heat oil over medium-high heat; tilt skillet to coat surface with oil. Add garlic and reduce heat to medium; after 30 seconds, add eggplant mixture and cook for 5 minutes, stirring constantly. Taste and adjust seasoning. Serve in shallow bowl garnished with remaining mint and finely chopped egg (if using).

MAKES 4 SERVINGS AS PART OF RICE MEAL.

SPICY FISH CURRY WITH COCONUT MILK

This Lao freshwater fish dish is a kind of curry—moist and savoury, but with relatively little sauce. The original recipe, from which this is adapted, appears in the cookbook of Pia Sing, long ago the head chef to the last king of Laos. Remind your guests that the wild lime leaves, like bay leaves in other cuisines, are not to be eaten. Serve with plain jasmine rice and a plate of sliced cucumber or other crisp raw vegetables.

1 lb fish fillet (catfish, tilapia or other freshwater fish)
½ tsp salt
¼ tsp pepper
2 dried red Thai hot peppers, soaked in ¼ cup warm water until softened
5 small to medium green onions
2 small shallots, chopped
1½ cups canned or fresh-pressed coconut milk
2 tbsp minced pork fat*, or peanut or vegetable oil
2 tbsp Thai fish sauce
3 to 5 whole wild lime leaves, fresh or frozen**
Pepper
½ cup coarsely chopped fresh coriander

**Use fat reserved from pork in Chicken Soup with Tofu Cubes recipe, page 40.*
***Available in Asian supermarkets.*

Slice fish into pieces less than ½ inch thick. In medium bowl, toss fish with salt and pepper to coat. Cover and set aside.

Drain peppers, reserving soaking water. Mince peppers, discarding any tough stem ends. Place in mortar with pinch salt, or in blender. Cut green part off green onions (leaving about 2 inches of tender green stem and bulb). Finely chop green part; measure ½ cup and set aside. Trim off roots, then finely chop bulbs and tender green stems. Place onion and shallots in mortar or blender with peppers; blend until paste forms, adding a little of the reserved pepper soaking water as necessary to reach consistency of paste. Set aside in bowl.

If using canned coconut milk, measure out 1 cup of the thickest part into bowl and set aside. Measure out another ½ cup of thinner (more watery) coconut milk and set aside. If using fresh pressed, set aside 1 cup of the first pressing and ½ cup of second pressing.

Heat wok or heavy skillet over medium-high heat. Add pork fat; when melted, add fish pieces. Fry for 3 minutes per side or until browned. Transfer to plate and set aside.

Place wok over high heat; add 1 cup thick coconut milk and reduce heat to medium-high. Bring to boil; cook for 3 minutes, stirring occasionally. Stir in spice paste; cook for 3 to 5 minutes or until mixture begins to smell fragrant. Add remaining coconut milk and fish sauce. When liquid returns to simmer, add fried fish pieces and lime leaves, stirring fish gently to coat with sauce. Add most of the reserved chopped green onion leaves; cook for 30 seconds. Serve on platter topped with pepper, remaining green onion and coriander.

MAKES 4 SERVINGS.

FOOD PRODUCT DEVELOPER

As the landscape of Canadian grocery shopping evolves, so does the field of product development. A constant, dizzying stream of new food products is appearing on supermarket shelves daily. Not surprisingly, many WCN members are involved in this field. They are the brains behind the new products that either capture the market, busting previous sales records or, more ignominiously, die silently on the shelves, never to return.

Most product developers are part of a team that analyzes market trends, identifies a need, then develops a product to meet those needs. A good product developer creates something that appeals to the senses, budget and sometimes even the conscience. The idea can originate at the marketing level or through research, whether it's travelling the world (as the President's Choice motto proclaims) or sleuthing local food markets, restaurants, food shows or cooking classes.

Depending on the product, it may be identified and developed in food plants abroad or locally. Regardless of where it is made, any new product will undergo extensive testing for flavour, appearance, texture, freezing stability, shelf life, and so on. It's not uncommon for a product to go through dozens of prototypes until a final version is defined. Plus, taste tests will be conducted, often involving elaborate tasting panels.

Creativity and persistence are requirements for this type of job, not to mention a pure love of food—a common thread found throughout the WCN.

M.G.

NANCY LEWIS

NANCY LEWIS IS AN ANTHROPOLOGIST, EDUCATOR AND FOOD ENTHUSIAST WHO LEARNED TO LOVE THAI FOOD DURING THE FIVE YEARS SHE LIVED IN THAILAND. NANCY HAS BEEN TEACHING THAI AND INTERNATIONAL COOKING IN THE TORONTO AREA FOR MANY YEARS.

THAI GRILLED BEEF SALAD

This delicious room-temperature salad is perfect for hot summer days. It's also a great way to use up leftovers; substitute 2 cups of leftover cooked beef, pork or chicken, cut into bite-size slices, for the steak. Serve with steamed Thai jasmine rice.

¾ lb steak (sirloin or flank) or beef tenderloin
1 tbsp long-grain white rice, uncooked
2 tbsp lime juice
2 tbsp fish sauce or soy sauce
2 tbsp water
1 tsp hot pepper flakes
1 tsp packed brown sugar
2 shallots, chopped
2 green onions, white and green parts, chopped
½ cup coarsely chopped fresh coriander leaves
½ cup coarsely chopped mint leaves

On greased grill over medium-high heat, grill beef for 6 minutes per side for medium rare or until desired doneness. Let cool. Slice into lengthwise strips about 2 inches wide, then cut strips into bite-size pieces. Transfer to bowl.

In small skillet over medium heat, toast rice, stirring often, for 5 minutes or until golden. Let cool. Using mortar and pestle, spice grinder or food processor, grind rice until powdery but with partial grains still visible. (This adds a pleasant toasted flavour, and thickens the sauce.)

In small saucepan, combine ground rice, lime juice, fish sauce, water, hot pepper flakes and brown sugar; cook, stirring, for 1 to 2 minutes or until slightly thickened. Pour over beef. Stir in shallots. Let cool to room temperature. (Can be prepared to this point, covered and refrigerated for up to 8 hours.)

Before serving, stir in green onions, coriander and mint. Toss to combine.

MAKES 4 SERVINGS.

HEATHER EPP

HEATHER EPP IS A FREELANCE RECIPE TESTER AND DEVELOPER. SHE ATTENDED THE STRATFORD CHEFS SCHOOL AND FOCUSED HER EARLY FOOD WORK ON SPA CUISINE AND HEALTH-RELATED SPECIAL DIETS. WHEN WORKING IN THE CANADIAN LIVING TEST KITCHEN, HEATHER CAME TO LOVE RECIPE TESTING AND DEVELOPMENT. SHE HAS WORKED FREELANCE ON A NUMBER OF COOKBOOKS AS WELL AS FOR THE *TORONTO STAR.*

MY INTEREST in cuisine stemmed from a curiosity about diet and physical health but has evolved into a broader curiosity about the role of food in *emotional* health. In other words, what foods are soul-satisfying, fun, elegant, guilt-inducing, cleansing, celebratory or memory-invoking? They all have their place and season.

My favourite meal to serve is brunch—placed at that perfect time in the middle of the day. Brunch can be incredibly versatile, with numerous menu possibilities, and usually leading to a great nap afterward.

For me, much of the pleasure of food is cooking with, and for, other people. When I worked at King Ranch Spa, north of Toronto, I met wonderful women chefs who inspired and challenged my cooking knowledge. Several of us eventually formed the Women's Culinary Network to maintain our supportive connections and to invite other women in the industry to join us. The WCN has grown tremendously since those days, and I'm constantly amazed at, and inspired by, the variety of food industry professions represented among the membership.

A LUNCH THAT COULD BE BRUNCH

• SQUASH AND PEAR SOUP •
• WILD MUSHROOM AND ONION TART WITH PECAN CRUST •
• WARM SEASONAL VEGETABLE SALAD •
• AUTUMN FRUIT PARFAIT •

SQUASH AND PEAR SOUP

This hearty yet soothing soup is a great make-ahead for leftovers or for freezing. I use hubbard squash for its deep orange colour, dry texture and full flavour, but turban or butternut are good, too. Adjust the liquid added to make the consistency you like.

5 lb hubbard squash (or turban or butternut squash), halved and seeded
2 sweet potatoes (about 1¼ lb)
2 tbsp butter
1 onion, chopped
2 pears, peeled, cored and chopped
2 tbsp finely chopped fresh ginger
6 cups vegetable stock
4 cups water
½ cup white wine
Salt and pepper

Place squash halves, cut side down, on greased baking sheet. Bake in 350°F oven for about ½ hour. Add whole sweet potatoes to baking sheet; bake for 1 hour. Test squash and sweet potatoes with a fork to ensure they are very soft. Let stand until cool enough to handle. Scoop out squash flesh; discard hull. Peel and thickly slice sweet potatoes.

In large saucepan, melt butter over medium heat; cook onion, stirring, for about 3 minutes or until beginning to soften. Stir in pears and ginger; cook, stirring, for 3 minutes. Add squash, sweet potatoes, stock, water and wine; bring to boil. Reduce heat and simmer, covered, for about 25 minutes to allow flavours to blend. In batches, purée soup in blender or food processor. Add a little more water if soup seems thick. Season to taste with salt and pepper.

Serve in shallow soup bowls with crusty bread.

MAKES 8 TO 10 SERVINGS.

WILD MUSHROOM AND ONION TART WITH PECAN CRUST

I first served a version of this tart as part of an autumn wedding meal; it was such a hit that the bride and groom sent out my recipe with their thank-you notes. To reduce costs, I sometimes make it using half button mushrooms and half oyster mushrooms—and it still tastes great.

CRUST:

2 cups all-purpose flour
1 cup finely chopped pecans
⅓ cup cold butter, cubed
½ tsp salt
1 egg yolk
3 to 4 tbsp cold water

FILLING:

1 tbsp each olive oil and butter
4 medium onions, chopped
1 lb mushrooms (oyster, chanterelle, portobello, shiitake), stems trimmed and sliced
1 cup light sour cream
½ lb Gruyère cheese, shredded
¼ cup finely sliced green onions
2 tbsp finely chopped fresh thyme
2 tbsp finely chopped fresh parsley
Salt and pepper

CRUST: In food processor, combine flour, pecans, butter and salt; pulse for a few seconds until mixture resembles coarse crumbs. In measuring cup, lightly beat together egg yolk and 3 tbsp water. Pour into flour mixture; pulse just until dough begins to clump together. If dough looks dry, add another 1 tbsp water. Do not overmix or dough will be tough.

Press evenly over bottom and sides of 12-inch tart pan with removable bottom. Prick bottom of pastry all over with fork. Freeze for 30 minutes. (If making crust ahead of time—up to 3 days—cover well with plastic wrap or plastic bag before freezing.) Bake crust directly from freezer in 350°F oven for about 25 minutes or until light golden. Let cool slightly.

FILLING: In large, heavy skillet, heat oil and butter over medium heat; cook chopped onions, stirring occasionally, for about 25 minutes or until golden. Add mushrooms; cook for about 10 minutes or until softened.

In bowl, combine onion mixture, sour cream, cheese, green onions, thyme and parsley. Season to taste with salt and pepper. Pour over baked tart shell. Bake in 350°F oven for about 35 minutes or until top is deep brown. Let cool for about 5 minutes before serving.

MAKES 8 TO 10 SERVINGS.

WARM SEASONAL VEGETABLE SALAD

For this colourful side dish, feel free to vary the ingredients depending on what your garden or market has available. Sometimes I substitute rapini or collard greens for the kale. Sweet peppers are a nice addition, too.

1 bunch kale (about 1 lb)
Salt
½ cup olive oil
1 bunch broccoli, trimmed and cut into florets
1 small head cauliflower, cut into florets
4 large carrots, peeled and sliced into matchsticks
¼ cup water
2 cloves garlic, minced
4 plum tomatoes, quartered
⅓ cup finely chopped fresh basil
⅓ cup lemon juice
Pepper

Trim hard stems from kale leaves; wash thoroughly and slice into 1½-inch wide strips. Place in large saucepan over boiling water; steam for about 10 minutes or until dark green and tender. Sprinkle with pinch salt and set aside.

Meanwhile, heat 2 tbsp of the oil in large skillet over medium heat; cook broccoli, cauliflower and carrots, stirring, for about 2 minutes. Add water, cover and steam for 6 to 8 minutes or until tender but still a bit crisp. Uncover; allow any remaining liquid to evaporate.

Stir in garlic; cook, stirring, for about 1 minute. Add tomatoes, basil, lemon juice, remaining oil, and salt and pepper to taste; toss to combine.

Place kale leaves around outer edge of large platter. Pile vegetables in centre. Drizzle any liquid from vegetable mixture over kale. Serve immediately.

MAKES 8 SERVINGS.

AUTUMN FRUIT PARFAIT

I have a green gage plum tree in my front yard, and some years it produces oodles of fruit. I have found that these plums, despite their unusual colour, are wonderful for eating fresh as well as for cooking. If you can't find green gage, any type of fresh, ripe plum will do.

1 lb plums, pitted and sliced (about 12)
1 lb sweet apples, cored and sliced (about 4)
¾ lb Bartlett pears, cored and cubed (about 3)
¼ cup water
2 tbsp good-quality marmalade
2 tbsp lemon juice
6 cups plain yogurt
¾ cup icing sugar
1 tbsp finely grated orange zest
1 tbsp finely grated lemon zest
1 tsp vanilla

In large saucepan over medium-high heat, combine plums, apples, pears, water, marmalade and lemon juice; bring to boil. Reduce heat and simmer, covered, for about 5 minutes. Remove from heat. Let cool completely.

Place yogurt in sieve or colander lined with clean tea towel or cheesecloth; place sieve over bowl. Let stand in refrigerator for 3 to 4 hours or until thickened slightly. Discard liquid in bowl. In clean bowl, gently stir together yogurt, icing sugar, orange and lemon zest, and vanilla.

Divide fruit and yogurt mixtures among 8 parfait glasses. Beginning with fruit and ending with yogurt, make 2 layers of each. Serve immediately or chill for up to 1 hour before serving.

MAKES 8 SERVINGS.

JANICE FRIIS

JANICE FRIIS IS AN ARTIST, WRITER AND SOLE PROPRIETOR OF JANART CREATIVE SERVICES. SHE'S THE AUTHOR OF *THE BREAKFAST COMPANION* (WORD OF MOUTH PUBLISHING, 1998), A COOKBOOK CONTAINING MORE THAN 200 RECIPES PERTAINING TO THE FIRST MEAL OF THE DAY. WHEN NOT COOKING OR PAINTING UP A STORM, SHE WRITES A QUARTERLY NEWSLETTER ON CREATIVITY, ENTITLED *THE JANART TIMES*.

DO-AHEAD CHEESE SOUFFLÉ

Soufflé means "breath," and just as we cannot hold ours for very long, so too a baked soufflé does not keep its puff for long. This recipe is very easy and can be prepared three hours ahead. It will hold its "breath" a little longer than most soufflés, which is why it's always a spectacular success.

½ cup sifted all-purpose flour
1½ tsp salt
½ tsp paprika
¼ tsp cayenne pepper
¼ tsp nutmeg
½ tsp pepper
½ cup butter
2 cups milk
2 cups shredded old Cheddar cheese
8 eggs, separated

Have the ingredients at room temperature. In small bowl, combine flour, salt, paprika, cayenne, nutmeg and pepper; set aside. In large saucepan, melt butter over medium heat; whisk in flour mixture until well blended. Gradually pour in milk and cook, whisking constantly, for about 5 minutes or until sauce is smooth and thickened. Add cheese, stirring constantly, until sauce is smooth; remove from heat. Beat egg yolks on high speed for 1 minute or until light and frothy. Return sauce to medium heat and gradually pour yolks into sauce; cook, stirring constantly, for about 5 minutes or until thickened. Remove from heat and set aside.

In large bowl, beat egg whites until very stiff but not dry; whisk one-third into cheese sauce. Fold in remaining whites. Pour mixture into greased 10-inch soufflé dish. (Can be refrigerated up to 3 hours before baking.) Bake on bottom rack of 475°F oven for 10 minutes. Reduce heat to 400°F; bake for 25 minutes longer or until puffed and golden and top is firm to the touch. Serve immediately.

MAKES 4 TO 6 SERVINGS.

MADELEINE GREEY

MADELEINE GREEY IS A FOOD WRITER, COOKING TEACHER AND COOKBOOK AUTHOR. SHE WAS A COLUMNIST FOR *THE TORONTO STAR* FOR EIGHT YEARS AND A FOOD COLUMNIST WITH *FOREVER YOUNG* AND *DOCTOR'S REVIEW*. HER BOOK, *GET FRESH! HOW TO COOK A KUMQUAT AND OTHER USEFUL TIPS FOR MORE THAN 100 FRUITS AND VEGETABLES*, WAS PUBLISHED BY MACMILLAN CANADA IN 1999. SHE ALSO AUTHORED AND DEMONSTRATED COOKING FOR TWO CD-ROMS ON CHINESE COOKING. MADELEINE'S FOOD WRITING CAN BE FOUND IN THE PAGES OF *TORONTO LIFE, CANADIAN LIVING, CHATELAINE, HOMEMAKER'S, ZELLER'S MAGAZINE, TODAY'S PARENT* AND *AIRBORN*.

IT WASN'T UNTIL I lived in Asia that I fell in love with food. In Canada, food was fuel. In Taipei, Taiwan, it was an adventure. I remember my first bowl of dan dan noodles, the eery nighttime call of the sweet potato vendor and the sweet, floral smell of fresh mangoes in summer. Every day offered another chance to taste something new.

After four years, it was time to go home. My heart called out for the maple leaf but my palate craved the Orient. So bottles of hoisin sauce and chili bean paste shadowed my return and have never left my kitchen since. The following recipes reflect my passion for Chinese food. You might need to shop in Chinatown for some of these ingredients, but if you're like me, that only helps ignite the appetite.

The Women's Culinary Network offers me another venue where I can sate my culinary curiosity. Every time I attend a meeting, I learn something new—whether it's a tip on quince growing in Don Mills or a new way to make sourdough starters.

EASY (AND EXOTIC) CHINESE

•SPRING ROLLS STUFFED WITH SHRIMP, JICAMA AND CARROT•
•STIR-FRIED EDAMAME WITH PICKLED CABBAGE•
•CHAYOTE STIR-FRIED WITH SHIITAKE MUSHROOMS•
•RED-BRAISED PORK RIBS WITH CHESTNUTS•

SPRING ROLLS STUFFED WITH SHRIMP, JICAMA AND CARROT

These spring rolls are bursting with luscious, moist shrimp. The jicama and carrot matchsticks add a little crunch. Jicama looks like a tan-skinned turnip, averaging about 6 inches in diameter. Look for fresh jicama in Asian and Latin American stores. A good substitute is canned water chestnuts.

1 pkg (7 oz/200 g) frozen small spring roll wrappers (6- x 6-inch squares)
1 lb shrimp, peeled and deveined
4 tsp cornstarch
2 tsp Chinese cooking wine or sherry
1 tsp finely grated ginger
1 tsp salt
1 tsp granulated sugar
1 tsp sesame oil
¼ tsp white pepper
½ cup jicama matchsticks (¼ x ¼ x 1½ inches)
½ cup carrot matchsticks
1 tbsp all-purpose flour
4 tsp water
Hot mustard, soy sauce or plum sauce

Thaw spring roll wrappers for 30 minutes at room temperature. Once thawed, cover with damp paper towels.

Finely chop shrimp. In medium bowl, combine shrimp, cornstarch, wine, ginger, salt, sugar, sesame oil and pepper. Add jicama and carrots; mix well.

In small bowl, whisk together flour and water to create runny paste. Working with 1 wrapper at a time, position wrapper on work surface with a corner facing you; place 1 tbsp of the shrimp mixture about ½ inch from corner, forming mixture into 3-inch long log. Using fingertips, wet edges of opposite corner with flour paste. Roll up halfway; fold in sides, then finish rolling to create 4-inch long rolls. Press to secure edges. Repeat with remaining wrappers and filling.

In large deep saucepan, heat 4 inches of oil to 350°F; fry shrimp rolls, in small batches, for 3 minutes or until golden brown. Remove with slotted spoon; drain on paper towels. Serve warm with desired mustard or sauce.

MAKES 20 ROLLS.

STIR-FRIED EDAMAME WITH PICKLED CABBAGE

This is a popular appetizer or side dish served in Taipei restaurants, and it makes use of those 39-cent yellow-and-orange cans of pickled cabbage sold under the Ma Ling label in every Asian supermarket. There's no need to thaw; just add the frozen soybeans (edamame) directly to the wok.

2 tbsp vegetable oil
1 tbsp grated fresh ginger
1 can (7 oz/200 g) pickled cabbage, rinsed, drained and finely chopped
1 lb bag frozen shelled soybeans
1 cup shredded bamboo shoots
½ cup chicken stock

1 tsp granulated sugar
1 tsp soy sauce

Heat wok or large frying pan over high heat; add oil and swirl to cover surface. Add ginger and pickled cabbage; stir-fry for 2 minutes. Add soybeans, bamboo shoots, stock, sugar and soy sauce; cook, covered and stirring occasionally, for 8 minutes or until tender.

MAKES 4 TO 6 SERVINGS.

CHAYOTE STIR-FRIED WITH SHIITAKE MUSHROOMS

All you need is a sharp vegetable peeler and the joys of chayote will become yours. This easy dish can be served alongside meat or chicken, or as a yummy, vegetarian sauce for rice noodles.

10 dried shiitake mushrooms
1 tbsp vegetable oil
3 green onions, chopped
2 chayote, peeled and sliced
1 tsp chicken bouillon powder
1 tbsp dry sherry
1 tsp light soy sauce
1 tsp sesame oil
Salt

In medium bowl, soak mushrooms in warm water for 20 minutes or until softened and pliable. Drain, reserving soaking liquid. Rinse mushrooms under running water to remove any dirt or grit. Drain again. Strain soaking liquid through cheesecloth or coffee filter to remove dirt or grit. Set liquid aside.

In wok or large frying pan, heat oil over high heat; stir-fry green onions for 30 seconds. Add chayote; stir-fry until wok becomes noticeably dry. Add 1 cup of the reserved mushroom soaking liquid, the bouillon powder, sherry and soy sauce; stir-fry until boiling. Reduce heat to simmer; cover and cook for 10 to 15 minutes or until chayote is tender. Add sesame oil. Season with salt to taste. Serve immediately.

MAKES 4 SERVINGS.

RED-BRAISED PORK RIBS WITH CHESTNUTS

This rich Chinese stew can be cooked in one hour (in a pinch), but it's best to braise for up to two hours. Serve it over rice or noodles. Both dark and light soy sauces can be found in any Asian food store and most supermarkets, too. Chinese black vinegar has a complex, smoky flavour—look for Chinkiang or Tientsin varieties in Chinese stores. While you're there, purchase your pork ribs, asking the butcher to cut the rib strips in half lengthwise to produce 2 long strips of short ribs. To peel chestnuts, use a sharp knife to slice an X into the flat side of the chestnut, then cook in boiling water for 3 to 5 minutes or until skin starts to peel back; alternatively, roast in a 350°F oven for 10 minutes. Chestnuts seem to peel best when still scorching hot—ouch!

2 lb short pork ribs
3 cups water
⅓ cup packed brown sugar
4 tbsp dark soy sauce
2 tbsp light soy sauce
2 tbsp Chinese black vinegar or balsamic vinegar
5 whole star anise
1 tbsp freshly grated ginger
3 cups peeled chestnuts (canned or fresh)

Trim fat from pork. In large pot over medium heat, combine ribs, water, sugar, dark and light soy sauces, vinegar, star anise and ginger; bring to boil, stirring constantly. Boil for 5 minutes, stirring constantly to prevent scorching. Reduce heat to low; simmer, covered, for at least 1 hour or until meat starts to fall off bone.

Add chestnuts; cover and simmer for 15 minutes.

MAKES 4 SERVINGS.

FLORENCE KWOK

FLORENCE KWOK IS A COOKING INSTRUCTOR SPECIALIZING IN AUTHENTIC ASIAN CUISINE. FLORENCE TEACHES AT LOBLAWS, THE PEEL BOARD OF EDUCATION IN MISSISSAUGA AND OFFERS PRIVATE CLASSES. SHE HAS APPEARED ON CITYTV'S "BREAKFAST TELEVISION."

BEEF SATAY STIR-FRY

This rich, coconut-infused stir-fry is wonderful served over steamed white rice or noodles—be they rice, egg or even spaghetti.

1 lb sirloin (grilling) or beef tenderloin
4 tbsp fish sauce
1 tsp cornstarch
3 tbsp vegetable oil
2 tbsp water
1 onion, chopped
½ cup chopped fresh coriander
3 tbsp lime juice
2 cloves garlic, chopped
1 hot pepper, chopped (or ½ tsp hot pepper flakes)
1 tsp ground cumin
1 tsp ground turmeric
½ cup coconut milk
2 tbsp crunchy peanut butter
1 tbsp packed brown sugar
¼ cup unsalted peanuts, chopped
2 green onions, thinly sliced diagonally

Cut beef across the grain into thin strips. In bowl, stir together 2 tbsp of the fish sauce, cornstarch, 1 tbsp of the oil and water. Stir in beef and marinate for 30 minutes.

Meanwhile, in food processor or blender, purée onion, coriander, lime juice, garlic, hot pepper, cumin and turmeric until smooth paste, adding a little water if necessary.

In wok or large deep skillet, heat 1 tbsp of the oil over high heat; stir-fry beef for 3 minutes or until browned but still pink inside. Transfer to bowl.

Add remaining oil to wok; stir-fry onion mixture for 6 minutes or until onions are softened. Add coconut milk, peanut butter, remaining fish sauce and sugar; bring to boil. Reduce heat to medium-low and simmer for 5 to 8 minutes. Stir in beef. Garnish with peanuts and green onions.

MAKES 4 SERVINGS.

GAIL HALL

GAIL IS A CATERER AND ENTREPRENEUR. HER AWARD-WINNING CATERING COMPANY, GOURMET GOODIES, WHICH SHE STARTED IN 1985, IS THE LARGEST OFF-PREMISE CATERING COMPANY IN EDMONTON AND ONE OF THE LARGEST IN CANADA. GOURMET GOODIES ALSO RUNS CULINARY TOURS, A COOKING SCHOOL AND A RETAIL-TO-GO STORE SUPPLYING FRESH FOODS, SAUCES AND CONDIMENTS FROM ACROSS THE COUNTRY. GAIL IS ACTIVELY INVOLVED ON THE BOARDS OF LOCAL, REGIONAL AND NATIONAL FOOD ASSOCIATIONS AND IS A FORMER CHAIRPERSON OF CUISINE CANADA.

I BEGAN Gourmet Goodies catering in 1985, at a turning point in my career as a civil servant. With only the love of cooking guiding my way, I changed careers and started a catering business.

My inspiration to delve into a career in which I had no formal training was simple: I feel enormous satisfaction feeding people the freshest and highest-quality foods. My catering company has allowed me to teach others, uncover wonderful food stories and discover unique ingredients. I share many of these ingredients in the following recipes from America's southwest.

The Women's Culinary Network had a small Edmonton branch for two years in the '90s, and our meetings were always more about food than socializing! There were always new ideas generated and tips shared. I have made many lasting friendships and hired a few employees through this networking group.

SOUTHWEST SENSATIONS

• BARBECUED CHIPOTLE CHICKEN CALZONE •
• TENDER GREENS WITH SPICED PECANS AND ORANGE SHERRY VINAIGRETTE •
• TAMARIND-GLAZED PORK LOIN •

BARBECUED CHIPOTLE CHICKEN CALZONE

Canned chipotle peppers in adobo sauce are available in Latin grocery stores and many fine food stores. Empty the contents into a blender, blend well, measure 2 tsp and freeze the remainder in ice cube trays. If you have any leftovers from this recipe, simply wrap each calzone tightly in plastic wrap and store in a freezer bag for up to two months.

DOUGH:

3½ cups all-purpose flour
1 pkg quick-rising (instant) dry yeast (or 1 tbsp)
1 tsp salt
1 tsp granulated sugar
1½ cups lukewarm water
1 tbsp olive oil

FILLING:

3 tbsp olive oil
1 lb boneless, skinless chicken breasts, thinly sliced
2 tsp Potlach Seasoning (recipe follows)
1 each sweet red and yellow pepper, thinly sliced
1 tbsp minced garlic
2 tsp chipotle peppers in adobo sauce
2 cups shredded Monterey Jack cheese

2 tbsp chopped fresh coriander
Olive oil

DOUGH: In bowl, combine flour, yeast, salt and sugar. With wooden spoon, gradually stir in water and oil. Mix until pulls together into soft, pliable dough, using hands if necessary. Turn out onto lightly floured surface; knead for 5 minutes or until smooth and elastic. Place in lightly greased bowl, turning to grease all over. Cover loosely with towel and set aside in warm place for 1 hour or until doubled in size.

FILLING: Meanwhile, in medium skillet, heat oil over medium heat; add chicken and sprinkle with Potlach Seasoning, stirring to coat. Cook for 5 minutes or until chicken is no longer pink inside. Transfer to bowl. Add sweet peppers and garlic to skillet; cook, stirring, for 5 minutes or until peppers are tender. Add to bowl; let cool for a few minutes. Stir in chipotle peppers, cheese and coriander.

Divide dough into 12 equal portions; roll out each into 6-inch circle. Spoon filling onto centre of each circle. Wet edge with water or lightly beaten egg; fold rounds in half, pinching edges to seal.

Brush both sides of calzones lightly with olive oil; grill over medium heat for 4 to 5 minutes per side or until dough is cooked and golden brown.

MAKES 12 SERVINGS.

POTLACH SEASONING

This mixture of spices produces a great combination to shake or rub onto fish, pork or beef. It makes a great gift item, so go ahead and double, triple or even quadruple this recipe.

4 tsp salt
3 tsp chili powder
2 tsp ground cumin
1 tsp garlic powder
1 tsp dried oregano
1 tsp celery salt
½ tsp white pepper
½ tsp paprika
¼ tsp turmeric

In bowl, combine salt, chili powder, cumin, garlic powder, oregano, celery salt, white pepper, paprika and turmeric. Store in airtight container for up to 2 months.

MAKES ABOUT ¼ CUP.

TENDER GREENS WITH SPICED PECANS AND ORANGE SHERRY VINAIGRETTE

Inspired by the flavours of Santa Fe, this salad features crunchy, spicy pecans.

6 cups mixed greens, washed and drained
1 small red onion, thinly sliced
2 small seedless oranges, peeled and sliced into rounds
½ cup Spiced Pecans, chopped (recipe follows)

DRESSING:

¼ cup frozen orange juice concentrate, thawed
¼ cup olive oil
2 tbsp sherry vinegar
¼ tsp each salt and pepper

DRESSING: In small bowl, whisk together orange juice, oil, vinegar, salt and pepper; set aside.

In large bowl, combine greens, red onion and orange slices. Pour dressing over salad. Add Spiced Pecans; toss lightly.

MAKES 6 SERVINGS.

SPICED PECANS

This recipe can be made ahead. Store in an airtight container in a dark cool cupboard. If you'd like extra to munch on as a snack or to give away as host/hostess gifts, double or triple the recipe.

1 tsp salt
¼ tsp granulated sugar
⅛ tsp chili powder
Pinch each cayenne pepper, cinnamon and nutmeg
¾ cup pecans, halved
1 tsp olive oil

In bowl, combine salt, sugar, chili powder, cayenne, cinnamon and nutmeg; set aside. Spread nuts on baking sheet and toast in 300°F oven for 3 to 4 minutes or until fragrant. In bowl, toss pecans with oil; sprinkle with spice mixture and toss again. Spread nuts on baking sheet and bake for 3 minutes longer. Remove from oven and let cool to room temperature. Store in airtight container for up to 2 months.

TAMARIND-GLAZED PORK LOIN

A sweet-and-sour basting sauce is the secret to adding rich colour and flavour to this pork loin. Tamarind is available in dried blocks or, less commonly, as a bottled paste in some large supermarkets, fine food stores and Asian stores. If you can't find the bottled paste, simply make your own from dried tamarind. Soak 2 heaping tbsp of dried tamarind in ¼ cup hot water for 15 minutes, then press through a sieve, reserving paste and discarding pits.

1 cup packed brown sugar
1 cup red wine vinegar
1 cup chicken stock
½ cup plum tomatoes, chopped
2 tbsp tamarind paste
5 lb boneless pork loin, trimmed
Salt and pepper
1 cup fresh basil leaves
½ cup each sun-dried red and yellow tomatoes
½ cup water

In medium saucepan over medium heat, combine sugar, vinegar, chicken stock, tomatoes and tamarind paste; cook for 15 to 20 minutes, stirring occasionally, or until thickened. Strain through sieve into small mixing bowl. Set aside to let cool.

Slice pork lengthwise down centre almost but not all the way through; open like book. Season with salt and pepper. Place basil leaves evenly over cut side of pork and top evenly with sun-dried tomatoes. Roll up and tie at both ends and centre with kitchen string. Season with salt and pepper and coat with reserved sauce. Place on rack in shallow roasting pan; roast in 425°F oven for 20 minutes. Reduce heat to 375°F; add water and cook, basting every 15 minutes, for 45 minutes or until meat thermometer inserted in centre reads 160°F. Transfer to cutting board; tent with foil and let stand for 10 minutes before slicing.

MAKES 6 SERVINGS.

MARSHA ROSEN

MARSHA ROSEN IS A REGISTERED DIETITIAN WITH A PARTICULAR FONDNESS FOR GOOD FOOD. DURING HER CAREER, SHE HAS TRAVELLED MANY ROADS, RANGING FROM NUTRITION COUNSELLING IN SPAS, TO PRODUCT DEMOS OF FOODS WITH A HEALTH FOCUS, TO NUTRITION WRITING FOR THE POPULAR PRESS, TO WORKING WITH SENIORS.

PISTACHIO FINGERS

These cigar-shaped phyllo creations are crispy and easy to make—a simple, yet popular addition to any sweet table. They freeze well; once thawed, reheat in 350°F oven for five minutes before serving.

1 cup shelled, unsalted pistachio nuts, finely chopped
¾ cup granulated sugar
2 tsp orange blossom water or almond extract or rose water
8 sheets phyllo pastry, thawed
½ cup unsalted butter, melted
Icing sugar

In medium bowl, mix together pistachios, sugar and orange blossom water.

Cut phyllo sheets into rectangles, about 4½ x 7 inches. Stack 2 rectangles on work surface, keeping remainder covered with sheet of waxed paper topped with damp tea towel to prevent drying out. Brush top sheet lightly with melted butter. Place 1 heaping tsp of filling at narrow end of buttered sheet. Lightly fold in each side (about ½ inch) and roll up into a tight cylinder. Place on lightly greased baking sheet and brush lightly with melted butter. Repeat with remaining phyllo, butter and filling. Bake in centre of 350°F oven for 12 to 15 minutes or until pale golden. Let cool on rack. Lightly dust with icing sugar.

MAKES ABOUT 36 PIECES.

BARB HOLLAND

BARB HOLLAND IS A PROFESSIONAL HOME ECONOMIST AND FOOD WRITER. SHE IS FOOD EDITOR OF *HOMEMAKER'S* MAGAZINE AND, FOR MANY YEARS A REGULAR FOOD COLUMNIST WITH THE *TORONTO STAR*. BARB HAS DONE COUNTLESS LIVE AND TELEVISION COOKING DEMONSTRATIONS FOR A VARIETY OF CLIENTS, AS WELL AS RECIPE DEVELOPMENT AND FOOD STYLING.

I LOVE living in old Markham, Ontario. Rapid development notwithstanding, we are still close enough to farmers' fields and roadside stands to get daily-picked corn, baskets of field tomatoes and hand-picked veggies in the summer. We also have terrific grocers and butchers, plus the convenience of a first-class supermarket.

And what area has expanded so much as the world of food? Each trip to the market brings new ingredients and foods to discover. The global grocery basket is ours for the tasting and testing. I love cooking and eating, and being in the communications business, I get to teach consumers about the new and old, often resulting in the marriage of both.

I believe in shopping in season and enjoy every season—even winter. The following casual dinner menu would be good for après skating or tobogganing or even a tree-trimming party. Seasonal and colourful, many of its elements can be made ahead, so you too can enjoy the party.

A SNOW-TIME SUPPER

• ROASTED RED PEPPER AND CHÈVRE SPREAD •
• GOLDEN SQUASH, POTATO AND LEEK PHYLLO TART •
• WARM BROCCOLI AND RED PEPPER SALAD •
• CHOCOLATE CLEMENTINE CAKE •

ROASTED RED PEPPER AND CHÈVRE SPREAD

So easy, so delicious—it will become a keeper. The spread is best made the day before to allow the flavours to blend and the texture to firm up. Serve with crostini or crackers and wonderful black olives.

1 sweet red pepper, roasted, peeled and coarsely chopped
1 small clove garlic, minced
5 oz goat cheese
4 oz cream cheese, softened

In food processor, blend together red pepper, garlic, goat cheese and cream cheese. Spoon into serving dish; cover and chill for several hours or overnight.

MAKES ABOUT 1½ CUPS.

GOLDEN SQUASH, POTATO AND LEEK PHYLLO TART

If you are pastry challenged, try phyllo. It's not difficult to work with and makes an attractive and light-textured pastry, terrific for this creamy potato, squash and feta cheese filling. Remember to transfer phyllo from the freezer to the fridge to thaw overnight before starting this recipe.

1 lb potatoes, such as Yukon Gold (about 3 medium), peeled and cut into chunks
1 clove garlic, crushed
1 cup milk
½ cup finely crumbled feta cheese (2 oz)
2 eggs, lightly beaten
2 tbsp extra-virgin olive oil
3 leeks, well rinsed and chopped
2 cloves garlic, minced
2 cups peeled and shredded butternut squash
½ tsp salt
½ tsp dried oregano
¼ tsp pepper
4 sheets phyllo pastry
2 tbsp melted butter
1 tbsp fine dry bread crumbs

In medium saucepan, combine potatoes and crushed garlic; cover with cold water. Bring to boil; cover and cook for 15 to 20 minutes or until potatoes are tender. Drain well. Using potato masher, mash potatoes with garlic. Stir in milk, feta and eggs until smooth. Transfer to large bowl.

Meanwhile, in large skillet, heat oil over medium-high heat; cook leeks and minced garlic for about 2 minutes or until leeks are slightly softened. Add squash and cook for 1 minute, stirring constantly. Add to potato mixture. Season with salt, oregano and pepper; stir well to combine. Set aside.

Cut phyllo into 13- x 13-inch squares. Brush top phyllo sheet lightly with butter. Gently place in 10-inch tart pan with removable bottom. Sprinkle with ½ tsp of the bread crumbs. Lightly butter second phyllo sheet and place on top so corners do not align; sprinkle with ½ tsp bread crumbs. Continue with remaining sheets, butter and bread crumbs, rotating around pan.

Spoon filling into phyllo base, spreading evenly. Place tart pan on baking sheet. Leave edges of phyllo in free-form style, if desired, trimming any edges that hang over more than 1½ inches, or trim phyllo close to pan edge.

Bake in bottom third of 375°F oven for 25 to 30 minutes or until filling is set and phyllo is golden brown. Let stand for about 10 minutes before serving.

MAKES 6 SERVINGS.

WARM BROCCOLI AND RED PEPPER SALAD

Cook broccoli just before serving and serve warm. To help retain its colour, cook uncovered. If you want, make the dressing the day before you serve it.

⅓ cup olive oil
1 tbsp balsamic vinegar
1 tbsp lemon juice
½ tsp Dijon mustard
½ tsp salt
Pinch pepper
2 bunches (4 stalks) broccoli (about 2 to 2½ lb)
1 sweet red pepper, cut in strips
2 shallots, peeled, sliced and separated into rings

In small bowl, whisk together oil, vinegar, lemon juice, mustard, salt and pepper; set aside.

Trim broccoli into florets with 3-inch stems. In large pot of boiling water, cook broccoli, uncovered, for 2 minutes or until bright green and barely tender. Drain, rinse in cold water and drain well, squeezing out excess moisture. In large bowl, combine broccoli, red pepper and shallots; toss with dressing. Serve warm.

MAKES 6 SERVINGS.

CHOCOLATE CLEMENTINE CAKE

Chocolate and orange are a delicious duo. And, clementines are as seasonal as shortbread and Christmas trees. Serve with a dollop of whipped cream or vanilla ice cream, if desired. This cake can be made up to a day before serving.

4 oz bittersweet or semisweet chocolate, coarsely chopped
½ cup butter
1 cup finely chopped peeled clementines (about 4)
1 cup all-purpose flour
½ tsp each baking powder and baking soda
¼ tsp salt
2 eggs
½ cup granulated sugar
1 tsp vanilla

CHOCOLATE ICING:

4 oz bittersweet or semisweet chocolate, coarsely chopped
2 tbsp butter
½ cup sifted icing sugar

2 tbsp thawed orange juice concentrate (not diluted)
White chocolate leaves and/or clementine segments covered with white and dark chocolate (optional)

Line bottom of 8½-inch springform pan with circle of parchment paper. Grease sides of pan. Place on baking sheet.

In double boiler over hot water, melt together chocolate and butter (or microwave at medium for 2 to 3 minutes); stir until smooth. Add clementines. Set aside.

In bowl, combine flour, baking powder, baking soda and salt.

In mixing bowl with electric mixer, beat eggs and sugar until light; beat in vanilla. On low speed, add flour mixture, then chocolate mixture, beating just until ingredients are mixed.

Pour batter into prepared pan. Bake in centre of 350°F oven 45 to 50 minutes or until cake tester inserted in centre comes out clean. Transfer to rack to cool. Remove outer ring; invert cake onto rack to cool completely.

CHOCOLATE ICING: In double boiler over hot (not boiling) water, melt chocolate (or microwave at Medium for 3 to 4 minutes). Stir to melt completely; add butter and beat until smooth. Beat in icing sugar and orange juice.

Place cooled cake on serving dish with strips of parchment or waxed paper under bottom edges. Spread icing over top and sides of cake. Let set at room temperature, then remove paper strips. Garnish with chocolate leaves or clementine segments, if desired.

MAKES 8 SERVINGS.

JENNY KONIUK

JENNY KONIUK IS A FOOD WRITER, RECIPE DEVELOPER AND RECIPE TESTER. HER ARTICLES HAVE BEEN PUBLISHED IN THE *TORONTO STAR, HOMEMAKER'S* AND *PRESIDENT'S CHOICE MAGAZINE*.

CARROT CRUMBLE

Whirl a piece of seven-grain, rye or whole wheat bread in the food processor to make fresh bread crumbs. If making ahead, keep crumble mixture separate from carrots and sprinkle on top just before baking.

12 medium carrots, peeled and chopped into ½-inch pieces
1 tbsp butter
1 tsp packed brown sugar
Pinch ground ginger

TOPPING:

¼ cup toasted sunflower seeds
¼ cup ground almonds
2 tbsp sesame seeds
½ cup fresh whole-grain bread crumbs
⅛ tsp salt
2 tbsp butter, softened

In medium saucepan over medium-high heat, cook carrots in lightly salted water for 7 to 10 minutes or until tender but firm.

TOPPING: Meanwhile, in small bowl, mix together sunflower seeds, almonds, sesame seeds, bread crumbs and salt. Using back of spoon, work in butter until mixture is crumbly.

Drain carrots; return to saucepan along with butter, brown sugar and ginger. Mix gently and pour into greased 6-cup baking dish. Spoon topping evenly over carrots. Bake in 350°F oven for 15 to 20 minutes or until hot.

MAKES 6 SERVINGS.

KAREN JULL

KAREN JULL, A UNIQUE PRODUCT DEVELOPER FOR LOBLAW BRANDS LTD., HAS WORKED IN OVER 150 FOOD PLANTS IN NORTH AMERICA AND EUROPE. KAREN STRIVES TO CREATE QUALITY PRODUCTS THAT PROVIDE CONSUMERS WITH MEANINGFUL FOOD ALTERNATIVES. SOME OF HER MOST INNOVATIVE PRODUCTS INCLUDE PC ORGANIC COFFEE, TEA, JUICES AND JAMS, PC WILD BLUEBERRY COCKTAIL, AND PC QUESADILLAS.

I HAVE always been passionate about food quality. I developed a taste for organic vegetables at my grandparents' sustainable farm in the Laurentians in Quebec. At age 17, I lived in Paris for one yummy year of seeking traditionally handcrafted and artisanal eats. My favourite culinary trip was to Guatemala with the world's best coffee cuppers in search of the highest-quality, fairly traded organic coffees. This experience fuelled my interest in sustainable practices and a quest for fairly traded foods where farmers and consumers are more closely linked and directly supported. The following recipes reflect my passion for quality sustainable cuisine that has nutritional meaning and functional attributes.

The Women's Culinary Network has provided me with an empowering environment for exchanging information. The diverse culinary knowledge and breadth of experience are the main ingredients that make this community so vibrant.

NATURALLY GOOD-FOR-YOU BREAKFAST

• MUESLI •
• CRANBERRY-SCENTED BAKED APPLES •
• WATERMELON-ADE •

MUESLI

This is a very nourishing and satisfying breakfast. You can substitute your favourite fruit for the berries. To toast the seeds, preheat a skillet over medium heat, add seeds to pan and cook, stirring often, for 3 to 4 minutes or until seeds start to pop and turn golden brown.

2 cups rolled oats (not instant)
1¼ cups orange juice
1 cup plain yogurt with active cultures
2 tbsp pure maple syrup
2 tbsp cold-pressed hemp or flax oil
1 tbsp toasted pumpkin seeds
1 tbsp toasted sunflower seeds
1 tbsp toasted sesame seeds
½ cup raspberries or blueberries

In large serving bowl, stir together oats and orange juice. Cover and refrigerate for at least 30 minutes or overnight.

Stir in yogurt, maple syrup, hemp oil, and half each of the pumpkin, sunflower and sesame seeds. Sprinkle with berries and remaining seeds. Serve immediately.

MAKES 4 SERVINGS.

CRANBERRY-SCENTED BAKED APPLES

Northern Spy, Mutsu, Granny Smith and Golden Delicious apples all work well in this recipe. While I prefer to use 100% cranberry juice, you can use cranberry cocktail or even apple juice in a pinch—but pure cranberry juice creates a lovely pink colour. These apples can be made ahead and reheated in a saucepan or microwave. Serve with muesli.

- 4 apples
- ¼ cup unsalted butter, softened
- 2 tbsp packed brown sugar
- 1 tsp cinnamon
- ½ tsp ground ginger
- ½ cup dried cranberries
- 2 tbsp pure maple syrup
- ½ cup cranberry juice

Wash and core apples, leaving a little apple at base. Peel top third of each apple. Place apples in shallow baking dish. In small bowl, stir together butter, brown sugar, cinnamon and ginger; stuff into centre of each apple. Divide cranberries evenly among apples, pushing into butter mixture. In small bowl, combine maple syrup and cranberry juice; drizzle over apples.

Bake in 350°F oven, basting occasionally, for 50 to 60 minutes or until apples are tender when pierced with toothpick. Using slotted spoon, transfer apples to plate. Pour sauce into saucepan over medium heat and reduce for 13 to 15 minutes or until thickened. Pour sauce over warm apples to serve.

MAKES 4 SERVINGS.

WATERMELON-ADE

This is a refreshing, thirst-quenching drink. Watermelon juice made from the pulp, seeds and *peel is very nutritious, containing vitamins A and C and chlorophyll. If you do not have a juicer, use just the pulp to create juice in a blender (if there are seeds, simply strain through sieve).*

- 4 cups fresh watermelon juice (pulp, seeds and peel) or 2 lb watermelon, peeled, cubed and puréed in blender
- ¾ cup lemon juice
- 20 drops clear liquid stevia extract* (optional)
- 4 sprigs fresh mint
- 4 lemon wedges

Pour watermelon juice into large jug. Add lemon juice and sweeten with stevia (if using). Serve in glasses over ice. Garnish with mint and lemon.

MAKES 4 SERVINGS.

**Stevia is a natural herb native to Paraguay, and is approximately 250 to 300 times sweeter than sugar. It is a natural sweetener that has no calories, which makes it ideal for diabetics. Stevia extract can be found in health food stores and some supermarkets.*

NORENE GILLETZ

COOKBOOK AUTHOR NORENE GILLETZ HAS WRITTEN FOR THE KOSHER (OR NOT!) COOK WITH *THE FOOD PROCESSOR BIBLE* AND *MEALLEANIYUMM!* NORENE IS A CERTIFIED CULINARY PROFESSIONAL WITH THE INTERNATIONAL ASSOCIATION OF CULINARY PROFESSIONALS (IACP) AND A CUISINE CANADA MEMBER. SHE'S ALSO A FOOD CONSULTANT, COOKING TEACHER, FREELANCE FOOD WRITER AND COOKBOOK EDITOR.

CHICKEN SOUP WITH MATZO BALLS

You don't have to be Jewish to love chicken soup! A steaming bowl of golden broth is sure to cure colds or flu. Not surprisingly, it's often called "Jewish penicillin." Use a kosher chicken for maximum flavour. This soup freezes and reheats well.

4 lb chicken pieces
10 cups cold water (approx)
4 tsp salt
2 medium onions
4 to 6 medium carrots
3 or 4 stalks celery
1 parsnip (optional)
2 cloves garlic
12 sprigs fresh dill
½ tsp pepper
Matzo Balls (recipe follows) or cooked noodles

Trim excess fat from chicken (but don't remove the skin as it adds flavour). In stockpot, bring chicken, water and salt to boil; skim off foam. Add onions, carrots, celery and parsnip (if using); simmer, partially covered, over medium-low heat for 1¼ hours. Add garlic and dill; simmer for 15 minutes. Add pepper and more salt if necessary.

Remove chicken and carrots and transfer each to separate bowl; cover and refrigerate. Discard onions, celery, parsnip, garlic and dill. Strain stock into large bowl; refrigerate for 8 hours or until fat congeals on surface. Lift off and discard fat.

In large saucepan, bring stock to simmer. Remove chicken meat from bones and discard skin; chop and add to soup. Chop carrots coarsely and add to soup. Serve with Matzo Balls or noodles.

MAKES 8 GENEROUS SERVINGS.

MATZO BALLS

¾ cup matzo meal
¾ tsp salt
¼ tsp pepper
3 eggs
3 tbsp club soda or cold water
2 tbsp vegetable oil
2 tbsp minced fresh dill (or parsley)
16 cups water plus 2 tsp salt

In large bowl, combine matzo meal, ¾ tsp of the salt and pepper. Add eggs, club soda, oil and dill to matzo mixture, stirring until moistened. Cover and refrigerate for at least 1 hour. (Mixture will become thick.)

In large saucepan, bring water to boil; add remaining salt. Wetting hands for easier shaping, form mixture into 1-inch balls. Carefully add matzo balls to pot; cover tightly and simmer for 45 minutes. (No peeking allowed!) Using slotted spoon, carefully transfer matzo balls to hot chicken soup.

MAKES 16 TO 18 MATZO BALLS.

COOKING TIPS: *Matzo Balls can be cooked in advance, then frozen in chicken soup. You can also freeze them on a baking sheet until firm, then transfer to plastic freezer bags and store in freezer. You don't need to thaw them before using; just reheat from frozen in soup. If you prefer firmer matzo balls, add 1 or 2 tbsp additional matzo meal.*

ANNE LINDSAY

ANNE LINDSAY HAS BEEN HELPING CANADIANS FIND HEALTHIER WAYS TO ENJOY GOOD FOOD FOR OVER 25 YEARS. HER FIVE BEST-SELLING COOKBOOKS HAVE BEEN PUBLISHED IN FIVE LANGUAGES IN 14 COUNTRIES. DURING THE 1990S, SHE WAS THE NUTRITION EDITOR OF *CANADIAN LIVING* MAGAZINE. ANNE APPEARS REGULARLY ON TELEVISION AND TRAVELS THE COUNTRY PROMOTING HEALTHY EATING. SHE IS CHAIR OF THE BOARD OF DIRECTORS FOR BREAKFAST FOR LEARNING, CANADIAN LIVING FOUNDATION, THE ONLY NATIONAL NONPROFIT ORGANIZATION DEDICATED TO SUPPORTING CHILD NUTRITION PROGRAMS IN CANADA.

I'VE ALWAYS been interested in food and cooking. As a very young child, I remember pushing a chair to the kitchen counter, climbing up and trying to help my mother roll pastry for a pie or drop cookie dough onto a baking sheet. My mom taught me a great deal about cooking and entertaining, and my father made sure we had the best-tasting ingredients to work with. He grew vegetables, planted fruit trees, smoked fish, pickled herrings, made marmalade and bought the freshest of fish and seafood from fishermen at the docks in Vancouver.

At school, I became interested in nutrition. It was exciting to combine my love of food and cooking with healthy eating and nutrition. Through writing my cookbooks, I've been privileged to work with many wonderful volunteers and to travel around the world.

I thank the WCN for inviting me to participate in this book. The combined knowledge of the members is staggering, and they are all generous in sharing it with others.

SUMMER ALFRESCO DINING

• BALKAN BEET SOUP •
• SALMON AND SCALLOP SKEWERS •
• GARLIC GREEN BEANS •
• NO-BAKE CHOCOLATE GINGER COOKIES •

BALKAN BEET SOUP

This is one of my favourite summer soups because it's full of fresh vegetables and totally refreshing. I love it for lunch or as a first course for dinner.

3 cups buttermilk
¾ cup light (5%) sour cream
½ English cucumber, diced
3 medium beets, cooked, peeled and diced
2 hard-cooked eggs, peeled and chopped
½ cup coarsely chopped fresh parsley
⅓ cup coarsely chopped radishes
3 tbsp chopped fresh chives or green onions
Salt and pepper

In bowl, whisk buttermilk and sour cream until smooth. Stir in cucumber.

Refrigerate for 30 minutes or for up to 1 day. Just before serving, divide beets among serving bowls. Stir egg, parsley, radishes and chives into buttermilk mixture. Season to taste with salt and pepper. Pour over beets. Serve cold.

MAKES 8 SERVINGS.

SALMON AND SCALLOP SKEWERS

This is one of my all-time favourite barbecue recipes. It is delicious and quick and easy to prepare. Serve with jasmine rice or couscous and Garlic Green Beans (recipe follows).

1 lb salmon fillet (about ¾ inch thick)
1 lb medium to large scallops
1 small sweet red pepper
1 small sweet green or yellow pepper

MARINADE:

⅓ cup hoisin sauce
2 tbsp chopped fresh coriander
2 tbsp soy sauce
1 tbsp minced ginger
1 tbsp minced garlic
½ to 1 tsp Asian hot sauce (or pinch hot pepper flakes)

MARINADE: In bowl, whisk together hoisin sauce, coriander, soy sauce, ginger, garlic and Asian hot sauce.

Remove skin from salmon; cut salmon into cubes. Add salmon and scallops to marinade; stir to coat. Cover and refrigerate for up to 8 hours.

Cut red and yellow peppers into 1-inch pieces. Thread scallops, salmon and peppers onto soaked wooden skewers. Place on greased grill over medium heat; close cover and grill, turning once or twice, for 8 to 12 minutes or until scallops and salmon are opaque.

MAKES 6 TO 8 SERVINGS.

GARLIC GREEN BEANS

This simple vegetable dish suits just about any menu. You can serve it hot, warm or at room temperature. In the spring, I use asparagus instead of green beans.

1½ lb green beans
1 clove garlic, chopped
1 tsp coarse salt
1 tbsp balsamic or red wine vinegar
1 tbsp extra-virgin olive oil
¼ cup finely chopped sweet red pepper or tomato

Remove stem ends from beans. In large pot of boiling water, cook beans for 4 to 5 minutes or until tender; drain well. (To serve cold, refresh beans under cold running water.)

Meanwhile, on serving platter and using pestle or back of fork, crush garlic with salt to form paste; stir in vinegar then oil.

Just before serving, add green beans; stir to coat. Sprinkle with red pepper.

MAKES 8 SERVINGS.

NO-BAKE CHOCOLATE GINGER COOKIES

I'm not sure whether these are a candy or a cookie, but I do know they are perfect to serve with fresh strawberries or any fresh fruit and ice cream for dessert.

1 cup whole almonds
1½ cups semisweet chocolate chips
½ cup dried cranberries
⅓ cup finely chopped crystallized ginger

Spread almonds on baking sheet and toast in 350°F oven for 7 minutes or until golden and fragrant.

In large glass measuring cup, microwave chocolate chips at Medium-Low for about 5 minutes, stirring after 2 minutes, until chocolate is just melted. Stir in almonds, cranberries and ginger until well coated. Drop by teaspoonfuls onto waxed paper–lined baking sheet. When firm, store in cool place. (Can be layered between sheets of waxed paper in an airtight container and frozen for up to 2 months.)

MAKES ABOUT 30 COOKIES.

DEBORAH MURRAY

DEBORAH MURRAY IS A GRADUATE OF THE STRATFORD CHEFS SCHOOL AND CURRENTLY ONE OF THE EXECUTIVE CHEFS OF THE WESTOVER INN IN ST. MARYS, ONTARIO. THIS IS THE FIRST TIME ONE OF HER RECIPES HAS BEEN PUBLISHED IN A COOKBOOK, AND SHE LOOKS FORWARD TO FUTURE ENDEAVOURS IN FOOD WRITING AND RECIPE TESTING.

GRILLED PEAR, PINEAPPLE AND MANGO SALSA

This salsa is versatile: serve as an appetizer, mix it with pasta for a main course, or present as an after-dinner condiment for a cheese plate. For an appetizer, I sometimes serve the salsa on thin oatmeal toasts, inside hollowed-out cherry tomatoes or on slices of grilled pear or pineapple.

2 Bosc pears
3 tbsp olive oil
1½ tbsp lemon juice
½ cup diced peeled mango
½ cup diced pineapple
4 tbsp finely diced sweet red pepper
2½ tbsp diced red onion
½ tbsp minced jalapeño pepper
1 tbsp orange juice
1 tsp lime juice
1½ tbsp finely chopped fresh mint
1 tbsp chopped fresh coriander
¼ tsp salt
Pinch pepper

Peel and core pears; cut into 8 equal pieces. Whisk 2 tbsp of the olive oil with ½ tbsp of the lemon juice; brush over pears. Cook on grill over medium-high heat for 1 to 2 minutes per side. Let cool. Chop into chunks the same size as mango and pineapple. In bowl, toss together pears, mango, pineapple, red pepper, onion and jalapeño pepper. In small bowl, whisk together remaining olive oil and lemon, orange and lime juices; toss with pear mixture. Stir in mint, coriander, salt and pepper.

MAKES 3 CUPS.

JENNIFER LOW

JENNIFER LOW IS A JOURNALIST, TRAINED COOK AND FOOD EDITOR OF THE AWARD-WINNING MAGAZINE *CANADIAN HOUSE & HOME*, WHERE SHE DEVELOPS RECIPES AND PRODUCES FOOD FEATURES. JENNIFER ALSO APPEARS ON THE COMPANION TELEVISION SHOW ON HGTV. SHE HAS WRITTEN FOOD STORIES FOR THE *NATIONAL POST* AND *THE TORONTO STAR*, WAS A RECIPE DEVELOPER FOR AN INTERNATIONAL FOOD COMPANY AND HAS COOKED FOR TORONTO'S ELITE CATERERS. SHE IS WORKING ON HER DEBUT COOKBOOK.

I SPENT nine years as a journalist covering business before I decided I was more interested in writing about pasta and pastry than profit margins. So how to switch gears? First, I enrolled in formal culinary training. I felt right at home from the first day, when we purchased chef's uniforms and got our lesson on how to handle a chef's knife. Every day, I was pulled deeper into a world of culinary experience leap years away from my former "comfort zone"—in front of the keyboard pecking out stories. But I found my second spiritual home in front of the stove.

After graduation, it was back to the real world. Food writing became my mission and, happily, I caught a few lucky breaks—chief among them was writing food articles for the *Toronto Star.*

Food is definitely my beat now—designing recipes, covering stories, occasional food styling and, most important, getting to know the vibrant people in the food community. I feel privileged to be part of a group that loves its work.

As a member of the WCN, I see the joy and camaraderie shared by people passionate about food. It's been a great common bond, whether the members are from the media, commercial kitchens or corporate backgrounds. The WCN reminds us all why we chose our line of work in the first place.

SIMPLY ELEGANT

• SHERRIED TIGER SHRIMP STARTER •
• CINNAMON CORNISH HENS WITH BALSAMIC GLAZE •
• POTATO AND CELERY ROOT MASH •
• DOUBLE-STRENGTH ICE CREAMS AND SWEETS PLATE •

SHERRIED TIGER SHRIMP STARTER

These shrimp turn out much better if cooked on a grill pan—rather than directly on the barbecue—to prevent flares that can dry them out. Herbes de Provence is a French dried herb mixture consisting of thyme, rosemary, bay leaf, basil and savoury; look for it in fine food stores or some supermarkets.

30 large tiger shrimp (5 per person), peeled and deveined
2 shallots, minced
¼ cup dry sherry
1 tbsp sesame oil
1 tbsp olive oil
½ tsp herbes de Provence
½ tsp minced garlic
Pinch each salt and pepper
Baby greens for dressing serving plates (optional)

In large bowl, combine shrimp, shallots, sherry, sesame and olive oils, herbes de Provence, garlic, salt and pepper. Let stand for at least 10 minutes or refrigerate for use later in day.

Thread shrimp onto 6 bamboo or metal skewers. In grill pan or on barbecue over high heat, cook shrimp for about 3 to 4 minutes per side or until pink and browning at edges, basting frequently with marinade from bowl. Stop basting about 1 minute before shrimp are done and turn over once more.

Serve on small plates dressed with baby green leaves as garnish, if desired.

MAKES 6 SERVINGS.

CINNAMON CORNISH HENS WITH BALSAMIC GLAZE

Slice and trim the hens, then premeasure all the ingredients before your guests arrive. The rest is a cinch, especially if you do everything but the roasting earlier in the day or even the day before.

3 Cornish game hens, each 1 lb
1½ tsp cinnamon
1½ tsp dried marjoram
1½ tsp paprika
1 tsp coarse sea salt
½ tsp pepper
1 tbsp butter
1 tbsp olive oil
12 pearl onions, peeled, roots removed and halved
8 large shallots, peeled, roots removed and quartered
1-½ cups seedless green grapes
½ cup dry white wine
1 cup balsamic vinegar (inexpensive varieties will work fine)

Split hens in half lengthwise between breasts, removing and discarding backbones. Slice off tips and wings (but leave portion that looks like a little drumstick). Trim off excess fat. Set aside.

In small bowl, mix together cinnamon, marjoram, paprika, salt and pepper; pat generously over hen skins.

In large nonstick skillet, heat butter and oil over medium heat. Place hen halves, skin side down, in pan; gently press down all parts to ensure browning all over. Fry for 5 to 6 minutes or until skins and spices are golden. Transfer, skin side up, to baking dish just large enough to hold hens in single layer.

Add onions, shallots and grapes to skillet; cook for 3 to 4 minutes or until softened. Stir in wine; cover and cook for 7 to 8 minutes or until grapes begin to yellow and wrinkle. Uncover and cook, stirring, for 2 minutes longer or until juices thicken slightly.

Pour onions, shallots, grapes and any pan juices over hen halves. (Can be prepared to this point; covered tightly and refrigerated for up to 1 day.) Roast in 400°F oven, uncovered, for 20 to 25 minutes or until juices run clear when hens are pierced.

Meanwhile, in small non-aluminum saucepan over medium heat, bring vinegar to low simmer and reduce by three-quarters or until syrupy. Serve Cornish hens drizzled with some of the balsamic glaze. Pour remaining glaze into small bowl to pass at the table.

MAKES 6 SERVINGS.

POTATO AND CELERY ROOT MASH

Skip the food processor or mixer. Using an old-fashioned potato masher gives this mash just the right body.

2 lb potatoes, peeled and cut into 1-inch cubes
2 lb celery root, peeled and cut into 1-inch cubes
1 tsp salt
½ cup milk (or cream, if desired)
¼ cup butter
Salt and white pepper

In large saucepan, cover potatoes and celery root with cold water. Add salt and bring to boil; cook for about 15 minutes or until tender. Drain.

Add milk and butter; mash with potato masher, leaving some slightly large bits. Season to taste with salt and pepper.

MAKES 6 TO 8 SERVINGS.

DOUBLE-STRENGTH ICE CREAMS AND SWEETS PLATE

Making your own little glasses of intensely flavoured ice creams is a fun and simple thing to do for dessert. Just be sure you get heavy, freezer-proof glasses. Note that the juice concentrate must be completely frozen for this to work well. Provide small spoons for eating ice creams.

1 can (350 mL) frozen juice concentrate in desired flavour
1 cup whipping cream
Assorted dainty store-bought cookies
Assorted small fruits such as strawberries, figs and apricots

Working quickly, break up frozen juice concentrate into large pieces in bowl of food processor. Add whipping cream and process until smooth. Pour into freezer-proof shot glasses or small juice glasses. Freeze until serving.

Place 1 or 2 glasses of ice cream on each of 6 decorative small plates. Garnish with 2 or 3 cookies and pieces of fruit.

MAKES ABOUT 10 SERVINGS, DEPENDING ON GLASS SIZE.

VARIATION: *Apple Pie Ice Cream: In food processor, combine apple juice concentrate, whipping cream and ½ tsp ground cinnamon.*

BARBARA ACKERMAN

BARBARA ACKERMAN IS THE OWNER OF THE COOK'S PLACE, A RETAIL KITCHENWARE STORE ON DANFORTH AVENUE IN TORONTO THAT OPENED IN 1998. SHE CARRIES AN ECLECTIC SELECTION OF FINE KITCHEN EQUIPMENT. BARB HAS HAD A LIFE-LONG LOVE OF COOKING—ESPECIALLY BREAD BAKING.

MEDITERRANEAN DINNER ROLLS

These flavourful rolls can be prepared the night before and left to rise in the refrigerator, or you can bake them the same day, just an hour before you serve dinner.

1 cup warm water
1 pkg active dry yeast (or 1 tbsp)
½ tsp honey
½ cup whole wheat flour
⅓ cup buttermilk
4 tbsp olive oil
1 tsp salt
2½ cups all-purpose flour
1 cup crumbled feta cheese
½ cup quartered pitted kalamata olives
1 cup chopped baby spinach leaves
1 egg, beaten

In large bowl, whisk together water, yeast and honey; let stand for 10 minutes or until frothy.

Stir in whole wheat flour, buttermilk, 3 tbsp of the oil, and salt. Using wooden spoon, gradually stir in all-purpose flour, ½ cup at a time, stirring well after each addition until dough forms ball. Turn out onto lightly floured surface; knead for 10 minutes or until smooth and elastic, adding more flour as necessary to prevent sticking. Place dough in greased bowl, turning to grease all over. Cover with plastic wrap and let rise in warm, draft-free place for 1 to 1½ hours or until doubled in bulk.

Punch dough down and let rest for 10 minutes. Turn out onto lightly floured surface and roll out to 15- x 12-inch rectangle. Spread evenly with feta, olives and spinach, leaving 1-inch border at edges. Starting at 1 long edge, roll up dough tightly and pinch to seal. Cut off ends to ensure that all rolls have stuffing. Slice dough into 12 equal pieces. Place in greased 13- x 9-inch baking dish. Cover and let rise for 45 to 60 minutes or until doubled in bulk. (Can be covered and left to rise in refrigerator 24 to 48 hours. Rolls may be baked directly from the refrigerator.)

Lightly brush tops of rolls with beaten egg. Bake in centre of 375°F oven for 30 minutes or until thermometer inserted into bread reads 190°F to 200°F. Let cool slightly before serving.

MAKES 12 ROLLS.

DIETITIAN OR NUTRITIONIST?

The titles dietitian and nutritionist are frequent entries in the WCN's directory, and many people use the terms interchangeably, but there's a big difference between the two.

The titles registered dietitian (RD), professional dietitian and dietitian are all protected by law. These titles can only be used by those who meet national standards.

Nutritionist is not an accredited profession protected by law—in other words, people with different levels of training and knowledge can call themselves a nutritionist. (Much confusion arises when dietitians call themselves nutritionists, but that's another story!)

Dietitians are trained to give advice on food, diet and nutrition. All dietitians have a bachelor's degree specializing in food and nutrition, and have completed an accredited internship or a graduate degree. Practicing dietitians are regulated in every province.

Many RDs work in hospitals, community health facilities and for home care organizations, counselling patients and developing special eating plans. In the community, public health dietitians offer nutrition programs and healthy eating resources. Dietitians who work in food service manage food preparation and distribution. Dietitians operating private practices consult individuals, groups, workplaces, institutions and the media. Many dietitians are involved in product development, marketing and consumer education within the food industry. And finally, dietitians who work in the government and in education develop food and nutrition policies, teach others and make new discoveries about nutrition and health.

M.G.

BARBARA-JO McINTOSH

AUTHOR OF THE BEST-SELLING *TIN FISH GOURMET*, BARBARA-JO MCINTOSH HAS DEVOTED HER PROFESSIONAL LIFE TO VARIOUS ASPECTS OF THE FOOD AND HOSPITALITY INDUSTRY. FORMERLY THE PROPRIETOR OF BARBARA-JO'S ELEGANT HOME COOKING—A MUCH LOVED VANCOUVER EATERY WITH A SOUTHERN FLAIR—SHE NOW OWNS BARBARA-JO'S BOOKS TO COOKS, A SPECIALTY COOKBOOK STORE IN VANCOUVER'S YALETOWN DISTRICT. BARBARA-JO IS CURRENTLY WORKING ON HER SECOND COOKBOOK FOR RAINCOAST BOOKS, *WHAT WE EAT HERE: SIMPLE RECIPES FROM FOOD GROWN IN B.C.*

I DISCOVERED a lot of wonderful things around the age of six—everything from the thrill of reading to the hard-earned satisfaction of shucking oysters for the benefit of family and friends. Looking back, it's no accident that I'm the proprietor of a cookbook store with a fully functioning kitchen surrounded by shelves. My life has always revolved around the many pleasures of food, books and good company. I've simply found a way to blend my three loves into a recipe that works.

Remove a vintage book from my shelf at home and you may find a smudged tribute to the magic of an especially fine sentence in the form of a floury thumb print or a stray crumb. I will sometimes pass on these cherished books to others, making the circle of my three favourite things complete: food, books, friends. I believe that the creation of each has its own special music. Put them together in a book of recipes and you inevitably get a kind of three-part harmony—the flip of a spoon, the turn of a page, the happy laughter around a shared table. Listen to it long enough, and it becomes the music of the heart.

WEST COAST DELIGHTS

• MOREL MUSHROOM AND ASPARAGUS RAGOUT •
• BEET AND KOHLRABI SALAD WITH ENGLISH PEAS AND QUAIL'S EGGS •
• CELERIAC AND LEMON RISOTTO •
• RHUBARB ROASTED WITH ROSEMARY AND HONEY •

MOREL MUSHROOM AND ASPARAGUS RAGOUT

I like this dish as an appetizer, but it's also very nice served over toast for lunch. Morel mushrooms have an upright, conical body resembling a honeycomb. Look for fresh or dried morels in fine food stores and farmers' markets.

8 large fresh morel mushrooms (or dried, soaked in boiling water for 5 minutes)
1 tbsp butter
1 small leek, washed well and sliced into thin rings (about ½ cup)
2 tbsp dry white wine or vegetable stock
½ cup whipping cream
6 stalks asparagus, sliced into 2-inch pieces and lightly steamed
Sea salt and pepper

Cut 6 of the morels in half lengthwise; set aside.

In medium skillet over high heat, melt butter until foaming; cook leek for 1 minute. Add morels; cook for 1 to 2 minutes or until softened. Add wine; cook for 1 minute or until almost evaporated; stir in cream. Simmer for 3 to 5 minutes or until thickened. Add steamed asparagus and heat through. Season to taste with salt and pepper. Garnish each serving with remaining whole morel.

MAKES 2 SERVINGS.

BEET AND KOHLRABI SALAD WITH ENGLISH PEAS AND QUAIL'S EGGS

Kohlrabi is a "mid-spring" veggie, a member of the cabbage family that tastes like a mild sweet turnip. If fresh peas are not available, substitute frozen. While quail's eggs add allure to this dish, you can substitute three chicken eggs.

3 medium beets, boiled until tender, peeled and sliced into quarters
1 medium kohlrabi, steamed and cut into ½-inch cubes (about 1 cup)
½ cup fresh peas, lightly steamed
6 hard-cooked quail eggs, sliced in half
2 green onions, sliced diagonally into ½-inch pieces
1 stalk celery (including leaves), chopped

DRESSING:

⅓ cup mayonnaise
1 tbsp lemon juice
1 tbsp grated lemon zest
Sea salt and pepper

DRESSING: In bowl, whisk together mayonnaise, lemon juice and lemon zest. Season to taste with salt and pepper.

On large platter, attractively arrange beets, kohlrabi, peas, eggs, onions and celery; drizzle with dressing.

MAKES 2 SERVINGS.

CELERIAC AND LEMON RISOTTO

While knobbly celeriac may look foreboding in the market, it's easy to prep. To start, simply cut a thin slice off the top and bottom. Place it firmly on your cutting board and cut long, vertical strokes along the outer edge to remove the skin. Once peeled, rub with lemon to prevent discolouring.

2 ½ cups vegetable or chicken stock
1 tbsp olive oil
1 small onion, grated (about ⅓ cup)
2 cloves garlic, minced
1 cup finely grated celeriac
¾ cup arborio rice
½ cup dry white wine
½ cup freshly grated Parmesan cheese
1 tbsp grated lemon zest
1 tbsp lemon juice
1 tbsp butter
Pepper
2 tbsp chopped celery leaves or fresh parsley

In small saucepan, bring stock to simmer over medium heat; reduce heat to low and keep warm.

In medium saucepan, heat olive oil over medium heat; cook onion and garlic, stirring, for 5 minutes or until softened without browning. Stir in celeriac and rice until well coated. Add wine and stir until absorbed. Reduce heat to medium-low. Stir in ¼ cup of the warm stock at a time, stirring after each addition until completely absorbed, for about 20 minutes or until rice is creamy and tender.

Remove from heat; stir in Parmesan, lemon zest, lemon juice and butter. Cover and let stand for 5 minutes.

Season to taste with pepper. Garnish with chopped celery leaves.

MAKES 2 SERVINGS.

RHUBARB ROASTED WITH ROSEMARY AND HONEY

Traditionally, rhubarb was used as a spring tonic to dispel the ills of winter. Add some honey and rosemary and you not only enjoy good medicine but great flavour as well. The cream—well, that is just a pleasurable indulgence.

¼ cup water
4 tbsp honey
1 large sprig rosemary, broken into 4 pieces
2 large stalks rhubarb, cut into 2-inch pieces
⅓ cup whipping cream
1 tbsp packed brown sugar

In shallow casserole dish over medium-low heat, bring water, honey and rosemary to simmer; cook for 5 minutes to allow rosemary to infuse. Place rhubarb in casserole dish in single layer. Roast in 350°F oven for 15 minutes or until rhubarb is tender and juices are thickened. Discard rosemary.

Whip cream with brown sugar until soft peaks form. Spoon rhubarb into 2 dessert bowls. Top with whipped cream and drizzle with rhubarb juices.

MAKES 2 SERVINGS.

WENDY BLACKWOOD

WENDY BLACKWOOD IS THE MANAGER OF LOBLAWS COOKING SCHOOLS, LOCATED UPSTAIRS AT LOBLAWS IN 20 STORES ACROSS ONTARIO. AN AVID GARDENER AS WELL AS A CHEF, WENDY HAS BEEN GROWING A VARIETY OF FRUITS AND VEGETABLES IN HER DOWNTOWN TORONTO BACKYARD, AND AT HER HOUSE NEAR KINGSTON, FOR THE PAST 15 YEARS.

SWEET POTATO AND CARROT GRATIN WITH GINGER

The trick to this pretty, saffron-coloured gratin is all in the slicing—you may want to use a mandoline or Benriner for this. Serve as part of a vegetarian meal or try it with roast beef or chicken.

1 cup whipping cream
1 piece (1 inch) fresh ginger, peeled and sliced into 3 pieces
½ cup chicken stock
2 sweet potatoes, peeled and thinly sliced (about 1½ lb)
Salt and pepper
2 green onions, finely chopped
3 large carrots, thinly sliced lengthwise (about ¾ lb)

In small heavy saucepan, heat cream with ginger over medium-high heat until boiling; reduce heat and simmer for about 5 minutes or until cream is reduced by half. Discard ginger; stir in stock.

Pour ¼ cup of the cream mixture into shallow 6-cup gratin or baking dish. Layer one-third of the sweet potatoes on top. Season with salt and pepper. Sprinkle with half of the green onions. Cover with half of the carrots and ¼ cup of the cream mixture. Repeat layers, finishing with layer of sweet potatoes and ¼ cup of cream.

Cover, set on baking sheet to catch drips and bake in 350°F oven for 1 hour. Uncover, spoon any liquid over top of potatoes and bake for 8 to 10 minutes longer or until lightly browned and vegetables are tender. Let stand for 5 minutes before serving.

MAKES 6 TO 8 SERVINGS.

JAN MAIN

JAN MAIN IS A PROFESSIONAL HOME ECONOMIST WHO HAS BEEN TEACHING, CATERING AND WRITING ABOUT FOOD FOR OVER 20 YEARS. SHE HAS WRITTEN THREE COOKBOOKS; THE MOST RECENT, *THE BEST FREEZER COOKBOOK* (ROBERT ROSE, 2001), REFLECTS HER BELIEF THAT GOOD FOOD SHOULD BE MANAGEABLE BY ALL. JAN CURRENTLY TEACHES COOKING AT AN INNER-CITY SCHOOL FOR GIRLS WITH SPECIAL NEEDS.

THE FIRST inkling of food mania hit me at the mature age of eight. I had written a detailed composition about squirrels dining by candlelight on nut loaf. My teacher commented on my romantic notions. I remember feeling puzzled. Romance be darned! The story wasn't about romance. It was all about nut loaf!

Home ec classes of the '60s taught me an initial understanding of recipes and the opportunity to see a career path. (At that time, chef school and the hospitality world were in mere infancy.) Initially, as a newly graduated home economist, I used my cooking skills as a focus to get women on low incomes together for cooking classes. I loved it! However, I soon realized what I loved best was sharing my passion for food with others, so I decided to start my own cooking school. Twenty-five years later, Jan Main's Kitchen continues as a cooking school and catering business. Writing about food was a natural extension—another means of teaching and sharing culinary ideas with others.

WCN, as a vital food network, offers this same opportunity to share food interests with other kindred spirits.

SIMMER UP STEW

• POLISH SAUSAGE STEW •
• LAMB STIFADO •
• TOFU VEGETABLE STEW •
• BOURRIDE •

POLISH SAUSAGE STEW

A great casual winter party dish, this Polish stew—called bigos*—was originally made with the hunter's catch. You can use your favourite meats. For best flavour,* bigos *is made at least one day ahead of serving. Serve with sour cream and rye bread.*

2 lb Polish sausage, sliced into ½-inch rounds
1 lb pork butt, stewing beef, ground pork or ground beef (if using stewing meat, cut into 1-inch cubes)
½ lb side bacon, chopped
3 onions, chopped
3 cloves garlic, minced
4 apples, peeled, cored and sliced
1 small cabbage, shredded
1 can (28 oz/796 mL) sauerkraut, rinsed and drained
1 can (28 oz/796 mL) diced tomatoes, with juice
1 can (5½ oz/156 mL) tomato paste
1 cup dry red wine, apple cider or apple juice
¼ cup packed brown sugar
1 bay leaf
2 tsp chopped fresh thyme
Salt and pepper

In large heavy saucepan over medium-high heat, brown sausage, pork butt and bacon. Drain fat. Stir in onions and garlic; cover and simmer for 5 minutes or until onions are softened.

Add apples, cabbage, sauerkraut, tomatoes, tomato paste, wine, sugar, bay leaf and thyme; bring to boil. Reduce heat and simmer, covered, for about 1½ hours or until meat and vegetables are very tender. Stir stew occasionally adding more wine if necessary. Discard bay leaf. Season to taste with salt and pepper. Let cool and refrigerate. Before reheating, remove any accumulated fat from surface of stew. (Can be covered and refrigerated for up to 3 days. Or freeze for up to 2 months.)

MAKES 10 TO 12 SERVINGS.

LAMB STIFADO

This aromatic Greek stew is especially delicious served with orzo.

2 tbsp olive oil
3 lb lamb leg or shoulder, trimmed and cut into 1-inch cubes
4 cloves garlic, minced
2 onions, chopped
1 can (28 oz/796 mL) diced tomatoes, with juice
1 can (5½ oz/156 mL) tomato paste
1 cup dry red or white wine
½ cup currants, rinsed in warm water
½ cup dried apricots, halved (or prunes, chopped)
2 tbsp honey
2 bay leaves
1 stick cinnamon
1 strip (2 inches) orange peel

1 tsp ground ginger
½ tsp salt
¼ tsp pepper
½ cup chopped fresh parsley

In large heavy saucepan, heat oil over medium-high heat; brown lamb. Stir in garlic and onions; cook, covered, for 5 minutes or until onions are tender.

Stir in tomatoes, tomato paste, red wine, currants, dried apricots, honey, bay leaves, cinnamon stick, orange peel, ginger, salt and pepper; bring to boil. Reduce heat to medium-low and simmer, covered, for 1 to 1½ hours or until meat is tender. Discard bay leaf and orange peel.

Stir in parsley. Taste and adjust seasoning if necessary. Serve immediately or cool, cover and refrigerate. (Can be refrigerated for up to 2 days. Or freeze for up to 2 months.)

MAKES 6 SERVINGS.

TOFU VEGETABLE STEW

Here's a healthy stew bursting with calcium, especially if you buy tofu that has calcium chloride or calcium sulfate included on the label's ingredient list. Napa cabbage looks like regular cabbage except it is oblong and up to 12 inches long. Both bok choy and napa cabbage are available in most large supermarkets. Serve this over Chinese noodles or rice.

2 tbsp vegetable oil
2 cloves garlic, crushed
1 large onion, sliced
2 tbsp grated fresh ginger
1 pkg (12 oz/375 g) firm or extra-firm tofu, sliced into ½-inch cubes
8 oz mushrooms, sliced
2 cups broccoli florets
2 cups shredded napa cabbage
2 cups bok choy
½ sweet red pepper, cut in thin strips

SAUCE:

½ cup chicken stock
¼ cup dry sherry or white wine
3 tbsp soy sauce
2 tsp cornstarch
2 tsp sesame oil
2 tbsp sesame seeds
2 tbsp chopped fresh coriander

In wok or large saucepan, heat oil over medium-high heat; stir-fry garlic, onion and ginger for about 30 seconds. Add tofu; stir-fry for 30 seconds. Add mushrooms, broccoli, napa cabbage, bok choy and red pepper. Reduce heat to medium; cover and cook for about 1 minute.

SAUCE: Meanwhile, whisk together stock, sherry, soy sauce, cornstarch and sesame oil. Pour over vegetable mixture and cook, uncovered, for about 5 minutes or until sauce has thickened slightly and vegetables are tender-crisp. Serve immediately garnished with sesame seeds and coriander.

MAKES 4 SERVINGS.

BOURRIDE

Traditionally, this fish stew from the Provence region of France is made with monkfish. However, any firm white fish will do nicely. Serve with fresh French bread to mop up the juices.

2 tbsp olive oil
3 cloves garlic, minced
1 each onion and leek, chopped
1 can (28 oz/796 mL) diced tomatoes, with juice
1 cup dry white wine
1 strip (2 inches) orange zest
2 bay leaves
½ tsp salt
½ tsp dried thyme
¼ tsp pepper
¼ tsp ground fennel
Pinch cayenne pepper
2 lb firm-fleshed fish such as halibut or haddock, cut into 1-inch cubes
½ cup chopped fresh parsley

AIOLI:

½ cup mayonnaise
3 cloves garlic, minced
2 tsp each white wine vinegar and olive oil

In large saucepan, heat oil over medium-high heat; stir in garlic, onion and leek. Cover and cook for about 5 minutes or until onions are softened.

Add tomatoes, wine, orange zest, bay leaves, salt, thyme, pepper, fennel and cayenne; bring to boil. Reduce heat to medium and simmer for 20 minutes.

Discard bay leaves and orange zest. Add fish cubes and parsley; reduce heat to medium and cook, stirring occasionally, for 10 to 15 minutes or until fish flakes easily with fork.

AIOLI: Meanwhile, in small bowl, whisk together mayonnaise, garlic, vinegar and oil.

Ladle stew into bowls and top with dollop of aioli.

MAKES 6 SERVINGS.

DEBBIE DIAMENT

DEBBIE DIAMENT IS A COMMERCIAL MENU CONSULTANT, AUTHOR, COOKING TEACHER AND RECIPE DEVELOPER. THROUGH HER COMPANY, MY PLACE FOR DINNER, SHE TEACHES HANDS-ON WORKSHOPS THROUGHOUT ONTARIO, AND APPEARS REGULARLY ON TELEVISION. MORE INFORMATION ABOUT DEBBIE AND HER COMPANY CAN BE FOUND AT WWW.MYPLACEFORDINNER.COM.

PAD THAI

This recipe captures the rich flavours of Pad Thai but is lower in fat than most restaurant versions. If you wish to add chicken, stir-fry boneless pieces until cooked with the tofu. Leftovers are wonderful and can be heated in the microwave (but don't nuke the cucumber!).

1 lb wide rice stick noodles
½ cup fish sauce
½ cup canned crushed tomatoes
½ cup granulated sugar
¼ cup lime juice

1 tbsp hot pepper flakes
2 tbsp vegetable oil
4 cloves garlic, minced
6 oz extra-firm tofu, cubed
2 eggs, lightly beaten
12 large raw shrimp, peeled and deveined
4 cups bean sprouts
4 green onions, thinly sliced diagonally
¼ cup unsalted roasted peanuts, coarsely chopped
½ cup peanut sauce

GARNISH:

½ cup chopped fresh coriander
¼ cup unsalted roasted peanuts, coarsely chopped
1 lime, sliced
½ English cucumber, thinly sliced

In large bowl, soak noodles in warm water for 30 minutes; drain and set aside.

In small bowl, combine fish sauce, crushed tomatoes, sugar, lime juice and hot pepper flakes. Set aside.

In wok or large skillet, heat oil over medium-high heat; cook garlic until fragrant. Add tofu and cook for 1 minute. Add egg and shrimp; stir-fry for about 3 minutes or until shrimp are pink.

Stir in noodles until beginning to soften, about 1 minute. Pour in sauce mixture; stir-fry for about 3 minutes or until noodles are tender.

Add bean sprouts, green onions and peanuts; mix well. Stir in peanut sauce; stir-fry for about 2 minutes or until heated through. Serve garnished with coriander, peanuts, lime and cucumber.

MAKES 6 TO 8 SERVINGS.

DANA McCAULEY

DANA McCAULEY IS A SEASONED COOKBOOK AUTHOR AND A CONSULTANT TO MANY NORTH AMERICAN FOOD COMPANIES. SHE IS MARRIED TO THE DEVILISHLY HANDSOME AND TERRIFICALLY TALENTED MARTIN KOUPRIE, CHEF AND CO-OWNER OF TORONTO'S PANGAEA RESTAURANT. MORE INFORMATION ABOUT DANA'S COOKBOOKS AND CORPORATE WORK CAN BE FOUND AT WWW.DANAMCCAULEY.COM.

I GREW UP in a house that often had two grandmothers knocking around in the kitchen at once. Both these women were former farmer's wives who, between them, raised 14 children. Their experience as mothers didn't include Internet grocery shopping, in-store bakeries or even convenience stores. To run their active households required daily bread baking, churning out a pie or cake for both lunch and dinner and possibly throwing together squares for evening snackers.

We lived within walking distance of a grocery store, but my Ukrainian grandmother still baked almost daily during her long stays at our house. I was usually at her elbow, learning how to tell when the dough was moist and pliable enough to be put to rest and how to make an apple upside-down cake using a tea cup with a broken handle for measuring. With Baba, it was all about feel and look; measuring was never discussed.

In fact, although I'd been baking for over 15 years, it wasn't until I was an adult at chef's school and then a recipe tester at *Canadian Living* magazine that I learned how to measure ingredients properly when baking! Luckily for you, I've learned those lessons now and can assure you that these dessert recipes, inspired by my childhood, will work as well for you as they do for me.

COFFEE BREAK CLASSICS

• FOUR-TIER RIBBON CAKE •
• APPLE CRANBERRY COBBLER •
• CHOCOLATE-COATED SHORTBREAD FINGERS •
• SOUR CREAM AND LEMON COFFEE CAKE •

FOUR-TIER RIBBON CAKE

Although this pretty dessert features four layers of cake, only two pans are needed to create it. A wedge of this wonderful cake is nice served with coffee or a glass of milk, but it truly sings when enjoyed with a cup of Earl Grey tea.

3 eggs
2 tsp vanilla
3 cups cake-and-pastry flour
1½ cups granulated sugar
4 tsp baking powder
¾ tsp salt
¾ cup butter, softened
1 cup milk
1 cup redcurrant or seedless raspberry jelly, melted
1½ cups whipping cream

In small bowl, whisk eggs with vanilla; set aside. In large bowl, stir together flour, sugar, baking powder and salt. In another large bowl, beat butter until creamy. Gradually add milk, beating until fluffy, for about 1 minute. Beat in egg mixture, alternating with flour mixture, in 3 additions, scraping down bowl between each addition.

Scrape batter into 2 greased 8-inch round cake pans. Bake in 350°F oven for 30 to 35 minutes or until golden and cake springs back when lightly touched in centre. Let cool on rack for 10 minutes. Turn out onto rack and let cool completely.

Using serrated knife, cut each cake layer in half to make 4 layers. Set aside ¼ cup of the jelly. Place 1 cake layer on cake plate, cut side up. Brush evenly with one-third of the remaining jelly. Top with another layer. Repeat with remaining layers.

Stir cream with reserved jelly. Beat until very thick and spreadable. Spread over top and sides of cake. Refrigerate until serving.

MAKES 10 TO 12 SERVINGS.

APPLE CRANBERRY COBBLER

Equally suited for a brunch or dinner dessert, this cobbler is big enough to feed a crowd. Make sure the cranberries are completely thawed, patted dry with paper towels and at room temperature before you start. If you bake the cranberries when still frozen, the topping will be gooey on the underside.

8 Northern Spy or Spartan apples
4 cups frozen cranberries, thawed
½ cup all-purpose flour
¾ cup packed brown sugar
1 tbsp finely grated orange zest
1 tsp cinnamon

TOPPING:

2 cups all-purpose flour
¾ cup granulated sugar
1 tbsp baking powder
1 tsp salt

¾ cup cold butter, cut into pieces
1 cup milk
1 tsp vanilla
½ cup sliced almonds (optional)

Peel apples and slice thickly. In large bowl, toss apples with cranberries. Stir together flour, brown sugar, orange zest and cinnamon until evenly combined; toss with apple mixture. Spread in greased 13- x 9-inch baking dish.

TOPPING: In medium bowl, combine flour, granulated sugar, baking powder and salt. Using pastry blender or 2 knives, cut in butter until mixture resembles coarse crumbs. In small bowl, stir milk with vanilla; pour over top of dry ingredients and stir just until thick dough forms.

Drop small spoonfuls of topping evenly over fruit mixture; with back of lightly buttered spoon, smooth out until topping is even and touches sides of pan. Sprinkle with almonds (if using).

Bake in 400°F oven for 30 to 35 minutes until topping is golden brown. Lift topping at one corner with fork and check if it is cooked on underside; if necessary, cook for up to 10 minutes longer. Let stand for 15 minutes before serving.

MAKES 6 TO 8 SERVINGS.

CHOCOLATE-COATED SHORTBREAD FINGERS

Even though these cookies are partially coated in chocolate, the delicate taste of the butter is still an important part of the flavour. Use only room-temperature unsalted butter, not margarine or shortening.

1½ cups unsalted butter, softened
1 cup icing sugar
2 tbsp granulated sugar
3¼ cups all-purpose flour
1 tsp vanilla
¼ tsp salt
8 oz semisweet chocolate
2 oz white chocolate (optional)

In large bowl, beat together butter, icing sugar and granulated sugar until light and fluffy. Stir in flour, vanilla and salt. Shape dough into smooth disc.

Roll out dough on lightly floured surface into ¼-inch thick rectangle. Cut into fingers about ¾ inch wide by 2 inches long. Bake on parchment paper–lined cookie sheet in 350°F oven for 10 to 12 minutes or until bottoms are pale golden. Let cool on rack.

Melt semisweet chocolate in deep, microwave-proof bowl at medium until softened; stir until melted. Brush over cooled cookies. Refrigerate until set. Meanwhile, melt white chocolate (if using); using tines of fork, drizzle white chocolate over dark chocolate. Refrigerate until set.

MAKES ABOUT 5 DOZEN COOKIES.

SOUR CREAM AND LEMON COFFEE CAKE

Sky-high and featuring a crunchy, nutty topping, this moist coffee cake keeps wonderfully well—if you can keep your hands off it long enough to have leftovers! Before removing the pan from the oven, test the cake with a long wooden skewer or metal testing rod to be sure that the centre is not gooey.

¾ cup packed brown sugar
1 tbsp all-purpose flour
1 tsp cinnamon
2 tbsp butter

1 cup slivered almonds
1 tbsp lemon juice

CAKE:

2 cups all-purpose flour
1 tsp each baking powder and baking soda
¼ tsp salt
½ cup butter, softened
1 cup granulated sugar
2 tbsp finely grated lemon zest
3 eggs
1 cup sour cream
½ cup raisins

In bowl, combine brown sugar, flour and cinnamon. Using rubber spatula, rub in butter. Stir in almonds and lemon juice. Set aside.

CAKE: Grease 8-inch round springform pan. Line bottom with square of waxed or parchment paper. In bowl, combine flour, baking powder, baking soda and salt. In another bowl, beat butter until creamy; beat in sugar and lemon zest until fluffy. Add eggs, 1 at a time, beating until light. Add flour mixture alternately with sour cream in 3 additions. Stir in raisins.

Scrape half of the batter into prepared pan. Sprinkle half of the almond mixture evenly over top. Top with remaining batter, smoothing with spatula. Sprinkle remaining almond mixture evenly over top. Bake in 325°F oven for 65 to 70 minutes or until tester inserted in centre comes out clean. Let cool in pan on rack.

MAKES 10 SERVINGS.

LENORE LOCKEN

LENORE LOCKEN IS A WRITER AND EDITOR SPECIALIZING IN BOTH FOOD AND COMPUTERS. SHE IS EDITOR OF THE COOKING NEWSLETTER, *ALPHABET SOUP*, AND IS ALSO THE MANAGING EDITOR OF *WE COMPUTE MAGAZINE*. HER ARTICLES HAVE APPEARED IN MANY PUBLICATIONS. OBSESSED WITH FOOD HISTORY, SHE IS AN AVID COLLECTOR OF PRE-1960S COOKBOOKS, RECIPE PAMPHLETS AND NEWSPAPER CLIPPINGS.

NANA'S CLAM CHOWDER

Chowders don't have to be laced with cream. Try this Manhattan-style version based on an original recipe by my paternal grandmother, Vivian Severud. It's comfort food at its best. The bacon drippings add flavour, but leave them out if you're strict about fat intake. It's not necessary to thicken the soup, but my grandmother always did, so I have included that step. Serve the chowder with fresh bread.

4 potatoes, peeled and cubed
2 onions, chopped
2 garlic cloves, minced
1 tsp dried oregano
½ tsp dried thyme
1 tsp salt
½ tsp pepper
4 slices bacon
2 tbsp bacon drippings (optional)
1 can (28 oz/796 mL) tomatoes
1 can (5 oz) baby clams
2 tbsp all-purpose flour
2 tsp water

In large heavy saucepan, combine potatoes, onions, garlic, oregano, thyme, salt and pepper. Cover with water and bring to boil. Reduce heat and simmer for 20 minutes or until potatoes are tender.

In skillet over medium-high heat, fry bacon for about 8 minutes until crisp. Drain on paper towel. Crumble and stir into potatoes along with drippings (if using). Stir in tomatoes and clams with their liquid. Using wooden spoon, press tomatoes against side of pan to break up; simmer, covered, for 15 minutes.

Whisk flour with water to make smooth paste. Remove pan from heat; whisk in flour mixture. Return to heat and simmer, covered, for 5 minutes.

MAKES 8 SERVINGS.

JOAN MOORE

JOAN MOORE IS A COOKING INSTRUCTOR AND PROFESSIONAL CATERER. HER FOCUS IS ON TRADITIONAL CARIBBEAN COUNTRY COOKING AND THE HISTORY OF REGIONAL COUNTRY CUISINE. SHE IS ALSO A DEDICATED GARDENER WHO GROWS AN ARRAY OF NATURAL FOODS, HERBS AND SPICES. A GRADUATE OF CULINARY MANAGEMENT AT GEORGE BROWN COLLEGE SCHOOL OF HOSPITALITY, MOORE'S ARTICLES HAVE BEEN PUBLISHED BY THE CULINARY HISTORIANS OF ONTARIO AND HER RECIPES HAVE APPEARED IN THE *TORONTO STAR,* THE *TORONTO SUN* AND VARIOUS COMMUNITY NEWSPAPERS.

MY ROMANCE with food started in the hills of my native Jamaica, when I visited my grandmother, Mrs. Anetta Moyston, a.k.a. "Ma'Neta," during summer vacations. Her kitchen was simple but effective. Above a fire of pimento embers, she smoked meats for soups and stews. In heavy iron cauldrons, she transformed white coconut milk into golden, savoury oil. Ripe bananas or sugar cane juice was made into the best vinegar for preserving the produce of a bountiful garden. From the bubbling brooks and rivers nearby, we caught crayfish to be made into "pepper shrimp," and from natural springs below her house, we picked tangy watercress for salads. The aromas from her kitchen drew everyone to the fireside, and the ease with which she prepared the meals revealed a genius at work. I have always wanted to cook like her.

As a member of the Women's Culinary Network, I get to explore the world of food with other professionals. Each meeting expands my horizons, whether it's information on food history conventions or going to a laboratory to learn how food is tested for marketing. And if there are business or job opportunities, there is always someone willing to share.

The following recipes are dedicated to Ma'Neta (she died in February 2001, just three months before her 100th birthday) and the art of Jamaican country cookery. All ingredients are available in large supermarkets or Caribbean food stores.

A TASTE OF JAMAICA

• PEPPER SHRIMP AND WATERCRESS SALAD WITH LEMON DRESSING •

• JAMAICAN-STYLE FRICASSEE CHICKEN, •

• RICE 'N' PEAS •

• TROPICAL FRUIT SORBET •

Penne with Olives, Capers, Sun-dried Tomatoes and Chickpeas (page 24)

Squash and Pear Soup (page 46)

Orange Ginger Baby Back Pork Ribs (page 9)

Cinnamon Cornish Hens with Balsamic Glaze (page 67)

Lamb Tagine (page 123)

Pepper Shrimp and Watercress Salad with Lemon Dressing (page 83)

Caramelized Peaches with Sweet Wine Sabayon (page 34)

Chocolate Fudge Tarts (page 108)

PEPPER SHRIMP AND WATERCRESS SALAD WITH LEMON DRESSING

This makes an elegant appetizer but also works as a wonderful snack (without the watercress) for Super Bowl parties and other casual get-togethers. Dried annatto seeds can be found in Caribbean, East Indian and Asian stores; paprika is a good substitute if you can't find them.

½ cup vegetable oil
1 tsp dried annatto seeds
6 allspice berries
2 whole dried hot peppers
1 lb large raw shrimp, peeled and deveined (about 20)
½ tsp each salt and pepper
5 cups watercress (about 2 bunches)
2 tbsp chopped green onions

DRESSING:

¼ cup lemon juice
1 tbsp vegetable oil
1 tsp granulated sugar
½ tsp each salt and pepper
½ tsp minced garlic

In small saucepan, heat oil over medium-high heat until hot but not smoking. Remove pan from heat and add annatto and allspice. Break up peppers and add to hot oil. Let stand at room temperature overnight. Strain pepper oil into small bowl and discard annatto, allspice and peppers.

In large heavy skillet, heat pepper oil over medium-high heat until hot but not smoking; cook shrimp, in batches, until starting to turn pink. Drain on paper towel. Sprinkle with salt and pepper.

DRESSING: In small bowl, whisk together lemon juice, oil, sugar, salt, pepper and garlic. Set aside.

Rinse watercress and pat dry. Remove and discard tough stems. Divide watercress among 4 plates. Top each plate with 5 shrimp and drizzle with dressing. Garnish with green onions.

MAKES 4 SERVINGS.

JAMAICAN-STYLE FRICASSEE CHICKEN

Fricassee chicken is a favourite dish at the Jamaican Sunday dinner table, usually served with rice 'n' peas, but plain steamed rice is acceptable. In Canada, creamy mashed potatoes will do justice to the dish. Fricassee chicken freezes well. Thaw overnight in refrigerator and reheat in the microwave.

3 lb chicken pieces
2 tbsp dark soy sauce
1 tbsp packed brown sugar
2 tsp minced garlic
1 tsp chopped fresh thyme
½ tsp minced Scotch bonnet pepper
1 tsp ground allspice
1 tsp pepper
½ tsp salt
½ cup vegetable oil
1½ cups canned diced tomatoes with juice
1 cup diced onion
1 cup diced sweet red pepper
½ cup diced sweet green pepper

Remove and discard excess fat from chicken. Rinse under cold running water, pat dry and place in large bowl. Add soy sauce, sugar, garlic, thyme, Scotch bonnet pepper, allspice, pepper and salt. Turn chicken pieces to coat evenly. Cover with plastic wrap and refrigerate for at least 2 hours or for up to 1 day, turning once.

In large deep skillet, heat oil over medium-high heat until hot but not smoking; brown chicken, in batches. Transfer to platter and set aside. Add diced tomatoes, onion, and red and green peppers to skillet; reduce heat to medium and cook, stirring occasionally, for 5 minutes.

Return browned chicken to skillet. Spoon mixture over chicken. Cook, covered, over medium heat for about 1 hour or until chicken is cooked through, very tender and sauce has thickened. Taste and adjust seasoning if desired.

MAKES 4 SERVINGS.

RICE 'N' PEAS

Serve this side dish—another Jamaican Sunday dinner standard—with chicken, roast beef or other meats, along with a rich gravy and steamed vegetables such as callaloo, okra, chayote, pumpkin or carrots. Fried ripe plantains and sometimes boiled yams often accompany the meal, too.

¾ cup dried red kidney beans
1 small onion, peeled
2 cloves garlic, peeled
2 tbsp coconut cream
2 sprigs fresh thyme
1 green onion, crushed
½ tsp ground allspice
½ tsp each salt and pepper
1 green Scotch bonnet pepper
1½ cups parboiled rice

Remove any grit from beans and wash in sieve under cold running water. Place washed beans in bowl with 4 cups cold water. Cover and let soak for 8 hours or overnight; drain.

In medium saucepan, cover soaked beans with 6 cups cold water. Add onion and garlic; bring to boil. Reduce heat to medium and cook, partially covered, until beans are tender and water is reduced by about half. Do not allow to boil over.

Add coconut cream, thyme, green onion, allspice, salt, pepper and Scotch bonnet pepper; simmer, covered, for about 15 minutes.

Add rice and stir well; return to boil. Reduce heat to low; cook, covered, for about 20 minutes or until water is absorbed and rice is tender. Turn off heat. Remove Scotch bonnet pepper. With fork, carefully fluff rice and beans. Remove onion, green onion, garlic and thyme. Cover and let stand for 15 minutes.

MAKES 4 SERVINGS.

TROPICAL FRUIT SORBET

Here's a refreshing backyard treat for a hot summer day. Substitute very ripe peaches (peeled) if mangoes are not available. Sorbet can be prepared and frozen up to a week ahead; transfer to refrigerator about an hour before serving.

½ cup granulated sugar
½ cup water
1 cup diced ripe mango (about 1)
1 cup diced fresh pineapple
1 cup diced ripe banana (about 2)
1 tsp grated lime zest
1 tbsp lime juice
4 sprigs mint

In small heavy saucepan over low heat, combine sugar and water, stirring until sugar is dissolved; simmer for 1 minute. Remove from heat and set aside to cool.

In non-aluminum bowl, combine mango, pineapple, banana, and lime zest and juice. Stir in cooled sugar syrup.

Transfer to food processor or blender; process until smooth. Return to bowl, cover with plastic wrap and refrigerate, preferably overnight, until well chilled.

Freeze in ice cream maker following manufacturer's instructions. Sorbet will be soft. To harden, place in freezer-safe container and freeze for 2 to 3 hours. Serve in chilled glass garnished with mint.

MAKES 4 SERVINGS.

KASIA LUCKEVICH

KASIA LUCKEVICH GRADUATED FROM THE UNIVERSITY OF GUELPH WITH A DEGREE IN CHEMISTRY AND FOOD SCIENCE, THEN CONTINUED STUDIES AT THE STRATFORD CHEFS SCHOOL. SHE HAS WORKED AROUND THE WORLD, INCLUDING TWO YEARS OF COOKING ON PRIVATE YACHTS IN THE CARIBBEAN, A STINT AS PRIVATE CHEF FOR NORMAN JEWISON, AND A YEAR IN TASMANIA, AUSTRALIA, DISCOVERING THE LOCAL CUISINE. KASIA NOW WORKS IN TORONTO AS A PRODUCT DEVELOPER FOR THE PRESIDENT'S CHOICE PRIVATE LABEL.

GAZPACHO

Gazpacho is a fresh and crunchy summer soup, and here, I've enlivened it with Bloody Caesar cocktail flavours. Try it with a shot of vodka for an extra kick!

6 cups clam-flavoured tomato juice
1 cup diced celery
1 cup diced sweet red pepper
1 cup diced fresh tomato
1 cup diced English cucumber
1 cup finely chopped fresh coriander
½ cup finely diced onion
½ cup diced sweet yellow pepper
2 tbsp Worcestershire sauce
2 tbsp finely chopped jalapeño pepper or 1 tsp hot pepper sauce
Salt and pepper
Celery stalks

In large bowl, combine clam-flavoured tomato juice, celery, red pepper, tomato, cucumber, coriander, onion, yellow pepper, Worcestershire and jalapeño pepper. Season to taste with salt and pepper. Refrigerate for 4 to 6 hours before serving. Serve in large cocktail or margarita glasses with celery stalk as garnish.

MAKES 10 TO 12 SERVINGS.

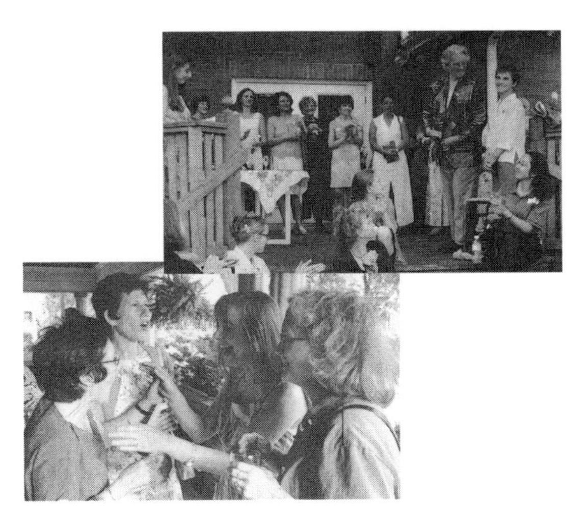

RECIPE DEVELOPER

How is a recipe born? The answer is found among those creative WCN individuals who develop recipes for food companies, the media or cookbooks. A successful recipe developer has a good sense of taste, an insatiable desire to create and a firm understanding of food science. If she's a cookbook author, she's probably well versed in food trends or simply possesses an innate understanding of good flavours. Corporate recipe developers keep their clients happy by delivering recipes that reflect corporate objectives. Food writers for magazines and newspapers design recipes that reflect the tone of the publication and draw in readers with their appeal. But most of all, a good recipe developer creates original, concise recipes that work every time and taste delicious.

How do they do it? Most recipe developers draw inspiration from a variety of sources—be it travel, restaurant dining, market sleuthing or a large library of cookbooks and food magazines. Many consider culinary education an ongoing process, constantly upgrading skills through cooking classes. But no doubt the biggest factor in successful creativity is endless time spent working (many call it "playing") in the kitchen.

Beyond creativity, recipes that work rely on sound science. Recipe developers measure, time and weigh everything, wielding pen and paper alongside knives and spoons. While creative concepts behind the recipes often arrive spontaneously, the final product is usually laboriously rewritten and tested numerous times before completion.

M.G.

ANTOINETTE PASSALACQUA

ANTOINETTE PASSALACQUA MANAGES THE EXECUTIVE DINING FACILITIES AT SCOTIA CAPITAL IN DOWNTOWN TORONTO AND IS AN ACTIVE VOLUNTEER WITH SECOND HARVEST CHARITABLE FOOD ORGANIZATION. IN 2001, ANTOINETTE RECEIVED THE WOMAN OF THE YEAR AWARD FROM THE WOMEN'S CULINARY NETWORK.

MY PASSION for the food business and traditional Italian recipes began at a very young age, when I began working in my family's trattoria and salumeria in the town of Entratico, northeast of Milan, in the Lombardy region of Italy.

Back in the early days, the luxury of going to the supermarket to search out any ingredient imaginable did not exist. Meals were prepared according to the seasons, with the land and climate dictating what would be on our plates. For this reason, I believe that the best dishes are those that are kept simple based on common household ingredients.

The Women's Culinary Network allows me to share my experiences with like-minded individuals and to hear how they started in the business. We all come from different culinary traditions yet seamlessly converge through the common elements of good taste and presentation.

REAL ITALIAN COOKING

• LASAGNA AL FORNO WITH BOLOGNESE AND BÉCHAMEL SAUCES •
• VEAL PICCATA AL MARSALA •
• ARUGULA, RADICCHIO AND CURLY ENDIVE SALAD WITH BALSAMIC VINAIGRETTE •
• ZABAGLIONE FREDDO WITH FRESH BERRIES •

LASAGNA AL FORNO WITH BOLOGNESE AND BÉCHAMEL SAUCES

This is a hearty dish that can be used as a main course. Prepare the Bolognese Sauce a day ahead and assemble and bake the lasagna the day the guests arrive. For a vegetarian version, replace the meat in the Bolognese Sauce with two bags of spinach, steamed and drained. Leftovers freeze well.

1 pkg (12.3 oz) fresh lasagna noodles, cut in half lengthwise (or about 15 dry noodles)
2 cups Bolognese Sauce (recipe follows)
2 cups shredded mozzarella cheese
1 cup freshly grated Parmesan cheese
¾ cup butter, cut into very small cubes
1 tbsp fresh bread crumbs

BÉCHAMEL SAUCE:

1½ cups milk
1 bouquet garni (1 bay leaf, 1 sprig each fresh oregano and rosemary, 1 slice onion, tied up in cheesecloth)
½ tsp salt
3 tbsp butter

3 tbsp all-purpose flour
¼ tsp nutmeg
¼ tsp pepper

In large pot of boiling salted water, cook noodles, a few at a time, for 1 minute or until pasta rises to surface. Rinse noodles under cold running water and lay on tea towel. (If using dried pasta, cook according to package directions.)

BÉCHAMEL SAUCE: In saucepan, bring milk, bouquet garni and salt to boil; turn off heat. In another saucepan, melt butter over medium heat; whisk in flour and cook, stirring, for 2 minutes without browning. Remove from heat and gradually whisk in milk mixture until smooth. Return to heat and bring to boil; reduce heat to low and cook, stirring constantly, for 10 minutes or until thickened. Stir in nutmeg and pepper. Taste and adjust seasoning.

Spread about ½ cup Bolognese Sauce over bottom of greased 13- x 9-inch baking dish. Place 3 noodles very loosely on top of sauce. Stir together mozzarella cheese and all but ¼ cup of the Parmesan cheese. Cover first layer of noodles with ½ cup Bolognese Sauce, ½ cup of the cheese mixture and a few cubes of butter. Loosely cover with another layer of noodles and spread with Béchamel Sauce. Sprinkle with ½ cup of the cheese mixture and a few cubes of butter. Continue layering lasagna, criss-crossing noodles and alternating layers of Bolognese and Béchamel Sauces until lasagna reaches top of baking dish ending with Bolognese Sauce and remaining cheese mixture. Sprinkle top with reserved Parmesan cheese, bread crumbs and remaining cubes of butter. Bake in 375°F oven for 40 minutes or until bubbling. Let stand for 10 minutes.

MAKES 8 SERVINGS.

BOLOGNESE SAUCE:

¼ cup olive oil
1 small red onion, finely chopped
½ stalk celery, finely chopped
½ sweet green pepper, finely chopped
3 cloves garlic, minced
2 cans (each 28 oz/796 mL) whole tomatoes with juice, chopped
3 tbsp tomato paste
1 bay leaf
1 tsp minced hot pepper
1 bouquet garni (3 whole cloves, 6 peppercorns, 1 sprig each fresh rosemary, basil and oregano, tied up in cheesecloth)
1 lb lean ground beef
Salt and pepper
1½ cups chicken stock (approx)

In large saucepan, heat half of the oil over medium heat; cook onion, celery and green pepper for 2 to 3 minutes. Add garlic; cook for 1 minute. Add tomatoes, tomato paste, bay leaf, hot pepper and bouquet garni. Remove from heat.

In skillet, heat remaining oil over high heat; add beef and season with salt and pepper. Cook until browned, about 5 minutes. Drain off any excess fat from beef; add beef to sauce. Pour in 1 cup of the stock; bring to boil. Reduce heat and simmer for 1 hour. Remove bay leaf, hot pepper and bouquet garni; taste and adjust seasoning. Sauce must be quite thin, and tomatoes and meat chunks quite small. If too thick, add as much of remaining stock as necessary.

MAKES 7 CUPS.

VEAL PICCATA AL MARSALA

This recipe is very versatile; use chicken, turkey or pork loin instead of the veal. The Marsala wine can be replaced with red, white or sweet wine, lemon or orange juice or 18% real cream.

8 thin veal cutlets (about 1½ lb)
Salt and pepper
Seasoned Flour (recipe follows)
1½ tbsp olive oil
1½ tbsp butter
½ cup chicken stock
¼ cup dry Marsala
1 tbsp chopped fresh parsley

Pat veal dry with paper towels. If too thick, pound between 2 pieces of waxed paper. Dust lightly with Seasoned Flour.

In skillet, heat oil and butter over medium-high heat; cook veal, in batches, for 1 to 2 minutes per side, being careful not to overcook or veal will get tough. Transfer to plate. Add stock and Marsala to pan; simmer for 2 minutes or until sauce is slightly thickened. Return veal to pan and cook for 1 minute. Transfer to platter or individual plates and garnish with parsley.

MAKES 8 SERVINGS.

SEASONED FLOUR:

½ cup all-purpose flour
½ tsp sea salt
¼ tsp dried thyme
¼ tsp dried sage
Pinch pepper
Pinch freshly grated nutmeg

In small bowl, combine flour, salt, thyme, sage, pepper and nutmeg.

MAKES ABOUT ½ CUP.

ARUGULA, RADICCHIO AND CURLY ENDIVE SALAD WITH BALSAMIC VINAIGRETTE

Here's a mix of nutty and bitter lettuces, rounded out by a simple vinaigrette. Break leaves into bite-size pieces by hand to prevent browning.

1 bunch arugula
1 head radicchio
1 small head curly endive

VINAIGRETTE:

½ cup extra-virgin olive oil
2 tbsp balsamic vinegar
1 tsp salt
¼ tsp pepper

Wash and pat dry arugula, radicchio and endive. Break leaves into bite-size pieces and toss together in bowl.

VINAIGRETTE: In small bowl, whisk together oil, vinegar, salt and pepper. Toss with greens to coat.

MAKES 6 TO 8 SERVINGS.

ZABAGLIONE FREDDO WITH FRESH BERRIES

Anyone who loves berries and cream is likely to relish this gorgeous Italian version. Be sure to gently heat the egg yolks so that a smooth custard forms, not scrambled eggs!

2 cups berries (strawberries, blueberries, raspberries or combination)
1 cup whipping cream
4 tbsp granulated sugar
4 large egg yolks
4 tbsp water
4 tbsp Marsala, or other sweet wine
½ cup lemon juice

Wash berries and drain well. Reserving 8 berries for garnish, divide remaining among 8 tall wine or dessert glasses; set aside in refrigerator. Whip cream with ½ tsp sugar of the sugar until soft peaks form; refrigerate.

In bowl large enough to fit in large saucepan, whisk together egg yolks, water, Marsala, lemon juice and remaining sugar. Set bowl in saucepan of barely simmering water (do not allow water to boil). Using whisk or electric beaters, beat until mixture thickens to custard consistency. Remove bowl from heat and place over ice; whisk mixture to cool. Fold in whipped cream. Pour over berries. Refrigerate until serving.

MAKES 8 SERVINGS.

IRENE RICHARDS

IRENE RICHARDS IS A CHEF AND FOOD STYLIST WITH A LOVE OF TRAVEL. WORKING IN THE FILM INDUSTRY, IRENE HAS CATERED FOR THE CAST AND CREW OF "THE X-FILES" TV SERIES AND NUMEROUS FEATURE FILMS. SHE HAS STYLED FOR COOKING SHOWS AND MOVIES—INCLUDING THE FILM *A WRINKLE IN TIME*—SOMETIMES UNDER CHALLENGING CONDITIONS. IRENE CURRENTLY ENJOYS SPENDING HER WINTERS IN THE CARIBBEAN AS A PRIVATE CHEF ON YACHTS.

LEMON ORZO WITH DEEP-FRIED CAPERS

This is one of my favourite comfort food recipes. It can be served hot, warm or cold, in winter or summer, and embellished as you like. It is amazingly simple to produce!

1 cup vegetable oil
1 cup capers, drained and patted dry on paper towel
8 cups water
1 cup orzo pasta
1 tsp salt
1 tbsp olive oil
2 tbsp butter
Grated zest and juice of 1 lemon
¼ cup finely chopped fresh parsley
¼ cup finely chopped fresh dill
Salt

In small deep saucepan or skillet, heat oil over medium-high heat. Drop 1 caper in oil to test temperature; oil should be hot enough for caper to expand like flower. Gently add remaining capers. Shake pan until capers "blossom" or "pop" and are slightly golden. Remove from heat; drain in sieve then on paper towel. Set aside.

In large pot of boiling salted water, cook orzo with olive oil for 8 to 10 minutes or until just tender. Drain. Return to pot and stir in butter to coat. Stir in lemon zest and juice to taste. Stir in herbs and fried capers. Season to taste with salt.

MAKES 6 SERVINGS.

DAPHNA RABINOVITCH

DAPHNA RABINOVITCH IS A CLASSICALLY TRAINED CHEF AND PASTRY CHEF, FOOD WRITER AND RECIPE DEVELOPER. DAPHNA IS CO-HOST OF "CANADIAN LIVING COOKS" (FOOD NETWORK CANADA) AND TEACHES COOKING CLASSES ACROSS THE COUNTRY. SHE STARTED HER COOKING CAREER AS A PASTRY CHEF AND WORKED AT *CANADIAN LIVING* MAGAZINE FROM 1990 TO 2002. SHE IS THE AUTHOR OF THE AWARD-WINNING COOKBOOK *CANADIAN LIVING COOKS STEP BY STEP* (RANDOM HOUSE, 1999).

I FEEL passionate about Italian food. After completing my chef training in San Francisco, I had the good fortune to live and work in Tuscany, where I discovered the Italian gusto for fine food and reverence for simple ingredients. That pretty much sums up the way I feel about food. Whether you are cooking or consuming it, the process should be relished and filled with pure joy.

I love all different kinds of foods and am particularly interested in the history and sociology of food. It's the simplest things, such as the intoxicating aroma of an aged balsamic vinegar, the heady perfume of a straw-coloured Parmigiano-Reggiano or the sweet succulence of a perfectly ripe fig, that speak to me and fill me with a sense of satisfaction and wonder.

It's that sense of adventure, love of eating and mutual quest for constant learning that I find so enthralling about the Women's Culinary Network. There's nothing more welcoming than a room, home or auditorium full of like-minded individuals who are as passionate about food as I am.

NORTHERN ITALIAN FLAIR

• OSSO BUCO •

• RISOTTO MILANESE •

• CHOCOLATE FIG CAKE WITH GIANDUJA GLAZE •

OSSO BUCO

These melt-in-your-mouth veal shanks literally fall off the bone after a long, slow bake in the oven. While you can cook this ahead (up to a day), don't garnish with gremolata until just before serving.

6 thick pieces (1½ inches) veal shanks
3 tbsp all-purpose flour
½ tsp each salt and pepper
2 tbsp extra-virgin olive oil
1 tbsp butter
1 onion, chopped
⅔ cup each chopped carrot and celery
3 cloves garlic, minced
2 strips lemon zest

¾ tsp dried sage
½ tsp dried thyme
6 sprigs fresh Italian parsley
1 cup dry white wine
1½ cups (approx) canned tomatoes, coarsely chopped
1 cup beef stock
2 bay leaves

GREMOLATA TOPPING:

¼ cup finely chopped fresh Italian parsley
1 tbsp finely grated lemon zest
1 clove garlic, minced

Using kitchen string, wrap each veal shank firmly but not overly tightly to prevent them from falling apart. On plate or shallow pie plate, combine flour with half each of the salt and pepper; dredge shanks in flour mixture, coating both sides well. Reserve any remaining flour mixture.

In pot large enough to accommodate all shanks in single layer, heat oil and butter over medium-high heat; cook shanks in batches until browned on both sides. Using tongs, transfer to plate.

Reduce heat to medium. Add onion, carrot, celery, garlic, lemon zest, sage, thyme and parsley to pan; cook, stirring often, for about 10 minutes or until softened. Stir in reserved flour; cook, stirring, for 1 minute. Stir in wine, scraping up any brown bits. Bring to boil; boil until reduced by half.

Stir in tomatoes, stock, bay leaves and remaining salt and pepper; bring to boil. Nestle shanks in mixture, adding any juices accumulated on plate. (Tomato mixture should come about two-thirds of the way up to top of shanks. If it does not, add another ¼ to ½ cup of tomatoes.) Cover tightly and bake in centre of 350°F oven for 2 hours, basting every 20 minutes.

Transfer shanks to deep platter. Cut off string and tent with foil to keep warm. Remove parsley sprigs and bay leaves from sauce; discard. Place pan over medium-high heat; bring to boil. Boil, stirring constantly, for about 5 minutes or until sauce is thickened; pour over shanks.

GREMOLATA TOPPING: Meanwhile, stir together parsley, lemon zest and garlic. Sprinkle over shanks and sauce.

MAKES 6 SERVINGS.

RISOTTO MILANESE

Although a bit time-consuming, risotto is worth every minute it takes to create that creamy indulgence. It's great with osso buco but also lovely with veal or pork chops or even an Italian-flavoured roast. Or make a meal of it, served with a refeshing green salad as the sole accompaniment.

4 cups chicken stock
1 cup water
¼ tsp saffron threads, crumbled
2 tbsp extra-virgin olive oil
1 tbsp butter
3 tbsp chopped pancetta
1 small onion, finely chopped
2 cups arborio rice
1 cup dry white wine
⅔ cup freshly grated Parmesan cheese

In saucepan, bring stock, water and saffron to simmer over medium heat; keep warm over low heat.

In separate large heavy-bottomed saucepan, melt oil and butter over medium heat; cook pancetta and onion, stirring, for 5 minutes or until softened. Stir in rice until well coated.

Stir in ½ cup of the warm stock; cook, stirring constantly, until stock is absorbed. Stir in wine; cook, stirring constantly, until all wine is absorbed. Continue to add stock, ½ cup at a time, stirring after each addition until absorbed, for about 25 minutes. (Rice should be creamy and tender but still a little firm to the bite, with a little flow to sauce.) Stir in Parmesan cheese.

MAKES 6 SERVINGS.

CHOCOLATE FIG CAKE WITH GIANDUJA GLAZE

Gianduja (pronounced jon-DOO-ya) is a creamy blend of pulverized hazelnuts and milk chocolate that is very popular in Italy and available in specialty food stores. If unavailable, substitute any hazelnut-flavoured chocolate. For an extra-special presentation, place five or six blanched sliced almonds under each hazelnut on top of the cake to resemble the petals of a nut "flower."

½ cup dried figs, coarsely chopped
½ cup Armagnac or cognac
4 oz bittersweet chocolate, coarsely chopped
1¼ cups toasted hazelnuts, skins rubbed off
¼ cup vanilla wafer crumbs
½ cup unsalted butter, softened
⅔ cup granulated sugar
Pinch salt

GLAZE:

¾ cup whipping cream
4 oz bittersweet chocolate, coarsely chopped
3 oz Gianduja chocolate, coarsely chopped

In small saucepan, over medium-high heat, combine figs and Armagnac; bring to boil. Remove from heat; let cool.

In small bowl set over saucepan of hot (not boiling) water, melt chocolate. Remove from heat; let cool.

Reserving 8 of the best hazelnuts, grind remaining hazelnuts in food processor with vanilla wafer crumbs to fine powder.

Using electric beaters, beat butter with sugar until light and fluffy. Beat in eggs, 1 at a time, beating well after each addition (mixture may look a little separated). Fold in melted chocolate. Fold in hazelnuts, then figs. Scrape into greased and floured 8-inch cake pan; spread evenly. Bake in centre of 375°F oven for about 30 minutes or until sides of cake are set but centre looks a little underdone. Let cool in pan on rack for 15 minutes. Turn out onto rack and let cool completely. (Cake can be wrapped in plastic wrap, overwrapped in foil and frozen for up to 2 weeks.)

GLAZE: Bring whipping cream to boil; pour over bittersweet and Gianduja chocolate, whisking until melted and smooth. Pour half of the glaze over cake; refrigerate for 30 minutes. If necessary, rewarm remaining glaze over saucepan of hot water until pourable; pour over cake. Refrigerate for 20 to 30 minutes or until set. Garnish with reserved hazelnuts. (Cake can be refrigerated for up to 24 hours.)

MAKES 8 TO 12 SERVINGS.

LINDA HAYNES

LINDA IS CO-FOUNDER AND CO-OWNER OF ACE BAKERY LIMITED, A SPECIALTY GOURMET BAKERY PROVIDING FRESHLY BAKED, ARTISANAL, EUROPEAN-STYLE BREADS IN ONTARIO. TEN PER CENT OF ACE'S PROFITS IS DONATED TO CHARITABLE ORGANIZATIONS IN THE PRINCIPAL CENTRES WHERE ACE BREADS ARE SOLD. THE FOCUS IS ON FOOD AND NUTRITION PROGRAMS THAT ASSIST LOW-INCOME MEMBERS OF THE COMMUNITY. LINDA, A FORMER TV PRODUCER, HAS BEEN ACTIVE SERVING ON BOARDS OF ARTS AND CHILD-CENTRED AGENCIES.

BREAD AND TOMATO SOUP

Depending on the occasion, or your mood, you can serve this soup in different ways. For a rustic soup, keep it chunky, adding a few toasted bread cubes to each bowl before serving. For a more sophisticated soup, purée in batches, reheat and garnish each bowl with a few croutons.

3 tbsp olive oil
1 medium onion, roughly chopped
1 bay leaf
1 clove garlic, chopped
3½ cups cubed Italian bread
1 can (28 oz/796 mL) tomatoes
4 cups vegetable or chicken stock
1 tbsp chopped fresh oregano (or 1½ tsp dried)
1 tsp chopped fresh thyme (or ½ tsp dried)
Salt and white pepper

In large saucepan, heat oil over medium-high heat; cook onion and bay leaf until onions are light golden. Add garlic and cook for 1 minute. Stir in 2 cups of the bread cubes; cook for 5 to 7 minutes or until bread is well coated with oil and lightly toasted.

Drain tomatoes, reserving 1 cup juice. Add to pot along with stock, oregano and thyme; cook for 10 minutes, stirring occasionally. Add reserved juice if soup is too thick. Season to taste with salt and pepper. Discard bay leaf. Purée if desired

Arrange remaining bread cubes in single layer on baking sheet; bake in 350°F oven for 10 minutes or until lightly toasted. Ladle soup into bowls. Stir a few bread cubes into each bowl of soup before serving.

MAKES 6 TO 8 SERVINGS.

ROSE REISMAN

ROSE REISMAN IS THE AUTHOR OF 12 COOKBOOKS, WITH OVER 750,000 COPIES IN PRINT. SHE HAS RAISED OVER ONE MILLION DOLLARS FOR BREAST CANCER RESEARCH AND EDUCATION THROUGH COOKBOOK SALES. ROSE APPEARS DAILY ON HER HEALTH NETWORK SHOW "LIGHTEN UP WITH ROSE REISMAN." SHE WRITES A MONTHLY COLUMN FOR THE *POST* NEWSPAPERS, RUNS A COOKING SCHOOL AND IS A MOTIVATIONAL SPEAKER ON HEALTHY LIVING.

I HAVE to be honest and tell you that I never learned to cook from my wonderful Eastern European mother. (My love of food must have skipped a generation because my grandmother was an incredible cook.) It wasn't until after I had two young babies at home and was completing two post-graduate degrees that I realized it was time to start experimenting in the kitchen! I actually found cooking relaxing and almost meditative, so I cooked my heart out during any spare time I had. One morning I awoke and stated, "I think I'll write a cookbook." That was 15 years ago, and I just recently completed my 12th cookbook, entitled *The Art of Living Well.*

Low-fat recipes have been my focus for the past few years. Eight of my 12 cookbooks feature light, healthy recipes with wonderful taste. Here, I've provided some of my favourite salad recipes, which can be served as appetizers or a complete meal.

Lesleigh Landry of the Women's Culinary Network has been my recipe tester for several cookbooks. She introduced me to the association, and I've been amazed to meet so many members who, like me, can talk about food all day long! Everyone has a special niche market in the food world, and it's fascinating to hear from so many experts at our meetings.

LOW-FAT SALADS

• WHEAT BERRY SALAD WITH SESAME DRESSING •

• TEX-MEX ROTINI SALAD •

• MANGO, LETTUCE AND FETA CHEESE SALAD •

• TOMATO, POTATO AND ARTICHOKE SALAD •

WHEAT BERRY SALAD WITH SESAME DRESSING

Wheat berries are unprocessed whole kernels of wheat sold in health food and bulk stores. They're tender, chewy and crunchy—great for salads and pilafs! Wheat berries are also extremely nutritious and make a great high-fibre substitute for meat in traditional meat loaf recipes.

DRESSING:

1 tbsp rice wine vinegar
1 tbsp sesame oil
1 tbsp light soy sauce
1 tbsp tahini
2 tsp honey
1 tsp lemon juice
1 tsp olive oil
1 tsp hot pepper sauce (optional)
1 tsp minced garlic
½ tsp minced fresh ginger
Salt and pepper

SALAD:

3½ cups chicken stock
1 cup wheat berries
½ cup thinly sliced green onions
½ cup thinly sliced carrots
½ cup each diced sweet green and red peppers
½ cup snow peas, sliced into thirds
8 oz boneless skinless chicken breasts
Salt and pepper
1 tbsp toasted sesame seeds

DRESSING: In bowl, whisk together vinegar, sesame oil, soy sauce, tahini, honey, lemon juice, olive oil, hot pepper sauce (if using), garlic and ginger. Season to taste with salt and pepper. Set aside.

SALAD: In saucepan over high heat, bring stock to boil. Add wheat berries; reduce heat to low. Cook, covered, for about 45 minutes or until wheat berries are tender but chewy. Drain any excess liquid; let cool. Stir in green onions, carrots, green and red peppers and snow peas. Set aside.

With mallet or underside of heavy frying pan, flatten chicken breast so that it cooks evenly. Season with salt and pepper. In nonstick skillet sprayed with vegetable spray or on grill, cook chicken over medium-high heat for 3 minutes or until no longer pink inside. Drain any excess liquid; dice chicken into 1-inch chunks.

In serving bowl, combine wheat berry mixture, chicken and dressing; toss to coat well. Sprinkle with sesame seeds. (Can be covered and refrigerated for up to 2 days.)

MAKES 4 TO 6 SERVINGS.

TEX-MEX ROTINI SALAD

Tortilla chips are a great low-fat snack food—but only if they're baked! The traditional deep-fried variety is much higher in fat and calories. For a great snack, melt some light Cheddar cheese over tortillas. Kids love them!

3 cups rotini pasta
1½ cups diced ripe plum tomatoes
1 cup canned red kidney beans, drained and rinsed
1 cup canned corn kernels, drained and rinsed
½ cup chopped fresh coriander
½ cup sliced green onions
8 oz sirloin steak (about ½ inch thick)
12 baked tortilla chips
1 lime, cut into 4 wedges

DRESSING:

⅓ cup barbecue sauce
2 tbsp cider vinegar
1 tbsp olive oil
1 to 2 tsp minced jalapeño pepper (optional)
1½ tsp ground cumin

In large pot of boiling water, cook pasta for 8 to 10 minutes or until tender but firm; drain. Rinse under cold running water; drain. In serving bowl, combine pasta, tomatoes, kidney beans, corn, coriander and green onions.

In nonstick skillet sprayed with vegetable spray or on grill, cook steak over medium-high heat for about 3 minutes per side or until desired doneness. Drain any excess liquid. Let steak cool slightly, then slice into 2-inch wide strips.

DRESSING: In bowl, whisk together barbecue sauce, cider vinegar, oil, jalapeño pepper (if using) and cumin; pour over salad. Add steak; toss to coat well. Arrange tortilla chips along perimeter of salad to use as scoops. Garnish with lime wedges.

MAKES 4 TO 6 SERVINGS.

MANGO, LETTUCE AND FETA CHEESE SALAD

Sweet fruit and a combination of lettuces make this a perfect salad. Any ripe fruit can replace mango. If you don't care for the bitter flavour of radicchio, use romaine or Bibb lettuce instead. If you don't want the salad to wilt, use a larger amount of romaine lettuce.

6½ cups red or green leaf lettuce, washed, dried and torn into pieces
1½ cups radicchio, washed, dried and torn into pieces
2 cups mango, diced into ½-inch chunks
2 oz feta cheese, crumbled (approx ½ cup)
⅓ cup sliced pitted kalamata or cured olives

DRESSING:

2 tbsp white wine vinegar
5 tsp extra-virgin olive oil
½ tsp minced garlic

DRESSING: In small bowl, whisk together vinegar, oil and garlic; set aside.

In serving bowl, combine leaf lettuce, radicchio, mango, feta and olives. Pour dressing over top; toss gently to coat.

MAKES 4 SERVINGS.

TOMATO, POTATO AND ARTICHOKE SALAD

This salad makes a great side dish or main course. If eaten the next day, it will appear wilted but will have richer flavour.

1 lb red-skinned potatoes (about 3)
3 plum tomatoes, seeded
1 can (14 oz/398 mL) artichoke hearts, drained and quartered
⅓ cup chopped red onion
⅓ cup thinly sliced, green onions
1 tbsp chopped fresh dill

DRESSING:

2 tbsp extra-virgin olive oil
2 tbsp cider vinegar
1 tbsp honey
1 tsp Dijon mustard
1 tsp minced garlic
1 tsp grated lemon zest
½ tsp salt

Scrub but do not peel potatoes; cut into 1-inch pieces and place in saucepan. Cover with water and bring to boil; reduce heat and simmer for about 20 minutes or until fork-tender. Rinse under cold water and drain.

Cut tomatoes into 1½-inch pieces. In serving bowl, combine potatoes, tomatoes, artichokes, red and green onions and dill.

DRESSING: In small bowl, whisk together oil, vinegar, honey, mustard, garlic, lemon zest and salt. Just before serving, pour over salad; toss to coat.

MAKES 4 TO 6 SERVINGS.

BARBARA SELLEY

BARBARA SELLEY ENJOYS PRESENTING AND INTERPRETING INFORMATION ABOUT FOOD. A REGISTERED DIETITIAN AND OWNER OF FOOD INTELLIGENCE, BARB HAS CALCULATED NUTRIENT PROFILES FOR SEVERAL COOKBOOKS—MANY AUTHORED BY WCN MEMBERS, INCLUDING NETTIE CRONISH, ANNE LINDSAY, JAN MAIN AND BONNIE STERN. BARB IS CO-AUTHOR OF *THE COMPLETE IDIOT'S GUIDE TO BEING VEGETARIAN IN CANADA* AND IS NUTRIENT DATA SPECIALIST FOR THE CANADIAN DIET AND BREAST CANCER PREVENTION STUDY.

GRAPEFRUIT, NAPA AND MESCLUN SALAD WITH A HINT OF MAPLE DRESSING

In this salad of flavour and textural contrasts, you can substitute Boston lettuce and baby spinach leaves if mesclun is unavailable. Sesame oil (the amber-coloured, toasted variety used widely in Chinese cooking) is found in most supermarkets and Asian stores.

8 cups mesclun (mixed baby) greens (about ¾ lb)
6 tender napa cabbage leaves, sliced thinly
2 red grapefruits
2 tbsp salted toasted sunflower seeds (optional)

DRESSING:

3 tbsp olive oil
3 tbsp maple syrup
1 tbsp rice vinegar
½ tsp soy sauce
¼ tsp sesame oil
1 tsp hot pepper sauce
Salt

In bowl, toss together mesclun and napa. Peel and segment grapefruit, reserving juice in measuring cup.

DRESSING: In bowl, whisk together ½ cup reserved grapefruit juice, oil, maple syrup, rice vinegar, soy sauce, sesame oil and hot pepper sauce. Season to taste with salt.

Toss salad with ¼ cup of the dressing. Scatter grapefruit segments and sunflower seeds (if using) on top. Serve remaining dressing on the side.

MAKES 6 SERVINGS.

ETTIE SHUKEN

ETTIE BENJAMIN SHUKEN IS A FOOD STYLIST FOR TELEVISION COMMERCIALS, PRINT ADVERTISING AND EDITORIAL. HER CLIENTS INCLUDE CAMPBELL'S SOUP, THE EGG MARKETING BOARD, *BON APPÉTIT*, *CHATELAINE* MAGAZINE, YOUR SOURCE AND KRAFT FOODS. ETTIE IS ALSO A COOKING INSTRUCTOR FOR LOBLAWS AND THE LCBO.

AFTER 20-ODD years in the interior design business, I was feeling a bit stale and tired of "schlepping" samples. Food had always been my passion. All the colours I chose for my clients were food linked: borscht and sour cream pink, banana yellow and green pea. When I named my paintings, they were "Cosmic Peaches," "Red Fruit" and "Purple Fruit."

My daughter Sarah was taking her culinary diploma at Toronto's George Brown College and was having such a good time I was jealous! My mom, who lives in New Jersey, intervened, saying, "Ettie, do it!" So, I followed Sarah to chef school.

Monda Rosenberg at *Chatelaine* encouraged me to style food, but I did recipe development and testing plus a year of catering before I was convinced. Not everything changes—I'm still carting around a lot of stuff for styling!

The WCN had a fabulous meeting at George Brown while I was a student there. The women were fun, helpful and inspiring—and they gave out chocolate! I was hooked and have been a member since 1994.

GREEK INSPIRATIONS

• BAMYA (GREEK-STYLE OKRA) •
• ATHENIAN CHICKEN •
• SAVOURY RICE •
• ITALIAN PURPLE PLUM TORTE •

BAMYA (GREEK-STYLE OKRA)

While I use frozen, not fresh, okra for this recipe, it still comes out succulent and firm, with a lovely, sweet peppery taste. Avoid overcooking and stir gently so it won't come out gluey. Grind whole coriander seeds in a peppermill or coffee grinder.

4 tbsp olive oil
2 medium onions, coarsely chopped

3 cloves garlic, finely chopped
1½ tsp coriander seeds, crushed
2 pkg (each 8 oz/250 g) frozen okra, thawed
2 cups canned tomatoes, roughly chopped with juice
3 bay leaves
2 tbsp honey
Juice of 1 small lemon (approx)
Salt and pepper

In large skillet, heat 2 tbsp of the oil over medium-high heat; cook onions for 2 to 3 minutes or until transparent. Add garlic and coriander; cook for 1 to 2 minutes or until coriander becomes fragrant. Reduce heat to medium and add okra; cook, stirring gently, for 3 to 5 minutes or until okra becomes slightly tender. Remove from heat and transfer to large skillet.

In same skillet, heat remaining oil over medium-high heat. Add tomatoes with their juice and bay leaves. When tomatoes begin to break up, stir in honey. Pour tomato mixture over okra with just enough tomato juice from can to almost cover. Add half of the lemon juice. Season to taste with salt and pepper. Simmer gently for about 30 minutes or until okra is tender. Taste and add more lemon juice if desired. Remove bay leaves before serving.

MAKES 8 SERVINGS.

ATHENIAN CHICKEN

This is an impressive company dish. Do the assembling in the afternoon and refrigerate on the cookie sheet. Put the chicken breasts in the oven when your guests arrive. They can be tied like a parcel with a leek ribbon or cut in half on the diagonal, with one half standing upright.

8 boneless skinless chicken breasts, pounded to ¼-inch thickness
1 cup white wine
½ cup olive oil
3 cloves garlic, chopped
2 bay leaves
1 tsp dried oregano
Salt and pepper to taste (check saltiness of feta—it can vary)
1 lb feta cheese, crumbled
1 egg
2 tbsp freshly grated Parmesan cheese
2 tbsp chopped fresh parsley
16 sheets phyllo pastry
½ lb butter, melted

Place chicken breasts in a 13- x 9-inch glass baking dish. In bowl, combine wine, oil, garlic, bay leaves, oregano and salt and pepper; pour over chicken. Cover and marinate in refrigerator for at least 8 hours or for up to 24 hours.

In small bowl, combine feta, egg, Parmesan, ¼ cup of the marinade and parsley.

Place 1 chicken breast flat on plate. Top with 2 generous tbsp of the cheese mixture and roll up, enclosing filling as best you can. Set aside, seam side down, and repeat with remaining chicken breasts and cheese mixture.

Place 1 sheet of phyllo on work surface, keeping remainder covered with damp towel to prevent drying out. Brush with melted butter; top with second sheet. Fold bottom of shorter side up about 2 inches and centre 1 rolled breast on fold. Fold in longer sides and roll up from the short end, creating a parcel. Repeat with remaining phyllo and chicken. Place parcels on greased baking sheet, seam side down; brush tops with more melted butter. Bake in 350°F oven for 1 hour or until tops are browned and chicken is no longer pink inside. If rolls are browning too quickly, tent with foil.

MAKES 8 GENEROUS SERVINGS.

SAVOURY RICE

Cardamom, bay leaves and lemon zest give this rice an exotic twist. Leftovers can be refrigerated for up to four days and reheated easily in the microwave oven.

1 tbsp olive oil
1 tbsp butter
1½ cups brown rice
1 cup sliced mushrooms
⅓ cup dry white wine
3 cups well-seasoned chicken stock
1 bay leaf
3 cardamom pods
2 tbsp chopped fresh parsley
1½ tsp grated lemon zest

In large saucepan over medium-high heat, heat oil and butter until hot but not smoking; add rice and stir to coat. Add mushrooms; cook for 3 minutes or until softened.

Add wine and stir for 2 minutes or until wine is reduced by half. Add stock, bay leaf and cardamom pods; bring to boil. Cover and reduce heat to low; cook for about 40 to 45 minutes or until stock is absorbed and rice is tender. (You will see little craters on surface of rice.) Remove from heat and let stand, covered, for 5 minutes. Discard bay leaf and cardamom pods. Gently stir in parsley and lemon zest.

MAKES 6 SERVINGS.

ITALIAN PURPLE PLUM TORTE

This sophisticated, chic-looking dessert is impressive and easy to prepare. Serve with vanilla ice cream, soft whipped cream or a custard sauce. You can make this in the winter using frozen plums. To freeze, simply halve and pit raw plums leaving skins on, then freeze in a sealed bag.

1 cup unsalted butter
1 cup granulated sugar
2 eggs
½ tsp almond extract or anise extract
1 cup all-purpose flour, sifted
1 tsp baking powder
Pinch salt
12 to 18 Italian prune plums, pitted and halved
½ tsp grated lemon zest
6 tsp granulated sugar

In large bowl, beat butter with sugar for about 2 minutes or until light and fluffy.

Beat in eggs, 1 at a time, beating well after each addition. Mix in almond extract. In another bowl, stir together flour, baking powder and salt; stir into creamed mixture until combined. Spread in lightly greased and floured 9-inch ceramic quiche pan, smoothing top. Cover entire surface with plums, skin side up. Sprinkle with lemon zest, then sugar.

Bake in 350°F oven for about 1 hour or until tester inserted in centre comes out clean.

MAKES 6 TO 8 SERVINGS.

KATE DOWHAN

KATE DOWHAN WORKS IN THE CANADIAN LIVING TEST KITCHEN ON A CONTRACT POSITION, TESTING AND DEVELOPING RECIPES. ALSO A FOOD WRITER, KATE CONTRIBUTES TO *SPA LIFE* MAGAZINE. SHE ATTENDED THE STRATFORD CHEFS SCHOOL AND GRADUATED WITH HONOURS IN 1997. KATE ALSO ENJOYS TEACHING COOKING AND GIVES CLASSES THROUGH VARIOUS LOBLAWS AND LCBO FACILITIES.

SPRING ASPARAGUS SALAD WITH RED NEW POTATOES, RED PEPPERS AND GOAT CHEESE

This is a beautiful spring appetizer. It is filled with colour and flavour and captures the season with each serving.

1 lb tiny new red potatoes
1 lb asparagus, woody ends removed
¼ cup olive oil
1 red onion, thinly sliced
1 sweet red pepper, thinly sliced
2 cloves garlic, minced
⅓ cup balsamic vinegar
2 oz goat cheese, crumbled
Salt and pepper
1 bunch watercress, washed, drained and thick stems removed

In saucepan of boiling salted water, cook potatoes for 10 to 15 minutes or just until tender. Using slotted spoon, transfer potatoes to colander and rinse under cold water to cool. Slice into thin rounds. Set aside.

In same saucepan of water, cook asparagus for 1 to 2 minutes or until bright green and tender. Remove and rinse under cold water.

In large skillet, heat 2 tbsp of the oil over medium-high heat; cook onion for about 2 minutes or until softened. Season to taste with salt and pepper. Add remaining oil, red pepper and garlic; cook for 2 minutes, stirring constantly. Add asparagus and sliced potatoes, tossing to coat with oil. Using slotted spoon, transfer vegetables to plate, leaving any liquid in pan to be used for the dressing.

Reduce heat to medium; add vinegar to skillet and cook for 1 minute, stirring well to combine with oil. (You may need to add more oil.) Return vegetables to skillet and sprinkle with goat cheese. Season to taste with salt and pepper. Serve on bed of watercress.

MAKES 6 TO 8 SERVINGS.

MAIRLYN SMITH

MAIRLYN SMITH IS AN ACTRESS, COOKING TEACHER, COOKBOOK AUTHOR, AND NOT THIN. HER LATEST BOOK, WHICH SHE CO-AUTHORED WITH DIETITIAN LIZ PEARSON, *THE ULTIMATE HEALTHY EATING PLAN WHICH STILL LEAVES ROOM FOR CHOCOLATE!* IS A NUTRITION GUIDE-COOKBOOK THAT IS JAM-PACKED WITH ALL THE LATEST INFORMATION ON POWERFUL FOODS LIKE FLAXSEED, SOY, EXTRA-VIRGIN OLIVE OIL AND SALMON, PLUS 120 RECIPES THAT TASTE TOO GOOD TO BE GOOD FOR YOU!

I FIRST got hooked on cooking at the ripe old age of four. My mom let me make brownies with her—one lick of the batter and I was a foodie for life!

They say that when you are 10 years old, you really know what you want to be when you grow up. I wanted to be an actress, a cooking show host, a cookbook author, a teacher and really thin! I became a home ec and drama teacher in the late '70s, an actress in the early '80s, a cooking show host in the early '90s, and a cookbook author in the mid '90s. I'm still working on that thin thing!

Growing up, I was a huge fan of the Galloping Gourmet because he was so funny and made it look so easy. I used to play "cooking show host" in the kitchen, talking to the wall. Heather Trim, food consultant and WCN member, once caught me talking to the wall at the Good Food Festival! Old habits die hard.

I am so thrilled to be a part of the Women's Culinary Network. To stand in a room full of smart, creative women—who all love what they do—is a wonderful high. I have received great advice, tips, hints and support from everyone who is a part of it. Being a member is one of the highlights of my culinary life.

FALL FEAST

• POMEGRANATE AND BLACKCURRANT SALAD DRESSING •
• BARLEY AND BROWN RICE RISOTTO WITH DRIED SHIITAKE MUSHROOMS •
• TURKEY BREAST STUFFED WITH DRIED CRANBERRIES AND WALNUTS WITH CRANBERRY JUS •
• PAN-FRIED AND OVEN-FINISHED FALL VEGETABLES •

POMEGRANATE AND BLACKCURRANT SALAD DRESSING

My grandmother was born in South Africa during the Boer War. One of her fondest memories of her days living there was the pomegranates! Gran wasn't allowed to wear makeup, so she and her sisters would cut a pomegranate in half and rub the stain onto their lips and cheeks! Serve this dressing over romaine or your favourite salad green mixture.

1 shallot, finely chopped
½ cup pomegranate seeds
⅓ cup blackcurrant concentrate
1 tbsp extra-virgin olive oil
1 tbsp balsamic vinegar
½ tsp Dijon mustard
¼ tsp pepper

In small bowl, whisk together shallot, pomegranate seeds, blackcurrant concentrate, oil, vinegar, mustard and pepper. Refrigerate for up to 4 days.

MAKES ¾ CUP.

BARLEY AND BROWN RICE RISOTTO WITH DRIED SHIITAKE MUSHROOMS

Barley and brown rice in a risotto? No way! Yes way! The creaminess of the barley and the short grain brown rice lend themselves to a healthy high-fibre version of the classic risotto.

12 dried shiitake mushrooms
1¼ cups boiling water
2 tbsp extra-virgin olive oil
1 onion, finely chopped

3 cloves garlic, minced
3 cups low-sodium chicken stock
½ cup pearl barley
½ cup short-grain brown rice
½ cup freshly grated Parmesan cheese

Soak shiitake mushrooms in boiling water for 30 minutes.

Meanwhile, in heavy-bottomed saucepan, heat oil over medium-high heat; cook onion and garlic, stirring, for 3 minutes or until softened. Add stock, barley and brown rice; bring to boil. Cover and reduce heat to low; simmer for 30 minutes, stirring occasionally.

Drain mushrooms, reserving liquid. Remove stems; discard. Coarsely chop mushroom caps. Add to barley mixture. Stir in 1 cup of the reserved liquid. Cover and simmer for 30 minutes or until barley and rice are tender. Stir in cheese.

MAKES 6 SERVINGS.

TURKEY BREAST STUFFED WITH DRIED CRANBERRIES AND WALNUTS WITH CRANBERRY JUS

I love to serve this dish for a really elegant but easy fall dinner party. You can make the stuffing and prep the turkey breast the morning of, then assemble and put the turkey into the oven 30 minutes before your company is expected. After the turkey comes out of the oven, cover it and let stand on the counter for 20 minutes before serving; this will give you enough time to cook your vegetables and make the jus.

2 boneless skinless single turkey breasts, each 1 lb
½ cup dry white wine
½ cup low-sodium chicken stock
¾ cup cranberry juice
1 tbsp hot pepper jelly

STUFFING:

2 tbsp olive oil
1 onion, finely chopped
½ cup dried cranberries
¼ cup walnuts, coarsely chopped
1 slice whole wheat or country-style bread, cubed
1 tbsp finely chopped fresh thyme
¼ cup dry white wine

STUFFING: In large skillet, heat 1 tbsp of the oil over medium-high heat; cook onion for 3 minutes or until transparent. Add cranberries and walnuts; cook for 1 minute. Stir in bread and thyme; cook until fat is absorbed. Add wine and stir until absorbed. Remove from heat.

Pat turkey breasts dry with paper towel. Use towel to grasp breast and turn thick side toward your knife. Holding knife horizontally, begin to cut midway through thick side toward thin side of each breast, stopping about 1 inch from thin edge. Breast will look like butterfly, with wings still connected at thin edge. Open up like book; flatten using a meat mallet or back of a heavy frying pan. Repeat with other breast. Cut four 12-inch pieces of string; arrange crosswise about 1½ inches apart on work surface. Place 1 breast, cut side down, on top of string. Pile stuffing on top, making sure it is evenly distributed. Place second breast, cut side up, over top, forming "sandwich." Tie strings around roast, trimming any excess. Rub with 1 tbsp of the remaining oil and place in roasting pan. Pour wine into bottom of pan. Roast in 350°F oven for 1 hour, basting occasionally.

Remove pan from oven; pour in stock. Roast for 20 to 30 minutes or until no longer pink inside. Transfer to cutting board; tent with foil and let stand for 20 minutes.

Place roasting pan with juices over medium heat. Stir in cranberry juice and hot pepper jelly; bring to boil. Boil until reduced by one third. Keep warm. Slice turkey breast into 6 equal servings. Spoon cranberry jus over top.

MAKES 6 SERVINGS.

PAN-FRIED AND OVEN-FINISHED FALL VEGETABLES

Here's a great side to serve with the turkey. You start this dish on top of the stove and finish it in the oven along with the turkey, 30 minutes after it goes in, so both are ready at the same time!

- 4 tbsp olive oil
- 8 red-skinned baby potatoes, halved
- 4 carrots, peeled and cut into 2-inch pieces
- 2 sweet potatoes, peeled and cut into 2-inch pieces
- 8 whole shallots, peeled
- 12 cloves garlic, peeled
- 1 tbsp balsamic vinegar
- 1 tbsp honey
- 2½ tbsp finely chopped fresh rosemary

In large ovenproof skillet or cast-iron frying pan, heat 3 tbsp of the oil over medium-high heat; cook potatoes, carrots and sweet potatoes, stirring often, for 5 minutes. Add shallots and garlic; cook for 1 minute. Add remaining oil, balsamic vinegar, honey and rosemary; toss to coat. Place skillet in 350°F oven and roast for 40 minutes or until vegetables are tender. (If the rest of dinner needs a few more minutes, cover with foil, turn off oven and let stand until everything else is ready to serve.)

MAKES 6 SERVINGS.

PAMELA STEEL

FOOD WRITER AND CHEF PAMELA STEEL HAS WRITTEN SEVERAL COOKBOOKS, INCLUDING *RECIPES FOR HOMEMADE LOVE*, *NICE TIMING* AND THE *GREAT CANADIAN* SERIES. SHE WAS A CONTRIBUTING EDITOR TO *PRESIDENT'S CHOICE MAGAZINE*, AND CONTRIBUTES TO SUCH PUBLICATIONS AS *THE TORONTO STAR* AND *TORONTO LIFE* MAGAZINE.

GARLIC FLAN

This sensuously creamy appetizer is ideally suited to serving on a bed of baby greens or by itself with plenty of good, chewy bread. As with all custards, temperature is very important in achieving success. Use an oven thermometer to confirm the internal temperature of your oven and use hot tap water for the water bath.

- 10 cloves garlic
- 1 cup whipping cream
- ¼ cup milk
- 2 eggs
- 1 tbsp chopped fresh thyme
- Pinch each salt and pepper
- Sprigs fresh thyme

Using side of knife, smash garlic cloves and discard peels. In medium saucepan over medium-high heat, heat cream, milk and garlic until small bubbles form around edge; remove from heat. In bowl, whisk eggs; slowly whisk in hot cream mixture. Gradually strain mixture through fine sieve into bowl. Stir in thyme, salt and pepper. Divide among 4 greased 6- or 8-oz ceramic ramekins. Place in shallow pan; pour enough hot water into pan to come halfway up sides of ramekins.

Bake in 325°F oven for 35 minutes or until edges are set but centres still jiggle. Remove from water and let cool on rack. To serve, run knife around edge of ramekins to loosen and invert onto plate. Garnish with fresh thyme.

MAKES 4 SERVINGS.

BONNIE STERN

BONNIE STERN LOVES TO COOK. SHE HAS OPERATED THE BONNIE STERN SCHOOL OF COOKING AND COOKWARE SHOP IN TORONTO SINCE 1973. SHE'S THE AUTHOR OF TEN BEST-SELLING COOKBOOKS AND WAS THE HOST OF TWO NATIONAL COOKING SHOWS. BONNIE WRITES A WEEKLY COLUMN FOR THE SATURDAY *NATIONAL POST* AND THE *CHICAGO SUN TIMES* AND IS A CONTRIBUTING FOOD WRITER TO *OUTLOOK* MAGAZINE. HER RECIPES ARE FEATURED ON NINE SONY "À LA CARTE" CLASSICAL MUSIC CDS. BONNIE IS A FOUNDING MEMBER OF THE WOMEN'S CULINARY NETWORK. HER WEBSITE IS WWW.BONNIESTERN.COM.

MY FAMILY says I got my love of cooking from my grandmother. She had 11 children and lived in Grand Valley, Ontario. Because they were not well off, my grandmother had to be very inventive to keep everyone fed. I don't know how much fun she had cooking, but her breads were always awarded first prize at the county fairs, winning her enough flour to keep the family in bread for another year.

To me, good food means using the freshest and best-quality ingredients. My favourite food is actually the food I cook for my family every day. I have two teenagers interested in good health (most of the time anyway) and a husband who is lactose intolerant, so it can be a challenge to find something for dinner that everyone likes. Chicken is often the answer, and I have a host of recipes that I can rotate. Here are four chicken recipes that take you through the seasons. I hope your family likes these as much as mine does.

FOUR-SEASON CHICKEN

• THAI MANGO CHICKEN •
• CHICKEN MEAT LOAF WITH CHIPOTLE TOMATO SAUCE •
• KNIGHTSBRIDGE CHICKEN SALAD •
• GRILLED CHICKEN IN PITA WITH TZATZIKI •

THAI MANGO CHICKEN

This autumn-appropriate recipe was adapted from my book HeartSmart Cooking for Family and Friends. *Unused coconut milk will last only three days in the refrigerator; or you can freeze it for up to a year. When using lemongrass, trim off the root end and use only the pale bottom part, mincing as finely as possible to eliminate coarseness. Serve this dish over steamed rice.*

1 egg white
1 lb boneless skinless chicken breasts, cut into 1-inch pieces
1 tbsp vegetable oil
1 tsp minced fresh ginger

2 cloves garlic, minced
2 green onions, chopped
2 tsp minced lemongrass (or ½ tsp grated lemon zest)
1 onion, cut into 1-inch chunks
2 sweet red peppers, cut into 1-inch chunks
1 cup broccoli florets
2 mangoes, peeled and cut into 1-inch chunks
2 tbsp chopped fresh coriander

SAUCE:

¼ cup hoisin sauce
2 tbsp soy sauce or Thai fish sauce
2 tbsp coconut milk
1 tbsp peanut butter
½ tsp hot pepper sauce

SAUCE: In small bowl, stir together hoisin, soy sauce, coconut milk, peanut butter and hot pepper sauce; set aside.

In medium bowl, beat egg white slightly and add chicken. In wok or large nonstick skillet, heat oil over high heat; stir-fry chicken for 5 minutes or until browned. Add ginger, garlic, green onions and lemongrass; stir-fry for about 30 seconds or until fragrant. Add onion and red peppers; cook for 2 minutes. Add broccoli; cook for 2 minutes longer. Add mangoes and sauce; bring to boil and cook for 2 minutes. Stir in coriander.

MAKES 4 TO 6 SERVINGS.

CHICKEN MEAT LOAF WITH CHIPOTLE TOMATO SAUCE

I serve the meat loaf plain for the kids and with the sauce for the adults. Chipotle chiles are smoked jalapeños that are commonly sold canned in adobo sauce. I purée the can's contents and freeze flattened in a resealable plastic bag, so that it is easy to just break off a small piece when I need some.

1 tbsp olive oil
1 onion, chopped
2 cloves garlic, minced
2 lb ground chicken
2 eggs
1 cup bread crumbs
½ cup ketchup plus 2 tbsp for glaze
1 tbsp Worcestershire sauce
1 tbsp Dijon mustard
2 tsp salt
½ tsp pepper
½ tsp hot pepper sauce
2 tbsp chopped fresh parsley

CHIPOTLE TOMATO SAUCE:

1 tbsp olive oil
1 onion, chopped
3 cloves garlic, minced
1 tsp puréed chipotle peppers (or more to taste)
3 cups chopped fresh tomatoes (preferably peeled before chopping)
1 tsp salt (or more to taste)
½ tsp pepper
2 tbsp chopped fresh coriander

In large nonstick skillet, heat oil over medium heat; cook onions and garlic for 5 minutes or until softened and fragrant. Let cool.

In large bowl, combine onion mixture, chicken, eggs, bread crumbs, ½ cup ketchup, Worcestershire sauce, mustard, salt, pepper and hot pepper sauce; knead together. Add parsley.

Pack mixture into 9- x 5-inch loaf pan that has been lined with parchment paper or foil. Cover with parchment or foil. Bake in 350°F oven for 1 hour. Uncover, brush with remaining ketchup and bake for 30 minutes longer. Drain off any juices and unmould.

TOMATO SAUCE: Meanwhile, in large deep skillet, heat oil over medium heat; cook onion and garlic for 5 minutes or until tender. Add chipotle peppers; cook for 30 seconds. Add tomatoes and bring to boil. Reduce heat and simmer for about 15 minutes or until thickened. Purée in blender. Stir in salt and pepper. Slice meat loaf and serve with sauce. Sprinkle with coriander.

MAKES 8 SERVINGS.

KNIGHTSBRIDGE CHICKEN SALAD

This is a beautiful-looking salad that makes a great main course in spring or summer. For a vegetarian version, simply hold the chicken.

2 tbsp olive oil
1 tsp each salt and pepper
1 lb boneless skinless chicken breasts
1 lb asparagus
2 sweet red peppers, halved
8 cups mixed greens
2 lb small potatoes, cleaned, halved and cooked
3 hard-cooked eggs, cut into wedges
½ cup pitted black olives

DRESSING:

⅓ cup olive oil (or more to taste)
¼ cup balsamic vinegar
1 clove garlic, minced
2 tbsp chopped fresh basil or tarragon
Salt and pepper

In small bowl, whisk together oil, salt and pepper; gently rub into chicken breasts. Place on hot grill and cook for 3 to 4 minutes per side or until no longer pink inside but not overcooked. Let cool. Slice thinly.

Meanwhile, brush asparagus with oil and grill for a few minutes or just until cooked. Cut into 2-inch lengths. Grill peppers, skin side down, for 5 to 7 minutes or until blackened. Let cool; rub off skins. Cut into large chunks.

Place salad greens on large platter. Place cooked potatoes on top. Arrange cooked asparagus, peppers, egg wedges and olives around potatoes. Arrange chicken slices on top of potatoes.

DRESSING: Whisk together oil, vinegar, garlic and basil. Season to taste with salt and pepper. Toss with salad just before serving.

MAKES 6 SERVINGS.

GRILLED CHICKEN IN PITA WITH TZATZIKI

Grilled chicken sandwiches are a summer favourite. Add grilled vegetables and/or sliced tomatoes and lettuce if you like. (Drained yogurt, or yogurt cheese, is often tolerated by those who are lactose intolerant.)

6 boneless skinless chicken breasts
2 tbsp olive oil
2 cloves garlic, minced
1 tbsp chopped fresh oregano
1 tbsp grated lemon zest

1½ tsp salt
¾ tsp pepper
Pinch hot pepper flakes
3 large pita breads, cut in half and gently opened

TZATZIKI:

2 cups plain yogurt
½ English cucumber, halved, seeded and thinly sliced
1 tbsp salt
2 cloves garlic, minced
2 tbsp chopped fresh mint
2 tbsp tahini
Salt

Trim any fat from chicken. Remove fillets and freeze for chicken fingers or stir-fries. Pound chicken breasts flat so that they will cook evenly.

In small bowl, combine oil, garlic, oregano, lemon zest, salt, pepper and hot pepper flakes; rub into chicken. Marinate in refrigerator for at least 10 minutes or for up to 2 hours.

TZATZIKI: Meanwhile, drain yogurt in cheesecloth- or paper towel–lined strainer set over bowl. Cover with plastic wrap. Refrigerate for a few hours or until yogurt is about twice as thick. At the same time, place thinly sliced cucumbers in strainer, toss with 1 tbsp salt and let drain for at least 30 minutes or for up to 2 hours. Rinse and pat dry. Just before serving, combine thick yogurt with cucumber, garlic, mint, tahini, and salt to taste.

On grill (or in grill pan) over medim heat, cook chicken for 3 to 5 minutes per side or until no longer pink inside. Place chicken breast in each pita half; top with tzatziki.

MAKES 6 SERVINGS.

DUFFLET ROSENBERG

DUFFLET ROSENBERG STARTED BAKING FOR LOCAL RESTAURANTS FROM HER MOTHER'S HOME IN 1975. HER BUSINESS HAS SINCE EXPANDED INTO A BAKERY LOCATION AND TWO RETAIL STORES. THE COMPANY CONTINUES TO GROW, SUPPLYING MORE THAN 400 RESTAURANTS, FINE FOOD SHOPS, CATERERS, HOTELS AND CAFÉS. DUFFLET DEMONSTRATES IN SOME OF TORONTO'S LEADING COOKING SCHOOLS, AND HER RECIPES HAVE BEEN FEATURED IN NUMEROUS PUBLICATIONS.

CHOCOLATE FUDGE TARTS

These chewy, not-too-sweet tarts are a treat for any occasion. The pastry can be made ahead of time, the filling is quick and easy to prepare, and most of the ingredients can be found in your pantry. Even easier, they can be made ahead and frozen, with the final garnish put on just before serving.

PASTRY:

2 cups all-purpose flour
½ cup granulated sugar
⅓ cup cocoa powder
1 cup unsalted butter, cubed and chilled
1 egg
1 tsp vanilla

FILLING:

½ cup granulated sugar
2 eggs
¼ cup cocoa powder
¼ cup corn syrup

¼ cup whipping cream
2 tbsp melted butter
½ tsp vanilla
⅛ tsp salt

TOPPING:

1 cup whipping cream
2 tbsp icing sugar
24 assorted berries

PASTRY: In bowl of food processor, pulse flour, sugar and cocoa powder to combine. Sprinkle butter over flour mixture; pulse until mixture is consistency of oatmeal. In small bowl, whisk together egg and vanilla. With motor running, pour egg mixture through feed tube. Process until dough forms ball. Turn out onto work surface and press into disc. On lightly floured surface, roll out pastry to ⅛-inch thickness. Using cookie cutter, cut pastry into 2-inch rounds. Press into 24 pastry tins or mini muffin tins and chill. (Scraps can be rolled out, cut out with decorative cutter, sprinkled with sugar and baked in 350°F oven for 8 to 10 minutes or until firm.)

FILLING: In bowl, whisk together sugar, eggs, cocoa, corn syrup, whipping cream, butter, vanilla and salt; mix well.

Spoon about 1 tbsp of the mixture into each pastry shell. Place pan on baking sheet and bake in 325°F oven for 15 to 20 minutes or until pastry is firm and filling is bubbling slightly. Carefully remove tarts from pan and transfer to rack to cool.

TOPPING: Whip cream with icing sugar until stiff peaks form. Using piping bag with decorative tip, pipe onto tarts. Top each with berry.

MAKES 24 TARTS.

ANITA STEWART

ANITA STEWART IS A CULINARY ADVENTURER. SHE'S BEEN OVER THE SIDE OF ICEBREAKERS INTO WORK BOATS IN THE NORTH PACIFIC TO VISIT EVERY MANNED (AND WOMANNED) LIGHT STATION ON THAT COAST; SHE'S TRAVELLED BY DOG SLED AND SNOWMOBILE TO CREE HUNT CAMPS IN NORTHERN QUEBEC; AND SHE'S HELICOPTERED OUT TO HIBERNIA, THE MOST EASTERLY BASTION OF CANADIAN CUISINE. IN 1994, SHE FOUNDED CANADA'S FIRST NATIONAL ORGANIZATION FOR FOOD PROFESSIONALS, CUISINE CANADA. SHE IS AN AUTHOR AND PHOTOJOURNALIST, AND CONSULTS FOR A VARIETY OF ORGANIZATIONS, INCLUDING AGRICULTURE AND AGRIFOOD CANADA, THE DEPARTMENT OF CANADIAN HERITAGE AND THE UNIVERSITY OF GUELPH, BRINGING REAL CANADIAN CUISINE TO BOTH THE NATIONAL AND INTERNATIONAL STAGE.

FROM MY vantage point in the small Wellington County village of Elora, Ontario, it's easy to put Canadian cuisine into perspective. All I have to do is drive up the highway toward Alma to see magnificent dairy farms and perfectly husbanded fields. Farther north, near Mount Forest, there's the land my grandparents cleared, part of what was once known as the Queens Bush. In summer, hedgerows line every back road with wild grapes, chokecherries and elderberries, which my mother and I used to pick to fill our fruit cellar. When I travel south, I go past land owned by the University of Guelph. It's here that some of our nation's leading-edge agricultural research occurs, with dozens of small plots growing thousands of varieties of grain and beans.

Sadly, the other side of the rural coin is also clearly visible in this region. I've watched family farms being destroyed by harsh economic realities and pressures for "development and progress."

It's experiences like these that mould a philosophy of eating. I have come to agree profoundly with Wendell Berry, who wrote that "Eating is an agricultural act."

A TASTE OF CANADA

•WARM AUTUMN SALAD WITH ST-BASILE CHEESE AND SAUTÉED CORTLAND APPLES •
•BRAISED QUEBEC LAMB SHANKS WITH WHITE BEANS •
•BUTTERY ONION MASHED POTATOES •
•MAPLE HAZELNUT SQUARES •

WARM AUTUMN SALAD WITH ST-BASILE CHEESE AND SAUTÉED CORTLAND APPLES

St-Basile-de-Portneuf, one of the most delicious cheeses in all of Canada, is produced from raw milk (lait cru) just west of Quebec City. Because it is made in small quantities, you may have to substitute a high-quality Quebec-made Brie in this recipe. Cortland or Northern Spy apples are preferred because they hold their shape well.

3 Cortland or other firm cooking apples, peeled and thinly sliced
½ cup unsalted butter, melted
6 sheets phyllo pastry
6 oz St-Basile-de-Portneuf (or good-quality Brie) cheese, divided into 6 portions
8 cups mixed salad greens

DRESSING:

⅔ cup vegetable oil
¼ cup apple cider vinegar
1 tsp Dijon mustard
½ tsp each salt and pepper

In small skillet, heat butter over medium heat; cook apples for 5 minutes or until tender. Remove from heat; divide into 6 equal portions and set aside to cool.

Place 1 sheet of phyllo on work surface, keeping remainder covered with damp towel to prevent drying out. Brush with butter. Fold in half on short side; brush with butter. Place 1 portion of apple in centre of folded sheet; top with 1 piece of cheese. Gather up pastry to form small purse, pinching tightly to seal. Place on lightly greased baking sheet. Repeat with remaining phyllo, butter, apples and cheese. Bake in 375°F oven for 15 minutes or until golden.

DRESSING: In small bowl, whisk together oil, vinegar, mustard, salt and pepper. Cover and refrigerate up to 1 week.

Divide salad greens among 6 plates. Top with phyllo purses; drizzle with dressing and serve immediately.

MAKES 6 SERVINGS.

BRAISED QUEBEC LAMB SHANKS WITH WHITE BEANS

Around Quebec, there are four distinct lamb-raising regions—l'Estrie (Eastern Townships); Charlevoix; Bas Saint-Laurent, including Kamouraska; and Mauricie-Bois-Francs, a huge area halfway between Montreal and Quebec City on the North Shore. Each region claims different tastes. Some, like Charlevoix, boast a pre-salée (slightly salty) flavour.

- 1 cup dried white beans
- 6 Quebec lamb shanks (about 4 lb)
- Salt and pepper
- 1 tbsp vegetable oil
- 4 garlic cloves, peeled
- 1 cup finely diced carrots
- ½ cup diced onion
- ½ cup diced celery
- 2 tbsp chopped fresh rosemary
- 1 tbsp minced fresh thyme
- 1 bay leaf
- 1 cup dry red wine
- ¼ cup tomato paste
- 4 cups beef stock

Rinse beans and sort, if necessary, discarding any blemished ones and any grit. In large saucepan, cover beans with 4 cups cold water and let soak for 8 to 10 hours or overnight. Bring beans and water to boil; cover and simmer over low heat for 30 minutes. Drain and set aside.

Season lamb lightly with salt and pepper. In large roasting pan, heat oil over medium-high heat; brown shanks on all sides, in batches if necessary. Transfer to plate. Drain fat from pan. Add garlic, carrots, onion and celery to pan; cook over medium heat, stirring constantly, for 3 to 5 minutes. Add rosemary, thyme and bay leaf. Stir in wine, tomato paste and beans; bring to boil over high heat, stirring constantly. Return shanks to pan, in single layer, along with stock; bring to boil. Cover and roast in 350°F oven for 1½ hours. Uncover and roast for 1½ hours longer or until meat is very tender and richly browned. Serve in heated rimmed soup bowls, ladling sauce over shanks.

MAKES 6 SERVINGS.

BUTTERY ONION MASHED POTATOES

Yukon Gold is the most famous potato Canada has ever produced, developed by the late Dr. Gary Johnston of the University of Guelph in 1966. The first Yukon Gold potato hill was dug at the University of Guelph's Research Station near Cambridge, Ontario.

- 1 large Spanish onion
- 2 tsp vegetable oil
- Salt and pepper
- 3 lb Yukon Gold potatoes, peeled and cut into quarters
- 2 tsp salt
- ½ cup buttermilk
- 2 tbsp butter

Cut onion into 8 wedges. Place in shallow roasting pan and sprinkle with oil, salt and pepper. Roast in 400°F oven for 40 to 45 minutes or until tender. Purée in food processor.

Place potatoes in large saucepan and cover with water. Add pinch salt; cover and bring to boil. Boil for about 20 minutes or until fork-tender. Drain and return to pot. Add buttermilk, butter and onion purée; mash until smooth. Season to taste with salt and pepper.

MAKES 6 SERVINGS.

MAPLE HAZELNUT SQUARES

The best hazelnuts I've tasted come from British Columbia. They are fat, round and particularly flavourful when roasted. The good news for Ontarians is that a substantial tree nut industry is springing up in the Niagara region. Use dark maple syrup; it's cheaper than first-run and well suited for baking.

BASE:

1 cup all-purpose flour
¼ cup packed brown sugar
½ cup butter, softened

TOPPING:

1 cup dark maple syrup
⅔ cup packed brown sugar
2 eggs, beaten
2 tbsp all-purpose flour
½ tsp vanilla
1½ cups hazelnuts, toasted and skins removed*

BASE: In small bowl and using fork, mix together flour, sugar and butter until mixture resembles coarse crumbs. Pat firmly into 9-inch square cake pan. Bake in centre of 350°F oven for 5 minutes. Let cool in pan on rack. Increase heat to 425°F.

TOPPING: In small saucepan, combine maple syrup and brown sugar; bring to boil over medium heat. Reduce heat and simmer for 5 minutes. Remove from heat and let cool for 10 minutes. Pour syrup mixture into medium bowl. Whisk in eggs, flour and vanilla until smooth. Stir in nuts. Pour evenly over baked base. Bake for 10 minutes. Reduce heat to 350°F and bake for 12 to 15 minutes or until firm and browned. Let cool. Slice into squares.

MAKES 20 TO 24 SQUARES.

**To remove hazelnut skins, spread hazelnuts on baking sheet and place in 350°F (180°C) oven. Shake or stir 2 or 3 times and when the nuts begin to turn dark brown and the skin cracks open (after about 15 minutes), turn them out onto a kitchen towel, wrapping them up to cool. While they are still in the towel, rub vigorously to remove the skins. Transfer roasted nuts to glass jar and cover tightly.*

CHARMAINE BROUGHTON

SINCE GRADUATING FROM THE CULINARY PROGRAM AT GEORGE BROWN COLLEGE, CHARMAINE BROUGHTON HAS GAINED WIDE EXPERIENCE IN THE FOOD INDUSTRY. SHE'S APPRENTICED AT SMALL FINE RESTAURANTS, LARGE UPSCALE HOTELS AND IN THE KITCHENS OF SPECIALTY GROCERY STORES. CHARMAINE CURRENTLY TEACHES COOKING AT LOBLAWS AND IS A FOOD CONSULTANT FOR BREWERY BAY FOOD COMPANY. IN THE SUMMER OF 2002, CHARMAINE AND SISTER MEAGAN LAUNCHED GOURMET ON THE LAKE, A SUCCESSFUL HORS D'OEUVRES AND CATERING COMPANY IN MUSKOKA.

WARM PASTA SALAD WITH SMOKED SALMON AND CURRIED MAYONNAISE

The smokiness of the salmon and the heat of the curry meld together beautifully. You can substitute good-quality canned salmon, but the flavour of the hot smoked salmon really makes this dish. Hot smoked salmon differs from cold smoked: it is usually made with Pacific salmon, has a firmer texture, flakes easily and can be found in some supermarkets and fine food stores.

1 tbsp butter
2 tbsp vegetable oil
1 medium onion, chopped
1 tbsp curry powder
½ tsp pepper
¾ cup dry white wine
4 cups medium-size shell pasta
7½ oz hot smoked salmon, chopped
¾ cup mayonnaise

2 roasted sweet red peppers, chopped
⅓ cup chopped fresh coriander
2 tbsp lemon juice
1 tbsp chopped fresh parsley
Salt

In medium skillet, heat butter and oil over medium-high heat; cook onion, stirring occasionally, for about 5 minutes or until golden. Add curry and pepper; cook for 1 minute or until pan becomes dry-looking. Add wine and cook for 3 to 5 minutes or until reduced by half.

In large pot of boiling salted water, cook pasta for 8 to 10 minutes or until tender but firm. Drain pasta and place in large mixing bowl along with onion mixture, smoked salmon, mayonnaise, roasted red peppers, ¼ cup of the coriander, lemon juice and parsley. Toss to combine. Taste and add salt if needed. Transfer to serving platter and sprinkle with remaining coriander. Serve immediately.

MAKES 4 TO 6 SERVINGS.

LILI SULLIVAN

SINCE GRADUATING FROM CULINARY MANAGEMENT AT TORONTO'S GEORGE BROWN COLLEGE IN THE EARLY '80S, LILI SULLIVAN HAS WORKED AT MANY OF THE CITY'S TOP RESTAURANTS. HER RECIPES HAVE BEEN PUBLISHED IN *MY FAVOURITE HERB* BY LAUREL KESER (CALLAWIND, 1999) AND *THE ORGANIC GOURMET* (ROBERT ROSE, 1998). A STRONG SUPPORTER OF ORGANIC FARMING AND REGIONAL AND SEASONAL COOKING, LILI SITS ON THE BOARD FOR ORGANIC ADVOCATES/FEAST OF FIELDS AND IS PART OF THE WCN'S EXECUTIVE STEERING COMMITTEE. LILI HAS APPEARED ON RADIO AND TELEVISION NUMEROUS TIMES AND HAS PUBLISHED THE CD-ROM "WORLD CUISINE BAKING" BY OASIS BLUE PRODUCTION. SHE TEACHES COOKING AT LOBLAWS.

AFTER EMIGRATING from Sweden at age 6, I graduated from mud pies in the backyard to my mother's kitchen. Thus began a lifelong passion for cooking and eating.

Since joining the WCN in the early '90s, I've been proud to serve on the executive committee for nine years. I enjoy meeting women in a relaxed social atmosphere and learning about the different fields of expertise represented by the membership.

I take a fresh, regional market approach to my cooking, often experimenting with traditional ideas. Here are some of my signature dishes, all popular in my cooking classes, where I focus on easy entertaining with restaurant-quality results.

WHEN SAVOURY TURNS SWEET AND VICE VERSA

• SMOKED SALMON BRÛLÉE •
• ROASTED RED PEPPER GOAT CHEESE CAKE •
• WILD MUSHROOM AND STILTON BREAD PUDDING •
• CHOCOLATE PRALINE PÂTÉ •

SMOKED SALMON BRÛLÉE

Serve this as an elegant appetizer or for a light brunch with a green salad and fresh, crusty bread.

- 8 large cloves roasted garlic*
- 4 oz smoked salmon, chopped
- 1½ cups chopped fresh spinach (loosely packed)
- 3 cups whipping cream
- 8 egg yolks
- 1 tsp salt
- ½ tsp ground white pepper
- 3 tbsp freshly grated Parmesan cheese

Lightly grease eight 6-oz ramekins or custard cups. Divide roasted garlic, salmon and spinach evenly among ramekins. Set aside.

In saucepan, heat cream over medium-high heat until steaming. In bowl, whisk egg yolks until light but not foamy; slowly whisk in cream until blended. Stir in salt and pepper. Divide among prepared ramekins. Place cups 1 to 2 inches apart in 2 large shallow pans. Pour enough hot water into pans to come halfway up sides of ramekins.

Bake in centre of 350°F oven for 30 to 40 minutes or until edges are set but centre is still a little loose. (Mixture will continue to set as it cools. Do not overcook as custard may separate.) Remove from water; let cool on racks. (Can be refrigerated at this point for up to 3 days.)

Place cups on rimmed baking sheet. Sprinkle Parmesan evenly over tops of custards to create thin layer. Bake in 350°F oven for 10 to 15 minutes or until tops are golden brown and centre is hot. Serve immediately.

MAKES 8 SERVINGS.

*TO ROAST GARLIC: *Toss cloves with 1 tbsp olive oil and 1 tsp salt. Wrap in foil and roast in 425°F oven for 20 to 30 minutes or until softened. Squeeze out pulp.*

ROASTED RED PEPPER AND GOAT CHEESE CAKE

I like to serve this savoury cheesecake with assorted breads and crackers or atop mixed greens tossed with a light vinaigrette and garnished with toasted pecans.

- 7 tbsp bread crumbs
- 1 tbsp melted butter
- 4 tsp freshly grated Parmesan cheese
- 2 tsp chopped fresh parsley
- 12 oz goat cheese
- 12 oz cream cheese
- 3 whole roasted sweet red peppers
- 1 tbsp chipotle pepper purée*
- 1 clove garlic
- ⅛ tsp salt
- 3 eggs
- ½ cup whipping cream

In bowl, combine bread crumbs, melted butter, Parmesan and parsley; pat into bottom of greased 10-inch springform pan.

In food processor, purée goat cheese, cream cheese, roasted peppers, chipotle pepper purée, garlic and salt; blend in eggs and cream. Pour into pan. Bake in 400°F oven for 40 to 60 minutes or until sides are puffy and centre is loosely set but not firm. Refrigerate for at least 8 hours or overnight.

MAKES 12 TO 16 SERVINGS.

**Chipotle peppers are smoked jalapeños canned with adobo sauce. They are sold at some supermarkets, and gourmet and Latin American stores. Purée the contents of the can in a blender; refrigerate for up to 1 week or freeze for up to 1 year.*

WILD MUSHROOM AND STILTON BREAD PUDDING

Serve this savoury pudding with roast beef and a port or Dijon-flavoured sauce. Or try it as a vegetarian entrée with a leafy green salad. You can assemble the pudding and refrigerate it for up to two days before baking. I prefer to let it stand in the refrigerator overnight to allow the bread to soak up all the liquid.

¼ cup butter
1 leek, halved lengthwise and sliced
1 tsp minced garlic
2 cups mixed mushrooms (such as shiitake, oyster and cremini)
3 cups whipping cream
3 cups milk
6 eggs
1 loaf sourdough or crusty French loaf
3 oz Stilton cheese
1 tsp salt
½ tsp white pepper

In skillet, heat 2 tbsp of the butter over medium heat; cook leeks and garlic for 8 to 10 minutes or until softened. Stir in mushrooms and cook for 5 minutes or until tender. Let cool to room temperature. In bowl, whisk together cream, milk and eggs. In another large bowl, break bread into chunks. Sprinkle with cheese, then leek mixture; pour custard mixture over top. Sprinkle with salt and pepper and stir until well mixed. Pour into greased 13- x 9-inch glass baking dish; dot with remaining butter. (Can be refrigerated at this point for up to 2 days.)

Bake in 350°F oven for 45 to 60 minutes or until set in centre and golden brown. (Pudding will rise up like a soufflé and then fall down as it cools.)

MAKES 12 TO 16 SERVINGS.

CHOCOLATE PRALINE PÂTÉ

This decadent dessert is best paired with fresh raspberries and whipped cream. Press the praline all around the outside instead of folding it in or, for a smooth truffle texture, omit praline and substitute your favourite liqueur for the Frangelico. Be adventurous and try bourbon with chopped pecans or port with candied figs.

PRALINE:

¼ cup granulated sugar
2 tbsp water
Pinch cream of tartar
¼ cup toasted hazelnuts

PÂTÉ:

8 oz bittersweet chocolate
3 egg yolks
2 oz Frangelico liqueur
1 tbsp maple syrup
¼ cup butter

¼ cup granulated sugar
¼ cup sifted cocoa powder
½ cup whipping cream

PRALINE: Line 8-inch square baking dish with parchment paper or coat with vegetable spray. In small heavy-bottomed saucepan, combine sugar, water and cream of tartar; stir over low heat until sugar is dissolved. Increase heat to medium-high and bring syrup to boil. Continue boiling, without stirring, until dark golden. Add hazelnuts and stir quickly with wooden spoon to completely coat nuts with caramel; immediately pour onto prepared pan. Let cool completely. Crush with rolling pin or grind in food processor until becomes coarse powder. Store in airtight container for up to 4 weeks.

PÂTÉ: Line 8- x 4-inch loaf pan with plastic wrap with 2-inch overhang. In bowl set over simmering water, melt chocolate. Remove from heat and whisk in yolks, Frangelico and maple syrup; set aside. Using electric mixer, beat butter, sugar and cocoa until smooth. In another bowl, whip cream until soft peaks form. Whisk one-quarter of the whipped cream into chocolate mixture. Fold in remaining cream along with crushed praline until well blended. Pour into prepared loaf pan. Fold over edges of plastic wrap to cover top; refrigerate for 8 to 12 hours or overnight. To unmould, unwrap top and invert serving platter over pan. Hold both platter and pan; quickly turn over and lift off pan. Remove plastic wrap. To serve, warm knife under hot water before slicing.

MAKES 8 SERVINGS.

GILLIAN TSINTZIRAS

GILLIAN TSINTZIRAS IS AN ART DIRECTOR AND COOKBOOK DESIGNER. SHE HAS EXTENSIVE EXPERIENCE PRODUCING PRINTED MATERIALS FROM CONCEPTION TO FINISHED PRODUCT, ART DIRECTING FOOD SHOOTS AND WORKING CLOSELY WITH FOOD EDITORS, PHOTOGRAPHERS, FOOD STYLISTS AND PROP STYLISTS. GILLIAN'S CLIENTS HAVE INCLUDED *HOMEMAKER'S*, CDG BOOKS, DAIRY BUREAU OF CANADA AND FIVE ROSES FLOUR.

GLAZED LEMON CRANBERRY LOAF

Cranberries add bite to this quick lemony loaf, which pairs beautifully with a steaming cup of Earl Grey tea.

2 cups all-purpose flour
1 tsp baking powder
¼ tsp salt
¼ cup margarine, softened
1¼ cups packed brown sugar
1 egg
1 egg white
½ cup skim milk
3 tbsp light sour cream
1 tbsp grated lemon zest
¼ cup dried cranberries, sliced

GLAZE:

2 tbsp lemon juice
¼ cup packed brown sugar

Grease and flour 8- x 4-inch loaf pan. Set aside.

In small bowl, combine flour, baking powder and salt;

set aside. In large bowl, beat margarine and sugar until fluffy. Stir in egg and egg white. Add milk, sour cream, lemon zest and cranberries, stirring well after each addition. Stir dry mixture into creamed mixture until smooth and creamy. Scrape batter into prepared pan.

Bake in 350°F oven for 1 hour or until tester inserted in centre comes out clean.

GLAZE: In small saucepan, whisk together lemon juice and sugar over medium heat until sugar is dissolved. Using toothpick, poke holes in top of loaf; pour lemon glaze over top. Let cool in pan for 10 minutes. Remove from pan and let cool completely on rack.

MAKES 12 SERVINGS.

THERESE TAYLOR

THERESE TAYLOR IS CO-OWNER OF DAN T'S INFERNO FOODS, AN AWARD-WINNING SAUCE MANUFACTURER. THERESE HAS DEMONSTRATED RECIPES AT FOOD SHOWS AND ON TELEVISION AND HAS SEARED TALK RADIO LINES. THE COMPANY'S PRODUCTS AND RECIPES HAVE BEEN FEATURED IN *THE TORONTO STAR, THE TORONTO SUN, CANADIAN BUSINESS, THE CALGARY HERALD* AND *THE OTTAWA CITIZEN. THE BEST SOUP COOKBOOK* BY MARILYN CROWLEY RECOMMENDS DAN T'S SPICED CAYENNE SAUCE AS THE PREFERRED HOT SAUCE. SINCE 1997, THERESE HAS BEEN A WCN EXECUTIVE MEMBER AND NEWSLETTER EDITOR.

SINCE OUR university days in London, Ontario, my husband, Dan, and I have been heating things up. Whether it was chilies on subs, fiery Chinese stir-fries or incredible curries cooked up by my dear sister Pat, it has all helped to fuel our never-ending appetite for cayenne. In fact, it was during those university days that Dan started making Buffalo-style chicken wings and created what later became Dan T's Inferno Spiced Cayenne Sauce.

Now approaching our 10th anniversary, Dan T's Inferno Foods markets 14 different spicy sauces across Canada and the world. Over the years, we've learned that every meal—including breakfast—can benefit from a kick of cayenne. The trick with heat, of course, is proper balance. When developing recipes, I'm careful not to mask the character of the other ingredients by overpowering with a heavy hand. A couple of my recipes here call for cayenne pepper sauce. This is different than the standard hot pepper sauce, and adds a wonderful subtle heat. If you do substitute, do so with care!

I'm very grateful to founding members Marilyn Crowley and Nettie Cronish, who have mentored me in my role as editor of the WCN newsletter and who have provided invaluable support for our company. Much of my work is done on my own, in the kitchen or at the computer. I've found friendship and support from the WCN executive and from members like Gina St. Germain, Debbie Diament, Antoinette Passalacqua and Helen Hatton. I don't know where I'd be in the food business without them! For more information and recipes, visit www.dants.com

ADD A LITTLE SPICE TONIGHT

• HEAVENLY LEMONY ARTICHOKES •
•FRAGRANT BASMATI RICE •
•CIDER GREENS RULE •
•PUMPKIN SEED BREADED CHICKEN •

HEAVENLY LEMONY ARTICHOKES

Here's a dish my family has been savouring for the past decade—everyone enjoys the lemony bite of the piquant artichoke sauce. Of course, I like to use our original Dan T's Spiced Cayenne Sauce in this recipe and in the chicken recipe, page 119.

4 medium artichokes
½ cup white wine
¼ cup freshly grated Parmesan cheese
Juice of 1 lemon
3 cloves garlic, minced
2 tbsp cayenne pepper sauce
1 tsp cornstarch
½ tsp dry mustard
¼ tsp each dried parsley, oregano and tarragon
⅓ cup olive oil

Trim bottoms of artichokes and cut 1 inch from tops. Trim sharp leaves if necessary. Steam for about 40 minutes or until tender. Remove choke.

Meanwhile, in blender, purée wine, Parmesan, lemon juice, garlic, hot pepper sauce, cornstarch, mustard, parsley, oregano and tarragon. With motor running, gradually add oil in thin stream.

In skillet over medium heat, combine artichokes and sauce. Simmer, occasionally spooning sauce over artichokes, for about 20 minutes or until sauce has thickened.

MAKES 4 SERVINGS.

FRAGRANT BASMATI RICE

Literally translated, basmati means the "queen of fragrance." Served simply on its own as a side dish, with its popcorn aroma and nutty flavour, it is anything but plain.

2 cups basmati rice
2½ cups water
2 tsp salt
2 tsp olive oil
Pepper

Wash rice 3 times quickly in cold water; drain. In heavy saucepan, combine rice, water, salt and oil. Let stand for 30 minutes. Bring to boil over high heat, partially covered. Cover with tight-fitting lid and reduce heat to low; simmer for 15 minutes or until tender and no liquid remains. Fluff with fork. Season to taste with pepper.

MAKES 4 SERVINGS.

CIDER GREENS RULE

Here's an easy salad with a piquant dressing. If you prefer a more mellow dressing, reduce the vinegar by 1 or 2 tbsp. This makes a little extra, so store the remainder in a tightly covered jar in the refrigerator for up to one week.

10 cups mixed greens such as dandelion, radicchio, arugula, Belgian endive, and red leaf lettuce, torn into bite-size pieces
½ small red onion, thinly sliced
1 pear, sliced (optional)

VINAIGRETTE:

½ cup extra-virgin olive oil
¼ cup apple cider vinegar

1 tsp Dijon mustard
½ tsp packed brown sugar
½ tsp salt

In large bowl, combine greens, onion, and pear (if using). **VINAIGRETTE:** In small bowl, whisk together olive oil, vinegar, mustard, brown sugar and salt. Toss greens with ⅓ cup vinaigrette, adding more if needed.

MAKES 4 SERVINGS.

PUMPKIN SEED BREADED CHICKEN

A wonderful, family-friendly version of chicken nuggets, this chicken is deliciously crunchy.

4 boneless, skinless chicken breasts (about 1½ lb)
½ cup toasted shelled pumpkin seeds (see Nettie's recipe, page 24)
½ cup bread crumbs
¼ tsp salt
1 egg
2 tbsp cayenne pepper sauce
½ cup olive oil (approx)

Trim any fat from chicken. Pound thicker parts with meat pounder to ensure breasts are uniform thickness. Place pumpkin seeds between 2 sheets of waxed paper; with rolling pin, roll to crush seeds. Transfer seeds to shallow dish and mix in bread crumbs and salt. In another shallow dish, lightly beat egg; stir in hot pepper sauce. One at a time, dredge breasts in egg mixture, then bread crumb mixture.

In skillet, heat oil over medium heat; cook breasts, 2 at a time, for 4 minutes per side or until crust is golden and chicken is no longer pink inside. Transfer to rack. Cook remaining breasts, adding more oil as necessary.

MAKES 4 SERVINGS.

MARY LOU HARRISON

MARY LOU HARRISON IS THE OWNER OF FOSTER'S FINE CATERING, A COMPANY SPECIALIZING IN PARTY FOOD FOR ALL KINDS OF CELEBRATIONS AND EVENTS. A DIABETIC, MARY LOU IS PARTICULARLY INTERESTED IN CREATING MENUS THAT ACCOMMODATE DIETARY RESTRICTIONS AND/OR HEALTHY LIFESTYLE CHOICES.

SUN-DRIED TOMATO PESTO DIP

This delicious yet healthful dip is a staple of my professional catering as well as my personal entertaining. Pair it with multicoloured crudités, toasted pita triangles or whole wheat pretzels.

2 cans (each 19 oz/540 mL) white kidney beans
1 cup oil-packed sun-dried tomatoes
3 cloves garlic, minced
½ cup freshly grated Parmesan cheese
½ cup lemon juice
¼ cup dried basil
½ tsp salt
Sprigs fresh basil and slices sun-dried tomatoes (optional)

Drain kidney beans, reserving liquid. Rinse beans under cold water and drain well.

In food processor, purée beans, sun-dried tomatoes, garlic, Parmesan, lemon juice, basil and salt. Add enough of the reserved liquid to reach soft, spreadable consistency.

Transfer dip to serving bowl; cover and refrigerate until serving. Garnish with fresh basil and slices of sun-dried tomatoes, if desired.

MAKES 4 CUPS.

HEATHER TRIM

IF SHE WERE TO DO IT ALL AGAIN, FOOD WRITER AND CONSULTANT HEATHER TRIM WOULD STILL HAPPILY CHOOSE A CAREER IN FOOD. SHE'S A FREQUENT CONTRIBUTOR TO *CHATELAINE, FOOD & DRINK, ZELLERS FAMILY* AND *FAMILY* MAGAZINES. AS WELL AS CONSULTING FOR FOOD COMPANIES, HEATHER ENJOYS TELEVISION WORK AS A SPOKESPERSON AND FOOD STYLIST. HEATHER HAS DEVELOPED FOOD PRODUCTS FOR MARKS AND SPENCER AND WAS ASSOCIATE FOOD EDITOR FOR *CHATELAINE* AND FOOD EDITOR FOR *MODERN WOMAN* MAGAZINE.

MY INTEREST in food started early with Easy Bake Oven creations, graduating to chocolate chip cookies and early Saturday morning eating jaunts to St. Lawrence Market in downtown Toronto with my dad. Through parents who enjoyed good food and a lot of worldly travel, I've been fortunate to enjoy, try and experiment with many new-to-me foods.

I chose this menu mostly because it's simple, but also because it features casual, "feel-good" food that I love to eat. Entertaining at home needn't be fancy—it's all about relaxing with friends and enjoying a meal and time together. Having children of my own, for the past number of years, dinner parties have no longer been formal affairs, as we have tended to entertain friends and their kids. À la minute cooking is a thing of the past—the whole meal needs to be prepared in advance and grocery shopping kept to a minimum. Since I won't do "kid" food or cook two meals, I try to serve food that is as satisfying for the adults as it is for the finicky two-year-old.

For me, going to the WCN meetings is about catching up with old friends who share a love of food.

FAMILY-STYLE ENTERTAINING

• MARINATED BOCCONCINI WITH BASIL AND CHILI •
• GARLIC AND HERB BREAD •
• FUSILLI WITH PANCETTA, TOMATO AND SAGE •
• APPLE CAKE WITH BUTTERSCOTCH DRIZZLE •

MARINATED BOCCONCINI WITH BASIL AND CHILI

Marinated bocconcini is perfect for the antipasto platter, piled high with other delectables, such as home-roasted sliced peppers tossed in olive oil, balsamic vinegar, salt and pepper; wedges of melon; long thin Italian bread-sticks wrapped in prosciutto; olives; thinly sliced salami; and fresh figs. I'll often throw in mini-carrots, as they're a perfect filler for the really picky eater.

8 small balls bocconcini cheese
3 tbsp olive oil
¼ tsp salt

Pinch hot pepper flakes
15 large fresh basil leaves

Drain bocconcini and cut into ¼-inch slices. Place in bowl and toss with olive oil, salt and hot pepper flakes. Let stand at room temperature for up to 1 hour or refrigerate up to 2 days. Let come to room temperature before serving. Just before serving, stack basil leaves on top of one another; slice into very thin strips. Toss with marinated cheese. Pile on platter along with at least 3 other antipasto choices.

MAKES 8 TO 10 SERVINGS AS PART OF AN ANTIPASTO PLATTER.

GARLIC AND HERB BREAD

This is an old-fashioned treat, but it's always loved. The butter can be prepared the day before, then covered and refrigerated. Leave a few slices at the end of the baguette plain, or spread with butter only, for the little ones who don't like "green things" on their bread.

¼ cup butter, softened
2 tbsp finely chopped fresh parsley or chives
2 cloves garlic, minced
Pinch salt
1 large baguette

In small bowl, mash butter with parsley, garlic and salt until blended. (Can be covered and refrigerated for up to 1 day.) Cut bread into ½-inch slices almost all the way through but leaving attached.

Spread butter mixture on one side of each slice. Wrap loaf in foil. Bake in centre of 400°F oven for about 10 minutes or until heated through. Serve hot.

MAKES 8 TO 10 SERVINGS.

FUSILLI WITH PANCETTA, TOMATO AND SAGE

The sauce can be made a couple of days in advance and refrigerated. It also freezes beautifully. Pancetta is an Italian-style bacon that is available in Italian grocery stores and some supermarkets in the deli section.

1 tbsp olive oil
3 oz pancetta, cut into ¼-inch pieces
2 medium carrots, chopped
1 stalk celery (including leaves), chopped
1 medium red onion, halved and thinly sliced
1 large sprig rosemary, halved
1 cup dry red wine
2 cans (each 28 oz/796 mL) plum tomatoes
10 large fresh sage leaves, finely chopped
4 garlic cloves, crushed
½ tsp salt
9 cups fusilli pasta
Freshly grated Parmesan cheese

In large saucepan or skillet, heat oil over medium heat; cook pancetta, stirring occasionally, for about 5 minutes or until crisp. Discard all but 2 tsp fat. Add carrots, celery, onion and rosemary; cook, stirring occasionally, for 7 to 10 minutes or until vegetables are softened. Stir in wine; bring to boil. Cook, stirring occasionally, for about 5 minutes or until wine has evaporated.

Add tomatoes, breaking up with spoon. Bring to boil; reduce heat to medium-low and simmer, uncovered, for about 1 hour or until sauce is thickened. Stir in sage, garlic and salt.

About 20 minutes before serving, bring large saucepan of salted water to boil. Add pasta and cook for

8 to 10 minutes or until tender but firm; drain and return to pot. (If some of the little guests like their pasta plain, set some aside.) Add sauce; toss to coat. Transfer to 1 or 2 warm serving dishes and serve at the table with Parmesan.

MAKES 8 TO 10 SERVINGS.

APPLE CAKE WITH BUTTERSCOTCH DRIZZLE

Empire, Spy or Cortland apples are especially good for this cake, but any apple will do in a pinch. If you're short on time, skip the drizzle and dust with icing sugar. Serve the cake with a dollop of whipped cream, if desired.

2½ cups all-purpose flour
2 tsp baking powder
2 tsp cinnamon
¾ tsp nutmeg
½ tsp baking soda
½ tsp salt
1 cup butter, softened
1 cup granulated sugar
2 eggs
2 tsp vanilla
1 cup sour cream
3 cups apple, peeled, cored and diced (about 3)

BUTTERSCOTCH DRIZZLE:

⅓ cup packed brown sugar
¼ cup whipping cream
2 tbsp butter
1 tbsp corn syrup

In medium bowl, stir together flour, baking powder, cinnamon, nutmeg, baking soda and salt; set aside.

In large bowl and using electric mixer, cream butter until light and fluffy. Beat in sugar until creamy, scraping down sides if necessary. Beat in eggs, 1 at a time, until well combined; beat in vanilla.

Reduce speed to low and mix in one-third of the flour mixture, then half of the sour cream. Scrape down sides. Repeat with another third of the flour and remaining sour cream. Stir in remaining flour mixture (batter will be thick). Stir in apples.

Scrape into greased 10-inch Bundt pan, smoothing top. Bake in centre of 350°F oven for 55 to 60 minutes or until cake tester inserted in centre comes out clean. Transfer to rack and let cool for 10 minutes. Run knife around edge of pan to loosen cake; turn out onto rack. Let cool completely. Place cake on a rack set over a rimmed baking sheet.

BUTTERSCOTCH DRIZZLE: In small saucepan, heat brown sugar, whipping cream, butter and corn syrup over medium heat, stirring often until butter is melted. Bring to boil; boil, stirring constantly, for 1 minute. Drizzle over cake, letting it run down sides.

MAKES 10 TO 12 SERVINGS.

SUSAN THOMPSON

SUSAN THOMPSON IS OWNER-OPERATOR OF FROM THE HERB GARDEN. SHE IS A PERSONAL CHEF, COOKING TEACHER AND PRODUCT DEVELOPER. SHE SPECIALIZES IN HELPING PEOPLE WITH DIETARY RESTRICTIONS. BASED ON HER OWN ALLERGIES TO GLUTEN AND DAIRY, SUSAN HAS DEVELOPED A LINE OF GLUTEN- AND DAIRY-FREE FOODS CALLED HONEST, IT'S GOOD.

LAMB TAGINE

Here's a rich and fragrant stew, perfect for entertaining since it actually tastes better the day after it's cooked. Lamb shoulder is less expensive than leg of lamb and just as moist and tender. To pit olives, smash on a cutting board with the flat side of a chef's knife. Serve this on a bed of couscous, basmati rice or even large, flat egg noodles.

- 2 or 3 cloves garlic, finely chopped
- 2 tsp ground ginger
- 1 tsp ground cumin
- 1 tsp paprika
- ½ tsp sea salt
- ½ tsp pepper
- 2 pinches saffron, crushed
- 3 lb boneless lamb shoulder or leg, cut into 1-inch cubes
- 3 tbsp extra-virgin olive oil
- 2 medium onions, thinly sliced
- 1 cup raisins (golden, sultana or green*)
- ½ cup dried apricots, sliced
- ¼ cup chopped fresh coriander
- ¼ cup chopped fresh parsley
- 2 sticks cinnamon
- 2 tbsp lemon juice
- 2 tsp preserved lemon peel, thinly sliced **
- 1 cup kalamata olives, pitted
- Chopped fresh coriander

In medium bowl, combine garlic, ginger, cumin, paprika, salt, pepper and saffron. Add lamb and combine well, rubbing spice mixture into meat. Set aside.

In large saucepan, heat oil over medium heat; cook onions for 3 minutes. Add lamb; brown for 8 minutes. Add raisins and apricots; cook for 3 minutes. Add coriander, parsley, cinnamon sticks and just enough water to cover ingredients; bring to boil. Reduce heat, cover and simmer gently for 1 hour or until meat is very tender.

Add lemon juice, preserved lemon peel and olives; simmer for 15 minutes. Garnish with chopped coriander.

MAKES 6 SERVINGS.

* **GREEN RAISINS:** *Long green raisins from Iran and China are an exotic treat; look for them in Middle Eastern, East Indian and Chinese food stores. These raisins puff up nicely and provide a sweet-and-sour flavour perfect for a tagine, curry or pilaf.*

** **PRESERVED LEMONS:** *Purchase preserved lemons at Middle Eastern food stores (at the deli section) or make them at home. These lemons need at least one week of curing before they are ready. Scrub 2 lemons (preferably organic and thin-skinned); dry well. Slice into 8 wedges. In medium bowl, toss with ⅓ cup coarse sea or kosher salt. Place salted lemons in sterilized 3-cup Mason jar. Cover with ½ cup fresh lemon juice (3 or 4 lemons), adding more juice if necessary to cover lemons. Screw on lid and let stand at room temperature for 7 days, shaking jar each day to redistribute salt and juice. Add enough olive oil to cover by ¼ inch; refrigerate up to 6 months. When using preserved lemons, rinse under water to remove pith and pulp (and excess salt), reserving peel only. Pat dry with paper towels. (Any recipes calling for preserved lemons may not need additional salt.)*

HOME ECONOMIST

Today's home economist is a far cry from the stereotypical home ec high school teacher many dreaded in their teen years. In fact, not only is the stereotype disappearing, but the profession appears to be disappearing as well! Colleges and universities in Canada no longer offer a degree in Home Economics.

But that doesn't mean that home economists aren't a big component of the WCN makeup. While they are likely to tell you that theirs is a "dying breed," home economists within the WCN are involved in a range of exciting food-related careers. Their knowledge of food preparation, food science and nutrition has meant employment in food companies and various branches of the government. The WCN includes home economists working in marketing, recipe development, advertising, public relations, media, food styling, consumer relations and recipe testing. Wherever there is food, there's likely to be a home economist involved.

M.G.

LUCY WAVERMAN

LUCY WAVERMAN WRITES THE SATURDAY FOOD COLUMN FOR THE *GLOBE AND MAIL* AND IS THE FOOD EDITOR OF THE LIQUOR CONTROL BOARD OF ONTARIO'S (LCBO) *FOOD AND DRINK* MAGAZINE. SHE IS ALSO THE FOOD CONSULTANT TO THE LCBO AND CONTRIBUTES TO CITYTV'S "CITYLINE." LUCY IS THE AUTHOR OF FIVE COOKBOOKS; HER LATEST, *THE CHEF'S TABLE*, IS A FUNDRAISER FOR SECOND HARVEST, AND HER NEWEST ONE IS *HOME FOR DINNER* (RANDOM HOUSE CANADA, 2002).

I COME from a long line of people for whom food is a passion. My grandmother owned a superb restaurant in Glasgow, Scotland. My mother had a cooking school and then a successful kitchen shop in Toronto.

When we first came to Toronto from Scotland, we were astounded by the lack of good food. Scottish home cooking was always outstanding, with top-quality ingredients like Tay salmon and Aberdeen Angus beef. But in Toronto, there was a distinct lack of fine food. My mother took on the challenge and opened one of the first cooking schools in Toronto, where I was often her unwilling assistant, because as a teenager I had "better" things to do!

My first career had nothing to do with food. I trained and worked as a journalist. Later, I became a grade school teacher. But the underlying food interest was always there. I loved to cook and entertain but had no training.

However, when I had my own family, we moved to London, England, and I was fortunate enough to attend Le Cordon Bleu. With my newfound skills, I became a cooking teacher with my own school, and over the years I have used my journalism background to become a successful food writer and author.

MOROCCAN MAGIC

• BAKED MOROCCAN LAMB CHOPS •
• SPICED VEGETABLE COUSCOUS •
• ONION, OLIVE AND ORANGE SALAD •
• PEARS WITH MAPLE CREAM •

BAKED MOROCCAN LAMB CHOPS

Serve harissa sauce (see recipe, page 127) on the side or use Asian hot sauce as a substitute. This is a different way of preparing lamb chops, but the result is always a tender and perfectly cooked dish.

2 tbsp olive oil
1 tbsp lemon juice
1 tbsp chopped fresh parsley
1 tbsp chopped fresh coriander
2 cloves garlic, chopped
1 tsp ground cumin
8 lamb loin chops (1 inch thick), trimmed
Salt and pepper
Spiced Vegetable Couscous (recipe follows)

In bowl, combine oil, lemon juice, parsley, coriander, garlic and cumin; brush onto both sides of lamb chops and season with salt and pepper. Place lamb chops on baking sheet and let stand for 30 minutes.

Bake in 500°F oven for 3 minutes. Turn off oven and let lamb chops stand in oven for 15 minutes for rare, 25 minutes for medium. (Do not open oven door.)

Remove from oven and arrange on bed of Spiced Vegetable Couscous.

MAKES 4 SERVINGS.

SPICED VEGETABLE COUSCOUS

This is a one-pot starch-and-vegetable side dish that may be served with a green salad as a main course for two.

½ cup canned chickpeas, drained and rinsed
½ cup finely chopped carrots
½ cup finely chopped zucchini
½ cup chopped green onions
2 tbsp olive oil
1½ cups chicken stock or water
2 tbsp chopped fresh parsley
1 tsp paprika
¼ tsp hot pepper flakes
Salt
1 cup couscous
½ cup raisins

In large saucepan, combine chickpeas, carrots, zucchini, onions and olive oil. Add stock, parsley, paprika, hot pepper flakes and pinch salt; bring to boil. Sprinkle in couscous; stir. Add raisins, cover and remove from heat. Let stand for 5 minutes. Uncover and fluff with fork; taste and adjust seasoning, if desired.

MAKES 4 TO 6 SERVINGS.

ONION, OLIVE AND ORANGE SALAD

This Moroccan-influenced salad is very pretty to look at as well as delicious.

1 head romaine lettuce, separated into leaves
1 cup red onion, halved and thinly sliced
1 cup pitted black olives
2 oranges

DRESSING:

½ cup olive oil
¼ cup lemon juice
1 tsp granulated sugar
¼ tsp ground cumin
½ tsp paprika
¼ cup chopped fresh Italian parsley

Spread romaine leaves on platter. Scatter red onion and olives over top. Remove skin and white pith from oranges and slice into sections. Arrange over onions.
DRESSING: In small bowl, whisk together oil, lemon juice, sugar, cumin and paprika; drizzle over salad. Garnish with parsley.

MAKES 4 TO 6 SERVINGS.

PEARS WITH MAPLE CREAM

Here's a surprisingly easy, rich dessert. Jars of preserved ginger come in a thick syrup and can be found in most grocery stores.

4 ripe Anjou or Bartlett pears, peeled
8 dates, chopped
2 tbsp minced ginger in syrup
2 tsp grated orange zest
1 cup whipping cream
½ cup maple syrup
¼ cup white wine
½ tsp nutmeg

Cut one-third from stem end of each pear and reserve. Scoop out core with melon baller. Combine dates, ginger and orange zest; stuff into pears and place reserved pear on top of filling. Stand pears in baking dish.

In bowl, combine whipping cream, maple syrup and

wine; pour over pears. Bake in 375°F oven, basting occasionally, for 20 minutes or until pears are tender. Sprinkle with nutmeg.

Reserve pears and, if necessary, pour basting sauce into saucepan and boil over high heat for 5 to 7 minutes or until thickened slightly. Place 1 pear in centre of each of 4 plates, spooning sauce around pears. Or serve pears in balloon wine glasses and pour sauce over top. Serve warm or at room temperature.

MAKES 4 SERVINGS.

KATHY WAZANA

CASABLANCA-BORN KATHY WAZANA HAS LIVED AND COOKED IN CANADA, FRANCE AND THE MIDDLE EAST. BASED IN TORONTO, SHE TEACHES AND WRITES ABOUT THE SEPHARDIC COOKING OF HER NATIVE MOROCCO. HER FOOD WRITING HAS APPEARED IN *FINE COOKING* AND *PRESIDENT'S CHOICE MAGAZINE*. KATHY IS ALSO A CONTRIBUTOR TO *EAT TO THE BEAT* (WHITECAP, 2002). SHE HAS TAUGHT COOKING AT GREAT COOKS IN TORONTO AND HAS PROVIDED PRIVATE CLASSES IN HER HOME.

HARISSA

This Moroccan hot sauce can be added to tagines or used in a spicy salad dressing for orange and olive salad or carrot salad. Although traditionalists will want to make it with a mortar and pestle and modernists in a food processor, I prefer the consistency obtained by puréeing through a meat grinder. By topping it with a generous layer of olive oil, your homemade harissa paste can be refrigerated for three months.

½ cup (2 oz) dried mild chili peppers, such as Aleppo, New Mexican, chipotle or a combination
2 tbsp cumin seeds
1 tbsp coriander seeds
3 tbsp chopped garlic
⅓ cup extra-virgin olive oil (or less, depending on desired consistency)
½ tsp salt

Remove stem and seeds from peppers; soak in hot water for 30 minutes. Drain and pat dry with paper towels.

In dry skillet over medium-high heat, toast cumin and coriander seeds for 2 to 3 minutes or until golden brown and fragrant. Let cool. Grind in coffee grinder or using mortar and pestle.

In food processor, mortar and pestle or meat grinder, combine chili peppers, cumin, coriander, garlic, olive oil and salt; purée until smooth.

Transfer to glass jar and top with more oil. Store in refrigerator for up to 3 months.

MAKES ½ CUP.

HOW WE TESTED THE RECIPES

WHEN THE Women's Culinary Network's cookbook team set out to test every recipe in *All Stirred Up*, we decided to rent the Incubator Kitchen in downtown Toronto, owned by Field to Table. We needed a commercial kitchen large enough to accommodate our eight testers, along with all the food and equipment required to test 35 recipes at a time. With its numerous stovetops, huge convection ovens, walk-in fridge and ample workstations, the Incubator looked like the right location for our project. Besides, rent for the day was attractively low, with one caveat: we would have to share the space with another tenant. On that first day of testing, we found ourselves working alongside the Afghan Women's Collective.

As we unpacked case after case of ingredients (from a shopping and supply list 10 pages long) and acquainted ourselves with the space and its equipment, our co-renters got established, too. We had a lot in common: we were both women's groups about to cook a lot of food. But our approaches to the task couldn't have been more divergent.

We of the Women's Culinary Network had arrived as a squad of scientists loaded down with measuring equipment: spoons and cups, scales and rulers, thermometers and timers, pens and papers. Our pace was slow and methodical as we followed instructions step by step. We chopped, we measured, we poured, we took notes, our rhythm dictated by computer-generated recipes. Delete spontaneity. No veering from the recipe. We stirred, always with a second eye on the clock for timing. We wrote incessant notes, scribbling down every detail of taste, time, size, flavour, method, appearance, texture and more. When the recipe was completed, we didn't just eat it. Oh no! We stared at it intensely, wrote more notes, photographed it, then methodically tasted it, and wrote more notes.

No wonder the Afghan ladies looked a little puzzled by our approach to cooking. There wasn't a written recipe among their group of 10 as they prepared to cater a meal for 220. Many wore shawls, some wore aprons, all worked at a constant pace, often giggling and chuckling while murmering away to each other in their Afghan dialect of Dari. While we were preparing 35 single recipes designed to serve two to six people each, they were cooking six big dishes in industrial sizes. They soaked vats of basmati rice, chopped hundreds of leeks, peeled a mountain of potatoes and unloaded huge boxfuls of chicken legs. Nary a measuring spoon was in sight as they poured a stream of turmeric into a marinade or filled a wonton wrapper with chopped coriander and leeks. Occasionally, as sauces simmered in huge cauldrons and smoke rose from the deep-frying oil, one of the women would quietly scurry out to the lockers, lay a small mat on the dirty concrete floor and pray.

We were fascinated by their food, their cooking and, above all, the aromas. They smiled and shyly offered a platter piled high with hot, crispy fried chicken, the meat made moist and flavourful by a yogurt, garlic and cayenne pepper marinade. In return, we brought out a ridiculously small bowl of freshly made tropical fruit sorbet. We reached for little plastic spoons to hand out, but they blushed and looked away, refusing our outstretched hands. It was Ramadan, and they were all fasting that day in the kitchen.

We learned a lot that day. Our tests spawned a list of changes to make to many of the recipes, calling for revisions to cooking times, yields, method and seasoning—all in the name of creating perfect recipes. At the same time, we happily verified that many of the recipes already produced delicious results and had sound methods, needing no tampering from us. Yes, we'd fussed and measured, worked and chopped all day long, but we were rewarded by a kitchen full of wonderful flavours. We lapped up warm spoonfuls of silky squash soup, fought over the remains of a mocha praline tart and rushed to taste a soufflé as it emerged from the oven as a golden puff of culinary magic.

Our goal was to ensure that every recipe in *All Stirred Up* was flawlessly written, resulting in the same tasty results each and every time the recipe was to be used. Meanwhile, the Afghan Women's Collective reminded us of the value of traditional cooking. All their recipes had been committed to memory, passed down orally throughout the generations. We smelled and tasted the results of those wonderful recipes, and the memory of working side by side with those women will probably remain with all our testers.

Not all of our testing for *All Stirred Up* was completed at the Incubator Kitchen. Loblaws Supermarkets Limited generously donated the President's Choice Test Kitchen to us for a day. Our testers loved the state-of-the-art equipment, sparkling appliances and airy, well-lit environs of this downtown corporate kitchen. Several members of the President's Choice team helped out in the kitchen that day, providing much-needed assistance and support. The team made us feel welcome in their kitchen, graciously offering an endless supply of PC organic juices and freshly roasted PC coffee. We'd like to thank all the members of the President's Choice team for helping to make this project happen.

M.G.

RECIPE INDEX

C

D

E

F

G

H

P

Q

R

S

T

V

W

Y

Z

GENERAL INDEX

Ackerman, Barbara, "Mediterranean Dinner Rolls." Copyright © 2003 Barbara Ackerman

Aitken, Julia, *A Spring Fling.* Copyright © 2003 Julia Aitken

Baird, Elizabeth, *A Quartet of Preserves.* Copyright © 2003 Elizabeth Baird

Bekker, Karen, "Red River Cheddar Walnut Muffins." Copyright © 2003 Karen Bekker

Blackwood, Wendy, "Sweet Potato and Carrot Gratin with Ginger." Copyright © 2003 Wendy Blackwood

Broughton-Dunn, Charmaine, "Warm Pasta Salad with Smoked Salmon and Curried Mayonnaise." Copyright © 2003 Charmaine Broughton-Dunn

Buckley, Laura, *Brunch with Flair.* Copyright © 2003 Laura Buckley

Chauhan, Arvinda, *A Vegetarian Feast from India.* Copyright © 2003 Healthy Gourmet Indian Cooking

Connolly, Susan, *Feeding the Athletic Family.* Copyright © 2003 Susan Connolly

Cronish, Nettie, *A Vegetarian Repast, Naturally.* Copyright © 2003 Nettie Cronish

Crowley, Marilyn Bentz, *Fresh Springtime Supper.* Copyright © 2003 Marilyn Bentz Crowley

Cushing, Christine, *Pleasures of Provence.* Copyright © 2003 Christine Cushing

Daley, Regan, *Four Sweet Endings.* Copyright © 2003 Regan Daley

David, Cynthia, *The Other White Meat.* Copyright © 2003 Cynthia David

Diament, Debbie, "Pad Thai." Copyright © 2003 My Place for Dinner

Dowhan, Kate, "Spring Asparagus Salad with New Potatoes, Red Peppers and Goat Cheese." Copyright © 2003 Kate Dowhan

Duguid, Naomi, *Soujourn into Southeast Asia.* Copyright © 2003 Naomi Duguid and Jeffrey Alford

Epp, Heather, *A Lunch that Could Be Brunch.* Copyright © 2003 Heather Epp

Friis, Janet, "Do-Ahead Cheese Soufflé. Copyright © 2003 Janart Creative Services

Gilletz, Norene, "Chicken Soup with Matzo Balls," Copyright © 2003 Norene Gilletz

Greey, Madeleine, *Easy (and Exotic) Chinese,* Copyright © 2003 Madeleine Greey

Hall, Gail, *Southwest Sensations.* Copyright © 2003 Gourmet Goodies Inc.

Harrison, Mary Lou, "Sun-Dried Tomato Pesto Dip." Copyright © 2003 Foster's Fine Catering

Haynes, Linda, "Bread and Tomato Soup." Copyright © 2003 Linda Haynes

Holland, Barb, *A Snow-Time Supper.* Copyright © 2003 Barb Holland, Ph.Ec

Jull, Karen, *Naturally Good-for-You Breakfast,* Copyright © 2003 Karen Jull

Katz, Miriam, "Orange Ginger Baby Back Pork Ribs." Copyright © 2003 Miriam Katz

Koniuk, Jenny, "Carrot Crumble." Copyright © 2003 Jenny Koniuk

Kwok, Florence, "Beef Satay Stir-Fry." Copyright © 2003 Florence Kwok

Langdon, Jane, "Crostini with Oven-Roasted Tomatoes and Goat Cheese." Copyright © 2003 Wine Country Cooking School

Leese, Joanne, "Mocha Praline Torte." Copyright © 2003 Joanne Leese

Lewis, Nancy, "Thai Grilled Beef Salad." Copyright © 2003 Nancy Lewis

Lindsay, Anne, *Summer Alfresco Dining.* Copyright © 2003 Anne Lindsay

Locken, Lenore, "Nana's Clam Chowder." Copyright © 2003 Lenore Locken

Low, Jennifer, *Simply Elegant.* Copyright © 2003 Jennifer Low

Luckevich, Kasia, "Gazpacho." Copyright © 2003 Kasia Luckevich

Magwood, Trish, "Frozen Lemon Soufflé." Copyright © 2003 dish cooking studio

Main, Jan, *Simmer Up Stew.* Copyright © 2003 Jan Main

McCauley, Dana, *Coffee Break Classics.* Copyright © 2003 Dana McCauley and Associates

McIntosh, Barbara-jo, *West Coast Delights.* Copyright © 2003 Barbara-Jo's Books to Cooks

Moore, Joan, *A Taste of Jamaica.* Copyright © 2003 Joan E. Moore
Murray, Deborah, "Grilled Pear, Pineapple and Mango Salsa." Copyright © 2003 Deborah Murray
Passalacqua, Antoinette, *Real Italian Cooking.* Copyright © 2003 Antoinette Passalacqua
Rabe, Kim, "Curried Lentil Soup." Copyright © 2003 Kim Rabe
Rabinovitch, Daphna, *Northern Italian Flair.* Copyright © 2003 Daphna Rabinovitch
Reisman, Rose, *Low-Fat Salads,* Copyright © 2003 Rose Reisman
Richards, Irene, "Lemon Orzo with Deep-Fried Capers." Copyright © 2003 Irene Richards
Rosen, Marsha, "Pistachio Fingers." Copyright © 2003 Marsha Rosen, RD
Rosenberg, Dufflet, "Chocolate Fudge Tarts." Copyright © 2003 Dufflet Pastries
Sajan, Sudha, "Curried Chickpeas with Coconut Flakes." Copyright © 2003 Sudha V. Sajan
Selley, Barbara, "Grapefruit, Napa and Mesclun Salad with a Hint of Maple Dressing." Copyright © 2003 Barbara Selley
Shneer, Adell, "Ginger White Chocolate Biscotti." Copyright © 2003 Adell Shneer
Shuken, Ettie, *Greek Inspirations.* Copyright © 2003 Ettie Benjamin Shuken
Smith, Mairlyn, *Fall Feast.* Copyright © 2003 Mairlyn Smith
Steel, Pamela, "Garlic Flan." Copyright © 2003 Pamela Steel
Stern, Bonnie, *Four-Season Chicken.* Copyright © 2003 Bonnie Stern Cooking Schools Ltd.
Stewart, Anita, *A Taste of Canada.* Copyright © 2003 Anita Stewart
Sullivan, Lili, *When Savoury Turns Sweet and Vice Versa.* Copyright © 2003 Lili Sullivan
Taylor, Therese, *Add a Little Spice Tonight.* Copyright © 2003 Dan T's Inferno Foods
Thompson, Susan, "Lamb Tagine." Copyright © 2003 Susan Thompson
Trim, Heather, *Family-Style Entertaining.* Copyright © 2003 Heather Trim
Trusler, Wendy, "Cinnamon Buns." Copyright © 2003 Wendy Trusler
Tsintziras, Gillian, "Glazed Lemon Cranberry Loaf." Copyright © 2003 Gillian Tsintziras
Vig, Michele, "Chicken and Fettucine with Pesto Pernod Cream Sauce." Copyright © 2003 Michele Vig
Waverman, Lucy, *Moroccan Magic.* Copyright © 2003 Lucy Waverman
Wazana, Kathy, "Harissa." Copyright © 2003 Kathy Wazana